UNITED STATES

ARAB LOBBY IN THE UNITED STATES HANDBOOK

ORGANIZATION, OPERATIONS, PERFORMANCE

International Business Publications, USA
Washington, DC USA

UNITED STATES
ARAB LOBBY IN THE UNITED STATES HANDBOOK
ORGANIZATION, OPERATIONS, PERFORMANCE

UPDATED ANNUALLY

Cover Design: International Business Publications, USA

We express our sincere appreciation to all government agencies and international organizations which provided information and other materials for this handbook

2015 Edition International Business Publications, USA
ISBN 1-4387-0226-4

This handbook provides basic information for starting or/and conducting business in the country. The extraordinary volume of materials covering the topic, prevents us from placing all these materials in this handbook. For more detailed information on issues related to any specific investment and business activity in the country, please contact Global Investment Center, USA
Please acquire the list of our business intelligence and marketing reports and other business publications. We constantly update and expand our business intelligence and marketing materials. Please contact the center for the updated list of reports on over 200 countries.

in the USA: **Global Investment Center, USA.**
P.O.Box 15343, Washington, DC 20003
Phone: (202) 546-2103, Fax: (202) 546-3275, E-mail: rusric@erols.com

For additional analytical, marketing and other information please contact Global Investment Center, USA

Printed in the USA

UNITED STATES

ARAB LOBBY IN THE UNITED STATES HANDBOOK

ORGANIZATION, OPERATIONS, PERFORMANCE

TABLE OF CONTENTS

LOBBYING AND LOBBYING PROCESS - IMPORTANT INFORMATION

Lobbying (also **lobby**) is the act of attempting to influence decisions made by officials in the government, most often legislators or members of regulatory agencies. Lobbying is done by many types of people, associations and organized groups, including individuals in the private sector, corporations, fellow legislators or government officials, or advocacy groups (interest groups). Lobbyists may be among a legislator's constituencies, meaning a voter or block of voters within his or her electoral district, or not; they may engage in lobbying as a business, or not. Professional lobbyists are people whose business is trying to influence legislation on behalf of a group or individual who hires them. Individuals and nonprofit organizations can also lobby as an act of volunteering or as a small part of their normal job (for instance, a CEO meeting with a representative about a project important to his/her company, or an activist meeting with his/her legislator in an unpaid capacity). Governments often define and regulate organized group lobbying that has become influential.

The ethics and morality of lobbying are dual-edged. Lobbying is often spoken of with contempt, when the implication is that people with inordinate socioeconomic power are corrupting the law (twisting it away from fairness) in order to serve their own interests. When people who have a duty to act on behalf of others, such as elected officials with a duty to serve their constituents' interests or more broadly the public good, stand to benefit by shaping the law to serve the interests of some private parties a conflict of interest exists. Many critiques of lobbying point to the potential for conflicts of interest to lead to agent misdirection or the intentional failure of an agent with a duty to serve an employer, client, or constituent to perform those duties. The failure of government officials to serve the public interest as a consequence of lobbying by special interests who provide benefits to the official is an example of agent misdirection.

In contrast, another side of lobbying is making sure that others' interests are duly defended against others' corruption, or even simply making sure that minority interests are fairly defended against mere tyranny of the majority. For example, a medical association may lobby a legislature about increasing the restrictions in smoking prevention laws, and tobacco companies lobby to reduce them: the first regarding smoking as injurious to health and the second arguing it is part of the freedom of choice

Governments often define and regulate organized group lobbying as part of laws to prevent political corruption and by establishing transparency about possible influences by public lobby registers.

Lobby groups may concentrate their efforts on the legislatures, where laws are created, but may also use the judicial branch to advance their causes. The National Association for the Advancement of Colored People, for example, filed suits in state and federal courts in the 1950s to challenge segregation laws. Their efforts resulted in the Supreme Court declaring such laws unconstitutional.

They may use a legal device known as *amicus curiae*, literally "friend of the court," briefs to try to influence court cases. Briefs are written documents filed with a court, typically by parties to a lawsuit. Amines curiae briefs are briefs filed by people or groups who are not parties to a suit. These briefs are entered into the court records, and give additional background on the matter being decided upon. Advocacy groups use these briefs both to share their expertise and to promote their positions.

LOBBYING IN THE UNITED STATES BASICS

Lobbying in the United States describes paid activity in which special interests hire well-connected professional advocates, often lawyers, to argue for specific legislation in decision-making bodies such as the United States Congress. It is a highly controversial phenomenon, often seen in a negative light by journalists and the American public. While lobbying is subject to extensive and often complex rules which, if not followed, can lead to penalties including jail, the activity of lobbying has been interpreted by court rulings as constitutionally-protected free speech and a way to petition the government for the redress of grievances, two of the freedoms protected by the First Amendment of the Constitution. Since the 1970s, lobbying activity has grown immensely in terms of the numbers of lobbyists and the size of lobbying budgets, and has become the focus of much criticism of American governance. Since lobbying rules require extensive disclosure, there is a large amount of information in the public sphere about which entities lobby, how, at whom, and for how much. The current pattern suggests much lobbying is done by corporations although a wide variety of coalitions representing diverse groups is possible. Lobbying happens at every level of government, including federal, state, county, municipal, and even local governments. In Washington, lobbying usually targets congresspersons, although there have been efforts to influence executive agency officials as well as Supreme Court appointments. It has been the subject of academic inquiry in various fields, including law, public policy, and economics. While the number of lobbyists in Washington is over twelve thousand, those with real clout number in the dozens, and a small group of firms handles much of lobbying in terms of expenditures. A report in *The Nation* in 2014 suggested that while the number of 12,281 registered lobbyists was a decrease since 2002, lobbying activity was increasing and "going underground" as lobbyists use "increasingly sophisticated strategies" to obscure their activity. Analyst James A. Thurber estimated that the actual number of working lobbyists was close to 100,000 and the industry brings in $9 billion annually

Political scientist Thomas R. Dye once said that politics is about battling over scarce governmental resources: who gets them, where, when, why and how. Since government makes the rules in a complex economy such as the United States, it is logical that various organizations, businesses, individuals, nonprofits, trade groups, religions, charities and others—which are affected by these rules—will exert as much influence as they can to have rulings favorable to their cause. And the battling for influence has happened in every organized society since the beginning of civilization, whether it was Ancient Athens, Florence during the time of the Medici, Late Imperial China, and the present-day United States. Modern-day lobbyists in one sense are like the courtiers of the Ancien Régime. If voting is a general way for a public to control a government, lobbying is a more specific, targeted effort, focused on a narrower set of issues.

The term *lobby* has etymological roots in the physical structure of the British Parliament, in which there was an intermediary covered room outside the main hall. People pushing an agenda would try to meet with members of Parliament in this room, and they came to be known, by metonymy, as *lobbyists*, although one account in 1890 suggested that the application of the word "lobby" is American and that the term is not used as much in Britain.

The term *lobbying* in everyday parlance can describe a wide variety of activities, and in its general sense, suggests advocacy, advertising, or promoting a cause. In this sense, anybody who tries to influence any political position can be thought of as "lobbying", and sometimes the term is used in this loose sense. A person who writes a letter to a congressperson, or even questions a candidate at a political meeting, could be construed as being a *lobbyist*.

However, the term "lobbying" generally means a paid activity with the purpose of attempting to "influence or sway" a public official - including bureaucrats and elected officials - towards a desired specific action often relating to specific legislation. If *advocacy* is disseminating information, including attempts to persuade public officials as well as the public and media to promote the cause of something and support it, then when this activity becomes focused on specific legislation, either in support or in opposition, then it crosses the line from *advocacy* and becomes *lobbying*. This is the usual sense of the term "lobbying." One account suggested that much of the activity of nonprofits was not *lobbying* per se, since it usually did not mean changes in legislation.

A lobbyist, according to the legal sense of the word, is a professional, often a lawyer. Lobbyists are intermediaries between client organizations and lawmakers: they explain to legislators what their organizations want, and they explain to their clients what obstacles elected officials face. One definition of a lobbyist is someone "employed to persuade legislators to pass legislation that will help the lobbyist's employer." Many lobbyists work in lobbying firms or law firms, some of which retain clients outside lobbying. Others work for advocacy groups, trade associations, companies, and state and local governments. Lobbyists can be one type of government official, such as a governor of a state, who presses officials in Washington for specific legislation. A lobbyist may put together a diverse coalition of organizations and people, sometimes including lawmakers and corporations, and the whole effort may be considered to be a *lobby*; for example, in the abortion issue, there is a "pro-choice lobby" and a "pro-life lobby".

An estimate from 2007 reported that more than 15,000 federal lobbyists were based in Washington, DC; another estimate from 2011 suggested that the count of registered lobbyists who have actually lobbied was closer to 12,000. While numbers like these suggest that lobbying is a widespread activity, most accounts suggest that the Washington lobbying industry is an exclusive one run by a few well-connected firms and players, with serious barriers to entry for firms wanting to get into the lobbying business, since it requires them to have been "roaming the halls of Congress for years and years."

Law in the United States is generally made by Congress, but as the federal government has expanded during much of the twentieth century, there are a sizeable number of federal agencies, generally under the control of the president. These agencies write often industry-specific rules and regulations regarding such things as automobile safety and air quality. Unlike elected congresspersons who are constantly seeking campaign funds, these appointed officials are harder to influence, generally. However, there are indications that lobbyists seek to expand their influence from the halls of Congress deeper into the federal bureaucracy.

President Obama pledged during the election campaign to rein in lobbying. As president in January 2009, he signed two executive orders and three presidential memoranda to help ensure his administration would be more open, transparent, and accountable. These documents attempted to bring increased accountability to federal spending and limit the influence of special interests, and included a lobbyist gift ban and a revolving door ban. In May 2009, the *Recovery Act Lobbying Rules*.[106] The Executive Branch Reform Act, H.R. 985, was a bill which would have required over 8,000 Executive Branch officials to report into a public database nearly any "significant contact" from any "private party." The purpose was to identify lobbying activity. The bill was supported by proponents as an expansion of "government in the sunshine" including groups such as *Public Citizen*.

But the proposals ran into serious opposition from various groups including the lobbying industry itself. Opponents argued that the proposed reporting rules would have infringed on the right to petition, making it difficult not just for lobbyists, but for regular citizens to communicate their views on controversial issues without having their names and viewpoints entered into a government database. Opposition groups suggested that although the proposed rules were promoted as a way to regulate "lobbyists," persons described as a "private party" could be practically anybody, and that anybody contacting a federal official might be deemed to be a "lobbyist". The U.S. Department of Justice raised constitutional and other objections to the bill. Opponents mobilized over 450 groups including the U.S. Chamber of Commerce and National Association of Realtors with letter writing campaigns against the proposed restrictions. Lobbyist Howard Marlowe argued in a "stern letter"that the restriction on gift-giving to federal employees would create "fear of retribution for political donations":

In 2011, there were efforts to "shift regulatory power from the executive branch to Congress" by requiring that any "major rule" which may cost the economy more than $100 million must be decided by Congress with an up-or-down vote. But skeptics think that such a move proposed by Republican lawmakers could "usher in a lobbying bonanza from industry and other special-interest groups" to use campaign contributions to reshape the regulatory milieu

DIFFERENT TYPES OF LOBBYING

Generally, lobbyists focus on trying to persuade decision-makers: Congress, executive branch agencies such as the Treasury Department and the Securities and Exchange Commission, the Supreme Court, state governments (including governors). Federal agencies have been targeted by lobbyists since they write industry-specific rules; accordingly, interest groups spend "massive sums of money" trying to persuade them to make so-called "carve-outs" or try to block specific provisions from being enacted. A large fraction of overall lobbying is focused on only a few sets of issues, according to one report. It is possible for one level of government to lobby another level; for example, the District of Columbia has been lobbying Congress and the President for greater power, including possible statehood or voting representation in Congress; one assessment in 2011 suggested that the district needed to rethink its lobbying strategy, since its past efforts have only had "mixed results".

Many executive branch agencies have the power to write specific rules and are a target of lobbying. Federal agencies such as the State Department make rules such as giving aid money to countries such as Egypt, and in one example, an Egyptian-American businessman named Kais Menoufy organized a lobby to try to halt U.S. aid to Egypt. Since the Supreme Court has the power of judicial review and can render a congressional law unconstitutional, it has great power to influence the course of American life. For example, in the *Roe v. Wade* decision, it ruled on the legality of abortion. A variety of forces use lobbying tactics to pressure the court to overturn this decision.

Lobbyists represent their clients' or organizations' interests in state capitols. An example is a former school superintendent who has been lobbying state legislatures in California, Michigan and Nevada to overhaul teacher evaluations, and trying to end the "Last In, First Out" teacher hiring processes; according to one report, Michelle Rhee is becoming a "political force."

State governments can be lobbied by groups which represent *other governments* within the state, such as a city authority; for example, the cities of Tallahassee and St. Petersburg lobbied the Florida legislature using paid lobbyists to represent the city's interests. There is lobbying activity at the county and municipal levels, especially in larger cities and populous counties. For example, officials within the city government of Chicago called aldermen became lobbyists after serving in municipal government, following a one-year period required by city ethics rules to abstain from lobbying.

PAID VERSUS FREE LOBBYING

While the bulk of lobbying happens by business and professional interests who hire paid professionals, some lobbyists represent non-profits pro-bono for issues in which they are personally interested. Pro bono publico clients offer activities to meet and socialize with local legislators at events like fundraisers and awards ceremonies.

SINGLE ISSUE VERSUS MULTIPLE ISSUE LOBBYING

Lobbies which push for a single issue have grown in importance during the past twenty years, according to one source. Corporations generally would be considered as *single issue* lobbies. If a corporation wishes to change public policy, or to influence legislation which impacts its success as a business, it may use lobbying as a "primary avenue" for this purpose. One research study suggested that *single issue* lobbies often operate in different kinds of institutional venues, sometimes bringing the same message to different groups. Lobbies which represent groups such as labor unions, business organizations, trade associations and such are sometimes considered to be *multiple issue lobbies*, and to succeed they must be somewhat more flexible politically and be willing to accept compromise.

INSIDE VERSUS OUTSIDE LOBBYING

Inside lobbying, or sometimes called *direct lobbying*, describes efforts by lobbyists to influence legislation or rule-making directly by contacting legislators and their assistants, sometimes called staffers or aides.

Outside lobbying, or sometimes *indirect lobbying*, includes attempts by interest group leaders to mobilize citizens outside the policymaking community, perhaps by public relations methods or advertising, to prompt them to pressure public officials within the policymaking community. One example of an outside lobbying effort is a film entitled *InJustice*, made by a group promoting lawsuit reform.

BUSINESS OF LOBBYING - IMPORTANT DEVELOPMENTS

KEY PLAYERS

The number of registered Washington lobbyists is substantial. In 2009, the *Washington Post* estimated that there were 13,700 registered lobbyists, describing the nation's Capitol as "teeming with lobbyists.". In 2011, *The Guardian* estimated that in addition to the approximately 13,000 registered lobbyists, thousands more unregistered lobbyists could exist in Washington. The ratio of lobbyists employed by the healthcare industry, compared with every elected politician, was six to one, according to one account. Nevertheless, the numbers of lobbyists actively engaged in lobbying is considerably less, and the ones occupied with lobbying full-time and making significant money is even less.

Law firms. Several law firms, including Patton Boggs, Akin Gump and Holland & Knight, had sizable departments devoted to so-called "government relations".One account suggested that the lobbying arms of these law firms were not held as separate subsidiaries, but that the law practices involved in government lobbying were integrated into the overall framework of the law firm. A benefit to an integrated arrangement was that the law firm and the lobbying department could "share and refer clients back and forth".Holland & Knight earned $13.9 million from lobbying revenue in 2011. One law firm employs so-called "power brokers" including former Treasury department officials such as Marti Thomas, and former presidential advisers such as Daniel Meyer. There was a report that two law firms were treating their lobbying groups as separate business units, and giving the non-lawyer lobbyists an equity stake in the firm.

Lobbying firms. These firms usually have some lawyers in them, and are often founded by former congressional staffers, legislators, or other politicians. Some lobbying groups have been bought by large advertising conglomerates.

CORPORATIONS

Corporations which lobby actively tend to be few in number, large, and often sell to the government. Most corporations do not hire lobbyists. One study found that the actual number of firms which do lobbying regularly is fewer than 300, and that the percent of firms engaged in lobbying was 10% from 1998 to 2006, and that they were "mainly large, rich firms getting in on the fun." These firms hired lobbyists year after year, and there was not much evidence of other large firms taking much interest in lobbying. Corporations considering lobbying run into substantial barriers to entry: corporations have to research the relevant laws about lobbying, hire lobbying firms, and cultivate influential people and make connections. When an issue regarding a change in immigration policy arose, large corporations currently lobbying switched focus somewhat to take account of the new regulatory world, but new corporations—even ones likely to be affected by any possible rulings on immigration—stayed out of the lobbying fray, according to the study.

Still, of all the entities doing lobbying in Washington, the biggest overall spenders are, in fact, corporations. In the first decade of the 2000s, the most lucrative clients for Gerald Cassidy's lobbying firm were corporations, displacing fees from the appropriations business. Wall Street lobbyists and the financial industry spent upwards of $100 million in one year to "court regulators and lawmakers", particularly since they were "finalizing new regulations for lending, trading and debit card fees." Firms are more likely to spend on lobbying if they were both large and concerned about "adverse financial statement consequences" if they did not lobby. Big banks were "prolific spenders" on lobbying; JPMorgan Chase has an in-house team of lobbyists who spent $3.3 million in 2010; the American Bankers Association spent $4.6 million on lobbying;[37] an organization representing 100 of the nation's largest financial firms called the *Financial Services Roundtable* spent heavily as well.

A trade group representing Hedge Funds spent more than $1 million in one quarter trying to influence the government about financial regulations, including an effort to try to change a rule that might demand greater disclosure requirements for funds. Amazon.com spent $450,000 in one quarter lobbying about a possible online sales tax as well as rules about data protection and privacy. Corporations which sell substantially to the government tend to be active lobbiers. For example, aircraft manufacturer Boeing, which has sizeable defense contracts, pours "millions into lobbying":

UNIONS

One report suggested the United Food & Commercial Workers International Union spent $80,000 lobbying the federal government on issues relating to "the tax code, food safety, immigration reform and other issues."

OTHER PLAYERS

Other possible players in the lobbying arena are those who might influence legislation: House & Senate colleagues, public opinion in the district, the White House, party leaders, union leaders, and other influential persons and groups. Interest groups are often thought of as "nonparty organizations" which regularly try to change or influence government decision-making.

LOBBYING METHODS AND TECHNIQUES

Lobbying has much in common with highly people-intensive businesses such as management consulting and public relations, but with a political and legal sensibility. Like lawmakers, many lobbyists are lawyers, and the persons they are trying to influence have the duty of writing laws. That the disciplines of law and lobbying are intertwined could be seen in the case of a Texas lawyer who had been seeking compensation for his unfairly imprisoned client; since his exonerated-prisoner client had trouble paying the legal expenses, the lawyer lobbied the Texas state legislature to raise the state's payment for unfairly imprisoned prisoners from $50,000 per year to $80,000 per year; it succeeded, making it possible for his newly freed client to pay the lawyer's fees.

Well-connected lobbyists work in Washington for years, know the issues, are highly skilled advocates, and have cultivated close connections with members of Congress, regulators, specialists, and others. They understand strategy and have excellent communication skills; many are well suited to be able to choose which clients they would like to represent. Lobbyists patiently cultivate networks of powerful people, over many years, trying to build trust and maintain confidence and friendships. When a client hires them to push a specific issue or agenda, they usually form coalitions to exert political pressure. Lobbying, as a result, depends on trying to be flexible to new opportunities, but at the same time, to act as an agent for a client.

Access is important and often means a one-on-one meeting with a legislator. Getting access can sometimes be difficult, but there are various avenues: email, personal letters, phone calls, face-to-face meetings, meals, get-togethers, and even chasing after congresspersons in the Capitol building

Lobbyists often assist congresspersons with campaign finance by arranging fundraisers, assembling PACs, and seeking donations from other clients. Many lobbyists become campaign treasurers and fundraisers for congresspersons. This helps incumbent members cope with the substantial amounts of time required to raise money for reelection bids; one estimate was that congresspersons had to spend a third of their working hours on fundraising activity.

PACs are fairly easy to set up; it requires a lawyer and about $300, roughly. An even steeper possible reward which can be used in exchange for favors is the lure of a high-paying job as a lobbyist; according to Jack Abramoff, one of the best ways to "get what he wanted" was to offer a high-ranking congressional aide a high-paying job after they decided to leave public office. When such a promise of future employment was accepted, according to Abramoff, "we owned them".This helped the lobbying firm exert influence on that particular congressperson by going through the staff member or aide. At the same time, it is hard for outside observers to argue that a particular decision, such as hiring a former staffer into a lobbying position, was purely as a reward for some past political decision, since staffers often have valuable connections and policy experience needed by lobbying firms. Research economist Mirko Draca suggested that hiring a staffer was an ideal way for a lobbying firm to try to sway their old bosses—a congressperson—in the future.

Lobbyists, according to several sources, strive for communications which are clear, straightforward, and direct. In a one-on-one meeting with a lobbyist, it helps to understand precisely what goal is wanted. A lobbyist wants action on a bill; a legislator wants to be re-elected. The idea is to persuade a legislator that what the lobbyist wants is good public policy. Lobbyists often urge lawmakers to try to persuade other lawmakers to approve a bill.

Still, persuasion is a subtle business, requiring a deft touch, and carelessness can boomerang. In one instance of a public relations reversal, a lobbying initiative by the Cassidy firm which targeted Senator Robert C. Byrd blew up when the Cassidy-Byrd connection was published in the *Washington Post*; this resulted in a furious Byrd reversing his previous pro-Cassidy position and throwing a "theatrical temper tantrum" regarding an $18 million facility. Byrd denounced "lobbyists who collect exorbitant fees to create projects and have them earmarked in appropriation bills... for the benefit of their clients."

Since it often takes a long time to build the network of relationships within the lobbying industry, ethical interpersonal dealings are important. A maxim in the industry is for lobbyists to be truthful with people they are trying to persuade; one lobbyist described it this way: "what you've basically got is your word and reputation". An untruth, a lie is too risky to the successful development of a long-term relationship and the potential gain is not worth the risk. One report suggested that below-the-belt tactics generally do not work. One account suggest that groping for "personal dirt" on opponents was counterproductive since it would undermine respect for the lobbyist and their clients. And, by reverse logic, if an untruth is told by an opponent or opposing lobby, then it makes sense to publicize it. But the general code among lobbyists is that unsubstantiated claims are bad business. Even worse is planting an informant in an opponent's camp, since if this subterfuge is ever discovered, it will boomerang negatively in a hundred ways, and credibility will drop to zero. The importance of personal relationships in lobbying can be seen in the state of Illinois, in which father-son ties helped push a smart-grid energy bill, although there were accusations of favoritism. And there is anecdotal evidence that a business firm seeking to profitably influence legislation has to pay particular attention to which lobbyist it hires.

Strategic considerations for lobbyists, trying to influence legislation, include "locating a power base" or a constituency logically predisposed to support a given policy. Timing, as well, is usually important, in the sense of knowing when to propose a certain action and having a big-picture view of the possible sequence of desired actions. Strategic lobbying tries to estimate the possible responses of different groups to a possible lobby approach; one study suggested that the "expectations of opposition from other interests" was a key factor helping to determine how a lobby should operate.

Increasingly, lobbyists seek to put together coalitions and use *outside lobbying* by swaying public opinion. Bigger, more diverse and deep pocketed coalitions tend to be more effective in outside lobbying, and the "strength in numbers" principle often applies. Interest groups try to build "sustainable coalitions of similarly situated individual organizations in pursuit of like-minded goals". According to one study, it is often difficult for a lobbyist to influence a staff member in Congress directly, since staffers tend to be well-informed and subject to views from competing interests. As an indirect tactic, lobbyists can try to manipulate public opinion which, in turn, can sometimes exert pressure on congresspersons.

Activities for these purposes include trying to use the mass media, cultivating contacts with reporters and editors, encouraging them to write editorials and cover stories to influence public opinion, which may have the secondary effect of influencing Congress. According to analyst Ken Kollman, it is easier to sway public opinion than a congressional staff member since it is possible to bombard the public with "half-truths, distortion, scare tactics, and misinformation." Kollman suggests there should be two goals: (1) communicate that there is public support behind an issue to policymakers and (2) increase public support for the issue among constituents. Kollman suggested outside lobbying was a "powerful tool" for interest group leaders. In a sense, using these criteria, one could consider James Madison as having engaged in *outside lobbying*, since after the Constitution was proposed, he wrote many of the 85 newspaper editorials arguing for people to support the Constitution, and these writings later became the *Federalist Papers*.

As a result of this "lobbying" effort, the Constitution was ratified, although there were narrow margins of victory in four of the state legislatures. Lobbying today generally requires mounting a coordinated campaign, using targeted blitzes of telephone calls, letters, emails to congressional lawmakers, marches down the Washington Mall, bus caravans, and such, and these are often put together by lobbyists who coordinate a variety of interest group leaders to unite behind a hopefully simple easy-to-grasp and persuasive message.

It is important for lobbyists to follow rules governing lobbying behavior. These can be difficult and complex, take time to learn, require full disclosure, and mistakes can land a lobbyist in serious legal trouble.

Gifts for congresspersons and staffers can be problematic, since anything of sizeable value must be disclosed and generally such gifts are illegal. Gifts under $5 are allowed. Another exception is awards, so it is permitted to give a congressperson a plaque thanking him or her for support on a given issue. Cash gifts payable by check can only be made to campaign committees, not to a candidate personally or to his or her staff; it is not permitted to give cash or stock.

Wealthy lobbyists often encourage other lobbying clients to donate to a particular cause, in the hope that favors will be returned at a later date.

The dynamics of the lobbying world make it fairly easy for a semi-skilled operator to defraud a client. This is essentially what happened in the Jack Abramoff Indian lobbying scandal. There was a concerned client—in this case, an Indian casino—worried about possible ill-effects of legislation on its gambling business; and there were lobbyists such as Jack Abramoff who knew how to exploit these fears. The lobbyists actively lobbied *against* their own casino-client as a way to ratchet up their fears of adverse legislation as well as stoke possible future contributions; the lobbyists committed other violations such as grossly overbilling their clients as well as violating rules about giving gifts to congresspersons. Numerous persons went to jail after the scandal. The following are factors which can make fraud a fairly easy-to-do activity: that lobbyists are paid only to *try to* influence decision-makers, and may or may not succeed, making it hard to tell if a lobbyist did actual work; that much of what happens regarding interpersonal relations is obscure despite rather strict disclosure and transparency requirements; that there are sizable monies involved—factors such as these almost guarantee that there will be future scandals involving fraudulent lobbying activity, according to one assessment. A fraud similar to Abramoff's was perpetrated in Maryland by lobbyist Gerald E. Evans, who was convicted of mail and wire fraud in 2000 in a case involving falsely creating a "fictitious legislative threat" against a client, and then billing the client to work against this supposed threat.

Lobbyists routinely monitor how congressional officials vote, sometimes checking the past voting records of congresspersons. One report suggested that reforms requiring "publicly recorded committee votes" led to more information about how congresspersons voted, but instead of becoming a valuable resource for the news media or voters, the information helped lobbyists monitor congressional voting patterns. As a general rule, lawmakers must vote as a particular interest group wishes them to vote, or risk losing support.

Strategy usually dictates targeting specific office holders. On the state level, one study suggested that much of the lobbying activity targeted the offices of governors as well as state-level executive bureaucrats; state lobbying was an "intensely personal game" with face-to-face contact being required for important decisions. Lobbying can be a counteractive response to the lobbying efforts of others.

LOBBYISTS AS EDUCATORS AND ADVISORS

Since government has grown increasingly complex, having to deal with new technologies, the task of writing rules has become more complex. "Government has grown so complex that it is a virtual certainty that more than one agency would be affected by any piece of legislation," according to one view. Lobbyists, therefore, spend considerable time learning the ins and outs of issues, and can use their expertise to educate lawmakers and help them cope with difficult issues. Lobbyists' knowledge has been considered to be an intellectual subsidy for lawmakers. Some lobbyists become specialists with expertise in a particular set of issues, although one study suggested that of two competing criteria for lobbyists—expertise or access—that access was far more important.

Lobby groups and their members sometimes also write legislation and whip bills, and in these instances, it is helpful to have lawyers skilled in writing legislation to assist with these efforts. It is often necessary to research relevant laws and issues beforehand. In many instances lobbyists write the actual text of the proposed law, and hire lawyers to "get the language down pat"—an omission in wording or an unclear phrase may open up a loophole for opponents to wrangle over for years. And lobbyists can often advise a lawmaker on how to navigate the approval process.

Lobbying firms can serve as mentors and guides. For example, after months of protesting by the Occupy Wall Street, one lobbying firm prepared a memo to its clients warning that Republicans may "turn on big banks, at least in public" which may have the effect of "altering the political ground for years to come." Here are parts of the memo which were broadcast on the MSNBC network.

A GROWING BILLION DOLLAR BUSINESS

Top lobbying sectors 1998-2010			
	Client	Amount Spent	%
1	Finance, Insurance & Real Estate	$4,274,060,331	15%
2	Health	$4,222,427,808	15%
3	Misc Business	$4,149,842,571	14%
4	Communications/Electronics	$3,497,881,399	12%
5	Energy & Natural Resources	$3,104,104,518	11%
6	Transportation	$2,245,118,222	8%
7	Other	$2,207,772,363	7%
8	Ideological/Single-Issue	$1,477,294,241	5%
9	Agribusiness	$1,280,824,983	4%
10	Defense	$1,216,469,173	4%
11	Construction	$480,363,108	2%
12	Labor	$427,355,408	1%
13	Lawyers & Lobbyists themselves	$336,170,306	1%
	Total	$28,919,684,431	99%
	Note: Amounts do not include campaign contributions.		

Since the 1970s, there has been explosive growth in the lobbying industry, particularly in Washington D.C.. By 2011, one estimate of overall lobbying spending nationally was $30+ billion dollars. An estimate of lobbying expenses in the federal arena was $3.5 billion in 2010, while it had been only $1.4 billion in 1998. And there is prodigious data since firms are required to disclose lobbying expenditures on a quarterly basis.

The industry, however, is not immune to economic downturns. If Congress is gridlocked, such as during the summer and early fall of 2011, lobbying activity dipped considerably, according to *The Washington Post.* Lobbying firm Patton Boggs reported drops in revenue during that year, from $12 million in 2010 to $11 million in 2011. To cope with the downturn, some law firms compensated by increasing activity in litigation, regulatory work, and representing clients in congressional investigations.

A sea-change in government, such as a shift in control of the legislature from one political party to the other, can affect the lobbying business profoundly. For example, the primarily Democratic-serving lobbying firm Cassidy & Associates learned that control of Congress would change hands from Democrats to Republicans in 1994, and the firm acquired Republican lobbyists before the congressional handover of power, and the move helped the lobbying firm stay on top of the new political realities

EFFECTIVENESS OF LOBBYING

There is general agreement that money is a key variable in lobbying.

The general consensus view is that lobbying generally works overall in achieving sought-after results for clients, particularly since it has become so prevalent with substantial and growing budgets, although there are dissenting views. A study by the investment-research firm Strategas which was cited in *The Economist* and the *Washington Post* compared the 50 firms that spent the most on lobbying relative to their assets, and compared their financial performance against that of the S&P 500 in the stock market; the study concluded that spending on lobbying was a "spectacular investment" yielding "blistering" returns comparable to a high-flying hedge fund, even despite the financial downturn of the past few years. A 2009 study by University of Kansas professor Raquel Meyer Alexander suggested that lobbying brought a substantial return on investment. A 2011 meta-analysis of previous research findings found a positive correlation between corporate political activity and firm performance.

There is widespread agreement that a key ingredient in effective lobbying is money. This view is shared by players in the lobbying industry.

Still, effectiveness can vary depending on the situational context. One view is that large multiple-issue lobbies tend to be effective in getting results for their clients if they are sophisticated, managed by a legislative director familiar with the art of compromise, and play "political hardball". But if such lobbies became too big, such as large industrial trade organizations, they became harder to control, often leading to lackluster results. A study in 2001 which compared lobbying activity in US-style congressional against European-style parliamentary systems, found that in congressional systems there was an advantage favoring the "agenda-setters", but that in both systems, "lobbying has a marked effect on policies".One report suggested that the 1,000 registered lobbyists in California were highly influential such that they were called the *Third House*.

Studies of lobbying by academics in previous decades painted a picture of lobbying being an ineffectual activity, although many of these studies were done before lobbying became prevalent in American politics. A study in 1963 by Bauer, Pool, & Dexter suggested lobbyists were mostly "impotent" in exerting influence. Studies in the early 1990s suggested that lobbying exerted influence only "marginally", although it suggested that when lobbying activity did achieve political impacts, that the results of the political choices were sufficient to justify the expenditure on lobbying. A fairly recent study in 2009 is that Washington lobbies are "far less influential than political rhetoric suggests", and that most lobbying campaigns do not change any views and that there was a strong entrenchment of the status quo.

But it depends on what is seen as "effective", since many lobbying battles result in a stalemate, since powerful interests battle, and in many cases, merely keeping the "status quo" could be seen as a victory of sorts. What happens often is that varying coalitions find themselves in "diametrical opposition to each other" and that stalemates result.

There is anecdotal evidence from numerous newspaper accounts of different groups battling that lobbying activity usually achieves results. For example, the Obama administration pledged to stop for-profit colleges from "luring students with false promises", but with this threat, the lobbying industry sprang into action with a $16 million campaign, and their efforts succeeded in watering down the proposed restrictions. How did the lobbying campaign succeed? Actions taken included:

- spent $16 million
- hired "all-star list" of prominent players including Democrats with White House ties
- plotted strategy
- worked with "fund-raising bundler" Jamie Rubin, a former Obama communications director
- won support from influential people including congressperson-turned-lobbyist Dick Gephardt, senator-turned-lobbyist John Breaux, lobbyist Tony Podesta, Washington Post CEO Donald E. Graham, education entrepreneur and University of Phoenix founder John Sperling, others
- key leaders made "impassioned appeals"
- mobilization effort produced 90,000 public documents to the Education department advocating against changes

And sometimes merely keeping the status quo could be seen as a victory. When gridlock led to the supposed supercommittee solution, numerous lobbyists from all parts of the political spectrum worked hard, and a stalemate resulted, but with each side defended their own special interests. And while money is an important variable, it is one among many variables, and there have been instances in which huge sums have been spent on lobbying only to have the result backfire. One report suggested that the communications firm AT&T failed to achieve substantial results from its lobbying efforts in 2011, since government antitrust officials rejected its plan to acquire rival T-Mobile.

Lobbying is a practical necessity for firms that "live and die" by government decisions, such as large government contractors such as Boeing. A study done in 2006 by *Bloomberg News* suggested that lobbying was a "sound money-making strategy" for the 20 largest federal contractors. The largest contractor, Lockheed Martin Corporation, received almost $40 billion in federal contracts in 2003-4, and spent $16 million on lobbying expenses and campaign donations. For each dollar of lobbying investment, the firm received $2,517 in revenues, according to the report. When the lobbying firm Cassidy & Associates began achieving results with earmarks for colleges and universities and medical centers, new lobbying firms rose to compete with them to win "earmarks of their own", a clear sign that the lobbying was exceedingly effective

ARAB LOBBY IN THE UNITED STATES - STRATEGIC INFORMATION AND DEVELOPMENTS

The **Arab lobby in the United States** is a collection of formal and informal groups that lobby the public and government of the United States on behalf of Arab interests

ORIGINS

Isaiah L. Kenen, the founder of what became American Israel Public Affairs Committee, says the Arab lobby has its roots in the "petro-diplomatic complex" that comprises the "oil industry, missionaries, and diplomats." Mitchell Bard, the American foreign policy analyst and historian who specializes in U.S.-Middle East policy, "from the beginning, the Arab lobby has faced not only a disadvantage in electoral politics but also in organization. There are several politically oriented groups, but many of these are one man operations with little financial or popular support."

FORMAL ARAB LOBBY

In 1951 King Saud of Saudi Arabia asked U.S. diplomats to finance a pro-Arab lobby to counter the leading formal Israel lobbying organization in the U.S., the *American Zionist Committee for Public Affairs* (AZCPA), the forerunner of the modern *American Israel Public Affairs Committee* (AIPAC). The result was the formation of the *National Association of Arab-Americans* which has since been disbanded. No cohesive Arab lobby has ever come to existence, with the closest being the American-Arab Anti-Discrimination Committee. This organization, which started in the 1970s, gained considerable support from politically active Arab Americans until the headquarters of the organization was bombed in the early 1980s. Even in its heyday it focused on serving the interests of Arab Americans within the confines of domestic politics. Today, this organization does little in terms of pressing to change foreign policy that is against "Arab" interests, though they do serve as a source of protection and advice for Arab Americans who fall victim to civil rights abuses and intimidation by government and private agents.

AMERICAN-ARAB ANTI-DISCRIMINATION COMMITTEE

The **American-Arab Anti-Discrimination Committee** (ADC) is a grassroots civil rights organization open to all regardless of background, faith and ethnicity committed to defending the rights of people of Middle Eastearn descent and promoting their rich cultural heritage. The ADC, which is non-sectarian and non-partisan, is the largest Arab-American grassroots civil rights organization in the United States. It was founded in 1980 by former United States Senator James Abourezk; and it has chapters nationwide, and members in all the 50 states. Advisory Board members include Muhammad Ali, Queen Noor of Jordan, several U.S. Congressmen and Casey Kasem. ADC has members in all 50 US states and is the largest Arab-American organization of its kind. AS of writing the ADC Communications Department has made over 3000 radio and television appearances.

With headquarters in Washington, DC, the ADC operates offices in Boston, Dearborn, Los Angeles, San Francisco, New York City, and San Diego. ADC welcomes members of all faiths, backgrounds, and ethnicities. Former US Congresswoman Mary Rose Oakar is the current president of ADC.

ADC is at the forefront in addressing discrimination and bias against Arab-Americans wherever it is practiced. It acts as a national and local framework through which Arab-Americans can channel their efforts toward making an impact in the public arena and also advocating a more balanced US policy towards the Middle East. By participating in a wide range of activities, ADC has made great strides in correcting the stereotypes of Arabs and Muslims, prejudice and fear. Consistent with its educational mission, ADC issues a bi-monthly newsletter; *Issue Papers* and *Special Reports* that study key issues of defamation and discrimination; community studies; and legal, media and educational guides. Additionally, ADC is an active member of the Leadership Conference on Civil Rights (LCCR) and the only Arab-American organization that is a member.

ADC's Communications Department challenges defamation, stereotyping and bias in films, television and news reporting. Staff have made thousands of appearances on major national and international media outlets. ADC spokespersons are widely recognized as the authoritative voice on Arab-American affairs, US foreign policy, Islam, civil rights and many other daily news items. The Communications Department's work has been featured in *Newsweek*, and also noted by the *New York Press* as "Outstanding Spokesperson" for the Arab-American cause. ADC Communications staff also frequently serve as editorial consultants for a wide range of documentaries and educational programs that have aired on PBS, the Discovery Channel, Nickelodeon, Showtime, HBO, and MTV. The Communications Department is also instrumental in organizing and promoting film festivals and cultural events celebrating Arab, Muslim, and Arab-American cinema, theatre, and the arts.

Through its Legal Department, ADC offers counseling in cases of discrimination and defamation, and provides assistance in selected litigation. Since September 11, ADC attorneys have been addressing hundreds of cases and have filed briefs and lawsuits against airlines for discrimination on the basis of ethnicity and national origin; against the United States government for discriminatory detentions of Arabs and Muslims without probable cause, and for discrimination against Arab Americans in the workplace, in addition to counseling and assisting victims of anti-Arab hate crimes. For these reasons, ADC's Legal Department was the recipient of the 2003 American Immigration Lawyers Association (AILA) Human Rights Award.

The Government Affairs affiliate of ADC works with Congress, the White House, the State and Justice Departments, as well as other elements of government to promote the interests of the community. ADC's testimony before Congress and elsewhere is impeccable, as ADC ensures that every assertion is documented and that a fair view of each situation is taken. ADC members, who are US citizens, can contribute to the NAAA-ADC PAC to support political candidates for federal office.

ADC's Organizing Department mobilizes the community by coordinating the efforts of chapters, local offices, and activists across the nation and directing ADC's national campaigns. As a grassroots organization, ADC's successes depend on the work of dedicated volunteers and activists. In order to ensure maximum efficiency in covering all dimensions of organizing and mobilizing the community, each ADC chapter includes membership, education, outreach, media, and fundraising committees. ADC's annual Convention draws participants from around the world and is the largest gathering of Arab Americans and their friends. The Convention features workshops, panel discussions, banquets, exhibits, and a two-day film festival.

The ADC Research Institute (ADCRI), which was founded in 1981, is a Section 501(c)(3) educational organization that sponsors a wide range of programs on behalf of Arab Americans and of importance to all Americans. ADCRI programs include research studies, seminars, conferences and publications that document and analyze the discrimination faced by Arab Americans in the workplace, schools, media, and governmental agencies and institutions. They also promote a better understanding of the rich Arab cultural heritage by the public and policy makers. A noteworthy achievement in this respect is ADC's Reaching the Teachers campaign, a program that provides lesson plans, background articles, fact sheets, bibliographies and other resources to educators to ensure an accurate, objective and fair portrayal of Arab history and culture in schools and empowers Arab Americans to become more actively involved in their local schools. ADC's intern program for undergraduate, graduate and law students trains a new generation of Arab-American leaders.

ADC is now celebrating 26 years of dedicated service to civil and human rights, and remains committed to building bridges with other communities and forging coalitions with organizations throughout the country on issues of mutual concern.

Board of Directors
Dr. Safa Rifka, Chairman
George Gorayeb, Vice-Chair
Assad Jebara, Treasurer
Ashley Mammo, Secratary
Nabih Ayad, Esq.
Asli Bali, Esq.
Thomas Tony George

Linda Mansour, Esq.
Albert Mokhiber, Esq.
Jamilah Shami
Naseem Tuffaha
Cheryl Feris, Esq.

ADC Regional Offices

ADC Michigan Office
13530 Michigan Ave. Suite 329
Dearborn, MI 48126
Tel: (313) 581-1201
ADCmidwest@adc.org

ADC NY Office
80 Wall St., Suite 718
New York, NY 10005
Tel: (212) 480-2955
Fax: (212) 480-2956
E-mail: outreach@adcnewyork.org

ADC LOCAL CHAPTERS

To contact any of the ADC local chapters, please e-mail: organizing@adc.org

ARIZONA	TUCSON PHEONIX
CALIFORNIA	LOS ANGELES ORANGE COUNTY SACRAMENTO SAN DIEGO SAN FRANCISCO
FLORIDA	MIAMI ORLANDO
GEORGIA	ATLANTA
ILLINOIS	CHICAGO
KENTUCKY	LOUISVILLE
LOUISIANA	NEW ORLEANS
MASSACHUSETTS	BOSTON
MARYLAND	BALTIMORE DC AREA
MICHIGAN	DETROIT WAYNE STATE UNIVERSITY UNIVERSITY OF MICHIGAN, ANN ARBOR KALAMAZOO

MINNESOTA	MINNEAPOLIS / ST. PAUL
MISSOURI	ST. LOUIS
NEVADA	LAS VEGAS
NEW HAMPSHIRE	MANCHESTER
NEW JERSEY	NORTHERN NEW JERSEY
NEW YORK	MANHATTAN ROCHESTER
OHIO	CLEVELAND
PENNSYLVANIA	PHILADELPHIA PITTSBURG
RHODE ISLAND	BROWN UNIVERSITY, PROVIDENCE
TENNESSEE	NASHVILLE
TEXAS	AUSTIN DALLAS HOUSTON
VIRGINIA	NORTHERN VIRGINIA
WASHINGTON, DC	DC METRO AREA
WASHINGTON	SEATTLE
WISCONSIN	MILWAUKEE

MISSION

THE AMERICAN-ARAB ANTI-DISCRIMINATION COMMITTEE (ADC) IS A CIVIL RIGHTS ORGANIZATION COMMITTED TO DEFENDING THE RIGHTS OF PEOPLE OF ARAB DESCENT AND PROMOTING THEIR RICH CULTURAL HERITAGE.

ADC, which is non-sectarian & non-partisan, is the largest Arab-American grassroots organization in the United States. It was founded in 1980 by former **U.S. Senator James Abourezk** and has chapters nationwide.

ADC's Advisory Committee is made up of an impressive group of people that include: Muhammad Ali, Her Majesty Queen Noor, U.S. Congressmen John Conyers (D-MI), Darrell Issa (R-CA), & Nick Joe Rahall (D-WV), as well as the Honorable Paul Findley, Clovis Maksoud, Casey Kasem, Archbishop Philip Saliba and others.

ADC is at the forefront in combating defamation and negative stereotyping of Arab

Americans in the media and wherever else it is practiced. In doing so, it acts as an organ-ized framework through which Arab Americans can channel their efforts toward unified, collective and effective advocacy; by promoting a more balanced U.S. Middle East policy and serving as a reliable source for the news media and educators. By promoting cultural events and par-ticipating in community activities, ADC has made great strides in correcting anti-Arab stereotypes and humanizing the image of the Arab people. In all these efforts, ADC coordinates closely with other civil rights and human rights organizations on issues of common concern.

Through its Department of Legal Services, ADC offers counseling in cases of discrimination and defamation and selected impact litigation in the areas of immigration.

In its efforts to educate the public and maintain regular communication with its members, the Media & Publications Department issues a bi-monthly newsletter, ADC Times, Issue Papers and Special Reports, which study key issues of defamation and discrimination; community studies, legal, media and educational guides; and action alerts, which call on members to act on issues necessitating grassroots response.

In the Department of Educational Programs of ADC, the Research Institute (ADCRI) publishes information on issues of concern to Arab Americans and sponsors ADC's Reaching the Teachers campaign, which aims at ensuring an accurate, objective and fair portrayal of Arab history and culture in schools. ADCRI also administers a year-round college internship program for Arab American students and others.

ADC's achievements demonstrate the success of Arab Americans in building vibrant institutions which not only draw on the strength of the Arab American community, but also engender the support of individuals and groups who are equally committed to deterring discrimination against all people.

NOTED LOBBYISTS

J. William Fulbright, former Chairman of the Senate Foreign Relations Committee .
Fred Dutton, former Assistant Secretary for Legislative Affairs and special assistant to President John F. Kennedy.
Clark Clifford, former Secretary of Defense under President Lyndon Johnson.
Richard Kleindienst, former Attorney General under President Richard Nixon.
William P. Rogers, former Secretary of State under President Richard Nixon.

National Arab American Organizations

The strong partnership with the most powerful Arab American organizations and associations helps us provide to our Clients a very powerful set of guaranteed outreach tools for public understanding, public awareness, dialogue or public relations. Most of these organizations communicate periodically to their members across different platforms: Media, Magazines, Brochures, Newsletters, Emails etc.
With one call, one service, one bill, Allied Media offers a general distribution of your message to all the members with a very high readership.
Allied Media gives you access to all the organizations and associations national and local events where millions of combined attendees.
Call us today to get a plan for your outreach program.
(703)-333-2008 or email at **info@allied-media.com**

WASHINGTON D.C.

Arab American Institute
Jim Zogby
1600 K St., Suite 601
Washington, DC 20006
(202) 429-9210
(202) 429-9214 (fax)

American-Arab Anti-Discrimination Committee
Hala Maksoud
4201 Connecticut Ave. NW, Suite 500
Washington, DC 20008
(202) 244-2990
(202) 244-3196 (fax)

Council on American-Islamic Relations
453 New Jersey Ave SE
Washington DC 20077-0839
202-488-8787
Fax: 202-488-0833

American Near East Refugee Aid (ANERA)
202-347-2558
anera@anera.org

United Palestinian Appeal
1330 New Hampshire Ave NW
Suite B1
Washington DC 20036
202-659-5007, or, 800-892-6183
FAX: 202-296-0224
upa@cais.com

Center for Policy Study Analysis on Palestine
2425-35 Virginia Ave NW
Washington DC 20037
202-338-1290
info@palestinecenter.org

DETROIT REGION

Arab Community Center for Economic and Social Services
Jeralda Hattar
2651 Saulino Court
Dearborn, MI 48120-1556
(313) 842-7010
(313) 842-5150 (fax)

ADC Detroit Regional Office
Imad Hamad
13530 Michigan Ave. No.220
Dearborn, MI 48126
(313) 581-1208

Chaldean Federation of America
18470 Ten Mile Road
Southfield, MI 48075
(248) 557-2362
(810) 788-0177 (fax)

Arab-American & Chaldean Council
28551 Southfield Road, No. 204
Lathrup Village, MI 48076-2723
(810) 559-1990
(810) 559-9117 (fax)

LOS ANGELES REGION

ADC West Coast Regional Office
Michel Shehadeh
12361 Lorna St.
Garden Grove, CA 92841
(714) 636-1232

Muslim Public Affairs Council
3255 Wilshire Boulevard, No. 603
Los Angeles, CA 90010
(213) 383-3443
(213) 383-9674 (fax)

Council on American-Islamic Relations
Hussam Ayloush
2115 West Crescent Avenue, Suite 228
Anaheim, CA 92801
(714) 776-1847
(714) 776-8340 (fax)

NEW YORK REGION

Arab American Family Support Center
Emira Habiby-Browne
88A Fourth Ave.
Brooklyn, NY 11217
(718) 643-8000
(718) 643-8167 (fax)

Arab American Council, Inc.
Majed Samarneh
69 Chestnut St.
Yonkers, NY 10701-3407
(914) 285-3385
(914) 963-6410 (fax)

DALLAS REGION

Arab American Community and Cultural Center Houston
Hatem Saqr, President

W. 2425 Loops
Houston, TX 77027-4205
(713) 621-2950
(713) 621-2139 (fax)
Yasmena Samahy
(713) 896-1630
(713) 937-6552 (fax)

PHILADELPHIA REGION

Philadelphia Association of Arab Americans
Marwan Kreidie, President
502 Hancock St.
Philadelphia, PA 19147
(215) 625-3732
(215) 972-8101 (fax)

Al-Aqsa Islamic Society
Imam Chukri Khorchid
2316 Holly Lane
Lafayette Hill, PA 19444
(610) 668-4649
(610) 941-0314 (fax)

CHICAGO REGION

Arab American Bar Association
PO Box 81325
Chicago IL 60681
312/946-0110
William Haddad, Executive Director
Review: One of the most dependable organizations in Chicagoland. Very active in local professional legal matters and events, supportive of all Arab American individuals, and active in reviewing the credentials of local judges in election campaigns.

Vanguards for Human Rights and Freedom
Ali Al-Arabi, President
PO Box 1224
LaGrange Park, IL 60526
708-442-8990
Fax: 708-442-9027
Review: Organizes meetings to address issues of bigotry and discrimination between victims, support groups and government agencies. Very effective as witnessed recently in Orland Park where dozens of Arab residents complained about bigotry there. Al-Arabi organized the meeting with Mayor McLaughlin and Police Chief McCarthy and the mayor vowed to create several community liaisons to address Arab American concerns.

Chicago Association of Arab American Journalist's and Communicators
Last updated July 21, 2001
PO Box 2127
Orland Park, IL 60462
708-403-3380 V/F

rayhanania@aol.com
Review: Sponsors the annual Arab American Writers Conference each year in Chicago. Sponsors bi-monthly meetings with journalists and communications professionals. A reorganization of the former

Association of Arab American Journalists founded in 1986 - 1990. The only professional writer's forum for Arab American's in the Chicago area. Has more than 71 members in Chicago.

Arab American Chicagoland Census Organization
7905 S. Cicero Ave
Suite 200
Chicago IL 60652
773-735-7755
Fax: 773-735-8466
Review: The official Arab American census effort in Chicago region. Works with the US Census office and Arab American Census Representative Anna Mustafa.

American Arab Anti-Discrimination Committee (ADC)
ADC Chicago Chapter
Shafic Budron, PHD, President
10005 Roberts Road, Suite B
Palos Hills, IL 60465 (847) 489-7999
adcChicago@turbotool.com
http://www.adcchicago.org/
Review: Very active Chicago chapter with a new board of directors. Visit the parent organization web site at http://www.adc.org/

United Holy Land Fund
6000 W. 79th Street
Lower Level
Burbank, IL 60543
708-430-9731
Review: Proven charitable source with an excellent reputation for supporting programs and needy projects in the Arab Countries, especially in Palestine.

The Lifta Association for Charity
Lifta Association for Charity
P.O. Box 528247
Chicago, IL 60652
Mofeed Bages, President
773-418-1564
Club House Location:
6000 W. 79th Street
Burbank, IL
708-599-3300
Review: The Lifta Association is a charitable organization working for the benefit of its members and the Arab community at large. It organizes educational, social and cultural activities. Its center is at 6000 W. 79th St., Lower Level in Burbank, IL and is open most evenings. A weekly tutoring program offers children instruction in Arabic language. Picnics and family outings are arranged throughout the year. Guest speakers have included: Dr. Bassam Jody (president of Mosque Foundation); Dr. Abdul-Atheem Siddiq; Dr. Ahmad Al-Kofahi; Imams from all mosques in the Chicagoland area; Joyce Murphy (attorney); Khalil Shannak (board member of the Lifta Arab Organization of Amman, Jordan); Anna Mustafa (US census); Dr. Rashid Khalidi (U of Chicago). These have all been open to the public.

ALSAC St. Jude Children's Research Hospital Assn.
PO Box 2190 Dept. JES
Oak Park, IL 60603
708-358-0330
FAX: 708-383-3992
Review: Charitable social service organization that helps raise funds and supports St. Jude's Children Hospital. Primarily Leanese and Syrian American, but has many board members of Palestinian and Jordanian heritage on its board.

AA Assn. of Engineers & Architects
P.O. Box 2160
Bridgeview, IL 60455

708-802-1148
Dr. Ahmad Hammad, President
E-mail: aaaea@aaaea.org
webpage: http://www.aaaea.org/
Review: Influential professional organization for engineers and architects of Arab American heritage.

Jordanian Arab American Business Assn
Ihsan Sweiss
PO Box 671
Oak Lawn, IL 60453
708-599-1300
FAX: 708-599-2121
E-mail: vojnews@aol.com
Review: An affiliate of the Voice of Jordan Newspaper.

The Ramallah Club of Chicago
Sam Salamy, President
2700 N. Central Ave
Chicago IL 60639
FAX 773-237-0214
Review: Palestinians from the Town of Ramallah constitute nearly 50 percent of all the Palestinians who live in the Chicago area. This is also a chapter of one of the largest national grassroots social organizations in the country, the Ramallah Federation of Palestine.

Turmus Siya Palestine Club
1257 N. Milwaukee Ave, 3rd Floor
Chicago, Il., 60613
Review: Organization of Americans originating from the Palestinian village of Turmus Siya.

Chicago Islamic Cultural Center
3357 W. 63rd Street
Chicago IL 60629
773-436-8083
773-436-8785 fax

Fuheis American Association of Chicago
http://fuheisclub.org/
Samih Ayed Sweis, President
7905 S. Cicero Ave, Ste 206
Chicago, IL 60652
telephone # 773-284-0201
fax# 773-284-0210.

Arab American Educational Council
Frank Bustany
708-243-7523

Illinois Coalition for Immigration and Refugee Rights
Juliette Abu-Ayoun
http://www.icirr.org/
36 S. Wabash Ave, Suite 1425
Chicago IL 60603
312/332-7360
FAX: 312/332-7044
info@icirr.org

Committee for a Democratic Palestine
Younis Al-Jazaran
773-672-1290

Palestine American Community Center
AbdelGhafer Al-Arouri, President
708-233-6623
6000 W. 79th Street
Burbank, IL 60453
Review: This is the largest organization representing Christian and Muslim Palestinians in the Chicagoland area.

Beitunia American Club
Kayyad Hassan, President
708-923-6312
708-923-7301 FAX
Miriam Zayed, Board member
708-349-4828
Background: Beitunia is the sister city of Ramallah located in the West Bank, Palestine. Palestinians from Beitunia and Ramallah make up about 90 percent of the Palestinians in the Chicagoland area, split equally.

Advisory Commission on Arab Affairs
Chicago Commission on Human Relations
740 N. Sedgwick St, Suite 300
Chicago IL 60610
312-744-4115
312-744-1081
Background: Created in the 1980s, basically takes direction from Mayor Daley and Commissioner Wood on practices of discrimination. Has never filed one suit on any issue of bigotry and is somewhat controversial concerning its effectiveness.

Muslim Americans for Civil Rights and Legal Defense
Kausar Ahmad
last updated May 10, 2001
7667 W. 95th St, Suite 2 W
Hickory Hills, IL 60457
708-598-6640
info@muslimcivilrights.com
www.muslimcivilrights.com
Background: Active in defending Arab Americans and Muslims targeted by bigoted and discriminatory practices by the Justice Department and INS. Very large constituency, including in the Southwest Suburbs. Has sponsored several programs and conferences in the past.

RAWI
Radius of Arab American Writers, Inc.
Leila Diab, co-founder/writer
P.O.B. 2164
Bridgeview, IL 60455
ldiab@aol.com
A professional network of writers of Arab heritage - writers, poets, novelists, editors, screen writers, filmmakers, journalists, translators, researchers, calligraphers, book illustrators, children's book designers - Membership $25 annually for writers; $10 for students - entitles members to RAWI 's quarterly newsletter, a members' directory and other services.

Now available RAWI's first anthology, A Different Path, (Ridgeway Press) edited by DH Melhem and Leila Diab - $12 plus $2 for shipping and handling.

Aqsa School
7361 W. 92nd Place
Bridgeview, Illinois

Information: The Aqsa School for Girl's, First Islamic all girl's school in Chicagoland, celebrating our 15th Year (by the way, if you would help publicize Saturday, 28th of April , 2001, our annual dinner, Sponsorship donations $1000.00, tickets$125.00). A registered not for profit organization, Board of Trustees, Chairman Mr. Tawfik Nassar, Sec.-Treasurer Dr. Mahmoud Ismail, Executive Director Mr. Faysal Mohamed, oversees operation of Administration and Staff. Principal Ms. Judy Maher. Fully accredited by State of Illinois, Classes taught, girls, preschool thru 4th year High School, boys, preschool thru 4th grade Elementary School, an independent institution funded only by tuition's and donations.

Midwest Federation of Syrian & Lebanese Clubs
PO Box 6835
Villa Park, IL 60181-6835
Emil Haddad, coordinator
Jackie Haddad, Chairman
Web page: http://www.midwestfederation.org/

Information: The Midwest Federation of Syrian and Lebanese Clubs is one of the longest existing organizations of Arab Americans in the country with chapters in cities throughout the United States, including in Chicago.

Arab American Republican Federation
12231 W. Lady Bar Lane
Orland Park, IL 60462-1085
Shibli Sawalha, Ph.D.

Information: Shibli Sawalha has been a leader in Arab American political activism for more than 36 years in the Southwest Suburbs, actively involved in the Republican Party and serving as a Precinct Committeeman in the 14th Congressional District.

Islamic Community Center of Illinois
Updated May 1, 2001
4003 W. Montrose Ave
Chicago IL 60641
773-725-5020
773-725-4103
Information: Yousif Marei hosts through the ICCI the very popular Arab Community Radio Show every Sunday at 4 pm on WCEV (1450 AM) radio. They are building a new center to be opened soon at 6435 W. Belmont Ave., Chicago.

American Islamic College of Chicago
640 W. Irving Park Rd
Chicago IL 60613
773-281-4700

Dr. Assad Busool
Information: Center of Islamic study and academic teaching on the Islamic religion

American Friends Service Committee
637 S. Dearborn, 3rd Floor,
Chicago, IL 60605.
Tele: 312-427-2533.

Jennifer Bing-Canar, Middle East program Director

Arab American Medical Association
Lilly Hussein, MD, President
11025 Terrace Lane
Hillside, IL 60102
312-633-7117

Arab American Family Services
Itedal Shalabi
Nareman
5440 W 87th Street Burbank, IL 60459

Phone: (708) 229-2314
Fax: (708) 229-2601
Information: One of the premier social service organizations in Chicago..

United Muslim Americans Association (UMAA)
Sabri Samirah
10661 S. Roberts Rd, # 202
Palos Hills, IL 60465
708-974-4472
FAX: 708-974-3389
http://www.theumaa.org/

Information: One of the premier social service organizations in Chicago..

Arab Business & Professional Assn (ABPA)
Talat Othman, President
3432 Monitor Lane
Long Grove, IL 60047
Information: Chicagoland business and professional organization

Institute for International & Cultural Studies
North Park University
3225 W. Foster Ave
Chicago IL 60625
773-244-5592
FAX: 773-583-0858
Robert Hostetter
773-244-5666
Information: Very active and strong program of Middle East studies and activities.

Lebanese Club of Chicago
PO Box 235
Gurnee, IL 60031
847-549-9417
www.leb.net/clc
M.htmaha Noujeme, President
Mark Bendok, VP
Doug Haddad, PR
Elie Dabdab, Treasurer
Nohra Masr, Secretary
Information: One of the leading Lebanese American organizations in the Midwest.

OHIO REGION

Greater Toledo Assn. of Arab Americans
2909 W. Central Ave
Toledo, Ohio 43606

Arab Americans of Central Ohio
PO Box 307112
Columbus, Ohio 43230-7112
614-470-2784
aaco@egroups.com

MASSACHUSETTS REGION

Institute of Near Eastern & African Studies (INEAS)

An independent, non-profit, tax-exempt organization with the mission to educate the public and inform the media on issues related to the Arab & Islamic worlds, Africa and the non-Arab Middle Eastern communities.
P.O. Box 425709
Cambridge, MA 02142 USA
Tel: (617) 86-INEAS (864-6327)
Fax: (617) 323-5950
Web site: http://www.ineas.org/

ARAB LOBBY GROUPS

The Arab lobby consists of those groups and individuals that directly and indirectly seek to influence American policy to support Arab interests both in the U.S. and abroad. While focusing on Arab concerns, by no means is this lobby composed exclusively of Arabs. The lobby is defined by its ideology, not the ethnicity of its active constituents. That ideology tends to be pro-Arab on the one hand, and anti-Israel on the other. The Arab lobby in America generally seeks to promote its agendas by characterizing them as beneficial to U.S. national interests; conversely, it depicts pro-Israel policies as harmful to those interests.

The roots of the Arab lobby in America can be traced back to 1951, when King Saud of Saudi Arabia asked U.S. diplomats to finance a pro-Arab lobby to serve as a counterweight to the American Zionist Committee for Public Affairs (later renamed the American Israel Public Affairs Committee, or AIPAC).

While the pace of the Arab lobby's growth was initially slow, there were nonetheless signs of increased assertiveness. After the 1967 Arab-Israeli war, for example, the Arabian American Oil Company (ARAMCO) set up a fund to present the Arab perspective on the conflict. In May 1970, ARAMCO representatives warned Assistant Secretary of State Joseph Sisco that American military sales to Israel would harm U.S.-Arab relations and jeopardize American oil supplies.

Driven by oil revenues, the Arab lobby's leverage in affecting American policy was demonstrated in early 1973 when Mobil published a pro-Arab advertorial in *The New York Times*. In July of that year, the chairman of Standard Oil of California (now called Chevron) distributed a letter asking the company's 40,000 employees and 262,000 stockholders to pressure their elected representatives to support "the aspirations of the Arab people." In a similar spirit, the chairman of Texaco urged the U.S. to reassess its Middle East policy.

When another Arab-Israeli war broke out in October 1973, the chairmen of the ARAMCO partners issued a memorandum warning the White House against increasing its military aid to Israel. Shortly thereafter, the OPEC oil embargo (enacted in retribution for Western support of Israel) ushered in an era where the Arab lobby became much more prominent and visible than ever before. "The day of the Arab-American is here," declared National Association of Arab Americans founder Richard Shadyac. "The reason is oil." Prior to October 1973 the price of oil had stood at $2.60 per barrel; within three months the price quadrupled to about $12 per barrel. Since then, it has risen to more than $60 -- for a commodity whose production costs are, at present, only $1.50 per barrel.

In 1977 President Jimmy Carter noted, in his diary, that the Arab lobby had pressured him mightily while he was involved in the peace negotiations between Egyptian President Anwar Sadat and Israeli Prime Minister Menachem Begin. "They [Arab Americans] have given all the staff, Brzezinski, Warren Christopher, and others, a hard time," wrote Carter.

Among the more notable individual members of the Arab lobby in recent decades was the late Clark Clifford (died October 1998), who *The New York Times* described as a key adviser to four U.S. presidents, and as an influential paid lobbyist for Arab sources. In his memoir, *Counsel to the President*, Clifford wrote that he advised his clients: "What we can offer you is an extensive knowledge of how to deal with the government on your problems. We will be able to give you advice on how best to present your position to the appropriate departments and agencies of the government."

Another key figure in the Arab lobby has been Fred Dutton, former Assistant Secretary for Legislative Affairs and special assistant to President John F. Kennedy. On July 19, 2005, *The Hill*, a newspaper about the U.S. Congress, reported that Dutton (a lobbyist for Saudi Arabia) had worked assiduously to persuade Congress to approve two major arms sales to that nation.

Axis Information and Analysis (AIA), which specializes in information about Asia and Eastern Europe, rated Prince Bandar Bin Sultan -- a Saudi ambassador to the U.S. from 1983 to 2005 -- as the single most influential foreigner in America. With links to high-ranking officials in the State Department, Pentagon, and CIA, Sultan was a key participant in many clandestine negotiations pertaining to U.S. interests in the Middle East. According to AIA, in 1990-91 it was Sultan who pushed President George H.W. Bush to launch the military campaign to drive Iraqi forces out of Kuwait. Moreover, his father -- Sultan Bin Abdul Aziz al Saud -- was a leading figure in the ruling Saudi dynasty. As such, he helped determine the extent of his nation's military cooperation with the U.S. in the Persian Gulf.

During a January 1998 U.S. Congressional Delegation briefing in Damascus, Syria, Congressman Nick J. Rahall (D - West Virginia), who is of Lebanese descent, said: "Our [Arab] lobby in the United States is growing in its influence and its participation in political campaigns across the spectrum. Our trip [was] sponsored by the Arab American Institute -- one of those most effective lobbying groups of the Arab groups in Washington -- and a relatively new group, the National Arab American Businessmen's Association. [Through] these groups ... we are increasing our influence, and we are increasing our participation."

Some members of the Arab lobby in America are heavily financed with money from the Arab world. Before his death in 2005, for instance, Saudi Arabia's King Fahd made several large donations to the Center, including a 1993 gift of $7.6 million. As of 2005, the king's nephew, Prince Alwaleed Bin Talal, had given at least $5 million to the Carter Center. In 2001 the United Arab Emirates (UAE) gave the Center $500,000. The previous year, ten of Osama bin Laden's brothers had jointly pledged $1 million, as did Sultan Qaboos bin Said of Oman in 1998. The Saudi Fund for Development has been another major contributor, as has the Kuwait Fund for Arab Economic Development. And Morocco's Prince Moulay Hicham Ben Abdallah has collaborated with the Carter Center on various initiatives.

It should be noted that the Arab lobby does not, by any means, speak for all Arab Americans. According to the Arab American Institute, there are approximately 3.5 million people of Arab heritage in the U.S. today, about half of them concentrated in five states -- California, Florida, Michigan, New Jersey, and New York. Nearly 40 percent of these Arab Americans are Lebanese, mostly Christians, who tend to be unsympathetic to the Arab lobby's anti-Israel perspectives. By contrast, only about 70,000Palestinian Americans reside in the United States -- a small percentage of the Arab American population. But because of their high level of political activism, their views and concerns have received hugely disproportionate attention from political leaders and the media alike. Indeed, the Palestinian cause heads the Arab lobby's list of concerns.

Because Arab Americans do not constitute a numerically large voting bloc, the Arab lobby has focused considerable effort on cultivating sympathies among the general public as a means of influencing U.S. policy. To further maximize its influence, the Arab lobby has also formed alliances with many anti-war, civil rights, civil liberties, and social justice organizations of the political left. The aforementioned Carter Center is but one of these.

For the reader interested in learning about the Arab lobby, a couple of definitions are in order. A lobby, strictly defined, is a group of persons -- be they volunteers or paid professionals -- engaged in an effort to persuade public officials to pass laws or implement programs that promote the lobbyists' goals. Lobbyists pursue their objectives in different ways: some (direct lobbyists) privately cajole legislators via telephone calls or face-to-face visits; others (grassroots lobbyists) urge the general public to contact their legislators; still others organize or participate in public actions such as mass demonstrations; and some employ a combination of all these approaches. In cases where a particular issue is to be decided through a ballot initiative or referendum, appeals to the public are technically classified as direct lobbying, because in those instances the public acts as the legislature.

Lobbyists are not necessarily members of groups or organized campaigns; they can also be independent individuals who feel strongly about the passage or the defeat of certain pieces of proposed legislation. Some are on the payroll of foreign governments.

There is technically a distinction between advocacy and lobbying. The former aims to influence some aspect of society, be it individual behavior (e.g., campaigns to discourage smoking or to encourage vegetarianism), employment policy (e.g., affirmative action in hirings and promotions), or legislation passed by elected government officials. Lobbying refers specifically to those advocacy efforts that attempt to convince legislators and public policy-makers to vote in a certain way.

This section of Discover The Networks profiles not only those pro-Arab organizations (both in the U.S. and abroad) that lobby to affect specific legislation, but also groups that engage in what might be defined, more precisely, as *advocacy* on behalf of Arab interests anywhere in the world. Through their press releases, official statements, publications, and direct actions, these organizations seek to shape public opinion as a means of influencing voter decisions and thereby indirectly affecting legislation passed by elected representatives.

According to terrorism expert Steven Emerson, "Assessing the influence and breadth of the Arab/Muslim lobby would be a difficult thing to do, since the metrics for assessing such things are not easily available. The lobby's real strength is felt on the local level, where its members receive community awards, participate in human relations councils, change the local educational curricula, persuade school districts to give them holidays off, and get local police and statewide officials to attend their events. Nationally, their influence is felt at the State Department in terms of their being invited to briefings, sponsored on road trips abroad, etc. The one recent time where they actually exacted an influence on President Bush was in persuading him to drop the use of the term 'Islamo-fascism.'"

While the Arab lobby has a few friends in Congress today, its effect is felt mainly as a result of its joint efforts with organizations like the American Civil Liberties Union to dilute anti-terror measures. The lobby, says Emerson, "is mainly in the process of building up a grassroots network around the United States, with the anticipation that, abetted by growing demographics, it will be in a position of political influence in the future."

ABOLITION 2000

c/o Polaris Institute
180 Metcalfe Street
Suite 500
Ottawa, ON K2P 1P5
Phone :613-237-1717
Email :
sstaples@polarisinstitute.org
URL: http://www.abolition2000.org/Nuclear disarmament lobbying group that excuses nuclear buildup by rogue countries while condemning the United States

"Even if Iraq is found to possess WMDs or their components, the U.S. approach is wrong."
Opposes sanctions against North Korea, but is willing to boycott U.S.

This organization was established in April 1995 by Alice Slater, President of the anti-nuclear group Global Resource Action Center for the Environment, with the grand aim of eliminating all nuclear weapons from the earth by the turn of the century. Abolition 2000 claims a membership of more than 2,000 supportive nongovernmental organizations (NGOs) in 95 countries.

Even as Abolition 2000 holds fast to the unequivocal goals set forth in its founding declaration -- "Our common security requires the complete elimination of nuclear weapons" -- the group has routinely settled for less ambitious initiatives like the "Mayors for Peace Emergency Campaign to Ban Nuclear Weapons" program. Working alongside other disarmament groups such as the Nuclear Age Peace Foundation, Abolition 2000 exhorted mayors from around the world to support negotiations for comprehensive nuclear disarmament by the year 2005. Although the "Mayors for Peace" initiative was intended as a first step toward the blanket elimination of nuclear arms, Abolition 2000 has now settled on what it deems a more pragmatic timetable: the year 2020.

In the short term, the group aims to mobilize anti-nuclear demonstrations, like its May 2005 rally in New York City, to gain the public's notice. Timed to correspond with the United Nations' review of the Non-Proliferation Treaty, the May 2005 event was meant to draw attention to Article 6 of the Treaty, which calls on nuclear weapons states to pursue good-faith negotiations designed to lead to eventual nuclear disarmament.

Perhaps impelled by its evident lack of success in securing the instant elimination of nuclear weapons, in recent years Abolition 2000 has diversified its interests, adopting resolutions endorsing other leftwing causes. In 1997, for example, it adopted the Moore Declaration, a signally vague statement of solidarity with "colonized and indigenous peoples." While unclear as to which particular peoples were the objects of its sympathy, Abolition 2000 stressed that they were, in any case, the victims of "environmental degradation and human suffering that is the legacy of fifty-two years of nuclear weapons usage, testing, and production." In a similar vein was the Saffron Walden Declaration. Adopted by Abolition 2000 in the year 2001, it detailed the obstacles to the organization's vision of a nuclear-free world. Chief among those obstacles was the United Sates, whose "drive to weaponize and nuclearize space," and whose "immoral and illegal quest for global domination," was allegedly placing an "increasing burden on the world's resources."
Equally hostile was Abolition 2000's assessment of modern Western nations. In a broad indictment of globalization, the Saffron Walden declaration stated, "The Western nuclear weapons states and their allies believe they can put a 'lid' on the rising tide of discontent at the economic inequity and lack of social justice

among the vast majority of the earth's people in order to maintain their access to world resources and their unsustainable levels of consumption."
Despite its professed opposition to all nuclear weapons, Abolition 2000 has frequently employed a double standard, condemning the possession of such weapons by Western nations while pointedly ignoring their possession by non-Western countries, including some of the most unstable rogue states in the world. The case of North Korea is instructive. When, in August 2003, international leaders pressed the Pyongyang government to disclose information about, and halt the buildup of, its nuclear arsenal, Abolition 2000, rather than applauding these efforts to disarm a militaristic regime with nuclear ambitions, condemned them.

After rejecting any "attempts to use force, sanctions, threats of sanctions, regime change, or talk of such measures" in dealing with North Korea, Abolition 2000 heatedly insisted in a letter that the attention of the international community was misdirected: "It must also be borne in mind that whatever the size and capabilities of the DPRK [Democratic People's Republic of Korea]nuclear arsenal, it in no way remotely compares with the 8,000 to 12,000 warheads of the U.S. arsenal, the approximately 22,000 warheads of the Russian arsenal, the roughly 400 warheads held by China and France, the 200-400 held by Israel, the 150-200 held by the UK, nor even with the arsenals held by India and Pakistan."

The real threat in the region, Abolition 2000 explained, came not from North Korea's communist regime but from the United States: "The DPRK has, from at least 1956, faced the threat of U.S. nuclear weapons, and up to 100 tactical nuclear warheads were stationed south of the DMZ until at least 1991." Condoning the North Korean regime's right to bear nuclear arms, Abolition 2000 stated, "The desire of the DPRK to defend itself may be understandable."
Parallel reasoning informed Abolition 2000's opposition to the U.S.-led war against Iraq's Baathist regime, which was widely believed to be in possession of an illicit nuclear weapons program. Omitting any mention of Saddam Hussein's past campaigns of mass murder, Abolition 2000 focused instead on the possibility of *American*-perpetrated atrocities. During the buildup to the 2003 war in Iraq, Abolition 2000 stated, "We are gravely concerned that conflict in the region might spiral out of control and that the U.S. would again use nuclear weapons." Unlike many critics of the war, Abolition 2000 also claimed that even the presence of Iraq's WMDs could not justify military intervention. "Even if Iraq is found to possess WMDs or their components, the U.S. approach is wrong," Abolition 2000 insisted, contending that "though nuclear weapons represent the ultimate form of violence, they cannot and should not be eliminated through the use of force." Abolition 2000 further insisted that Iraq, like North Korea, was the wrong target in the War on Terror: "While we condemn Iraq's record of human rights violations, the U.S. policy towards Iraq is selective and hypocritical. The U.S. continues to support Israel, which has nuclear weapons as well as a long record of noncompliance with U.N. Security Council resolutions, and which has occupied Palestine for decades."

In September of 2004, Abolition 2000 concentrated its energies on a project called "Boycott Bush," a grassroots organizing effort seeking to show that "the U.S. operates outside international law." And, notwithstanding its prior refusal to countenance talk of such measures, the organization expressed a willingness to support a boycott of U.S. products.
Abolition 2000 was a signatory to a petition of so-called "civil society" organizations that opposed globalization, big business in general, and "any effort to expand the powers of the World Trade Organization (WTO) through a new comprehensive round of trade liberalization." Members affiliated with some of the signers actively participated in the November 1999 riots in which some 50,000 protesters did millions of dollars worth of property damage in their effort to shut down the WTO Conference in Seattle. In fact, Medea Benjamin -- the leader of Global Exchange, which was another signatory to the petition -- is widely credited as having been a chief organizing force behind the riots.

A founding member of Abolition 2000 is the well known anti-war activist David Krieger, who also co-founded the Nuclear Age Peace Foundation and serves as the deputy chairman of the International Network of Engineers and Scientists for Global Responsibility.

Abolition 2000 is a member organization of the United for Peace and Justice anti-war coalition, which is led by Leslie Cagan, the longtime communist who proudly aligns her politics with those of Fidel Castro.

Funding for Abolition 2000 has been provided by the Seventh Generation Fund, the EarthWays Foundation, and the Lifebridge Foundation.

AL-AWDA (AKA PALESTINE RIGHT TO RETURN COALITION)

P.O. Box 131352
Carlsbad, CA
92013

Phone :760-685-3243
Email :
info@al-awda.org

Calls for the Palestinian "Right of Return"

Seeks the dissolution of Israel
Has quoted the Hamas slogan, "Palestine will be free from the river to the sea"

Co-founded by Mazin Qumsiyeh, Zahi Damuni, and Jess Ghannam, Al-Awda (a.k.a. the Palestine Right to Return Coalition) describes itself as "a broad-based, non-partisan, democratic, and charitable organization of grassroots activists and students committed to comprehensive public education on the rights of all Palestinian refugees to return to their homes and lands of origin, and to be granted full restitution of all their confiscated and destroyed property in accordance with the Universal Declaration of Human Rights." Viewing Israel as an illegitimate entity with no right to exist as a sovereign nation, Al-Awda condemns what it calls the "Zionist[s'] insatiable need for colonial expansion and the systematic destruction of the indigenous Arab population." "For almost sixty years," Al-Awda adds, "the genocidal Israeli government has been murdering, exiling and maiming innocent Palestinians who wished simply to be left to live on their land with dignity and peace."

The refugees on whose behalf Al-Awda agitates were never expelled from their homeland; they voluntarily (for the most part) left their homes during the period just before and shortly after the commencement of the 1948 Arab-Israeli war. They sought out safe haven during what they anticipated would be a brief war that the Arab allies would undoubtedly win, and fully expected to return to their homes once the fighting had stopped and the Jews had been exterminated. Instead, the Arab armies were defeated. Today Al-Awda calls for the readmittance not only of the relatively few survivors who were among the 725,000 original refugees, but also for the admittance of more than 7.2 million of their descendants.

Al-Awda lists the following "Points of Unity" as the key axioms upon which its mission is founded:

(a) "[T]he Palestinian Arab people, regardless of their religious affiliation, are indigenous to Palestine. Therefore, they are entitled to live anywhere in Palestine which encompasses present-day 'Israel,' the West Bank and Gaza Strip. Al-Awda regards the 'Israeli' definition of Jewish nationals, granting exclusive rights to citizenship and land to any Jew from anywhere in the world, as part of the racism and discrimination inherent in Zionist ideology which underlies the policies and laws of the settler state of 'Israel.'"

(b) "Al-Awda unequivocally supports the rights of all Palestinian refugees to return to their original towns, villages and lands anywhere in Palestine from which they were expelled. Al-Awda also unequivocally supports the rights of all Palestinian refugees to compensation for damages inflicted on their property and lives, and to restitution of all destroyed and confiscated property."

(c) "Al-Awda will work to educate the public about 'Israeli' injustices the U.S. government subsidizes with billions of dollars annually. Until the dismantlement of the exclusionary and racist character of 'Israel,' and until all Palestinians are granted the right to return and achieve equality, Al-Awda is united in working for and demanding: an end to all U.S. political, military and economic aid to 'Israel'; the divestment of all public and private entities from all 'Israeli' corporations and American corporations with subsidiaries operating within 'Israel'; an end to the investment of Labor Union members' pension funds in 'Israel'; the boycott of all 'Israeli' products; ... [and] the formation of an independent, democratic state for all its citizens in all of Palestine."

With thousands of members worldwide, Al-Awda has 17 local and regional chapters (in nine U.S. cities, two American universities, two Canadian cities, Italy, Spain, Egypt, and the United Kingdom). These chapters regularly sponsor anti-Israel exhibits, film festivals, lectures, and protests. In September and October of 2002, Al-Awda held anti-Israel rallies where its members sold t-shirts donning the famous Hamas quote, "Palestine will be free from the river to the sea."

A member organization of the United for Peace and Justice anti-war coalition, Al-Awda lists New Jersey Solidarity as one of its "Coalition Committee Members" and the Palestine Children's Relief Fund as a "partner organization."

On July 14-16, 2006, Al-Awda and the General Union of Palestine Students at San Francisco State University co-sponsored the Fourth International Al-Awda Convention, which highlighted two main themes: (a) "Political and material isolation of the Genocidal Zionist State of Israel"; and (b) "Political and material support of the Palestinian refugee population." A featured speaker at the event was Michel Shehadeh, the host of "Radio Intifada," a KPFK-FM Los Angeles radio program named in honor of the Palestinian terrorist campaign seeking to destroy the State of Israel.

AL-MAGHRIB INSTITUTE

318 John R Road
Suite 346
Troy, MI
48083

Phone :1-888-256-2447
Email :
info@almaghrib.org
URL: http://www.almaghrib.org/

College-level religious education program through which students can obtain a bachelor's degree in Islamic Studies

Course curriculum is characterized by extremism, anti-Semitism, Holocaust denial, and the preaching of militaristic *jihad*

All six of Al-Maghrib's instructors hold degrees from Saudi institutions controlled by Wahhabi extremism

The Michigan-based Al-Maghrib Institute is a college-level religious education program whose mission is to help its students "gain a deeper understanding of Islam"; to "build sincere, dedicated and brilliant students ... who will go on to become leaders, bringing their communities to new heights"; and to "make people better Muslims and bring people closer to Allah." The Institute seeks to achieve these objectives by offering "trademark double-weekend [six-day] university-style seminars carrying students toward a bachelor's degree in the Islamic Studies."

Al-Maghrib's classes are given at mosques in at least thirteen North American cities: College Park, Maryland; Fairfax, Virginia; Houston, Texas; New Brunswick, New Jersey; San Francisco Bay area, California; Seattle, Washington; Memphis, Tennessee; Sacramento, California; Detroit, Michigan; Chicago, Illinois; Ottawa, Canada; Montreal, Canada; and Toronto, Canada. Al-Maghrib also ran onsite seminars in Columbus, Ohio during 2006.

Characterized by Wahhabi-influenced extremism, rabid anti-Semitism, Holocaust denials, and the preaching of militaristic *jihad*, Al-Maghrib's courses are accredited by American Open University (AOU), which in turn is accredited by Al-Azhar University in Cairo -- the headquarters of the Muslim Brotherhood, the oldest and largest radical Islamic organization in the world.

A review of the course summary for Al-Maghrib's Islamic Studies degree program shows that the required reading list is dominated by the works of Muslim Brotherhood and Wahhabi theologians and theorists. In particular, the program requires students to read Sayyid Qutb's *In the Shade of the Quran.* Qutb, the Muslim Brotherhood thinker who was executed by Egyptian President Gamal Abdel Nasser in the 1960s, was influential in justifying terrorism and *jihad*, and in laying down the theoretical principles upon which al Qaeda was built.

Another Muslim Brotherhood theorist prominent in the Al-Maghrib curriculum is Sayyid Sabiq, who wrote his book *Fiqh-us-Sunnah* at the request of Muslim Brotherhood founder Hasan al-Banna. The two volumes of Sabiq's work are the only texts for Al-Maghrib's "Fiqh of Worship" course.

The Al-Maghrib reading list also features the works of Bilal Phillips, who in January 2007 gained notoriety as one of the radical preachers secretly videotaped for the *Undercover Mosque investigative program* aired on Britain's Channel Four. In that program, Phillips was shown lecturing in favor of forced Islamic marriages for prepubescent girls.

The justification of *jihad* and a call for Islamic dominance are promoted in the Al-Maghrib course titled "Islam Invulnerable: The Making of the Modern Muslim World." Tracing the rise of Islam as a global force from the initial Islamic invasions and occupations of the Near East, North Africa and the Iberian Peninsula, this class glories in the triumphs of the Ottoman, Safavid, Qajar and Mughal Empires. The Crusades are denounced, as are European "imperialist" and "colonialist" efforts in recent centuries, while Islamic conquests undergo "narrative reinterpretation" to explain how they differ from Western exploits. Moreover, the present-day Arab-Israeli conflict is blamed entirely on the "Zionists."

Other Al-Maghrib's courses rely on commentaries by 13th Century theologian Ibn Taymiyyah and Wahhabi sect founder Muhammad ibn Abd-al-Wahhab.

All six of Al-Maghrib's instructors hold degrees from Saudi institutions controlled by Wahhabi extremism:

> Muhammad Alshareef, the founder of Al-Maghrib Institute and a Canadian citizen, graduated from the Islamic University of Medina in 1999 with a degree in *Shari'a* (Islamic Law). The University of Medina was founded in 1961 by the ruling Saud family specifically for the propagation of Wahhabism worldwide. In an article titled "Why the Jews are Cursed," Alshareef charged that the international media are owned and controlled by Jews, and thus are biased against Muslims; that Jews were guilty of making blasphemous statements and murdering the Prophets; and that Muslims should never marry, befriend, or imitate Jews or Christians under any circumstances. Alshareef's father was an associate of Ahmed Said Khadr, a leading al Qaeda financier, the top al Qaeda agent in Canada, and a close personal associate of Osama bin Laden.
>
> Yaser Birjas, a Palestinian, graduated from the Islamic University of Medina as the 1996 class valedictorian. According to an announcement issued by the Al-Maghrib Institute, Birjas was arrested and detained by U.S. authorities in 2005 due to problems with his immigration visa.
>
> AbdulBary Yahya obtained his degree from the Islamic University of Medina. In March 2006 it was reported that Yahya was scheduled to speak at an event (sponsored by the University of Central Florida's Muslim Student Association) with Ibrahim Dremali, a Florida-based *Imam* who advocates suicide bombings. Yahya and Dremali had previously shared a podium at the 2005 Texas Dawah Convention, which also featured Siraj Wahhaj, an unindicted co-conspirator in the 1993 World Trade Center bombing.
>
> Yasir Qadhi, who graduated from the Islamic University of Medina, draws from the anti-Semitic fogery, *Protocols of the Elders of Zion*, to explain that Jews are not racially Semitic and therefore have no right to make a claim on the Holy Land. A Holocaust denier, Qadhi has stated: "Hitler never intended to mass-destroy the Jews." In August 2006 Qadhi revealed that he was on the U.S. Department of Homeland Security's terrorist watch list.
>
> Mohammed Faqih obtained his bachelor's degree from the Institute of Islamic and Arabic Sciences in Fairfax, Virginia, and then earned a degree in Koran Recitation and Memorization from the King Abdulaziz University in Jeddah, Saudi Arabia. This latter school was Osama bin Laden's alma mater and a haven for Muslim Brotherhood teachers who fled persecution from President Nasser's regime in Egypt during the 1950s and 1960s. Sayyid Qutb's brother, Mohammed, was a longtime instructor in the Jeddah university and was one of bin Laden's primary mentors.
>
> Waleed Basyouni attended the Al-Imam Muhammad ibn Saud Islamic University in the Saudi capital of Riyadh, where he studied under the Wahhabite ideologist Sheikh Abdelaziz bin Baz and obtained both a bachelor's degree and a master's degree.

Apart from their teaching duties, Al-Maghrib instructors appear regularly on a number of Islamic satellite television networks, and are in high demand as motivational speakers at Muslim organization events all over the world. The Institute is also active amongst the 150-plus campus chapters of the Muslim Students' Association of the U.S. and Canada, located at universities all over North America.

In addition to the courses it offers, the Institute sponsors the EmanRush Audio website, which sells Al-Maghrib audio and video course lectures, and the Khutbah.com website, which provides the texts of sermons and articles delivered by Al-Maghrib instructors and staff.

This profile is adapted from the article "Jihad U," written by Patrick Poole and published by ***FrontPageMagazine.com*** *on February 14, 2007.*

AMERICAN MUSLIM ALLIANCE (AMA)

39675 Cedar Blvd.
Suite 220 E
Newark, CA
94560

Phone :510-252-9858
Email :
civilrightsforall@sbcglobal.net
URL: http://www.amaweb.org/

- Works to get Muslims elected or appointed to policy-influencing positions at all levels of American government
- Opposes the Patriot Act
- Works with pro-Hamas and -Hezbollah groups

Founded in 1994, the American Muslim Alliance (AMA) is a political action committee that works to get Muslims elected and/or appointed to policy-influencing positions at all levels of political governance in the United States, from local city councils, to county and state representative governments, all the way to Washington, D.C. This organization currently has 101 chapters in 31 states, and aspires eventually to have chapters in all 435 U.S. congressional districts. One month after the 9/11 terrorist attacks, a delegate at the AMA convention in San Jose stated, "By the year 2020, we should have an American Muslim President of the United States."

To achieve these goals, AMA provides political education and leadership training for aspiring legislators; conducts campaign and issue research and analysis; maintains a comprehensive database of American Muslim candidates; develops political strategies and articulates policy positions; conducts voter-registration, -education, and -mobilization drives; organizes member participation at the national and state conventions of the Democratic and Republican Parties; establishes political clubs across the United States; and sponsors numerous workshops, seminars, and conferences.

AMA is an active member of the American Muslim Political Coordinating Council. It also is affiliated with Muslim groups -- such as the Council on American-Islamic Relations (CAIR) and the Muslim Public Affairs Council -- whose members have publicly supported Hamas and Hezbollah, or have been linked to the funding of terrorist activities. In 1998 AMA, along with CAIR and the American Muslim Council, sponsored a rally at Brooklyn College in New York City, where militant speakers advocated *jihad* and characterized Jews as "pigs and monkeys."

With regard to the Israeli-Palestinian conflict, AMA states, "As long as the Israeli government and Israeli settlers continue to kill Palestinian men, women, and children, we will continue to condemn their atrocities and to expose the hideous nature of this neo-colonial occupation."

In 2004, AMA was a signatory to a letter urging members of the U.S. Senate to vote against supporting Israel's construction of an anti-terrorist security fence in the West Bank, a barrier that the letter described as an illegal "apartheid wall" that violated the civil and human rights of Palestinians. In the United States,

AMA has taken a stand against the Patriot Act, characterizing it as an assault on civil liberties.

AMA chose not to endorse or participate in the May 14, 2005 "Free Muslims March Against Terror," an event whose stated purpose was to "send a message to the terrorists and extremists that their days are numbered . . . [and to send] a message to the people of the Middle East, the Muslim world and all people who seek freedom, democracy and peaceful coexistence that we support them."

AMA's National Chair is Dr. Agha Saeed, a professor of political science and speech at California State University.

AMERICAN MUSLIM ASSOCIATION OF NORTH AMERICA (AMANA)

183 North East 166 Street
Miami, FL
33162
Phone :305-945-0414
Email :
info@al-amana.org
URL: **American** Islamic Relations (CAIR) and the Islamic Society of **North America ...**
www.al-**amana**.org

Website contains numerous hate- and terror-related links
Supports Hamas

The American Muslim Association of North America (AMANA) is a self-described "civil rights" organization based in Miami, with separate offices in Pennsylvania, Georgia, and Puerto Rico. AMANA offers help to Muslims needing guidance in applying for food stamps, welfare, Medicaid, Social Security, and Medicare. It also provides tax and accounting services; immigration-related legal services; job-hunting assistance; free copies of the Koran, Islamic books, and Islamic audio and videotapes; marriage ceremonies and certificates for Muslims; and counseling for victims of domestic violence and child abuse. Moreover, AMANA plans to establish Islamic day care centers "to help the low income families looking for a job, and help the single parent not to worry about her children while working."

The slogan on the AMANA website reads, "Islam Honors Human & Civil Rights! We Honor them too!" That same website, however, once featured a link to the Al-Haramain Islamic Foundation, a Saudi charity that had its offices closed down all over the globe due to its fundraising activities for al Qaeda. In March 2004, AMANA condemned the assassination of the founder of the terrorist group Hamas, Sheikh Ahmed Yassin, calling him a "renowned Islamic scholar."

The Director of AMANA, Sofian Abdelaziz-Zakkout, is the former Vice President of the Health Resource Center for Palestine, a now-defunct charity which was linked to the Hamas front group Islamic Association for Palestine, and which openly admitted to having raised funds for *shuhada* (i.e., suicide bombers).

AMANA chose not to endorse or participate in the May 14, 2005 "Free Muslims March Against Terror," an event whose stated purpose was to "send a message to the terrorists and extremists that their days are numbered . . . [and to send] a message to the people of the Middle East, the Muslim world and all people who seek freedom, democracy and peaceful coexistence that we support them."

AMANA views the United States as a nation rife with bigotry and injustice aimed at Muslims. Thus the organization's website features a complaint form where people can report instances of perceived discrimination they encounter in the housing market, the business world, or elsewhere.

To disseminate its message and publicize its activities, AMANA publishes *The AMANA Voice* magazine, as well as numerous booklets and pamphlets.

In March 2007, AMANA posted on its website an article titled "To Muslims – Stop Apologizing." The piece read, in part:

"Stop apologizing for Al Qaeda. You didn't create them, the Central Intelligence Agency did. Stop apologizing for every act of violence perpetrated by Muslims -- unless you demand that every Christian and Jew apologize for the murderous acts of their co-religionists, too. ... Yes, the 9/11 terror attacks were a truly grotesque act of mass murder, leading to the deaths of 3,000 innocent men, women, and children. But their lives and their innocence was not greater than the hundreds of thousands of innocent Iraqi lives lost as a result of Western and Zionist aggression. How many 9/11s have been unleashed against the Iraqi people in the last four years alone, to say nothing of the countless victims generated as a direct result of US-led economic sanctions during the 8 years prior to the invasion?

"... When someone asks you to condemn Islamic violence, demand they first condemn Christian and Jewish violence and apologize for the disproportionate amount of death and destruction they have visited upon the world. ... When you are reminded of how Muslim financial support for terrorist organizations has led to thousands of deaths around the world, don't forget to remind them how Zionist Jewish bankers in New York, Germany, and England funneled millions of dollars to the Bolsheviks, who killed an estimated 20 million Russian Orthodox Christians between 1917 and 1945. You may also wish to remind them that $5 billion a year from the US has been funding Israel's 40-year occupation of the West Bank and Jerusalem, its construction of segregated Jewish supremacist settlements, and its continued violation of dozens of UN resolutions, to say nothing of its history of violence against innocent Arab civilians."

AMERICAN MUSLIM COUNCIL (AMC)

1005 W. Webster
Suite 3
Chicago, Ill
60614
Phone :773-248-3390
Email :
info@amcnational.org
URL: http://www.amcnational.org/new/index.asp

Former Chairman was Abdulrahman Alamoudi, who was imprisoned for terror-related convictions in 2003

Supports Hamas, Islamic Jihad and Hezbollah

Defended terror suspect and Palestinian Islamic Jihad operative Sami Al-Arian

Established in 1990 as a charity designed to protect the political and civil rights of Muslims in the United States, the American Muslim Council (AMC) developed into one of the most prominent Islamic organizations of recent times. Its importance has declined, however, since its founder and former Chairman Abdurahman Alamoudi was imprisoned in October 2003 on terrorism-related charges. Alamoudi was a supporter of Hamas, Hezbollah, Islamic Association for Palestine (IAP) founder Musa Abu Marzook, and Islamic Group leader Omar Abdel Rahman, mastermind of the 1993 World Trade Center bombing. Alamoudi also conducted business with Libya's "World Islamic Call Society," a sponsor of terrorism.

AMC's ties to Islamic terror are not limited to Alamoudi. In December 2000, the organization's Dallas chapter presented an award to IAP official Ghassan Dahduli, who would be deported eleven months later because of his connections to al Qaeda and Hamas.

In January 2002, AMC's then-Executive Director Eric Vickers publicly defended University of South Florida professor Sami Al-Arian, whose involvement with the terrorist group Palestinian Islamic Jihad had recently been uncovered. In June 2002, Vickers was asked on Fox News and MSNBC to denounce Hamas, Hezbollah, Islamic Jihad, and al Qaeda by name. He refused, asserting instead that al Qaeda was "involved in a resistance movement" against outside aggressors. Vickers has since been replaced as AMC Executive Director by M. Ali Khan. The organization's current President is Raied N. Abdullah, and its Vice President is Nedzib Sacrebey.

In March 2002, federal authorities raided the Virginia house and business of AMC Board member Jamal Barzinji in an anti-terrorism investigation. Moreover, according to a U.S. prosecutor, AMC Advisory Board member Soliman Biheiri served as "the Muslim Brotherhood's financial toehold" in the United States.

In November 2002, AMC publicly urged American Muslims to give money to Islamic relief organizations to aid refugees who had fled their homes in response to America's post-9/11 invasion of Afghanistan. Included in AMC's list of recommended charities was the Holy Land Foundation for Relief and Development (HLF), whose assets had recently been seized by the FBI and the Treasury Department because of its activities as a fundraising front for Hamas. AMC, which lauded HLF for its "strong global vision," called Bush's action against the charity "particularly disturbing ... unjust and counterproductive." AMC also exhorted Muslims to send money to the Global Relief Foundation, another charity that was shut down by the U.S. government for having "provided assistance to Usama Bin Ladin, the al Qaeda Network, and other known terrorist groups."

In February 2003, AMC formed a coalition with the Council on American-Islamic Relations, the American Muslim Alliance, and the Muslim Public Affairs Council to repeal and amend the Patriot Act -- alleging that it violated the civil liberties of Americans. AMC also endorsed the Civil Liberties Restoration Act of 2004, which was designed to roll back, in the name of protecting vital freedoms, national-security policies that had been adopted after the 9/11 attacks. In the aftermath of 9/11, AMC's website linked to a document titled "Know Your Rights," which advised: "Don't Talk to the FBI."

AMC is a member organization of the National Coalition to Protect Political Freedom (NCPPF), established in 1997 by Sami Al-Arian to litigate against U.S. counter-terrorism laws, to provide legal counsel to terrorist suspects, and to help overturn terrorist convictions. Fellow NCPPF members include the National Conference of Black Lawyers, the Center for Constitutional Rights, and the National Lawyers Guild.

Jamil Abdullah Al-Amin (the former H. Rap Brown), a one-time President of AMC's Executive Board, has been listed twice on the FBI's "Ten Most Wanted Fugitives" list. Today he is in prison, serving a life sentence without parole for murdering a policeman.

AMC created the National Islamic Prison Foundation, which has contributed to the proselytizing by radical Wahhabist Imams in U.S. prisons.

AMC is a longtime supporter of Sudan's National Islamic Front (NIF) government, which is on the State Department's list of terrorist organizations. In 1992, AMC hosted the NIF leader during his visit to the United States.
The American Muslim Council's national headquarters are located in Chicago. The organization also maintains branch offices in California, Florida, Georgia, Hawaii, Illinois, Indiana, Iowa, Michigan, New Jersey, New York, Ohio, Virginia, and Wisconsin.

AMERICAN MUSLIM UNION (AMU)

Paterson, NJ
http://www.muslimleadership.org/en/index.php

> New Jersey Islamic group associated with the Islamic Center of Passaic County, which was founded by a Hamas fundraiser

Based in Paterson, New Jersey, the American Muslim Union (AMU) is "dedicated to serving the American Muslim community and its unique needs." Five of AMU's current and former directors and executives have held, or still hold, leadership positions at the Islamic Center of Passaic County (ICPC), which was co-founded by Hamas fundraiser Mohammad El-Mezain. AMU's President, Mohamed Younes, is a member of ICPC's Board of Trustees.

At an October 2001 event, AMU hosted the pro-Hamas attorney Stanley Cohen. In March 2004, AMU's invitation to an interfaith event was revoked after two Jewish organizations complained about the group's ties to Islamic terrorism.

AMU views the post-9/11 anti-terror legislation passed by the U.S. government -- particularly the Patriot Act -- as a coordinated assault on the civil liberties of Americans, especially those of Muslim heritage. AMU Executive Director Waheed Khalid has called the Patriot Act "an extremely dangerous piece of legislation" that, "under the guise of 'national security,'" tramples on "our nation's more than 200-year-old Constitution."

In December 2001 -- three months after the 9/11 attacks -- AMU joined forces with the American Civil Liberties Union of New Jersey, the American Immigration Lawyers Association, the Human Rights Education & Law Project, and the Council of New Jersey Mosques in a campaign to provide immigration attorneys for any Muslims in New Jersey who were questioned by law-enforcement officials in connection with Justice Department terrorism investigations.

AMU chose not to endorse or participate in the May 14, 2005 "Free Muslims March Against Terror," an event whose purpose was to send "a message to radical Muslims and supporters of terrorism that we reject them and that we will do all we can to defeat them."

AMERICAN MUSLIMS FOR GLOBAL PEACE AND JUSTICE (AMGPJ)

2094 Walsh Avenue C-2
Santa Clara, CA
95050
Phone :408-988-1011
URL: http://www.bapd.org/gamlce-1.html
Founded by radical Islamist Mahboob Khan

> Former spokesman Yousef Al-Yousef supported Palestinian Islamic Jihad and the Holy Land Foundation

Founded in February 1998 and inactive since late 2002, American Muslims for Global Peace and Justice (AMGPJ) was a Washington, DC-based advocacy/activist group. It was created by Mahboob Khan, who died in 1999 at the age of 60. (A native of Madras, India, Khan also helped establish the Muslim Students' Association of the U.S. & Canada, and later became an official with the Islamic Society of North America.) AMGPJ described itself as "a non-profit grass-root organization established ... for the purpose of educating, aligning and mobilizing fellow Americans on issues of human dignity, freedom, peace and justice." Its volunteer members joined other peace and interfaith organizations and went on fact-finding and humanitarian missions to the Gulf region. These volunteers produced documentaries and videos "on the suffering of the Iraqi people due to eight years of economic sanctions" -- placing blame for that suffering entirely upon the United States.

AMGPJ characterized the U.S. as a nation rife with anti-Muslim bigotry and discrimination. In January 2002, the organization's chairman, Yousef Al-Yousef, stated that Muslims in America are routinely "deprived of their liberties." That same month, Al-Yousef wrote an article defending a Palestinian Islamic Jihad fundraiser on behalf of the Holy Land Foundation for Relief and Development, a Hamas front group that was shut down by the U.S. government for supporting terrorism.

The Outreach Coordinator for AMGPJ was Raeed N. Tayeh, who made headlines in 2001 when he accused Jewish lawmakers of exhibiting inappropriate loyalty to the State of Israel. "The Israeli occupation of all territories must end, including Congress," Tayeh said. He was subsequently fired from his job as a Congressional staffer for Cynthia McKinney.

AMERICAN MUSLIMS FOR JERUSALEM (AMJ)

208 G Street, NE
Washington, DC
20002
Phone :202-548-4200

> Supports Hamas and Hezbollah
> Routinely involved in anti-Zionist campaigns
> Has featured calls at its conferences for the killing of Jews

Incorporated in 1999, American Muslims for Jerusalem (AMJ) is a nonprofit organization headquartered near Capitol Hill. Publicly, AMJ defines its mission as: "to ensure [that] ... the concerns of the American-Muslim community regarding Jerusalem and its environs are understood and respected by the formulation of U.S. policy; to present accurate and timely information to the mass media and other interested parties; to educate, inform, and mobilize the American Muslim community; to raise the awareness of the American society in general and work for a just and comprehensive solution to the issue of Jerusalem; [and] to cooperate with other organizations having similar objectives." Appealing for "a Jerusalem that symbolizes religious tolerance and dialogue," AMJ advocates free access by all to the city's religious sites, rejects any form of sovereignty gained through force, and endorses the "right of return" for Palestinian refugees. The organization neither echoes the radical Palestinian assertion that Jerusalem is the capital of Palestine, nor denies Jewish historical ties to Jerusalem.

As Islam scholar Daniel Pipes points out, however, at private events AMJ adopts positions that are much more radical. For example, at the organization's first major event, a November 1999 fundraising dinner, featured speakers Nihad Awad (a founding member of the Council on American-Islamic Relations) and Abdurahman Alamoudi (founder and Executive Director of the American Muslim Council) derided the State of Israel and American Jews, blaming the latter for exerting undue influence upon U.S. politics and brainwashing American Christians. The keynote speaker, Issa Nakhleh, a Christian member of the Arab Supreme Council for Palestine, alleged that the Israel lobby spends $20 million annually to persuade members of Congress to legislate in a manner advantageous to Jews and Israel. Nakhleh advised Arabs and Muslims to counter this practice by dispatching fundraising delegations to Saudi Arabia and the emirates: "I am sure you will get $10 million from these two, and Iran will give you $10 million," he said.

In 1999 AMJ co-organized a boycott campaign against Burger King, in protest against the fast-food franchise's decision to build a restaurant in an Israeli settlement community, which AMJ called "Palestinian territory occupied by Israel." Said AMJ, "This settlement was built illegally on land seized from Muslims and Christians by Israel after it conquered the territory around Jerusalem in 1967." That same year, AMJ also pressured the Disney Corporation not to list Jerusalem as the "Jewish capital" of Israel at a World Expo in Florida.

Terrorism expert Steve Emerson has characterized AMJ as an organization that "routinely involves anti-Zionist campaigns and has featured calls at its conferences for the killing of Jews." The organization frequently publicizes stories about Christians and Muslims being discriminated against by Israel in Jerusalem, while behind the scenes it maintains close ties with the American Muslim Council, whose leader -- the aforementioned Abdurahman Alamoudi -- is a supporter of both Hamas and Hezbollah.

In February and April of 2001, a number of the world's most extreme Islamic terror groups held a pair of meetings in Beirut and Tehran, respectively, to set aside their differences and unite for *jihad* (holy war) against Israel and the United States. These unprecedented events, together dubbed "the Jerusalem Conference," drew more than 400 militants seeking to unite behind the Palestinians and win total Arab control over Jerusalem. The attendees agreed on the creation of an organization now known as "the Jerusalem Project," and crafted a document that stated: "The only decisive option to achieve this strategy is the option of *jihad* in all its forms and resistance ... America today is a second Israel." The participants in these meetings included leaders of al Qaeda, Hamas, Islamic Jihad, and Hezbollah, as well as militants from Egypt, Pakistan, Jordan, Qatar, Yemen, the Sudan, and Algeria. According to an August 8, 2001 report on the Jerusalem Cloakroom website, AMJ Executive Director Khalid Turaani attended the Jerusalem Conference.

AMJ was a signatory to a MAY 20, 2004 "Joint Muslims/Arab-American Statement on Israeli Violence in Gaza," which "strongly condemn[ed]" Israel's "indiscriminate killings of innocent Palestinians, including many children," and its "demolition of Palestinian homes."

AMERICAN TASK FORCE ON PALESTINE (ATFP)

815 Connecticut Avenue NW
Suite 200
Washington, DC
20006

Phone :202-887-0177
URL: http://www.americantaskforce.org/

Lobbies for a Palestinian state alongside Israel
Demands "right of return" for Palestinian refugees from 1948 Arab-Israeli war and their descendants

Established in 2003, the American Task Force on Palestine (ATFP), originally called the American Committee on Jerusalem, is a not-for-profit group whose goal is to persuade U.S. lawmakers to support the creation of a Palestinian state alongside Israel "in the territories occupied in 1967." ATFP favors "a two state solution, with a shared Jerusalem and a just solution for the refugee problem according to international law." "A resolution of the Palestinian refugee issue can only come about through direct negotiations between Israeli and Palestinian officials as an expression of their national policies," says ATFP. "No other parties are entitled to negotiate on this issue."

ATFP blames Israel for most, but not all, Palestinian suffering: "There are many parties responsible for the suffering of the Palestinian refugees. Responsible parties include first Israel for displacing the Palestinian refugees, refusing their return and confiscating their property without compensation. Some Arab states also bear varying degrees of responsibility; some for allowing generations of refugees to languish in camps under miserable conditions, or by placing various restrictions in terms of their legal status, employment and travel rights, and others for not having done enough to ease the suffering of refugees. Finally, the Palestinian leadership has been at fault for not communicating honestly and openly with the refugees on what they can expect for their future."

According to ATFP, the formation of a Palestinian state "would represent an absolute windfall for the interests of the United States." "As America continues the defense of its citizens and its freedoms in the global War on Terrorism," the organization explains, "a final and satisfactory resolution of the Mideast conflict, which is the single greatest source of anti-American sentiment throughout the Arab and Muslim worlds, would be an invaluable asset. ... At the same time, Israel's security and its integration in the Middle East depend firmly on the establishment of defined borders with its neighbors and a just solution for the Palestinian problem based on international legality."
"The ill will directed at the United States by its perceived support for Israeli conquests and for corrupt authoritarian regimes," adds ATFP, "has created serious security risks for our country, as demonstrated so horrifically on 9-11."

ATFP observes that a major obstacle to peace in the Middle East is the issue of the "right of return" for the Palestinian refugees who left their homes during the early phases of the 1948 Arab-Israeli war. (Seeking out a temporary safe haven during what they anticipated would be a brief conflict that the Arab invaders would undoubtedly win, those refugees fully expected to return to their homes once the fighting had stopped and the Jews had been exterminated. Instead, the Arab armies were defeated.) Today ATFP calls for the re-admittance not only of the relatively few remaining survivors who were among the 725,000 original refugees, but also for the admittance of more than 5 million of their descendants. "The right of return is an integral part of international humanitarian law," says ATFP, "and cannot be renounced by any parties. There is no Palestinian constituency of consequence that would agree to the renunciation of this right. There is also no Jewish constituency of consequence in Israel that would accept the return of millions of Palestinian refugees. ... The challenge for the Israeli and Palestinian national leaderships is to arrive at a formula that recognizes refugee rights but which does not contradict the basis of a two-state solution and an end to the conflict."

"As part of any comprehensive settlement ending the conflict," says ATFP, "Israel should accept its moral responsibility to apologize to the Palestinian people for the creation of the refugee problem. Palestinians should accept that this acknowledgment of responsibility does not undermine the legitimacy of the present-day Israeli state."

ATFP was a signatory to a MAY 20, 2004 "Joint Muslims/Arab-American Statement on Israeli Violence in Gaza," which "strongly condemn[ed]" Israel's "indiscriminate killings of innocent Palestinians, including many children," and its "demolition of Palestinian homes." The statement made no mention of the fact that the Israeli Defense Force's home demolitions are entirely related to anti-terrorist measures.

ATFP's President and Founder Ziad Asali was formerly President of the American-Arab Anti-Discrimination Committee. ATFP's Vice President is Columbia University professor of Middle East Studies Rashid Khalidi, the former Director of the PLO press agency and onetime moderator of the PLO Advisory Committee.

A notable member of the ATFP Board of Directors is George Salem, Co-Founder and Chairman of the Arab American Institute.

A senior fellow with ATFP is Hussein Ibish, who from 1998-2004 served as Communications Director for the American-Arab Anti-Discrimination Committee, and from 2001-2004 was Vice President of Sami Al-Arian's National Coalition to Protect Political Freedom.

ATFP Co-Founder Jesse Aweida contributed to Cynthia McKinney's 2004 congressional campaign.

AMERICAN-ARAB ANTI-DISCRIMINATION COMMITTEE (ADC)

1732 Wisconsin Avenue, NW
Washington, DC
20007

Phone :202-244-2990
Email :
adc@adc.org
URL: http://www.adc.org/

Civil rights and civil liberties group
Opposes U.S. aid to Israel
Opposes ethnic profiling of Arab Americans
Opposes Patriot Act and the U.S. war on terror
Supports Palestinian "martyrdom" campaigns in Israel

The American-Arab Anti-Discrimination Committee (ADC) was founded in 1980 by James Zogby and James Abourezk (a South Dakota Democrat who was the first Arab American to serve in the U.S. Senate, from 1973-79) as a non-religious civil rights group "which welcomes people of all backgrounds, faiths and ethnicities as members." It was created in imitation of, and even as a rival or counterweight to, the Anti-Defamation League, a Jewish civil rights organization.

In recent years, ADC's focus has broadened. As its Communications Director Hussein Ibish puts it, "We've decided that it's just not enough to be a civil-rights group. You have to lobby, get involved in campaigns, and give contributions. We have to become a presence." Putting Ibish's words into action, ADC in 2004 contributed $1,000 to the congressional campaign of Cynthia McKinney (D - Georgia). Samer Khalaf (Chairman of the ADC Political Outreach Committee in New Jersey) and Hareth Raddawi (a Board member of ADC's Chicago branch) made personal contributions to McKinney's campaign as well.

ADC originally concentrated its attentions on Christian Arab Americans, who make up a majority of the Arab American population, and established chapters on campuses and in communities across the U.S. The organization currently has at least 35 local offices in the United States. Its President since 2003 has been Mary Rose Oakar, whose predecessor was Dr. Ziad Asali. ADC's current Executive Vice President is Khalil Jahshan.

ADC identifies five major objectives that govern its activities:

(a) "*Empowering Arab Americans*": A key means of achieving this is voter registration in large numbers.

(b) "*Promoting civic participation*"

(c) "*Supporting freedom and development in the Arab World*"

(d) "*Defending the civil rights of all people of Arab heritage in the United States*": After the beginning of the U.S. war on terror, a perceptible shift occurred in the orientation and activities of ADC. It suddenly became a strident voice protesting what it said were plans by the Bush administration to curtail the civil liberties of Arab Americans. It depicted all anti-terrorism efforts by the Justice and Treasury Departments as unfair persecution based on ethnic discrimination. And it endorsed the Civil Liberties Restoration Act of 2004, which was designed to roll back, in the name of protecting civil liberties, vital national-security policies that had been adopted after the 9/11 terrorist attacks.

ADC was a co-plaintiff in the first major legal challenge to a section of the Patriot Act -- specifically Section 215, which allows for government access to such information as medical, educational, and library records pursuant to a terrorism investigation. The organization has also endorsed the Community Resolution to Protect Civil Liberties campaign, which tries to influence city councils to pass resolutions of noncompliance with the provisions of the Patriot Act. Moreover, ADC was a signatory to a March 17, 2003 letter exhorting members of the U.S. Congress to oppose Patriot Act II on grounds that it contained "a multitude of new and sweeping law enforcement and intelligence gathering powers ... that would severely dilute, if not undermine, many basic constitutional rights." Fellow signers included the American Civil Liberties Union, the American Immigration Lawyers Association, the American Library Association, the Arab American Institute, the Bill of Rights Defense Committee, the Center for Constitutional Rights, the Immigrant Defense Project of the New York State Defenders Association, the Immigrant Legal Resource Center, the Lawyers' Committee for Civil Rights, the League of United Latin American Citizens, the Mennonite Central Committee, the Mexican American Legal Defense and Educational Fund, the National Association for the Advancement of Colored People, the National Council of La Raza, the National Immigration Law Center, the National Lawyers Guild, People for the American Way, and Women Against War.

The Georgia and San Francisco chapters of ADC were signatories to a February 20, 2002 document composed by the radical group Refuse & Resist, condemning military tribunals and the detention of immigrants apprehended in connection with post-9/11 terrorism investigations. The document accused the U.S. government of rounding up and incarcerating large numbers of Arab, Muslim and South Asian immigrants without cause.

(e) ADC's fifth major objective is "*Encouraging a balanced U.S. foreign policy in the Middle East*": In effect, this means discouraging American support for Israel, which ADC views as an oppressor nation that routinely violates the human rights of Palestinians. In August 2006 ADC drew up, for its supporters to sign, a petition that read: "I strongly oppose sending Israel any weaponry ... If the United States is to be taken seriously as a peace making nation, it cannot continue to provide the weapons being used by Israel to kill hundreds of innocent people in such brutal and inhumane ways. ... It must also be remembered that sending Israel more arms will only serve to increase hostility towards U.S. citizens here and abroad." In ADC's view, America has more than once been guilty of genocide against foreign populations -- sometimes directly through the use of its own military might, and in other cases indirectly, through Israel.

ADC was a signatory to a MAY 20, 2004 Joint Muslims/Arab-American Statement on Israeli Violence in Gaza, which "strongly condemn[ed]" Israel's "indiscriminate killings of innocent Palestinians, including many children," and its "demolition of Palestinian homes." The organization has also expressed its view that Israel's security barrier in the West Bank is an illegal "apartheid wall." When Israel released hundreds of Hezbollah prisoners in early 2004, Imad Hamad, ADC's Midwest Regional Director, openly celebrated the freedom of "the Heroes." This sentiment was consistent with ADC's longstanding pattern of praising both Hezbollah and Hamas.

ADC's affinity for Islamic terrorist groups is further evidenced by the fact that the organization formerly ran ads in its publication *ADC Times* for the Holy Land Foundation for Relief and Development, which in 2001 President Bush shut down for funneling millions of dollars to Hamas.

ADC is composed of five major departments:

(a) The Legal Department is staffed by a team of full-time attorneys who provide advice and referrals "whenever Arab Americans face discrimination." "Since the attacks of September 11," ADC laments, "our ... community is becoming increasingly vulnerable. The documentation of hate crimes or discrimination based on ethnicity, nationality or religion is important to our community as a collective."

ADC is particularly opposed to law-enforcement making any distinctions on the basis of race or ethnicity, and thus "has been on the forefront working against racial profiling since the terrorist attacks of September 11, 2001." According to ADC, profiling has become so widespread in the post-9/11 era, that Arab Americans, Muslims, and South Asians can rightfully be considered "among the secondary victims of the attacks ..." ADC's opposition to profiling long predates 9/11, however. In 1993 the organization joined forces with the American Civil Liberties Union to sue Pan American World Airways for having detained a man of Iranian descent during the first Persian Gulf War. "Arab Americans will not tolerate such blatant acts of corporate discrimination which unfairly treat us as a suspect class of criminals and terrorists," said ADC

President Albert Mokhiber.

(b) The Education Department "works with schools, teachers and Arab-American parents across the country to combat discrimination and tensions in school and ensure that the curriculum does not perpetuate stereotypes or misinformation about the Arab world or Islam." Says ADC: "Popular culture aimed at children is replete with negative images of Arab women ... and Arab men ... American textbooks are often Eurocentric, while Arab points of view regarding such issues as the nationalization of resources or the Arab-Israeli conflict are presented inadequately or not at all."

To combat these perceived problems, ADC encourages teachers and administrators to "include Arab Americans and the Arab world in your multicultural curriculum"; to "teach students to appreciate the Arab world, one of the great cultures when Europe was still a backward, under-developed region on the periphery of world civilization"; to have students "write letters of concern about anti-Arab incidents and media stereotyping"; to "recognize Ramadan and other Muslim holidays"; to "arrange the state and school schedule to avoid Islamic holidays"; and "not to order pepperoni sausage for the class pizza party."

(c) The Organizing Department "mobilizes the [Arab American] community by coordinating the efforts of chapters, local offices and activists across the nation, and directing ADC's national campaigns."

(d) The Governmental Affairs Department "works with Congress, the White House, the State and Justice Departments, and other elements of government to promote the interests of the [Arab American] community." It has established a political action committee, to which members can contribute in support of candidates for public office.

(e) The Communications Department "combats defamation, stereotyping and bias in films, television and news reporting ..."

Just as ADC's domestic civil rights posture shifted dramatically after 9/11, so did its positions on foreign affairs. For example, before September 11th ADC had never seriously concerned itself with the suffering of Muslims in the Balkans or Chechnya. However, during the Afghan and Iraq interventions, the Committee became most outspoken in painting these military operations as conspiratorial intrigues controlled by Israel. To register its opposition to America's foreign wars, ADC became a member organization of the United for Peace and Justice and Win Without War anti-war coalitions. The Committee also became a leading defender of Palestinian "martyrdom" campaigns inside Israel; of Saudi Arabia, whose role in funding Wahhabism had come under scrutiny; and of Saddam Hussein's Iraqi regime, which it characterized as innocent of terrorist associations.

ADC receives financial backing from the Boston Foundation, the General Motors Foundation, the Public Welfare Foundation, the San Francisco Foundation, and the Joseph R. and Helen Shaker Family Foundation. The group has also received Saudi funds through third parties such as mosques and charitable organizations.

ADC is notable not only for its programs and campaigns, but also for its open expressions of support for some controversial figures. For instance, in 1987 the Committee honored filmmaker Michael Moore for his "courageous efforts in journalism." A decade and a half later, when University of South Florida professor Sami-Al Arian was indicted on terrorism-related charges, ADC's Hussein Ibish rushed to his defense, branding FBI investigations of Al-Arian "a political witch hunt, a vendetta, and a kind of very, very ugly post-9/11 McCarthyism."

AMERICANS FOR JUSTICE IN PALESTINE (AFJP)

Email :
mahmoudnmusa@yahoo.com
URL: http://www.one-democratic-state.org/articles/campbell.html

Anti-Israel group located in Oakland, California
Supports Palestinian "right of return"
Opposes U.S. aid to Israel

The Oakland-based Americans For Justice in Palestine (AFJP) is an anti-Israel group that lobbies for the so-called "right of return" for Palestinian refugees. The refugees on whose behalf AFJP works are the approximately 725,000 who left their homes during the early phases of the 1948 Arab-Israeli war. Seeking out a temporary safe haven during what they anticipated would be a brief conflict that the Arab invaders would undoubtedly win, those refugees fully expected to return to their homes once the fighting had stopped and the Jews had been exterminated. Instead, the Arab armies were defeated. Today AFJP calls for the re-admittance not only of the relatively few remaining survivors who were among the 725,000, but also for the admittance of more than 5 million of their descendants -- which would render Jews a permanent minority in their own country.

In an effort to end Israel's status as a predominantly Jewish state, AFJP exhorts the American government to cut off all economic funding to Israel, and to help force the latter into a "one-state solution" whereby Israel would become a secular country called "Palestine-Israel," or simply "Palestine." AFJP also lends its name to petitions calling for similar or related actions.

Americans For Justice in Palestine was founded by filmmaker Wendy Campbell, a veteran of the 1960s anti-war movement who contends that suicide bombers' actions "are taken out of context" by their critics, and that "one of the reasons that 9/11 happened was because of the injustices happening in the Middle East, most specifically the Israeli Occupation." Characterizing Israel as a "racist country" ruled by an "apartheid regime," Campbell calls hopes of achieving a two-state solution "obsolete."

Starting in June of 2003, Americans For Justice in Palestine organized a monthly anti-Zionist rally titled the Rachel Corrie Banner Project, named in honor of the late International Solidarity Movement activist Rachel Corrie, who was accidentally crushed by a bulldozer while she was protesting the Israeli Defense Force's demolition of a Palestinian suicide bomber's home in March 2003. The AFJP demonstrations were strategically planned to take place at political events and outside the offices of elected officials.

On March 16, 2004, AFJP participated in a large-scale National Day of Action for Rachel Corrie, urging supporters to organize vigils in Miss Corrie's remembrance, and to ask their Congressional representatives to co-sponsor a resolution calling upon the U.S. government "to undertake a full, fair, and expeditious investigation into the death of Rachel Corrie." Other participants in this event included: Al-Awda, the American-Arab Anti-Discrimination Committee, the American Friends Service Committee, Council for the National Interest, Jewish Voices Against the Occupation, Jews for a Just Peace, Jews for Peace in Palestine and Israel, Not in My Name, the Palestine Children's Welfare Fund, Palestine Media Watch, the Palestine Solidarity Committee, Partners for Peace, Pax Christi, Women in Black, Students for Justice in Palestine, SUSTAIN, US Campaign to End the Israeli Occupation, Veterans for Peace, and the Women's International League for Peace and Freedom.

AFJP co-sponsored a Palestine Solidarity Movement national conference at Ohio State University in November 2003. Other co-sponsors included Action LA, Al-Awda, the American-Arab Anti-Discrimination Committee, Amnesty International, Code Pink, Duke Divest, Friends of Sabeel, Jews Against the Occupation, Jews for a Free Palestine, Left Turn, MADRE, Malia - Collective of Italian American Women, the Middle East Children's Alliance, the Muslim Students' Association of the U.S. and Canada, SUSTAIN, US Campaign to End the Israeli Occupation, the Union of Arab Student Associations, and Women Against War.

A notable activist affiliated with AFJP is Huwaida Arraf, co-founder of the International Solidarity Movement.

AMNESTY INTERNATIONAL (AI)

5 Penn Plaza
14th Floor
New York, NY
10001

Phone :212-807-8400
Email :
admin-us@aiusa.org
URL: http://www.amnesty.org/

Aims a disproportionate share of its criticism for human rights violations at the United States and Israel

Opposed American invasions of Afghanistan and Iraq

Accuses the U.S. and Israel of war crimes

Amnesty International was founded by the British lawyer and activist Peter Benenson. In March 1961 Benenson, moved by a newspaper report of two Portuguese students incarcerated for criticizing the regime of their nation's dictator Antonio Salazar, published in a London newspaper an editorial titled "The Forgotten Prisoners." In it, Benenson urged readers to join his "Appeal for Amnesty in 1961" campaign to aid political dissidents and prisoners of conscience worldwide. As part of the campaign, groups were organized in several countries, including the United States. At a 1962 conference in Belgium, these groups formally joined as one organization, Amnesty International (AI).

Since the time of its founding, AI has presented itself as an ideologically disinterested and apolitical organization. AI maintains that it "does not support or oppose any government or political system, nor does it support or oppose the views of the victims whose rights it seeks to protect. It is concerned solely with the impartial protection of human rights."

During the Cold War, however, AI focused scant attention on the human rights abuses committed by the Soviet Union and its satellites via the Warsaw Pact. Only in 1975, fully 13 years after its formation, did the organization finally release a report -- "Prisoners of Conscience in the USSR" -- documenting the plight of political prisoners behind the Iron Curtain. In its own defense, AI maintained that its work was complicated by the lack of access to prisoners in the Communist world, and by the possibility that its activism might trigger retaliation against political prisoners by the ruling authorities.

The consequences of this approach were evident in AI's assessment of human rights in Communist Cuba, where throughout the 1970s the organization underestimated the number of political prisoners while offering only mild criticism of the Castro regime's persecution of political opponents. An AI annual report for 1976, for instance, noted that the "persistence of fear, real or imaginary, was primarily responsible for the early excesses in the treatment of political prisoners." This cautiously diplomatic approach to the Castro dictatorship did not prevent AI from being awarded the Nobel Peace Prize the following year. In his acceptance lecture, Mumtaz Soysal, a little-known professor from Turkey, hailed what he called AI's mission "to spotlight the victims in every society where imprisonment results from political or religious belief ..."

A grossly disproportionate share of Amnesty International's criticism is reserved for the United States. In the 1980s AI joined leftist non-governmental organizations like the Church World Service and Americas Watch in vocally opposing the Reagan administration's support for the Contra resistance movement against Nicaragua's Communist dictatorship.

In recent years, AI has emerged as a vocal critic of the U.S.-led war on terror, opposing especially the American-led invasions of Afghanistan and Iraq. AI's University of Oklahoma chapter endorsed a May 1, 2003 document titled "10 Reasons Environmentalists Oppose an Attack on Iraq," which was published by Environmentalists Against War.

AI has also condemned the U.S.-operated detention facilities in Guantanamo Bay, Cuba. In March 2005, Amnesty International-USA's then-Executive Director William Schulz alleged that the United States had become "a leading purveyor and practitioner" of torture and urged that senior American officials -- including President Bush, former Defense Secretary Donald Rumsfeld, former Undersecretary of Defense for Policy Douglas Feith, Attorney General Alberto Gonzales, former Central Intelligence Agency director George Tenet, and high-ranking officers at Guantanamo Bay -- face prosecution by other governments for violations of the Geneva Conventions and the U.N. Convention Against Torture. On May 25, 2005, Schulz announced that his organization "calls on foreign governments to uphold their obligations under international law by investigating all senior U.S. officials involved in the torture scandal." "The apparent high-level architects of torture," he added, "should think twice before planning their next vacation to places like Acapulco or the French Riveria because they may find themselves under arrest as Augusto Pinochet famously did in London in 1998." Schulz's remarks were echoed in May of 2005 by Amnesty International's Secretary General Irene Khan, who charged that "Guantanamo [Bay] has become the gulag of our times..."

In a 2002 report, AI admonished the Immigration and Naturalization Service for its policy, instituted after the 9/11 attacks, of "prolonged detention for minor immigration infractions" -- though it neglected to note that such a policy, had it been in place prior to September 11, 2001, might have exposed the three 9/11 hijackers who were in the United States illegally, including two who already had previous immigration violations). In its report, AI placed the word "terrorism" in scare quotes, suggesting that it questioned the serious nature of the phenomenon.

In AI's calculus, the PATRIOT Act counterterrorism legislation "undermines the human rights of Americans and non-citizens, and weakens the framework for promoting human rights internationally." In 2004 Irene Khan condemned the "security agenda promulgated by the U.S. Administration," calling it "bankrupt of vision and bereft of principle." Khan further claimed that America had "openly eroded human rights to win the 'war on terror.'"

Amnesty International was a signatory to a March 17, 2003 letter exhorting members of the U.S. Congress to oppose Patriot Act II on grounds that it "contain[ed] a multitude of new and sweeping law enforcement and intelligence gathering powers ... that would severely dilute, if not undermine, many basic constitutional rights." Fellow signers included the American-Arab Anti-Discrimination Committee, the American Civil Liberties Union, the American Immigration Lawyers Association, the American Library Association, the Arab American Institute, the Bill of Rights Defense Committee, the Center for Constitutional Rights, the Immigrant Defense Project of the New York State Defenders Association, the Immigrant Legal Resource Center, the Lawyers' Committee for Civil Rights, the League of United Latin American Citizens, the Mennonite Central Committee, the Mexican American Legal Defense and Educational Fund, the National Association for the Advancement of Colored People, the National Council of La Raza, the National Immigration Law Center, the National Lawyers Guild, People for the American Way, and Women Against War.

In addition, Amnesty International has given its organizational endorsement to the Community Resolution to Protect Civil Liberties campaign, which tries to influence city councils to pass resolutions of noncompliance with the provisions of the Patriot Act. Moreover, AI endorsed the Civil Liberties Restoration Act of 2004, which was designed to roll back, in the name of protecting civil liberties, vital national-security policies that had been adopted after the 9/11 terrorist attacks.

Local chapters of AI were signatories to a February 20, 2002 document, composed by C. Clark Kissinger's radical group Refuse & Resist (a front organization for the Revolutionary Communist Party), condemning military tribunals and the detention of immigrants apprehended in connection with post-9/11 terrorism investigations. The document charged that the U.S. government had indiscriminately "rounded up" and incarcerated without cause more than 1,500 Arabs, Muslims, and South Asians.

AI was a signatory to a November 1, 2001 document characterizing the 9/11 attacks as a legal matter to be addressed by criminal-justice procedures rather than by military retribution. Suggesting that the hijackers were motivated chiefly by a desire to draw attention to global injustices perpetrated by the United States, this document explained that similar future calamities could be averted only if America would finally begin to "promote fundamental rights around the world."

AI is an opponent, in all cases, of the death penalty, which it regards as the "ultimate form of cruel and inhuman punishment," and has repeatedly urged Congress to abolish it. Because the death penalty is currently a legally permitted punishment in the United States, a 2003 AI report characterized the U.S. as part of the "axis of executioners" along with China and Iran.

Another recurring target of disproportionate criticism from Amnesty International is Israel. For example, AI rushed to denounce Israel's April 2002 military campaign in the Jenin refugee camp. A November 2002 AI report on the events -- bearing the title "Israel and the Occupied Territories, Shielded from Scrutiny: IDF Violations in Jenin and Nablus" -- accused Israel of "serious violations of international human rights or humanitarian law." Among other criticisms, AI reproached Israel's allegedly ongoing "occupation" of Jenin, though control of the city had in fact been ceded by Israel to the Palestinian Authority in 1996. The AI report additionally accused the Israeli Defense Forces of using Palestinian civilians as "human shields," though it was later demonstrated that Palestinian terrorists, rather than Israeli soldiers, had exploited the camp's residents as shields against incoming fire. In 2004 Irene Khan singled out Israel -- along with Colombia, Indonesia and Pakistan -- as a state exhibiting an "appalling human rights record."

In the summer of 2006, AI issued a de-contextualized censure of Israel's retaliatory military campaign against the Lebanese-based terror group Hezbollah. In an August report, AI accused Israeli forces of engaging in "war crimes" such as the "deliberate destruction" of civilian infrastructure in Southern Lebanon, omitting to note that Hezbollah terrorists had initiated the conflict and then intentionally sought refuge amid residential areas.

In May 2007, NGO Monitor released the results of its quantitative analysis of Amnesty International's 2006 publications and alerts *vis a vis* human rights violations. According to the study, Israel had been the subject of 63 such Amnesty documents that year, more than any country in the Middle East except Iran. The corresponding numbers for other nations and notable entities in the region were as follows: Sudan (61 documents), Syria (51), Iraq (29), Hezbollah (20), Algeria (19), Tunisia (15), Egypt (13), Jordan (12), the Palestinian Authority (10), Libya (6), Saudi Arabia (6), and Morocco (5).

The current Executive Director of Amnesty International is Larry Cox, who succeeded William Schulz in January 2006.

AI has received funding from dozens of foundations, including the Columbia Foundation, the Ford Foundation, the Geraldine R. Dodge Foundation, the JEHT Foundation, the John D. & Catherine T. MacArthur Foundation, the Minneapolis Foundation, the Agape Foundation, the Bank of America Foundation, the Open Society Institute, the Rockefeller Brothers Fund, the Stewart R. Mott Charitable Trust, the Vanguard Public Foundation, the William and Flora Hewlett Foundation, and the Rockefeller Foundation.

APPLIED RESEARCH INSTITUTE OF JERUSALEM (ARIJ)

Caritas Street
P.O.Box 860
Bethlehem
Palestine

Phone :972-2-2741889
URL: http://www.arij.org/

NGO that accuses Israel of polluting Palestinian water supplies
Condemns Israel's construction of anti-terror barrier in West Bank
Accuses Israel of bringing "segregation, colonization and occupation to Palestine"

Founded in 1990, the Applied Research Institute of Jerusalem (ARIJ) is a "non-profit organization dedicated to promoting sustainable development in the occupied Palestinian territories and [promoting] the self-reliance of the Palestinian people through greater control over their natural resources." To accomplish this, ARIJ "works specifically to augment the local stock of scientific and technical knowledge and to introduce and devise more efficient methods of resource utilization and conservation, improved practices, and appropriate technology."

Though initially conceived to confront issues facing farmers (such as cultivation in marginal lands, livestock production, agro-industries, and water management), ARIJ has since broadened its agenda to include a wide spectrum of environmental concerns. In 1994 it established an Environmental Research Unit to assess the air and water quality in the West Bank and Gaza, and subsequently to help formulate strategy options, policy guidelines, and national standards and legislation. That same year, the organization established a Land Use Unit "with the aim of using up-to-date data and mapping technology for analysis planning and modeling of sustainable development in Palestine." Additionally, ARIJ has instituted a Resource Center that makes scientific data, literature, and periodicals on a wide range of subjects available to the local community. The Institute also maintains a data analysis center, laboratory, weather station, and hydroponics unit. In 1996 Al Quds University President Sari Nusseibeh and ARIJ Board President Daoud Istanbuli signed an agreement to "creat[e] a role model for institutional cooperation aimed at promoting the research capabilities in Palestine to meet the growing needs of the Palestinian society ..."

ARIJ's current projects include the following:

Update of the Palestinian Environmental Information System: "... to provide an update and comprehensive description and assessment of the state of the environment in the West Bank and Gaza strip as well as to show the trends of the major environmental indicators ... [a]nd to distribute the results in a digital format to the stakeholders including governmental and non-governmental organization[s] who are active in the field of environment."

Environmental Sustainability for a Better Life: "... aims at providing local authorities with the required support to create more sustainable communities ... by applying a more integrated participatory approach to local policy making ..."

Water Harvesting and Wastewater Reuse: "... to enhance [the] food security of 434 poor, marginalized and highly vulnerable people in 3 villages in the Bethlehem and Hebron Districts. The project is broken down into two complimentary action categories: Rainwater harvesting and Wastewater treatment and reuse."

Filtration System for Wastewater Treatment in the West Bank Activated Sludge: "... to contribute in the preservation of the environment and groundwater from the pollution due to wastewater collected in septic tanks"; "to find [an alternative] to the septic tanks used in the collection of wastewater in rural areas, by treating [the water] close to its source"; and "to save in the volume of the consumed drinking water used in irrigation, by replacing it with treated wastewater."

Improving Plant Production to Enhance Household Food Security in Marginalized Communities: "... to enhance the sustainability of the rain-fed farming system and improve food security ... [for] 79 poor and marginalized households in 10 villages of Bethlehem Governorate."

Improving Plant Production to Enhance Food Security of Farming Communities: "... aims to improve [the] food security of 287 poor and marginalized households (3.3% of total population community) in 10 villages of Bethlehem Governorate through engaging in dry-land farming improvement programs, water resource management, and [the construction of greenhouses] with increased capacities ..."

Characterizing Israel as an oppressor nation whose policies greatly damage the environment in Palestinian territories, the ARIJ website "monitors and assesses the magnitude of environmental degradation caused by politically induced changes to Palestine's land and natural resources." The organization condemns "individual and collective political activities such as expansion and fattening of Israeli colonies, land expropriation and closures, uprooting of trees, Israeli stone quarrying, house demolitions, sewage disposal from Israeli colonies, and several other relevant activities." Moreover, it produces a *Monthly Report* on Israel's "destruction of the Palestinian land" in the West Bank.

ARIJ strongly opposes Israel's construction of an anti-terrorism security barrier in the West Bank, dubbing it "the Segregation Wall." The organization also denounces Israel's practice of "house demolition" -- depicting it as a practice that maliciously targets the homes of innocent civilians rather than those of known terrorists. ARIJ's extreme distaste for Israel is reflected by its participation in the Divestment campaign against the Jewish State.

On December 23, 2004, ARIJ released a "Christmas Message" that read, in part, as follows: "In the Holy Land ..., Christmas is marred by the ongoing Israeli occupation of Palestinian land. The ancient hills which Jesus Christ once walked in the spirit of peace and compassion are now the site of an increasingly brutal military occupation and colonial enterprise perpetrated by the state of Israel and supported by the government of the United States of America. In the course of its 37-year occupation, Israel has appropriated increasing amounts of Palestinian land for the purpose of Israeli colonization. ... An analysis of Israeli actions on the ground ... reveals that the future will continue to bring segregation, colonization and occupation to Palestine. These are Israel's gifts to Palestine this Christmas season."
ARIJ receives financial support from the European Union, the Swiss Agency for Development and Cooperation, the Mennonite Central Committee, the Canadian government's International Development Research Center, and USAID.

ARAB AMERICAN ACTION NETWORK (AAAN)

3148 West 63rd Street
Chicago, IL
60629
Phone :773-436-6060
URL: http://www.aaan.org/

- Chicago-based organization established to promote the interests of the city's large Arab-American population
- Supports expanded rights for illegal aliens

Founded by anti-Israel professor Rashid Khalidi, former director of the PLO press agency and onetime moderator of PLO advisory committee

Established in 1995, the Arab American Action Network (AAAN) "seeks to empower Chicago-area Arab immigrants and Arab Americans through the combined strategies of community organizing, advocacy, education and social services, leadership development, and forging productive relationships with other communities ... [and] to be an active agent for positive social change." Its founders were Columbia University professor Rashid Khalidi (the former Director of the PLO press agency and onetime moderator of the PLO Advisory Committee) and his wife, Mona Khalidi.

Headquartered in the heart of Chicago's large Palestinian community, AAAN views the United States as a nation wherein Arab citizens are routinely maltreated. To remedy this perceived societal injustice, the organization aims "to challenge government policies that violate the civil, political and human rights of the Arab American and Arab immigrant community." Among these policies are "detentions, deportations and other attacks on immigrants that result from Homeland Security [measures]."

AAAN has worked closely with the Illinois Coalition for Immigrant and Refugee Rights, which seeks to promote open borders immigration policies, to advocate for a law giving illegal aliens who attend Illinois high schools (dubbed "undocumented students" by AAAN) "the opportunity to pursue higher education; to press the state for increased funding for immigrant services, such as English Language, Outreach and Interpretation, and Civics programs; and to support other beneficial immigrant rights legislation."

In December 2005, AAAN and numerous other Arab lobby groups composed a letter to New Mexico Governor Bill Richardson, characterizing a North Carolina/New Mexico joint initiative to deny driver's licenses to illegal immigrants as a "bigoted attack on Arabs and Muslims." At issue, said the letter, was "an inflammatory and misleading billboard campaign ... which contains extremely negative images of Arabs and Arab cultural symbols with the message, 'Don't License Terrorists.' The billboards unfairly conflate the question of immigration and national security and cast a shadow of suspicion on Arabs and Muslims, unfairly equating them with terrorism and encouraging an environment that can lead to prejudice and hate crimes. In doing so, the ads utilize false stereotypes and racist rhetoric to promote an anti-immigrant agenda."

AAAN is "committed to speaking out" against what it calls the pervasive "biased reporting, media stereotypes, and the criminalization of Arabs and Muslims." Its staff and Board have developed a Speakers' Bureau of experts on these issues from throughout the Chicago area, speakers who have made many presentations to audiences at schools, universities, churches, community centers, and corporations. Moreover, they facilitate workshops and "provide training to agencies on the provision of culturally appropriate human services to our community."

In early 2005, AAAN co-sponsored an art exhibit titled "The Subject of Palestine." Held at DePaul University and featuring the works of ten Palestinian artists, the exhibit's central theme was "the compelling and continuing tragedy of Palestinian life ... under [Israeli] occupation ... home demolition ... statelessness ... bereavement ... martyrdom, and ... the heroic struggle for life, for safety, and for freedom."

AAAN's hostile view of the Jewish state is further manifest in the organization's reference to Israel's creation in 1948 as *Al Nakba* ("The Catastrophe"). In collaboration with the American Friends Service Committee, AAAN recently initiated a project titled "*Al Nakba*: 1948 As Experienced by Chicago Palestinians." This venture solicits photographs, letters, and verbal accounts of local Palestinians' recollections about their sufferings immediately before, during, and after Israel's establishment.

Among the current luminaries of AAAN's staff are: (a) Vice President Ali Abunimah, who maintains the website ElectroicIntifada.com and is a Board member of the Sabeel Ecumenical Liberation Theology Center; and (b) Executive Director Hatem Abudayyeh, who has condemned "the Israeli government and its military killing machine."

AAAN actively collaborates with scores of leftist organizations nationwide. Among these are the American Arab Anti-Discrimination Committee, the American Friends Service Committee, Amnesty International, the Arab American Institute, the Council on American-Islamic Relations, the 8th Day Justice Center, MADRE, the Mosque Foundation, the National Lawyers Guild, Service Employees International Union, and Voices in the Wilderness.

AAAN has received donations from the Fry Foundation, the Tides Foundation, the Polk Brothers Foundation, and the Woods Fund of Chicago.

ARAB AMERICAN INSTITUTE (AAI)

1600 "K" Street NW
Suite 601
Washington, DC
20006

Phone :202-429-9210
URL: http://www.aaiusa.org/

Seeks to promote Arab American participation in the U.S. electoral system, both as voters and as candidates
Opposed ending Saddam Hussein's Ba'athist regime
Opposes Israel's security wall

A self-described "nonpartisan" group, the Arab American Institute (AAI) was established in 1985 to promote "Arab American participation in the U.S. electoral system" and to advocate for the "domestic and policy concerns" of that demographic. Toward that end, AAI developed a strong reputation for organizing "voter-education" campaigns and acting as a liaison between the Arab American community and the major national political parties.

Operating on an annual budget of about $1 million, AAI's major activities include the following: convening national and local organizations for "national leadership summits to respond to crisis situations"; holding meetings with policy-makers and U.S. government officials; helping establish Arab American Democratic and Republican leadership councils; hosting events at national and state party conventions; conducting get-out-the-vote drives and candidate forums; "registering and informing" Arab American voters in "key" states; producing a variety of issue briefs on topics of concern to Arab Americans; publishing an annual "congressional scorecard" detailing how elected officials have voted on various matters; periodically organizing member-mobilizations; conducting polling and research of Arab American voters; and organizing trips to the Middle East for members of Congress and other U.S. delegations.

AAI also conducts media outreach and provides public information via several regularly distributed publications, including: (a) its weekly e-newsletter *AAI Bulletin*; (b) *Countdown*, a weekly update that covers political developments in Congress and the White House; and (c) *AAInsider*, a seasonal magazine for Institute members.

Moreover, AAI co-founder, President, and leading spokesman James Zogby is the author of *Washington Watch*, a weekly column for the Arab World and the Arab American press. Zogby also hosts *Viewpoint*, a weekly policy program that airs on Abu Dhabi TV and Link TV. Formerly the Executive Director of the American-Arab Anti-Discrimination Committee, Zogby is a major figure in Democratic Party affairs. He advised Jesse Jackson's 1984 presidential campaign and was close to President Clinton.

James Zogby's brother John, who runs a polling business, is an AAI Board member, along with international marketing executive and AAI backup spokesperson Jean Abi Nader. The Institute's Executive Director is Nidal Ibrahim, formerly the founder and publisher of *Arab American Business Magazine.* AAI's Chairman is the Republican George Salem, a partner in the Washington, DC law office of Akin, Gump, Strauss, Hauer & Feld, a firm that has been prominent in defending Saudis accused of involvement in terrorism.

Subdivided into numerous community branches, AAI is extremely active on university campuses nationwide. Prior to September 11, 2001, the organization enjoyed immense popularity in the U.S. media, especially among liberal and peace-oriented American Jews, for its seemingly moderate position on the Arab-Israeli conflict. Following 9/11, however, the tone of AAI's public pronouncements underwent a striking change; with ever-increasing frequency, the Institute denounced its opponents as racists, extremists, and Zionist agents. Moreover, it vehemently denied charges that Saddam Hussein had ever supported terrorism. According to Islam scholar Stephen Schwartz, in the wake of September 11th AAI "moved from the center to the extreme left of the American public square."

Among the issues AAI is currently focused on are: opposition to America's war against Iraq; opposition to Israel's construction of a barrier in the West Bank to prevent would-be terrorists from entering areas populated by Israeli civilians; and the denunciation of former Israeli Prime Minister Ehud Barak's land-for-peace proposals at Camp David in 2000. Characterizing Israel as a brutal oppressor of the Palestinian people, AAI was a signatory to a May 20, 2004 Joint Muslims/Arab-American Statement on Israeli Violence in Gaza, which "strongly condemn[ed]" Israel's "indiscriminate killings of innocent Palestinians, including many children," and its "demolition of Palestinian homes."

AAI also denounces what it depicts as widespread civil liberties violations directed against Arab Americans in the post-9/11 period. "The USA Patriot Act and initiatives launched by the Attorney General in the aftermath of September 11," says James Zogby, "have endangered basic constitutionally protected rights of due process and judicial review."

"Since 9/11," Jean Abi Nader concurs, "Arab-Americans have watched their dream of being fully a part of American society subject to the stresses of federal initiatives ... that produce fear and intimidation in their community. ... Being an Arab has become a liability in this country. We are being told, essentially, that we are not good enough. ... The civil liberties of Arab-Americans and American Muslims came under attack, and we have been treated increasingly as second-class citizens in this country." Abi Nader further laments the "systematic degrading of Islam by conservative Christians, neoconservatives and the right wing," who he portrays as chief among those who view Islam as a "religion of liars and terrorists."

During a panel discussion at an October 2003 conference of the Arab American Institute, Marwan Kreidie of the AAI National Leadership Conference referred to "that lunatic [John] Ashcroft," the then-Attorney General who was the chief enforcer of the Patriot Act. "Anytime Ashcroft comes to Philadelphia, we hand him a copy of the Constitution," said Kreidie.

AAI was a signatory to a March 17, 2003 letter exhorting members of the U.S. Congress "to oppose ... 'Patriot [Act] II'" on grounds that it "contain[ed] a multitude of new and sweeping law enforcement and intelligence gathering powers ... that would severely dilute, if not undermine, many basic constitutional rights." In addition, AAI has given its organizational endorsement to the Community Resolution to Protect Civil Liberties campaign, which tries to influence city councils to be non-compliant with the provisions of the Patriot Act. AAI also endorsed the Civil Liberties Restoration Act of 2004, which was designed to roll back, in the name of protecting civil liberties, vital national-security policies that had been adopted after the 9/11 terrorist attacks.

AAI has received funding from the Open Society Institute and the Annie E. Casey Foundation, the Carnegie Corporation of New York, the ChevronTexaco Foundation, the Fannie Mae Foundation, the Ford Motor Company Fund, and the Seaver Institute.

ARAB ASSOCIATION FOR HUMAN RIGHTS (HRA)

Mary's Well Street
P.O. Box 215 - 16101
Nazareth - Israel

URL: http://www.arabhra.org/

- One of the oldest NGOs in the Arab sector of Israel
- Alleges that Arabs in Israel are "routine[ly]" victimized by Israeli-perpetrated, racially motivated attacks

Founded in 1988, the Nazareth-based Arab Association for Human Rights (HRA) seeks "to promote and protect the political, civil, economic, and cultural rights of the Palestinian Arab minority in Israel, and to further the domestic implementation of international human rights principles ..." HRA literature alleges that Arabs in Israel are "routine[ly]" victimized by Israeli-perpetrated, racially motivated attacks, and that Israeli authorities are oblivious to the plight of Arabs.

HRA's "core programs" include the following:

(a) *International Advocacy*: "The discourse about the ongoing violence in Israel/Palestine is dominated by the hostilities resulting from Israel's occupation of the West Bank and Gaza. ... Our main goal is to put the human-rights issues related to the Arab minority inside Israel on the international agenda and to impact the international discourse towards a more rights-based approach concerning Israel."

(b) *Human Rights and Civic Education Project*: Led by HRA-trained student facilitators, this program reaches more than 16,000 Palestinian Arab schoolchildren and teachers throughout Israel via semester-long courses, workshops, lectures, summer camps, and "human-rights days." The purpose of the program is to "raise [public] awareness" of HRA's contention that Israeli policies have caused Palestinian pupils to be "educated in a school system ... [that] offers fewer facilities and educational opportunities than its Jewish counterpart, which lead[s] to a general education deficit among the Palestinian minority citizens."

(c) *Working Group on Women's Rights*: "In the Arab community in Israel, women face violations to their rights on multiple levels: Their rights are violated in Israel as members of a minority in a Jewish state; their rights are violated as Arab women in a patriarchal society based on traditional authority; and they share the violations practiced against all women - Jewish and Arab - within the state. These sources of marginalization ... combine to make Arab women in Israel the lowest paid, least educated, and least represented portion of Israeli society."

(d) *Research and Reporting* (R&R): Launched in 2003, this program "monitor[s] human rights violations against the Palestinian minority in Israel. The methodology relies on field research -- interviews with victims, collection of testimonies -- and analysis of domestic and international law concerning human rights." R&R reports consistently portray Israel as an oppressor nation. In May 2004, for example, HRA published "'Let Them Suffocate' -- Police Brutality during House Demolition in Upper Galilee Village of al-Bea'neh," which charged that "the [Israeli] police continue to treat Palestinian citizens of Israel as an enemy that can only be addressed through the use of excessive force."
To supplement its R&R publications, HRA also produces Fact Sheets addressing various issues of relevance to Arabs in Israel. For instance, a fact sheet titled "Discrimination in Israeli Law" holds that Palestinian Arab citizens of Israel are "discriminated against in a variety of forms and denied equal individual rights because of their national belonging." Another fact sheet, titled "Land Planning and Policy in Israel," claims the following: "In 1948, the Palestinian Arab community owned and used most of the land within the State of Israel. Today it owns less than 3% of these lands. Palestinian Arab citizens' ability to own or use the rest is severely restricted by a series of discriminatory laws and practices ... a continual process of land expropriation from private (Arab) owners, that has systematically reduced Arab land ownership to cement Jewish control over all parts of the country."

An HRA press release of March 15, 2006 condemned Israel's seizure of Ahmed Saadat, the Popular Front for the Liberation of Palestine leader who ordered the 2001 assassination of Israeli Cabinet Minister Rehavam Zeevi. Making no mention of the fact that this seizure was prompted by the Palestinian Authority's Hamas-led government's announcement that it was contemplating releasing Saadat from prison, HRA accused the United States and United Kingdom of complicity in the operation, and called on the international community to "put pressure on Israel to retract from this illegal action and to return the prisoners to PA jurisdiction."

On July 31, 2006 -- in the midst of an intense Israeli military operation against the Lebanese-based organization Hezbollah -- HRA issued a press statement accusing Israel of perpetrating "war crimes," "violent massacres," "collective punishment," and "blatant breaches of international law." The press release further asserted that "more than 60 civilians" had been killed by an Israeli Air Force attack on the Lebanese village of Qana. The figures provided by the Red Cross on July 30 stated that 28 people had been killed, but HRA never issued a correction.

HRA's Executive Director is a well-known Israeli Arab politician Muhammad Zeidan, formerly the personal companion and confidant of the longtime Palestinian terrorist Abu Abbas.

HRA is a member organization of such NGO umbrella groups as the Euro-Mediterranean Human Rights Network and Ittijah. It has also collaborated with the Sabeel Ecumenical Liberation Theology Center and the Israeli Committee Against House Demolitions.
HRA receives funding from the Mertz Gilmore Foundation, the Moriah Fund, the European Union, and the Ford Foundation.

ASSOCIATION FOR THE DEFENSE OF THE RIGHTS OF THE INTERNALLY DISPLACED (ADRID)

Phone :972-4-600-1765
www.ittijah.org

Supports Palestinians' "Right of Return"
Falsely accuses Israel of committing atrocities against Palestinians

Based in Nazareth, the Association for the Defense of the Rights of the Internally Displaced (ADRID) is a member of the highly politicized NGO umbrella group known as Ittijah (Union of Arab Community-Based Organizations). According to Ittijah, ADRID's goal is to facilitate "the return of displaced Palestinians within the Green Line to their villages and homes which they were expelled from, in accordance with UN Resolution 194." (This Resolution, adopted in December 1948, was a complex package that included Arab recognition of Israel and formal peace agreements, and was never implemented.)

ADRID sponsors and organizes Land Day events in the Palestinian villages; holds lectures and panel discussions on issues of importance to Palestinians; seeks to disseminate its message in schools, libraries, universities, and through the media; helps restore damaged mosques and churches; supports research on "uprooted and destroyed" Palestinian villages since 1948; and collects statistics and information about displaced persons in Israel.

Although they are Israeli citizens, ADRID officials pursue a strong, overtly anti-Israel agenda. Ignoring the context and history of the 1947-1948 Arab-Israeli war and the violent Arab rejection of UN Resolution 181, ADRID simply claims, "The experience of Palestinians before, during, and after the 1948 *al-Nakba* [Arabic term meaning "the Catastrophe," a reference to Israel's creation] is the result of the Zionist policies of occupation, violence and military eviction." Further, ADRID claims that "consecutive Israeli governments have robbed refugee properties and homes, destroyed our villages, and confiscated our lands by means of discriminatory, ethnic legislation and by denying our right of return to our homeland." "The Palestinian refugees' right to return to their homeland and homes is a sacred right," the organization says, adding: "the refugee issue is the heart of the Palestinian cause and the Palestinian-Israeli conflict."
ADRID's manifesto of November 19, 1999 casts blame for the Palestinian refugee situation on "Zionist conspiracies," and claims that the establishment of the State of Israel was "gained with the support of international Zionist and imperialist forces."

ADRID does not have its own website and does not disclose sources of its funding.

BADIL RESOURCE CENTER FOR PALESTINIAN RESIDENCY AND REFUGEE RIGHTS (AKA BADIL)

P.O. Box 728
Bethlehem, West Bank
Palestine

Phone :972-2-277-7086
URL: http://www.badil.org

Jerusalem-based NGO that favors Palestinian "right of return" and refuses to recognize Israel as a Jewish state

A project of the NGO Alternatives, the Badil Resource Center for Palestinian Residency & Refugee Rights was established in Bethlehem in 1998 to "provide a resource pool of alternative, critical and progressive information and analysis on the question of Palestinian refugees and displaced persons." Badil (pronounced "*badeel*") is an Arabic word that means "alternative."

With an annual budget of more than $400,000, Badil receives funding from numerous sources, including Oxfam, the Mennonite Central Committee, the Canadian International Development Agency, the Norwegian Agency for Development Cooperation, the Swiss Foreign Ministry, and church groups.

A member organization of Al-Awda (a.k.a. the Palestine Right of Return Coalition), Badil refuses to recognize Israel as a legitimate state and actively promotes the "right of return" for 7 million Palestinian refugees whose influx into Israel would render Jews a permanent minority in that nation.

According to Badil, "There are five primary groups of Palestinian refugees and displaced persons. The largest group is comprised of those Palestinians displaced/expelled from their places of origin in 1948. ... The second major group ... is comprised of those Palestinians displaced for the first time from their places of origin in the West Bank, eastern Jerusalem, and the Gaza Strip (often referred to as '1967 displaced persons'). The third category ... includes those ... who are neither 1948 or 1967 refugees and are outside the Palestinian territories occupied by Israel since 1967 and unable due to revocation of residency, denial of family reunification, deportation, etc., or unwilling to return there owing to a well-founded fear of persecution. [The fourth group] includes internally displaced Palestinians who remained in the area that became the state of Israel in 1948. [The fifth group] includes Palestinians internally displaced in the West Bank, eastern Jerusalem, and the Gaza Strip."

"The majority of Palestinians became refugees during armed conflict and war in Palestine," says Badil. "Sources of flight include indiscriminate [Israeli] attacks on civilians, massacres, looting, destruction of property (including entire villages), and forced expulsion. Israeli military forces adopted 'shoot to kill' policies along the armistice lines to prevent the return of refugees."

Badil's activities are divided into two spheres:

(a) The Campaign Unit "facilitates partnership-based initiatives with local Palestinian and international organizations in order to strengthen refugee identity, promote refugee unity, and empower initiatives of refugee self-organization for Palestinian refugee rights. Activities include workshops on refugee rights, support for rallies and community lobbying, study tours to villages of origin, regional workshops, support for media initiatives including radio and TV series, English training courses for activists ..."

(b) The Research, Information and Legal Advocacy Unit publishes Arabic- (*Haq al-Awda*) and English-language (*Majdal*) magazines; conducts an annual Survey of Palestinian Refugees and Internally Displaced Persons; sponsors expert workshops; offers policy advice; and distributes advocacy materials, legal papers, and press releases.

BETSELEM (B'TSELEM)

P.O. Box 53132
Jerusalem
91531

URL: http://www.btselem.org

Anti-Israel NGO

Betselem (alternately "B'Tselem"), which dubs itself "The Israeli Information Center for Human Rights in the Occupied Territories," was established in 1989 by a group of academics, attorneys, journalists, and Knesset members. Betselem in Hebrew literally means "in the image of," and is taken from Genesis 1:27, which reads, "And God created humans in His image. In the image of God did He create him."

In Betselem's view, the state of Israel egregiously violates the injunction to treat people—in this case, the Palestinians, as though they were fashioned in the image of God. Therefore, Betselem's mission is "to document and educate the Israeli public and policymakers about human rights violations in the Occupied Territories, combat the phenomenon of denial prevalent among the Israeli public, and help create a human rights culture in Israel."

Toward this end, Betselem produces a large number of reports, published in both Hebrew and English, condemning Israel's purported human rights abuses. Originating from the West Bank and Gaza Strip, these reports are regularly cited by international NGOs such as Amnesty International, Human Rights Watch, Euro-Mediterranean Human Rights Network, Human Rights Watch, MIFTAH, and Christian Aid, as well as numerous Palestinian NGOs. Among the specific topics the reports address are the Separation Barrier under construction by Israel; the "Road Map to Peace"; Israeli medical personnel accused of being unresponsive to, and disrespectful of, Palestinians in need of their services; Israel's "punitive house demolitions"; "restrictions on movement" that prevent Palestinians from traveling freely; and Israeli "security force violence." In each case, Betselem's allegations of Israeli transgressions entirely ignore the context established by Palestinian terrorism.

To further disseminate its message, Betselem works extensively with the media, issuing press releases, accompanying journalists into the field, and giving interviews on the aforementioned topics -- efforts that have landed the organization's spokespeople hundreds of citations and appearances in the local and foreign press. Betselem also provides periodic updates to local policymakers and diplomats "on human rights developments in the Occupied Territories," and gives presentations to visiting foreign policymakers and delegations from around the world.

In contrast to other human rights NGOs that are based outside of Israel and thus have limited knowledge of the situation on the ground, Betselem is situated in Israel and its researchers speak both Hebrew and Arabic. The organization has a trilingual website that receives more than 1,500 visitors per day, and transmits a monthly email newspaper to some 8,500 subscribers.

Affiliated with blatantly anti-Israel political organizations such as the Palestine Center for Human Rights and Miftah, Betselem initiated a campaign in 2003 to deploy Israelis to IDF checkpoints to "document, intervene, and prevent human rights violations." These deployments frequently drew immense media attention.

Also in 2003, Betselem launched a major campaign against what it termed Israel's "siege policy," aiming to "raise awareness among the Israeli public and policymakers about the devastating effects of the checkpoints and roadblocks inside the West Bank."

The following year, Betselem released a music video titled "Eyes Wide Open," featuring performances by popular Israeli entertainers as a backdrop to film footage of alleged Israeli abuses that had occurred at West Bank roadblocks and checkpoints. Moreover, to coincide with the release of "a report on Israel's policy of punitive house demolitions," Betselem produced a video chronicling how Israel's demolition policy had harmed innocent children. More than 30,000 people viewed each of these videos on the Betselem website, and thousands more saw them in movie theaters across Israel.

In 2005 Betselem released four publications denouncing alleged Israeli injustices. They were titled: (a) *Under the Guise of Security: Routing the Separation Barrier to Enable the Expansion of Israeli Settlements in the West Bank*; (b) *Means of Expulsion: Violence, Harassment and Lawlessness Toward Palestinians in the Southern Hebron Hills*; (c) *Take No Prisoners: The Fatal Shooting of Palestinians by Israeli Security Forces during "Arrest Operations"*; and (d) *One Big Prison: Freedom of Movement to and from the Gaza Strip on the Eve of the Disengagement Plan.*

Betselem has an impressive range of funders, including the Ford Foundation; Christian Aid; the New Israel Fund; the Sheta Fund; the Commission of the European Communities; DanChurchAid; the International Commission of Jurists, the Mertz Gilmore Foundation, the Norwegian Foreign Ministry, Novib, and the Federal Department of Foreign Affairs of Switzerland.

BOSTON TO PALESTINE (B2P)

URL: http://www.bostontopalestine.org/

- Affiliated with the International Solidarity Movement
- Accuses Israel of human rights atrocities, and calls the Palestinian campaign of terrorism a "non-violent struggle"
- Seeks to obstruct Israeli security forces protecting Arab and Jewish Israeli citizens

Established in June 2002, Boston to Palestine (B2P) describes itself as "a group of Boston-based activists who work in solidarity with the Palestinian people in their non-violent struggle to resist and end the occupation of Palestine by the Israeli Defense Forces (IDF)." B2P seeks to achieve this objective "by sending delegates to work with International Solidarity Movement (ISM) and other peace and justice groups operating in Palestine." These delegates are equipped with still and video cameras "for the purposes of documenting life and events (including direct actions) in Palestine under occupation." B2P then creates "opportunities for them to relate their experiences to the public when they return."

Boston to Palestine has conducted dozens of what it terms "educational and outreach events" in Boston-area community and religious centers, high schools, and colleges, where returning delegates speak publicly about what they experienced and observed in the Middle East. The group has also organized demonstrations and vigils in and around Boston to protest "the ongoing atrocities conducted against Palestinians by the IDF, and to honor and commemorate ISM activists who have been killed or wounded by the IDF." B2P seeks to convey to the world "the horrors that are a feature of [the Palestinians'] daily lives at the hands of the IDF." Condemning the Israeli government's "lethal targeting and murdering of activists and journalists, and the detention and deportation of activists as a matter of policy," Boston to Palestine does not use the word "terrorist" -- either as a noun or an adjective -- to describe any Palestinian individual or deed.

In June 2006, B2P co-sponsored (with the American-Arab Anti-Discrimination Committee, Dorchester People for Peace, Friends of Sabeel, the Gaza Mental Health Foundation, Jewish Voice for Peace, Jewish Women for Justice in Israel/Palestine, Unitarian Universalists for Justice in the Middle East, and United for Justice with Peace) a protest against Israel's "Siege of the Palestinian People." The organizers urged participants to bring signs with messages demanding an end to: "the siege and starvation of Palestinians"; "punishing Palestinians for their democratic vote" (in favor of a Hamas-led government) ; "the denial of food and medicine to Palestinians"; and "Israel's 39-year-old military occupation."

Boston to Palestine is a member organization of the United for Peace and Justice anti-war coalition, led by Leslie Cagan.

CANADIAN INTERNATIONAL DEVELOPMENT AGENCY (CIDA)

200 Promenade du Portage
Gatineau, Quebec
K1A 0G4

Phone :819-997-5006
URL: http://www.acdi-cida.gc.ca

NGO created by the Canadian government in 1968
Funds numerous groups with strong ideological and political agendas that are hostile to the state of Israel

Created by the Canadian government in 1968 as the successor to the federal External Aid Office, the Canadian International Development Agency (CIDA) describes itself as "Canada's lead agency for development assistance" whose mandate is to "reduce poverty and ... contribute to a more secure, equitable, and prosperous world." In June 2004, the Canadian government allocated more than $2.2 billion of its federal budget to CIDA for projects involving social development, humanitarian assistance, environmental sustainability, and governance.

CIDA identifies seven priority campaigns:

Governance: CIDA supports its partner countries' efforts to promote "democratization, human rights, the rule of law, public-sector capcity building, and conflict prevention."

Health: This program assists countries "to improve health outcomes, particularly among the poorest, through a focus on: preventing and controlling high-burden, communicable, poverty-linked diseases (especially HIV/AIDS); strengthening the capacity of health systems; improving infant and child health; strengthening sexual and reproductive health; and improving food security."

Education: This program "supports initiatives that improve the quality, safety, and relevance of basic education; remove barriers that prevent closing the gender gap in education; provide education to prevent HIV/AIDS; and provide education for girls and boys in conflict, post-conflict, and/or emergency situations."

Environmental Sustainability: "The poor, who depend most directly on their natural environment for food, shelter and income, are ... at greatest risk from external factors such as climate change. ... "

Private Sector Development: This campaign seeks to cut in half the proportion of people living in poverty and suffering from hunger by 2015.

Gender Equality: "... [M]ost women worldwide ... continue to have fewer rights, lower education and health status, less income, and less access to resources and decision-making than men. ... CIDA promotes women's equal participation in decision-making, full realization of their human rights, and equal access to and control over the resources and benefits of development."

Millennium Development Goals: CIDA seeks to "eradicate extreme poverty and hunger; achieve universal primary education; promote gender equality and empower women; reduce child mortality; improve maternal health; combat HIV/AIDS, malaria and other diseases; [and] ensure environmental sustainability ... by 2015."

Africa and the Middle East receive about one-fourth of all CIDA funding. While CIDA professes a commitment to "focus on creating an environment favorable to sustainable development and peace" in the Middle East, much of its funding is earmarked for groups with ideological and political agendas that are hostile to the state of Israel. These organizations include Alternatives, BADIL, Doctors without Borders, Inter-Church Lutheran World Relief and Justice, Medical Aid for Palestinians, Medecins du Monde, the Mennonite Central Committee, Oxfam, Save the Children, and World Vision.

CARTER CENTER (CC)

One Copenhill
453 Freedom Parkway
Atlanta, GA
30307

Phone :800-550-3560
URL: http://www.cartercenter.org

Focuses on peace and health issues around the world
Heavily financed by Arab sources

Established in 1982 by former U.S. President Jimmy Carter and former First Lady Rosalynn Carter, the Center that bears their name works in partnership with Emory University to fight for "human rights and the alleviation of human suffering," and seeks "to prevent and resolve conflicts, enhance freedom and democracy, and improve health." The Carter Center describes itself as "nonpartisan" and "neutral in dispute-resolution activities." Located in a 35-acre park approximately two miles east of downtown Atlanta, over the course of its history the Center has been active in 65 countries around the world. Construction of its facilities was financed by private donations from individuals, foundations, and corporations. Today the Center employs 150 full- and part-time workers who are based primarily in Atlanta, with some field representatives stationed in Africa, South America, Eastern Europe, and Central America.

The Carter Center's programs fall broadly under two principal categories: Peace and Health.

1) *Peace Programs*: Says the Carter Center: "Peace with justice requires resolving conflict according to rules agreed to by all, beginning with the shared commitment to human rights and democratic values. Today, virtually all governments claim to share this belief. The Carter Center ... seeks practical ways to narrow the gap between the rhetoric and realities of government policies in countries striving to overcome legacies of oppression and deadly conflict by building more just societies of their own."

The Carter Center's Peace Programs include the following:

a) The Democracy Program is the Center's most well known initiative. It works for "the development of inclusive democratic societies and the empowerment of citizens through election observation, consensus-building for international standards for democratic elections, and democracy-strengthening activities in emerging democracies and regional organizations." To date, the Carter Center has monitored more than 50 of what Jimmy Carter calls "troubled democratic elections, all of them either highly contentious or a nation's first experience with democracy." Since 2000, Carter Center delegations have overseen local and national elections in Peru, the Dominican Republic, Venezuela, Nicaragua, Guyana, East Timor, Zambia, Sierra Leone, China, Kenya, Mozambique, Guatemala, Indonesia, Congo, and Ethiopia. In most of those cases, the Center opposed the use of independent exit polls to verify whether its assessments of the elections' integrity were accurate.

In 1996 Jimmy Carter himself headed a Carter Center delegation that monitored the Palestinian Authority elections, pronouncing them "democratic," "open," "fair," and "well organized." These were the elections about which former CIA director Jim Woolsey -- as cited in *National Review* by Jay Nordlinger -- wrote: "Arafat was essentially 'elected' the same way Stalin was, but not nearly as democratically as Hitler, who at least had actual opponents."

The Carter Center also monitored the Venezuelan recall referendum of 2004 (which was designed to determine whether President Hugo Chavez should be recalled from office). According to the Center for Security Policy, the Chavez regime "delayed and obstructed the recall referendum process at every turn. Once the regime was forced to submit to such a referendum, moreover, it used a fraud-filled voting process to ensure victory. The government did everything -- including granting citizenship to half a million illegal aliens in a crude vote-buying scheme and 'migrating' existing voters away from their local election office -- to fix the results in its favor. The outcome was then affirmed and legitimated by ... Jimmy Carter's near-unconditional support. ... Carter ignored pleas from the opposition and publicly endorsed the results, despite the fact that the government reneged on its agreement to carry out an audit of the results. Carter's actions not only gave the Venezuelan regime the legitimacy it craved, but also destroyed the public's confidence in the voting process and in the effectiveness of international observers."

b) The Human Rights Program "intervene[es] on behalf of victims of human rights abuses; strengthen[s] the voices of human rights defenders internationally; and build[s] capacity for rule of law in partnerships with civil society, governments, and international organizations." This program also calls for the worldwide abolition of the death penalty.

c) The Conflict Resolution Program focuses on "helping prevent deadly conflict, mediating differences, ... ensuring that peace processes become irreversible at the invitation of parties to disputes, and assisting capacity building for conflict resolution in regional organizations."

d) The Americas Program seeks to "improve[e] regional cooperation and the deepening of democracy within the Western Hemisphere; thwar[t] corruption; increas[e] transparency, and decreas[e] social inequities to ensure that free and fair elections lead to the consolidation of democratic institutions and rule of law."

e) The China Program advises China's Ministry of Civil Affairs on local elections practices, voter education, and data collection.

f) The Global Development Initiative aims to help developing countries "devise their own plans for sustainable development."

2) *Health Programs*: According to the Carter Center, "Many of the most severe [physical] afflictions are entirely preventable. Yet people living in developing nations die or are disabled because they do not have access to the services they need to treat their illness or avoid infection entirely. Every day our experts show people how they can take steps to transform their own lives." The Center's Health Programs focus on eradicating infectious diseases; improving sanitation and hygiene; developing drug-distribution systems; strengthening health-care delivery infrastructures; increasing access to trained health personnel; improving agricultural techniques; and reducing "stigma and discrimination against people with mental illnesses."

With an annual operating budget of $36 million, the Carter Center is supported by grants from many charitable foundations, including the Bank of America Foundation, the Boston Foundation, the Ford Foundation, the Freddie Mac Foundation, the Bill and Melinda Gates Foundation, the William and Flora Hewlett Foundation, the W.K. Kellogg Foundation, the Minneapolis Foundation, the Moriah Fund, the New York Community Trust, the Public Welfare Foundation, the Rockefeller Foundation, and the Turner Foundation. The four largest donations were from the Bill and Melinda Gates Foundation -- a $4 million grant in 2003; a $10 million grant, also in 2003; a $25 million grant in 2005; and a $10 million grant in 2006. From 2000 to 2003, the aggregate sum of foundation, corporate, and individual contributions to the Carter Center was more than $433 million.

The Carter Center has also been a longtime recipient of Arab funding. Before his death in 2005, Saudi

Arabia's King Fahd made several large donations to the Center, including a 1993 gift of $7.6 million. As of 2005, the king's nephew, Prince Alwaleed Bin Talal (whose post-9/11 offer of $10 million to New York City was rejected by then-mayor Rudolph Giuliani because it was accompanied by the suggestion that America should cut back its support of Israel), had given at least $5 million to the Carter Center. In 2001 the government of the United Arab Emirates gave the Center $500,000. The previous year, ten of Osama bin Laden's brothers had jointly pledged $1 million, as did Sultan Qaboos bin Said of Oman in 1998. The Saudi Fund for Development has been another major contributor, as have the Kuwait Fund for Arab Economic Development and the government of Nigeria. In addition, Morocco's Prince Moulay Hicham Ben Abdallah has collaborated with the Carter Center on various initiatives. Arab donations such as these are encouraged by Mr. Carter's consistently pro-Arab, anti-Israel perspective regarding the Mideast conflict. There are no corresponding contributions from Israeli sources.

Additional Arab ties to the Carter Center can be found in the form of a few of its founders: the king of Saudi Arabia, Bank of Credit and Commerce International's Agha Hasan Abedi, and Yasser Arafat's friend Hasib Sabbagh.

In December 2006, Kenneth Stein, a professor of Israeli Studies at Emory University and the first Executive Director of the Carter Center, stepped down from his position at the Center and issued a resignation letter in which he described Carter as an incompetent, a liar, and a fraud. Of Carter's 2006 book *Palestine: Peace Not Apartheid*, whose title he classified as "too inflammatory to even print," Stein said that it was "replete with factual errors, copied materials not cited, superficialities, glaring omissions, and simply invented segments." More troubling than Carter's attacks on Israel, Stein noted, were his outright misrepresentations. In particular, Stein called attention to "meetings where I was the third person in the room, and my notes of those meetings show little similarity to points claimed in the book."

On January 11, 2007, fourteen members of the Carter Center's 200-person Board of Councilors, responsible for building public support for the Center, also resigned to protest Carter's anti-Israel screed. "You have clearly abandoned your historic role of broker in favor of becoming an advocate for one side," they wrote in their letter of resignation. "It seems that you have turned to a world of advocacy, including even malicious advocacy," they added. "We can no longer endorse your strident and uncompromising position. This is not the Carter Center or Jimmy Carter we came to respect and support." Atlanta real estate developer Steve Berman, who was among those who resigned, said the Board members had "watched with great dismay" as Carter defended the book, especially as he implied that Americans were reluctant to discuss the Arab-Israeli conflict because they feared a powerful Jewish lobby.

In fiscal year 2004-05, the Carter Center took in $172 million in donations.

CENTER FOR CONSTITUTIONAL RIGHTS (CCR)

666 Broadway, 7th Floor
New York, NY
10012
Phone :212-614-6464
Fax :212-614-6499
URL: http://www.ccr-ny.org

Founded by pro-Castro radicals
Opposes post-9/11 anti-terrorism laws

The Center for Constitutional Rights (CCR) was co-founded in November 1966 by the radical attorneys Morton Stavis, Ben Smith, Arthur Kinoy, and William Kunstler, longtime members of the Communist and radical left. (Kinoy and Kuntsler were well known for their pro-Castro politics.) CCR characterizes itself as an organization that "uses litigation proactively to advance the law in a positive direction, to guarantee the rights of those with the fewest protections and least access to legal resources."

CCR is a core member of the open borders lobby, which seeks to effectively initiate an era of mass, unchecked immigration. In 2002, the Center filed a class action lawsuit on behalf of illegal alien detainees, seeking punitive damages and a declaratory judgment that the detentions were unconstitutional and violated customary international law.

Since 9/11, CCR has focused its efforts heavily on reining in the U.S. government's newly implemented anti-terrorism measures, which the Center depicts as having "seriously undermined civil liberties, the checks and balances that are essential to the structure of our democratic government, and indeed, democracy itself." "Perhaps the most disturbing aspect of the government's actions," explains CCR, "has been its attack on the Bill of Rights, the very cornerstone of our American democracy."

CCR was a signatory to a March 17, 2003 letter exhorting members of the U.S. Congress to oppose the Domestic Security Enhancement Act, also known as "Patriot Act II," which was then under consideration. The letter asserted that the new legislation "fail[ed] to respect our time-honored liberties," and "contain[ed] a multitude of new and sweeping law enforcement and intelligence gathering powers ... that would severely dilute, if not undermine, many basic constitutional rights." In addition, CCR supports the California-based Coalition for Civil Liberties, which tries to influence city councils to pass resolutions creating "Civil Liberties Safe Zones"; that is, to be non-compliant with the provisions of the Patriot Act.

On January 17, 2006, CCR filed a lawsuit against President George W. Bush, the head of the National Security Agency (NSA), and the heads of the other major security agencies, "challenging NSA's surveillance of persons within the United States." (The NSA program targeted communications between persons in the United States and persons abroad where one party was suspected of having connections to terrorism.)

When law-enforcement agencies attempted, in the wake of 9/11, to conduct voluntary interviews with several thousand Middle Eastern men who were in the United States on temporary visas, CCR denounced such "racial profiling"; it issued this same complaint in response to the government's detention of hundreds of non-citizens from the Middle East for possible terrorist connections. When Attorney General Ashcroft warned in 2002 that visa violators would henceforth be arrested, CCR characterized his comments as "chilling." When new regulations permitted the FBI, CIA, and INS to share information about possible terrorist plots with one another, CCR lamented such assaults on "our privacy."

CCR's views on the political and psychological roots of anti-American terrorism were summarized in March 2002 by the organization's President, Michael Ratner, who said: "If the U.S. government truly wants its people to be safer and wants terrorist threats to diminish, it must make fundamental changes in its foreign policies ... particularly its unqualified support for Israel, and its embargo of Iraq, its bombing of Afghanistan, and its actions in Saudi Arabia. [These] continue to anger people throughout the region, and to fertilize the ground where terrorists of the future will take root." Condemning America's post-9/11 "aggression" against Afghanistan, Ratner suggested that as an alternative to war, the U.S. ought to "treat the attacks on September 11 as a crime against humanity, establish a UN tribunal, extradite the suspects, or if that fails, capture them with a UN force, and try them."

CCR has been a strong supporter of radical attorney Lynne Stewart, who in February 2005 was convicted on charges that she had illegally "facilitated and concealed communications" between her client, the incarcerated "blind sheik" Omar Abdel Rahman, and members of his Egyptian terrorist organization, the Islamic Group, which has ties to al Qaeda. CCR called Stewart's indictment in 2004 "an attack on attorneys who defend controversial figures, and an attempt to deprive these clients of the zealous representation that may be required."

In March 2005, CCR joined with the parents of deceased anti-Israel activist Rachel Corrie (the International Solidarity Movement volunteer who was accidentally crushed to death while trying to obstruct the path of a bulldozer that was engaged in anti-terror operations by Israeli Defense Force soldiers in Gaza) in filing a federal lawsuit against Caterpillar Inc., the Illinois-based manufacturer of the bulldozers used for such purposes by the IDF. Arguing that Caterpillar had violated international and state laws by providing the IDF with this machinery, CCR sued the company, marking the first time that American citizens had filed suit against a U.S. corporation for alleged misdeeds in a foreign country.

CCR only defends clients whose political views it supports, among the more notable of whom was Tom Hayden. Other CCR clients have included members of the Black Liberation Movement, the Student Nonviolent Coordinating Committee, Students for a Democratic Society, Women's Strike for Peace, the Communist Party, the Black Panther Party, the Chicago Seven, and the Catonsville Nine. The organization has also taken up the cause of Leonard Peltier, an American Indian rights activist who was convicted of murdering two FBI agents in 1975, a crime for which he is currently serving a life sentence in prison.

Regarding international matters, CCR has argued in court that: the Vietnam War was unconstitutional and criminal; bombing North Vietnam was illegal; the Nuremberg war crimes laws should have been applied to

Americans involved in the Vietnam War; the American military should have been restrained from fighting in Cambodia; fighting the Communist onslaught in Vietnam was wrong; and the U.S. Navy should not be permitted to use the Puerto Rican island of Vieques for bombing exercises. In addition, the Center attacked America's anti-Communist foreign policies concerning El Salvador, Nicaragua, Chile, Cuba, and elsewhere in Central and South America.

Characterizing President Bush as a political leader who is "out of control" and engaged in the "reckless abuse of power," CCR in 2006 produced a book titled *Articles of Impeachment Against George W. Bush.* This screed accused Bush of "illegally spying on U.S. citizens, lying to the American people about the Iraq war, seizing undue executive power, and sending people to be tortured overseas." CCR exhorted likeminded people to sign its online impeachment petition.

In November 2006, CCR filed a criminal complaint requesting "an investigation and, ultimately, a criminal prosecution that will look into the responsibility of high-ranking U.S. officials for authorizing war crimes in the context of the so-called 'War on Terror.'" The defendants in the case included former Secretary of Defense Donald Rumsfeld, former CIA Director George Tenet, and former Chief White House Counsel (and current Attorney General) Alberto R. Gonzales. The complaint was brought on behalf of 12 Iraqi citizens who were held at Abu Ghraib prison and one Guantánamo detainee -- all of whom were, according to CCR, tortured by American authorities.

In July 2005, CCR joined a coalition "including individuals and organizations ranging from Eve Ensler, Gloria Steinem, Not In Our Name, Code Pink, the Culture Project, [and] United For Peace and Justice" -- who together demanded the closure of the Guantánamo Bay prison camp and an "immediate independent investigation into the widespread allegations of abuse taking place there."

In December 2006, CCR and the Humanitarian Law Project (HLP) jointly petitioned a federal judge to dismiss many of the charges brought against the Hamas-linked organization Holy Land Foundation for Relief and Development, which in 2001 was shut down by the U.S. government because of its terrorist ties. Defense attorneys argued that Executive Order 13224, the statute under which HLF was named as a financier of terrorism, is overly broad.

A member organization of the Abolition 2000 and United For Peace and Justice anti-war coalitions, CCR is supported, in part, by donations from the Ford Foundation, the JEHT Foundation, the Samuel Rubin Foundation, the Scherman Foundation, the Open Society Institute, the Public Welfare Foundation, the New World Foundation, the Stewart R. Mott Charitable Trust, the Tides Foundation, and the Vanguard Public Foundation.

CENTER FOR ECONOMIC AND SOCIAL RIGHTS (CESR)

162 Montague Street
Third Floor
Brooklyn, NY
11202
Phone :718-237-9145
URL: http://www.cesr.org/

> Anti-Israel NGO
>
> Produces reports that characterize Israel as an oppressor nation and Palestinians as its innocent victims

According to its mission statement, the Center for Economic and Social Rights (CESR) seeks to advance "social justice through human rights," and to promote "the universal right of every human being to housing, education, health, and a healthy environment, food, work, and an adequate standard of living." In its extensive activities related to Israel and the Palestinian Territories, CESR identifies "the discrimination and brutality inherent in the Israeli occupation" as "the root cause" of Palestinian hardship, calling for "alternatives that recognize and promote equal rights for all people living under Israeli rule."

CESR was co-founded in 1993 by two lawyers (Roger Normand and Sarah Zaidi) and a scientist from Harvard University (Christopher Jochnick). Following a 2004 change in leadership, CESR is now headed by Eitan Felner, a former Director of Betselem and the onetime Chair of the Israeli Section of Amnesty

International.

Established on a grant of just over $100,000 from the John D. and Catherine T. MacArthur Foundation and the Echoing Green Foundation, CESR currently operates on an annual budget of more than $500,000. Between 2001 and 2006, the organization received over $3 million in grants from the Ford Foundation. Other recent funders include the John D. and Catherine T. MacArthur Foundation, the Mertz Gilmore Foundation, the Lannan Foundation, the Samuel Rubin Foundation, the Life Foundation, and the Moriah Fund. CESR has also received substantial donations from private benefactors like Elizabeth Benjamin, Carol Bernstein Ferry, and Claude Welch.

In May 1996, CESR released a report (which based its claims almost entirely on figures provided by the Iraqi Ministry of Health) stating that as a direct result of the United Nations sanctions that had first been imposed against Iraq in 1990, the death toll of Iraqi children under age five was, by then, already "over half a million." This CESR estimate represented a significant inflation of even the mortality estimates furnished by the Iraqi government at that time. To stress the gravity of the situation, CESR implied that the UN sanctions amounted to genocide: "In simple terms, more Iraqi children have died as a result of sanctions than the combined toll of two atomic bombs on Japan."

In a May 12, 1996 report, Lesley Stahl of *60 Minutes* filmed a CESR fact-finding tour of Iraq. On camera, she confronted then-UN Ambassador Madeleine Albright with the following: "We have heard that a half million children have died. I mean, that's more children than died in Hiroshima. And -- and you know, is the price worth it?" A flustered Albright replied, "I think this is a very hard choice, but the price -- we think the price is worth it." Anti-sanctions activists took this as an admission by Albright that the grossly inflated CESR figures were accurate.

CESR produces articles, fact-sheets, and reports on the Israeli-Palestinian conflict, and organizes conferences and teach-ins with such titles as "Palestinian Refugees and the Right of Return," and "Great Expectations, Bitter Realities: Human Rights Abuse and Economic Decline under the Oslo Process." CESR publications invariably cast Palestinians as the innocent victims of Israeli oppression, entirely ignoring the context of Palestinian terrorism in the region. In addition, CESR's special consultative status with the UN Committee on Economic, Social, and Cultural Rights has enabled it, over the years, to provide reports and oral testimonies to the United Nations and its (now-defunct) Commission on Human Rights.

CESR coordinates research projects on the Israeli-Palestinian conflict from its New York City and Gaza regional offices with a number of organizations, including LAW, the Al-Mezan Center for Human Rights, Betselem, the Palestinian Ministry of Education, the United Nations Relief and Works Agency, Birzeit University, the Palestinian Center for Human Rights, Defense of Children International/Palestine Section, Caritas, the Center on Housing Rights and Evictions, and the Palestinian Environmental NGOs Network.

In October 2001 -- together with more than 200 NGOs and individuals, including Christian Peacemaker Teams, Grassroots International, the Israel Committee Against House Demolitions-USA, MADRE, US Campaign to Stop the Wall, and Friends of Sabeel-North America -- CESR helped to create U.S. Campaign to End the Israeli Occupation. This umbrella group spearheads a concerted effort to divest financial assets from Israel, and promotes the Palestinian "right of return."

CESR formerly employed Lucy Mair, who has written for Electronic Intifada and currently works for Human Rights Watch as a researcher on Israel/Palestine issues. Mair contributed to CESR reports to the UN, coordinated protests against Israeli officials, and organized events that promoted a one-sided and highly distorted view of the Arab-Israeli conflict.

A 2001 CESR report submitted to the United Nations Economic and Social Council, titled "Under Siege: Israeli Human Rights Violations in Palestine," asserts that "Israel's occupation is the underlying cause of the Israeli-Palestinian conflict," and that "the current systematic violations of economic, social and cultural rights in the OPT [Occupied Palestinian Territories] derive from Israel's interrelated policies of ... closure, curfew and siege."

CENTER FOR POLICY ANALYSIS ON PALESTINE (CPAP)

2425-35 Virginia Avenue, NW
Washington, DC
20037

Phone :202-338-1290
URL: http://www.thejerusalemfund.org

Self-described "non-profit humanitarian organization"
Accuses Israel of practicing "apartheid and ethnic cleansing"

Established in 1991, the Washington, DC-based Center for Policy Analysis on Palestine (CPAP) is a Palestinian-American think tank describing itself as "a non-profit humanitarian organization." CPAP pursues "the study and analysis of the relationship between the United States and the Middle East, with particular emphasis on Palestine and the Arab-Israeli conflict, [and] seeks to bring into focus the implications of specific U.S. policies with regard to Palestine and the broader region." Founded as a part of The Jerusalem Fund, CPAP holds periodic symposims and conferences to showcase speakers on the Arab-Israeli conflict.

In CPAP's calculus, Israeli transgressions and human rights violations are entirely to blame for that nation's ongoing state of war with the Palestinian people. At the organization's 2003 winter conference -- entitled "Israel's Policy of Apartheid and Ethnic Cleansing" -- CPAP Chairman Hisham Sharabi set the tone for the seminar with his opening remarks: "In the face of relentless Israeli force, the only weapon the helpless and desperate have is to fling their bodies against the beast. Suicide bombings are no longer the lone act of desperate fanatics, but have become a conscious weapon of resistance and war. The culture of death and self-sacrifice is spreading in many Arab and Muslim countries. With unprecedented force being unleashed [by Israel] against helpless people, the task of recruiting hundreds, if not thousands of men and women willing to die has become a routine organizational matter in the resistance process."

CPAP derives its revenues from investment income and from "community assistance grants" that are funded through donations from private individuals in the United States and abroad.

CENTER FOR THE STUDY OF ISLAM AND DEMOCRACY (CSID)

1050 Connecticut Avenue
Suite 1000
Washington, D.C.
20036

Phone :202-772-2022
URL: http://www.csidonline.org/

Seeks "to contribute to the promotion of democracy, good governance, freedom, and human rights in the Arab and Muslim world."
Closely linked to the American Muslim Council, which supports Hamas and Hezbollah

Founded in March 1999, the Center for the Study of Islam and Democracy (CSID) is an organization of academicians, professionals, and activists -- both Muslim and non-Muslim -- from across the U.S. who, as CSID Founder and President Radwan A. Masmoudi puts it, seek "to contribute to the promotion of democracy, good governance, freedom, and human rights in the Arab and Muslim world." According to Masmoudi, CSID has organized more than 30 seminars, conferences, and workshops on these topics in Morocco, Algeria, Tunisia, Egypt, Jordan, Yemen, Bahrain, Turkey, and Iran. "Our [Americans'] old policy of giving tacit (and sometimes not so tacit) support to dictators and oppressors in the Arab and Muslim world," says Masmoudi, "will only exasperate [*sic*] the situation and make the situation much worse."

CSID organized two major international conferences -- titled "What is *Shariah*?" -- in Nigeria and Sudan, seeking to identify ways that Islamic Law "can be modernized and updated, through the process of *Ijtihad*, to address the needs of the Muslims in the 21st century." "*Shariah* in Arabic simply means 'rule of law,'" says Masmoudi, "and therefore we cannot be against it. ... [Its] punishments (stonings and amputations) were not invented by Islam. ... The majority of Islamic legal scholars are now of the legal opinion that these punishments can be changed to more modern and/or culturally acceptable forms of punishments for ... crimes [such as] theft, rape, adultery, murder, drugs, etc."

CSID seeks to produce scholarship that will "spread knowledge in the Muslim community" and "improve the mainstream American community and policymakers' understanding of Islam's approach towards individual freedom, civil rights, and political pluralism" while countering "widely held prejudices and misconceptions."

CSID was created by Board members and former staffers of the American Muslim Council, a group whose leadership has declared its support for Hamas and Hezbollah. "Most of CSID's Muslim personnel are radicals," wrote Islam scholar Daniel Pipes in March 2004. One such individual is CSID fellow Kamran Bokhari, who, according to Pipes, "also happens to have served for years as the North American spokesman for Al-Muhajiroun, perhaps the most extreme Islamist group operating in the West."

Some CSID Board members are agents of the Saudi Arabian government, which spends enormous sums of money to spread Wahhabism, a radical and intolerant form of Islam, all around the globe. One of the Center's Founding Directors was Taha Jabir al Alwani, a Founder of the Council of the Muslim World League in Mecca, perhaps the most influential distributor of Saudi Arabian money on earth.

The Chairman of CSID's Board of Directors is Ali Al Mazrui, a State University of New York professor who in 2003 came to the defense of University of South Florida Professor Sami Al-Arian when the latter was arrested as an agent of the terrorist group Palestinian Islamic Jihad.

CSID maintains a close relationship with the Muslim Students' Association of the United States and Canada (MSA). For example, on October 12, 2005, Radwan Masmoudi was the featured speaker at a MSA-sponsored event titled "The Future of Democracy in the Muslim World," which was held at the University of North Carolina.

CSID receives funding from the Earhart Foundation.

COALITION FOR PEACE IN THE MIDDLE EAST (CPME)

www.palestinecampaign.org

Anti-war group
Condemns the governments of U.S. and Israel

Founded in 1990, the Coalition for Peace in the Middle East (CPME) is an anti-war network with numerous chapters across the United States -- most prominently in Los Angeles (California) and Youngstown (Ohio). The Coalition's original mission was to pressure the United States to reject the use of military force as a means of driving Iraq's invading army out of Kuwait in 1991. CPME's slogans at the time were "Sanctions, not War" and "Let the Sanctions Work." CPME further called for an end to the Israeli occupation of the West Bank, Gaza, and East Jerusalem -- favoring "a two-state solution ... and recognition of the PLO as the representative of the Palestinian people." Anti-war and anti-Israel campaigns remain foremost on CPME's agenda to this day.

On March 30, 2002, CPME co-sponsored a Washington, DC rally exhorting Israel to "End the Occupation, End the Violence." CPME's co-sponsors for this event included: the Council on American-Islamic Relations; the Islamic Association for Palestine; the American-Arab Anti-Discrimination Committee; the American Friends Service Committee; the American Muslim Council; the Muslim Public Affairs Council; Al-Awda; Jews Against the Occupation; the Muslim American Society; the International Action Center; the International Socialist Organization; the Women's International League for Peace and Freedom; the Council for the National Interest; Partners for Peace;
Solidarity USA; Christian Peacemakers Teams; American Muslims for Jerusalem; Peace Action; Pax Christi USA; American Muslims for Global Peace and Justice; the International Action Center; the International Socialist Organization; Queers For Racial & Economic Justice; the Muslim Students Association of the U.S. and Canada.

CPME has also worked closely with such groups as the Palestine Solidarity Committee; the International Jewish Peace Union; Fellowship of Reconciliation; Pledge of Resistance; the Gray Panthers; Committee in Solidarity with the People of El Salvador; and the Democratic Socialists of America.

COMMITTEE FOR JUSTICE IN PALESTINE (CJP)

Anti-Israel activist group based at Ohio State University

The Committee for Justice in Palestine (CJP) is an anti-Israel activist group based at Ohio State University (OSU). Opposed to what it calls Israel's "occupation" of "Palestine," CJP's ongoing Divestment Campaign exhorts OSU officials to sever all of the university's current financial ties to Israeli corporations and interests.

On October 18, 2003, CJP was a sponsoring organization of a United For Peace and Justice rally whose participants first gathered at Pennsylvania's York County Prison "to protest the continued illegal detention of immigrants following 9-11," and then marched to the nearby Caterpillar Parts Distribution Plant "to protest Caterpillar's continuing support for Israel's illegal occupation of Palestine." According to the promotional literature for this rally: "Caterpillar is responsible for the manufacturing of armored bulldozers, which they sell to the Israeli Defense Force. The IDF [Israeli Defense Force] uses these bulldozers in the occupied territories to demolish homes of families thought to be associated with Palestinian militants. This policy of collective punishment is specifically against the Geneva Conventions, and is considered a war crime under international law. It was with such a bulldozer that American Palestinian solidarity activist Rachel Corrie was murdered by the IDF last spring, while non-violently trying to prevent a home demolition. Rachel, while in plain sight, was viciously run over and then backed over again, by a bulldozer manufactured by Caterpillar."

In November 2003, CJP hosted the Palestine Solidarity Movement's (PSM) Annual Conference at Ohio State University. CJP also took part in PSM's Fourth Annual Conference, held at Duke University the following fall.

In 2004, CJP was a signatory -- along with more than 200 other leftist organizations -- to a letter exhorting members of the U.S. Senate to oppose Israel's construction of an anti-terrorist security fence in the West Bank. In CJP's view, the security barrier is an illegal "apartheid wall" that violates the civil and human rights of Palestinians.

In July 2006, CJP co-signed a letter to UN Secretary General Kofi Annan calling for the "Immediate International Protection for the Palestinian People in the Occupied Territory." This letter read, in part: "[T]he inexorable march of Israeli human rights violations continues with renewed savagery. The Israeli military has escalated its assault upon the Palestinian people, with dozens of Palestinians killed and wounded in recent months. ... [Israeli] forces continue illegally to arrest and detain thousands of Palestinians, confiscate Palestinian land, demolish homes, impose a deadly economic blockade, and build an annexationist Apartheid wall. ... We therefore call upon the United Nations to intervene to defend the Palestinian people ..." Among CJP's dozens of fellow co-signers were the International Solidarity Movement, the American-Arab Anti-Discrimination Committee, the Troops Out Now Coalition, the International Action Center, the Middle East Children's Alliance, the Workers World Party, Ittijah, and the Arab Association for Human Rights.

COUNCIL FOR THE NATIONAL INTEREST (CNI)

1250 4th Street SW
Suite WG-1
Washington, DC
20024

Phone :202-863-2951
URL: http://www.cnionline.org/Non-profit organization whose mission is "to restore a political environment in America in which voters and their elected officials are free from the undue influence and pressure of a foreign country, namely Israel."

"September 11 would not have occurred if the U.S. government had refused to help Israel humiliate and destroy Palestinian society."
Maintains ties to several supporters of Islamic terror

Established in 1989, the Council for the National Interest (CNI) is an offshoot of the Washington D.C.-based American Educational Trust (AET), an anti-Israel organization that publishes the academic journal

Washington Report on Middle East Affairs. CNI's founders included Paul Findley and Paul N. "Pete" McCloskey (both former U.S. congressmen), Andrew Killgore (former U.S. ambassador to Qatar), Eugene H. Bird (formerly with the U.S. foreign service), and Richard Curtiss (former U.S. Information Agency chief).

CNI describes itself as "a non-profit, non-partisan grassroots organization advocating a new direction for U.S. Middle East policy." CNI's mission is "to restore a political environment in America in which voters and their elected officials are free from the undue influence and pressure of a foreign country, namely Israel." As CNI Founding Chairman Paul Findley puts it, the organization seeks to "help advance the national interest in the Middle East and at the same time help repair the damage being done to our political institutions by the over-zealous tactics of Israel's lobby." "September 11 would not have occurred if the U.S. government had refused to help Israel humiliate and destroy Palestinian society," says Findley.

CNI enumerates its organizational goals as follows:

> Total withdrawal of Israel from all occupied territory ...
>
> A shared Jerusalem, the capital of two states, Israel and Palestine.
>
> An end to all acts of aggression, provocation, and retaliation by Israel and the end of all violence and attempts to solve the problem by military means. This includes terrorism committed against Israelis as well as the state terrorism committed by Israel against Palestinians.
>
> American recognition of a totally independent state of Palestine.
>
> An elimination of all unaudited U.S. aid to Israel.
>
> Normalized relations with Israel, her neighbors, and regional organizations such as the Arab League.
>
> A political atmosphere in which a fair and objective media covers the Middle East without fear of retaliation by advertisers and pro-Israeli groups; the American electorate is unafraid to debate the issues openly and frankly; and our elected officials vote their conscience.

CNI seeks to help achieve the foregoing objectives by coordinating its efforts with local and regional activist organizations; making use of "local and national full-page newspaper advertising and email lists to build the organization"; and sponsoring public hearings and seminars on Capitol Hill, for which it attracts big-name speakers such as Ralph Nader and Hanan Ashrawi.

CNI and its sister organization, the Council for the National Interest Foundation (CNIF), maintain close ties with numerous individuals linked to Islamic terror groups. One such person is CNIF Board Member Abdurahman Alamoudi, an open supporter of Hamas and Hezbollah. Alamoudi is currently serving a 23-year prison term for having illegally accepted hundreds of thousands of dollars from top Libyan officials, plotted to murder Saudi Crown Prince Abdullah (on behalf of Libyan President Muammar Qadhafi), and violated numerous tax and immigration laws.

A 1999 CNIF press release shows that during a tour of the Middle East, CNI President Eugene Bird was part of a delegation that met with Nabih Berri (the former head of Lebanon's Amal terrorist movement), an unnamed "leader in Hezbollah," and Mahmoud Al-Zahar (a senior official of Hamas). Also in 1999, CNI co-founder Richard Curtiss was the featured speaker at a Jerusalem Festival organized by the Islamic Association for Palestine, which has distributed Hamas communiqués, including a charter calling for *jihad* against Jews.

The CNI and CNIF websites share the same Internet domain, which registers back to Bayan Elashi and the Richardson, Texas-based Infocom Corporation, of which Elashi was the Chief Executive Officer. According to a Justice Department report, in April 2005 a federal court convicted Elashi and his four brothers "on charges of conspiracy to deal in the property of a specially designated terrorist [Hamas political leader Mousa Abu Marzook] and [of] money laundering. The activities were related to Infocom, an Internet Service provider believed to be a front for Hamas."

Dr. Laura Drake is another extremist with ties to CNI. In 1993 and 1994, Drake served as the organization's Director of Research. By 1998, she was Director of the United Association for Studies and Research, described by law enforcement as "the political command of Hamas in the United States." Speaking in December 2002 at the Islamic Circle of North America's and Muslim American Society's Annual Convention in Chicago, Drake voiced her feelings about Israelis: "So now the occupiers are whining to the U.S. that they are being hit back, that they are getting burned once in a while, that the settlers are being set aflame. Let them burn, I say, let them burn."

CNI has drafted a petition to support an Israel Accountability and Security Act, charging that "U.S. foreign policy continues to turn a blind eye to the continued violations of international law by Israel's right-wing government."

As noted earlier, CNI has close ties to the *Washington Report on Middle East Affairs* (*WRMEA*), whose content is intensely hostile to Israel. In the 1990s, *WRMEA* published numerous CNI articles and newsletters; the journal even shared the same office address as CNI for a number of years. Today Richard Curtiss and Andrew Killgore, a pair of self-described "outspoken Arabists," serve as *WRMEA*'s Executive Editor and Publisher, respectively.

CNI's operations are funded mostly by individual donations; it also receives a small amount of foundation support.
CNI rents space in its Washington, DC office to the anti-Israel organization Partners for Peace.

COUNCIL ON AMERICAN-ISLAMIC RELATIONS (CAIR)

453 New Jersey Avenue SE
Washington, DC
20003
Phone :202-488-8787
Fax :202-488-0883
URL: http://www.cair-net.org/Civil rights group partially funded by Saudi Wahhabi establishment

The Council on American-Islamic Relations (CAIR) describes itself as a "non-profit, grassroots membership organization ... established to promote a positive image of Islam and Muslims in America," to protect Muslims from hate crimes and discrimination, and to present "an Islamic perspective on issues of importance to the American public." According to the Council's Director of Communications, Ibrahim Hooper, "We are similar to a Muslim NAACP." As of June 2007, CAIR claimed 32 branch affiliates in the United States and one in Canada.

CAIR was co-founded in 1994 by Ibrahim Hooper, Nihad Awad, and Omar Ahmad, all of whom had close ties to the Islamic Association for Palestine (IAP), which was established by senior Hamas operative Mousa Abu Marzook and functioned as Hamas' public relations and recruitment arm in the United States. Awad and Ahmad had previously served, respectively, as IAP's Public Relations Director and President. Ibrahim Hooper was also an employee of IAP. Thus it can be said that CAIR was an outgowth of IAP.

CAIR opened its first office in Washington, DC, with the help of a $5,000 donation from the Holy Land Foundation for Relief and Development (HLF), a self-described charity founded by Mousa Abu Marzook. In May 1996, CAIR coordinated a press conference to protest the decision of the U.S. government to extradite Marzook for his connection to terrorist acts performed by Hamas. CAIR characterized the extradition as "anti-Islamic" and "anti-American." Shortly after 9/11, the CAIR website featured a picture of the World Trade Center in flames and below it a call for donations that was linked to the HLF website. When President Bush closed HLF in December 2001 for collecting money "to support the Hamas terror organization," CAIR decried his action as "unjust" and "disturbing."

From its inception, CAIR has sought to portray itself as a moderate, mainstream organization, and as early as 1996 its officials became frequent guests at State Department and White House events. In the aftermath of 9/11, when the Bush administration tried to reassure American Muslims that Islam was not the target of the war on terrorism, CAIR officials were prominent among the invitees. CAIR was the main Islamic group to gain U.S. media access in the post-9/11 period, providing the "Muslim view" of the terrorist attacks and of America's response to them. As self-acclaimed Muslim spokesmen, CAIR officials typically refused to "simplify the situation" by blaming Osama bin Laden for the attacks on America. Moreover, while they were eventually induced by journalists to condemn Palestinian suicide terror in a *pro forma* manner, they hedged their disavowals by describing it as an understandable response to Israeli brutality.

Contending that American Muslims are the victims of wholesale repression, CAIR has given sensitivity training to police departments across the United States, instructing law officers in the art of dealing with Muslims respectfully.

CAIR further claims that U.S. foreign policy is dictated largely by Zionist extremists. As Evan McCormick of the Center for Security Policy puts it: "By convincing moderate Muslims that they are being targeted unfairly by the Bush administration's [anti-terror] policies, CAIR incites fear in members of that demographic. If innocent Muslims are then convinced that they will be the target of government action, then they have no incentive to reject an extremist ideology that resists the government's anti-terror policies. ... This is the essence of CAIR's strategy: shock moderate Muslims about the motivations of the U.S. Government, turn them into post-[9/11] victims, and then recruit them as supporters for your political agenda when they are ripe for the taking."

Along the same lines, a civil suit filed by the estate of 9/11 victim and former high-ranking FBI counter-terrorism agent John O'Neill, Sr. asserted that CAIR's goal "is to create as much self-doubt, hesitation, fear of name-calling, and litigation within police departments and intelligence agencies as possible so as to render such authorities ineffective in pursuing international and domestic terrorist entities."

CAIR endorsed an October 22, 2002 "National Day of Protest" whose premise was: "Since September 11th thousands of Muslims, Arabs and South Asians have been rounded up, detained and disappeared. ... Hard-won civil liberties and protections have been stripped away as part of the government's 'war on terrorism.' The USA-PATRIOT Act brings in a new set of repressive laws and restrictions on people and grants even greater power to law enforcement agents of all kinds." Moreover, this document explicitly defended the convicted murderers Mumia Abu-Jamal and Leonard Peltier, as well as Lynne Stewart and Jose Padilla, who were convicted on terrorism-related charges -- depicting all four as persecuted political prisoners of a repressive American government.

CAIR was a signatory to a February 20, 2002 document, composed by C. Clark Kissinger's radical group Refuse & Resist, condemning military tribunals and the detention of immigrants apprehended in connection with post-9/11 terrorism investigations. The document lamented that "the denial of any due process for Arab[s], Muslim[s], South Asians and others" bore "chilling similarities to a police state."

In February 2003, CAIR joined the American Muslim Council, the American Muslim Alliance, and the Muslim Public Affairs Council in forming a coalition to repeal and amend the Patriot Act -- alleging that it violated the civil liberties of Americans, particularly Muslims. CAIR also endorsed the Civil Liberties Restoration Act of 2004, which was designed to roll back, in the name of protecting civil liberties, vital national-security policies that had been adopted after the 9/11 terrorist attacks.

CAIR promotes a radical Islamic vision, as evidenced by the fact that its co-founder Omar Ahmad told a Fremont, California audience in July 1998: "Islam isn't in America to be equal to any other faith, but to become dominant. The Koran ... should be the highest authority in America, and Islam the only accepted religion on Earth." In a similar spirit, Ibrahim Hooper told a reporter in 1993: "I wouldn't want to create the impression that I wouldn't like the government of the United States to be Islamic sometime in the future." In 2003 Hooper stated that if Muslims ever become a majority in the United States, they will likely seek to replace the U.S. Constitution with Islamic law, which they deem superior to man-made law. In the late 1980s, Ihsan Bagby, who would later become a CAIR Board member, stated that Muslims "can never be full citizens of this country," referring to the United States, "because there is no way we can be fully committed to the institutions and ideologies of this country."

CAIR receives considerable funding from Saudi Arabia. In 1999, the Saudi embassy in Washington announced a $250,000 grant by the Islamic Development Bank to CAIR for the purchase of land in Washington, DC to be used in the construction of "an education and research center."

In 2003 CAIR invested, according to its own Form 990 filed with the Internal Revenue Service, $325,000 from its California offices with the North American Islamic Trust (NAIT). According to *Newsweek*, authorities say that over the years "NAIT money has helped the Saudi Arabian sect of Wahhabism—or Salafism, as the broader, pan-Islamic movement is called—to seize control of hundreds of mosques in U.S. Muslim communities." A recent study by the Center for Religious Freedom found that a very large number of American mosques teach hatred of Jews and Christians, coupled with doctrines of Islamic supremacism.

Writes Islam scholar Stephen Schwartz: "CAIR should be considered a foreign-based subversive organization, comparable in the Islamist field to the Soviet-controlled Communist Party USA, and the Cuban-controlled front groups that infiltrated 'Latin American solidarity' organizations in the U.S. during the 1980s. It has organized numerous community branches and has had immense success in gaining position as an 'official' representative of Islam in the U.S."

Notable facts about CAIR's *pas de deux* with Islamic extremism and terrorism include the following:

Co-founder Nihad Awad asserted at a 1994 meeting at Barry University, "I am a supporter of the Hamas movement." Awad wrote in the *Muslim World Monitor* that the 1994 trial which had resulted in the conviction of four Islamic fundamentalist terrorists who had perpetrated the previous year's World Trade Center bombing was "a travesty of justice."

On February 2, 1995, U.S. Attorney Mary Jo White named CAIR Advisory Board member and New York imam Siraj Wahhaj as one of the "unindicted persons who may be alleged as co-conspirators" in Islamic Group leader Omar Abdel Rahman's foiled plot to blow up numerous New York City monuments.

On June 6, 2006, CAIR's Ohio affiliate held a large fundraiser in honor of Siraj Wahhaj. Following the event, CAIR-OH issued a press release heralding the more than $100,000 that Wahhaj had helped raise that evening for the organization's "civil liberties work."

In October 1998, CAIR demanded the removal of a Los Angeles billboard describing Osama bin Laden as "the sworn enemy," asserting that this depiction "offensive to Muslims."

In 1998, CAIR denied bin Laden's responsibility for the two al Qaeda bombings of American embassies in Africa. According to Ibrahim Hooper, the bombings resulted from "misunderstandings of both sides."

In September 2003, CAIR's former Community Affairs Director, Bassem Khafagi, pled guilty to three federal counts of bank and visa fraud and agreed to be deported to Egypt. Federal investigators said that a group Khafagi founded, the Islamic Assembly of North America, had funneled money to activities supporting terrorism and had published material advocating suicide attacks against the United States. Khafagi's illegal activities took place while he was employed by CAIR.

In July 2004, Ghassan Elashi, a founding Board member of CAIR's Texas chapter, was convicted along with his four brothers of having illegally shipped computers from their Dallas-area business, InfoCom Corporation, to Libya and Syria, two designated state sponsors of terrorism. That same month, Elashi was charged with having provided more than $12.4 million to Hamas while he was running HLF. In April 2005, Elashi and two of his brothers were also convicted of knowingly doing business with Hamas operative Mousa Abu Marzook, who was Elashi's brother-in-law. Elashi's illegal activities took place while he was employed by CAIR.

On September 6, 2001, the day that federal agents first raided Infocom's headquarters, CAIR Executive Director Nihad Awad denounced the government for "tak[ing] us back to the McCarthy era." Similarly, CAIR's Dallas-Fort Worth chapter depicted the Elashis' indictment as "a war on Islam and Muslims" and alleged that the brothers had been convicted "for their crime of being Muslims in America."

Randall Todd Royer, who served as a communications specialist and civil rights coordinator for CAIR, trained with Lashkar-I-Taiba, an al Qaeda-tied Kashmir organization that is listed on the State Department's international terror list. He was also indicted on charges of conspiring to help al Qaeda and the Taliban battle American troops in Afghanistan. He later pled guilty to lesser firearm-related charges and was sentenced to twenty years in prison. Royer's illegal activities took place while he was employed by CAIR.

Onetime CAIR fundraiser Rabih Haddad was arrested on terrorism-related charges and deported from the United States due to his subsequent work as Executive Director of the Global Relief Foundation, which in October 2002 was designated by the U.S. Treasury Department for financing al Qaeda and other terrorist organizations.

During the 2005 trial of Sami Al-Arian, who was a key figure for Palestinian Islamic Jihad in the United States, Ahmed Bedier of CAIR's Florida branch emerged as one of Al-Arian's most vocal advocates.

The foregoing terrorist connections have drawn the notice of numerous commentators:

Steven Pomerantz, the FBI's former chief of counter-terrorism, has stated that "CAIR, its leaders and its activities effectively give aid to international terrorist groups."

The family of John P. O'Neill, Sr., the former FBI counter-terrorism chief who died at the World Trade Center on 9/11, named CAIR in a lawsuit as having "been part of the criminal conspiracy of radical Islamic terrorism" responsible for the September 11 attacks.

Terrorism expert Steven Emerson, citing federal law enforcement sources and internal documents, characterizes CAIR as "a radical fundamentalist front group for Hamas."

U.S. Senator Richard Durbin has said, "CAIR is unusual in its extreme rhetoric and its associations with groups that are suspect."

On September 17, 2003, U.S. Senator Charles Schumer stated that CAIR co-founders Nihad Awad and Omar Ahmed have "intimate links with Hamas." He later remarked that "we know [CAIR] has ties to terrorism."

During September 2003 hearings held by the Senate Judiciary Subcommittee on Terrorism, Technology, and Homeland Security, Chairman Jon Kyl noted the connections between such groups as CAIR and the Saudi government, stating: "A small group of organizations based in the U.S. with Saudi backing and support is well advanced in its four-decade effort to control Islam in America -- from mosques, universities and community centers to our prisons and even within our military. Moderate Muslims who love America and want to be part of our great country are being forced out of those institutions."

A number of American Muslims have made similar observations:

The late Seifeldin Ashmawy, who published *Voice of Peace*, called CAIR the champion of "extremists whose views do not represent Islam."

Tashbih Sayyed of the Council for Democracy and Tolerance (CDT) called CAIR "the most accomplished fifth column" in the United States. Jamal Hasan, also of CDT, said that CAIR's goal is to spread "Islamic hegemony the world over by hook or by crook."

According to Kamal Nawash of the Free Muslim Coalition Against Terrorism, CAIR and similar groups "condemn terrorism on the surface while endorsing an ideology that helps foster extremism," and adds that "almost all of their members are theocratic Muslims who reject secularism and want to establish Islamic states."

In 1998, CAIR co-hosted a rally at Brooklyn College where Islamic militants exhorted the attendees to carry out "*jihad*" and described Jews as "pigs and monkeys." The crowd chanted: "No to the Jews, descendants of the apes." Referring to Israel as a "racist country and state," CAIR was a signatory to a MAY 20, 2004 "Joint Muslims/Arab-American Statement on Israeli Violence in Gaza," which "strongly condemn[ed]" Israel's "indiscriminate killings of innocent Palestinians, including many children," and its "demolition of Palestinian homes." In August 2006 CAIR accused Israel of practicing state terrorism in its war against the Lebanese terrorist organization Hezbollah. Said CAIR Communications Director Ibrahim Hooper, "Our [American] government must end it support for Israel's campaign of terror in Lebanon and join an international effort to protect and bring humanitarian aid to the civilian population of that devastated nation."

CAIR officials have displayed a double standard for denouncing violence. For example, Ibrahim Hooper in a *Pittsburg Post-Gazette* interview refused to denounce the terrorism of Hamas and Hezbollah, stating, "we're not in the business of condemning." By contrast, when Israeli troops killed Hamas leader Ahmed Yassin, CAIR condemned "the assassination of a wheelchair-bound Palestinian Muslim religious leader," calling the operation "an act of state terror."

According to terrorism expert Steven Emerson: "Hussam Ayloush, the Executive Director of the Southern California chapter of [CAIR] ... is known to use the term 'Zionazi' to refer to Israelis, and [he] compare[s] Zionism to Nazism, once writing in an e-mail, 'Indeed, the Zionazis are a bunch of nice people; just like their Nazi brethren!'"

CAIR chose not to endorse or participate in the May 14, 2005 "Free Muslims March Against Terror," an event whose stated purpose was to "send a message to the terrorists and extremists that their days are numbered ... [and to send] a message to the people of the Middle East, the Muslim world and all people who seek freedom, democracy and peaceful coexistence that we support them."

CAIR states that it "works in close cooperation with other civic and civil liberties groups such as the American Civil Liberties Union, Amnesty International, NAACP, Hispanic Unity, Organization of Chinese

Americans, Japanese American Citizens League, Sikh Mediawatch and Resource Task Force, among many others." CAIR also identifies the National Council of Churches as a "partner" organization.

On December 12, 2006, CAIR Board Chairman Parvez Ahmed called the war in Iraq a "pure unadulterated projection of raw power" and said the U.S. should withdraw its forces immediately.

Another notable CAIR official is Altaf Ali, the organization's Florida Director. Ali alleges that America unfairly responded to the 9/11 attacks by trampling on the civil liberties of all Muslims, and he has wavered on the question of whether or not the victims who died in the World Trade Center on 9/11 could be classified as innocents whose killings were unjustified.

In 2007 CAIR became involved in the infamous "flying imams" lawsuit, a case that centered around six Muslim clerics aboard a November 2006 US Airways flight from Minneapolis to Phoenix. Shortly before takeoff, they began engaging in bizarre behaviors eerily reminiscent of those that had been used by the 9/11 hijackers: shouting slogans in Arabic; leaving their assigned seats to position themselves in different places; requesting seat belt extenders that they positioned on the floor, rather than using them to secure themselves. Responding to the concerns of alarmed passengers and the flight crew, authorities removed the imams from the plane. Soon thereafter the imams filed a lawsuit against US Airways, claiming that they had been removed from the flight for no reason other than anti-Muslim discrimination. It has also been reported that the imams plan to sue the passengers whose complaints resulted in their removal from the plane. The lawyer for the imams is Omar T. Mohammedi, who as of 2006 was President of CAIR's New York chapter.

In February 2007, CAIR endorsed a call by the American Muslim Taskforce for Civil Rights and Elections, for a worldwide "rolling fast" in support of the incarcerated Sami Al-Arian, who had initiated a hunger strike on January 21 to protest his detention and treatment by federal authorities. Participants in the campaign agreed to fast every Monday, Wednesday, and Friday for as long as Al-Arian continued his hunger strike.

On June 4, 2007, the *New York Sun* reported that CAIR had been named as an unindicted co-conspirator in an alleged criminal conspiracy to support both Hamas and the Holy Land Foundation for Relief and Development. The federal prosecution document, in naming CAIR as an unindicted co-conspirator, described the organization as a present or past member of the U.S. Muslim Brotherhood's Palestine Committee.

According to a June 2007 *Washington Times* report, CAIR's membership had declined more than 90 percent since the September 11, 2001 terrorist attacks, from approximately 29,000 in 2000 to fewer than 1,700 in 2006. As a result, CAIR's annual income from dues dropped from $732,765 in 2000 (when yearly dues cost $25 per person), to $58,750 in 2006 (when dues cost $35). As of 2007, the majority of CAIR's $3 million annual budget derived from about two dozen individual donors.

M. Zuhdi Jasser, Director of the American-Islamic Forum for Democracy, said in June 2007 that the decline in CAIR's membership contradicted the organization's claim that it represents the interests and concerns of 7 million American Muslims. "This is the untold story in the myth that CAIR represents the American Muslim population," said Jasser. "They only represent their membership and donors."

CAIR is funded by the Community Foundation for Greater Atlanta and by the New York Foundation.

DEFENSE FOR CHILDREN INTERNATIONAL/PALESTINE SECTION (DCI-P)

PO Box 55201
Jerusalem

Phone :972 2 240 7530
URL: http://www.dci-pal.org/

Anti-Israel NGO

Established in 1992, Defense for Children International / Palestine Section (DCI/PS) is affiliated with the Geneva-based Defense for Children International, whose roots date back to 1979. DCI/PS describes itself as "an independent, Palestinian non-governmental organization which develops its programs and acts according to Palestinian children's needs and Palestinian priorities." The programs and projects of DCI/PS are implemented within the framework of four main units:

Legal Aid and Representation: "DCI/PS defends the rights of Palestinian children through providing free legal services and consultations to children and families in need. DCI/PS attorneys represent Palestinian children who are detained and brought before Israeli military courts, and the Legal Unit monitors and documents child arrests, the treatment of child prisoners and detention conditions for Palestinian children under 18. Additionally, DCI/PS attorneys intervene in defense of children's rights in areas under the jurisdiction of the Palestinian Authority, and, where necessary, represent children brought before Palestinian courts."

Documentation of Children's Rights: "DCI/PS ... specializes in documenting violations of Palestinian children's rights, both individual and collective, using a team of fieldworkers around the West Bank and Gaza Strip."

Research and International Advocacy: "DCI/PS regularly produces research reports, publications, information briefs and press releases on the status of Palestinian children's rights ... On the advocacy level, DCI/PS lobbies and reports to UN bodies."

Training and Social Mobilization: "A key component of DCI/PS projects and programs is direct work with Palestinian children, including programs to increase children's life skills, awareness of their rights, and to promote their active participation in the community. ... In addition, DCI/PS implements awareness campaigns and training courses for the local community, in order to deepen public understanding of children's rights and to strengthen the sense of collective responsibility for promoting and safeguarding these rights. Educational booklets, posters, stickers, and other rights-awareness materials are produced to further this goal."

Characterizing Israel as an unrepentant violator of Palestinian human rights, DCI/PS regularly condemns the Jewish state's "war crimes," its "collective punishment" of Arabs living within its borders, and its "gross violation of child rights."

DCI/PS bitterly opposes Israel's construction of an anti-terrorism barrier along its border with the West Bank, depicting the barrier as an "Apartheid Wall" that is an affront to the dignity of Palestinians in the region. Says DCI/PS: "Palestinian children report ... that the Wall prevents them from going to school, from seeing family and friends, and from getting health care. They say they feel insecure and afraid of the Wall, and that their families are poorer and have lost their lands because of it."

DCI/PS's official statements and press releases commonly make reference to Palestinian children who allegedly have been killed without cause by Israeli soldiers. In a September 29, 2005 statement, for example, the organization denounced "the systematic and daily violations of the rights of Palestinians in general and of Palestinian children in particular." "Children too young to walk or speak have been shot dead," the statement added, "thousands have been injured, still more have looked on horrified as friends and family members have been killed, maimed, arrested, humiliated. Schools and homes have been demolished, hospitals destroyed. A vast array of discriminatory and illegal movement restrictions including closures, curfews, checkpoints and roadblocks have been imposed on the Palestinian residents of the OPT [Occupied Palestinian Territories], plunging the Palestinian economy further and further into crisis. ... Israel bears full responsibility for the appalling circumstances in which many Palestinians find themselves ..."

Condemning also Israel's targeted killings of terrorist leaders, to whom DCI/PS refers as "Palestinian activists," the organization was a co-signatory to a public statement that read: "This targeted assassination policy not only circumvents the fundamental right to due process but also risks the further destabilization of an already volatile political situation. ... Inevitably, bystanders -- including women and children -- are killed or injured in such operations. Targeted assassinations and other forms of extrajudicial executions violate the fundamental right to life, protected under international human rights and humanitarian law." Additional signers of this document included such anti-Israel NGOs as Adalah, Al-Haq, the Al-Mezan Centre for Human Rights, and the Palestinian Center for Human Rights.

In the summer of 2006, when Israel was engaged in simultaneous military conflicts against the Hamas and

Hezbollah terrorist organizations, DCI/PS condemned Israel's "grave violations and massacres against Palestinian and Lebanese civilians, especially children, through [its] ongoing military offensive in the Gaza Strip ... and Lebanon."

ECUMENICAL ACCOMPANIMENT PROGRAMME IN PALESTINE AND ISRAEL (EAPPI)

WCC/EAPPI
International Coordination Team
International Affairs, Peace and Human Security
World Council of Churches
150, route de Ferney
PO Box 2100
CH-1211 Geneva 2
Phone :4122 791 63 13
URL: http://www.eappi.org/Anti-Israel NGO

Established in August 2002, the Ecumenical Accompaniment Programme in Palestine and Israel (EAPPI) is an initiative of the World Council of Churches (WCC), which is a major supporter of the campaign to divest financially from all Israeli business entities. Asserting that it was "developed as a response to Israel's violation of internationally accepted norms and principles of human rights and the rule of law," EAPPI seeks to: "expose the violence of the [Israeli] occupation"; "end the brutality, humiliation and violence against civilians"; "influence public opinion in [the] home country and affect foreign policy on [the] Middle East in order to end the occupation and create a viable Palestinian State"; "express solidarity with Palestinian and Israeli peace activists and empower local Palestinian communities/churches"; and "be an active witness that an alternative, non-violent struggle for justice and peace is possible to end the illegal occupation of Palestine."

Toward these ends, EAPPI organizes internships and three-month visits to Palestinian villages, where activists monitor "violations of human rights and international humanitarian law, suppor[t] acts of non-violent resistance alongside local Christian and Muslim Palestinians and Israeli peace activists, offe[r] protection through non-violent presence, engag[e] in public policy advocacy and, in general, stan[d] in solidarity with the churches and all those struggling against the occupation." Thereafter, they return to their communities in Europe and North America, where they join anti-Israel political campaigns.

EAPPI's activities are managed by Salpy Eskidjian, an Armenian Cypriot whose anti-Israel agenda is reflected in the organization's Ecumenical Campaign to End the Illegal Occupation of Palestine, a program that sends "Ecumenical Accompaniers" to Palestinian villages for three-month periods "to try to reduce the brutality of the Occupation and improve the daily lives of both peoples." Since the program was launched, accompaniers have participated from churches in 14 countries: Canada, Denmark, Finland, France, Germany, Iceland, Ireland, New Zealand, Norway, South Africa, Sweden, Switzerland, the United Kingdom, and the United States.

Despite its claims of balance and fairness, EAPPI consistently employs such terms as "apartheid" and "war crimes" in reference to Israel's treatment of Palestinians, and cooperates with such radical Palestinian NGOs as the Union of Palestinian Medical Relief Committees.

ELECTRONIC INTIFADA (EI)

MECCS/EI Project
1507 E. 53rd Street, #500
Chicago, IL
60615
URL: http://electronicintifada.net/

Website that reports on the Arab-Israeli Mideast conflict "from a Palestinian perspective"

Launched in February 2001, Electronic Intifada (EI) is a not-for-profit, independent website focusing on "the question of Palestine, the Israeli-Palestinian conflict, and the economic, political, legal, and human dimensions of Israel's ... occupation of Palestinian territories." Specifically, EI seeks to provide an alternative to what it deems "the prevailing pro-Israeli slant in U.S. media coverage by offering information from a Palestinian perspective." With close ties to the International Solidarity Movement (ISM), Electronic Intifada refers to Israel's 1948 creation as *Al Nakba* (Arabic for "The Catastrophe"). While EI typically draws a quarter-million visitors to its website each month, that figure soars to approximately one million per month during times of acute crisis in the Middle East, such as Israel's war with Lebanon in the summer of 2006.

EI's Executive Director (and co-founder) is Ali Abunimah, who is also a member of ISM and currently serves as Vice President of the Arab American Action Network. In Abunimah's view, Palestinian violence and terrorism is caused entirely by Israel's "land confiscation," its "ongoing orgy of violence," and its "routine human-rights abuses" that have "made life under a seemingly endless occupation so intolerable."

Another EI co-founder is Arjan El Fassed, a former researcher at the Nablus-based Center for Palestine Research & Studies, a contributor to the Palestinian Independent Commission for Citizens' Rights in Ramallah, and the author of the 1999 book *Institutional Design and Prospects for Palestinian Democratic Transition*. El Fassed is also affiliated with Al-Awda (a.k.a. the Palestine Right to Return Coalition).

A third EI co-founder is Laurie King-Irani, former coordinator of the International Campaign for Justice for the Victims of Sabra and Shatila, and former editor (from 1998-2000) of *Middle East Report* Magazine. Holding a Ph.D. in Sociocultural Anthropology, King-Irani specializes in "the political identity and participation of Palestinian citizens of Israel."

A fourth co-founder is Nigel Parry, the former webmaster for BirZeit University which is located in the West Bank.

EI reveres the memory of Rachel Corrie, an American member of ISM who in March 2003 was accidentally killed while trying to block an Israeli bulldozer from destroying a Palestinian home that was concealing a tunnel through which Hamas and Islamic Jihad terrorists were receiving smuggled weapons. In her article "Of broken Bodies and Unbreakable Laws" (published a week after Corrie's death), Laurie King-Irani wrote: "Time and again Rachel ... put her body in the path of the instruments of a brutal military occupation in order to defend and protect those rights and their holders: Palestinian men, women, and children, all of whom lack even the most basic legal protection of citizenship, since they also lack a state."

EI has two sister websites -- Electronic Iraq and Electronic Lebanon -- which focus principally on alleged American and Israeli transgressions in those two nations.

According to the Marxist, anti-American journalist Alexander Cockburn: "There are a number of excellent news outlets for those who want unjaundiced reporting ... The Electronic Intifada ... is trusted." In 2003, EI received the "Voices for Peace" award from the American-Arab Anti-Discrimination Committee, in recognition of its commitment "to bringing the concerns, voices, and experiences of the Iraqi and Palestinian peoples to audiences the world over via the Internet."

Notable contributors to EI include Ali Abunimah, George Bisharat, Ilan Pappe, Omar Ahmad, Charlotte Kates, Tanya Reinhart, and Joseph Massad.

EURO-MEDITERRANEAN HUMAN RIGHTS NETWORK (EMHRN)

Strandgade 56
DK-1401 Copenhagen K
Denmark

Phone :45 32 69 88 88
URL: http://www.euromedrights.netAnti-Israel NGO

The Euro-Mediterranean Human Rights Network (EMHRN) describes itself as a "network of more than 80 human rights organizations from over 30 countries in the Euro-Mediterranean region." It was formed in 1997 to "contribute to the protection and promotion of the human rights principles embodied in the Barcelona Declaration of November 1995." Essentially a funding and development arm of the European Union (EU), EMHRN is heavily funded by the EU Commission and also receives money from the Swedish Agency for International Development Cooperation and the Ford Foundation.

Regarding the Israeli-Palestinian conflict in particular, EMHRN has exhibited a well-documented trend of bias against Israel. Its "country reports" -- such as "Tightened Spaces for Human Rights - Palestinian NGO Work" in March 2004 and "Migrant Workers in Israel - A Contemporary Form of Slavery" in August 2003 -- concentrate on criticisms of Israel. EMHRN has frequently condemned Israel for "acts of harassment, intimidation, threats, and deliberate attacks on human rights defenders in the OPT [Occupied Palestinian Territory]."

EMHRN has a "Working Group on Palestine, Israel, and Palestinians" whose stated objective is "to strengthen coordination of activities to promote respect for international human rights standards and international human rights norms as a foundation for peace in the region." Its members include representatives of such NGOs as Al-Haq, the International Commission of Jurists, the Arab Association for Human Rights, and the Palestinian Center for Human Rights -- all of which have demonstrated strong and consistent biases against Israel. Numerous EMHRN member groups label Palestinian acts of terrorism as "resistance," and condemn them only when they cause Palestinian casualties. EMHRN denounced Israel's March 22, 2004 targeted killing of Hamas leader Sheikh Ahmed Yassin.

EMHRN's October 21, 2005 press release described the findings of a delegation it had sent to the Gaza Strip earlier that month. The mission was hosted by EMHRN member Palestine Center for Human Rights (PCHR). Co-sponsored by the Interchurch Organization for Development Co-operation (ICCO) in the Netherlands, the mission included representatives of the International Commission of Jurists (Sweden), the Bruno Kreisky Foundation (Austria), and EMHRN (Denmark). All of these organizations were part of the working group that contributed to the EMHRN report, "A Human Rights Review on the EU and Israel 2003-2004," which accused Israel of "systematic human rights violations" and violation of "international humanitarian law."

Following Israel's 2005 withdrawal from Gaza, an EMHRN press release titled "The Gaza Strip is still occupied" attacked Israel for "separating families that live on different sides of borders" but omitted any mention of the continued Kassam rocket attacks emanating from the Gaza Strip. It implied that Israel was to blame for "the investment environment [being] highly risky."

EUROPEAN COUNCIL FOR FATWA AND RESEARCH (ECFR)

19 Roebuck Road
Clonskeagh, D 14
Dublin, Ireland

Phone :00351-1 208 0004
URL: www.ecfr.org

> Promotes militant Islam and justifies *jihad* for Muslim youths
> "Martyrdom operations are not suicide and should not be deemed as unjustifiable means of endangering one's life."

A Dublin-based private foundation, founded in London on 29 March - 30 March 1997 on the initiative of the Federation of Islamic Organisations in Europe, the European Council for Fatwa and Research ('ECFR') is a largely self-selected body, composed by Islamic clerics and scholars, presided by Yusuf al-Qaradawi, and considered as belonging to the islamist tendency within the Islamic world community, the Ummah.

Established in March 1997 in the United Kingdom by the Federation of Islamic Organizations in Europe, the European Council for *Fatwah* and Research (ECFR) is a private foundation whose stated objectives are fourfold: (1) to unify Europe's differing views of *Fiqh* (Islamic jurisprudence); (2) to apply *Fiqh* in European societies where Muslims live; (3) to conduct studies of various issues related to Islamic Law (*Sharia*) in Europe; and (4) to guide "Muslims in Europe generally and youth particularly, through spreading authentic concepts of Islam and its noble principles."

The fourth precept refers specifically to the promotion of militant Islam, with its justifications for *jihad* and terrorism, among young European Muslims. The World Assembly of Muslim Youth, which was shut down in the U.S. because of its role in funding terrorism, promotes ECFR's mission on one of its websites.

In ECFR's view, all Muslims should live not under the laws enacted by legislators and democratic institutions, but under *Sharia*, which "cannot be amended to conform to changing human values and standards," and which represents "the absolute norm to which all human values and conduct must conform."

One of ECFR's leaders, Sheik Faysal Mawlawi, issued a *fatwah* (religious legal ruling) following a Palestinian suicide bombing in Israel that killed forty people, including four Americans. His *fatwah* asserted that "martyrdom operations are not suicide [which Islam purportedly prohibits] and [thus] should not be deemed as unjustifiable means of endangering one's life." "Whoever is killed in such missions is a martyr," explained Mawlawi. "[M]ay Allah bless him with high esteem."

Shortly thereafter, at a Stockholm, Sweden conference on *jihad*, ECFR President Yousef Al-Qaradhawi agreed that "martyrdom operations ... are not in any way included in the framework of prohibited terrorism, even if the victims include some civilians." A supporter of Osama bin Laden, Al-Qaradhawi is also active in the Muslim Brotherhood.

Statutory ambitions

The ECFR aims "to present to the Muslim World and the Muslim minorities in the West particularly" its interpretation of "the manifestation of Allah's infinite mercy, knowledge and wisdom". For the ECFR, the shariah clearly embodies the superior rules in life. The sharia should therefore be respected as superior to civil law and to the democracy: "the Shari'ah cannot be amended to conform to changing human values and standards, rather, it is the absolute norm to which all human values and conduct must conform; it is the frame to which they must be referred; it is the scale on which they must be weighed." .
It wants to achieve these through:

1. bringing together Islamic scholars who live in Europe
2. attempting to unify the jurisprudence views between them in regards with the main Fiqh (islamic law) issues, especially with regard to the minority stats of Muslims in Europe;
3. issue collective fatwas which meet the needs of Muslims in Europe, solve their problems and regulate their interaction with the European communities, all according the shariah;
4. research how arising issues in Europe can be resolved with strict respect for the shariah.

The ECFR is one of the main channels for the publications of fatwa's by Yusuf al-Qaradawi, and his main English-language channel.
Among others, it wants to promote, and control, the local education of native imam's for the Muslim minorities in European countries. Amongst others, it participates in such initiatives in France (in cooperation with the European Institute for Humanitarian and Islamic Studies and the United Kingdom.
It also strives to become an approved religious authority before local governments and private establishments in all countries where Muslims are a minority.

Evaluation of the positions of the ECFR

The ECFR clearly wants to assume a leading role in all dogmatic and accordingly also in all worldly issues in the worldwide Islamic community, the Ummah. Among others, it wants to address the younger Muslim generations living in outside Islamic countries, especially those in Europe and the United States. It wants to project a relatively contemporary position, all through it is heavily criticized for some very undemocratic and non-contemporary positions:

> Its fatwas often rely on the four classical Islamic law schools (four schools of Fiqh), as well as all other schools of the people of Islamic law (Fiqh) knowledge, although with exclusion of modernist Islamic scholars in Europe as French great-imam from Marseille, Soheib Bencheikh and Zaki Badawi, president of the London-based Muslim College and a keen promotor of interfaith dialogue (among other publishing regularly together with the Archbishop of York and the British Chief Rabbi).
> Its fatwas also insist on a strong priority for religious law over secular law.

On the other hand, it regularly pleads for mutual respect for non-Muslims, and for respect for civil procedures; e.g. marriage is considered valid only if the rights of both spouses are respected and if the civil procedure is followed to (any marriage which is conducted purely in the mosque is not considered Islamic).

Aside from the exclusion of non-Sunni Muslims, and more importantly, other people criticize the ECFR for its fierce refusal to accept separation of church and state as an element of democracy, as well as several principles of democracy. The fatwa's of the ECFR's chairmain, Yussuf al-Qaradawi, are clear on how this tendency in Islam sees democracy and universal human rights:

> On the separation of state and church (secularism): *"Since Islam is a comprehensive system of `Ibadah (worship) and Shari'ah (legislation), the acceptance of secularism means abandonment of Shari'ah, a denial of the Divine guidance and a rejection of Allah's injunctions. (...) the call for secularism among Muslims is atheism and a rejection of Islam. Its acceptance as a basis for rule in place of Shari'ah is a downright apostasy."* . At the same time, he appears to know very well this is a crucial element in democracy.
>
> On equal rights for women: *"Those misguided people cudgel their brains in finding out lame arguments that tend to give both males and females equal shares of inheritance ... it's the nature of woman to be maintained and cared for by man ... irrespective of whether she is poor or rich."* .
>
> On democracy -where per definition a majority vote might differ from the commands in the Qur'an and Sunnah,: *"the Shari'ah cannot be amended to conform to changing human values and standards, rather, it is the absolute norm to which all human values and conduct must conform ..."* .
>
> On the freedom of religion: *"All Muslim jurists agree that the apostate is to be punished. However, they differ regarding the punishment itself. The majority of them go for killing; meaning that an apostate is to be sentenced to death."* .

Also, in August 2005, the Wall Street Journal reported that the Council had used the infamous anti-Semitic forgery known as the Protocols of the Elders of Zion in its theological deliberations. The Journal also reported that "the council is part of a web of organizations that spread ideology close to the Muslim Brotherhood throughout Europe." .

COOPERATION WITH OTHER ISLAMIC ORGANISATIONS IN EUROPE:

1. Al-Maktoum Charity Organisation, Dublin, Ireland
2. Milli Görüs (German and other sections)
3. Federation of Islamic Organisations in Europe

MEMBERS OF THE ECFR

1. Professor Yusuf Al-Qaradawi, President of ECFR (Egypt, Qatar)
2. Judge Sheikh Faisal Maulawi, Vice-President (Lebanon).
3. Sheikh Hussein Mohammed Halawa, General Secretary (Ireland)
4. Sheikh Dr. Ahmad Jaballah (France)
5. Sheikh Dr. Ahmed Ali Al-Imam (Sudan)
6. Sheikh Mufti Ismail Kashoulfi (UK)
7. Ustadh Ahmed Kadhem Al-Rawi (UK)
8. Sheikh Ounis Qurqah (France)
9. Sheikh Rashid Al-Ghanouchi (UK)
10. Sheikh Dr. Abdullah Ibn Bayya (Saudi Arabia)
11. Sheikh Abdul Raheem Al-Taweel (Spain)
12. Judge Sheikh Abdullah Ibn Ali Salem (Mauritania)
13. Sheikh Abdullah Ibn Yusuf Al-Judai, (UK)
14. Sheikh Abdul Majeed Al-Najjar
15. Sheikh Abdullah ibn Sulayman Al-Manee' (Saudi Arabia)
16. Sheikh Dr. Abdul Sattar Abu Ghudda (Saudi Arabia)
17. Sheikh Dr. Ajeel Al-Nashmi (Kuwait)
18. Sheikh Al-Arabi Al-Bichri (France)
19. Sheikh Dr. Issam Al-Bashir (Sudan)
20. Sheikh Ali Qaradaghi (Qatar)

21. Sheikh Dr. Suhaib Hasan Ahmed (UK)
22. Sheikh Tahir Mahdi (France)
23. Sheikh Mahboub-ul-Rahman (Norway)
24. Sheikh Muhammed Taqi Othmani (Pakistan)
25. Sheikh Muhammed Siddique (Germany)
26. Sheikh Muhammed Ali Saleh Al-Mansour (UAE)
27. Sheikh Dr. Muhammed Al-Hawari (Germany)
28. Sheikh Mahumoud Mujahed (Belgium)
29. Sheikh Dr. Mustafa Cerić (Bosnia)
30. Sheikh Nihad Abdul Quddous Ciftci (Germany)
31. Sheikh Dr. Naser Ibn Abdullah Al-Mayman (Saudi Arabia)
32. Sheikh Yusf Ibram (Switzerland)
33. Dr. Salah Soltan (Egypt, USA)

FOCUS ON AMERICAN AND ARAB INTERESTS AND RELATIONS (FAAIR)

17300 W. Ten Mile Rd.
Suite 200
Southfield, MI
48075

Phone :248-298-9199
URL: http://www.faair.org/index.html

Anti-Israel, anti-American, anti-war organization
"The U.S. has no legal justification for launching an unprovoked war on Iraq."

Shortly after the 9/11 terrorist attacks, the Detroit-based organization Focus on American and Arab Interests and Relations (FAAIR) was founded by two Iraqi expatriates, Mohammed Alomari and Muthana al-Hanooti, "to promote fair policies and a better understanding of the issues pertaining to the Arab World." This organization has joined forces with a handful of anti-war groups to take the U.S. to task for its policies in Iraq.

Before co-founding FAAIR and becoming a spokesman for Iraqi nationals in the U.S., Alomari wrote a book titled *The Secrecy of Evil: The Qabala and Its Followers*, which denounced Jews and their alleged scheme to create a New World Order. Today he charges that the U.S. and Israel "organized" the 9/11 attacks.

Prior to the 2003 Iraq War, FAAIR's website featured an essay by Alomari entitled "Twelve Years of Siege on Iraq," which depicted the U.S. -- because of its role in leading the UN economic sanctions against Iraq -- as the cause of that nation's social and economic troubles. (Alomari expanded upon this theme in his book *The Blockade and Destruction of Iraq: Crimes Against Humanity*.) He argued that America's justifications for going to war against the "besieged nation" of Iraq were very weak. "Unfortunately," he wrote, "... none of these arguments [justifications] stand on any basis of fact or legality. Iraq never had any ties or links whatsoever with the September 11, 2001 terrorist attacks or with Al-Qaeda group. In fact, Iraq actually offered to help the U.S. in tracking down the culprits behind the 9-11 terrorist attacks." Charging that the United States deceptively used "old regurgitated and unsubstantiated rhetoric claiming that Iraq somehow poses a threat to the world," FAAIR has called the Iraq War not only illegal but also "a crime against humanity." The organization blames America's invasion of Iraq on anti-Arab "extremists" and "pro-Israeli fanatics" in the Bush administration.

FAAIR has aligned itself with a number of organizations that share its hatred for Israel and the United States. These allies include: (a) Campaign of Conscience for the Iraqi People (CCIP), which was formed jointly by the American Friends Service Committee (AFSC) and Fellowship of Reconciliation; (b) Iraq Action Coalition, an organization founded in 1993 by Rania Masri, a Media Director for Al-Awda (Palestine Right of Return Coalition) and a Board Member of Peace Action Network; (c) United For Peace and Justice, an anti-war coalition led by Leslie Cagan, a longtime committed socialist who aligns her politics with those of Fidel Castro's Communist Cuba; and (d) Peace Action Network, which demands that America "end its shameful status as arms merchant to the world."

FAAIR's lobbying efforts are directed mainly by Muthana al-Hanooti, the former Public Relations Director for the Islamic Relief Association (IRA), a militant Islamic group which, according to terrorism expert Steven Emerson, is a money-laundering front operation for Hamas and al-Qaeda.

FREE PALESTINE ALLIANCE (FPA)

c/o International Action Center
39 West 14th Street
Room 206
New York, NY
10011

Phone :212-633-6646
Email :
iacenter@action-mail.org
URL: http://www.iacenter.org/

Blames the Bush Administration "for the carnage carried out against our steadfast [Palestinian] people"
Many members are affiliated with the Workers World Party, a Marxist-Leninist group
Shares the same contact information as Ramsey Clark's International Action Center

Based in San Francisco, the Free Palestine Alliance (FPA) is a pro-Hamas organization that supports the dissolution of the State of Israel and the "unconditional liberation" of Palestinians in the Occupied Territories and in Israel proper. It is a member of the International ANSWER steering committee, and its contact information is identical to that of Ramsey Clark's International Action Center. Many individuals involved with the FPA are also members of the Marxist-Leninist Workers World Party. In addition, the FPA is closely affiliated with Al-Awda and the American-Arab Anti-Discrimination Committee.

Advocating "justice and liberation" for the Palestinian people, the FPA impugns the U.S. for its support of Israel, and thus "hold[s] the Bush Administration responsible for the carnage carried out against our steadfast [Palestinian] people in heroic Janin, Nablus, Bethlehem, Ramallah, Doura, Qalqilia, Tulkarem, Rafah, Jabalia, and every town and camp in our beloved land."

The FPA affirms that "the Palestinian Arab people constitute an indivisible unit naturally bound to the land of Palestine despite the passage of time and the onset of colonial rules"; that "all constituent sectors of the Palestinian people -- regardless of imposed demarcation borders inside Palestine and including all Palestinians in exile -- constitute one inseparable collective national unit"; that "the struggle for Palestine is a joint responsibility of the Arab people as a whole"; and that there exists a "unique symbiotic relationship of the reciprocal political-economic-military interests between Western colonialism in general, the U.S. Empire, [and] the Zionist movement and its material manifestation -- the racist Apartheid State of Israel."
In addition, the FPA "fully recognizes the emerging Arab-American character of our community in the United States, and seeks to establish programs and projects to empower, safeguard, and develop our cultural, linguistic and political identity."

Viewing America as a nation rife with bigotry and discrimination, the FPA "values its partnership role in the struggle within constitutional means for a just society in the United States in shaping political agenda and defending civil rights and liberties of all; and fully recognizes the struggle for justice of oppressed communities and movements." In the FPA's estimation, America's allegedly inequitable society is in need of a radical transformation.

Free Palestine Alliance's Political Program consists of the following tenets:

> "The ... establishment of a democratic secular state on all of historic Palestine that would end all forms of Apartheid, colonial power structures, racial & religious segregation, [is] a just, inevitable,

and realistic imperative ..." ["All of historic Palestine" is a reference to the area that curently constitutes the State of Israel.]

"Ending the occupation of the West Bank and the Gaza Strip is a right due to the Palestinian people within the larger context of the struggle for a secular democratic state on all of historic Palestine."

"... Palestinians have the national, historic, human, and absolute individual and collective inalienable right to return to their homeland, homes of origin, and property in Palestine; and ... they have the absolute right to restitution for all property, reparation for damages, and retribution for their suffering, displacement, and dispossession for more than half a century."

"[T]he Palestinian struggle for self-determination and return [is] universal, and ... primarily rooted in the historic, cultural and political inextricable belonging of the people of Palestine to their homeland, also affirmed by international law."

"The struggle against Zionist colonialism is the responsibility of all justice-seeking people, primarily the Arab people, equally as it is the responsibility of the Palestinian people."

"The struggle for Palestine is inseparable from the struggle against underdevelopment, dictatorial rule, racism, imperial hegemony and globalized control."

"The FPA is fully cognizant of the intertwined relationship between national, gender, class and racial inequities, and hence seeks to empower the most affected and dispossessed sectors of our people and community through social transformation and democratic and institutional empowerment."

"Recognizing that the Palestinian struggle is also a struggle of narratives, the FPA seeks to support and establish programs that would directly serve this end through grassroots and community-oriented social, cultural, and political activities."

"To achieve these goals, the FPA formulates immediate and long-term community and grassroots programs on various levels and in harmony with the requirements of any given historical period. The formulated programs are within the larger context of the struggle of Arab-American and marginalized communities, and in partnership with peace and justice movements across all sectors of society in the United States."

"... [T]he implementation of a full divestment program in the United States coupled with effective corporate boycotts [is] a necessary material formulation of the overarching goal of ending all forms of governmental and private economic, political, and military support to the Apartheid State of Israel."

"... [T]he struggle of the Palestinian people is natural to all movements seeking peace and justice worldwide; and emphasizes the inextricable centrality of Palestine in all formulations against war, subjugation and empire."

On March 20, 2004, the FPA participated in a Global Day of Action (GDOA) aimed at raising public support for a movement to "Bring the Troops Home Now" and to "End Colonial Occupation from Iraq to Palestine to Haiti and Everywhere." Initiated by the International ANSWER coalition, this GDOA was observed in more than 60 countries worldwide. In the United States, demonstrations took place in some 300 cities, including actions in New York, San Francisco, and Los Angeles, which drew one hundred thousand, fifty thousand, and twenty thousand participants, respectively. FPA contingents attended the rallies in all three of those cities, where the featured speakers included actor Woody Harrelson, United Farm Workers co-founder Dolores Huerta, Gloria La Riva of the National Committee to Free the Cuban Five, Richard Becker of the ANSWER Coalition, and California Congresswoman Maxine Waters. The FPA helped coordinate the New York City GDOA, along with ANSWER, Al-Awda, the Arab Muslim American Federation, the Muslim American Society Freedom Foundation, and the Muslim Students' Association of the U.S. and Canada.

On November 11, 2004 -- the day of Yasser Arafat's death -- the FPA eulogized the Palestinian Authority President with a statement titled "In Memory of a Fallen Leader," which exhorted "our people in Palestine and throughout exile" as well as "all peace and justice loving people in the United States" to observe "3 full days of national mourning, remembrance, and a steadfast of reciprocal solidarity and unity." Added the FPA: "We call on all to display on their homes, institutions and property Palestinian flags, scarfs, or other symbols of the Palestinian national movement for liberation and justice. ... The legacy of Yasser Arafat is inextricable from that of the entirety of not only the Palestinian people, but all those struggling for freedom."

The FPA's nominal leader is Elias Rashmawi, who also serves as the national coordinator for the National Council of Arab Americans. Other notable FPA officials include Michael Shehadeh, Eyad Kishawi, and Hanna Hanania.

GISHA: CENTER FOR THE LEGAL PROTECTION OF FREEDOM OF MOVEMENT (GCLPFM)

Seeks to help Palestinians "exercise their right to freedom of movement"
Works for "systemic change in military practices and abuses at Israeli border-crossings and checkpoints"

Established in 2005 and based in Tel Aviv, Gisha: Center for the Legal Protection of Freedom of Movement describes itself as "an Israeli not-for-profit organization that seeks to protect the fundamental rights of Palestinians living in the Occupied Territories by imposing human rights law as a limitation on the behavior of Israel's military." According to Gisha (whose name means both "access" and "approach"): "Since Israel's 1967 occupation of the West Bank and Gaza Strip, its military has developed an elaborate system of rules and sanctions to control the movement of the 3.4 million Palestinians who live there. Every day, infringements on the right to mobility compromise the ability of thousands of Palestinian residents to carry out the ordinary tasks crucial to a person's physical health, economic sustenance, developmental needs, and human dignity." Portraying Israel as an oppressor nation, Gisha engages "in litigation and advocacy that aim to help individuals exercise their right to freedom of movement while working for systemic change in military practices and abuses at Israeli border-crossings and checkpoints."

On numerous occasions Gisha has petitioned the Israeli Supreme Court to allow particular Palestinian students to study at Israeli or West Bank universities, and campaigned "for removal or reduction in restrictions on movement of people and goods in and out of Gaza." In these campaigns, Gisha fails to mention the context of Palestinian terrorism and the logic of Israeli border-crossings and checkpoints.

In one instance, Gisha petitioned the Court to repeal a November 19, 2006 directive -- which Gisha characterized as an "apartheid order" -- prohibiting Israelis without a special permit from transporting by car any Palestinian residents of the West Bank. In a another petition to the Supreme Court, Gisha accused Israel of implementing the "ideology of segregation": "We cannot claim a patent on the establishment of a legal system of segregation, since human history is familiar with methods of racial or other 'segregation' as was the case in South Africa during the apartheid and in the Southern US States until the 1960s."

In 2005 and 2006, Gisha -- in conjunction with such organizations as Yesh Din, the Association for Civil Rights in Israel, the Committee against Torture in Israel, Physicians for Human Rights-Israel, HaMoked, and Betselem -- took part in a number of public expressions of condemnation against Israel. In 2005, for instance, Gisha and some of the aforementioned groups jointly placed an advertisement in the Israeli daily newspaper *Haaretz* referring to Israel as an "apartheid" regime. On July 11, 2006, Gisha and five other political NGOs called on the Israeli government to keep open the crossings into Gaza for essential supplies, characterizing Israel's current restrictive policies as "collective punishment" while ignoring the security threat at the Gaza crossings. And on November 9, 2006, Gisha and several other groups placed another ad in *Haaretz*, this time charging that Israeli authorities had routinely and indiscriminately fired their guns into crowded Palestinian civilian areas.

In January 2007, Gisha produced a much-publicized report titled "Disengaged Occupiers: The Legal Status of Gaza," which claimed that "Israel continues to control Gaza through an 'invisible hand': control over borders, airspace, territorial waters, population registry, the tax system, supply of goods and others." Gisha's report accused Israel of regulating "movement within the Gaza Strip through sporadic troop presence and artillery fire from positions along its border with Gaza," and called on the Jewish state to "fulfil its obligations toward the people of Gaza ... namely: to open Gaza's borders to the free passage of people and goods, [and] to refrain from inflicting damage on Gaza's infrastructure ..." The authors of this report made no mention of the 2,127 Palestinian rocket attacks launched from Gaza during 2005 and 2006.

Gisha's Director is Sari Bashi, an attorney educated at Yale Law School and a former Israeli Supreme Court clerk. Prior to founding Gisha, Bashi worked at the Association for Civil Rights in Israel. Professor Kenneth Mann, a law professor at Tel Aviv University and a former Chief Public Defender, serves as Gisha's Legal Adviser and Chairman of its Advisory Committee.

Gisha receives funding from the Dutch and Norwegian Foreign Ministries, the Foundation for Middle East Peace, the New Israel Fund, and George Soros's Open Society Institute. Gisha also receives support from Echoing Green, a "social change" organization that has granted fellowships to such individuals as Gisha Director Sari Bashi, International Solidarity Movement co-founder Huwaida Arraf, and the former Operations Manager of the Israeli Committee Against House Demolitions, Fred Schlomka.

GRADUATE SCHOOL OF ISLAMIC AND SOCIAL SCIENCES (GSISS)

750-A Miller Drive SE
Leesburg, VA
20175

Phone :703-779-7477
Fax :703-779-7999
URL: http://www.siss.edu/

Front group for Wahhabi-Saudi money movers
Was raided by the U.S. Treasury in March 2002 for allegedly funding terrorism

Affiliated with Cordoba University in Ashburn, Virginia, the Graduate School of Islamic and Social Sciences (GSISS) is the only educational institution that the U.S. Defense Department has approved to both train and endorse Muslim chaplains for the American military. Characterizing itself as "the first Muslim-run graduate-level Islamic studies institution of higher education in the United States," GSISS seeks "to link the modern social sciences to the traditional classical Islamic sciences in a serious and scientific way," so as to "assist in discovering an intellectual direction that bridges the potential conflict in paradigms between Western civilization and the classical Islamic legacy."

GSISS offers a Master of Arts degree in its Social Studies/Islamic Studies program, which students can complete in a ten-month period. Graduates of this program commonly go on to become imams, academics, non-profit directors, and military, hospital, and prison chaplains. GSISS owns a library of 30,000 volumes in the English, Farsi and Arabic languages. The school's first graduating class completed its studies in 1999.

Shortly after 9/11, as the U.S. prepared to invade Afghanistan, Muslim American military chaplain Abdul-Rashid Muhammad asked GSISS leader Taha Jabir Alwani (who would be named as an unindicted co-conspirator of Palestinian Islamic Jihad operative Sami Al-Arian in early 2003) for his authoritative opinion as to whether American Muslim soldiers were morally permitted serve in a war against an Islamic enemy. Alwani, in turn, conveyed the inquiry to the Qatar-based Wahhabi cleric Yousef al-Qaradhawi, who vacillated before ultimately calling on Muslims worldwide to "support the Afghans who stand firm against the American invasion," which he blamed on justifiable Muslim anger over U.S. support for Israel.

Islam scholar Stephen Schwartz has called GSISS "a front group for Wahhabi-Saudi money," and the federal government has long suspected the organization of maintaining ties to Islamic terrorism. On March 20, 2002, U.S. law-enforcement agents raided the offices of key GSISS personnel, including Board member Jamal Barzinji, who was involved with a total of nine organizations raided in connection with terrorist financing -- among them the World Assembly of Muslim Youth and the International Institute for Islamic Thought. On the day of the raids against GSISS, Barzinji appeared on television claiming that he was unaware of any questionable activities by any of the targeted groups.

In March 2003, the ChevronTexaco Foundation awarded GSISS a $100,000 grant for a program "designed to empower members of the Muslim community to respond to prejudice expressed against many individuals and communities, especially South Asians, Muslims and Arabs after the September 11th tragedy." Founded on the premise that American society is rife with anti-Muslim bias, this project trained 40 Muslims from 10 mosques in techniques of "conflict resolution" and "identifying bigotry"; the participants were then dispatched to various locations in metropolitan Washington, DC to give small-group presentations on the evils of anti-Muslim prejudice.

GRASSROOTS INTERNATIONAL (GRI)

179 Boylston Street
4th floor
Boston, MA
02130
Phone :617-524-1400
URL: http://www.grassrootsonline.org/

Assets: $3,008,937 (2006)
Grants Received: $2,750,865 (2006)
Grants Awarded: $1,531,854 (2006)

Grassroots International (GRI) defines itself as a "human rights and development organization that channels funds to small community groups around the world that are working for peace and social justice." Since its founding in 1983, Grassroots has disbursed $20 million to its partner organizations and engaged in what it characterizes as "campaigns for positions on equality, development, independence, and self-reliance."

The GRI website states, "Grassroots International was born out of a commitment to justice for Palestinians. In the nearly two decades since then, the cause of Palestinian rights remains central to GRI and its supporters." In 2001, GRI formed a partnership with the Advocacy Project (AP), an NGO which draws a moral equivalence between Palestinian terrorism and Israeli counter-terror measures, and which accuses Israel of practicing "apartheid" and "racism." In her 1999 book *Hell to Pay*, the late Susan Olson wrote that GRI has "had direct ties to the PLO" (Yasser Arafat's Palestine Liberation Organization).

In 2004, GRI was a signatory -- along with more than 200 other leftist groups -- to a letter exhorting members of the U.S. Senate to oppose Israel's construction of an anti-terrorist security fence in the West Bank, a barrier that GRI characterizes as an illegal "apartheid wall."

Grassroots International was a signatory to a May 30, 2000 document denouncing globalization and the World Trade Organization (WTO). GRI is a member of OneWorld Network, an umbrella of more than 1,500 leftist groups that seek "to promote sustainable development, social justice, and human rights." Grassroots is also a member organization of the International Human Rights Funders Group (IHRFG), a network of more than six-dozen grantmakers dedicated to funding leftist groups and causes.

GRI opposes what it calls "the so-called 'war on terrorism'" which has "sacrifice[d] our cherished civil liberties in the tragically ironic quest to eliminate 'enemies of democracy and our way of life.'" It is a member organization of the United for Peace and Justice anti-war coalition led by Leslie Cagan, a longtime committed socialist who aligns her politics with those of Fidel Castro's Communist Cuba.

Grassroots International was founded by Dan Connell, a lecturer in journalism and African politics at Simmons College, Boston and a two-time MacArthur Foundation grantee. GRI's Board of Advisors includes the "antiracist essayist" Tim Wise; socialist professor Dessima Williams; and Michael Ratner, President of the Center for Constitutional Rights and former President of the National Lawyers Guild.

The Executive Director of GRI is Nikhil Aziz, a contributor to RightWeb who, in a December 2003 article he co-wrote with Chip Berlet (of the National Lawyers Guild and the Southern Poverty Law Center), condemned "Christian evangelical rightists" who are distinguished by "their unqualified support for Israel and their Islamophobic opposition to Palestinian self-determination." Aziz ascribed the U.S. invasion of Iraq to a dual quest for "control of global oil resources" and "military hegemony" – a quest he says is motivated by the "[i]mperialism and racism" that "have deep roots in U.S. history and foreign policy."

GRI produces an online newsletter that features many anti-capitalist, anti-U.S., anti-Israel themes. For example:

> GRI laments "the catastrophic results of ten years of the World Trade Organization," whose "'liberalization' of agricultural trade has resulted in a world-wide rural depression with millions of farmers and peasants … rising unemployment, stagnating growth … and a growing gap between rich and poor people all over the world, destruction of the environment, hunger and massive displacement of rural peoples."

> GRI claims "the U.S. food system benefits agribusiness, shipping companies and private voluntary organizations while either ignoring or exacerbating the long term causes of food insecurity."

> GRI supported a "shareholder resolution calling for Caterpillar to investigate whether their sale of bulldozers to Israel [for the demolition of Palestinian terrorists' homes and bases of operation] violates the CAT 'good global citizen' code of conduct."

> GRI stated in October 2004: "The Israeli attacks on civilians in Gaza -- often with U.S.-made weapons, payed [sic] for by American tax dollars -- are in clear violation of the Arms Export Control Act."

Grassroots International maintains a Speakers Bureau of individuals to publicly address issues of concern to the organization. It has also established a "Resource Rights for All" initiative to counteract what it calls the "neo-liberal, market-based [economic] model" that has enabled "international development banks and the corporations that control much of world agriculture … to wrest control of what have traditionally been community decisions: how best to use local resources to meet the needs of local people."

GRI has received funding from the Public Welfare Foundation, the Boston Foundation, the Moriah Fund, the John Merck Fund, the Fund for Nonviolence, the Pond Foundation, Working Assets, the Ben & Jerry's Foundation, and the New World Foundation.

HABITAT INTERNATIONAL COALITION (HIC)

7 Mohammad Shafiq Street, No. 8
Muhandisin, Giza
Egypt

Phone :20 02 347-4360
URL: http://www.hic-mena.org

> "Housing rights" NGO which publishes anti-Israel literature
> Has received funding from the Ford Foundation

Habitat International Coalition (HIC) describes itself as "an independent, international, nonprofit movement of some 400 organizations and individuals working to support campaigns for housing rights." The movement is "coordinated geographically" by way of regional focal points, and maintains offices in Africa, Asia, Europe, Latin America, Middle East/North Africa (MENA), and North America.

HIC identifies four "perspectives" as central to its work:

(a) The *social production and management* perspective "concerns practices that affirm people as active agents of change" in addressing problems of "global and local deprivation." Deeming capitalism an unjust economic system, HIC supports a socialist model featuring people's "own regulation of the ends, means and relations of production, and the sharing of habitat goods and services …"

(b) The *human dignity and rights* perspective "seeks to enhance the implementation of international consensus, commitments and obligations, including those relating to the universal entitlements of individuals and groups -- women, men, youth and children ... specifically the right to adequate housing, which includes secure tenure."

(c) The *sustainable environment* perspective aims "to ensure social, economic and environmental sustainability of 'habitat as human settlements' and 'habitat as planet Earth.'"

(d) The *gender equality* perspective seeks "to ensure the elimination of all forms of discrimination against women, including domestic violence in all situations."

HIC originally grew out of an NGO committee that was formed to help organize and coordinate the NGO input into the United Nations Conference on Human Settlements in Vancouver in 1976. During the 1980s and 1990s, HIC led fact-finding missions to "denounce violations of the right to housing" in Santo Domingo (1988); Seoul (1990); Hong Kong (1990); Narmada (1992); Panama (1992); Managua (1992); Israel and the Occupied Palestinian Territories (1993); Rio de Janeiro (1994), Kobe (1995); Istanbul (1996) and Lima (1998). HIC has been active in the World Urban Forums in Nairobi (2002) and Barcelona (2004), in the pro-socialist World Social Forums, and in many other UN conferences.

HIC's major programs include the following:

(a) The *Housing and Land Rights Network* is "a specialized group of HIC members who cooperate to develop methods and share strategies for using human rights to promote and defend adequate housing and land for deprived persons and groups ... [and] to promote ... the human right to adequate housing as [a] right for everyone ..."

(b) The *Women and Shelter Network*, which has had a formal consulting relationship with UN-Habitat since 1989, seeks "to unite, promote and support women and their organizations in the development of human settlements that improve women's and a community's quality of life."

(c) The *Habitat and Sustainable Environment Network aims* "to establish linkage between issues of habitat and environmentally sustainable development in order to improve the quality of peoples' living conditions ..."

In addition to these Netwotks, HIC also maintains several informal working groups that arise periodically from the initiatives of members "with a common interest in the social production of habitat." In 2005, HIC members created: (a) the Task Force on Housing and Land Rights in War, Conflict and Foreign Occupation; and (b) the Working Group on Privatization and Globalization of Habitat, which focused the negative impact of free trade agreements on habitat.

The Middle East/North Africa section of the HIC website is replete with articles that are strongly critical of Israel. In a section that lists the countries where HIC is actively engaged, there is no link for "Israel"; instead, reports and other materials pertaining to housing issues inside Israel are found in the "Palestine" section.

The HIC website also features a "historical overview" that likens the "legal mechanisms in Israel" to those of "the apartheid regime in South Africa," claiming that such mechanisms "reflect the racism at the base of the state's colonial ideology."

In February 2003, the "News" section of the HIC website featured an article charging that the "Zionist Entity" -- the piece did not call Israel by its name -- was planning "the demolition of 50,000 Arab houses in the Negev, Galilee and Triangle areas." The article also quoted Dr. Amer Al-Hazeel, a member of the regional council for "unrecognized villages," accusing "Tel Aviv" of "plotting a settlement plan on the lands of unrecognized [Arab villages] in the Negev." Another article lamented that "the state has a policy of demolishing Arab houses inside Israel."

HIC is financed by the Ford Foundation, the Rockefeller Foundation, the Netherlands-based Interchurch Organisation for Development Cooperation, and the Dutch and other European governments.

HAMOKED -- CENTER FOR THE DEFENSE OF THE INDIVIDUAL

URL: http://www.hamoked.org/

mail@hamoked.org.il

Anti-Israel NGO that aims to "assist Palestinians whose rights are violated by the Israeli authorities"

Established by Dr. Lotte Salzberger in 1988, HaMoked is a registered Israeli NGO whose broad objective is to "provide assistance to persons who have fallen victim to acts of violence, abuse, or deprivation of basic rights by governmental authorities (including local government), especially those needing assistance in conveying their complaints to these authorities, and also to protect basic rights." Vis a vis the Middle East in particular, HaMoked aims to "assist Palestinians whose rights are violated by the Israeli authorities or as a result of Israeli policy."

Hamoked alleges that Israeli authorities systematically oppress and abuse innocent Palestinians by means of beatings, torture, murder, harassment and threats, unwarranted detention, theft and confiscation of property, and damage to the Palestinian Authority's infrastructure. HaMoked further objects to Israel's demolition and seizure of Palestinian houses (an activity directed against terrorists and their abettors); Israel's construction of an anti-terrorism separation barrier in the West Bank; roadblocks and curfews imposed on Palestinians; and the deportation of suspected Palestinian terrorists. HaMoked regularly publishes reports condemning Israel for such alleged transgressions.

HaMoked works closely with other highly politicized NGOs, including: Al-Haq, Betselem, the Public Committee Against Torture in Israel, Adalah, Machsom Watch, the International Solidarity Movement, the Palestinian Prisoner's Club, LAW, Amnesty International, Physicians for Human Rights - Israel, and Human Rights Watch.

Hamoked's major funders include the European Commission; the Ford Foundation; the International Commission of Jurists; the New Israel Fund; the Dutch Foreign Ministry; the Swiss Federal Department of Foreign Affairs; and the British, Norwegian, Danish, and Finnish embassies in Tel Aviv.

Staffed by approximately 30 employees, HaMoked deals regularly with Palestinians claiming to have been abused by Israeli authorities. In such cases, the organization contacts the relevant authorities and, when necessary, files legal claims and submits petitions to the High Court of Justice. The NGO also works to introduce policy changes and legislative amendments "that would improve the status of human rights in the Occupied Territories." Since its inception, HaMoked has handled more then 50,000 complaints on various subjects.

HEALTH, DEVELOPMENT, INFORMATION AND POLICY INSTITUTE (HDIPI)

PO Box 1351
Ramallah, Palestine

Phone :972 2 298 5372
URL: http://www.hdip.org/Palestinian, anti-Israel NGO

Established in 1989 by a group of researchers and health practitioners in Ramallah, the Health, Development, Information and Policy Institute (HDIPI) defines itself as "an independent non-profit Palestinian organization [that specializes] in policy research and planning regarding the Palestinian health care system in the West Bank and Gaza Strip." It focuses on enhancing "coordination and cooperation between the different health care providers in Palestine, particularly ... between Palestinian NGOs and the Palestinian Authority."

HDIPI serves as a "resource for policy makers, development agencies, health care organizations, individual researchers and students who require quality, up-to-date information, research and ideas about health care and other development issues in the West Bank and Gaza Strip." It also "coordinate[s] with a large network of health care NGOs working on development activities in all of the urban and rural areas of the country, providing it with first-hand knowledge of the health and infrastructure conditions on the ground in Palestine."

HDIPI's current projects include the following:

(a) *Women's Empowerment*: "... to increase household income, reduce malnutrition in children and improve living conditions in rural and isolated Palestinian communities, cut off from their sources of employment and social services, through the empowerment of women as wage-earners and the creation of jobs."
(b) *Adoption*: "... to provide direct help and assistance to children who belong to needy [Palestinian] families and live under poverty line." As of December 2006, HDIPI had found adoptive parents for 36 children from the Jenin and Ramallah areas. Most were either orphans or belonged to unemployed families with little income.

(c) *Laws*: HDIPI's legislative unit "plays a major role in advocating and lobbying for effective legislation, and provides this type of support to other organizations interested in formulating laws that promote society's varied interests."

(d) *Voter Registration*: This program recruits teenagers and young adults to motivate residents of the West Bank and Gaza to register for, and then vote in, political elections.

HDIPI views Israel as an oppressor nation that is the principal cause of Palestinian suffering. On May 17, 2006, the organization published an article stating the following: "The Palestinians are facing one of the most vicious assaults in their history against their right to self-determination, their economic livelihood and their very future as an independent people. Israel ... is inexorably tightening its military, political and economic blockade against the Palestinian people ... thereby destroying the prospect of peace on the basis of a two-state solution. Even if Mother Theresa were brought back to life and made president of the Palestinian people, Israel would still refuse to recognize a Palestinian negotiating partner. ... [W]e must defend the fate of our children and ourselves ..."
HDIPI periodically produces "fact sheets" on Israel's alleged transgressions in various realms, including the following:

(a) *Children*: "All violations perpetrated by Israel against the Palestinians over the last decades -- ranging from torture and illegal killings to expulsion, the prevention of access to medical treatment, discrimination, and the destruction of homes and livelihoods -- have had a disproportionate effect on the children of Palestine. ... Palestinian children arrested, detained or imprisoned by Israeli authorities routinely face violations of their rights. ... Palestinian children experience constant discrimination as a result of living under Israeli military occupation."

(b) *Apartheid Wall*: "Israel maintains that the Wall is a temporary structure to physically separate the West Bank from Israel and thus to prevent suicide attacks on Israeli citizens. However the [W]all's location ... and projected length ... suggest it is more realistically an additional effort to confiscate Palestinian land, facilitate further colony expansion and unilaterally redraw geopolitical borders, all the while encouraging an exodus of Palestinians by denying them the ability to earn a living from their land, reach their schools or work places, access adequate water resources, or reach essential health care. ... If Israel is truly interested in its security it will ... withdraw completely from all of the territories it occupied in 1967 ... Israel has long had the formula for peace and security -- end the occupation."

(c) *Water*: "... 75% of the Occupied West Bank & Gaza Strip renewable water resources are used by Israel. ... Many villages in the Jenin Governate are suffering from serious water shortage due to the Israeli siege."

HOLY LAND TRUST (HLT)

Manger Street
Bethlehem
Palestine
P.O. Box 737

Phone :972-2-2765930
URL: http://www.holylandtrust.org/Anti-Israel humanitarian organization

The Holy Land Trust (HLT) was founded in Bethlehem as a non-profit humanitarian NGO in 1998, "with the aim of strengthening, encouraging and improving the Palestinian community through working with children, families, youth, and the [NGO] community." In its quest to help Palestinians achieve "political independence" through "nonviolent resistance approaches towards ending the [Israeli] occupation," HLT has launched a number of "comprehensive community awareness programs" and "local and international advocacy initiatives." The organization's major projects include the following:

Palestinian Center for the Study of Nonviolence (*PCSN*): This program "works on parallel levels: developing nonviolent approaches to resisting the Israeli occupation and using nonviolence to build the social infrastructure that will lead to the creation of a healthy and vibrant society. ... Work begins with young children through programs that seek to plant the principles of peace, nonviolence and conflict resolution in their lives; then move[s] to adolescents to develop their skills to take on more leadership roles and increase their involvement in serving their communities; [and] finally [works] with adults in developing their capacity to be agents of nonviolence and conflict transformation, in their families, organizations, universities, neighborhoods, villages, cities and nation."

Palestine News Network: PNN "was initially established as a web-based news service in Palestine in the year 2002 to provide direct and accurate news and reports from Palestine in the Arabic language. In the year 2003, Holy Land Trust adopted the PNN website, provided administrative and technical support, and add[ed] an English language page in addition to Arabic. ... PNN works with a network of professional reporters dispersed throughout the West Bank and the Gaza Strip. Some of these reporters also work for local Palestinian stations or international press agencies. ... PNN also produces documentaries; assisting filmmakers in their efforts by contributing producers, filming, editing and directorial services, and facilities needed for production work. Future plans for PNN include the launching of the first web-based Palestinian radio station."

Travel and Encounter: Founded in 2000, this program organizes tours (religious pilgrimages, fact-finding missions, and reality tours) to the Middle East for members of large evangelical congregations in the United States -- to provide them with "cross-cultural experiential learning opportunities in Palestine and Israel." "The purpose of our programs," says HLT, "is to build personal relationships between the peoples of the Middle East and the rest of the world. It is only through face-to-face dialogue that we can achieve mutual understanding between diverse groups of people."

To those participating in the Travel and Encounter program, HLT enumerates a litany of alleged Israeli atrocities while obscuring the truth about the large-scale persecution of Christians living under Palestinian Authority rule. For example, the travelers are not told about such widespread Palestinian transgressions as: the desecration of Christian churches in the region; the forced evictions of monks and nuns from monasteries and convents; the use of Christian homes, hotels, schools and churches as terrorist bases; the kidnapping of Christian clergy and nuns; the vandalism of Christian cemeteries; the burning of Christian businesses; and the targeted raping of Christian women. Rather, Palestinians are depicted as the uniformly peaceful victims of Israeli injustices and aggression.

Joseph Farah, Editor of *World Net Daily*, has written the following about HLT: "The lies this group tells in the name of Christianity are big and bold. They include the standard lines about Jews robbing the homes of Arabs, stealing their land and brutalizing them in a repressive state of military occupation. These so-called Christians even rationalize terrorism."

On its website, HLT features The History of Palestine: a Timeline, which states: "Palestine is the land upon which the Palestinian people were born. It is the land on which they grew and on which they developed as a culture and as a people. Palestine is also a land rich in history. There is evidence that Palestine has been inhabited for nearly two hundred thousand years." Exhorting readers to cultivate a "respectful acknowledgement of the rights of the indigenous Palestinian people," the timeline begins with the "Arab conquest of Palestine" in the year 638 A.D. -- omitting any mention of the fact that the Jewish presence in the region predated that of the Arabs by some two-and-a-half millennia.

HUMAN APPEAL INTERNATIONAL (HAI)

Victoria Court
376 Wilmslow Road
Fallowfield
Manchester M146AX
England

Phone :44 0161 225 0225
URL: http://www.hai.org.ae/Dubai-based Islamic charity that funded the terrorist group Hamas and possibly also Iraqi insurgents in war against U.S.

Based in Dubai, (United Arab Emirates), Human Appeal International (HAI) is an Islamic charity and a registered Non-Governmental Organization established in 1991 to: "provide relief to victims of natural disasters, wars and social hardship"; "improve the quality of life of underprivileged communities through ... projects that aim to provide education, health and social development"; "facilitate secure provisions for orphans"; and "cooperate and coordinate with other relief organizations working in the same field." As of December 2006, HAI's work extended to the following countries: Egypt, Ethiopia, Kenya, Niger, Somalia, Sudan, Afghanistan, Bangladesh, China, India, Indonesia, Kyrgyzstan, Pakistan & Kashmir, Sri Lanka, Bosnia, Kosovo, Iraq, Iran, Jordan, Lebanon, Yemen, and "Palestine." (Notably, HAI does not list Israel as one of the nations wherein it is active, but instead identifies "Palestine" as an independent state.)

To accomplish the foregoing objectives, HAI solicits donations from the public. The organization's current appeals include the following:

Middle East Crisis Appeal: Blaming Israel for the 2006 military conflicts with Hezbollah (in Lebanon) and Hamas (in Gaza), HAI stated: "Bombardment [by Israel] of Lebanon and Palestine has claimed the lives of more than 1100 people, mostly innocent civilians and children. ... The infrastructure of Lebanon has been completely destroyed ... The economy is being strangled ..."

Palestine Food Appeal: "The current situation in the holy land of Palestine is in a dire state. ... [O]ver half of the population is living below the poverty line ... Curfews and checkpoints [imposed by Israel] have deprived the vast majority of Palestinians to work and earn a living. ... The current unemployment rate is over 70%. Families have nothing to rely on for the basic need such as food, water and shelter."

Horn of Africa Appeal: "Short rainfalls have resulted in the population of east Africa to be on the brink of starvation due to huge food shortages. Kenya, Ethiopia, Uganda and Somalia are worst affected."

HAI's major ongoing projects include the following:

Education: This program seeks to "restore and improve educational institutions such as schools and day centers which are affected by natural disasters and war; ... eliminate illiteracy ...; reduce unemployment rates by providing specialized adult courses which will increase employment opportunities; ... [and build and furnish] schools, providing students with schoolbooks, bags and accessories ..."

Food: HAI ships food parcels to people in need. Valued at approximately $50 apiece, each parcel "provides enough food for a family for one whole month," and contains flour, rice, tea, sugar, oil, lentils, dry baby milk, cheese, canned meat, beans, and tomatoes.

Medical: "Many people do not have access to hospitals, clinics, etc, while in some rural areas medical aid is 50 miles away and, with no transport, [it] can take days before treatment is given." To address this problem, HAI has set up numerous medical convoys, mobile clinics, land clinics, and hospital sponsorships.

Water: This program "has helped tens of thousands of people benefit ... through the installation of small hand-pumps, bore tube wells, and large tankers catering [to] villages of over 20,000 people."

The U.S. Senate Committee on Finance is currently investigating HAI for suspected ties to international Islamic terrorism. According to the FBI, Hamas operations in Jordan are carried out through HAI. As early as 1996, a CIA document linked HAI to the now-defunct Saudi-based charity Muwafaq, which the U.S. identified as an al Qaeda front organization. That document further named HAI as a fundraiser for Hamas.

HAI's Dubai website makes reference to an HAI donation of $27,000 to a hospital in the Palestinian Authority that is believed to have ties to Hamas; the website also solicits aid for Palestinians in Rafah and Jenin, where the Israeli army is trying to stop the flow of terror weapons via underground tunnels from Egypt. In November 2005 it was reported that millions of dollars in donations to HAI had been funneled directly to Hamas, where they helped fund suicide bombing operations in Israel.

HUMAN RIGHTS WATCH (HRW)

350 Fifth Avenue
34th Floor

New York, NY
10118

Phone :212-290-4700
URL: http://www.hrw.org/Human rights organization founded in 1978

Directs a disproportionate share of its criticism at the United States and Israel

Human Rights Watch (HRW) was founded in 1978 as "Helsinki Watch," to monitor the Soviet Union's compliance with the human rights provisions of the Helsinki Accords. Among its founders were Bob Bernstein, CEO of Random House publishers; Aryeh Neier, the current President of the Open Society Institute, a former Executive Director of the American Civil Liberties Union, and a co-founder of Students for a Democratic Society in 1959; Orville Schell, Dean of the University of California at Berkley graduate school of journalism and a leftwing journalist; and Jeri Laber, a writer and political activist. In the 1980s, the organization developed a number of "Watch" committees, including Americas Watch, Asia Watch, and Africa Watch, which ultimately united under the umbrella of the U.S.-based HRW in 1988. Today HRW states that its "principle advocacy strategy is to shame offenders by generating press attention and to exert diplomatic and economic pressure on them by enlisting influential governments and institutions" on a wide array of issues.

Even as it documented abuses in the Soviet Union, HRW directed much of its censure in the 1980s at the United States. Particularly, the organization denounced the Reagan administration's policy of combating Soviet expansionism in Latin America by aiding anti-Communist governments and opposition forces. In her autobiography, *The Courage of Strangers,* Jeri Laber noted that "Americas Watch reports ... were eagerly read in the United States by people who deplored the Reagan policies." Aryeh Neier, who served as Executive Director of HRW for 12 years, would later write that Americas Watch (AW) could deflect charges of political bias against the Reagan administration's policies because it was also critical of Communist regimes. Neier explained that this "made it difficult for [the Reagan administration] to portray us as Soviet dupes."

In stark contrast to AW's roundly critical appraisal of American policies in Latin America and anti-Communist movements allied with the United States, was its comparatively indulgent assessment of Communist regimes in the region. In Nicaragua, AW routinely portrayed anti-Communist guerillas, the Contras, as the leading threat to human rights while giving short shrift to the abuses of the Communist Sandinista regime. Moreover, AW charged that the Reagan administration was unfairly maligning the Sandinistas.

Symptomatic of this preferential treatment of the Sandinistas was a 1985 AW report titled "Human Rights in Nicaragua: Reagan, Rhetoric and Reality." While allowing that the Sandinistas had committed human rights abuses, the report reposed the greatest share of the blame on the Reagan administration, claiming that "U.S. officials have built and edifice of innuendo and exaggeration" about the Sandinista regime and were guilty of the "misuse of human rights data." More favorable was the report's view of the Sandinistas. Whereas other non-governmental organizations, backed by eyewitness reports from Nicaraguan exiles, had identified a widespread pattern of state-sponsored repression, murder and torture, AW's report dismissed such concerns, averring that "[i]n Nicaragua, there is no systematic practice of forced disappearances, extrajudicial killings ..." Despite a government crackdown on political dissent, the AW report claimed that "debate on major social and political questions is robust." Noting that "emergency legislation" had imposed censorship in the country, the AW report discounted its impact on free-speech rights. Overall, the report concluded, the "description of a totalitarian state bears no resemblance to Nicaragua in 1985."

Human Rights Watch purports to be "strictly non-partisan" in orientation and maintains that it "does not favor any political force." In practice, HRW has often operated as a partisan organization, dressing up its decidedly leftwing political preferences in the language of human rights.
In the United States, HRW regularly interjects itself into domestic political disputes in support of left-liberal positions. For example, the organization maintains that "equitable access to safe abortion services is first and foremost a human right." HRW also has sided against traditionalist opponents of gay marriage. Said HRW Executive Director Kenneth Roth in 2003: "It is discriminatory to refuse to recognize marriages on the basis of sexual orientation." The following year, HRW was a signatory to an amicus brief to the Supreme Judicial Court in Massachusetts, urging it to affirm the legality of same-sex marriage.

HRW is an opponent, "in all circumstances," of the death penalty. In defense of this position, HRW claims that capital punishment is incompatible with "human rights" because it is "a form of punishment that is unique in its barbarity and finality." Consistent with this absolutist stance, HRW condemned the December 31, 2006 execution of former Iraqi dictator Saddam Hussein, calling his death sentence "indefensible." Richard Dicker, Director of HRW's International Justice Program, stated that the "test of a government's commitment to human rights is measured by the way it treats its worst offenders," adding, "History will judge these actions harshly."

With recourse to the rhetoric of human rights, HRW also opposes all enforcement of American immigration laws. In 2005, the organization urged Congress to oppose the "Border Protection, Antiterrorism, and Illegal Immigration Control Act," which provided for a number of measures to strengthen border security. Referring to illegal immigrants as "undocumented workers," HRW has defended the "right" of illegals to organize unions and has condemned employers who "threaten to call immigration authorities if workers seek to organize or make claims for labor law protection." HRW has also called on the U.S. government to enact legislation conferring the rights of full citizenship to individuals "regardless of their immigration status," and "prohibiting any inquiry into ... immigration status."

Human Rights Watch is a vocal supporter of institutions like the International Criminal Court (ICC). A 1998 HRW report, titled "The Danger of Indulging Great Power Arrogance on Human Rights," took issue with America's refusal to cede authority to the ICC. Scolding the United States for exhibiting "great power arrogance toward international human rights institutions," the report declared: "If the U.S. government persists in its current attitude toward international human rights law, the international community should simply leave the United States behind."

While professing neutrality in matters of war and peace, HRW has been a staunch foe of the American-led war on Terror. The organization was a signatory to a November 1, 2001 document characterizing the 9/11 attacks as a legal matter to be addressed by criminal-justice procedures rather than military means. Ascribing the hijackers' motives to alleged social injustices against which they were protesting, this document explained that "security and justice are mutually reinforcing goals that ultimately depend upon the promotion of all human rights for all people," and called on the United States "to promote fundamental rights around the world." Similarly, in 2002 HRW claimed that the United States and its coalition allies "have substituted expediency for the firm commitment to human rights that alone can defeat the rationale of terrorism." Moreover, HRW warned that "the coalition risks reinforcing the logic of terrorism unless human rights are given a far more central role." That is, unless coalition forces followed HRW's distinctive definition of human rights, they were only reinforcing the "view that anything goes in the name of a cause."

HRW endorsed the Civil Liberties Restoration Act of 2004, which was designed to roll back, in the name of protecting civil liberties, vital national-security policies that had been adopted after the 9/11 terrorist attacks.

With regard to the military conflicts in Afghanistan and Iraq, HRW has consistently judged the actions of coalition forces to be contrary to human rights. Several HRW reports have alleged an "excessive use of force by U.S. troops," even as the organization has conceded that it has only incomplete information about the facts on the ground in Iraq. In one such instance, when Americans battled insurgent forces in the city of Fallujah in April of 2004, the organization reported that it was "deeply concerned about the consistent reports we are getting about women, children and unarmed civilians being killed" by American forces. At the same time, HRW admitted that it had no clear knowledge "whether any crimes have been committed" by the military.

Connected with its criticism of the war effort, Human Rights Watch has routinely condemned American interrogation and detention policies. Among other objections, HRW claims that a form of coercive interrogation known as "waterboarding" constitutes "torture."

A leading opponent of military commissions created by the United States to try detainees suspected of terrorist activities, Human Rights Watch has criticized the U.S. for not granting the "fundamental right" of *habeas corpus* to those prisoners. In addition, HRW has denounced the American detention facility in Guantanamo Bay, Cuba, as a violation of international law.

HRW also directs a disproportionate share of its criticism at Israel. Following an April 2002 counterterrorism operation by the Israeli military in the Palestinian refugee camp of Jenin, the organization issued a report charging that "IDF [Israeli Defense Forces] military attacks were indiscriminate," and that "Israeli forces committed serious violations of international humanitarian law, some amounting *prima facie* to war crimes."

Contrary to HRW's charges, which echoed Palestinian propaganda, a United Nations report later exonerated the Israeli forces.

HRW released an equally one-sided attack in August of 2006, amid Israel's war with Hezbollah terrorists in southern Lebanon. Titled "Israel's Indiscriminate Attacks Against Civilians in Lebanon," this report repeated many of the same charges that the organization had leveled against Israel during the Jenin controversy. Among other claims, the document asserted that Israel was guilty of "consistently failing to distinguish between combatants and civilians," and that "the extent of the pattern and the seriousness of the consequences indicate the commission of war crimes."

Human Rights Watch has denounced Israel's construction of an anti-terrorism security barrier in the West Bank as a violation of Palestinians' human rights. Joe Stork, the acting Director of HRW's Middle East and Africa Division, claims that the barrier "seriously impedes Palestinian access to essentials of civilian life, such as work, education and medical care."

HRW has a full-time staff of 190 employees worldwide and a budget of approximately $22 million per year. The organization has received funding from many foundations, including the Ahmanson Foundation; the Carnegie Corporation of New York;the Columbia Foundation; the Ford Foundation; the William and Flora Hewlett Foundation; the John D. & Catherine T. MacArthur Foundation; the Nathan Cummings Foundation; the JEHT Foundation; the Joyce Foundation; the J.M. Kaplan Fund; the Open Society Institute; the David and Lucile Packard Foundation; the Righteous Persons Foundation; the Rockefeller Brothers Fund; the Rockefeller Foundation; and the Scherman Foundation.

I'LAM

POB 101
Attn. Haneen Zoubi
16000 Nazareth, Israel

Phone :972 04 600 1370
URL: http://www.ilamcenter.org/Anti-Israeli NGO

Founded in 2000 and based in Haifa, I'lam
describes itself as "the only not-for-profit Palestinian Media Center in Israel." The organization's mission is "to develop and empower the Arab media and to give voice to Palestinian issues"; to contribute "to the development of a plural and unbiased media landscape"; and "to serve primarily the Palestinian citizens in Israel through the improvement of their mass media system with training, documentation, advocacy, cooperation, and outreach." In I'lam's estimation, the Israeli media "is to a large extent controlled by the national government, which uses it to ... manipulate public knowledge and opinion." Consequently, says I'lam, "the media in Israel fails to satisfy [its] fundamental responsibility ... to disseminate balanced and accurate information and to promote democratic values, civil society, and pluralism."

I'lam views Israel as a nation whose government abuses and oppresses its Palestinian citizens and neighbors. The organization's December 2000 report, titled "The Israeli Media and the *Intifada*," stated: "The [Arab-Israeli] war is taking place on the territories of the party [the Palestinians] who is completely under siege and possesses mere rocks and rifles, whereas, the other party [Israel] possesses the largest military arsenal in the Middle East." This document traced the roots of the latest *Intifada* (which had erupted three months earlier) exclusively to Prime Minister Ariel Sharon's visit to the Temple Mount, and criticized the Israeli media for taking what I'lam deemed a one-sided approach to its reporting on the violence.

In April 2002 the I'lam website directed readers to an article from the daily publication *Al-Itihad,* entitled "Report from Jenin Refugee Camp: Even Flies Reveal What the Israeli Army Wants to Hide." Claiming that the Israeli Defense Forces had massacred Palestinian civilians in Jenin earlier that month, the author wrote: "I imagine the picture: The soldiers are the grandchildren of the Nazis' victims, the Nazis' survivors. They have come here to consume food quickly and consume life quickly. This is the true image of Israel. The real Israel is not in the clean, lofty suburbs of Northern Tel-Aviv ... It is not in the literary cafes and journalists' clubs ... It is not its High Court. I saw the real Israel, its ugliness in the Jenin Refugee Camp on Monday, April 15, 2002. The rest remains decor for murder."

On August 5, 2005, I'lam published a six-page report on Israel's television coverage of the murder of four

Arab citizens by an Israeli soldier (who was absent without leave) in Shafa'amr. The report alleged that the four victims had "paid with their lives for 'the political culture' that the official policies of Israel have nurtured for over 50 years." I'lam also charged that the Israeli media had "contributed to preparing the groundwork for the terrorist attack in Shafar'amr" by allegedly ignoring, on a consistent basis, racist commentary and racially motivated attacks aimed against Arabs. No specific facts or statistics were presented to support this claim.

In a March 2005 communiqué, I'lam condemned the renewal of Israel's Citizenship Law which restricts the automatic granting of Israeli citizenship to Palestinian residents of the West Bank and Gaza who marry Israelis. I'lam described the law as a "blatantly discriminatory" form of "collective punishment."

In a May 2005 news release, I'lam implicitly accused the State of Israel of restricting Muslims' right to freedom of religion when Sheikh Abd Al-Rahman Bakirat was indicted on charges of committing "incitement to violence or terror." Calling on the international community and media to show solidarity for "the right of individuals ... to freedom of expression and freedom of worship," I'lam declined to mention that a police investigation found that a column recently penned by Bakirat had included "praise, sympathy and encouragement for an act of violence or terror," and that there was "a tangible possibility that it would lead to [such] an act."

In 2002, I'lam's major projects included the production and dissemination of video documentaries, the facilitation of awareness-raising sessions aimed at high-school students, and the convening of public policy roundtable discussions with members of the local media community. The following year was a period of transition for I'lam, during which the organization reworked its infrastructure, made personnel changes, and acquired additional financial resources. In May 2004 I'lam launched its "Responsible and Professional Media" project, seeking "to develop respect for press freedom and responsibility, media professionalism and ethics, and media rights for Arabs inside Israel." Throughout 2004 and the first half of 2005, I'lam focused its resources on "improving the coverage of Arab citizens of Israel in the Hebrew media, and at democratizing media laws and regulations in Israel." During the second half of 2005 and 2006, the organization's focus was on "developing and consolidating [its] work with the community and the local Arabic media."

I'lam receives financial backing from the New Israel Fund, the British Council (Israel), the European Union (through the European Initiative for Democracy and Human Rights), the Swiss Federal Department of Foreign Affairs, the Heinrich Boell Foundation, and the Open Society Institute Development Foundation.

IF AMERICANS KNEW (IAK)

914 Westwood Blvd. #235
Los Angeles, CA
90024

Phone :310-441-8580
URL: http://www.ifamericansknew.org/Tax-exempt research institute focusing on alleged "pro Israel bias" in the American media

Charges Israel with war crimes and human rights abuses

If Americans Knew (IAK) describes itself as a "research and information-dissemination institute, with particular focus on the Israeli-Palestinian conflict, U.S. foreign policy regarding the Middle East, and media coverage of this issue." The organization was founded in 2001 by freelance journalist Alison Weir to counter what she deemed a pro-Israel bias coloring U.S. media coverage of Mideast events.

The group's website contains a number of glaring inaccuracies. It states, for example: "When the inevitable (1948) war broke out, the outcome was never in doubt ... The Zionist army consisted of over 90,000 European-trained soldiers and possessed modern weaponry, including up-to-date fighter and bomber airplanes. The Arab forces, very much a Third World army, consisted of approximately 30,000 ill-equipped poorly trained men." Actually the reverse is true. The Arab League -- representing five neighboring Arab states, several of which had fought alongside Hitler -- declared war on Israel on the day of its creation. Armed with modern weaponry and aiming to destroy the new Jewish state, those five Arab armies invaded Israel.

If Americans Knew also mischaracterizes the 1967 Six Day War as a conflict that erupted when "Israeli forces launched a highly successful, Pearl Harbor-like surprise attack on Egypt [and thereafter] occupied the additional 22 percent of Palestine that had eluded it in 1948 -- the West Bank and the Gaza Strip." In reality, Egyptian dictator Gamel Abdel Nasser, who had declared Israel's existence "an aggression," blockaded the Port of Eilat and moved two tank battalions and 150,000 troops right up to Israel's western border -- an unambiguous act of war. For three weeks Israel tried, to no avail, to negotiate for peace. On June 5, 1967, after receiving military intelligence that Egypt was within hours of launching an invasion via the Gaza Strip, Israel launched its defensive pre-emptive strike, an air attack that destroyed the air forces of Egypt and its allies Jordan and Syria while they were still on the ground.

On its website, If Americans Knew provides statistics indicating that during the current Intifada (which was launched in September 2000), Palestinian civilians have suffered significantly greater numbers of deaths and injuries than have their Israeli counterparts. But IAK entirely omits the context in which those deaths have occurred. It does not mention the waves of Palestinian suicide bombings and other terrorist attacks deliberately targeting Israeli civilians; nor does it acknowledge that Israel's military efforts have been aimed entirely at terrorist operations, many of which use private homes and civilian areas as bases for their operations, thereby placing civilians in harm's way.

Calling for an end to U.S. aid to Israel, If Americans Knew states, "Empowered by American money, Israel is occupying land that doesn't belong to it, is breaking numerous international laws and conventions of which it is a signatory, and is promulgating policies of brutality that have been condemned by the United Nations, the European Union, the National Council of Churches, Amnesty International, the International Red Cross, and numerous other international bodies." U.S. support for Israel, says IAK, "interferes with: American relations with the oil-producing nations, with whom we previously had friendly ties; with Muslim consumers ... and removes much-needed money from domestic American requirements — tax revenues that could be addressed to domestic needs are instead sent abroad to prop up a system of discrimination that is antithetical to American principles of equality and democracy."

In its "Synopsis of the Current Situation," IAK charges: "Israeli forces regularly confiscate private [Palestinian] land; imprison individuals without process - including children - and physically abuse them under incarceration; demolish family homes; bulldoze orchards and crops; place entire towns under curfew; destroy shops and businesses; shoot, maim, and kill civilians - and Palestinians are without power to stop any of it."

Paul Findley, a former eleven-term Illinois Congressman, is a board member of If Americans Knew. Findley has stated that President Bush "overreacted" to the September 11th terrorist attacks, and claims that Americans "have been misled by the American media, which is controlled by the Jewish lobby." These views have been endorsed by such institutions as Harvard Law School, Stanford University, Columbia University, the Fletcher School of Law and Diplomacy, the University of California at Berkeley, Northwestern University, the Center for Policy Analysis on Palestine, and the National Press Club -- all of which have made use of written materials and guest speakers provided by If Americans Knew.

If Americans Knew also produces annual "Media Report Cards" that evaluate major media outlets across the United States on their coverage of the Israeli-Palestinian conflict.

INSTITUTE FOR POLICY STUDIES (IPS)

733 15th St NW
Suite 1020
Washington DC
20005

Phone :202-234-9382
URL: www.**ips**-dc.org

America's oldest leftwing think tank

Has long supported Communist and anti-American causes around the world

The Institute for Policy Studies (IPS) was founded in 1963 as a tax-exempt 501(c)(3) organization with seed money (derived from a fortune made in cosmetics sales under the Faberge trade name) from the Samuel Rubin Foundation. Samuel Rubin (1901-1978) was a Russian Bolshevik and the father of Cora Weiss, who headed the Samuel Rubin Foundation from its inception and is currently the principal financier of IPS. Weiss' husband, Peter, is Chairman of the IPS Board of Trustees. He is also a member of the National Lawyers Guild and the National Emergency Civil Liberties Committee, both of which were created as Communist Party fronts. The Weisses selected Richard J. Barnet and Marcus Raskin to be the first Co-Directors of IPS, with the aim of transforming the United States by altering public attitudes, changing laws, and reversing foreign policy through an Academy that reached every nexus of the national nervous system.

Throughout its history, IPS has committed itself to the task of advancing leftist causes. It worked with agents of the Castro regime and championed environmentalist and anti-war positions in the 1960s and 1970s; it declared against the Reagan administration's efforts to roll back communism in the 1980s; it joined the vanguard of what IPS hails as the "anti-corporate globalization movement" in the 1990s; and, most recently, it has furnished policy research assailing the U.S.-led war in Iraq.

IPS's Washington, DC headquarters quickly became a resource center for national reporters and a place for KGB agents from the nearby Soviet embassy to convene and strategize. Cora Weiss headed one of the IPS's most successful forays -- into Riverside Church in Manhattan. She was invited there in 1978 by the Reverend William Sloane Coffin to run the church's Disarmament Program, which sought to consolidate Soviet nuclear superiority in Europe -- in the name of "peace." In 1982 Weiss helped organize the largest pro-disarmament demonstration ever held. Staged in New York City, the rally was attended by a coalition of communist organizations. During her decade-long tenure at Riverside, which became home to the National Council of Churches, Weiss regularly received Russian KGB agents, Sandinista friends, and Cuban intelligence agents. Weiss became infamous for her role in the psychological warfare conducted against U.S. prisoners of war held in the infamous "Hanoi Hilton" during the Vietnam War.

The Liberation News Service, which is a news source for hundreds of "alternative" publications nationwide (with antiwar, Marxist-oriented perspectives), was founded in 1967 with IPS assistance.
The Center for Security Studies was a 1974 IPS spinoff and strove to compromise the effectiveness of U.S. intelligence agencies. The mastheads of two anti-FBI and anti-CIA publications, *Counterspy* and the *Covert Action Information Bulletin*, were heavy with IPS members.

The Middle East Research and Information Project (MERIP) was begun in 1971 by IPS fellow Joe Stork, who is now a Director with Human Rights Watch. The magazine *Mother Jones* was founded in 1975 by the IPS spinoff Foundation for National Progress. *In These Times*, established in 1976 as a leftwing tabloid, was financed by the IPS until 1982.

Also spawned by IPS were: (a) the North American Congress on Latin America, created in 1966 as a New Left intelligence-gathering agency; (b) the Holland-based Transnational Institute, a major source of anti-American, anti-capitalist literature; (c) the Institute for Food and Development Policy (a.k.a. Food First), which has spent years finding fault with the quality of America's food gifts to the Third World and helped to give rise to Medea Benjamin's organization Global Exchange; (d) the Data Center in Oakland, a major database that cross-indexes the annual reports of more than 1,000 corporations to detect any signs of incipient monopoly; (e) the Institute for Southern Studies, which has compiled a similar database on more than 400 Southern corporations; (f) the Council on Economic Priorities, which received IPS money with a view to exposing corporate skullduggery and passing judgment on companies' social conscience; and (g) the Interfaith Council on Corporate Responsibility.

IPS is also linked to the phalanx of leftist anti-war groups, either through funding or leadership. Among these are the Committee for a Sane Nuclear Policy (SANE); Fellowship of Reconciliation; Promoting Enduring Peace; and Business Executives for National Security. Moreover, IPS is a member organization of the United for Peace and Justice anti-war coalition, and it endorsed a May 1, 2003 document titled "10 Reasons Environmentalists Oppose an Attack on Iraq," which was published by Environmentalists Against War. In 2003 it was reported that IPS, in conjunction with the National Organization for Women, made some of its Washington DC office space available (at no charge) to the feminist antiwar organization Code Pink, headed by the longtime communists Medea Benjamin and Jodie Evans.

IPS has consistently tried to derail American efforts to combat Communism. In 1985, for instance, as President Reagan pressed Congress to fund the Contras in Nicaragua, IPS fellow Peter Kornbluh arranged for Senators John Kerry and Tom Harkin to fly to Managua to meet with Communist Sandinista leaders. Convinced by the Kerry-Harkin report on the allegedly happy atmosphere in Managua, Congress denied the funds, though it reversed itself a few weeks later when Sandinista President Daniel Ortega met with his Soviet friends in the Kremlin.

The consistently anti-American positions adopted by IPS are frequently expressed in tandem with condemnations of Israel. In February 2005, for instance, IPS Fellow Phyllis Bennis published a commentary depicting the United States as a cynical manipulator seeking only to extract favorable deals for its ally, Israel, no matter how negatively they might affect Palestinians. Bennis further denounced Israel's efforts to "demolish Palestinian homes"; Israel's "assassination policy" (a reference to the targeted killings of Palestinian terrorist leaders); and the "land-grab known as the Apartheid Wall" (a reference to the anti-terror security fence designed to stem the tide of suicide bombers from the West Bank).

Central to the IPS worldview is the think tank's unyielding opposition to free markets particularly and capitalism broadly. Viewing capitalism as a breeding ground for "unrestrained greed," IPS seeks, through its reports and programs, to provide a corrective to "unrestrained markets and individualism." One such initiative is the Global Economy Project, overseen by Sarah Anderson and IPS Director John Cavanagh, which seeks to: (a) undercut the Free Trade Area of the Americas; (b) foment grassroots resentment against the World Trade Organization; (c) incite opposition to the North American Free Trade Agreement; and (d) promote "economic alternatives" to globalization.

In their 2004 book *Alternatives to Economic Globalization: A Better World Is Possible*, John Cavanagh and Jerry Mander (President of the IPS Board of Directors and a longtime critic of globalization) contend that capitalism is "a system in crisis," and they appeal to "an alliance of leading activists, scholars, economists, researchers, and writers" to take up the ideological cudgel against globalization.

IPS professes an unquestioning faith in the righteousness of the United Nations, as evidenced by its "New Internationalism" project, which was introduced in 1996 and is directed by Phyllis Bennis. Working in concert with the Congressional Black Caucus and the Progressive Caucus, this project seeks to hamstring American foreign policy and bring it under the control of the UN. In recent years, it has condemned NATO military intervention in the former Yugoslavia; denounced the "unilaterally imposed" U.S.-British no-fly-zones in Iraq; sought to spark public opposition to pre-war economic sanctions against Iraq; attempted to align U.S. policy toward Israel more closely with the ritually critical stance of the UN; and impugned unilateralism in combating terror, viewing it as hostile to the function of the United Nations.

A corollary of the New Internationalism campaign advises European nations to assume a more assertive role in the Middle East. Toward this end, IPS contends, European nations must "challenge more directly U.S. control of the diplomatic process." Underlying this proposal is the core IPS belief that the United States is itself a rogue nation that poses a grave threat to international peace and stability. Phyllis Bennis made this point succinctly in a July 2004 article wherein she asked, "Haven't we -- and the rest of the world -- had enough of Washington's rogue behavior?"

Similar sentiments are purveyed by the Institute's in-house team of scholars, which in recent years has featured such radical activists as Noam Chomsky, Barbara Ehrenreich, Gore Vidal, Norman Birnbaum, and Richard Falk.

One of the more notable figures in IPS history is Robert Borosage, who served as the organization's Director from 1979 to 1988.

Financial support for IPS comes from such foundations as the Ford Foundation, the Ploughshares Fund, the Charles Stewart Mott Foundation, the Arca Foundation, the Ben & Jerry's Foundation, the Compton Foundation, the Educational Foundation of America, the Energy Foundation, the David and Lucile Packard Foundation, the Rockefeller Brothers Fund, the Nathan Cummings Foundation, the Foundation for Deep Ecology, the John D. and Catherine T. MacArthur Foundation, the Tides Foundation, the Open Society Institute, the Turner Foundation, and many others.

INSTITUTE OF ISLAMIC AND ARABIC SCIENCES IN AMERICA (IIASA)

8500 Hilltop Road
Fairfax, VA
22031

Phone :703-641-4890
URL: http://www.iiasa.org/Virginia-based satellite campus of Saudi Arabia's Ibn Saud Islamic University

The Institute of Islamic and Arabic Sciences in America (IIASA) was established in 1988 as a nonprofit organization in Fairfax, Virginia. A satellite of Ibn Saud Islamic University in Riyadh, Saudi Arabia, IIASA's objectives are to: (a) "educate the American society about Islamic studies and Arabic language and culture"; (b) "provide continuing undergraduate and graduate education in Islamic Studies and diplomas in Arabic language"; (c) "conduct scholarly research in the filed of Islamic studies"; (d) "collaborate with American educational institutions interested in Islamic studies, and ... assist them to spread (*sic*) the Arabic language and Islamic civilization"; (e) "promote public dialogue and education about Islamic teachings and Muslim culture"; and (f) "use all manner of legal communications to accomplish these goals."

IIASA is funded by, and serves as an arm of, the Saudi embassy's Religious Affairs Department. The Institute's Board Chairman is the former Saudi ambassador to America (from 1983 to 2005), Prince Bandar Bin Sultan. Axis Information and Analysis (AIA), which specializes in information about Asia and Eastern Europe, rated Bin Sultan as the single most influential foreigner in America. With links to high-ranking officials in the State Department, Pentagon, and CIA, Bin Sultan was a key participant in many clandestine negotiations pertaining to U.S. interests in the Middle East. According to AIA, in 1990-91 it was he who pushed President George H.W. Bush to launch the military campaign to drive Iraqi forces out of Kuwait. Moreover, his father -- Sultan Bin Abdul Aziz al Saud -- was a leading figure in the ruling Saudi dynasty.

IIASA has been a major center for Saudi-sponsored Islamic outreach in America, training imams for local mosques in addition to at least 75 Muslim lay chaplains for service in the U.S. armed forces. Its 400 students pay no tuition. In late 2002, Ali al-Ahmed, a prominent Saudi dissident then based in Washington, DC, charged that IIASA, in its instruction on Islam, hewed to an ultra-radical line. Al-Ahmed analyzed literature produced by IIASA, including an Arabic-language textbook titled *A Muslim's Relations with Non-Muslims, Enmity or Friendship* by Dr. Abdullah al-Tarekee, who wrote: "Unbelievers, idolaters and others like them must be hated and despised ... *Qur'an* forbade taking Jews and Christians as friends, and that applies to every Jew and Christian, with no consideration as to whether they are at war with Islam or not." Based on his findings vis a vis IIASA's role as a distributor of extremist literature, al-Ahmed called on U.S. and Saudi authorities to close the school and repatriate its staff.

According to the Foundation for Defense of Democracies, "[IIASA] is the largest source of Saudi hate literature in the Washington area. The Institute is ... managed and staffed by Saudi diplomats. [It] practices gender segregation against its women students who are confined to a small part of the building and forced to use a back entrance. It also practices religious supremacy and bars Shi'a students, teachers, and books. [It represents Shi'a beliefs] as Jewish manipulations, not as an Islamic tradition. The Institute teaches Wahhabi Islam to over 400 students, ... training them to serve as imams in U.S. mosques, i.e. as community leaders infected with extremism."

On December 22, 2003, Senator Charles Grassley of the Senate Finance Committee included IIASA in a list of U.S.-based, Saudi-established nonprofits and charities suspected of laundering funds used for terrorism. This move was prompted in part when American authorities revoked the diplomatic visa of Jaafar Idris, a Sudanese national with Saudi documents who was one of the most influential clerics in IIASA. Idris, who was eventually deported by the United States, is a proponent of Wahhabist Islam, which encourages *jihad* (holy war) against the West.

In July 2004, agents from the FBI, Internal Revenue Service, and Bureau of Immigration and Customs Enforcement shut down and searched IIASA for evidence of links to terrorism. When they failed to turn up enough evidence to warrant the Institute's permanent closure, IIASA reopened its doors.

INTERNATIONAL FEDERATION OF HUMAN RIGHTS (FIDH)

FIDH
17, passage de la main d'or
75011 Paris
France
fax + 33 1 43 55 18 80
www.**fidh**.org

Pro-Palestinian, anti-Israel federation of human rights organizations

Established in 1922, the Paris-based International Federation of Human Rights (*Fédération Internationale des ligues des Droits de l'Homme*, or FIDH) is a union of 141 human rights organizations in nearly 100 countries; it coordinates and supports its members' activities, and provides them with a voice at the international level. FIDH asserts that its mandate is "to contribute to the respect of all the rights defined in the Universal Declaration of Human Rights," and to "[obtain] effective improvements in the protection of victims, the prevention of Human Rights violations and the sanction of their perpetrators."

FIDH identifies 4 Statutory Priorities that guide its activities:
Protecting Human Rights, Assisting Victims: Activities in this category include judicial enquiry, trial observation, research, advocacy, and litigation. FIDH reports that from 2001 to 2003, it carried out 111 fact-finding and observation missions, published 201 reports covering more than 80 countries, and initiated some 1,300 specific interventions on cases or situations.

Mobilizing the Community of States: FIDH guides and supports its member organizations and other local partners in their dealings with inter-governmental organizations. From 2001 to 2003, FIDH filed and supported more than 500 cases before international governmental bodies, "with actions ranging from written appeals to the UN Commission on Human Rights, to monitoring global conferences."

Supporting Local NGOs' Capacity for Action: "FIDH organizes legal cooperation programs jointly with its member leagues and local partners ... to strengthen ... the capacity for action of Human Rights defenders and the credibility of their organizations, through training and dialogue with authorities. From 2001 to 2003, judicial cooperation action programs were pursued in 30 African, 16 Latin American, and 12 countries from the North Africa/Middle Eastern region."

Raising Awareness: FIDH publicizes its research findings and eyewitness accounts of Human Rights abuses via press releases, press conferences, open letters to Heads of States, mission reports, urgent appeals, petitions, publicity, and regular website updates; during 2004, Internet traffic to its website (www.fidh.org) amounted to approximately 1 million pages visited.

FIDH also enumerates 5 Thematic Priorities:

Protecting Human Rights Defenders and the Implementation of the 1998 UN Declaration: In 2004, FIDH and the World Organization Against Torture jointly addressed 1,154 cases in more than 90 countries, with the collaboration of approximately 200 Human Rights organizations.

Defending Women's Rights: FIDH "fights against the secondary status treatment of women in nearly all societies and the flagrant persistence of gender-based discrimination," via its Action Group for Women's Rights, which is headed by the 2003 Nobel Peace Prize winner and FIDH League President, Shirin Ebadi."

Justice for Victims Fighting Impunity: In this area, FIDH, which made a significant contribution to the establishment of the International Criminal Court, "gives daily support to victims by accompanying them throughout the entire course of their legal proceedings."

Promoting Respect of Human Rights in the Fight Against Terrorism: "Since 2002, FIDH initiated or supported key proceedings before domestic courts ... in cases concerning arbitrary measures and practices in the fight against terrorism." According to FIDH, "Terrorism can only be effectively combated by and through the respect of Human Rights."

Advocating Economic Globalization Respectful of Human Rights: "FIDH actively seeks to ensure the justiciability of economic, social and cultural rights, the responsibility of economic actors, the primacy of Human Rights over trade law, and the participation of civil societies in globalization organizations."

Professing nonpartisanship, FIDH claims that it is "linked to no party, no religion, and is independent *vis-a-vis* all governments." It does, however, accuse the United States of having fostered, by means of its military response to the attacks of 9/11, a worldwide atmosphere of disregard for human rights: "Fanatical ideologists, proselytes, and murderers have found an echo in the action of the leading world power, which is responding to the deep wound of its people with a brutal and arbitrary expansionistic nationalism. Good and Evil, as well as the illegal use of force, deception and opportunism are just so many 'concepts' and methods on which American policy is now based. The American base in Guantanamo, the Abu [Ghraib] prison, and the American intervention in Afghanistan and Iraq are symbols of its perversion: now, the ends justify the means, contracted international obligations are neglected to the benefit of security imperatives."

FIDH also follows a strong pro-Palestinian, anti-Israel political agenda, as evidenced by the fact that its member organizations include the Palestinian Center for Human Rights and Al-Haq. On May 27, 2003, FIDH and five other prominent NGOs issued a joint press release entitled "International Rights Groups Decry Increased Harassment of Monitors," which accused the Israeli government of intimidating, harassing, and even killing foreign national humanitarian workers in the Gaza Strip. Taking umbrage at the fact that such workers must sign a waiver form when they enter Gaza, FIDH made no mention of the fact that this policy was necessitated by the fact that many self-identified "humanitarians" (such as the late Rachel Corrie) are in fact political activists intent on aggressively interfering with the anti-terrorism activities of the Israeli Defense Force. Nor did the FIDH press release note the recent spate of incidents where individuals purportedly engaged in humanitarian enterprises were in fact terrorists. One such case took place in April 2003, when two suicide bombers posing as human rights workers traveled to Gaza on British passports. To provide cover, they met with members of the Palestinian-run International Solidarity Movement. One of them later blew himself up -- killing three civilians and injuring 50 more -- in a midnight attack in a popular Tel Aviv jazz bar.

FIDH has received funding from the Ford Foundation.

INTERNATIONAL INSTITUTE OF ISLAMIC THOUGHT (IIIT)

500 Grove Street
Herndon, VA
20170

Phone :703-471-1133
Fax :703-471-3922
Email : iiit@iiit.org
URL: http://www.iiituk.com/indexlo.htm

Islamic institution with ties to the extremist Saudi-Wahhabi movement
Seeks to portray Wahhabism as peaceful
Partner organization to the Graduate School of Islamic and Social Sciences

A partner organization to the Graduate School of Islamic and Social Sciences, the International Institute of Islamic Thought (IIIT) defines itself as "a private, non-profit, academic and cultural institution, concerned with general issues of Islamic thought." Giving "special emphasis to the development of Islamic scholarship in contemporary social sciences," it works "from an Islamic perspective to promote and support research projects, organize intellectual and cultural meetings and publish scholarly works" that will help "the *Ummah* [Muslim nation] to deal effectively with present challenges." Established in 1981, IIIT is headquartered in Herndon, Virginia (near Washington, DC), and has set up branch offices in a number of capital cities worldwide.

The Institute seeks to achieve its objectives by: "directing research and studies to develop Islamic thought and the Islamization of knowledge"; "holding specialized scholarly, intellectual and cultural conferences, seminars and study circles"; supporting researchers and scholars in universities and research centers, and publishing selected scholarly, cultural and intellectual works, in English, Arabic and several other languages"; and signing agreements of cooperation with various universities, research centers and academic institutions throughout the world to carry out activities of mutual interest."

Controlled by the extremist, Saudi-based Wahhabi movement, IIIT maintains that reports about mosques distributing hate-filled literature are untrue, and claims that the concept of *jihad* in no way condones or connotes violence. As an IIIT public-relations flyer puts it: "*Jihad* does not mean 'holy war.' Literally, *jihad* in Arabic means to strive, struggle and exert effort. It is a central and broad Islamic concept that includes struggle against evil inclinations within oneself, struggle to improve the quality of life in society, struggle in the battlefield for self-defense or fighting against tyranny or oppression." The back of the flyer contains a list of recommended websites and books on Islam. Among the authors of these books are such apologists for extremism as John Esposito, Karen Armstrong, Hassan Hathout, and Bill Baker.

IIIT has numerous documented links to terrorism. According to court documents, in the early 1990s the organization donated at least $50,000 to a think tank run by Sami al-Arian, the World Islam Study Enterprise, which served as a front group for Palestinian Islamic Jihad. IIIT is also named as a defendant in two class-action lawsuits brought by victims of the 9/11 attacks. One alleges that the Institute received the bulk of its operating expenses from the SAAR network, whose component groups are accused in another class-action suit of being "fronts for the sponsor of al Qaeda and international terror." The same suit lists IIIT and nearly all of its officers as supporters of the SAAR network.

Moreover, IIIT's 2003 tax-exempt IRS filing lists a $720 donation to the al-Haramain Islamic Foundation of Ashland, Oregon, which was designated as a terrorist-funding entity by the U.S. government in 2004.

INTERNATIONAL PROGRESS ORGANIZATION (IPO)

Postal address: Kohlmarkt 4, A-1010 Vienna, Austria, Europe
Telephone: +43-1-5332877
Telefax: +43-1-5332962
E-mail: info@i-p-o.org
Editorial office: ipo@i-p-o.org
President's office: pres@i-p-o.org

Human rights NGO that monitors and condemns alleged Israeli abuses of Palestinians

Founded in 1972 in Innsbruck, Austria by students from Austria, India, and Egypt, the International Progress Organization (IPO) is a non-profit, non-governmental, and nominally "non-partisan" group that claims to promote "cultural and academic exchange between all nations; ... cultural self-realization ...; tolerance towards other cultures that are not yet included in cultural exchanges; realization of political, social and economic human rights; establishment of a new international economic order; [and] development of international law."

Currently based in Vienna, IPO sponsors international conferences and research seminars on democracy, human rights, conflict resolution, international law, and economic development; it monitors elections and human rights situations in various countries; it works jointly with academic institutions and international NGOs around the world; and it publishes the series "Studies in International Relations." It also produces books, papers, and monographs that are largely critical of American and Israeli policies. Recently published titles include: *Global Justice or Global Revenge? International Criminal Justice at the Crossroads*; *The Iraq Crisis and the United Nations: Power Politics vs. the International Rule of Law*; and *9/11 - Discrimination in Response*.

IPO enjoys consultative status with UNESCO (United Nations Educational, Scientific and Cultural Organization) and is affiliated with the United Nations Department of Public Information. It has permanent representation at the UN in New York City, Vienna, and Geneva, as well as at UNESCO in Paris and in Beirut. Additionally, IPO serves as the Secretariat of the NGO Committee on Development, a collection of NGOs in consultative status with the United Nations. IPO claims to have "a regular budget based solely upon contributions from its members and from individual donors," but does not divulge its sources of funding on its website.

IPO is one of the primary NGOs supporting the "Durban strategy" to delegitimize Israel as an alleged human rights violator. Its website features an inflammatory August 28, 2001 speech by Dr. Hanan Ashrawi at Durban. In that address, Ashrawi referred to "Palestine" as "a land besieged and repeatedly violated by a most brutal Israeli military occupation"; a "tortured nation" suffering "exclusion, denial, racism, ... national victimization ... oppression, violence, cruelty, and injustice."

Since its founding, IPO has been headed by Dr. Hans Koechler, a professor of philosophy at the University of Innsbruck who also serves as Coordinator for the International Committee for Palestinian Human Rights, a division of IPO. Koechler participated in a July 2002 conference at the Zayed Center for Coordination & Follow-Up in Abu Dhabi, entitled "War Victims and International Law. The Zayed Center was closed in August 2003 after international attention was focused on the extremist nature of its agendas, its guest speakers, and the anti-Semitic and conspiracy theory literature it published.

Koechler also appeared at a September 2002 International Ecumenical Conference on "Terrorism in a Globalized World" in the Philipines. There he spoke on the "War on Terror, its Impact on the Sovereignty of States and its Implications for Human Rights and Civil Liberties." The Conference Declaration abjured the "Israeli state terrorism against Palestine [that] forms part of the U.S. agenda in the Middle East." On November 29, 2005 (the "International Day of Solidarity with the Palestinian People"), Koechler addressed the UN General Assembly's Committee on the topic of the "Exercise of the Inalienable Rights of the Palestinian People." His speech was an excoriation of Israel, including demands for an international investigation into Yasser Arafat's "mysterious" death.

In its reports on the Israeli-Palestinian conflict, IPO often denounces Israel's allegedly gratuitous violence while casting Palestinian terrorism as an understandable response to that violence. In a 2002 statement titled "War In Palestine: A Declaration of the International Progress Organization," Hans Koechler asserted: "[T]he problem of terrorism can only be solved if the root causes of the suicidal attacks are addressed: namely the ongoing illegal occupation of Palestinian land ... and the permanent subjugation of the entire people of Palestine to Israeli rule."

INTERNATIONAL SOLIDARITY MOVEMENT (ISM)

Phone :202-494-0471
URL: http://www.palsolidarity.org/Radical, anti-Israel organization that recruits westerners to travel to Israel to obstruct Israeli security operations

Justifies Palestinian terrorism against Israeli civilians

The International Solidarity Movement (ISM) was founded in August 2001 by Adam Shapiro, Huwaida Arraf; Ghassan Andoni, and George Rishmawi. The organization describes itself as "a Palestinian-led movement committed to resisting the Israeli occupation of Palestinian land using nonviolent, direct-action methods and principles."

ISM's activities fall under three major categories, which the organization describes as follows:

Direct Action: "challenging crippling checkpoints and curfew, confronting tanks and demolition equipment, removing roadblocks, participating in nonviolent demonstrations, accompanying farmers to their fields and protecting families whose homes are threatened with demolition"
Emergency Mobilization: "escorting ambulances through checkpoints, delivering food and water to families under curfew or house arrest, assisting the injured or disabled to access medical care and walking children to school"

Documentation: "documenting and reporting to local and international media about the daily life under occupation and the countless human rights and international law violations by the Israeli military"
Though professing, as noted above, a commitment to nonviolence, ISM members openly advocate the "liberation" of Palestinians "by any means necessary," including "legitimate armed struggle."

Led by Palestinians working closely with American recruiters, ISM invites American volunteers to travel to the Palestinian territories and disrupt the actions of the Israeli Defense Force (IDF), which is engaged in anti-terror operations in the region. ISM maintains a continual, low-level presence in the territories year-round, punctuated by occasional large, episodic campaigns. At various times, ISM members have temporarily taken over Israeli military checkpoints, interfered with the arrests of Palestinians charged with terrorism, and attempted to prevent the destruction of Palestinian homes containing subterranean tunnels for weapons smuggling.

Among ISM's most well known members was the late Rachel Corrie, a 23-year-old volunteer who, in March 2003, was crushed beneath a bulldozer in Rafah when its operator failed to see her trying to block the destruction of a Palestinian home that was concealing a tunnel through which Hamas and Islamic Jihad terrorists were receiving smuggled weapons.

ISM is an uncompromising supporter of the Palestinian "right of return" not only for the few remaining survivors who were among the 725,000 Palestinians who fled Israel during the 1948 war (when eight Arab armies attacked Israel on the very day of its creation), but also for all their descendants born since 1948. Thus ISM places the number of refugees who should be permitted to "return" to Israel at approximately 6 million.

ISM also opposes what it dubs "Israel's Apartheid Wall," the recently constructed anti-terror barrier bordering the West Bank. According to ISM, this wall is an affront to Palestinian dignity and a violation of their human rights. As of July 2004, one of the ISM officials leading the protests against the security barrier was Hisham Jam Joun, a veteran of the Marxist-Leninist terror group Popular Front for the Liberation of Palestine.

The Chicago chapter of ISM has endorsed the "Declaration Regarding Caterpillar Violations of Human Rights," a document that impugns the U.S.-based Caterpillar Corporation for selling its machinery to the Israeli army, which in turn uses that equipment to demolish Palestinian terrorists' homes and bases of operation. This Declaration characterizes the Israeli actions as malicious and unprovoked acts of indiscriminate destruction that constitute "grave abuses of human rights and humanitarian law."

In the wake of two April 29, 2003 suicide bombings in an Israeli bar that killed three people and wounded more than 50, Israeli officials discovered that the bombers, both British nationals, had been hosted by ISM just prior to carrying out their deed. This prompted the Israeli government in June 2003 to formally accuse ISM of maintaining ties with Palestinian terrorism. "For us," said the Foreign Ministry's Information Chief Gideon Meir, "that was the turning point. Defying army bulldozers was one thing; providing cover for suicide bombers to slip into the country quite another." Israeli officials immediately announced that all foreign nationals seeking to enter Gaza would thenceforth be required to sign a form swearing they were not members of ISM, and absolving Israel of responsibility should they be killed or injured in what the army defined as a "war zone." To this day, ISM remains the only organization specifically mentioned on the waiver form. "We have nothing against the internationals," says a senior IDF officer. "But, as far as we are concerned, ISM is not an international organization or a peace organization. It's a pro-Palestinian organization, set up by Palestinians, funded by Palestinians and linked to Palestinian terror."

ISM also lobbies for the release of Marwan Barghouti — an Al-Aqsa Martyrs' Brigades leader who was captured by Israel in April 2002 and was charged with terrorism and the murders of 26 people. Ultimately he was convicted of five counts of murder, each carrying a sentence of life in prison.

In addition, ISM raises funds for the Palestine Children's Welfare Fund and the Palestine Children's Relief Fund.

A member organization of the United for Peace and Justice anti-war coalition, in the post-9/11 era ISM has taken a stand against the U.S. war on terror, the Patriot Act, and the American military incursions in Afghanistan and Iraq.

ISLAMIC ASSEMBLY OF NORTH AMERICA (IANA)

PMB #270
3588 Plymouth Rd.
Ann Arbor, MI
48105

Phone :734-528-0006
URL: http://www.iananet.org/Michigan-based Islamic organization which has been described as a "glorified al Qaeda recruitment center"

The Islamic Assembly of North America (IANA) was created in 1993 by American and Canadian representatives of various Muslim centers and organizations. Its mission is to "unify and coordinate the efforts of North America's *dawah*-oriented organizations" [groups that perform missionary work for Islam]; to spread the "correct knowledge of Islam ... and to assist its dissemination among Muslim Americans and immigrants"; to analyze current events in the Muslim world; to assist oppressed Muslim workers and scholars; to produce "a serious and effective media institute to serve the Islamic presence in North America"; and to "create a *dawah* program ... that will protect the Islamic presence in North America." To achieve these objectives, as well as its "final goal of reviving the Islamic nation to its proper state and condition," IANA uses conventions, general meetings, *dawah*-oriented institutions and academies, books, magazines, and youth programs.

In February 2003, four individuals associated with IANA were indicted for illegally sending millions of dollars to Iraq through a Syracuse, New York charity called Help the Needy. In addition, a University of Idaho student named Sami Omar Al-Hussayen (who was a member of IANA's Technical Committee) was arrested for knowingly failing to mention his affiliation with IANA on his visa application when he entered the United States. The *Seattle Post-Intelligencer* quotes one federal source saying that Al-Hussayen was "in touch with people who could pick up the phone, call UBL [Usama bin Laden], and he would take the call."

According to court papers filed by Idaho prosecutors in 2003, IANA's mission included the "dissemination of radical Islamic ideology, the purpose of which was indoctrination, recruitment of members, and the instigation of acts of violence and terrorism." In *National Review Online*, IANA has been described as a "glorified al Qaeda recruitment center."

IANA's Vice Chairman, Rafil Dhafir, in 2005 was convicted of illegally laundering money to Iraq. Moreover, Sami Omar Al-Hussayen was indicted for routing to IANA thousands of dollars he had received from overseas sources, and for providing computer expertise and website services to the organization.

According to Dore Gold's book *Hatred's Kingdom*, in May 2001 -- four months before the 9/11 terrorist attacks -- IANA's main website featured justifications for "martyrdom operations," including crashing an airplane "on a crucial enemy target." In 2003 the IANA website posted the *fatwas*, or religious rulings, of two radical Saudi sheiks who maintain close ties to al Qaeda and provide religious justification for acts of Islamic terrorism. Radical proselytization, both written and spoken, was a common theme on the website. Considerable attention was given, for instance, to the teachings of Osama bin Laden's mentor Abdullah Azzam.

The IANA website also hosts recruitment videos for *jihad*, with clips displaying the corpses of *mujahedeen* warriors killed in terrorist operations. One such video shows deceased al Qaeda-funded "martyrs" from Chechnya, eulogizing them as heroes who had given their lives in service to Allah.

IANA has created additional websites to disseminate its message. One such site, Azzam.com, was named for the aforementioned Abdullah Azzam, and was shut down by the FBI in 2002. Another IANA website, Islamway.com, promoted the Saudi charity Al-Haramain, whose Bosnia and Somalia branches supported al Qaeda and in 2002 were raided by American and Saudi government authorities. The link to al-Haramain never appeared on the English-language version of the website. As a rule, IANA has published its most radical content -- glorifying suicide missions and *jihad* -- solely in Arabic; its English products and publications do not contain terrorist propaganda.

Since 2002, IANA's Inmates Program has shipped at least 530 packages of Islamic indoctrination materials to prisons across the United States. Each package consists of seven different Islamic books, twelve audio cassettes, one copy of the Koran, and a videotape on Muslim prayers and rituals.

According to a *New York Times* interview with former IANA Director Mohammed al-Ahmari, approximately half of the organization's funding derives from the Saudi government, and the other half from mostly Saudi private donors.

ISLAMIC ASSOCIATION FOR PALESTINE (IAP)

P.O. Box 1163
Bridgeview, IL
60455

Phone :708-974-1488
http://**iap**.orgNow-defunct Illinois-based front group for the terrorist organization Hamas

Islamic Association of Palestine (**IAP**) was an Islamist organization that raised money in the United States for Hamas. It purported to write articles of a factual nature on issues that "Zionist controlled" westernized media failed to report. It called itself "a not-for-profit, public-awareness, educational, political, social, and civic, national grassroots organization dedicated to advancing a just, comprehensive, and eternal solution to the cause of Palestine and suffrages of the Palestinians." For a time it also used the name **American Muslim Society**.

Founders include

> Mousa Mohammed Abu Marzook, funder and 1989 member of IAP Board of Directors, Specially Designated Global Terrorist.
> Sami Al-Arian, cofounder of Islamic Society of North America and supporter of Palestinian Islamic Jihad.

It published a magazine, *Tareeq Filistine (Road to Palestine)*, *Ila Filastin*, and newspapers *Al-Zaytuna* and *Muslim World Monitor.*

It had been accused of issuing anti-Semitic propaganda and having links to terrorists by the ADL.
The U.S. government considers the IAP a front for Hamas in the United States.
In December 2004, a federal judge in the U.S. city of Chicago ruled that the IAP (along with the Holy Land Foundation) was liable for a $156 million dollar lawsuit for aiding and abetting the terror group Hamas in the death of a 17-year-old David Boim, an American citizen. Though IAP has already had its assets frozen by the U.S. executive branch of the government, this was the first time a U.S. court officially linked IAP to Hamas.

The organization was the parent organization of Council on American-Islamic Relations, or CAIR
Defunct since 2005, the Islamic Association for Palestine (IAP) was established in 1981 by Hamas operative Mousa Abu Marzook. IAP identified itself as "a not-for-profit, public-awareness, educational, political, social, and civic, national grassroots organization dedicated to advancing a just, comprehensive, and eternal solution to the cause of Palestine and suffrages [sic] of the Palestinians." The organization sought to advance this goal by producing what it characterized as factual articles on issues that the "Zionist-controlled" Western media allegedly failed to report.

IAP was the parent organization of the Council on American-Islamic Relations (CAIR), which was co-founded in 1994 by Nihad Awad (IAP's President), Omar Ahmad (IAP's Public Relations Director), and Ibrahim Hooper (an IAP employee).

According to an August 14, 2001 Immigration and Naturalization Services report, IAP's work consisted of "publishing and distributing HAMAS communiqués printed on IAP letterhead, as well as other written documentation to include the HAMAS charter and glory records [a list of terrorist attacks that HAMAS had carried out against Israeli civilians], which are tributes to HAMAS' violent 'successes.'" The same report also stated that IAP had received "approximately $490,000 from [Mousa Abu] Marzook during the period in which Marzook held his admitted role as a HAMAS leader."
Terrorism expert Steven Emerson characterized IAP as Hamas' "primary voice in the United States." The former chief of the FBI's counter-terrorism department, Oliver Revell, called IAP "a front organization for Hamas that engages in propaganda for Islamic militants."

In December 2004, a federal judge in Chicago ruled that IAP (along with the Holy Land Foundation for Relief and Development, or HLF), was liable for a $156 million lawsuit for having aided and abetted Hamas in the West Bank killing of a 17-year-old American citizen named David Boim. IAP thereafter had its assets frozen by the U.S. government and was shut down on grounds that it was funding terrorism.
IAP's worldview and politics were reflected in the attitudes and activities of its founders and leaders, among whom were the following individuals:

> Mousa Mohammed Abu Marzook: This IAP founder also established the Holy Land Foundation for Relief and Development, whose assets were blocked by the U.S. government in 2001 because it was funding Hamas. In addition, Marzook is the founding President of the United Association for Studies and Research (UASR), a prominent Islamist think tank with close ties to Hamas. In 1997 Marzook was extradited by the United States to Jordan. From there he went to Syria, where he currently serves as the Deputy Chief of Hamas' Political Bureau.

Sami Al-Arian was an IAP co-founder who would later go on to become a leader of Palestinian Islamic Jihad's North American operations.

Rafeeq Jaber served as IAP President. He was also a co-founder of the American-Arab Anti-Discrimination Committee's Chicago chapter, a founder of CAIR's national office, and a Board member of the Bridgeview, Illinois Mosque Foundation.

Emad Sarsour was a Wisconsin-based Board member of IAP. In 1993 he co-founded the Al Aqsa Educational Fund, a fundraising "charity" for Hamas, with Abdelhaleem Hasan Abdelraziq Ashqar. In a 2002 court ruling, U.S. District Judge Gladys Kessler labeled Ashqar "a senior Hamas activist." In October 2003, Ashqar was indicted for refusing to testify before a Chicago grand jury investigating Hamas fundraising.

Sufian An-Nabhan was a Michigan-based Board member of IAP. In November 2002 he admitted to having personally sent money to the Holy Land Foundation for Relief and Development.

Raeed N. Tayeh was a member of the IAP's Executive Board. He was also a research fellow for the aforementioned United Association for Studies and Research. Tayeh called Yasser Arafat "an honorable Palestinian leader"; called Ariel Sharon "an irresponsible terrorist, murderer and war criminal"; and excused suicide bombings by saying, "The young Palestinians who commit crimes by exploding themselves, in some way, may have been affected by Israeli crimes."

ISLAMIC CENTER OF AMERICA (ICA)

19500 Ford Road
Dearborn, MI
48128

Phone :313-593-0000
Email :
info@icofa.com
URL: http://www.icofa.com/Michigan-based Islamic organization founded in 1963

The Dearborn, Michigan-based Islamic Center of America (ICA) was established in 1963 by the Muslim cleric Mohamad Jawad Chirri. Its mission is to "receive, administer and distribute funds; preserve and teach the religion of Islam; perpetuate the social, moral, and religious standards of Muslims in the United States; teach the Arabic language; [and] educate the American society about Islam and the Arab culture."

ICA further seeks to give Muslims "an opportunity to benefit from ... University-style sermon[s] with a broad mix of religious practices, science, ethics, current events, and tradition all with a common sense approach." These sermons are delivered by ICA's leading mullah, Hassan al-Qazwini, who commonly officiates at ecumenical functions attended also by Jewish rabbis and Christian ministers and priests, and who maintains that the misguided politics of militant Islamists should not be confused with the peaceful teachings of Islam itself. Al-Qazwini, who has invited Louis Farrakahn of the Nation of Islam to be a guest speaker at the ICA mosque, is also a Board Member of the American Muslim Council.

ICA chose not to endorse or participate in "Free Muslims March Against Terror," a May 14, 2005 event whose purpose was to "send a message to the terrorists and extremists that their days are numbered ... [and to send] a message to the people of the Middle East, the Muslim world and all people who seek freedom, democracy and peaceful coexistence that we support them."

ISLAMIC CIRCLE OF NORTH AMERICA (ICNA)

166-26 89th Avenue
Jamaica, NY
11432
Phone : http://www.icna.org/New York-based Islamic organization which has been probed by the FBI for ties to terrorism

Works closely with radical Islamic organizations and invites radical speakers to its conferences

The Islamic Circle of North America (ICNA) was founded in 1971 as a "non-ethnic, non-sectarian, open-to-all, independent" grassroots organization. Its goal is "to seek the pleasure of Allah ... through the ... establishment of the Islamic system of life as spelled out in the *Qur'an* and the *Sunnah* of Prophet Muhammad." Toward this end, ICNA endeavors to: "invite mankind to submit to the Creator by using all means of communications"; "motivate Muslims to perform their duty of being witnesses unto mankind by their words and deeds"; "organize those who agree to work for this cause in the discipline of ICNA"; offer educational and training opportunities to increase Islamic knowledge, to enhance character, and to develop skills for all those who are associated with ICNA"; "oppose immorality and oppression in all forms, and support efforts for civil liberties and socio-economic justice in the society"; "strengthen the bond of humanity by serving all those in need anywhere in the world, with special focus on our neighborhood across North America"; and "cooperate with other organizations for the implementation of this program and unity in the *ummah* [Muslim community]."

Based in Queens, New York, ICNA's activities include training camps, study circles, speakers' forums, night vigils, seminars, and retreats.

ICNA has established a reputation for bringing anti-American radicals to speak at its annual conferences. Moreover, experts have long documented the organization's ties to Islamic terrorist groups. Yehudit Barsky, a terrorism expert at the American Jewish Committee, has said that ICNA "is composed of members of Jamaat e-Islami, a Pakistani Islamic radical organization similar to the Muslim Brotherhood that helped to establish the Taliban." (Pakistani newspapers have reported that Khalid Shaikh Mohammed, a leading architect of the 9/11 terrorist attacks, was offered refuge in the home of Jamaat e-Islami's leader, Ahmed Quddoos.) On September 27, 1997, another Pakistani Islamist leader, Maulana Shafayat Mohamed, played host to an ICNA conference at his Florida-based fundamentalist *madrassa* (religious school), which served as a recruitment center for Taliban fighters.

In 2000, CNSNews.com made public a press release, originally posted on a Middle Eastern website, from a July 2000 ICNA meeting, which read: "Jamaat e-Islami's supporters have an organization in America known as ICNA ..." The press release also recounted some of the views expressed at the aforementioned ICNA meeting. These included an exhortation that "Islam must be translated into political dominance"; pleas for support for "*jihad*" in "Chechnya, Kashmir, Palestine, Iraq [against U.S. forces], southern Sudan, and ... in Bosnia/Kosova [sic]"; an appeal for unity among Pakistani Muslims against "Hindu Brahmins and Zionist Jews"; and an endorsement of Muslim women's inclusion in carrying out *jihad.* One Islamic leader present at the ICNA event complained about "human rights violations" being carried out by the U.S. government against the terrorist mastermind Omar Abdel Rahman, spiritual leader of Egypt's Islamic Group.

In part because of such revelations, ICNA is now under investigation by U.S. authorities for possible connections to terrorist groups. In December 2003, the U.S. Senate Finance Committee requested that the Internal Revenue Service provide detailed information on 25 U.S. Muslim organizations, including ICNA.

In March 1996, U.S. Senator Mitch McConnell stated, "One of the groups with Hamas ties is the Dallas-based Islamic Association for Palestine in North America, which, in turn, apparently is allied with the Islamic Circle of North America in New York." The *New York Daily News* reports that ICNA has been "probed by FBI counter-terrorism agents" for "terror ties." Terrorism analyst Steven Emerson claims that ICNA has close ties to the Muslim Brotherhood, the ideological forebear of all radical Islamic movements -- including Hamas and al-Qaeda. Documents show that Hamas officials have participated in previous ICNA events. "The ICNA's hatred of the Jews is so fierce," writes Emerson, "that it taunted them with a repetition of what Hitler did to them." In his book *American Jihad*, Emerson expounds: "The ICNA openly supports militant Islamic fundamentalist organizations, praises terror attacks, issues incendiary attacks on western values and policies, and supports the imposition of Sharia [Islamic law]."

ICNA works closely with the Muslim American Society (MAS). Speaking at a December 2002 conference sponsored by ICNA and MAS, Muslim cleric Shaker Elsayed complained in Arabic "about the subject unfairly named suicide bomber, homicide bomber, murderers, or killers. Our answer to this issue is simple ... The Islamic scholars said whenever there is an attack on an Islamic state or occupation, or the honor of the Muslims has been violated, the *Jihad* is a must for everyone, a child, a lady and a man. They have to make *Jihad* with every tool that they can get in their hand ... and if they don't have anything in their hand then they can fight with their hand without weapons."

A cognate view was expressed at an Islamic conference in Orlando, Florida, co-sponsored by ICNA. The keynote speaker at this event expressed support for suicide bombers, dismissed the notion that Muslims had any involvement with the 9/11 terrorist attacks, asserted that the U.S.-led war on terror was a Zionist plot intended to wipe out Muslims and Islam, and argued that attacks on affirmative action programs were attributable to "the rise of the Jewish cracker."

In 2000, ICNA held its 25th national convention in Baltimore. One of the featured speakers was Tayyib Yunus, head of ICNA's youth section, who used the occasion to appeal to American Muslims to send their children to Chechnya in order to wage *jihad*. Said Yunus: "We all want to see our youth to succeed to become doctors, to become engineers; but how many of you can actually say that you want to send your sons to *jihad*, to Chechnya? How many of you can actually say that you want to send your youth to fight in *jihad*?"

In the post-9/11 era, ICNA has taken a strong stand against the U.S. war on terror, the American military incursions in Afghanistan and Iraq, and the Patriot Act (characterizing it as an assault on the civil liberties of Americans, particularly Muslims). A member organization of the United for Peace and Justice anti-war coalition, ICNA in 2001 received a $100,000 grant from the Rockefeller Foundation.

ICNA chose not to endorse or participate in the May 14, 2005 "Free Muslims March Against Terror," an event whose stated purpose was to "send a message to the terrorists and extremists that their days are numbered . . . [and to send] a message to the people of the Middle East, the Muslim world and all people who seek freedom, democracy and peaceful coexistence that we support them."

ICNA reports that its "representatives visit public schools sharing knowledge of Islam as an attempt to correct the misrepresentations often found in secular reading materials." In pursuit of this objective, ICNA has formed an affiliation with the website DawaNet, which advocates turning public schools into forums for Islamic proselytizing. Among the suggestions offered to Islamic activists on that website is the following: "It is highly recommended that all Muslim students carry Dawa flyers in their schoolbags and purses to pass them on to their friends at school. To obtain free Islam brochures for distribution, contact the Islamic Circle of North America."

On numerous occasions, ICNA has explicitly excluded non-Muslims from its public gatherings. In September 2004, for example, ICNA sparked widespread controversy when, in cooperation with the management of the Great Adventure Theme Park in New Jersey, it organized a "Great Muslim Adventure Day" that barred non-Muslims from the park on that day. This annual tradition is still observed.

ICNA is listed as an endorser of C. Clark Kissinger's revolutionary communist movement World Can't Wait, and as a signatory of the latter's mission statement, entitled "Call to Drive out the Bush Regime." This statement alleges that the U.S. government "is waging a murderous and utterly illegitimate war in Iraq, with other countries in their sights"; "is openly torturing people, and justifying it"; "puts people in jail on the merest suspicion"; and "is moving each day closer to a theocracy, where a narrow and hateful brand of Christian fundamentalism will rule."

ICNA has many subdivisions throughout the United States. One of these is ICNA South East Region, currently based in Atlanta but originally founded as a Florida enterprise. Its current website is devoted to announcements of the organization's various events and projects. But the old website, which was abandoned as a result of public criticism, featured links to the official websites of Hezbollah and Hamas. Also appearing on the old website (from March 1, 2000 through September 27, 2001) was the following message: "Remember Your Fellow Chechnyan Muslims. ICNA requests all Muslims around the world to include Chechnyan Muslims in their daily and Qunut prayers. We must show our spiritual and material support for our brothers and sisters being oppressed by the brutal Russian forces." Directly under the message was a link to the website, www.Qoqaz.net (a.k.a. "Jihad in Chechnya"), which was a project of *Azzam Publications*, an organization named for Osama bin Laden's mentor, Abdullah Azzam. Qoqaz.net was created specifically to raise finances and recruit fighters for al Qaeda-related groups and the Taliban.

In 1993, ICNA strongly condemned the Oslo accord which sought to establish peace between the Palestinians and Israel. In a joint statement with the Islamic Association for Palestine, the Islamic Committee for Palestine, the Islamic Society of North America, the Muslim Arab Youth Association, the Muslim Public Affairs Council, and the Muslim Students' Association, ICNA charged that Israel's creation in 1948 "had involved the unjust and illegal usurpation of Muslim and Christian lands and rights," and declared that "to recognize the legitimacy of that crime is a crime in itself and any agreement which involves such recognition is unjust and untenable."

ISLAMIC COMMITTEE FOR PALESTINE (ICP)

Philanthropic advocacy group founded by terrorist Sami al-Arian
Responsible for funding Palestinian terrorists and organizing anti-American, anti-Israeli rallies in the U.S.

Established in 1986 by Sami Al-Arian and Hussam Jubara, the Islamic Committee for Palestine (ICP) was promoted as a philanthropic advocacy group devoted to alleviating the suffering of Palestinian women and children. In reality, the organization served as an American front for the terrorist organization Palestinian Islamic Jihad. At a 1991 conference in Cleveland, Ohio, a lecturer introducing Al-Arian as the ICP President candidly called the Committee "the active arm of the Jihad movement in Palestine." "We like to call it the Islamic Committee for Palestine here for security reasons," he added. Shortly after being introduced that evening, Al-Arian declared, "Let us continue the protests. Let us damn America. Let us damn Israel. Let us damn their allies until death."

In addition to financing Palestinian suicide bombers, ICP organized rallies and sponsored a number of conferences throughout the United States in the late 1980s and early 1990s. PIJ materials and emblems were prominently displayed at these events, where known terrorists were among the attendees and keynote speakers alike. Featured speakers at ICP conferences included: Sheikh Omar Abdel Rahman, leader of the Islamic Group and mastermind of the 1993 World Trade Center bombing; Sheikh Abdel Aziz Odeh, the spiritual leader of Palestinian Islamic Jihad (PIJ); Mohammad Al-Asi, a Hezbollah-linked radical imam who used an ICP event as a forum to exhort Muslims to create a "war front for the Americans in the Muslim world"; Abd Al-'Aziz Al'Awda, Islamic Jihad's "spiritual leader"; and Muhammad 'Umar, whose Islamic Liberation Party seeks to overthrow secular government institutions throughout the Middle East.

ICP also invited several guest speakers who could not attend its conferences, including PIJ's then-leader Fathi Shikaki, and Osama bin Laden's ideological mentor and al Qaeda co-founder Abdullah Azzam.

ICP functioned as a sister organization to another Sami Al-Arian creation: the World Islam Study Enterprise (WISE). Through ICP's and WISE's pretense of legitimacy, Al-Arian was able to secure visas for terror-related individuals seeking to gain entry into the United States. Among these was Ramadan Abdullah Shallah, who served as WISE's Director of Administration and became PIJ's worldwide leader in 1995 (when Fathi Shikaki was assassinated).

Shallah's elevation within PIJ prompted a federal investigation into ICP and WISE. In a 1995 affadavit, William West of the Immigration and Naturalization Service wrote: "I have probable cause to believe that ICP and WISE were utilized by Sami Al-Arian and Ramadan Abdullah Shallah as 'fronts' in order to enable individuals to enter the United States, in an apparent lawful fashion, despite the fact that these individuals were international terrorists."
ICP and WISE were financed by the Virginia-based SAAR Network, which was the target of U.S. federal raids in March 2002, on suspicion that it was funding terrorism.

ISLAMIC SOCIETY OF NORTH AMERICA (ISNA)

P.O. Box 38
Plainfield, IN
46169
Phone :317-839-8157
Fax :317-839-1840
URL: http://www.isna.net/Enforces extremist Wahhabi theological writ in America's mosques

Established in 1963 by the by the Saudi-funded Muslim Students' Association of the U.S. and Canada, the Islamic Society of North America (ISNA) calls itself the largest Muslim organization on the continent. Its annual convention draws more attendees -- usually over 30,000 -- than any other Muslim gathering in the Western Hemisphere. ISNA's mission is to function as "an association of Muslim organizations and individuals that provides a common platform for presenting Islam, supporting Muslim communities, developing educational, social and outreach programs and fostering good relations with other religious communities, and civic and service organizations."

ISNA focuses heavily on providing Wahhabi theological indoctrination materials to a large percentage of the 2,500+ mosques in North America. Many of these mosques were recently built with Saudi money and are required, by their Saudi benefactors, to strictly follow the dictates of Wahhabi imams -- an edict that affects the tone and content of the sermons given in the mosques, the selection of books and periodicals that may be read in mosque libraries or sold in mosque bookshops, and the policies governing the exclusion or suppression of dissenters from the congregations.

Through its affiliate, the North American Islamic Trust -- a Saudi government-backed organization created to fund Islamist enterprises in North America -- the Saudi-subsidized ISNA reportedly holds the mortgages on 50 to 80 percent of all mosques in the U.S. and Canada. Thus the organization can freely exercise ultimate authority over these houses of worship and their teachings.

Writes Kaukab Siddique, the editor of *New Trend*, an Islamic periodical of extremist views that is nonetheless opposed to Wahhabi domination of American Islam: "ISNA controls most mosques in America and thus also controls who will speak at every Friday prayer, and which literature will be distributed there."

Islam scholar Stephen Schwartz describes ISNA as "one of the chief conduits through which the radical Saudi form of Islam passes into the United States."

According to Sufi leader Sheikh Muhammad Hisham Kabbani's testimony before a State Department Open Forum on January 7, 1999, extremists have taken over "more than 80 percent of the mosques in the United States ... This means that the ideology of extremism has been spread to 80 percent of the Muslim population, mostly the youth and the new generation." Kabbani based his statement on his personal investigation of 114 American mosques. "Ninety of them," he said, "were mostly exposed, and I say exposed, to extreme or radical ideology, based on their speeches, books and board members." This is largely due to the efforts of ISNA.

According to terrorism expert Steven Emerson, ISNA "is a radical group hiding under a false veneer of moderation"; "convenes annual conferences where Islamist militants have been given a platform to incite violence and promote hatred" (for instance, al Qaeda supporter and PLO official Yusuf Al-Qaradhawi was invited to speak at an ISNA conference); has held fundraisers for terrorists (after Hamas leader Mousa Marzook was arrested and eventually deported in 1997, ISNA raised money for his defense); has condemned the U.S. government's post-9/11 seizure of Hamas' and Palestinian Islamic Jihad's financial assets; and publishes a bi-monthly magazine, *Islamic Horizons*, that "often champions militant Islamist doctrine."

Adds Emerson: "I think ISNA has been an umbrella, also a promoter of groups that have been involved in terrorism. I am not going to accuse the ISNA of being directly involved in terrorism. I will say ISNA has sponsored extremists, racists, people who call for *Jihad* against the United States."

WTHR, an Indianapolis television station located close to ISNA's Plainfield, Indiana headquarters, said it had found "about a dozen charities, organizations and individuals under federal scrutiny for possible ties to terrorism that are in some way linked to ISNA."

In December 2003, U.S. Senators Charles Grassley and Max Baucus of the Senate Committee on Finance listed ISNA as one of 25 American Muslim organizations that "finance terrorism and perpetuate violence." ISNA is known to have permitted the Holy Land Foundation for Relief and Development (and a number of other Islamic charities with terror connections) to set up booths at its conventions, and in some cases has helped raise money for them.

Upon learning of the arrest of Sami Al-Arian, the University of South Florida computer science professor eventually found guilty of conspiring to fund the terrorist organization Palestinian Islamic Jihad, ISNA issued a statement criticizing the U.S. government for its prosecution of Al-Arian.

ISNA was a signatory to a February 20, 2002 document, composed by C. Clark Kissinger's revolutionary communist group Refuse & Resist, condemning military tribunals and the detention of immigrants apprehended in connection with post-9/11 terrorism investigations. In ISNA's estimation, the Patriot Act constitutes an assault on the civil liberties of Muslim Americans and ought to be repealed.

ISNA endorses the Immigrant Workers Freedom Ride Coalition, which seeks to secure amnesty and civil liberties protections for illegal aliens, and policy reforms that diminish or eliminate restrictions on future immigration.

ISNA chose not to endorse or participate in the May 14, 2005 "Free Muslims March Against Terror," an event whose purpose was to "send a message to the terrorists and extremists that their days are numbered . . . [and to send] a message to the people of the Middle East, the Muslim world and all people who seek freedom, democracy and peaceful coexistence that we support them."
Among ISNA's more prominent members and affiliates (past and present) are Mohammed Nur Abdullah, Muzammil Siddiqi, Siraj Wahhaj, Ihsan Bagby, Jamal A. Badawi, Abdullah Idris Ali, Hadia Mubarak (a former President of the Muslim Students' Association who now sits on ISNA's Board of Directors), and Omar J. Siddiqui (the Muslim Youth of North America Chairman who is also a member of the ISNA Board).

ISNA's current President is Ingrid Mattson, professor of Islamic Studies at the Macdonald Center for Islamic Studies, and of Christian-Muslim Relations at Hartford Seminary in Connecticut.

Also affiliated with ISNA is Abdurahman Alamoudi, who in 1982 founded the Islamic Society of Boston under ISNA's tax-exempt umbrella.

In July 2006, ISNA Secretary General Sayyid M. Syeed joined Sojourners leader Jim Wallis and National Council of Churches (NCC) General Secretary Robert Edgar in opposing any U.S. military action against Iran's nuclear weapons program -- instead advocating "direct negotiations" with Tehran.

At ISNA's 44th annual convention (held in Rosemont, Illinois) in August 2007, NCC's Interfaith Relations office sponsored an Ecumenical Study Seminar for "reflecting and learning together."

ISRAEL POLICY FORUM

National Office - New York

Israel Policy Forum
165 East 56th St. 2nd Floor
New York, NY 10022
Tel: 212.245.4227
Fax: 212.245.0517
www.ipforum.org

Contact National Office

Media and Publications
Washington, DC -

Israel Policy Forum - DC
122 C St. NW, Suite 820
Washington, DC 20001
Tel: 202.347.3811
Fax: 202.347.6130

Israel

Israel Policy Forum - Jerusalem
43 Emek Refaim Street, Suite 10
Jerusalem 93141
Tel: 972.2.561.7258
Fax: 972.2.561.7437

Contact Israel Office American Jewish organization that encourages Israeli concessions to Palestinian militants

Founded in 1993, the New York-based Israel Policy Forum (IPF) is an American Jewish organization "dedicated to mobilizing American Jews in support of sustained U.S. diplomatic efforts in the Middle East." It describes itself as "a central clearinghouse for policymakers seeking to more effectively engage the United States in the resolution of the Israeli-Palestinian conflict." IPF was created, as Kenneth Levin notes in *The Oslo Syndrome*, "at the behest of Israel's Labor-Meretz coalition government and placed under the leadership of ... Jonathan Jacoby, who had earlier in his career signed a *New York Times* ad accusing Israel of 'state terrorism.'" Jacoby resigned as Executive Director in 2006 and was succeeded by Dr. David M. Elcott, Director of U.S. Interreligious Affairs for the American Jewish Committee.

IPF's current President is Seymour D. Reich, a Senior Partner at the New York City law firm of Gallet, Dreyer & Berkey LLP. Mr. Reich has also served as Chairman of the Conference of Presidents of Major American Jewish Organizations, President of B'nai Brith International, President of the American Zionist Movement, and Chairman of the International Jewish Committee on Interreligious Consultations.

According to IPF, "a two-state solution to the Israeli-Palestinian conflict" will create a "more secure, prosperous and stable" Middle East. "To achieve this goal," adds IPF, "... the United States must remain a consistent and fully engaged partner in the Middle East peace process."

The Israel Policy Forum's activities fall under the following four categories:

Advocacy: "IPF meets regularly with key U.S. policymakers -- in Congress and the Executive Branch -- and with Middle East leadership to continue building the foundation for a two-state solution to the Israeli-Palestinian conflict. IPF works with other organizations, community leaders and the average citizens to mobilize support for these efforts."

Fact-Finding: "IPF leads delegations to Israel, the Palestinian territories, Jordan, Egypt and elsewhere in the Middle East to meet with political and opinion leaders. IPF also conducts research on key issues related to U.S. Mideast policy and incorporates its findings into IPF materials."

Education: "IPF works with scholars, policymakers, security specialists and other regional expers; conducts regular meetings and conference call briefings on development in Israel and the region; distributes weekly publications *IPF Friday* and *IPF Focus*; and maintains a website. All of IPF's education programs promote the vision of a two-state solution." The organization also produces opinion surveys that purportedly "document American Jewish support for active U.S. involvement in peace diplomacy."

Network: IPF has created a network of leaders in business, politics, and Jewish philanthropy from across the United States.

Vis a vis the Arab-Israeli war, IPF has consistently urged the U.S. government to press Israel into making ever-greater concessions to Palestinian militants -- in the belief that such a course of action would help bring peace to the region. IPF bases many of its recommendations on the results of polls it conducts of American Jews. According to the Zionist Organization of America, these polls commonly use "vague and deceptive language," "misus[e] statistical evidence," and constitute a "reprehensible misuse of ... polling."

In November 2005, U.S. Secretary of State Condoleezza Rice met in Washington, DC with IPF leaders who exhorted the United States to take "aggressive" action in brokering peace between Israelis and Palestinians. After the meeting, IPF followed up by sending a policy paper to Rice, stating: "The three steps that should be implemented in tandem, rather than in sequence, are as follows: Unambiguous and effective efforts by the PA [Palestinian Authority] to control terror and prevent attacks on Israelis; an Israeli freeze on extending existing settlements, including roads and other associated infrastructure, and removal of unauthorized settlement outposts; and efforts to help grow the Palestinian economy so the Palestinian Authority can provide jobs and basic services for Palestinians. This effort would help strengthen the PA's position among the various Palestinian factions, including Hamas." "The U.S. should embark on these steps immediately and vigorously," IPF emphasized.

Influenced by IFP's recommendations, the U.S. thereafter applied intense pressure on Israel to sign with the Palestinian Authority a new deal that contained the following stipulations: (a) At the Rafah crossing between Egypt and Gaza, incoming traffic of Palestinians and others from the Sinai would thenceforth be monitored not by Israelis, but by Egyptians on the one side and Palestinians on the other; (b) Palestinians had permission to build a seaport in Gaza; and (c) At the Karni crossing from Gaza to Israel, which had permitted the passage of 35 Gazan export trucks per day since the Israeli withdrawal from Gaza in August 2005, would, by the end of 2006, allow for the passage of more than 400 trucks per day. "The result is easy to see," said former Prime Minister Binyamin Netanyahu. "Kassam rockets and mortars will be transported through Judea and Samaria to be launched at Israel."

IPF President Seymour Reich, who participated in the meeting with Rice, said, "I have no doubt that we bolstered the Secretary of State's instinct and strengthened her opinion that aggressive American involvement was needed to achieve practical results."

ISRAELI COMMITTEE AGAINST HOUSE DEMOLITIONS (ICAHD)

P.O. Box 2030
Jerusalem, Israel
91020

Phone :919-277-0632
URL: http://www.mennonitechurch.ca/programs/peace/icahd/Anti-Israel NGO that opposes the destruction of Palestinian terrorists' homes and facilities

Based in Jerusalem and composed of members of many Israeli peace and human rights organizations, the Israeli Committee Against House Demolitions (ICAHD) describes itself as "a non-violent, direct-action group originally established to oppose and resist Israeli demolition of Palestinian houses in the Occupied Territories." "As our activists gained direct knowledge of the brutalities of the Occupation," ICAHD elaborates, "we expanded our resistance activities to other areas -- land expropriation, settlement expansion, by-pass road construction, policies of 'closure' and 'separation,' the wholesale uprooting of fruit and olive trees and more."

ICAHD's activities extend into three interrelated spheres:

> Resisting the demolition of Palestinian homes: "ICAHD members physically block [Israeli] bulldozers sent to demolish homes. We also mobilize hundreds of Israelis and Palestinians to rebuild them as acts of resistance." (No mention is made of the fact that these demolitions target the homes and operating bases of Palestinian terrorists.)
>
> Disseminating information and networking: ICAHD conducts "informational tours of the Occupied Territories from a critical peace perspective," sends speakers on these tours to "educate" the participants, and is active in international conferences and gatherings that address Mideast issues.
>
> Providing strategic practical support to Palestinian families and communities: ICAHD "aids Palestinians in filing police claims, in dealing with the Israeli authorities, in arranging and subsidizing legal assistance, and in general coping with the traumas and tribulations of life under Occupation. ... ICAHD also cooperates with other human rights organizations to present legal challenges to Israeli actions and policies in the Occupied Territories."

In the United Kingdom and the United States, ICAHD has established regional affiliates whose activities include: conducting conference workshops and community and church presentations on "the Israel-Palestine conflict"; maintaining an active Speakers Bureau; gaining media exposure for their perspective on Arab-Israeli relations; publishing op-ed pieces and other articles; co-sponsoring educational and cultural events; networking with other likeminded organizations; raising money to support ICAHD's house-building and educational work; and providing materials, speakers and other support for house party fundraising events.

ICAHD's Coordinator is Jeff Halper, an Israeli professor of anthropology who frequently refers to Israel as an "apartheid" state that is guilty of "war crimes"; who advocates sanctions and boycotts against Israel; and who supports a "one-state solution." ("A Jewish state has proven politically and, in the end, morally untenable," he says.)

Affiliated with the Mennonite Church, ICAHD works in close cooperation with such NGOs as Christian Aid, LAW, and Christian Peacemaker Teams.

In tandem with Al-Haq, Al-Mezan, Badil, and Ittijah, ICAHD authored a Joint NGO submission in May 2006 to the UN Committee on the Elimination of Racial Discrimination (UN CERD). ICAHD's contribution to CERD was a set of "statistics" on the numbers of Palestinian homes demolished in the West Bank. No sources or evidence for these statistics are provided, making independent verification of ICAHD's allegations impossible.

Sabeel, which leads international church divestment campaigns against Israel, is another of ICAHD's main partners. In 2006, Jeff Halper appeared at Sabeel's Kansas City Conference with Phyllis Bennis, co-founder of the U.S. Campaign to End the Israeli Occupation and a fellow at the Institute for Policy Studies. Halper also spoke at a conference on divestment from Israel sponsored by the Canadian Friends of Sabeel, and at the 2006 Sabeel Washington DC Conference where he called for "the use of boycott, divestment and sanctions." In February 2007, Halper joined the founder of Sabeel, Rev. Dr. Naim Ateek at a "public hearing" sponsored by the Council for the National Interest, where Israel was accused of being an "apartheid" state.

In May 2006, ICAHD joined War on Want, Friends of Sabeel UK, Interpal, and Pax Christi in writing to the Church of England's Commissioners to reiterate their support for disinvestment from all companies that do business with Israel.

ICAHD also works cooperatively with the International Solidarity Movement, which sends volunteers to participate in ICAHD house-rebuilding campaigns.

Regarding the 2006 war between Israel and Hezbollah in Lebanon, ICAHD stated: "We recognize Israel's ever-repressive Occupation as the main source of conflict and instability in our region ... Israel seeks to break the will of the Palestinian people and destroy any resistance to the imposition of an apartheid regime."

In October 2006, ICAHD published an article titled "The Struggle for Palestine's Soul," which argued that Israel "has not for one moment renounced violence against Palestinian resistance to occupation." The article added that if Hamas were to emerge victorious from its political and military battles with Fatah, "then the Palestinians will have the chance to re-energize the intifada, and launch a proper, consensual fight to end the occupation."

ICAHD regularly publishes articles on its website by British-born journalist Jonathan Cook, who has written for Al Jazeera's online English edition and Electronic Intifada. In a December 1, 2006 article, Cook describes a suicide bombing as a choice between "death and resistance over powerlessness and victimhood."

In past years, ICAHD received considerable financial support from the Ford Foundation and the New Israel Fund, but neither of those organizations fund ICAHD today. The Committee's current funding derives largely from the European Union.

ITTIJAH

P.O. Box 9577
Haifa 31095
Israel

Phone :972 4 850 7110
URL: http://www.ittijah.org/Network of anti-Israel, Palestinian NGOs

> Played a prominent role in the anti-American, anti-Israel U.N. World Conference Against Racism in 2001
> Has received funding from the Ford Foundation and the European Union

Established in 1995 and based in Haifa, Ittijah describes itself as "the network for Palestinian non-governmental organizations [NGOs] in Israel." Its mission is "to strengthen and empower the Palestinian Arab citizens of Israel by promoting the development of Palestinian civil society and advocating for political, economic, and social change." Among Ittijah's more than 50 member organizations are the Arab Association for Human Rights and the Association for the Defense of the Rights of Internally Dispaced Persons in Israel. Itself a member of the Palestinian NGO Network (PNGO), Ittijah cooperates with Adalah, a leading proponent of the pro-Palestinian militant political agenda.

Ittijah has received funding and support from numerous sources, including the Ford Foundation, the European Union, and NGOs such as the New Israel Fund and Christian Aid. In its January 16, 2004 newsletter, Ittijah backed PNGO's campaign against USAID's anti-terrorism clause, the latter of which stated that foundations should not "provide material support or resources to any individual or entity that advocates, plans, sponsors, engages in, or has engaged in terrorist activity." Similarly, Ittijah officials convened on February 10, 2004 to formulate a response to the Ford Foundation's new regulations for grant contracts, wherein Ford stipulated that recipients of funding "will not promote or engage in violence, bigotry or the destruction of any state, nor ... make sub-grants to any entity that engages in these activities." According to Ittijah's February 13 newsletter, the organization's leaders "agreed that they should insist on the maintenance of their independence, and on the fact that they are the owners of their own agenda. They would not be able to agree on political conditionality on financial support."

Ittijah has three principal areas of focus:

Advocacy: "Ittijah works on local (inter-Palestinian), regional (Arab), and international advocacy to promote the unique status of Palestinian citizens of Israel, to highlight their social, political and economic needs ..." Toward this end, the organization sponsors regular Ambassadorial study days, conferences, and solidarity delegations; it also publishes fact sheets that present its perspectives on Middle East affairs.

Capacity Building: "Ittijah strives to increase the human, technical, financial and educational resources of its member organizations, through facilitating access to knowledge transfers, volunteer staff, technical and educational resources, and fundraising support."

Networking: "Ittijah fosters field-based networking (such as women, youth, etc.) on [local, regional, and international] levels to encourage specialized contact between civil society organizations with similar platforms, skills, expertise and experiences." Under the auspices of this category is Ittijah's Youth Program, whose establishment was based on the premise that "the Israeli educational system discriminates systematically against Arab youth. ... In virtually every way, the quality of education provided to Israel's Palestinian citizen children is inferior to that provided to the state's Jewish children."

At the Durban World Conference Against Racism in 2001, Ittijah played a prominent role in promoting accusations of "Israeli-state racism towards Palestinian citizens," and of "the apartheid [which] the State [of Israel] practices in the West Bank and Gaza Strip."

In a May 19, 2004 press release titled "Rafah Appeal, Ittijah and PNGO Call for Support to the Population of Rafah", Ittijah claimed that the Israeli government had carried out "massacres, ethnic cleansing and war crimes" in Gaza.

In its "Fact Sheet about Palestinians in Israel", Ittijah charges that "[d]iscrimination and racism are endemic in Israeli society" -- in the realms of law, citizenship regulations, requirements for participation in the political process, land rights, budget allocations, basic infrastructural and government services, education, and health care.

Strongly opposed to the 2003 U.S. invasion of Iraq, in May 2004 Ittjah circulated a document titled "Petition of the Arab Associations: Who will put an end to the American-British occupation's crimes?"

Ittijah's General Director is the Palestinian political analyst Ameer Makhoul.

JERUSALEM MEDIA AND COMMUNICATIONS CENTER

Nablus Road #7
Sheikh Jarrah
P.O. Box 25047

URL: http://www.jmcc.org/Jerusalem-based news agency that displays anti-Israel bias

Established in 1988 by a group of Palestinian journalists and researchers, the Jerusalem Media and Communications Center (JMCC) is a Jerusalem-based news agency whose mission is to "provide a wide range of services to journalists, researchers, international agencies, individuals and organizations interested in obtaining reliable information on the Palestinian territory." It publishes the weekly *Palestine Report*, which provides updates "on the latest news concerning Palestinians." In practice, JMCC routinely defames Israel and advocates a one-state solution to the Arab-Israeli conflict.

JMCC has produced a manual -- based on workshops it has conducted -- teaching "Palestinian policymakers and media professionals" how to slant stories in a pro-Palestinian, anti-Israel manner. The manual quotes Alison Weir, Executive Director of If Americans Knew, stating that the *San Francisco Chronicle*'s coverage of the Palestinian *Intifada* was heavily biased in favor of Israel. Advises the manual: "What Palestinians fail to do is to assert their agenda. It is not simply enough to say a hundred Palestinians have been killed and so many houses have been destroyed. What the Israelis will say is: yes, but we have to do this because you are firing into our cities. In other words, it becomes a neutral position. What Palestinians can do more of is to say that violence in Gaza by Palestinians is in self-defense, that the reason for the mortar attacks inside Israel is a response to systematic Israeli incursions and systematic destruction by Israel and a systematic policy attempt to define the new borders in Gaza. In that way, you give journalists a different way of looking at the reality: that Israel is propagating its occupation."

JMCC's distortion of news events was displayed in early November of 2006, when Israeli troops seized the Gaza town of Beit Hanoun in an effort to rescue a kidnapped soldier and to stop Palestinian militants from firing Qassam rockets into Israel. All told, the Israeli military destroyed approximately 30 Gazan houses, damaged 100 more, and killed 52 people in this anti-terrorism operation that lasted for 9 days. JMCC depicted the events as "a massacre and genocide" directed by Israel against the people of Gaza, and characterized the Palestinian militants who had been killed as "martyrs."

Each year, JMCC conducts several public opinion polls of Palestinian attitudes (and less frequently, Israeli attitudes) regarding various issues of concern, including elections, military engagements, political affairs, legislative matters, the *Intifada*, Palestinian living conditions, peace negotiations, and the status of refugees.

The organization also produces research reports on the foregoing topics. For example, a December 2001 JMCC study titled "*The Israeli Assassination Policy in the Aqsa Intifada*" condemned Israel's targeted killings of Palestinian terrorist leaders. "Israeli assassination policy," said the report, "violates the right to life, the most fundamental of all human rights enshrined in religious, international and even Israeli law. There is no legal basis for these killings. The Israeli army plays the role of informer, attorney, judge and executioner and the decision to kill is implemented with no legal process whatsoever. ... Today, one of the roles of assassination ... is to prevent the possibility for political compromise. ... Assassination against Palestinians is carried out ... through their complete dehumanization. It is this very same dehumanization and cultural differentiation that was the driving force behind the many massacres committed by the Zionist movement in 1948, which lead [sic] to the ethnic cleansing of Palestine."

JMCC receives financial backing from the Ford Foundation, including a recent grant of $365,000.

JEWISH ALLIANCE FOR JUSTICE AND PEACE

11 E. Adams
Suite 707
Chicago, IL
60603

Phone :312-341-1205
URL: http://www.btvshalom.org/

- Believes that security for Israel "can only be achieved through the establishment of an economically and politically viable Palestinian state."
- Calls for the evacuation of Israeli settlements in the Occupied Territories and the withdrawal of Israeli military forces from the West Bank
- Condemns the construction of an Israeli security barrier
- Denounced the strategic killing of Palestinian terrorist leader Sheikh Ahmed Yassin

The Jewish Alliance for Justice and Peace (JAJP), also referred to by its Hebrew name, *Brit Tzedek v'Shalom*, is an organization of American Jews whose mission is "to educate and mobilize American Jews in support of a negotiated two-state resolution of the Israeli-Palestinian conflict." JAJP believes that security for Israel "can only be achieved through the establishment of an economically and politically viable Palestinian state, necessitating an end to Israel's occupation of land acquired during the 1967 war and an end to Palestinian terrorism."

At the heart of JAJP's efforts is its call for the evacuation of Israeli settlements in the Occupied Territories, and for the withdrawal of Israeli military forces from the West Bank. "These settlements," says JAJP, "are a major obstacle to peace, a tremendous financial burden to Israel, and do little, if anything, to enhance Israel's security. The settlements constantly expose to danger the settlers themselves and the Israeli soldiers sent to defend them, and they bring grave harm to the Palestinians living under Occupation."

JAJP has developed an online petition titled "A Call to Bring the Settlers Home to Israel," which asks the U.S. government "to provide generous foreign assistance" and financial incentives to those settlers willing to evacuate. The petition -- which was signed by such notables as Eric Alterman, Gordon Fellman, Ed Asner, Morton Halperin, Stanley Hoffman, Michael Lerner, Eli Pariser, and Gloria Steinem -- calls for $3 billion in cash incentives to be given to 16,000 settler families as a payoff for moving back inside Israel's pre-1967 border.

JAJP's President is Marcia Freedman, a former member of Israel's parliament and currently a member of the *Coalition of Women for a Just Peace* and *Women in Black*. According to Freedman, "The Palestinians have been living under Israel's illegal military occupation of the West Bank, Gaza Strip and East Jerusalem for 34 years ... [and] this is an enormous injustice that the world has turned its back on."

JAJP has condemned Israel's construction of a 480-mile security fence in the West Bank aimed at keeping Palestinian terrorists out of the country. Says JAJP: "With every additional kilometer that the barrier extends into the West Bank, creating a new de facto border for Israel, the prospects for a peaceful negotiated settlement recede further. The barrier is not a security barrier, but rather a political barrier to progress towards peace."

Whereas some pro-Palestinian groups in the U.S. demand divestment from Israel and the withholding of monies from that country, JAJP instead advocates giving such funds directly to the Palestinian people: "Donating to organizations that invest in Palestinian businesses, loan money to development banks involved in micro-lending, help rebuild the infrastructure of the West Bank, invest in promot[ing] dialogue and understanding or provide humanitarian relief for victims of violence are a few examples of how individuals, corporations, organizations and the United States government can support the Palestinian people and activists for a just peace."

Although JAJP has denounced Palestinian terrorism, the organization has also condemned the strategic killing of terrorist overlords. Following the 2004 assassination of Hamas leader Sheikh Ahmed Yassin by Israeli helicopter gun ships, JAJP released a press statement deploring the assassination, and stating that it "can only increase hatred of Israel and the U.S. throughout the Islamic world, and could constitute a danger not only for Israelis, but for Americans as well."

On the "Resources" page of its website, JAJP links to the websites of a number of anti-Israel organizations. These include: Israel Policy Forum; the American Task Force on Palestine; the Arab American Institute; B'Tselem; Adalah; Al Haq; the Holy Land Trust; MIFTAH; Physicians for Human Rights - Israel; and the New Israel Fund.

Headquartered in Chicago, JAJP also has 37 chapters in 24 states and Washington, DC. Its membership consists of approximately 27,000 individuals. The organization has received funding from the Ford Foundation; the Nathan Cummings Foundation; the Shefa Fund; the Samuel Rubin Foundation; the Tides Foundation; and The Funding Exchange.

The Executive Director of JAJP is Diane Cantor, who formerly spent nine years as Executive Director of Coastal Empire Habitat for Humanity (the largest non-profit homebuilder in Savannah, Georgia) and four years as President of the Savannah-Chatham County Board of Education.

JEWS AGAINST THE OCCUPATION (JATO)

Prince Street Station
P.O. Box 494
New York, NY
10012

Phone :212-539-6683
URL: http://www.jatonyc.org/Anti-Israel Jewish organization

Seeks the end of American aid to Israel

Jews Against the Occupation (JATO) describes itself as "an organization of progressive, secular, and religious Jews of all ages throughout the New York City area advocating peace through justice for Palestine and Israel." Its "points of unity" include the following:

No Occupation in Our Name: "We ... reject the Israeli government assertion that it is 'necessary' to subjugate Palestinians for the sake of keeping Jews safe. We assert that security can only come from mutual respect, and that the occupation of Palestine is only worsening the position of Jews in the Middle East and around the world."

Restore Human and Civil Rights: "The Israeli military fires bone-crushing rubber bullets and live ammunition at unarmed Palestinian civilians engaged in peaceful protest, failing to distinguish between peaceful and violent resistance. The Israeli government has been demolishing Palestinian houses and crops in the Occupied Territories, while allowing Jewish settlers -- many of them American -- to illegally occupy the same land."

End U.S. Aid to Israel: "The U.S. government provides more aid to Israel than to any other country -- the vast majority of this is for military purposes. Billions of U.S. taxpayer dollars have propped up the occupation and fueled the Israeli government's war machine ... This aid must end."

Stop Economic Attacks on Palestine: "The Israeli government has attacked the Palestinian economy by: closing Palestinian banks; imposing extreme taxes on business; withdrawing operating licenses; destroying industrial equipment; bulldozing farmland and banning fishing; restricting workers' movement; controlling the export of Palestinian goods; closing the borders of the Occupied Territories; and refusing to fund infrastructure like water and electricity -- even in Arab villages within Israel."

Let Palestinians Return Home: "Thousands of Palestinians were driven out of their houses and off of their farms during and after the creation of Israel. They must be allowed to return to their homeland." In JATO's calculus, the "right of return" should not be restricted only to the surviving Palestinians who were among the 725,000 Arabs who actually fled the slivers of the British Mandate when the 1948 war broke out, but should be extended to all their descendants as well. Thus JATO places the number of potential returnees at 5 million.

According to JATO, "Judaism is a cultural and religious identity which must not be equated with Zionism, a political movement. Criticism of the state of Israel, its policies, or the idea of a Jewish state does not by itself constitute anti-Semitism."

JATO makes no mention, anywhere in its literature, of Palestinian terrorism against Israel. Nor does it express concern that terrorism may be a potential impediment to the establishment of a Palestinian state or to the feasibility of a "right of return."

To summarize its positions and demands, JATO has composed the following petition, addressed jointly to the Israeli government and to "international public opinion":

"We, concerned Jews from around the world, continue to view with horror the consequences of military repression and economic blockade of the Palestinians by Israel. Israel and the Palestinians are not equal partners in a peace process. Israel is a nation state equipped with an army and highly sophisticated weaponry; the Palestinians are a dispossessed people, living under Israeli military, political and economic control ... We support the co-existence, on equal terms, of Palestinians, Israelis, and all other peoples of the region and call for an end to Israeli aggression and oppression. We urge Israel to uphold the human rights of Palestinians by: immediate, total and unconditional withdrawal from all of the territories taken by force and occupied in 1967; recognition of the Palestinian right to national self-determination, to return and to compensation ...; redistribution of resources and a massive program of international aid to rehabilitate Palestinian communities."

JATO is an endorser of Wheels of Justice, a group that accuses Israel of ethnic cleansing and human rights violations against the Palestinians, and calls for an end to all American aid to Israel. Fellow endorsers include Veterans For Peace, September 11th Families for Peaceful Tomorrows, Traprock Peace Center, and Pax Christi USA.

In September of 2003, the President of Rutgers University's JATO chapter, Abe Greenhouse, was arrested for hitting Israeli Cabinet Minister Natan Sharansky in the face with a pie.

JEWS FOR A FREE PALESTINE

www.studentorg.vcu.edu

Anti-Israel group based in the San Francisco Bay area
Supports Palestinian "right of return"

Based in San Francisco, Jews For a Free Palestine (JFFP) is an organization of nominally Jewish activists who support what they call "Palestine liberation solidarity efforts." In conjunction with its partner organization, Renounce Aliyah, JFFP says: "[W]e denounce the continued racist and inhumane policies of the Israeli government. There can be no safety for Jews internationally as the Israeli government continues in the role of occupier and oppressor, while falsely claiming to represent us all."

JFFP's preferred *modus operandi* is to stage disruptive protests in a variety of public venues. On the eve of Passover in April 2003, for example, the organization led a group of 50 protestors in taking over the lobby of the building that housed the Israeli Consulate of San Francisco. Twelve JFFP demonstrators who were blocking the flow of traffic into and out of the building were arrested for trespassing.

In a March 2003 anti-war rally, JFFP protested side-by-side with such groups as International ANSWER, United For Peace and Justice, Al-Awda, the International Solidarity Movement, If Americans Knew, the Muslim Students' Association of the U.S. and Canada, and the Council on American-Islamic Relations.

Jews for a Free Palestine calls on Jews to actively oppose U.S. economic aid to Israel, and to "affirm the Palestinian Right of Return." JFFP places the number of Arabs who ought to be granted this "Right of Return" to Israel at 5 million. This is more than *ten* times the number of Arabs who actually left the Jewish portions of the British Mandate in 1948, most of whom are now deceased.

JFFP also condemns the Israeli government's destruction of many Palestinian dwellings, making no mention of the fact that these demolitions are targeted specifically at the homes of terrorists and their collaborators. Similarly, the organization denounces the Israeli security fence that was erected in the West Bank to stem the tide of suicide bombing attacks aimed at Israeli civilians, calling it an "Apartheid Wall" whose existence has consigned Palestinians to "a radical form of exclusion." Again, no mention is made of the waves of terrorism that necessitated the barrier's construction. Consistent with the foregoing positions, JFFP condemns the Israeli government's targeted assassinations of known Palestinian terrorist leaders and their operatives.

When the Israeli Action Committee, in an effort to raise American public awareness of the horrors of Arab terrorism, acquired and displayed in Berkeley, California a bus that had been blown up by a Palestinian suicide bomber in Jerusalem, JFFP President Susan Green complained: "It's meant to demonize Palestinians and deflect the American people away from the fact that millions of our tax dollars are spent daily to support the illegal Israeli occupation of Palestine."

In July 2006, JFFP co-sponsored (along with Break the Silence and Jewish Voice for Peace) a rally where more than 400 people demonstrated in front of the Israeli Consulate in San Francisco to protest Israel's ongoing military campaigns against Hamas in Gaza, and against Hezbollah in Lebanon. During this event, more than a dozen Jewish activists blocked Montgomery Street (in front of the Israeli Consulate) "in solidarity with the people of Palestine and to call for an and to the siege of Gaza, to the bombing of Lebanon, and to the occupation of Palestine." After they had shut down the street for over an hour, they were all arrested.

JEWS FOR A JUST PEACE

www.jewsforajustpeace.com
info@jewsforajustpeace.com

- Anti-Israel Jewish group based in Vancouver, Canada
- Has demanded that the Canadian government recognize the Islamic terrorist group Hamas as legitimate political entity
- Condemned Canada's Prime Minister for justifying Israel's war against Hezbollah in 2006

Jews for a Just Peace (JFJP) is a Vancouver, Canada-based organization of Jews whose mission is to work "for a fair and just solution to the Israeli-Palestinian conflict." Central to the organization's vision of justice is its unyielding opposition to any and all measures taken by the Israeli government to thwart Arab terrorism against its citizens.

For example, JFJP condemns Israel's "military attacks against civilian populations" and its destruction of Palestinian homes and farms -- ignoring, at least in its public rhetoric -- the fact that these operations are targeted specifically at Palestinian terrorists and their collaborators. Similarly, the organization denounces such Israeli anti-terror measures as the imposition of curfews for Palestinians and the construction of physical barriers like the separation wall (which essentially brought suicide bombings to an end) in the West Bank. Says JFJP: "We do not believe that such actions, in contravention of the 1949 Geneva Convention accords to which Israel was signatory, serve genuine security needs."

A notable JFJP steering committee member is Vancouver resident Stephen Aberle, who supports the Palestinian "right of return" and has worked cooperatively with the Israeli Committee Against House Demolitions.

On February 16, 2006, JFJP demanded that the government of Canada recognize the terrorist group Hamas (whose founding Charter is specifically dedicated to Israel's destruction) as the legitimate, democratically elected government of the Palestinian people, and that Canada support the imposition of sanctions against Israel if the latter refused to negotiate politically with Hamas. Said JFJP: "Hamas received the overwhelming support of the Palestinian people in free and fair elections. That population has suffered a cruel occupation for decades. The new Palestinian government deserves our recognition."

JFJP officially endorses StopWar.ca, formerly known as the November 17th Peace Coalition, a broad-based alliance of more than 180 anti-war organizations, labor unions, and individuals that oppose not only the U.S. military presence in Iraq, but also the profiling of immigrants and refugees in North America. Fellow endorsers of StopWar.ca include: Direct Action Against Refugee Exploitation; the War Resisters Support Campaign; the Trade Union Committee for Justice in the Middle East; the Arab Palestine Association; the Canada Palestine Association; Coalition In Solidarity with the People of Iraq; Palestine Solidarity Group; Veterans Against Nuclear Arms; the Communist Party of Canada; International Socialists; Lawyers Against the War; Artists Against War; Global Justice; Oxfam Canada; Queers United Against Kapitalism; and the Women's International League for Peace and Freedom.

In July 2006, JFJP published a joint statement with StopWar.ca expressing outrage over Canadian Prime Minister Stephen Harper's justification of Israel's military action against Hezbollah forces in Lebanon. The statement read, in part: "We would remind Mr. Harper that Palestinians have a right under international law as an occupied people to engage with the Israeli military and to take their soldiers as prisoners of war. ... While Hezbollah's initial attack on an Israeli military target and the subsequent attacks on civilian areas in Israel is in contravention of international law, these actions can never constitute a justification for Israel to ignore the Geneva Conventions and to launch the massive attacks on civilian populations that we have witnessed ..."

JFJP also endorsed the "Combatant's Letter" crafted in 2002 by Courage to Refuse, an organization of IDF (Israeli Defense Force) combat officers and soldiers accusing Israel of trying to "dominate, expel, starve and humiliate an entire people," and demanding that Israelis evacuate all Jewish settlements located outside their country's pre-1967 borders.

JFJP identifies the International Solidarity Movement, Noam Chomsky, and Norman Finkelstein as "like-minded groups and people."

KAIROS: CANADIAN ECUMENICAL JUSTICE INITIATIVES

129 Saint Claire Ave. West
Toronto, Ontario
Canada
M4V 1N5

Phone :416-463-5312
URL: http://www.kairoscanada.org/NGO that takes takes a blatantly political anti-Israel position on the Israeli-Palestinian conflict

Founded in July 2001, KAIROS: Canadian Ecumenical Justice Initiatives describes itself as "a coalition of churches and religious organizations devoted to justice in the community, nationally and internationally." The word *kairos*, the organization explains, "comes to us from the Greek word for time. Contrasting with *chronos*, meaning ordinary or chronological time, *kairos* means holy or God-given time, time laden with meaning and choice. *Kairos* signals a time of crisis and new possibilities, a time of repentance, renewal and decisive action." (The group capitalizes all the letters in its name.)

KAIROS runs programs in the following areas:

Aboriginal Rights: "Through public education and action campaigns, KAIROS aims to change federal Aboriginal policy by calling for recognition of Aboriginal title and nationhood, and the implementation of Aboriginal land, treaty and inherent rights."
Anti-Poverty: "KAIROS believes that poverty in Canada is neither inevitable nor acceptable. This country has abundant resources, and sharing these fairly must be our first priority. We ... can begin to end poverty by placing priority on: good jobs with good wages, income security, affordable housing, [and] support for families, including strategies aimed at ending child poverty."

Corporate Issues: "As shareholders, the churches use their investments to engage corporations in dialogue. Through shareholder activism, the churches apply direct pressure on corporations to improve their social and environmental performance."

Ecology: "Sustainable communities ... require a just and moral economy where people are empowered to participate in decisions affecting their lives, where public and private institutions are held accountable for the social and environmental consequences of their activities, and where the Earth is honoured rather than exploited or degraded."

Education and Animation: "We are committed to building an ecumenical movement for justice and peace ... We organize campaigns, produce resources, and provide training to KAIROS organizers across the country."

Global Economic Justice: "Inequalities between and within nations are growing ever wider, with disastrous effect on basic services such as health care, education, access to clean water. KAIROS believes that trade agendas and economic policy must serve the good of all peoples and the earth. We believe that powerful decision makers, such as national governments, international financial institutions and corporations, must be accountable for the impacts of their economic policy."

International Human Rights: "KAIROS believes that human beings are created in the image of God, and as such deserve the utmost dignity and respect. Our commitment to human rights is an expression of this. Whether human rights are civil, political, economic, social or cultural, we contend that they must be protected by international law."

Partnerships: "The Global Partnerships Program works with approximately 35 partners in Africa, Asia-Pacific, the Caribbean/Latin America, and the Middle East. Together we address global, national and local peace and justice issues. Many of these partners are church-related organizations, while others are citizens' groups and coalitions. All share the KAIROS goal of bringing about social transformation ..."

Refugees and Migration: "While Canada prides itself on welcoming refugees and migrants, we are often far less welcoming than we want to believe. Recent federal initiatives threaten the basic human rights of refugee claimants, and everywhere refugees and migrants continue to face suspicion and discrimination. ... The Bible calls us to 'welcome the stranger' ... To counter the many myths and stereotypes about refugees and migrants, we offer resources, media advocacy, and workshops."

Particularly vocal about Middle Eastern affairs, KAIROS draws a moral equivalence between Palestinian suicide bombings aimed at Israeli civilians on the one hand, and Israel's targeted killings of Palestinian terrorists on the other. For instance, on March 22, 2004 -- immediately after the Israeli military's assassination of Hamas leader Ahmed Yassin -- KAIROS expressed, in a letter to Canadian Prime Minister Paul Martin, its objections to Israel's action: "Like suicide bombings, targeted assassinations destroy the fragile trust between Israelis and Palestinians." In the same letter, KAIROS claimed that "the Israeli occupation is the root cause of the violence."

KAIROS's Basic Affirmations are similarly bereft of any moral distinctions between terrorists who target civilians, and governments that target terrorists. "Both Palestinians and Israelis must be held to a common human rights standard which includes the protection of civilians," says this document, which also claims falsely that Israel's legitimacy has been accepted by neighboring states."

In a November 3, 2003 letter to Canadian Minister of Foreign Affairs Bill Graham, KAIROS refers to Israeli house demolitions (of terrorists' homes and bases of operation) as "war crimes"; the letter further condemns "the Occupation," the "wall" [designed to prevent would-be suicide bombers from entering Israeli towns], and a multitude of other alleged Israeli transgressions.

In a June 28, 2002 analysis of President Bush's Middle East policy, KAIROS featured the perspectives of Jeff Halper, Coordinator of the Israeli Committee Against Housing Demolitions. Halper claimed that Israel's security barrier was "electrified," and he described then-Prime Minister Ariel Sharon's plans as "reminiscent of the South African apartheid system where Palestinians will essentially become prisoners of their homes." Halper added, "Many believe that Sharon's eventual plan ... is to transfer the Palestinians out of the West Bank." In the same piece, KAIROS attributed the failure of Israeli peace efforts with Yasser Arafat to Sharon's "long feud" with him.

KAIROS has produced an education packet on the Arab-Israeli conflict; it lacks citations, sources, and a bibliography, and contains numerous examples of historical distortion and politicization. For instance (a) It questions the very legitimacy of, and Jewish connection to, the State of Israel: "...[O]f the approximately 15 million Jewish people in the world today, just 5 million live in Israel -- meaning 2 out of 3 Jewish people choose not to live in Israel." (b) Depicting Israel as the aggressor in its 1948 war against several Arab states, the education packet claims that the Israeli army was "a well-coordinated force several times the size of the combined Arab troops." But in fact, the troops from the eight Arab armies that united to attack Israel on the very day of its creation outnumbered the IDF troops by about five to one. (c) The education packet's "Psychological Impact" section ignores Israeli rights and the effect of terrorism on that nation's civilian population; it refers only to the suffering of Palestinians. (d) It also makes the unsubstantiated claim that Palestinian "workers attempting to harvest the olives are shot at and sometimes killed by [Israeli] settler residents."

KAIROS, whose Board Chair is a Catholic priest named Paul Hansen, works closely with the Mennoninte Central Committee of Canada.

KAIROS receives substantial funding from the Canadian International Development Agency, as well as from its constituent church members and other individual donors.

LAW

P.O.Box 20873
Jerusalem
Israel

Phone :972 2 583 3430
URL: http://www.law-society.orgJerusalem-based anti-Israel NGO

Active participant in the anti-American, anti-Israel U.N. World Conference Against Racism in 2001
Accuses Israel of widespread human rights violations against Palestinians

Founded by a group of Palestinian lawyers in 1990, LAW is a Jerusalem-based NGO that identifies itself as a "Palestinian human rights organization." Its stated goals are to "promote human rights and further the principles of the rule of law, ... to defend Palestinian rights in accordance with international human rights law and United Nations declarations, ... [and to] protect human rights through an intensive program of documenting and following up abuses, and through providing legal and financial help to people in need." The organization's full name is the Palestinian Committee for the Protection of Human Rights and the Environment. The acronym LAW is derived from the name of its predecessor activist organization, Land And Water.

LAW organizes workshops and conferences "in order to raise human rights awareness and to strengthen community involvement." It also produces a journal so as "to participate in the building of a democratic civil society through bringing human rights issues to the attention of the Palestinian community."

Politically and ideologically, LAW sides entirely with the Palestinian side in the Arab-Israeli conflict. It was an active participant at the Durban World Conference Against Racism in 2001, playing a central role in the steering committee and pre-conference organizing. LAW press releases regularly depict Israel as an oppressive nation that engages in widespread human rights violations against Palestinians. For example, LAW refers to the security fence that Israel is building to prevent future terror attacks in the West Bank as an "apartheid wall" that "will restrict Palestinian freedom of movement, Palestinian livelihoods, and Palestinian access to land -- a wall which divides upon ethnic, national, and religious identity."

LAW also makes frequent references to Israeli "war crimes" and "crimes against humanity," accusing the Jewish state of engaging in "a policy to deliberately target civilians [via] indiscriminate attacks [that] cause excessive losses to civilians in deaths, injuries, and property."

LAW was a signatory to a May 15, 2002 petition calling for the creation of a Friends of the Earth Palestine Campaign, to combat the alleged "environmental violations" of the Israeli army. The petition read, in part: "Often times, daily environmental violations such as massive land sweeping have reached proportions that equal decades of similar crimes. ... We [Palestinians] continue to watch as our land and our future are destroyed, and we continue to engage the world—to demand for witnesses and voices—amidst our travesty."

MACHSOM WATCH

URL: http://www.machsomwatch.orgHuman Rights NGO that monitors and reports on Israeli Defense Force checkpoints

Machsom Watch (a.k.a. Women for Human Rights) was established in January 2001 by three Israeli women -- Ronnee Jaeger, a longtime human rights activist in Guatemala and Mexico; Adi Kuntsman, a feminist scholar who emigrated to Israel from the former Soviet Union in 1990; and veteran activist Yehudit Keshet, an orthodox Jew. They formed Machsom Watch "in response to repeated reports in the press about human rights abuses [against] Palestinians crossing army and border police checkpoints." The word "machsom" is Hebrew for "checkpoint," a reference to Israeli Defense Force (IDF) checkpoints designed to prevent West Bank-based Palestinian terrorists from entering Israel.

With a membership composed exclusively of Israeli women, Machsom Watch identifies its goals as: "to monitor the behavior of soldiers and police at checkpoints"; "to ensure that the human and civil rights of Palestinians attempting to enter Israel are protected"; and "to record and report the results of our observations to the widest possible audience, from the decision-making level to that of the general public." Perhaps the most notable of Machsom Watch's 400 current members is Israeli Prime Minister Ehud Olmert's daughter Dana.

Machsom Watch condemns what it calls "[t]he excessive Israeli response to the El Aksa [a.k.a. Al Aqsa] Intifada," and Israel's "prolonged closure and siege of [Palestinian] villages and towns on the West Bank." The organization produces regular reports that, according to NGO Monitor, use "emotive and politically charged language that contributes to the demonization of Israel." In June 2006 Machsom Watch reported: "Over the past five years we have seen that restricting freedom of movement doesn't stop at the checkpoints. It also comes into play each time Palestinians encounter the state authorities. ... With time, we've realized that [Israeli] state entities are being recruited to enforce bureaucratic regulations that are aimed solely at impeding the Palestinians' lives."

The IDF has accused Machsom Watch of disrupting the operation of checkpoints, and of making false, (often) profanity-laced accusations against the Israeli troops stationed there.

Though Machsom Watch does not make public its sources of funding, it is known to accept donations through the Bat Shalom organization; it is also a member of the Coalition of Women for Peace, which takes donations through the New Israel Fund.

MEDICAL AID FOR PALESTINIANS

33a Islington Park Street
London N1 1QB
United Kingdom

Phone :44 0 20 7226 4114
URL: http://www.map-uk.org/Pro-Palestinian British charity

Works in conjunction with several anti-Israeli organizations

Medical Aid for Palestinians (MAP) describes itself as "a British charity dedicated to the health and humanitarian needs of the Palestinian people." Established in 1984, MAP currently operates in the West Bank, the Gaza Strip, and Lebanon.

Claiming to be "non-political and non-partisan," MAP receives some 39 percent of its annual budget from the European Union. Other funders include the British government's Department for International Development, the European Community Humanitarian Office, EuropeAid, and the Linbury Trust.

MAP ascribes most of the political, economic, and health-related problems affecting Palestinians to Israel's allegedly brutal and repressive rule over the "Occupied Territories." In July 2006, after Israel responded militarily to the kidnappings of three Israeli soldiers by the Gaza-based organization Hamas and the Lebanon-based group Hezbollah, MAP accused Israel of having responded with "excessive and disproportionate force." MAP's partner organizations include the highly politicized, anti-Israel NGOs Ard et-Aftal, Ard el-Insan, and the Union of Palestinian Medical Relief Committees.

MAP's program areas include the following:

Environmental Health: This program is directed toward "Palestinians living in some of the most over-crowded places in the world. ... In some areas, the lack of water and sanitation systems is a result of appalling, over-crowded living conditions. In other areas, water and sanitation systems have been destroyed by military activity."

Public Health Awareness: "Sexual and reproductive health, accident prevention and the health implications of early marriage are among the areas where MAP is currently working to increase public health awareness."

Mobile Clinics: "The ... impediments of checkpoints, the [anti-terrorism] Wall, settler-only roads and frequent closures mean that access to health care remains elusive for many. For this reason, MAP has given its support to mobile clinics ... that now deliver care to some of the West Bank's most needy Palestinian communities."

Training: "There are still very significant unmet primary health care needs in Lebanon, in the Occupied Palestinian Territories and among Bedouin communities inside Israel. Particularly disadvantaged communities can be found in both rural and acutely stressed urban areas due to a combination of factors that include poverty, exclusion, and lack of access."

Counseling: "Many Palestinian children have been exposed to extreme violence, killings, bereavement, displacement and house destruction. Problems such as sleep disorders, nervousness, lack of appetite, frustration and abnormal thoughts of death are common."

Disability: "There exist high levels of disability in the Occupied Palestinian Territories, both congenital ... and as a result of trauma. Disabled people tend to be marginalized by society and there are insufficient care facilities or trained staff, particularly in Gaza."

Income Generation: "Poverty and unemployment are critical problems in the Occupied Palestinian Territories and within Palestinian refugee camps in Lebanon. Restrictions on movement and the Wall in the West Bank cut many people off from their lands and jobs ..."

Nutrition: "Food insecurity ... is a very real issue for many Palestinian households. ... The restrictions on movement imposed by the occupation contribute to unemployment and poverty in the OPT and have a direct bearing on nutritional standards."

MENNONITE CENTRAL COMMITTEE (MCC)

General inquiries
21 South 12th Street, PO Box 500
Akron, Pennsylvania, 17501-0500
(717) 859-1151
1-888-563-4676
www.mcc.org

Pennsylvania-based NGO
Promotes anti-Israel propaganda

Established on September 27, 1920 and based in Akron, Pennsylvania, the Mennonite Central Committee (MCC) has offices located throughout the United States and Canada. The Committee was formed as the result of a meeting held two months earlier, when 13 church leaders had met in Elkhart, Indiana to discuss ways that North American Mennonites could respond to the needs of hungry people in the former Soviet Union. Today MCC's self-defined mission is "to demonstrate God's love by working among people suffering from poverty, conflict, oppression and natural disaster; [and to serve] as a channel for interchange by building mutually transformative relationships ... by sharing our experiences, resources and faith in Jesus Christ." The organization seeks to achieve these objectives by: (a) "send[ing] people, food and material goods to communities recovering from war and natural disasters"; (b) "support[ing] local churches and community groups in their efforts to provide food, health care, education, employment and social services"; (c) help[ing] people develop skills for creating peace in their families, neighborhoods, villages, towns and nations"; and (d) "encourage[ing] exchanges of visits, gifts and prayers between supporters and those with whom we work around the world."

MCC describes itself as "a relief, service, and peace agency of the North American Mennonite and Brethren in Christ churches." Its overseas work includes development work such as education, health and agriculture, peace and justice issues, relief work, and job creation. In North America, MCC's work is with "immigration, refugee assistance, job creation, people with disabilities, offenders and victims of crime, and more." As of July 2006, MCC personnel were stationed in 53 countries; 26 countries received material and/or food assistance from MCC; and 70 countries received financial support from the organization.

MCC's relief work in the Middle East started in 1949 -- as its website puts it, "following [the] war and the creation of the state of Israel, which left 700,000 Palestinians as refugees." Today MCC's Washington office promotes the "Bridges Not Walls" campaign exhorting U.S. politicians "to call upon Israeli and Palestinian leaders to build bridges for peace, not walls that divide" -- a reference to the anti-terror security barrier constructed by Israel in the West Bank.

MCC's July-September 2004 *Peace Office Newsletter*, produced by the organization's Middle East leadership, contains highly vitriolic attacks on Israel. The newsletter features a number of articles relating to Israel's security barrier, including one by Alain Epp Weaver -- MCC's co-representative for Palestine, Jordan and Iraq -- who argues that the 1948 creation of the state of Israel constituted "a violent imposition on the native population." Weaver likens the barrier to the Berlin Wall and compares its effects to those of South African apartheid. Another contributor to the *Peace Office Newsletter* is Jeff Halper, Coordinator of the Israeli Committee Against House Demolitions.

The newsletter's list of resources betrays an extremist political bias, including books by Uri Davis (*Apartheid*

Israel: Possibilities for the Struggle Within) and the radical academic Ilan Pappe. MCC's links to other websites include those of Al-Haq, the Palestine Center for Human Rights, the Applied Research Institute (Jerusalem), Electronic Intifada, and the Stop the Wall Campaign.

MCC's annual income exceeds $60 million, mainly from individual contributions. Other sources of revenue include relief sales, thrift shops, and donations of food grains. The grain donation is matched by the Canadian government through the Canadian International Development Agency, which contributes as much as four dollars for every dollar of grain donated.

MERCY CORPS

Dept. W
P.O. Box 2669
Portland, OR
97208
Phone :888-256-1900
URL: http://www.mercycorps.org/Anti-Israel NGO

Blames Israel for Palestinian poverty and suffering

Established in 1981, Mercy Corps provides humanitarian assistance to people living in regions beset by war, internecine violence, and natural disasters. From 1981 through 2006, Mercy Corps provided $1 billion in assistance to people in 82 nations. Maintaining headquarters in North America, Europe, and Asia, the organization's unified global programs employ 3,200 staff worldwide and reach nearly 10 million people in more than 40 countries. As of 2006, Mercy Corps' projects extended to Eritrea, Ethiopia, Liberia, Niger, Somalia, Sudan, Uganda, Zimbabwe, Colombia, Guatemala, Honduras, Nicaragua, Bosnia and Herzegovina, Kosovo, Serbia, Azerbaijan, Georgia, Kyrgyzstan, Tajikistan, Uzbekistan, China, East Timor, Indonesia, Kiribati, Mongolia, North Korea, Iran, Jordan, Lebanon, West Bank/Gaza, Afghanistan, India, Nepal, Pakistan, Sri Lanka, and the Gulf Cast of the United States.

With regard specifically to the Arab-Israeli conflict, Mercy Corps places all blame for Palestinian poverty and suffering directly on Israel. In one report, Mercy Corps claims: "As a result of the severe restrictions placed on Palestinians in the West Bank and Gaza, the UN and other agencies have identified serious micronutrient deficiencies among Palestinian children." The report provides no evidence that this situation is due to Israeli policies, and makes no effort to examine Israeli measures aimed at alleviating Palestinian suffering. In a second example, Mercy Corps claims: "Over the past decade, the Israeli Defense Forces (IDF) began implementing a closure system in the West Bank to regulate Palestinian movement ... through a series of roadblocks and military checkpoints. In the past three years access and movement for Palestinians within the West Bank has been crippled by more than 700 IDF barriers and checkpoints. The massive wall the Israeli Government is building will further separate Palestinian communities, sever social and economic links and block access to critical health and education services."

Mercy Corps objects to the fact that Hamas' landslide victory in the political elections of January 2006 triggered a halt in Israeli tax transfers and a moratorium on most international aid to the Palestinian Authority. “As a result,” said Senior Director of Program Operations Jim White in June 2006, “wages to 73,000 teachers, healthcare workers, policemen and other municipal workers in Gaza — more than one-third of its workforce — haven't been paid since February. Poverty rates are expected to hit 74 percent without these salaries ... Tightened borders have added to Gaza's economic woes. ... Stocks of wheat flour are ‘critically low’ and there are fears that basic commodities will soon dry up, according the World Food Program ... The looming humanitarian catastrophe threatens the well-being and security of most of Gaza's 1.3 million residents, as well as the prospects for Middle East peace.”

The founder of Mercy Corps is Dan O'Neill, who in 1999 co-founded the Save the Refugees Fund, an emergency relief task force to assist Cambodian refugees. He also served on the White House Cambodian Crisis Committee at the request of Rosalynn Carter, wife of former U.S. President Jimmy Carter.

Neal Keny-Guyer has been Mercy Corps' Chief Executive Officer since 1994. He was formerly a Field Coordinator for CARE/UNICEF, and spent nine years as Director of Save the Children's Middle East, Europe and North Africa programs.

Nancy Lindborg has been the President of Mercy Corps since 1996. She also currently serves as Vice President of the Board of Directors for the U.S. Global Leadership Campaign, a Board member of the ONE Campaign, Co-Chair of the National Committee on North Korea, and Chair of the InterAction North Korea working group.

Mercy Corps receives funding from numerous foundations, including the American Express Foundation, the Carnegie Corporation of New York, the Nathan Cummings Foundation, the Bill and Melinda Gates Foundation, the Andrew W. Mellon Foundation, and the Open Society Institute.

MIDDLE EAST CHILDREN'S ALLIANCE

901 Parker Street
Berkeley, CA
94710

Phone :510-548-0542
Fax :510-548-0543
URL: http://www.mecaforpeace.org/Pro-Palestinian, anti-Israeli organization

> Founder Barbara Lubin is allied with Workers World Party, a Marxist-Leninist sect aligned with Communist North Korea

Founded in 1988 by Barbara Lubin, the Middle East Children's Alliance (MECA) describes itself as "a non-profit organization working for justice in the Middle East, focusing on the Occupied Palestinian Territories, Israel and Occupied Iraq." Viewing the Iraqi and Palestinian peoples, respectively, as victims of American and Israeli oppression, MECA claims that since its inception it has "brought over $8 million of much needed relief to besieged communities in Iraq and Palestine through emergency medical aid and direct aid to families and communities." Among the projects funded by this organization are: children's clinics and family mental health projects in various refugee camps throughout what MECA calls the "Occupied West Bank and Gaza," as well as various community projects for children including, playgrounds, libraries, and youth centers.

"Our work in the United States," says MECA (which calls the U.S. occupation of Iraq "illegal" and accuses the U.S. of "purposefully" targeting civilian areas), "is centered ... on educating North Americans about U.S. foreign policy in the Middle East, the affect it has on children, families and communities there, and the connection these policies have to our own communities. Through public lectures, audio-visual, presentations, teach-ins, demonstrations, and community work we dispel the myths and raise awareness about the history behind the Israeli-Palestinian conflict, the current situation in the Occupied Palestine and Occupied Iraq and the role of U.S. policy in maintaining and perpetuating instability and conflict in the Middle East. ... We stand in solidarity with the Palestinian people as they seek freedom from oppression and we support the right of Palestinian refugees to return to their homes."

MECA is a member organization of International ANSWER's steering committee, the United For Peace and Justice antiwar coalition, the U.S. Campaign to End the Israeli Occupation, the Palestine Solidarity Movement's divestiture project, the Justice in Palestine Coalition, and the Middle East Policy Advisory Committee. MECA is also the fiscal sponsor for the International Solidarity Movement USA.

MECA's Board of Directors and Board of Advisors have at one time or another included such individuals as Leonard Weinglass; Noam Chomsky; Ramsey Clark; Maxine Waters; Ron Dellums (a socialist who is the current Mayor of Oakland, California, and who served as a U.S. Congressman in that state from 1971 to 1998); Gus Newport (MECA's current President, the former Mayor of Berkeley, and the onetime General Manager of Pacifica Radio affiliate KFPA); Maudelle Shirek (a former Berkeley City Council member suspected of having close ties to the Communist Party); Father William O'Donnell (a liberation theologian who was sentenced to a six-month jail term for protesting the School of the Americas); Fathi Arafat (the brother of Yasser Arafat), Edward Said (the late Columbia University professor and a member of the Palestine National Council); Ibrahim Abu Lughod (currently a member of the Palestine National Council); and the co-founders of the American-Arab Anti-Discrimination Committee, James Abourezk and James Zogby.

MECA supports the Ibaada Center in the West Bank, which the *Jerusalem Post* describes as an indoctrination center that teaches Arab children to reject Israel's existence and to support Palestinian terrorism aimed ultimately at conquering Israel by violence. The Center's walls are festooned with scenes of terrorist "resistance."

MECA has also promoted a clinic in Gaza, the Union of Health Work Committees, whose former manager was a member of the Popular Front for the Liberation of Palestine, which is classified as a terrorist organization by the U.S. State Department.
MECA spokeswoman Penny Rosenwasser and Executive Director Barbara Lubin are both allied with the Marxist-Leninist Workers World Party. MECA's Political Education Coordinator is Uda Walker, who has visited American high-school campuses with the organization Voices in the Wilderness during school hours, and who has denounced U.S. foreign policy before audiences in the United Kingdom.

The Middle East Children's Alliance's recent activities include the following:

- a 24-hour "Support Cindy Sheehan" vigil in San Francisco in August 2005
- a September 24, 2005 antiwar march in San Francisco, where every conceivable aspect of American foreign policy came under attack. The rally's themes included: "End Colonial Occupation: Iraq, Palestine, Haiti..."; "Support the Palestinian People's Right of Return"; "Military Recruiters Out of Our Schools"; "Stop the Racist, Anti-Immigrant and Anti-Labor Offensive"; "U.S. Out of the Philippines, Puerto Rico and Afghanistan"; and "Stop the Threats Against Iran, Cuba, Venezuela and North Korea."
- a "Wheels of Justice Bus Tour," where MECA members joined their counterparts from Voices in the Wilderness, Al-Awda, and the International Solidarity Movement in a two-year "nonviolent educational tour against war and occupation in Iraq and Palestine and for justice and universal human rights."

In 2004, MECA was a signatory -- along with more than 200 other leftist organizations -- to a letter exhorting members of the U.S. Senate to oppose Israel's construction of an anti-terrorist security fence in the West Bank, characterizing the barrier as an illegal "apartheid wall" that violated the civil and human rights of Palestinians.

MIDDLE EAST NGOS GATEWAY PROJECT (MENGOS)

URL: http://www.mengos.net/

The Middle East NGOs Gateway Project [MENGOS] is an Internet gateway containing information about non-governmental organizations, funding agencies, events, projects, success stories of individuals as well as organizations, and other topics relevant to nongovernmental organizations across the Arab Middle East. It hopes to establish an electronic forum linking nonprofits to facilitate exchange of experiences, best practices, material resources, and other valuable information regarding the usage of IT primarily in Arabic. MENGOS is a project of **Virtual Activism** and its branch **Center for Knowledge Society** in Cairo, Egypt.

MENGOS aims at disseminating information and promoting human rights and development initiatives in the Arab Middle East. In particular, MENGOS focuses on progressive, under represented and marginalized NGOs to give them voice and presence on the Internet. The Gateway therefore is essentially a database of NGOs who are both online and offline, in countries that are members of the Arab League, and who work on progressive human rights and development issues.

The database is a multi-lingual database [Arabic/English/French] that allows internet users to identify NGOs by name, region, area of focus, or primary contact person in three languages. It opens channels for donors to identify potential grantees, and opens channels of communication and networking among nonprofit organizations throughout the Middle East and beyond.

Mission:

MENGOS is a gateway that encourages networking among civil society organizations in the Arab Middle East, and is committed to harnessing the potential of information and communication technologies (ICTs) for sustainable and equitable development and for the promotion of human rights and democracy. MENGOS enables the sharing of information, experiences and resources to help highlight initiatives that reduce poverty, empower people, and promote democracy and human rights.

Objectives:

Form an evolving network of Arab public, private and not for profit organizations.

Promote broad access to - and effective use of - knowledge and information as tools of equitable sustainable development and promotion of democracy and human rights.

Increase knowledge sharing, experiences and resources to realize the potential of information and communication technologies to improve lives, reduce poverty, promote democracy, and empower people.

Build local IT capacity to enable civil society in the Arab World to recognize and use the IT tools available to enhance their work.

Internet website featuring information on Islamic and Arab NGOs and organizations

Provides links to anti-Israel articles and reports

An initiative of Virtual Activism, the Middle East NGOs Gateway Project (MENGOS) describes itself as "an Internet gateway containing information about non-governmental organizations, funding agencies, events, projects, success stories of individuals as well as organizations, and other topics relevant to nongovernmental organizations across the Arab Middle East." It is a multi-lingual (Arabic/English/French) database of NGOs based in countries that are members of the Arab League -- NGOs that "work on progressive human rights and development issues." The database allows Internet users to search for NGOs of interest by name, region, area of focus, or primary contact person -- in three languages -- making it easier for donors to identify potential grantees.

Moreover, MENGOS "encourages networking among civil society organizations in the Arab Middle East, and is committed to harnessing the potential of information and communication technologies for sustainable and equitable development and for the promotion of human rights and democracy." MENGOS is registered in the United States, and its branch office -- called the Center for Knowledge Society -- is based in Cairo, Egypt.

The MENGOS website makes available a number of reports on topics of political import. Among these titles are:

Fatal Strikes: Israel's Indiscriminate Attacks Against Civilians in Lebanon (an April 2006 report by Human Rights Watch): "By consistently failing to distinguish between combatants and civilians, Israel has violated one of the most fundamental tenets of the laws of war: the duty to carry out attacks on only military targets. The pattern of attacks during the Israeli offensive in Lebanon suggests ... the commission of war crimes."

A Preliminary analysis of the Humanitarian impact of the Barrier in the West Bank (an August 2006 report by the Office for the Coordination of Humanitarian Affairs): This document discusses the hardships which Palestinians face as a result of Israel's construction of the anti-terrorism fence in the West Bank.

Command's Responsibility: Detainee Deaths in U.S. Custody in Iraq and Afghanistan (a February 2006 report by Human Rights First): "Since August 2002, nearly 100 detainees have died while in the hands of U.S. officials in the global "war on terror." According to the U.S. military's own classifications, 34 of these cases are suspected or confirmed homicides; Human Rights First has identified another 11 in which the facts suggest death as a result of physical abuse or harsh conditions of detention."

Save Jerusalem from the Apartheid Wall and Ethnic Cleansing: "[This] comprehensive fact sheet on Jerusalem shows the dramatic process of Judaization that the city is undergoing. [The analysis begins with] the historical, cultural and spiritual role the Palestinian capital played before the *Nakba* [Arabic word meaning "the catastrophe," a reference to Israel's creation] in '48 until today."

Beyond Abu Ghraib: Detention and Torture in Iraq (a March 2006 report by Amnesty International): "Nearly three years after United States and allied forces invaded Iraq and toppled the government of Saddam Hussein, the human rights situation in the country remains dire. The deployment of U.S.-led forces in Iraq and the armed response that engendered has resulted in thousands of deaths of civilians and widespread abuses amid the ongoing conflict."

The Israel Lobby and U.S. Foreign Policy **(a** March 2006 report by John J. Mearsheimer and Stephen M. Walt): "... [T]he Bush Administration's attempt to transform the region into a community of democracies has helped produce a resilient insurgency in Iraq, a sharp rise in world oil prices, and terrorist bombings in Madrid, London, and Amman. ... The combination of unwavering U.S. support for Israel and the related effort to spread democracy throughout the region has inflamed Arab and Islamic opinion and jeopardized U.S. security."
Access to Jerusalem: New Military Order Limits West Bank Palestinian Access (March 2006): "As the Barrier nears completion around Jerusalem, recent Israeli military orders further restrict West Bank Palestinian pedestrian and vehicle access into Jerusalem."

MIFTAH

P.O.Box 38588
Jerusalem 97800
Israel

Phone :972-2-585 1842
URL: http://www.mecaforpeace.org/Jerusalem-based, anti-Israel NGO

Founders and board members include prominent anti-Israel Palestinians, including Hanan Ashrawi, Rashid Khalidi, and the late Edward Said

Established in 1999 and based in Jerusalem, MIFTAH (the Palestinian Initiative for the Promotion of Global Dialogue and Democracy) describes itself as an "independent institution committed to fostering the principles of democracy and effective dialogue based on the free and candid exchange of information and ideas ... to ensure democratic practice, the rule of law, and respect for human rights."

The organization's stated objectives include:

Reinforcing the Palestinian state-building process through ensuring democratic practices, the rule of law, and respect for human rights
Providing a forum for innovative public discourse and free debate on issues of Palestinian concern
Increasing global awareness and knowledge of Palestinian realities by providing reliable, accurate and comprehensive information, policy analysis, strategic briefings and position papers

In practice, MIFTAH seeks, through its press releases and reports, to undermine Israel's legitimacy while making virtually no reference to Palestinian terrorism. Producing biased reports wrapped in human rights terminology, MIFTAH regularly condemns Israeli efforts to imprison or kill Palestinian "activists." For example, on May 6, 2006, MIFTAH reported: "The Israeli army shelled a training camp in Gaza City belonging to the Popular Resistance Committees [PRCs], killing [five]." It did not mention that the PRCs are classified as terrorist organizations by the U.S. and Israel; that they consist of ex-Fatah members and current members of Hamas, Islamic Jihad, and the Al-Aqsa Martyrs' Brigades; or that the PRCs' *modus operandi* is to plant roadside bombs and vehicle explosives targeting Israeli military and civilian convoys in the Gaza Strip.

MIFTAH also "cautions" the international community "against Israel's clear attempt to provoke the

Palestinian resistance movement to retaliate and further inflame an already volatile situation in the occupied Palestinian territories." It expresses "alarm" over "Israel's clear adoption of a 'preventive strikes' policy, which justifies the extra-judicial killing of any Palestinian activist with impunity." And it "re-asserts the need for international protection to the Palestinian people, particularly at a time in which the Israeli government is clearly bent on inflicting the maximum amount of pain on the Palestinians."

MIFTAH refers to the 1948 creation of Israel as "al Nakba," or "the Catastrophe," lamenting "the dispossession, displacement, and uprooting of almost 1 million Palestinians ... from their original homes in what is [now] Israel."

Hanan Ashrawi, a member of the Palestinian Legislative Council and a frequent spokesperson for the Palestinian cause, founded MIFTAH and served as its Secretary General from its inception through January 2006. Lily Feidy, who also serves as a Board member of the Ramallah-based human rights organization Al-Haq, assumed the role of MIFTAH Secretary General in May 2006.

MIFTAH's Board of Trustees includes, among others: Khalil Jahshan, who is the President of the Washington, DC-based National Association of the Arab Americans; Rashid Khalidi, a prominent Columbia University Middle East Studies professor; Mustafa Bargouthi, President of the Union of Palestinian Medical Relief Committees and Director of the Health Development Information and Policy Institute; Ziad Abu-Amr, President of the Palestinian Council on Foreign Relations and a member of the Palestinian Legislative Council; and Azmi Bishara, a professor at the University of Haifa and a former Prime Ministerial candidate in Israel. Bishara, who describes himself as a human-rights campaigner, first drew public attention when he lionized Syrian President Bashar al-Assad, a notorious human-rights abuser who has called for the intensification of violence against Israel.

Until his death in 2003, MIFTAH's Board also included Columbia University professor Edward Said.

Because of the international prominence of its leaders, MIFTAH's name has become well known in human-rights circles, and its reports have been widely circulated. MIFTAH engages in heavy networking with diplomats, international agencies, institutions of civil society, and the media. Its website points out that "currently, an international Advisory Board is being established to include global personalities whose lives and work embody these shared goals."

MIFTAH has received considerable funding from the Ford Foundation, which gave the organization $550,000 in grants between 2001 and 2005.

MUSLIM ALLIANCE OF NORTH AMERICA (MANA)

Address:
MANA Office
P.O. Box 910375
Lexington, KY 40591

Tel: 858-296-0206
Fax: 859-257-3743
Email: mana@manaoffice.net
http://www.mana-net.org/

Muslim Alliance in North America (MANA) is an organization committed to Muslim issues and concerns that especially impact indigenous Muslims—issues and concerns that we feel have been largely neglected. With the launch of this web site we are inviting masjids, organizations and individuals to join MANA.

> African-American Muslim organization
>
> Headed by Siraj Wahhaj, believed to be a co-conspirator to the 1993 bombing of the World Trade Center

A predominantly African American organization representing Muslims indigenous to the United States, the Muslim Alliance of North America (MANA) was founded in February 2001 by Siraj Wahhaj and Ihsan Bagby. The latter is currently MANA's General Secretary.

MANA is part of the American Muslim Task Force on Civil Rights and Elections (AMTF), a national coalition of some of the largest Muslim organizations in the U.S., whose common objectives are to "[m]ainstream the American Muslim community" and work for "the empowerment of [that] community and for the protection of its rights." MANA's fellow AMTF members include the American Muslim Alliance, the Council on American-Islamic Relations, the Islamic Circle of North America, the Islamic Society of North America, the Muslim American Society, the Muslim Public Affairs Council, the Muslim Students' Association of the U.S. and Canada, the Muslim *Ummah* of North America, Project Islamic Hope, and United Muslims of America.

MANA's Director of Governmental Affairs is Johari Abdul Malik, who likens the Israeli anti-terror separation barrier to South African apartheid; advocates divestiture from Israel; urges a boycott of all entertainers who perform in Israel; and accuses the Israeli government of engaging in a "scorched earth policy" against the Palestinians. At an anti-Israel rally in April 2004, Abdul Malik lamented the Israeli army's recent killing of Hamas leader Sheik Ahmed Yassin, describing him as "a poor paraplegic in a wheelchair."

MANA chose not to endorse or participate in the May 14, 2005 "Free Muslims March Against Terror," an event whose purpose was to "send a message to the terrorists and extremists that their days are numbered ... [and to send] a message to the people of the Middle East, the Muslim world and all people who seek freedom, democracy and peaceful coexistence that we support them."

MUSLIM AMERICAN SOCIETY (MAS)

3602 Forest Drive
Alexandria, VA
22303
Phone :703-998-6562
URL: http://www.masnet.org/Founded in 1992 for the purpose of promoting "Islam as a total way of life"

Has stated that American foreign policy is to blame for the 9/11 attacks

Founded in 1992, the Muslim American Society (MAS) describes itself as "a charitable, religious, social, cultural and educational, not-for-profit ... Islamic organization." MAS's mission is to promote "Islam as a total way of life"; to "encourage the participation of Muslims in building a virtuous and moral society"; to "offer a viable Islamic alternative to many of our society's prevailing problems"; to "promote family values in accordance with Islamic teaching"; to "promote the human values that Islam emphasizes: brotherhood, equality, justice, mercy, compassion, and peace"; and to "foster unity among Muslims and Muslim organizations and encourage cooperation and coordination amongst them." MAS identifies the Muslim Students Association and the Islamic Society of North America as Muslim organizations that are rooted in the same "Islamic revival movement" as MAS.

In May 2005, Daveed Gartenstein-Ross reported in *The Weekly Standard* that MAS is a U.S. front group for the Muslim Brotherhood and, as such, wishes to see the United States governed by *sharia*, or Islamic law. "The message that all countries should be ruled by Islamic law," writes Gartenstein-Ross, "is echoed throughout MAS's membership curriculum. For example, MAS requires all its adjunct members to read Fathi Yakun's book *To Be a Muslim.* In that volume, Yakun spells out his expansive agenda: 'Until the nations of the world have functionally Islamic governments, every individual who is careless or lazy in working for Islam is sinful.'"
MAS's ties to the Muslim Brotherhood were confirmed on August 14, 2007, as The Investigative Project on Terrorism reported:

"As the terror-support trial of the Holy Land Foundation (HLF) continued today, FBI agent Lara Burns testified that a phonebook found at the home of Ismail Elbarrasse -- un-indicted co-conspirator and former assistant to HAMAS leader Musa Abu Marzook -- listed the names and numbers of the Muslim Brotherhood leadership in the United States. On the first page of the phonebook under the title 'Members of the Board of Directors' were fifteen names. Among those names are Ahmad Elkadi, Jamal Badawi, and Omar Soubani: the founding incorporators of the Muslim American Society (MAS)."

The Investigative Project continued:

"This evidence confirms ... Matthew Levitt's expert testimony that MAS is the representative of the Muslim

Brotherhood in the United States, and is substantiated by a [2004] *Chicago Tribune* article that outlined the history of MAS.

"Ahmad Elkadi, who told the *Chicago Tribune* that he was the leader of the Brotherhood in the U.S. from 1984-1994, worked with Mohammed Mahdi Akef, head of the Egyptian Muslim Brotherhood since 2003, to advocate for the founding of MAS. According to the *Tribune* report, Akef and Elkadi pushed for more openness for the Muslim Brotherhood through MAS. Akef himself 'says he helped found MAS by lobbying for the change during trips to the U.S.'
"In fact, MAS does not deny its Muslim Brotherhood foundations. In 2004, then-Secretary General of MAS Shaker Elsayed stated to the *Tribune* that 'Ikhwan [Brotherhood] members founded MAS…' Elsayed even went so far as to admit that about 45 percent of MAS's active members belong to the Brotherhood. Federal officials have confirmed this, noting continued ties between MAS and the Muslim Brotherhood."

MAS is described by Stephen Schwartz, author of *The Two Faces of Islam*, as "a major component" of the "Wahhabi Lobby" that channels money from and advances the policies of Muslim-fundamentalist Saudi Arabia.

MAS publishes *The American Muslim* magazine. In a July 2003 article titled "Reaching the Roots of Terrorism," author Omer bin Abdullah blames America's "forceful" foreign policy for having provoked the 9/11 attacks. "Terrorism enables the weak to confront the strong," he writes, "and thus has an enduring appeal to those who are dissatisfied with the status quo. … Its causes usually can be traced to political oppression, cultural domination, economic exploitation, ethnic discrimination, and religious persecution. … The U.S. has placed itself in a corner: It insists that other governments stop, prevent, and even help it to fight terrorism, and yet arms such practitioners of state terrorism as Tel Aviv. Today, terrorism refers to those whom the U.S. dislikes, especially Muslims."

In 2002 Randall Royer was the Communications Director of MAS. The following year, federal agents arrested Royer and charged him with conspiring with a Pakistani Wahhabist group -- Lashkar-I-Taibi, or "Army of the Righteous" -- to commit terrorism in Kashmir, Chechnya and elsewhere.

Closely linked to MAS is the Muslim American Society Freedom Foundation, whose Executive Director is Mahdi Bray, a former Students for a Democratic Society activist now affiliated with International ANSWER, an anti-war front group for the Communist World Workers Party. "Our mission," Bray has written, "is to build an integrated empowerment process for the American Muslim community." Toward this end, Bray and MAS have been involved in a voter-registration drive and an effort to train 1,000 "activists" in the "skills necessary for effective activism."

MAS also has close ties to Islamic American University, an unaccredited university in the Detroit suburb of Southfield, which teaches Islamic law and other subjects. (One IAU faculty member is Sheikh Yousef Al-Qaradhawi, who until at least June 2003 was also the Chairman -- in abstentia -- of the university's Board of Trustees.)

In addition, MAS operates programs for educating the young, providing fellowship for Muslim youth, creating its own network of Islamic schools, and sustaining a nationwide Council of Imams.

MAS was a signatory to a February 20, 2002 document, composed by the radical group Refuse & Resist, condemning military tribunals and the detention of immigrants apprehended in connection with post-9/11 terrorism investigations.

MAS strongly opposes the Patriot Act, which it says "strips away the fundamental checks and balances that safeguard many of our basic civil liberties," and has "drastically infringed upon every American's rights by giving the government expanded powers to invade privacy, imprison and deport people without due process, and punish political dissent."

As of early June 2007, the Minnesota chapter of MAS featured the following anti-Semitic, pro-*jihad* quotes on its website, www.masmn.org:
- "The Holy Prophet (and through him the Muslims) has been reassured that he should not mind the enmity, the evil designs and the machinations of the Jews ..."
- "In view of the degenerate moral condition of the Jews and the Christians, the Believers have been warned not to make them their friends and confidants."
- "If you gain victory over the men of Jews, kill them."

 "The Hour will not be established until you fight with the Jews, and the stone behind which a Jew will be hiding will say, 'O Muslim! There is a Jew hiding behind me, so kill him.'"
 "May Allah destroy the Jews, because they used the graves of their prophets as places of worship."
 "A Muslim must always worship Allah and wage jihad until death in order to reach his ultimate goal ... Regularly make the intention to go on *jihad* with the ambition to die as a martyr."

MUSLIM ARAB YOUTH ASSOCIATION (MAYA)

Muslim Arab Youth Association (MAYA)
P.O. Box 741 Stn,
Ottawa, ON K1P 5P8, CANADA
Ph: 745-0837
Fax: 234-4775
www.**maya**.org

Now-defunct organization that sponsored conferences featuring known Islamic terrorists as guest speakers
Placed by the U.S. government on a list of organizations that "finance terrorism and perpetuate violence"

The Muslim Arab Youth Association (MAYA) was established in the 1970s and incorporated in Plainfield, Indiana in 1989. Until it became inactive in early 2004, MAYA was listed on various Islamic reference websites as an organization set up to sponsor Muslim youth conferences and matrimonial services. The preface of the official MAYA constitutions read: "In the heart of America, in the depths of corruption and ruin and moral deprivation, an elite of Muslim youth is holding fast to the teachings of Allah." A companion MAYA publication stated, "Western civilization is based upon the separation of religions from life [whereas] Islamic civilization is based upon fundamentals opposed to those of Western civilization," and warned Muslim women to be "conscious of the evils of Western civilization."

MAYA first came to public attention when it co-financed and sponsored a December 1989 conference in Kansas City, Missouri that invited, as a guest speaker, a known Hamas terrorist named Sheikh Mohammed Siyyam, who called for violent *jihad* against Israel, Jews, and Christians. Another conference attendee was Nasser Himdi, who took weapons training classes in Chicago under the aegis of Mohammad Salah, an Arab-American who was ultimately arrested and imprisoned in Israel for supplying weapons that killed Israeli civilians in a terrorist attack. The conference exhorted those in attendance to participate in, or otherwise support, the Palestinian *Intifada* against Israel. The keynote speaker wore a veil and was introduced as a man who had proudly killed 16 Israelis in a bus attack. His speech was enthusiastically greeted with chants of "*Allahu Akhbar!*" ("God is great!")

Co-sponsoring the Kansas City conference with MAYA was the Holy Land Foundation for Relief & Development, which was closed down by the U.S. government in 2001 because it had funded terrorism. Another co-sponsor of the conference was the Islamic Association for Palestine (IAP), which was co-founded by Sami Al-Arian, who headed the U.S. operations of the terrorist organization Palestinian Islamic Jihad.

The Kansas City conference was just one of many MAYA events at which prominent members of Hamas and other terrorist groups were featured speakers. Another MAYA conference was keynoted by Sheikh Yousef Al-Qaradhawi, the influential Sunni jihadist cleric with close ties to the Muslim Brotherhood. In his 2002 book *American Jihad*, Steven Emerson wrote that MAYA conferences "have regularly attracted a parade of top Islamic militants."
In the aftermath of 9/11, the U.S. government placed MAYA on its list of organizations that "finance terrorism and perpetuate violence."

MUSLIM PUBLIC AFFAIRS COUNCIL (MPAC)

3010 Wilshire Boulevard, #217
Los Angeles, CA
90010

Phone :213-383-3443

Fax :213-383-9674
URL: http://www.mpac.org/Los Angeles-based Muslim organization whose leadership defends extremist violence

Opposes the shutdown of Muslim charities suspected of supporting terrorism
Opposes the Patriot Act

Founded in 1988, the Muslim Public Affairs Council (MPAC) describes itself as "a public service agency working for the civil rights of American Muslims, for the integration of Islam into American pluralism, and for a positive, constructive relationship between American Muslims and their representatives." The organization consists of eight chapters in California, and one each in Texas, Kansas, Nevada, and Iowa.

MPAC's vision is "to establish a vibrant Muslim American community that will enrich American society through promoting the Islamic values of Mercy, Justice, Peace, Human Dignity, Freedom, and Equality for all." In an effort to achieve this objective, the Council's mission consists of: "effect[ing] positive change in public opinion and in policy with the purpose of realizing our vision"; "promoting an American Muslim identity"; "fostering an effective grassroots organization"; "training a future generation of men and women who share our vision"; "promoting an accurate portrayal of Islam and Muslims in mass media and popular culture"; "educating the American public, both Muslim and non-Muslim, about Islam"; "building alliances with Muslim and non-Muslims groups"; and "cultivating relationships with opinion- and decision-makers."

From its inception, MPAC presented itself as more inclusive, and more open to peaceful coexistence with Jews and Christians, than other Arab and Muslim groups, and sought to make Americans comfortable with Islam by showing how much the religion embraced core American values. Throughout the 1990s, MPAC nurtured this image of moderation by organizing Muslim-Jewish dialogues in Los Angeles. Its members received invitations to the Clinton White House and appointments on federal commissions; they were similarly courted by the Bush campaign as the Clinton presidency drew to a close. MPAC's Senior Advisor, Maher Hathout, who has close ties to the Muslim Brotherhood and espouses the radical brand of Islam known as Wahhabism, was invited to address the Democratic Convention in Los Angeles in 2000. Shortly thereafter, however, MPAC endorsed George W. Bush for U.S. President.

MPAC's centrist public image unraveled after the September 2000 launching of the Second Palestinian Intifada, when the Council severed its ties to the Jewish community and issued one-sided condemnations of Israel's response to the Arab violence.

MPAC's support for President Bush similarly disintegrated after 9/11, when the Council actively opposed Bush's military incursions into Afghanistan and Iraq, as well as his "excesses" in the war on terror. In February 2003, MPAC joined the Council on American-Islamic Relations, the American Muslim Council, and the American Muslim Alliance in forming a coalition to repeal and amend the Patriot Act, which these organizations depicted as an assault on the civil liberties of Americans, particularly Muslims. Seven months earlier (on July 14, 2002), MPAC National Director Ahmed Younis had stated that "if Thomas Jefferson or Madison or the like were alive today, they would go to John Ashcroft's house and just shoot him." (Ashcroft was the Attorney General who sought to enforce the Patriot Act.)

MPAC claims that Islam is a religion of peace and moderation, and contends that Muslim extremists are no more numerous or dangerous than fundamentalists in any other faith. "There are radical Christian, Jewish and Hindu movements, too," says MPAC, "which are also capable of slaughtering innocents." On occasion, MPAC has publicly condemned Islamic suicide bombings. These condemnations, however, are invariably accompanied by endorsements of Muslim "resistance" and "armed struggle" which MPAC frames as justified retribution against prior Israeli or Western transgressions.

Holding Israel entirely responsible for the "pattern of violence" in the Middle East, MPAC asserts that Hezbollah "could be called a liberation movement." The Council likens Hezbollah members to American "freedom fighters hundreds of years ago whom the British regarded as terrorists." In a November 1997 speech at the University of Pennsylvania, MPAC Co-Founder and Executive Director Salam Al-Marayati steadfastly refused to call Hezbollah a terrorist organization; he justified the existence of Hamas as a political entity and a provider of social programs and "educational operations"; and he equated *jihad* with the sentiments of the American statesman Patrick Henry, whose "Give me liberty or give me death" declaration was, in Al-Marayati's view, "a way of looking at the term *jihad* from an American perspective." In a 1999 position paper, MPAC justified Hezbollah's deadly 1983 bombing of the American Marine barracks in

Lebanon as a "military operation" rather than a terrorist attack. As Maher Hathout puts it: "Hezbollah is fighting for freedom, an organized army, limiting its operations against military people, this is a legitimate target against occupation. ... this is legitimate, this is an American value -- freedom and liberty."

MPAC's worldview is further revealed by its many additional public statements on a wide array of issues and events:

> According to MPAC: "Israel was established by terrorism"; its founding "involved the unjust and illegal usurpation of Muslim and Christian land and rights"; and "to recognize the legitimacy of that crime is a crime in itself."
>
> MPAC characterizes Israel as a "racist, chauvinistic and militaristic" state that is prosecuting "a war to steal land from Palestinians, to decimate their leadership, to humiliate the Palestinian people."
>
> Condemning Israel's "apartheid-like ideology," MPAC warns: "History shows that Muslim and Christian religious rights are not safe under Israeli occupation."
>
> Israelis are "the worst terrorists in the world," says MPAC, "... Yet Israel is not found on the list of state sponsors of terrorism in the [U.S.] State Department Report on Terrorism."
>
> MPAC co-sponsored pro-Palestinian rallies in the fall of 2000, where MPAC speakers chanted "Khaybar, Khaybar, oh Jews, the Army of Muhammed is coming for you!" The rally featured literature and many placards calling for the annihilation of the Jews and Israel.
>
> A few hours after the 9/11 terrorist attacks, MPAC Co-Founder Salam Al-Marayati told a Los Angeles talk radio audience: "If we're going to look at suspects, we should look at the groups that benefit the most from these kinds of incidents, and I think we should put the state of Israel on the suspect list because I think this diverts attention from what's happening in the Palestinian territories so that they can go on with their aggression and occupation and apartheid policies."
>
> On November 30, 2002, MPAC Vice Chairman Aslam Abdullah said: "Those who are part of the political Zionist movement in America ... know it very well that without the support of the United States ... their country, namely Israel, would not be able to pursue its apartheid and racist policies in the Middle East. They will use every means possible to ensure that American administration stays on their side. They will create false enemies, they will distort facts, they will manipulate events; and they will concoct and fabricate lies. They have taken America hostage."
>
> MPAC was a signatory to a MAY 20, 2004 Joint Muslims/Arab-American Statement on Israeli Violence in Gaza, which "strongly condemn[ed]" Israel's "indiscriminate killings of innocent Palestinians, including many children," and its "demolition of Palestinian homes" -- but made no mention of Arab terrorism.
>
> On March 23, 2005, MPAC National Director Ahmed Younis spoke at a Muslim Students' Association-sponsored event, where he explained that because Adolf Eichmann was himself a Jew, it could accurately be said that Jews had killed themselves in the Holocaust.
>
> MPAC endorsed a November 1, 2001 document characterizing the 9/11 attacks as a legal matter to be addressed by criminal-justice procedures rather than military means. Ascribing the hijackers' motives to alleged social injustices against which they were protesting, this document called on the United States "to promote fundamental rights around the world."
>
> MPAC speakers regularly complain that the U.S. is "dominated" by Zionists and favors Jews over Muslims.
>
> Opposed to efforts to shut down Islamic charities that fund terrorism -- alleging that such efforts interfere with freedom of religion and the exercise of the Muslim obligation to give to charity -- MPAC states that the U.S. government should instead investigate what it terms Jewish "terrorists"

like the Jewish Defense League. The Council signed and sponsored a petition to reinstate the assets of Hamas' charitable front, the Holy Land Foundation for Relief and Development, after it was designated as a front for terrorist financing.

According to MPAC, "A major threat to the safety of the Muslim community is the Islam-bashing that has been very evident since 9/11. There has been a steady stream of attacks on the *Quran* ... These attacks are vicious, mean-spirited, and politically motivated. ... [T]he most sustained and vitriolic [attacks] are from right-wing Christian groups led by Jerry Falwell and Pat Robertson."

The MPAC 2002 Annual Banquet featured Ali Al-Mazrui, a SUNY-Binghamton professor who said: "There is also suspicion that some members of the Bush administration in collusion with Israel are more than ready to plunge the Middle East into turmoil in the hope that the final outcome would be to the territorial advantage of Israel and the strategic advantage of the United States. All this is part of the emerging external sadism of the United States, a readiness to hurt others abroad."

In a May 7, 2004 statement, MPAC said: "The scandal of Abu Ghraib was not an isolated incident but a manifestation of hate rooted in a distortion of American culture. The soldiers charged for torturing and sexually humiliating Iraqi prisoners were reflecting, among other things, an irrational hatred against Arabs and Muslims. Hatred in Abu Ghraib is inextricably linked with hatred increasingly fostered by some elements of our government, our media, and other major national institutions."

After a series of arrests made in connection with an August 2006 airline terror scare in London, President Bush called the uncovered plot "a stark reminder that this nation is at war with Islamic fascists who will use any means to destroy those of us who love freedom, to hurt our nation." MPAC spokeswoman Edina Lekovic reacted, "When the people we need most in the fight against terrorism, American Muslims, feel alienated by the President's characterization of these supposed terrorists, that does more damage than good."

In September 2005, MPAC joined with the anti-war organization Code Pink for Peace to sponsor a Culver City, California event promoting a new book by UC-Irvine professor Mark LeVine, who contends that an "Axis of Empathy" is the only strategy that can bring about a long-term solution to the war between radical Islam and the West. MPAC has also worked closely with International ANSWER, which has intimate ties to Ramsey Clark's International Action Center and the Marxist-Leninist Workers World Party.

MUSLIM STUDENTS' ASSOCIATION OF THE U.S. AND CANADA (MSA)

P.O. Box 18612
Washington, DC
20036
Phone :703-820-7900
Fax :703-820-7888
URL: http://www.msa-natl.org/Network of some 150 campus Muslim Students' Associations

A key lobbying organization for the Wahhabi sect of Islam

Established in January 1963 at the University of Illinois Urbana-Champaign, the Muslim Students' Association of the United States and Canada, or MSA (also known as MSA National) currently has chapters on nearly 240 college campuses across North America. (The relationship between MSA National and the individual university chapters is not a fixed hierarchy, but rather a loose connection. Thus the policies and views of the national organization may differ from those of some of the local chapters.)

Founded by members of the Muslim Brotherhood, MSA's mission is "to serve the best interest of Islam and Muslims in the United States and Canada so as to enable them to practice Islam as a complete way of life." Offshoots of MSA include the Islamic Medical Association, the Muslim Arab Youth Association, the Association of Muslim Social Scientists, the Islamic Circle of North America, and the Islamic Society of North America.

According to author and Islam expert Stephen Schwartz, MSA is a key lobbying organization for the Wahhabi sect of Islam. From its inception, MSA had close links with the extremist Muslim World League, whose chapters' websites have featured not only Osama bin Laden's propaganda, but also publicity-recruiting campaigns for Wahhabi subversion of the Chechen struggle in Russia. MSA solicited donations for the Holy Land Foundation for Relief and Development, whose assets the U.S. government seized in December 2001 because that organization was giving financial support to the terrorist group Hamas. MSA also has strong ties to the World Assembly of Muslim Youth.

Charging that U.S. foreign policy is driven by militaristic imperialism, MSA steadfastly opposes the American military incursions into both Afghanistan and Iraq. The organization is also harshly critical of Israel's allegedly oppressive policies *vis a vis* the Palestinian people residing in the West Bank and Gaza. In MSA's view, for example, the anti-terrorist security fence that Israel has built in the West Bank is an illegal "apartheid wall" that violates the civil and human rights of Palestinians.

An influential member of International ANSWER's steering committee, MSA maintains a large presence at ANSWER-sponsored demonstrations. By supporting ANSWER, MSA tacitly endorses the agendas of the Marxist-Leninist Workers World Party which dominates ANSWER. At a March 15, 2003 anti-war rally in San Francisco, MSA representatives manned several booths where they displayed and distributed anti-Israel publications, banners, and placards. Many of these items contained the word "Israel" with the "s" replaced by a swastika; others likened a swastika to the Star of David.

Local chapters of MSA were signatories to a February 20, 2002 document, composed by the radical group Refuse & Resist (a creation of the Revolutionary Communist Party's C. Clark Kissinger), condemning military tribunals and the detention of immigrants apprehended in connection with post-9/11 terrorism investigations. The document read, in part: "[T]hey [the U.S. government] are coming for the Arab, Muslim and South Asian immigrants. ... The recent 'disappearances,' indefinite detention, the round-ups, the secret military tribunals, the denial of legal representation, evidence kept a secret from the accused, the denial of any due process for Arab, Muslim, South Asians and others, have chilling similarities to a police state."

MSA strongly opposes the Patriot Act, which it describes as an "infamous" piece of legislation. The organization's chapters across the United States have similarly denounced virtually every other national security initiative implemented by the U.S. government since the 9/11 attacks.

MSA chose not to endorse or participate in the May 14, 2005 "Free Muslims March Against Terror," an event whose stated purpose was to "send a message to the terrorists and extremists that their days are numbered ... [and to send] a message to the people of the Middle East, the Muslim world and all people who seek freedom, democracy and peaceful coexistence that we support them."

MSA's President as of September 2006 was Mohamed Sheibani, a fourth-year student attending the University of Ottawa; from 2003-2004, he served as President of the Muslim Youth of Ottawa.

Noteworthy news items related to MSA include the following:

On October 22, 2000, Ahmed Shama, then-president of the UCLA Muslim Students' Association, led a crowd of demonstrators at the Israeli consulate in chants of "Death to Israel!" and "Death to the Jews!" One guest speaker at the event was Hamid Ayloush, a member of the Council on American-Islamic Relations (CAIR), which co-sponsored the rally. In his speech, Ayloush solicited contributions for the aforementioned Holy Land Foundation.

At a January 21, 2001 MSA event, guest speaker Imam Abdul Alim Musa declared: "If you were to say that the Soviet Union [would be] wiped off the face of the earth ... people would have thought you were crazy, right? The people of Afghanistan didn't have the intellect or historical knowledge to know that they wasn't supposed to wipe out the Soviet Union, is that right? ... We saw the fall of one so-called superpower; Old Sam [the U.S.] is next."

In recent years, MSA members at UCLA raised money for Hamas and Hezbollah terrorists at their annual "Anti-Zionist Week."

In March 2003, speaker Muammad Faheed told an MSA meeting at Queensborough Community College in New York, "The only relationship you should have with America is to topple it!"

At its Annual Conference in 2003, the Iowa Muslim Student Association invited, as a guest speaker, CAIR Executive Director Nihad Awad, who had told a college audience in 1994, "I am a supporter of the Hamas movement."

The University of Southern California MSA invited Taliban ambassador Sayyid Hashimi to speak on campus six months before 9/11.

The MSA chapter at California State University Northridge held a fundraiser for Islamic Relief, an organization that received a $50,000 contribution from a pro- Osama bin Laden front group based in Canada.

In 2002, James Madison University's MSA sponsored a "Jihad" panel that included Dr. Abdulrahman Hijazi, who had once extolled an Islamic suicide bomber as a "martyr" whose actions were animated by a hope of securing "the mercy of Allah" by means of "one of the greatest good deeds, which is *jihad.*"

In 2003, University of Idaho MSA President Sami Omar Al-Hussayen was ordered deported because he worked for the Islamic Assembly of North America, which has ties to al Qaeda. While on campus, Al-Hussayen had sought access to a chemical lab containing nuclear material.

A notable former member of MSA is Asan Akbar, an American Muslim extremist who attended the MSA-controlled student mosque at the University of California, Davis. After college, Akbar joined the U.S. Army and, in the early hours of March 23, 2003, he intentionally detonated a grenade amidst sleeping members of his 1st Brigade of the 101st Airborne Division stationed in Kuwait -- killing two and wounding fifteen. Not long before this incident, Akbar, who had been reprimanded for insubordination, reportedly had told his mother that he felt the military was persecuting him because he was a Muslim.

MUSLIM WORLD LEAGUE

http://saudinf.com

Islamic NGO based in Saudi Arabia that advances Wahhabi extremism

Organization's Pakistan office employed al Qaeda operatives

Oversaw Rabita Trust, a charity that knowingly funded terrorist groups

Oversees the World Assembly of Muslim Youth, which teaches religious hatred to Islamic children

Enjoys observer status in the United Nations

Founded in 1962 by Islamic representatives from 22 countries, the Muslim World League (MWL), also called Rabita, is an Islamic non-governmental organization based in Saudi Arabia and controlled and funded by the Saudi government. Its objectives are "to disseminate Islamic Dawah and expound the teachings of Islam," and "to defend Islamic causes in a manner that safeguards the interests and aspirations of Muslims, solves their problems, refutes false allegations against Islam, and repels inimical trends and dogma which the enemies of Islam seek to exploit in order to destroy the unity of Muslims and to sow seeds of doubt in our Muslim brethren." All MWL leaders are of Saudi descent, and the organization's current Secretary General is Dr. Abdullah Al-Turki.

MWL promotes Wahhabism, the extremist form of Islam practiced in Saudi Arabia. In the 1980s, the League's Pakistan office was run by Mohammed Jamal Khalifa, a senior member of the Muslim Brotherhood and brother-in-law of Osama bin Laden. Khalifa was the co-founder of the Benevolence International Foundation and he helped to finance Operation Bojinka, a foiled 1995 plot that would have simultaneously detonated bombs aboard eleven U.S.-bound airliners, blowing them up in mid-flight over the Pacific Ocean and the South China Sea.

In addition, two members of an al Qaeda sleeper cell based in Boston worked at MWL's Pakistan office. One worker, Nabil al-Marabh, number 27 on the FBI's list of wanted terrorists, was arrested by federal agents in Detroit shortly after 9/11; it was reported that he "intended to martyr himself in an attack against the United States." The other operative, Raed Hijazi, was apprehended and tried in Jordan on charges that he planned to blow up a hotel filled with Americans and Israelis on New Year's Eve in 2000.

In his book *The Two Faces of Islam*, Stephen Schwartz reports: "In 2000, the Muslim World League (a provider of funds to Osama bin Laden) hosted 100 prominent American Islamic personalities on *hajj* [a pilgrimmage to Mecca]. They were accompanied by a delegation of 60 Latin American 'academics and specialists.' All expenses for the latter were paid by Prince Bandar, Saudi ambassador to the United States."

MWL at one time oversaw Rabita Trust, a now-defunct charity whose professed purpose was to give aid to Afghani refugees in Pakistan. The Trust came under investigation by the U.S. Senate Finance Committee based on evidence that it had knowingly funded terrorist groups.

Today MWL oversees the World Assembly of Muslim Youth (WAMY), one of the vehicles through which the Saudi government finances Islamic extremism and international terrorism.

In January 2006, MWL called for United Nations Secretary General Kofi Annan to denounce a derisive cartoon of the Prophet Mohammed that had recently appeared in Danish and Norwegian newspapers. A letter sent by MWL Secretary General Al-Turki to Annan noted that Muslims around the world were offended by the cartoon and that international laws "prohibited scorning religions and other hatred-provoking practices."

MWL is an observer member of the Organization of Islamic Conferences, an inter-governmental coalition dedicated to "liberating Jerusalem and Al-Aqsa from Zionist occupation." MWL also has "Category A" observer status in the United Nations, and consultative status in the UN Economic and Social Council. Moreover, MWL is a member of the UN Educational, Scientific, and Cultural Organization (UNESCO) and the UN International Children's Emergency Fund (UNICEF). The League is also a founding member of the International Supreme Council for Dawah and Relief, an Islamic recruiting center based in Cairo.

MUSLIM YOUTH OF NORTH AMERICA (MYNA)

P.O. Box 4647
Chicago, IL
60680

Phone :866-566-6962
URL: http://www.mynaevents.com/Charitable organization affiliated with the Islamic Society of North America

Affiliated with the Islamic Society of North America (ISNA), Muslim Youth of North America (MYNA) defines itself as a charitable organization "dedicated to youth programming and issues." Geared to youngsters aged 12 to 18, MYNA's goals are to: "strengthen the faith and practice of Muslim youth, allowing them to develop an Islamic identity"; "help Muslim youth and communities plan and carry out educational training, and spiritual, recreational, and charitable Islamic activities"; "develop Islamic leadership for the future"; and "establish a positive and healthy image of Islam in North America."

MYNA was the brainchild of ISNA's Youth Committee, which in 1985 proposed the creation of a continental organization for young Muslims. The ISNA policy-making body endorsed the idea, and as a result MYNA was formally approved and introduced at the First Annual Muslim Youth Winter Conference in December of 1985. The first programs sponsored by MYNA were held at ISNA conferences and conventions.

According to a former official of the Indian government, MYNA is believed to be closely associated with Tablighi Jamaat, a jihadist organization that serves as a recruiting ground for al Qaeda. MYNA's past conferences have featured such radicals as Siraj Wahhaj, who is believed to have been a co-conspirator in the 1993 bombing of the World Trade Center.

MYNA's National Advisor is Riyad Shamma, a member of the the Majlis Youth Committee that oversees the operations of ISNA's Youth Programming and Services Department.
MYNA's Chairman Omar J. Siddiqui is also a member of the ISNA Board of Directors.

Some MYNA members recently initiated "MYNA Raps," a project of Muslim youth "who write songs about Islam and the struggle as young Muslims in America" (sic). MYNA Raps has produced a few tapes featuring the rap songs of numerous contributors. These tapes have been sold internationally, with all proceeds going directly to MYNA, helping to fund the organization's camps and conferences.
MYNA Raps artists use no wind or string instruments in their compositions. Says the project's website: "Some scholars such as Sheikh Yousef al-Qaradhawi say that if the lyrics of the music is Islamic, then any type of musical instrument is permissible. However there are others that say that wind and string instruments must be avoided and only percussion (drums) instruments can be used. There other scholars that say that

only the duff (tambourine) can be used. Even others say no instruments at all are allowed. Since this is such a hot debate, we tried to use the least amount of instruments possible and still give the sound most American Muslim youth are used to. ... We pray to Allah that our intentions are accepted in this matter and we have made a correct decision."

MUSLIMS IN AMERICAN PUBLIC SQUARE (MAPS)

Center for Muslim-Christian Understanding
Edmund A. Walsh School of Foreign Service
Georgetown University
37th & "O" Streets NW
Washington, D.C.
20057
Phone :202-687-0291
URL: www.project**maps**.com Georgetown University-based scholarly organization whose membership consisted of numerous individuals involved with radical Islamic organizations

Based within Georgetown University's Center for Muslim-Christian Understanding, Muslims in American Public Square (MAPS) was a five-year initiative (1999-2004) whose mission was to "examine the role and contribution of Muslims in the American civic life." MAPS's research on this topic was funded by a $1.25 million grant from Pew Charitable Trusts.

MAPS was composed of numerous scholars, some of whom were involved in radical Islamic organizations such as the Council on American-Islamic Relations, the American Muslim Alliance, the International Institute of Islamic Thought, and the United Association for Studies and Research.

Notable members of the MAPS Advisory Board were professors John Esposito and Ali al-Mazrui. Other scholars affiliated with MAPS included Ihsan Bagby and Aminah Beverly McCloud.

In May 2001, MAPS sponsored a National Leadership Focus Group which included the participation of representatives from the Muslim American Society, the Islamic Society of North America, the Islamic Circle of North America, the Muslim Alliance of North America, the Islamic Center of America, the Council on American-Islamic Relations, the American Muslim Council, the American Muslim Alliance, the Muslim Public Affairs Council, the Muslim Students' Association of the U.S. and Canada, and the Islamic Assembly of North America. Among the representatives in attendance were Muzammil Siddiqi, Wallace Deen Muhammad, Abdullah Idris Ali, Zulfiqar Ali Shah, Shaker Elsayed, Souheil Ghannouchi, Ihsan Bagby, Eric Vickers, Nihad Awad, and John Esposito.

MAPS's major projects included:

(a) publishing two volumes wherein thirty commissioned scholars discussed "research on the participation, contribution and role of the Muslim community in American civic life."
(b) publishing a *Directory of Muslim Civic Organizations and Centers/Mosques*, and *Who's Who Among American Muslims*: The latter includes biographical information on approximately 1,000 Muslim civic leaders in America who have achieved prominence in public affairs, academia, science and technology, media, business and commerce, sports and entertainment, and civic organizations.

(c) arranging four one-day regional seminars in New York, Atlanta, Chicago, and Los Angeles, to bring commissioned scholars together with Muslim religious and community leaders to exchange ideas on Muslim participation in American civic life

(d) conducting a national survey to gain insight into the views of Islamic centers/mosques, community leaders, and Muslim congregants:

The Executive Summary of this survey, published in 2004, states the following:

"In a few short years [since 2000], [American Muslims] have undergone massive political shifts ... Muslims are a politically active group. A high proportion of registered Muslim voters (95%) plan to vote in national elections ... [There has been a] dramatic shift away from the Republican Party and President Bush versus the 2000 election. ... In the post-9/11 world, Muslim identity is key in voting decisions. Nearly seven-in-ten Muslim voters say being a Muslim is important in their voting decision. ... [T]hree-in-five American Muslims are dissatisfied with the way things are going in American society today ... Muslims also have a strong desire for political unity within their religion. ...A majority of American Muslims say that American Muslims should vote as a bloc for president this year. ... Muslims overwhelmingly back changing U.S. policy in the Mideast as the best way to way wage the war on terror. Muslims would prefer the government backed a Palestinian state and was less supportive of Israel. ... Slightly more than a third of Muslims say that in their own experience, Americans have been respectful of Muslims, but that American society overall is disrespectful and intolerant of their culture."

NATIONAL COUNCIL OF ARAB AMERICANS

National Council of Arab Americans (NCA)
1719 Jefferson Blvd,
Oakland, CA 94612;
Ph. 510-268-8595
Fx. 510-268-8592.
www.**arab**-american.ne

Activist Arab American organization
Coalition Partner with International ANSWER
Radical, anti-Israel and anti-American group

Established on November 29, 2003 in Washington, DC by a nationwide group of activists, the National Council of Arab Americans (NCAA) is a consortium of grassroots organizations professing a desire to help Arab Americans assert their "national presence as a community from coast to coast." "Our belonging in the United States," says NCAA, "can only be complete if our Arab heritage, culture, and identity are fully respected and cherished." Viewing the U.S. as a nation rife with discrimination against ethnic minorities, NCAA calls for an end to the "collective criminalization of Arab Americans and Muslims," and fights for what it considers the currently unprotected "civil rights and liberties" of that demographic. NCAA currently has chapters in New York, Los Angeles, San Diego, Sacramento, Chicago, and Massachusetts.

Asserting that "We are unequivocal in our rejection of war," the Council's 2003 anti-war manifesto calls for America's immediate, unilateral withdrawal from Iraq, and exhorts the U.S. to renounce its "militarism and colonial expansions." Any suggestion that Western nations may sometimes have a right to intervene in Middle Eastern affairs is anathema to NCAA, which issued a pre-Iraq War declaration that read: "Regardless of the source, the notion that the people of Iraq 'need some form of Western intervention,' even if temporary, to secure their very own stability is overtly racist and a real threat to civilization."

The NCAA's 2003 manifesto is also decidedly hostile to Israel -- advocating the suspension of all forms of economic, political, and military support for that nation, and demanding that Palestinians be granted a full "right of return" without further delay. Moreover, NCAA has allied itself with International ANSWER to campaign against the construction of the Israeli security fence in the West Bank, which they dub an "Apartheid Wall." NCAA's Chairman and National Coordinator is the radical Palestinian activist Elias Rashmawi.

The National Council of Arab Americans currently oversees the following projects:

Defense of Civil Rights in Academia: This initiative is aimed at "proactively defending and securing the rights of the Arab American academic community, students, faculty and staff." Notable supporters of the program include Hatem Bazian, Mazin Qumsiyeh, Michael Shehadeh, Khalid Turaani.

Legal Defense Project: This consists of a Legal Assistance Program "aimed at networking attorneys with those in need of legal consultation"; a Legal Hotline that provides information in Arabic and English "on immigration policies and procedures that may directly affect the Arab-American community"; a Volunteer Legal Advice program where participating attorneys make themselves available for free initial consultations with Arab American clients; a Civil Rights Defense Project "to safeguard and promote the civil rights of the more than 1.2 million Arab Americans living in the United States"; and a Nationwide Speakers Bureau "devoted to bringing civil rights issues faced by Arab Americans to the fore."

Al-Kitab Educational Project: This program promotes education about Arabs and Arab Americans on the K-12 academic levels. This is done through textbooks, curricula, and educational materials. The program also sponsors seminars for Arab American parents.
Arab American History Project: "Under the supervision of an experienced committee of academics and community activist, 100 students across the country will engage in documenting the experience of 100 personalities representing the cumulative experience of our people in the US."

On September 13, 2005, NCAA co-sponsored (along with the Traprock Peace Center, the International Socialist Review, and The Nation Institute, among others) a Boston appearance by British Member of Parliament George Galloway, who, during the course of his address, condemned American support for Israel, praised antiwar activist Cindy Sheehan, laid blame for the Hurricane Katrina disaster on President Bush, impugned America for having "created the swamp of radical Islam" from which the 9/11 attackers arose, blamed the Bush administration's War on Terror for creating "hundreds of thousands" of "new terrorists"; and accused the U.S. of "going around the world occupying countries and stealing their things."

Other speakers that evening included the following: (a) Eriko Nagai (of the counter-recruitment group Campus Anti-War Network) said that both race and class played a major role in determining the fate of people in post-Katrina New Orleans; (b) Annie Zirin (artist, schoolteacher, and International Socialist Organization member) made a similar charge; (c) Boston City Councilman Chuck Turner said, "We need to acknowledge the obscenity that America is. We need to acknowledge that [in the eyes of] people around the world ... we are obscene, we are a joke ..."; (d) Brown University's socialist professor of English Literature William Keach urged the crowd to confront the "war criminals in the Oval Office"; and (e) NCAA member Naseer Aruri alleged that the existence of Israel, coupled with U.S. support for the Jewish state, had created the "so-called terrorists" of the Muslim world. Aruri castigated the Bush administration for denying terrorist suspects their "human rights," housing them in "gulags," and allegedly creating many more terrorists than had existed before the invasions of Afghanistan and Iraq.

On August 12, 2006, NCAA participated in a large-scale protest against "the U.S.-Israeli assault" on "Lebanon and Palestine" -- a reference to Israel's then-raging war against Hezbollah and Hamas, organizations that had recently initiated a two-front attack on Israel by kidnapping and murdering a number of Israeli soldiers, and then had perpetuated the conflict by firing thousands of rockets into the midst of Israeli cities. The protesters chanted, "Occupation is a crime, from Lebanon to Palestine!" Other participating organizations included International ANSWER, the Muslim American Society, the Council on American-Islamic Relations, the National Lawyers Guild, the Green Party, Project Islamic Hope, Women in Black, the Islamic Shura Council of Southern California, Al-Awda, the Alliance for Just and Lasting Peace in the Philippines, Korean Americans for Peace, the Party for Socialism and Liberation, and the Farabundo Martí National Liberation Front (FMLN) of El Salvador.

That same day, NCAA Vice Chair Mounzer Sleiman addressed more than 30,000 demonstrators at a parallel rally on the streets around the White House. His fellow speakers included Ramsey Clark, Mahdi Bray, Mara Verheyden-Hilliard, Brian Becker and Dr. Clovis Maksoud.

NATIONAL COUNCIL OF CHURCHES (NCC)

475 Riverside Drive
Suite 880
New York, NY
10115
Phone :212-870-2227
URL: http://www.ncccusa.org/Largest coalition of leftist religious denominations in the United States

Has long record of financial support for Communist regimes

At its founding in 1950, the New York City-based National Council of Churches (NCC) absorbed its predecessor, the communist front-group known as the Federal Council of Churches. At one time an overt supporter of the communist cause, NCC has today recast itself as a leading representative of the "religious Left." It claims a membership of 35 Protestant, Anglican and Orthodox Christian denominations, and some 50 million members in over 140,000 congregations.

In the 1950s and 1960s, under the rubric of charity, NCC provided financial assistance to the communist regimes in Yugoslavia and Poland, funneling money to both through its relief agency, the Church World Service. In the 1970s, working with its Geneva-based parent organization, the World Council of Churches (WCC), NCC earmarked money for Soviet-sponsored guerrilla incursions - which it characterized as "liberation movements" - into Zimbabwe, Namibia, Mozambique, and Angola. Other beneficiaries of NCC philanthropy included El Salvador's Sandinista guerrillas.

A staunch supporter of Communist Cuba, NCC has pushed for the United States to normalize relations with the Castro regime since 1968. In 1977, after heading a delegation of American church officials to Cuba, the Methodist bishop James Armstrong, who would be elected NCC President the following year, stated: "There is a significant difference between situations where people are imprisoned for opposing regimes designed to perpetuate inequities, as in Chile and Brazil, for example, and situations were people are imprisoned for opposing regimes designed to remove inequities, as in Cuba."

An advocate of "liberation theology" in the 1980s, NCC was silent about the depredations of Ethiopia's Marxist government, which left 10,000 dead and shuttered 200 churches. Nor did it criticize the Soviet Union's 1978 invasion of Afghanistan. Not until after the Soviet Union's collapse did NCC speak out on the subject of Communist oppression, when in 1993 Joan Brown Campbell, a former NCC General Secretary, said: "We did not understand the depth of the suffering of Christians under Communism. And we failed to really cry out under the Communist oppression."

Nonetheless, to this day NCC's human rights charges are aimed mostly at the U.S. and Israel. One study, conducted by the Institute of Religion and Democracy in September 2004, found that "of the seven human rights criticisms [NCC] issued from 2000-2003, Israel received four, the United States two, and Sudan one."

NCC was a signatory to a November 1, 2001 document characterizing the 9/11 terrorist attacks as a legal matter to be addressed by criminal-justice procedures rather than military reprisals. Ascribing the hijackers' motives to alleged social injustices against which they were protesting, this document explained that "security and justice are mutually reinforcing goals that ultimately depend upon the promotion of all human rights for all people," and called on the United States "to promote fundamental rights around the world."

NCC claims that the Patriot Act, instituted shortly after 9/11, tramples on the civil liberties of Americans. "We believe it is time for us to stop and think about where we should draw the line in our search for security," said the NCC in 2004. "... Only a self-obsessed society pursues security at all costs."

On December 8, 2003, NCC General Secretary Robert Edgar asked the Department of Defense for permission to send a small interfaith delegation to visit the prisoners being held at the U.S. Naval Base at Guantanamo Bay. When his request was denied, Edgar vowed that the Council would "continue to advocate for the due process rights of Guantanamo Bay detainees." On January 14, 2004, NCC was part of what it called "a broad coalition of domestic and international religious, legal and human rights organizations that filed a friend of the court brief with the U.S. Supreme Court ... asserting that foreign nationals being held at the U.S. Naval Base at Guantanamo Bay have the right to challenge the legality of their detention."

Citing the counsel of the New Testament — "Blessed are the peacemakers, for they will be called children of God" (Matthew 5:9) — in 1991, the NCC played a central role in opposing the first Gulf War, claiming that the risks of such an action were "out of proportion to any conceivable gain." Its assessment of the second Gulf War was identical. In January 2003, NCC's President, the Methodist Bishop Thomas L. Hoyt, Jr., joined 46 other religious leaders in signing a letter to President Bush expressing "continuing uneasiness about the moral justification for war on Iraq." NCC is a member organization of the Win Without War and United for Peace and Justice anti-war coalitions.

In February 2005 NCC condemned Israel for having "established hundreds upon hundreds of checkpoints, roadblocks, and gates across the Occupied Territories, making daily life and travel extremely difficult for ordinary Palestinians." Proclaiming that "[s]tereotypes of all Palestinians as terrorists must be broken," the Council explained that "[t]he crushing burden of Israel's occupation of Palestinian territory contributes to deep anger and violent resistance, which contributes to fear throughout Israeli society."

In March 2006 NCC General Secretary Robert Edgar joined other prominent Christian and Jewish religious leaders in Washington, DC to support legislation that would legalize illegal aliens in the United States.

While proclaiming the virtues of the Kyoto Protocol in 1998, NCC's then-General Secretary, Rev. Joan Brown Campbell, insisted that an acceptance of the radical environmentalist movement's assertions about global warming ought to be made a "litmus test for the faith community." In 2002 NCC was a party to "What Would Jesus Drive?" — a campaign that exhorted car manufactures to embrace stricter emissions standards.

NCC has been plagued by a history of financial mismanagement. The organization's leadership has long spent beyond its means, and gifts from member denominations dropped throughout the 1980s and 1990s. By 1998, the Council faced a deficit of $1.5 million. The following year, its expenses exceeded total revenues by some $4 million. These budgetary shortfalls compelled NCC to appeal to its member denominations—seven of which account for 90 percent of NCC's budget—to step up their contributions. For instance, in 1999 NCC requested that its chief sponsor, the United Methodist Church, increase its yearly contribution of $2.5 million by an additional $700,000. But the Council's member donations nonetheless continued to drop -- by 40 percent between 2001 and 2005.

In an effort to offset this decline, General Secretary Edgar sought out new income from secular foundations and other non-church sources. As a result of his efforts, NCC's "other" income grew from $800,000 in fiscal year 2000-2001, to $2.9 million in 2004-2005. During the fiscal year ending in June 2005, NCC received slightly more money from non-church sources than from its member communions.

Recent contributors to NCC include the Sierra Club, TrueMajority, ACORN, People For the American Way, MoveOn.org, and the Connect US Network, which has ties to George Soros' Open Society Institute. Foundation contributions to NCC have come from the Annie E. Casey Foundation, the Beldon Fund, the Carnegie Corporation of New York, the Lilly Endowment, the Rasmussen Foundation, the Rockefeller Brothers Fund, the W.K. Kellogg Foundation, the United Nations Foundation, the Tides Foundation, and the Ford Foundation.

According to the Institute on Religion and Democracy (IRD), the Council "is more dependent financially upon the Ford Foundation than upon 32 of its 35 member denominations." Says IRD: "Most of the NCC-supporting groups share several characteristics: (a) They are not affiliated with an NCC member communion, or any other church body; (b) Christian unity and common witness to the Gospel of Jesus Christ do not appear to be among their principal aims; (c) They have a much stronger interest in addressing social and political issues; (d) Their positions on those issues, insofar as they can be discerned, lean overwhelmingly toward the left."

In August 2007, NCC's Interfaith Relations office sponsored an Ecumenical Study Seminar for "reflecting and learning together" at the 44th annual convention of the Islamic Society of North America (ISNA), held in Rosemont, Illinois.

NATIONAL LAWYERS GUILD (NLG)

143 Madison Avenue, 4th Floor
New York, NY
10016
Phone :212-679-5100
URL: http://www.nlg.org/Active affiliate of the International Association of Democratic Lawyers, which served as a Soviet front group during the Cold War

Seeks to weaken America's intelligence-gathering agencies

The National Lawyers Guild (NLG) states that it is "dedicated to the need for basic and progressive change in the structure of our [American] political and economic system." Identifying "economic and social justice" as its ultimate concerns, the organization aims to "eliminate racism"; "safeguard and strengthen the rights of workers, women, farmers and minority groups"; and "maintain and protect our civil rights and liberties in the face of persistent attacks upon them." With more than 8,000 members, the NLG has chapters in every major U.S. city and in nearly every state; it also has tens of thousands of active supporters worldwide.

The NLG was founded in 1937 by Communist Party USA attorneys and liberal fellow-travelers as a pro-New Deal, progressive alternative to the segregated and comparatively conservative American Bar Association (ABA). Many have alleged that the Communist International (Comintern) spearheaded the Guild's creation. While there were elements within the early Guild that were dedicated communist revolutionaries -- NLG founding member David Freedman candidly advocated socialism as a desirable alternative to American capitalism -- these were by no means the only actors within the fledgling organization: future Supreme Court Justices, New Deal supporters, civil libertarians, and other liberals were among its earliest members.

A watershed moment for the organization occurred in its third year, when its National Executive Board chose not to adopt an amendment to the NLG Constitution condemning dictatorship and supporting democracy -- an amendment its Communist organizers called "divisive." During the McCarthy era, Guild members represented the Hollywood Ten, the Rosenbergs, and thousands of victims of what the NLG termed "the anti-communist hysteria."

In a 1950 report titled "Report on the National Lawyers Guild: Legal Bulwark of the Communist Party," the House Committee on Un-American Activities Committee (HUAC) declared: "The real aims of the National Lawyers Guild, as demonstrated conclusively by its activities, ... are not specified in its constitution or statement of avowed purpose. In order to attract non-Communists to serve as a cover for its actual purpose as an appendage to the Communist Party, the National Lawyers Guild poses benevolently as 'a professional organization which shall function as an effective social force in the service of the people.'" The report accused the Guild of attacking the FBI as "part of an overall Communist strategy aimed at weakening our nation's defenses against the international Communist conspiracy." The document also recommended that Guild members be barred from federal employment, and that the ABA consider whether it should permit its members to belong to the Guild in light of the latter's "subversive" character.

Decimated by the HUAC report, and viewed by many non-members with deep distrust, the Guild survived the 1950s by limiting the scope of its projects and otherwise concentrating on issues related to the practice of law rather than to societal transformation.

As the 1960s began, the Guild focused heavily on fighting for civil rights for black Americans. (One of the NLG's black members, John Conyers, was elected to Congress in 1964.) The Guild defended rioters and others involved in civil unrest as the 1960s progressed, and "helped" the U.S. war effort in Vietnam by encouraging young men to become draft evaders and then defending them. NLG lawyers were active in defending those arrested during the 1968 Chicago Democratic Convention riots and members of the Black Panther Party. Guild President Victor Rabinowitz (1967-1970) -- a Communist who represented Fidel Castro's Cuban dictatorship -- openly advocated a Marxist future. Repudiating the idea that incremental reforms were sufficient for committed leftists, the NLG's 1967 Statement of Policy and Program argued that "basic structural changes in society" were needed.

Prominent Guild member Arthur Kinoy argued that the proper role of the radical lawyer was to facilitate the coming anti-capitalist revolution by weakening the law's ability to function effectively against law-breaking radicals. Future Guild President Paul Harris quoted Lenin in arguing that a successful revolution required a "legal struggle" that coincided alongside illegal, militant revolutionary activity. And Doris Brin Walker, who served as NLG President from 1970-1971 (and who would later remark that she was "so proud to be a member of the Communist Party"), eagerly anticipated a "Second American Revolution."

Throughout the Cold War, the NLG embraced pro-Soviet agendas while systematically opposing the foreign policies of the United States. It promoted Marxist "liberation" movements in the 1970s, including the Palestine Liberation Organization (which the Guild recognized as the "sole legitimate representative of the Palestinian people"); the Viet Cong; the African National Congress; pro-Soviet Angolan and Mozambican factions; the Puerto Rican FALN; and the Philippine New People's Army (the military wing of the Communist Party of the Philippines). The Guild also launched an effort to end the U.S. embargo on communist Cuba, a longtime friend of the organization.

In the 1980s the NLG supported the Sandinistas in Nicaragua and the FMLN in El Salvador. It embraced the church-based Sanctuary movement and "began working systematically on immigration issues," spurred by what it called "the need to represent Central American refugees and asylum activists fleeing U.S.-sponsored 'terror.'" The Guild also supported the anti-nuclear movement of the 1980s.

After Iraq invaded Kuwait in 1990, the NLG "mobilized opposition" to Gulf War I. It similarly opposed the second war in Iraq as an "illegal preemptive" invasion of a sovereign state, exhorting Americans to engage in acts of "civil disobedience" to register their outrage. Said the Guild: "U.S. government officials forfeit legitimacy and the power to enforce laws against non-violent trespass and 'disorder' when they pursue policies that result in war crimes."

In 1999, NLG member Chip Berlet, who is also an activist with Morris Dees's Southern Poverty Law Center, described the Guild's saturation with Communist and far-left ideologies: "The cacophony at some [Guild] meetings ... [arises from] debates featuring cadres from Leninist, Trotskyist, Stalinist, and Maoist groups, along with Marxists, anarchists, libertarians, and progressive independents -- interacting with a preponderance of reluctant Democrats -- all intertwined with multiple alternate identities as lawyers, legal workers, labor organizers, tribal sovereignty activists, civil liberties and civil rights advocates, environmentalists, feminists, gay men and lesbians, and people of color."

The NLG today is an active affiliate of the International Association of Democratic Lawyers, which in 1978 the CIA described as "one of the most useful Communist front organizations at the service of the Soviet Communist Party, [an organization that] has so consistently demonstrated its support of Moscow's foreign policy objectives, and is so tied in with other front organizations and the Communist press, that it is difficult for it to pretend that its judgments are fair or relevant to basic legal tenets."

In 2003 the NLG initiated its Korean Peace Project (KPP), which dispatched a delegation to develop "personal and professional relationships" with leaders in North Korea, to "replace demonizing with dialogue," and to determine the "real situation," politically and economically, of life in that country. In a report summarizing their observations in North Korea, the KPP delegates noted that "this was not the Orwellian society George Bush and much of the media is [sic] trying to portray." "The contrast," added the report, "between North Korea and its lack of policeman, and North America in which armed police in bulletproof vests are commonplace, was more than striking -- it was startling. If the presence or absence of armed policemen is a criterion for a free society then it speaks volumes about the nature of the two societies." The report praised North Korea's free health care and education systems, and the fact that capital punishment was nonexistent in its criminal-justice system. It noted that women are not "objectified in the same ways they sometimes are in the West," and observed that "[t]he absence of other [political] parties is not considered a failing, as the entire society is socialist." Chastising the U.S. "for its failure to deal fairly and in good faith" with North Korea, the report stated that "the U.S. government cannot advocate the rule of law and democracy, when it fails to model it itself." The report also recorded a North Korean general's "astute" comment that his country does not "oppose the American people," but only America's "hostile policy and its efforts to exercise control over the whole world and inflict calamity on its people." "Unresolved pain still exists about the Korean war where millions of Koreans were killed," says the Korean Peace Project. "Nearly the entire North, including cities, was leveled to the ground by U.S. bombers."

The Korean Peace Project is in keeping with the NLG's propensity to blame the United States for any international conflicts that arise. Four hours after the 9/11 terrorist attacks, for instance, John Wheat Gibson (the Guild's Texas-Oklahoma Region Co-Vice President) claimed that the U.S. and Israel were most likely responsible for the atrocities of that day.

In July 2006, the NLG's Middle East Subcommittee issued a condemnation of "Israel's crimes against humanity and brutal aggression against Palestine and Lebanon." This subcommittee has formulated a "Resolution to Divest, in Practice and Principle, from Israel"; a "Resolution to Stop and Dismantle the Wall" (a reference to the anti-terrorism barrier constructed in the West Bank); and a "Resolution Affirming the Individual and Collective Palestinian Right of Return." In March 2006 the NLG urged "support for the boycott of Israeli goods."

Running anti-military-recruitment campaigns in U.S. schools, the NLG's Military Law Task Force complains that "an inordinate percent of [America's] wealth is directed away from the citizenry and its social needs, and into a military/industrial clique that saps the wealth of the nation."

The NLG's National Immigration Project seeks "to recognize the contributions of immigrants in this country, to promote fair immigration practices, and to expand the civil and human rights of all immigrants, regardless of their status in the United States." In short, it advocates amnesty for all illegals currently residing in the U.S., and unchecked immigration across open borders henceforth. The Guild further rejects "all deportations and manipulations of the border carried out in the interests of capitalism," encouraging local NLG chapters to "develop training programs and legal clinics to support mass defense efforts against deportations." According to the Guild, government raids against "undocumented working people" constitute "an effort to terrorize and silence immigrant communities."

The NLG endorsed the December 18, 2001 "Statement of Solidarity with Migrants," drawn up by the National Network for Immigrant and Refugee Rights, which called upon the U.S. government to "[r]ecognize the contribution of immigrant workers, students, and families, and [to] end discriminatory policies passed on the basis of legal status in the wake of September 11."

In recent decades, the NLG has stood at the forefront of efforts to weaken America's intelligence-gathering agencies. By effectively pushing such legislation as the Foreign Intelligence Surveillance Act of 1978, the NLG helped limit U.S. law-enforcement and counter-intelligence capabilities. Post-9/11, the NLG launched a national campaign to repeal the Patriot Act -- arguing that the Act's provisions trample on the civil liberties of Americans. The NLG similarly opposes the Domestic Security Enhancement Act and the use of military tribunals for captured combatants in the War on Terror.

In April 2004, the NLG announced that it had joined "a broad coalition of groups" challenging "the executive branch's claim to un-checked wartime powers." Said the organization: "While the [Supreme Court] Justices will not rule on the constitutionality of the hundreds of detainees that are being held at Guantanamo Bay, the National Lawyers Guild believes the U.S. is unlawfully occupying the base because the treaty between the U.S. and Cuba limits its use to a 'coaling or naval station,' and not a prison or a concentration camp. The Lawyers Guild therefore calls for the immediate closure of the concentration camp at Guantanamo Bay and the release of the prisoners. If probable cause exists for charging these prisoners with criminal offenses, they should be charged and immediately be provided with access to legal counsel, human rights organizations and their families."

The San Francisco/Bay Area Chapter of the NLG co-signed a February 20, 2002 document, composed by C. Clark Kissinger's radical group Refuse & Resist, condemning military tribunals and the detention of immigrants apprehended in connection with post-9/11 terrorism investigations. The Guild was also a signatory to a March 17, 2003 letter exhorting members of the U.S. Congress to oppose Patriot Act II, on grounds that it "fail[ed] to respect our time-honored liberties," and "would severely dilute, if not undermine, many basic constitutional rights."

The NLG endorses the Community Resolution to Protect Civil Liberties campaign, a project of the California-based Coalition for Civil Liberties, which seeks to influence city councils to pass resolutions pledging noncompliance with the Patriot Act's provisions. The Guild also endorsed the Civil Liberties Restoration Act of 2004, which was designed to roll back, in the name of protecting civil liberties, vital national-security policies that had been adopted after the 9/11 terrorist attacks.

Following 9/11, the NLG released flyers, posters, and CDs entitled "Know Your Rights," which provided legal advice -- translated into several Middle Eastern languages -- for immigrants contacted by the U.S. government during its anti-terrorism initiatives. These materials advised immigrants to refuse to talk to investigators -- because "[t]he FBI is not just trying to find terrorists, but is gathering information on immigrants and activists who have done nothing wrong."

Consistent with the NLG's view that nonwhite immigrants and minorities are routinely harmed by America's allegedly rampant racism, sexism, and intolerance, the Guild's United People of Color Caucus was created to counter these purported societal defects. The Caucus impugns "the capitalist United States" as a place "where economic prowess is dependent on the furthered and continued subjugation of people of color, women, the poor, queers and other oppressed people."

Rejecting capitalism as a viable economic system, the NLG was a signatory to a May 30, 2000 document denouncing globalization, big business in general, and the World Trade Organization (WTO) in particular. A co-signer was Medea Benjamin -- the leader of Global Exchange.

In recent years, the NLG has defended a number of notorious individuals and organizations:

> On February 17, 2005, the Guild called for a "national day of outrage" to protest the prosecution and conviction of NLG member Lynne Stewart, the self-proclaimed "radical attorney" who had illegally facilitated communication between her incarcerated client Omar Abdel Rahman and his Egypt-based terrorist organization, the Islamic Group. The Guild ascribed Stewart's conviction to a Bush administration effort "to deter lawyers from representing politically unpopular clients, particularly individuals charged with terrorism-related crimes."
>
> The NLG aggressively defended Sami Al-Arian, who for several years was the North American head of the terrorist organization Palestinian Islamic Jihad. (Former NLG Executive Vice President Kit Gage replaced Al-Arian as President of the National Coalition to Protect Political Freedom after al-Arian's February 2003 arrest on a number of terrorism charges.)

- The NLG supports Lori Berenson, a New Yorker who was arrested in 1995 [and was later convicted] in Peru for her active involvement with the terrorist group known as MRTA (or "Tupac Amaru Revolutionary Movement").
- The Guild supports cop-killer Mumia Abu-Jamal (naming him as one of its National Vice Presidents); Symbionese Liberation Army member Sara Jane Olson; and Leonard Peltier, an American Indian Movement activist who was convicted of murdering two FBI agents.
- On June 12, 2006, the NLG denounced an FBI crackdown on domestic terror groups like the Earth Liberation Front and the Animal Liberation Front, complaining that prosecuting such organizations for their use of explosives and high-caliber weapons evidenced a "disturbing trend of targeting protesters engaged in dissent, and in imposing draconian sentences for expressing such dissent."

The Guild also has ties to the onetime Weather Underground terrorist (currently a professor of law) Bernadine Dohrn, who once worked as an NLG staffer.

A member organization of the United for Peace and Justice anti-war coalition, the NLG co-sponsored large-scale anti-war rallies in Washington, DC on October 26, 2002 and April 12, 2003. The Guild partially controls the Los Angeles chapter of the Workers World Party front group, International ANSWER. Additionally, the Guild co-founded the anti-war organization Not in Our Name; other co-founders included the Revolutionary Communist Party, the All-African Peoples Revolutionary Party, Refuse and Resist!, and the International League of Peoples' Struggle.

The NLG has received funding from the Open Society Institute, the John D. & Catherine T. MacArthur Foundation, the Nathan Cummings Foundation, the Overbrook Foundation, and the Ford Foundation.

On October 20, 2006, Professor Marjorie Cohn assumed the presidency of the National Lawyers Guild.

NETUREI KARTA

www.**nk**usa.org

- Ultra-orthodox Jewish group that opposes Israel's existence
- Membership consists of no more than 5,000 people, mainly in Jerusalem and New York
- Has strong links to the PLO and the Palestinian Authority

Neturei Karta (NK), Aramaic for "Guardians of the City," is an ultra-orthodox Jewish group which holds that Israel's existence is "contrary to Jewish law." According to NK, God punished the Jews with exile for their indiscretions, and consequently they are forbidden to establish a Jewish state in the holy land before the coming of the Messiah.

NK was founded in Jerusalem in 1938 when it broke away from another ultra-orthodox group, Agudas Yisorel, over the question of Zionism. Contrary to NK's claim that it represents several hundred thousand orthodox Jews throughout the world, informed estimates place NK membership at no more than 5,000 people, most of them located in Jerusalem and New York.

Declares NK: "Among its [Zionism's] fruits are the persecution of the Palestinian people and the spiritual and physical endangering of the Jewish people"; "[Zionism] encourages treasonous, dual loyalty among unsuspecting Jews throughout the world"; and "The so-called 'state of Israel' stands rejected on religious grounds by the Torah."

A prominent NK member, the Rabbi David Weiss, summarizes his organization's creed as follows: "Zionism, from its inception, advocated and urged cruelty towards the Palestinian people. ... Zionism advocates and executes war against all nations. ... Zionism sadistically abuses [the poor and suffering]. ... There is no excuse for the Zionist takeover of the Holy Land. It was achieved only after a series of wars and incessant brutality. ... The Palestinian people have graciously agreed to participate in a so-called peace process with the Israeli government. That is most kind of them. However, we must warn them that it is our belief that until the scourge of Zionism, incarnated in the state of Israel, is removed from the Middle East there can be no peace. We are a people in exile. We are forbidden to attempt to reconquer the Holy Land. ... We call for a peaceful dismantling of the Israeli state without violence or bloodshed. ... We look forward to the day when Jews and Palestinians may live together under a Palestinian government."

In its effort to bring about Israel's destruction, NK cooperates with frankly anti-Semitic groups such as the Nation of Islam (NOI). At the invitation of Louis Farrakhan, Rabbi Weiss spoke at the NOI annual convention in 2000, where he denounced Zionism and the Jewish state.

Moreover, recently discovered information has linked NK to the late Yasser Arafat and the Palestine Liberation Organization. Among the many documents seized by the Israeli Defense Forces in Arafat's compound were allotments of money from Arafat to Neturei Karta's "foreign minister," Rabbi Moshe Hirsch. The money amounted to $55,000 over a two-month period for "expenses for activities."

Rabbi Hirsch, NK's leader in Israel, works closely with the Palestinian Authority (PA) and currently holds a position as its Minister of Jewish Affairs. He staged a graveside memorial service for Arafat in the West Bank shortly after the Palestinian leader's death in November 2004.

In December 2006, eight Neturei Karta rabbis traveled to Tehran to meet with Iranian President Mahmoud Ahmadinejad, a Holocaust denier, embracing him and endorsing his stance that Israel has no right to exist. "We tried to appease them [the Iranians]," Rabbi David Weiss told the New York *Daily News*. "We explained how the Holocaust is used to intimidate people who want to speak against the unjust Zionist regime."

This was not Neturei Karta's first visit to Tehran. In March 2006 the organization had also sent a delegation to meet with senior Iranian officials and express support for Ahmadinejad's calls to eliminate Israel. In a statement to Iran's official IRIB radio, the group called for "the disintegration of the Zionist regime" and said that it "is a dangerous deviation to pretend that the Iranian president is an anti-Jewish or anti-Semitic personality." Neturei Karta added that it was "upset about the recent ploys, propaganda and tensions which have been created by the West regarding the statements of the Iranian president Mahmoud Ahmadinejad about a world free of Zionism, since this is nothing more than wishing for a better world dominated by peace and calm."

NEW ISRAEL FUND (NIF)

1101 14th Street NW
Sixth Floor
Washington, DC
20005

Phone :202-842-0900
URL: http://www.nif.org/

> Founded in 1979 for the purpose of providing "justice and equality for all Israel's citizens"
> Allocates grants to such anti-Israeli NGOs as Hamoked, I'lam, and Ittljah

Established in 1979, the New Israel Fund's (NIF) mission is to "strengthen Israel's democracy and to promote freedom, justice and equality for all Israel's citizens." From its inception through 2005, NIF granted over $120 million to more than 700 Israeli organizations that share its political and social objectives -- which focus heavily on the redistribution of wealth and the radical transformation of an allegedly oppressive society. To complement its grant-making, in 1982 NIF established Shatil (a word meaning "seedling" in Hebrew) to provide technical assistance and training to leftist social change organizations in Israel. Among the major beneficiaries of NIF grants are the Arab Association for Human Rights, Hamoked, I'lam, Adalah, Ittijah, the Ahali Center for Community Development, the Arab Association of Human Rights, and Mossawa. These NIF-supported NGOs regularly produce reports that accuse Israel of human rights violations and religious persecution.

NIF's Program Areas include the following:

Arab and Bedouin Citizens: "Arab citizens of Israel occupy the lowest rung on the socioeconomic ladder and suffer pervasive discrimination, unequal allocation of resources and violation of their legal rights."

Social and Economic Justice: "Israel's economic policy over the past decade has involved massive cuts to education, health and social welfare budgets. This once-egalitarian society now has a gap between rich and poor second only to that of the U.S. among industrialized nations. [NIF] aims to reduce the social and economic gap between rich and poor in Israel ... [by] investing $3.2 million annually in its work to achieve social and economic justice for Israel 's disadvantaged citizens."

Civil and Human Rights: "1.3 million Arab citizens of Israel ... face pervasive discrimination and unequal allocation of resources in housing, planning and education ... NIF works to ... safeguard the legal rights of disadvantaged populations [and] educate and mentor the next generation of civil rights advocates."

Religious Pluralism and Tolerance: In an effort "to move Israeli society toward ... promoting religious pluralism, tolerance and social cohesion," NIF each year invests $800,000 in grants to 23 organizations "enhancing the links between Jewish life and social activism among all streams of Judaism."

Education: "The Israeli education system has not yet met the challenges of providing equal educational opportunity to rich and poor, native and immigrant, Jew and Arab. Massive government budget cuts have exacerbated these inequalities ..." To address this issue, NIF invests $1.2 million each year in education and youth activities, through grants to 21 nonprofit organizations. The Fund also petitions the courts for the implementation of the Long School Day Law and the Hot Lunch Law to cover (with taxpayer dollars) the costs of food and after-school programs for children whose mothers work fulltime jobs.

Environment: "Environmental degradation is endangering the health of Israel 's citizens - particularly disempowered groups and those living in the geographic periphery ... Israel's recreational and pristine areas are being devoured by unfettered development ..." NIF invests some $300,000 per year in the Green Environment Fund (GEF), the largest funder of environmental NGOs in Israel. Other major contributors to GEF include the Nathan Cummings Foundation, the Andrea and Charles Bronfman Philanthropies, and the Pratt Foundation. NIF also administers a Training and Empowerment Center for Social Change Organizations, which seeks to strengthen environmental activist groups by providing assistance with strategic planning, management, fundraising, advocacy, public relations, and media.

Immigrants: "Massive immigration to Israel over the past 25 years brought nearly one million people from the former Soviet Union (FSU) and another 90,000 from Ethiopia , increasing the country's total population by 20 percent. ... [These immigrants] are still grappling with day-to-day issues of unemployment and under-employment, housing, youth at-risk, and social alienation. Draconian cutbacks in government assistance since 2001 have further exacerbated problems. NIF is investing an average of $800,000 annually to 22 nonprofit immigrant organizations ..."

Women's Rights: "Women ... still confront a situation of profound inequality. Social institutions, traditions and religious laws have kept girls and women at a disadvantage in schools, in the workplace, in divorce cases, and as victims of violence." NIF provides grants to a variety of organizations working to promote women's rights. A special NIF initiative, launched in partnership with the Nathan Cummings Foundation, aims to promote social change for Orthodox and Arab women. A major objective of NIF's Women's Rights program is to "advocat[e] for increased government funds to address the needs of poor women."

NIF has received funding from: the Nathan Cummings Foundation; the Ford Foundation; and the Public Welfare Foundation.

NEW JERSEY SOLIDARITY -- ACTIVISTS FOR THE LIBERATION OF PALESTINE

SAC Box 52
613 George Street
New Brunswick, NJ
08901

URL: http://www.njsolidarity.org/Pro-Palestinian militant organization that calls for the destruction of Israel

Openly calling for the destruction of Israel, New Jersey Solidarity Activists for the Liberation of Palestine (NJS) declares that its mission is to "support ... the Palestinian struggle for justice, national liberation, human rights and self-determination"; to "stan[d] firmly against racism and all forms of oppression"; and to work "in solidarity with liberation struggles of people around the world against imperialism and colonialism."

NJS demands "an immediate end to the Israeli occupation of all Palestinian territories, the recognition of the full, non-negotiable human right of return for all Palestinian refugees, and full political, social and economic equality under law for all people in historic Palestine." It condemns "the existence of the apartheid colonial settler state of Israel, as it is based on the racist ideology of Zionism and is an expression of colonialism and imperialism." And NJS "stand[s] for the total liberation of all of historic Palestine" -- meaning the area comprising the entirety of present-day Israel, plus the West Bank and Gaza. NJS embraces the slogan, "From the River to the Sea, Palestine will be Free!" -- a reference to the Jordan River and the Mediterranean Sea, precisely the territory that currently constitutes the state of Israel.

NJS seeks to help achieve the foregoing objectives by sponsoring educational events and activities; delegations and report-backs; film showings; cultural events; musical and artistic events; rallies and demonstrations; direct actions and displays; outreach; coalition building; anti-Israel divestment campaigns; and study groups.

In the fall of 2003, NJS hosted a conference at Rutgers University promoting divestment from Israel and the "celebrat[ion] [of] Palestinian resistance." Among the organizations to endorse this conference were: International ANSWER, Al-Awda, the Al-Bireh Palestine Society, the American-Arab Anti-Discrimination Committee, Amnesty International, the Free Palestine Alliance, the International Action Center, the International Socialist Organization, the Islamic Association for Palestine, Jews for a Free Palestine, the Korea Truth Commission, La Raza Unida Party, the Middle East Children's Alliance, the Muslim Student Association, the National Lawyers Guild, the Nicaragua Network, the Palestine Children's Welfare Fund, the Palestine Solidarity Group, Students for Justice in Palestine, SUSTAIN, Women Against War, and the Workers World Party.
NJS reports that it has a particularly close working relationship with Ramsey Clark's International Action Center, International ANSWER, and the Palestine Children's Welfare Fund. Al-Awda lists NJS as one of its "Coalition Committee Members."

Lifelong communist Charlotte Kates, spokesperson for NJS, wrote an op-ed which she titled "Israel Has No 'Right to Exist'" for the Rutgers University newspaper, the *Daily Targum*, whose editors retitled the piece "Palestine Roots in Land Proven Through History" prior to publication. Kates characterizes Israel as "an oppressive, racist state."

NJS is an uncompromising supporter of "the right of return for Palestinian refugees to their homes and their homeland." Palestinian authorities place the number of Arabs who ought to be granted a "right of return" to Israel at 5 million. This is more than *ten* times the number of Arabs who actually left the Jewish portions of the British Mandate in 1948, most of whom are now deceased. The incorporation of five million Arabs into Israel would render Jews a permanent minority in their own country, and would thus spell the end of Israel. Understanding this, NJS supports this fundamental demand.

NJS views Israel's main ally, the United States, as a nation whose foreign policies are founded on oppression, injustice, and imperialism. Thus the organization seeks to "expos[e] and highligh[t] the role of the United States in furthering injustice and oppression in Palestine," and calls "for an immediate end to all U.S. aid--political, military and economic--to Israel."

In September 2006 NJS sponsored a Brooklyn, New York rally called "Stop the War Against the Arab People," which demanded the following: "Immediate & Unconditional Right to return for all Palestinian refugees"; "End the occupation of historic Palestine, Lebanon, Iraq and everywhere"; "End all U.S. aid to apartheid Israel"; "Release all political prisoners"; and "Support the people's right to resist."

ORGANIZATION OF SOLIDARITY OF THE PEOPLES OF AFRICA, ASIA AND LATIN AMERICA

www.ospaaal.com

Anti-Israel NGO

The Organization of Solidarity of the Peoples of Africa, Asia, and Latin America (OSPAAAL) was established in 1966 -- following the Tricontinental Conference held in Havana -- to promote "solidarity with the Third

World people's struggles, claims, and most precious desires." OSPAAAL holds Special Consultative Status with the United Nations Economic and Social Council (UNESCO). It also organized the first "International Conference of Solidarity with the Palestinian People" held in Greece in 1999, and the second Conference, which was held in Mexico in 2002.

Particularly outspoken about the Arab-Israeli conflict in the Middle East, OSPAAAL characterizes Zionism as racism, and in 2002 portrayed the Palestinians as a "heroic ... people that, deprived of its national rights for 54 years and led by the Palestine Liberation Organization, its sole and legitimate representative, fights for its self-determination and for the restoration of its national rights, including that to establish its own independent State on the soil of Palestine, with Jerusalem as its capital."

In May 2004 a German diplomat at the UNESCO Committee on NGOs rebuked, and threatened sanctions against, OSPAAAL for its "anti-Semitic activities" and its role in the lead-up to the Durban World Conference Against Racism in 2001. This marked the first time that a UN-accredited NGO had been rebuked for anti-Semitic or anti-Israel activity.

OXFAM INTERNATIONAL (OI)

Oxfam Supporter Services
Oxfam House
274 Banbury Road
Oxford
OX2 7DZ

Phone :0870 333 2700
URL: http://www.oxfam.org.uk/International relief organization that condemns Israeli defensive measures against terrorism

Supports boycotts of Israeli products

Oxfam International describes itself as "a confederation of 12 organizations working together in more than 100 countries to find lasting solutions to poverty, suffering, and injustice." "We seek to help people organize so that they might gain better access to the opportunities they need to improve their livelihoods and govern their own lives," says Oxfam. "We also work with people affected by humanitarian disasters, with preventive measures, preparedness, as well as emergency relief." Oxfam is active in 26 countries representing seven major geographic regions: the United States; Central America, Mexico and the Caribbean; South America; West Africa; the Horn of Africa; Southern Africa; and East Asia.

Oxfam lists the following as the major issues on which it focuses:

Making a Living: "Working largely with rural communities, Oxfam helps people understand their rights, build skills and assets, and find new ways of working—to move beyond poverty towards greater security."

Natural Resources: "With powerful interests vying for some of the world's most valuable commodities, many natural resources are being polluted or dangerously depleted. Oxfam empowers farmers, fishers, and others to defend their right to life-sustaining resources."

Peace & Security: "Oxfam helps communities analyze the root causes of conflict and find creative ways to build peace."

Equality of Women: "About 70 percent of the 1.2 billion people who live in extreme poverty are women and girls. Oxfam ... promotes investments in women as an investment in families and communities."

Indigenous & Minority Rights: "Diversity should be a social asset, but in many places there is little respect for indigenous people and minorities. Oxfam specializes in strengthening organizations to overcome racism and discrimination."

Trade: "World trade could be a powerful force for reducing poverty, if poor people could sell their products at a decent price. Oxfam and our partners are joining together to ensure international trade provisions benefit all people."

Operating with an annual budget of over $300 million, Oxfam regularly issues political condemnations of Israel while remaining silent about Palestinian-perpetrated human rights abuses and acts of terror. The British branch of Oxfam denounces also Israel's security policies against terror attacks. Oxfam Belgium recently produced a poster, in both Flemish and French, calling on Belgian consumers to boycott Israeli products; the poster declared that "Israeli fruits have a bitter taste," and depicted blood dripping from an Israeli fruit.

Oxfam International was a signatory to a 1999 petition of so-called "civil society" organizations that opposed globalization, big business in general, and "any effort to expand the powers of the World Trade Organization (WTO) through a new comprehensive round of trade liberalization." A notable cosigner of this petition was Global Exchange Director Medea Benjamin, who was a chief organizing force behind the November 1999 riots in Seattle, where some 50,000 protesters destroyed millions of dollars worth of property in their effort to shut down the WTO Conference in that city. Oxfam also endorsed a recent "Our World is Not for Sale" campaign similarly condemning the WTO.

Oxfam America was a signatory to a November 1, 2001 document characterizing the 9/11 attacks as a legal matter to be addressed in courtrooms rather than by military means. Ascribing the hijackers' rage to alleged American injustices against which they sought to strike a blow, this document explained that "security and justice are mutually reinforcing goals that ultimately depend upon the promotion of all human rights for all people," and called on the United States "to promote fundamental rights around the world."

Oxfam International is a member of OneWorld Network, an umbrella organization of more than 1,500 leftist groups that, according to the OneWorld website, seek "to promote sustainable development, social justice, and human rights."

Oxfam has received funding from: the AT&T Foundation, the William and Flora Hewlett Foundation, the Ford Foundation; the Bill and Melinda Gates Foundation; the John D. & Catherine T. MacArthur Foundation; the Minneapolis Foundation; the Public Welfare Foundation; and the Rockefeller Brothers Fund, the Rockefeller Foundation, and many others.

PALESTINE CHILDREN'S RELIEF FUND

P.O. Box 1926
Kent, OH
44240
Phone :330-678-2645
URL: http://www.pcrf.net/first.htmlEstablished in 1991 "to address the medical and humanitarian crisis facing Palestinian youths in the Middle East"

Considered terrorist-fundraising groups like the Holy Land Foundation for Relief and Development and the Global Relief Foundation to be its "assisting organizations"

A self-described "non-political organization" established in 1991, the Palestine Children's Relief Fund (PCRF) states that its founders were "concerned people in the U.S. [wishing] to address the medical and humanitarian crisis facing Palestinian youths in the Middle East." PCRF helps to secure free medical care for children in the region who are unable to get the specialized treatment they need in their homeland. Says PCRF: "We locate, sponsor and run volunteer medical missions to the Middle East in adult and pediatric cardiac surgery, pediatric cardiology, plastic and reconstructive surgery, maxillofacial surgery, pediatric urology, ophthalmology, vascular surgery, pediatric orthopedic surgery, occupational therapy, and other specialties. We also locate abroad free medical care for children who cannot be adequately treated in the Middle East."

PCRF focuses its efforts heavily on the Palestinian people living in the West Bank and Gaza Strip -- sending them medical supplies and equipment, training Palestinian surgeons to perform procedures with which they may be unfamiliar, and sending American medical personnel to the region to treat especially difficult cases.

Considered a "Partner Organization" of Al-Awda, PCRF is headed by Stephen Sosebee, who depicts Israelis as murderous Zionist terrorists who Palestinians must resist by means of "armed struggle" (i.e., suicide bombings). Sosebee charges that the U.S. government, citizenry, and media are manipulated by a "Zionist lobby" and "Zionist influence." He speaks extensively at universities and other political

"solidarity meetings," where he consistently delivers a virulently anti-Semitic, anti-Israel message; one of his speaking venues was
the Zayed International Centre for Coordination and Follow-up.

On June 24, 2003, *NGO Monitor* reported: "PCRF received assistance from [t]he Holy Land Foundation for Relief and Development, Global Relief Foundation, and [t]he International [Islamic] Relief Organization -- all of which were closed down by the U.S. government for funding terrorist groups. Yet, PCRF proudly claims on its website that it "works with these organizations" and acknowledges their 'support and cooperation.'"

In addition, PCRF received thousands of dollars from the American-Arab Anti-Discrimination Committee (ADC). According to the December 17, 2001 edition of *Insight m*agazine: "Throughout the 1980s, the [ADC] lent its name to political-support campaigns for Soviet-backed guerrilla organizations around the world from the Palestine Liberation Organization (PLO) and the PFLP [Popular Front for the Liberation of Palestine] to Marxist revolutionaries in Latin America."

On March 17, 2001, Stephen Sosebee spoke on behalf of PCRF at a "Conference on Palestine" held at the University of Michigan. The event was co-sponsored by the Global Relief Foundation, the International Action Center (the parent of International ANSWER), the Islamic Association for Palestine, the Council on American-Islamic Relations (CAIR), and others. Also speaking at the event was Ibrahim Hooper, the National Communications Director for CAIR. The conference began with the showing of a video entitled "The New Uprising," a reference to the Second Palestinian *Intifada* against Israel.

Sosebee, who claims not to have "any political designs," also represented PCRF at an antiwar rally held at Kent State University on May 4, 2002. Other organizations represented at this event included the All-African People's Revolutionary Party and the Revolutionary Communist Youth Brigade, the youth wing of the Revolutionary Communist Party.

PALESTINE CHILDREN'S WELFARE FUND (PCWF)

www.**pcwf**.org

Anti-Israel Islamic children's charity

With branches and volunteers in more than ten countries, the Palestine Children's Welfare Fund (PCWF) describes itself as "an enterprise that was established by a group of individuals whose goals are to improve the living standards of the children of Palestine in the refugee camps inside Palestine." The organization's mission is "to provide the children of the refugee camps with better educational opportunities, health facilities and a bright future without violence, hatred and discrimination." PCWF professes to be "not connected with any militant or political association of any kind, ... a non-political, non-religious enterprise whose aspirations are purely humanitarian."

PCWF was founded by Bob Rossi, who along with Margaret Stephens (a.k.a. Margaret Phillips), published the *Northwest Ethnic Voice*, a now-inactive Oregonian newsletter that endorsed a "Call to Action" by the anti-war group International ANSWER, which is closely tied to Ramsey Clark's International Action Center and the Marxist-Leninist Workers World Party.

In January 2002, PCWF initiated a "Book Campaign" to collect donated educational books, videos, cassettes, and software for Palestinian students of all ages, particularly in the fields of mathematics, natural science, and social studies.
Through PCWF's "Sponsor a Child" program, sponsors send $10 per month to help pay for a given Palestinian child's food, education, clothing, and medical services. This program is coordinated by the Holy Land Trust, a Christian nonprofit organization through which all money received on behalf of the children is processed. According to *World Net Daily* Editor Joseph Farrah, Holy Land Trust not only promotes such anti-Semitic themes as "the standard lines about Jews robbing the homes of Arabs, stealing their land and brutalizing them in a repressive state of military occupation," but "even rationalize[s] terrorism."

PCWF also oversees a Union of Health Workers Committees project, which "provides medical services to needy children in Gaza and all other Palestinian cities." This program recruits "experienced medical personnel to go to Gaza and other Palestinian cities to work and train the existing staff and provide professional and moral support" on a volunteer basis for periods ranging from two weeks to six months. It also solicits donations of medical equipment and supplies, ambulances, medicine, and any material relevant to the operation of emergency rooms and hospitals.

Another PCWF program sells embroidery and clothing fashioned by Palestinian women in order to raise funds for the necessities of life in Gaza and the West Bank. Among the items that PCWF has sold was a T-shirt inscribed with a poem in praise of suicide bombers, which read as follows:

My Homeland
The youth will not get tired
Their goal is your independence
Or they die
We will drink from death
But will not be slaves to our enemies
We do not want
An eternal humiliation
Nor a miserable life
We do not want
But we will return
Our great glory
My homeland
My homeland

PCWF Director Riad Hamad, who the FBI has investigated on a number of occasions, has called it a misconception to assume "that most of us Arabs recognize the right of Israel to exist."

To help finance the education of deserving Palestinian children, PCWF has established a "Rachel Corrie Scholarship Fund" in honor of its namesake, a young International Solidarity Movement volunteer who was accidentally killed in April 2003 while attempting to interfere with Israeli anti-terror activities.
The PCWF website provides links to the websites of such anti-Israel organizations as Holy Land Trust, Betselem, SUSTAIN, Electronic Intifada, Palestine Media Watch, Al-Awda Chicago, Northwest Ethnic Voice, and Women in Black.

PCWF praises the Palestinian-American rapper Iron Shiek as "one of the most brilliant new artist/activist[s] to take his message to the microphone." "His bold and insightful rap-style challenges traditional views on Palestinians," says PCWF. Maintaining that Israel's influence in the Palestinian territories is far more objectionable than are suicide bombings, Iron Sheik accuses Israel of practicing "apartheid," and graphically describes his desire to physically assault former Israeili Prime Minister Ariel Sharon. PCWF ordered 100 of Iron Shiek's CDs for a recent fundraiser.

In 2002, PCWF sponsored a drawing contest for children between the ages of six and fourteen, entitled, *Why I love Palestine.* The clear objective of the contest was to support the destruction of the Jewish state. Almost without exception, the judges rewarded entries that featured fierce and violent hatred of Israel. The overall winner was Bushra Ahed, whose picture depicted a bonfire, in the shape of a map of Israel and the Palestinian Authority, consuming the Star of David with the word "Israel" written inside the flag. Another entry, that of Jihad Alajarmeh, depicted a Palestinian flag dropping flames on an Israeli flag and immolating Israelis standing next to it.

PCWF identifies as its "Affiliated Groups" such anti-Israel organizations as Rabbis for Human Rights and the Union of Health Workers Committees in Gaza -- the latter of which accuses Israel of maliciously destroying Palestinian ambulances without cause (making no mention of the frequent exploitation of ambulances to transport Palestinian terrorists into Israel).

PALESTINE MEDIA CENTER

Al Quds-Nablus Street.
National Insurance Co. Bldg - Third Floor
Al Bireh/ Ramallah
Palestine

URL: http://www.palestine-pmc.comPalestinian news outlet that offers propagandistic accounts of all pertinent stories relating to the Israeli-Palestinian conflict

The Palestine Media Center (PMC) was established in 2001 by Palestine National Authority Minister of Cabinet Affairs, Yasser Abed Rabbo. According to its mission statement, PMC was formed "to provide a reliable and professional media source that will cater the media with accurate, timely, and informative news relevant to the Palestinian reality."

PMC presents news stories involving the Arab-Israeli conflict in a manner that depicts Israel as a tyrannical oppressor of innocent, peace-seeking Palestinians. The organization commonly characterizes Israeli military actions targeting specific terrorists as acts of "manslaughter" and "murder," but classifies Palestinian suicide bombers as "activists."

PMC produces Daily Situation Reports on various issues in "the Occupied Territories." These reports quantify the number of allegedly unjustified deaths, assaults, injuries, arrests, air attacks, raids, detentions, house demolitions, checkpoint conflicts, road closures, and incidents of property destruction or confiscation for which Israeli authorities are responsible each day. The reports also provide updates on Israel's progress in building the anti-terror separation barrier (which PMC terms an "Apartheid Wall") in the West Bank.

The consistently anti-Israel tone of PMC's reports was displayed in a November 5, 2006 article titled "PLO condemns the bloody attacks against Gaza," which read, in part, as follows: "The Israeli military forces ... are escalating ... vicious attacks on the town of Beit Hanon and the surroundings. ... Witnesses add that massive destructions for [*sic*] the infrastructure, houses and mosques in the neighborhoods are still ongoing. ... The Israeli troop's [*sic*] immoral crimes would [*sic*] only help to drag the region towards more violence and instability." This article was composed by the Palestine Liberation Organization's Department of Arab and International Relations.

A November 30, 2006 PMC article, titled "Israelis adopt what South Africa dropped," stated the following: "Many aspects of Israel 's occupation surpass those of the apartheid regime. Israel's large-scale destruction of Palestinian homes, leveling of agricultural lands, military incursions and targeted assassinations of Palestinians far exceed any similar practices in apartheid South Africa. No wall was ever built to separate blacks and whites. ... And the United States and the European Union ... have in effect imposed economic sanctions on the Palestinian people for having, by democratic means, elected a [Hamas-led] government deemed unacceptable to Israel and the West. ... In these circumstances, the United States should not be surprised if the rest of the world begins to lose faith in its commitment to human rights."

PMC also posted an October 29, 2006 article titled "Israel's scandalous siege of Gaza," which said: ""Israel has killed 2,300 Gazans over the past six years ... How long will the "international community" allow the slaughter to continue? The cruel repression of the occupied territories, and of Gaza in particular, is one of the most scandalous in the world today. It is the blackest stain on Israel's patchy record as a would-be democratic state. ... Far from reining in the Israeli hawks, messianic settlers, Arab-killers and expansionists, [President] Bush gave them a completely free hand -- and continues to do so."

PMC receives funding from the European Union.

PALESTINE MEDIA WATCH

P.O. Box 62
Dunn Loring, VA
22027
Phone :866-342-5769
URL: http://www.pmwatch.orgPalestinian-allied group seeking to shape news media coverage of the Arab-Israeli conflict

The mission of Palestine Media Watch (PMW) is to "help media outlets with [i.e., gain] access to pro-Palestinian points of view and voices for interviews, op-eds, or background discussions." PMW seeks to minimize media references to Palestinian terrorism and corruption, while promoting images of Palestinians as victims of Israeli oppression. (This group is not connected to the Jerusalem-based, similarly named but pro-Israel media monitoring group "Palestinian Media Watch.")

A donation based, all-volunteer organization with 42 U.S. chapters, PMW was founded in October 2000 by Philadelphia-based activist Ahmed Bouzid, an Algerian-born computer engineer and software developer who remains the organization's President. Bouzid established PMW as a result of what he perceived to be the *Philadelphia Inquirer*'s biased coverage of Middle East issues.

PMW focuses on disseminating e-mail action alerts, submitting opinion columns to newspapers, meeting with newspapers' foreign and opinion page editors, teaching activists how to write letters to editors, and providing basic talking points from a pro-Palestinian perspective.

The organization analyzes the writings of various media outlets, compiling statistics on how many sentences, quotes and photographs depict the Palestinians, and, conversely, the Israelis in a favorable light. One PMW media critique "quick sheet" gives the following instructions:

> "When critiquing a news story about the Palestinian-Israeli conflict, ask yourself the following questions: How many times were UN reports/findings/resolutions mentioned? How many times were Human Rights reports/findings/statements mentioned?"
>
> "How many times were the words 'terror/terrorist' used to describe Palestinians/Palestinian actions vs. Israelis/Israeli actions? How many times was the word 'violence' used to describe Palestinian actions vs. Israeli actions?"
>
> "Were Palestinian actions described in context (e.g., 'Palestinians launched a mortar attack after Israelis bulldozed a row of houses')? Were Israeli actions described in context (e.g., 'Israelis bulldozed a row of houses after Palestinians launched a mortar attack')? Did the story describe official Palestinian denials/pleas of ignorance and innocence in violent acts?"
>
> "Did the story describe official Israelis' denials/pleas of ignorance and innocence in violent acts? How much personal detail about Palestinian victims did the story go into? How much personal detail about Israeli victims did the story go into?"

Typical of PMW's work was a March 2005 report -- produced jointly with two other Palestinian-allied groups, If Americans Knew and Americans United for Palestinian Human Rights, charging that Oregon's largest daily newspaper, the Portland-based *Oregonian*, had provided biased coverage of the Arab-Israeli conflict. According to the report, *Oregonian* news pages from May through October of 2004 were characterized by "clear double standards when it comes to reporting Palestinian deaths compared to Israeli deaths. ... Analysis of *The Oregonian* news articles showed that 100% of all Israeli deaths were report[ed] during the analysis. ... By contrast, only 61% of all Palestinian deaths [were reported]." The PMW web page headline read, "*Oregonian*: Some lives are more equal than others."

To brief activists on the background and basic facts of the Arab-Israeli conflict, PMW uses the book *Understanding the Palestinian-Israeli Conflict: Primer*, by anti-Israel researcher Phyillis Bennis of the Institute for Policy Studies. Palestine Media Watch also sponsors speaking engagements by activist-lecturers Rania Awwad and Rima Mutreja.

PMW urges media outlets to use, in their coverage of Palestinian-Israeli affairs, terminology favorable to the Arab perspective. For example, it encourages the use of "anti-occupation" rather than "pro-Palestinian"; "extra-judicial liquidation" rather than "targeted killing" [of terrorists]; "Israeli colonizers" rather than "Israeli settlers"; "Israeli Occupation Forces" rather than "Israeli Defense Forces"; "Israeli-only colonies" rather than "settlements"; "Israeli assault against Palestinian civilians" rather than "military operation"; "occupied Arab Jerusalem" rather than just "Jerusalem"; "Palestinian armed resistance" rather than "Palestinian violence"; "Palestinian resistance fighters" rather than "Palestinian militants"; "Palestinian struggle for self-determination" rather than "Palestinian-Israeli conflict"; and "pro-occupation" rather than "pro-Israel."

PMW proudly embraces quotes of praise it has received from such noted anti-Israel critics as Noam Chomsky and Norman Finkelstein. "I have been impressed with the care and sophistication of the work of PMWatch, and its constructive achievements," says Chomsky. "This worthy project [PMW] deserves the support of everyone seeking a just and durable peace," Finkelstein agrees.

PALESTINE SOLIDARITY MOVEMENT (PSM)

Phone :202-494-0471
URL: http://www.palsolidarity.org/Student arm of the International Solidarity Movement

Supports the dissolution of Israel

The Palestine Solidarity Movement (PSM) is the student arm of the International Solidarity Movement (ISM). PSM describes itself as "an umbrella group of Palestine-related groups, primarily on campuses, across North America." It was established in February 2002 at a UC Berkeley event co-sponsored by Students for Justice in Palestine and the San Francisco chapter of the American-Arab Anti-Discrimination Committee. This conference resulted in the adoption of a resolution affirming PSM's unreserved support for the Palestinian *Intifada*: "We, the national student movement for solidarity with Palestine, declare our solidarity with the popular resistance to Israeli occupation, colonization, and apartheid."

PSM members demand that their respective colleges and universities "divest from Israel all financial holdings until Israel ends its system of occupation and apartheid in Palestine." Moreover, the organization calls for "ending U.S. aid to Israel"; supports "the Right of Return of Palestinian refugees"; and endorses "education, public demonstrations and rallies, and non-violent direct action for the purpose of encouraging awareness of Palestine issues and of the above campaigns."

PSM has declined to condemn acts of terrorism against Israelis, stating that "as a solidarity movement, it is not our place to dictate the strategies or tactics adopted by the Palestinian people in their struggle for liberation."

An honored guest at PSM's October 2002 conference at the University of Michigan in Ann Arbor was former University of South Florida Professor Sami al-Arian, who has acknowledged his intimate ties to the terrorist organization Palestinian Islamic Jihad. Representatives of Al-Awda sold T-shirts bearing the inscription "*Intifada*! Palestine will be free from the river to the sea." Delegates in attendance chanted "Kill the Jews!"

The October 2003 PSM conference in North Brunswick, New Jersey was hosted by New Jersey Solidarity -- Activists for the Liberation of Palestine, and was supported by Al-Awda and the Islamic Association for Palestine. Resolutions adopted during the conference included reaffirmations of PSM's commitment to the anti-Israel divestment campaign; its support for the Palestinian Right of Return; and its demand for the cessation of "Israeli occupation of ... all Arab lands." Refusing to denounce Palestinian terrorism, PSM conference organizer Charlotte Kates stated: "Why is there something particularly horrible about 'suicide bombing' -- except for the extreme dedication conveyed in the resistance fighter's willingness to use his or her own body to fight?"

PSM's November 2003 conference at Ohio State University was hosted by the local Committee for Justice in Palestine, and reaffirmed PSM's equation of Zionism with racism.

In October 2004, PSM held its conference at Duke University. One attendee, Stephen Miller, describes what he witnessed there:

"During one of the workshops I attended at the conference, eager students were fed outrageous lies about Israel by ISM representatives, which then tried to convince students to join the ISM, attend a one-week training session in Palestine, and then begin fighting the evil Israelis, by building human walls in front of IDF Bulldozers, interfering at security checkpoints, and tearing down the security wall. Naturally, the bulldozers were not described as targeting terrorists and bomb-making facilities, but the homes of innocent Palestinians to "even out demographics." The security checkpoints were described not as being used to prevent explosives for suicide bombers from getting into Israel, but for the purpose of "humiliating and degrading Palestinians." And the security wall was described not as for keeping out terrorists, but for maintaining "and apartheid state," which, as we were told during the conference's opening lecture, was actually not a fair comparison, as what the Israelis were doing was far worse than the South Africans. One of the recruiters at this session was none other than the co-founder of the ISM, who admitted that the organization worked with Islamic Jihad and Hamas ..."

The Palestine Solidarity Movement has endorsed the "Declaration Regarding Caterpillar Violations of Human Rights," a document that impugns the U.S.-based Caterpillar Corporation for selling its machinery to the Israeli army, which in turn uses that equipment to demolish Palestinian terrorists' homes and bases of operation. This Declaration characterizes the Israeli actions as malicious and unprovoked acts of indiscriminate destruction and, in some cases, murder. The document reads, in part: "The Caterpillar Corporation's machinery is directly implicated in grave abuses of human rights and humanitarian law by the Israeli army ... causing widespread economic hardship and environmental degradation in rural areas of Palestine ... leaving tens of thousands of men, women, and children homeless."

PALESTINE-ISRAEL JUSTICE PROJECT (PIJP)

URL: www.commondreams.org Minnesota-based anti-Israeli organization

Accuses Israel of committing human rights violations against Palestinians

The Palestine-Israel Justice Project (PIJP) is part of the Missions Ministry Team of the Minnesota Annual Conference of The United Methodist Church. Accusing Israel of committing gross "violations of human rights," PIJP focuses "primarily on supporting Palestinians in various ways."

In October 2003, PIJP Chairman Ric Koehn spoke out against Israel's demolition of a Palestinian house wherein terrorist activities were being organized. The house had been dedicated, by its occupants, to the memory of the late Rachel Corrie of the International Solidarity Movement, a group that invites Westerners to obstruct the anti-terrorist activities of the Israeli Defense Force.

PIJP has endorsed the Declaration Regarding Caterpillar Violations of Human Rights, which reads, in part: "The Caterpillar Corporation's machinery is directly implicated in grave abuses of human rights and humanitarian law by the Israeli army. ... Since 1967, the Israeli army has used Caterpillar equipment ... to destroy over 12,000 houses in the West Bank, Gaza Strip and East Jerusalem, leaving tens of thousands of men, women and children homeless. ... The Israeli army [also] uses Caterpillar bulldozers to build a separation wall with significant portions of it inside the Occupied Palestinian Territory. ... We call on Caterpillar to stop selling bulldozers to Israel until Israel stops using these machines to destroy Palestinian lives and livelihoods ..." Fellow endorsers of this Declaration include: Al-Awda, the American-Arab Anti-Discrimination Committee, Amnesty International, United For Peace and Justice, Christian Peacemaker Teams, Code Pink, Global Exchange, the International Solidarity Movement, Jews Against the Occupation, the Middle East Children's Alliance, the Palestine Solidarity Movement, Pax Christi, Peace Action, SUSTAIN, U.S. Campaign to End the Israeli Occupation, Veterans for Peace, the War Resisters League, and the Women's International League for Peace and Freedom.

During the 1990s, PIJP's Reverend John Darlington, a Methodist minister, was the pastor to Sara Jane Olson, the onetime member of the Symbionese Liberation Army (SLA) terrorist group. When Olson in 1999 was finally arrested for her SLA involvement, after having lived many years as a fugitive, Darlington publicly defended her. He said that Olson had been a great benefactor to her community, "feeding the hungry, helping to house the homeless, reading to the blind, helping people learn English as their second language. ... She loved children, and she wanted to make a difference in their lives." "Sara is involved in every peace and justice issue that comes along," added Darlington. "She served meals at a peace camp, played host to a Somali refugee family and performed instructive dramatizations of biblical scenes at church. Her impression upon me and the church is indelibly positive because of her caring and courageous nature."

In addition to its anti-Israel positions, PIJP also opposes the U.S. military action in Iraq.

PALESTINIAN ACADEMIC SOCIETY FOR THE STUDY OF INTERNATIONAL AFFAIRS (PASSIA)

18 Hatem Al-Ta'i Street
Wadi Al-Joz
Jerusalem
Phone :972 -2 - 626-4426
URL: http://www.passia.org/Jerusalem-based NGO that claims to "present the Palestinian Question ... through academic research"

Participates in the global campaign to boycott Israeli goods
Member of Palestinian NGO Network

Established in 1987 in Jerusalem, the Palestinian Academic Society for the Study of International Affairs (PASSIA) is an Arab non-profit institution headed by its founder, Dr. Mahdi Abdul Hadi. PASSIA describes itself as a "financially and legally independent" entity "not affiliated with any government, political party or organization." Its mission is "to present the Palestinian Question ... through academic research" and to ensure "that research ... be specialized, scientific and objective [as well as] ... open, self-critical and conducted in a spirit of harmony and cooperation."

PASSIA's Research Studies Program has produced more than 90 separate studies -- performed by researchers commissioned by the organization -- on a wide range of subjects relating to the Palestine question. PASSIA publishes the results of these studies and distributes them both locally and internationally to academics, diplomats, professionals, and libraries. Some recent titles include: *Economic Aspects of the Intifada* by Dr. Andrew Rigby; *Economic and Social Conditions During the Intifada* by Dr. Hazem Shunnar; *Israeli Planning and House Demolishing Policy in the West Bank* by Rasem M. Khameyseh; *The Intifada: Causes and Factors of Continuity* by Dr. Ziad Abu-Amr; *The Intifada: The Struggle Over Education* by Dr. Andrew Rigby; *The Intifada and the Arab Press* by Ali Khalili; *The Palestinian Islamic Movement and the New World Order* by Dr. Iyad Al-Barghouthi; *Palestinian Refugees* by Najeh Jarrar; and *From Religious Salvation to Political Transformation: The Rise of Hamas in Palestinian Society* by Dr. Hisham H. Ahmed.

PASSIA commonly hosts seminars on Diplomacy and Protocol, Strategic Studies, the European Community, and Education on Democracy. The organization also sponsors workshops that address various issues *vis a vis* Jerusalem, such as the city's holy sites and its viability "as [a] capital for the two [Israeli and Palestinian] States."

Funding for PASSIA's projects is provided by the Rockefeller Foundation, USAID, the Canadian Embassy in Tel Aviv, and the British and U.S. Consulates in Jerusalem.

PASSIA is a member organization of the Palestinian NGO Network, which was instrumental in producing many of the preparatory documents for the 2001 Durban Conference, including the document calling for embargoes against Israel. PASSIA is an active participant, along with many other anti-Israel groups, in the global campaign to boycott Israeli goods. It also trains professionals to lobby legislators on Capitol Hill for the PLO cause.

A notable member of PASSIA's Board of Directors is Dr. Sari Nusseibeh, a professor of Islamic Philosophy and the president of Al Quds University in Jerusalem.

PALESTINIAN CENTER FOR HUMAN RIGHTS (PCHR)

29 Omar al-Mukhtar St
P.O. Box 1328
Gaza City
Gaza Strip
Israel

URL: http://www.pchrgaza.org/Gaza City-based Palestinian rights organization

Condemns Israeli anti-terror measures

Founded in 1995 by Palestinian lawyers and human rights activists, the Gaza City-based Palestinian Center for Human Rights (PCHR) defines itself as "an independent legal body ... dedicated to protecting human rights, promoting the rule of law, and upholding democratic principles in the Occupied Palestinian Territories."

Headed by attorney Jonathan Kuttab, PCHR has Special Consultative Status with the United Nations Economic and Social Council, and is an affiliate of the International Commission of Jurists, the International Federation of Human Rights, and the Euro-Mediterranean Human Rights Network.

PCHR receives funding from the Ford Foundation; NOVIB (Holland); the Open Society Institute; Christian Aid; the Canadian Auto Workers' Social Justice Fund; Dan Church Aid (Denmark); Grassroots International; the European Commission; the Royal Danish Representative Office; the Representative Office of Norway; and Ireland Aid.

Depicting Palestinians as innocent victims of relentless Israeli brutality, PCHR press releases regularly accuse Israel -- often on scanty evidence -- of perpetrating "extrajudicial executions"; "mass arbitrary arrests and humiliation"; "harassment and violence"; "war crimes"; "torture"; "inhumane treatment"; and "gross violations of international humanitarian and human rights law." Conversely, they make no mention of Palestinian acts of violence, and fail to criticize the Palestinian Authority for its corruption and its complicity in organized terrorism.

On March 16, 2004, for instance, PCHR issued a press release entitled "Israel Occupying Forces Destroy a Branch Campus of al-Aqsa University in Gaza," which accused Israel of waging "continuous belligerent military attacks on Palestinian educational institutions." Though the press release implied that the Israeli Defense Forces (IDF) had entirely decimated a university and its infrastructure, PCHR itself admitted that those charges were based only upon "preliminary investigations," unconfirmed reports by "a number of residents of the area," and unnamed "university sources." It was later learned that the Israeli military operation had actually taken place in the al-Zaytoun neighborhood of Gaza, and was not at all a direct attack on the al-Aqsa University.

In an April 24, 2006 press release, PCHR referred to the IDF killing of Al-Aqsa Martyrs' Brigades operatives in Bethlehem as "extra-judicial executions" of "activists." In another press release three days later, PCHR condemned an IDF attack on Islamic Jihad terrorists who were on their way to launch Qassam rockets at Israel, and called on the international community to "intervene to stop such crimes."

In 2005, PCHR joined other Palestinian NGOs in supporting the short-lived British Association of University Teachers' boycott of Israeli universities, calling the move "an historic moment in the global movement to isolate Apartheid Israel ... [which] steals our land and ghettoizes us behind Walls in a project aimed at the expulsion of Palestinians from their land."

PALESTINIAN ENVIRONMENTAL NGOS NETWORK (PENGON)

PO Box 25220
Beit Hanina, Jerusalem
Palestine
URL: http://www.pengon.org/Anti-Israel NGO

Accuses Israel of perpetrating atrocities against Palestinians

Formed in 1998, the Palestinian Environmental NGOs Network (PENGON) describes itself as "a coordinating body between the different Palestinian NGOs working in the field of environment[alism]." PENGON's 21 member organizations -- among which are the Union of Palestinian Medical Relief Committees, the Applied Research Institute of Jerusalem, and LAW -- focus their efforts on the following domains: developing and sustaining natural resources; environmental awareness; protecting wildlife; preventing desertification; combating environmental pollution; developing and maintaining archeological sites; eco- and environmental tourism; and developing alternative and renewable energy uses.

In PENGON's view, Palestinian environmental problems are largely "due to violent Israeli occupation practices on the ground, including the confiscation of land, illegal settlement activities, the uprooting of trees, the destruction of Palestinian agricultural land, the use of Palestinian occupied lands by Israel as dumping ground for poisonous industrial waste, and the exhausting of water resources and the polluting of the water ground reservoirs by settlements."

PENGON actively promotes the false notion that massive Israeli "massacres" of Palestinians took place in Jenin in April 2002. One PENGON publication about this topic -- titled "Jenin Refugee Camp Massacre: The Atrocities Must Be Revealed" -- claims that it "was rare to find anyone ... who lost only one family member. Most lost several loved ones, if not their entire families. ... Witnesses recounted how people were buried alive by the soldiers in graves and holes dug in the ground, rows of injured people were laid flat on the ground and were then crushed to death by a tank that drove over their bodies, men were tied and made to face the wall and killed, execution style." PENGON ignores the fact that Israel's Jenin incursion was in response to a massive wave of Palestinian terrorist activity that had originated there. The organization has further failed to acknowledge that the "massacre" accusations aimed at Israel have been proven to be false. The Palestinian Authority itself has placed the official death toll from the Jenin battle at 56, of whom 48 were armed combatants.

PENGON administers an Apartheid Wall Campaign designed to discredit and disrupt Israel's construction of an anti-terrorism barrier in the West Bank. The campaign calls for "the immediate cessation of the building of the Wall"; "the dismantling of all parts of the Wall and its related zones already built"; "the return of lands confiscated for the path of the Wall"; and "the compensation of damages and lost income due to the destruction of land and property." According to PENGON, "[T]he Wall is an integral and large scale part of Israel's plans to confiscate and annex Palestinian lands, isolate Palestinian communities, and deny any prospects for survival in their villages and homes. The Wall is therefore not only the negation of Palestinian national aspirations and right to self-determination, but also a tool in the creeping 'transfer' of the population and the realization of the Zionist/Israeli expansionist plans."

In July 2006, when Israel was engaged in a military conflict against Gaza-based Hamas militants who were firing rockets into Israel, PENGON drew up a petition titled "Stop Israel's Siege and Attacks on Gaza; Stop the Environmental and Humanitarian Disaster." The petition read, in part: "The economy of Gaza is destroyed for years to come. ... The aim of the Occupation is clear to all that want to see: breaking Palestinian determination to resist within the Bantustans in Gaza or the West Bank and weakening opposition to the Israeli apartheid system faced on a daily basis."

PALESTINIAN NGO NETWORK (PNGO)

P.O. Box 2322
Ramallah, Palestine
URL: http://www.pngo.net/Anti-Israel, Palestinian umbrella organization composed of 92 member groups

Funded by the Ford Foundation

A project of the NGO Alternatives, this Palestinian NGO umbrella was established in September 1993. It is composed of 92 member organizations, among which are the Al-Mezan Center for Human Rights, the Palestine Center for Human Rights, the Al-Haq Institute, Miftah, and the Union of Palestinian Medical Relief Committees.
According to its own literature, "PNGO is guided by the network's clear mission, where the national, developmental roles of NGOs go alongside with the building of a Palestinian democratic, civil society based on social justice, the sovereignty of law, and the respect of human rights."
PNGO produces 3 publications: *Palestine Monitor*, *Palestine Observatory*, and *Grassroots International Protection for the Palestinian People*. It is also the recepient of hundreds of thousands of dollars in Ford Foundation money, and was instrumental in producing many of the preparatory documents for the 2001 Durban World Conference Against Racism, including a document calling for embargoes on Israel.

PALESTINIAN YOUTH ASSOCIATION FOR LEADERSHIP AND RIGHTS ACTIVATION (PYALARA)

Flat 12, 4th floor
Julani Building
Ar-Ram, Jerusalem
P.O. Box 54065
Jerusalem
URL: http://www.pyalara.org/Anti-Israel NGO that justifies Palestinian suicide bombings against Israeli civilians

Formed in 2000, the Palestinian Youth Association for Leadership and Rights Activation (PYALARA) describes itself as a "communication and media-oriented Palestinian NGO established for Palestinian youth." Claiming to be "non-political," PYALARA is an officially registered NGO at the Palestinian Ministry of Interior Affairs and works closely with a wide network of Palestinian schools and colleges. It also works with the Palestinian Ministries of Education, Information, and Youth and Sports.

PYALARA's objectives are to: "give a voice to Palestinian youngsters through specialized media focusing on youth"; "increase awareness among youth concerning issues pertaining to their rights"; "increase awareness concerning one's roots and identity, environment and culture, as well as awareness pertaining to the situation of youth in other countries and the world at large"; "create a lively Palestinian youth culture"; and "encourage the development of one's community and people."

According to PYALARA, the Palestinian people are consistently victimized by Israeli oppression and injustice. Seeking "to prevent young Palestinians from becoming thoroughly frustrated as a result of the harsh conditions under which they are forced to live," PYALARA encourages them "to express themselves through writing, talking, and other forms of communication in order to maintain a connection with the community." The resulting written and verbal contributions appear in *The Youth Times* (*TYT*), the only Palestinian monthly newspaper for young people. Contributors range in age from 14 to 25. Established in 1997, *TYT* is a 24-page bilingual publication that distributes some 20,000 copies each month -- many of them to schools run by the Palestinian Authority and by the United Nations Relief and Works Agency. *TYT* is funded by UNICEF, CORDAID, the Friedrich Naumann Stiftung/German Fund for Palestinian NGOs, and the European Union.

Since December 2000, PYALARA has produced, with the support of UNICEF and the cooperation of Palestine TV, a weekly two-hour television program called "Alli Sowtak" ("Speak Up"), which is viewed by an average of 300,000 Palestinian children and teenagers. Each episode focuses on a major theme, such as education, children's talents, health, and children's awareness concerning their various rights.

PYALARA has established a "Program for the Well-Being of Youth," which consists of three branches: (a) *Psychosocial Well-Being*: "The 'We Care Project' was developed by PYALARA in response to the negative psychological impact the present-day political situation is having on Palestinian youth. The essence of this particular project is youth-to-youth counseling"; (b) *Physical Well-Being*: "One of the main objectives of the 'Youth 4 Health Program' is to improve the health of Palestinian families through raising awareness concerning health practices by resorting to the youth-to-youth approach"; and (c) *Socio-Political Well-Being*: "The 'Youth 4 Change Program' aims at spreading awareness among Palestinian youth in underprivileged areas concerning how to become a 'good citizen,' concepts of democracy, youth rights and duties, etc."

In 2002, PYALARA published an article about Abu Ali Mustafa, a Popular Front for the Liberation of Palestine terrorist leader who was killed by Israeli forces in 2001. The article called Mustafa "a political leader ... whose history prides his nationalistic activism." Describing Mustafa as "a human being who has a family that awaits his arrival every day," the report added that "the Israelis could have turned to [him] to talk peace if peace were what they truly wanted." (PYALARA did not mention that Mustafa was famous for his uncompromising refusal to engage with the Israelis.)

A section on the PYALARA website, entitled *Dear World*, tacitly justifies Palestinian suicide bombings: "The world talks a lot about the young Palestinians who have willingly sacrificed their lives in the name of their homeland and condemns their actions, but one has to remember that we are talking here about a new generation whose innocence was taken from them the minute they were born. The youth in question were raised amidst evil war crimes and exposed to the most terrible acts of violence, and as their ears were deafened by numerous explosions and their lungs filled by gas and smoke, they were expected to settle for ruins for playgrounds and missiles and spent bullets for toys. Tell me, in all honesty, who is to 'blame' for their actions?"

PYALARA maintains close ties to the Palestinian Authority. PYALARA's Director, Hania Bitar, has a picture of Yasser Arafat displayed above her desk. She has been a candidate for the Palestinian Legislative Elections.

The Palestinian Youth Association for Leadership and Rights Activation receives considerable funding from UNICEF, which considers the PYALARA "a major strategic partner in Palestine." PYALARA also gets financial support from the International Red Cross and various European groups. Its current annual budget is approximately $144,000.

PARTNERS FOR PEACE

1250 4th St. SW
Suite WG-1
Washington, DC
20024
Phone :202-863-2951
URL: http://www.partnersforpeace.org/Anti-Israel organization

Founded in 1998, Partners for Peace (PFP) is a Washington, D.C.-based, Palestinian-allied nonprofit group which also is listed as a United Nations Non-Governmental Organization (NGO). The group's start-up working committee merged with another non-profit, the American Alliance for Palestinian Human Rights, retaining the Partners for Peace name for the two merged entities. PFP today has the same Washington address as another Palestinian-allied group, the Council for the National Interest. PFP's founder and current President is Jerri Bird, wife of retired State Department Foreign Service Officer Eugene Bird (a career diplomat with many Middle East postings).

PFP generates publicity for Palestinian causes, partly via media interviews, and partly through its regular speaking tours in U.S. cities -- usually by trios of Middle Eastern women who are presented as interfaith peace activists from Jewish, Muslim and Christian backgrounds. The PFP-sponsored tours are called "Jerusalem Women Speak: Three Women, Three Faiths, One Shared Vision." One of the more notable participants in these events is Nina Mayorek, who charges that "Since its foundation, Israel has lived by its sword." In the spring of 2005, PFP lecture venues included Washington's Georgetown and American Universities; an African-American congresswoman's Capitol Hill office; the University of Virginia; the Chicago Council of Foreign Relations; and Islamic centers, Protestant churches, seminaries, synagogues, colleges, law schools, and public libraries in North Carolina, Maryland, Michigan, Minnesota, and Wisconsin. Some of these events received media coverage from C-SPAN television.

The PFP website presents an "Introduction" to the organization's worldview and agenda. Written by PFP President Jerri Bird, this piece begins as follows: "It may come as an unpleasant surprise for many of you to learn that for over 30 years, Israel has repeatedly detained, tortured and incarcerated Americans of Arab origin, without suffering any sanctions or even a public reprimand from Washington. Of course the Palestinians have been suffering this torture for 35 years on a scale that is truly unimaginable." The PFP website encourages likeminded activists to: "Get acquainted with the editor of the Letters to the Editor section and establish yourself as a credible, knowledgeable citizen"; "Call in [to radio talk shows] whenever the subject relates to the Middle East"; and "[A]rrange an event at your church, mosque, synagogue, or elsewhere that includes food, music, and educational material from the region."

Partners for Peace also highlights what it believes are cases of Israeli government abuse of Arab-Americans in the Occupied Territories, though Israeli and U.S. courts generally have not sided with PFP's position in these cases.

The Partners for Peace Board of Directors includes anti-Israel activist Adam Shapiro, who also heads the International Solidarity Movement (ISM). PFP has posted, on its website, ISM press statements about alleged Israeli military harassment of ISM activists. Moreover, PFP echoes ISM's description of the Israeli security barrier as an "Apartheid Wall."

The PFP Board of Advisors includes George McGovern, the former Democratic presidential candidate, and Betty Bumpers, wife of former U.S. Senator Dale Bumpers (D-Arkansas). The group's Executive Director, Michael Brown, previously worked as a pro-Palestinian activist in Gaza.

PFP rents its office space from Council for the National Interest, inside the latter's Washington, DC headquarters.

PAX CHRISTI INTERNATIONAL (PCI)

Pax Christi International
Rue du Vieux Marché aux Grains, 21
B-1000 / Brussels, Belgium
Tel. ++32 (0)2.502.55.50 Fax. ...
www.**paxchristi**.netCatholic peace movement

Highly critical of America and Israel
Opposes American foreign policy and the War on Terror

Pax Christi International (PCI) is a Catholic peace movement whose name means "Peace of Christ" in Latin. The organization traces its origins to a group of Catholics in France and Germany "who wanted to promote reconciliation" in the immediate aftermath of World War II. Pax Christi identifies in particular "two seeds of inspiration" that were central to its formation: (a) the French bishop Pierre-Marie Théas who in 1944 was arrested for speaking out against the deportation of Jews to forced labor camps, and who counseled his fellow prisoners to "love [their] enemies" and pray for their Nazi jailers; and (b) Marthe Dortel-

Claudot, a teacher in southern France who in 1944 persuaded Bishop Théas to lead a "Crusade of Prayer" aimed at helping Germany "be healed of the spiritual and moral effects of twelve years of Nazism" -- on grounds that "Jesus died for everyone. Nobody should be excluded from one's prayer." This project was given the name "Pax Christi." Since 1945, the organization has grown to include some 60,000 members in more than thirty countries on five continents.

PCI today has representation status at the United Nations in New York and Vienna, UNESCO in Paris, UNICEF in New York, and the Council of Europe. It also enjoyed representation status at the now-defunct UN Human Rights Commission in Geneva. Claiming that its work "is based in spirituality," Pax Christi does not limit its membership solely to Catholics "but welcomes all religious groups and strives for dialogue and co-operation with non-governmental organizations and movements working in the same field -- Christian, Jewish, Muslim and non-religious."

Viewing military action as immoral and unjustified in every circumstance, PCI's work "is focused in the fields of demilitarization and security, justice, human rights, ecology, development, non-violence, economic justice and reconciliation." Pax Christi considers capitalism to be a chief cause of the international inequity and discord that give rise to poverty, oppression, and war.
PCI's activities fall broadly under five categories:

Solidarity: "visits and fact-finding missions to areas affected by violence in order to report, document and educate the wider world"

Dialogue: "offering opportunities for leaders of religious communities, especially in conflict areas, to listen and learn from one another so together they can help their different faith communities to find a way toward reconciliation"

Training: "exchanges and experiences where people can confront old prejudices and develop new skills as future peacemakers"

Advocacy: "speaking up for human rights, justice and disarmament in the UN and other international institutions where decisions are made"

Networking: "with those in every country who are working for peaceful alternatives to violence"

Pax Christi International is part of the Abolition 2000 anti-war coalition and the National Coalition for Peace and Justice. Its subsidiary Pax Christi USA is a member of the Win Without War coalition; and a few regional Pax Christi branches belong to the United for Peace and Justice anti-war coalition.

Alleging that America and Israel are responsible for a large share of international disharmony, PCI participates regularly in anti-war demonstrations, candlelight vigils, and teach-ins. At those events, the group works closely with such organizations as Al-Awda, Stop The War Coalition, JustPeaceUK, UNISON, People Against Oppression and War, Jews for Justice for Palestinians, and the Black Radical Congress.

Since 1999 the International President of PCI has been the Reverend Michel Sabbah, who also holds the title of Latin Patriarch of Jerusalem. At a pre-Christmas press conference in 2003, Sabbah offered his opinion *vis a vis* who was most culpable for the ongoing Israeli-Palestinian conflict. "The one who occupies the land of the other," said Sabbah, "is more responsible."
Funding for PCI comes from foundation grants, sales of publications and newsletter subscriptions, and contributions from its national chapters.

PAX CHRISTI USA

National Office:
Pax Christi USA
532 West Eighth Street
Erie, PA 16502
Phone: 814/453-4955; Fax: 814/452-4784
Email: info@paxchristiusa.org

Washington D.C. Office:
Pax Christi USA Washington, D.C. Office
415 Michigan Ave NE
Washington, DC 20017
Fax: 202-832-5195
Phone: 202-319-5543
E email: jean@paxchristiusa.org

PCUSA Regional/Local Group Contacts:
Email: johnnypcusa@yahoo.com
Phone: 352-219-8419

www.**paxchristiusa**.org

Subsidiary of the Catholic peace movement Pax Christi International
Depicts America as a nation plagued by racism, militarism, and economic injustice
Views military action as immoral and unjustified in every circumstance
Favors open borders; opposes efforts to curb illegal immigration

Founded in 1972 by Bishop Thomas Gumbleton and a small group of American (mostly lay) Catholics, Pax Christi USA is a prominent subsidiary of the Catholic peace movement Pax Christi International. Dedicated to creating "a world that reflects the Peace of Christ by exploring, articulating, and witnessing to the call of Christian nonviolence," PCUSA seeks to "transform structures of society" -- one of those being the capitalist economic system that allegedly spawns racism, militarism, economic injustice, and international strife.

Viewing military action as immoral and unjustified in every circumstance, PCUSA promotes "nuclear, conventional and domestic disarmament," and "rejects war, preparations for war, and every form of violence and domination." All international disputes, says the organization, can be reconciled "through the United Nations and other channels."

PCUSA's major Programs and Campaigns include the following:

Called to the Common Good: This program derides America for its involvement in "a war that seems to have no end"; its alleged absence of concern for "children who live in poverty within our own borders"; its lack of a universal, taxpayer-funded health care system for all U.S. residents; its culpability for "the increasing threat of global climate change"; its "rampant greed and materialism"; and its shameless "profiteering."
Brothers and Sisters All: Launched in 1998, this program is "a 20-year initiative to transform Pax Christi USA into an anti-racist, multicultural Catholic peace and justice movement." The organization's commitment "to embrace this new identity and do all its work from an anti-racist perspective" is founded upon its "conviction that personal and systemic racism continues to perpetrate deep spiritual and social brokenness" in the United States. The solution to this problem, says PCUSA, is to "transform structures and cultures of violence and domination" so as to better serve "people of color" and other "oppressed and marginalized people struggling for dignity" all over America.

Beatrice Parwatikar, Vice-Chair of PCUSA's National Council, explains the rationale for this initiative: "Law in the U.S. protects white skin privilege because White male landowners created the laws to protect their rights, their culture and their wealth. In communities of color, White privilege has kept White men in power as gatekeepers—they control the banks for loans and home mortgages, insurance for cars and homes ... The PCUSA analysis of racism (Racism = Prejudice + Institutional Power) can [also] be applied when we look at countries in the Global South—especially in looking at institutions like the World Bank, International Monetary Fund, and the World Trade Organization, as well as the lasting effects of colonization on the Global South. ... We must not forget the arrogance of how U.S. government officials deal with governments in the Global South—we have observed that same arrogance when we advocate for [people of color] and the poor in the United States."

People's Peace Initiative: This project condemns "the suffering and death happening at the U.S.-Mexico border" when would-be illegal border-crossers occasionally succumb to the desert heat. In PCUSA's calculus, the unlawful migrations of impoverished Central Americans are no less morally justifiable than the relocations of "Appalachian ... mountain people forced to leave their homes in search of work." PCUSA endorses the Immigrant Workers Freedom Ride Coalition, which seeks to secure amnesty for illegal aliens, and policy reforms that diminish or eliminate future restrictions on immigration.

The People's Peace Initiative also laments the "widening gap between rich and poor" in the United States, which it characterizes as "a superpower in a world of globalization"; "a nation of wealth and poverty, [of] extravagant consumerism amid struggles for basic survival"; a land whose "national culture [is] too often characterized by fear, individualism, and domination"; and the perpetrator of widespread "economic violence" against African Americans.

PCUSA demonstrated its pro-socialist leanings when it endorsed the Earth Charter, a document that blames capitalism for many of the world's environmental, social, and economic woes. The Charter maintains that "the dominant patterns of production and consumption are causing environmental devastation, the depletion of resources, and a massive extinction of species. The benefits of development are not shared equitably and the gap between rich and poor is widening."
Global Restoration: Reasoning from the premise that human industrial activity is largely responsible for environmental problems, PCUSA impugns America's "reliance on non-renewable energy sources that contribute to the degradation of the air, water and land."
Conscientious Objection: "For two thousand years, some people who identify themselves as Christians have refused to participate in war and the taking of other human lives. They have given themselves to the service of life, not the work of death. ... They are ... motivated by conscience, which forbid their participation in war."

PCUSA has given its organizational endorsement to the following campaigns:

(a) *Justice for Immigrants: A Journey of Hope*: This initiative seeks to bring about "a broad-based legalization (permanent residency) of the undocumented of all nationalities"; "to allow family members [of illegal aliens] to reunite with loved ones in the United States"; to end "the border 'blockade' enforcement strategy"; and to restore "due process protections for [illegal] immigrants."

(b) *The International Shadow Project* (ISP): Founded on the axiom that the United States' atomic bombings of Hiroshima and Nagasaki in 1945 constituted grievous and unwarranted crimes against humanity, this project encourages Americans each August 6th (the anniversary of the first bombing) to draw chalk silhouettes of human figures on paved surfaces in their neighborhoods to represent the Japanese innocents who lost their lives to American aggression. ISP is endorsed by singer Bonnie Raitt, actor Martin Sheen, and author Barbara Kingsolver, and by such organizations as Physicians for Social Responsibility, Veterans For Peace, Women's Action for New Directions, and the Women's International League for Peace and Freedom.

(c) *Abolition! Now*: A project of the anti-war group Abolition 2000, this campaign "aims to create the political will, though the mobilization of civil society, for the complete abolition of nuclear weapons by 2020."
(d) *Alternatives for Simple Living*: This project is a critique of capitalism generally, and of American consumerism particularly.

(e) *Oak Ridge Environmental Peace Alliance*: This initiative sponsors "Stop the Bombs," a series of protests aimed mainly at the Nuclear Weapons Plant in Oak Ridge, Tennessee.
(f) *Nonviolent Peaceforce*: This anti-war NGO deploys its members to disrupt military actions in areas of conflict around the world.

(g) *National Network to Oppose the Militarizaiton of Youth*: A project of the American Friends Service Committee, this anti-military recruitment program strives "to halt the growing influence of the military in U.S. schools."

Pax Christi USA is a member organization of the Win Without War coalition; Pax Christi International is part of the Abolition 2000 anti-war coalition; and a few regional Pax Christi branches are members of the United for Peace and Justice anti-war coalition.

In the immediate aftermath of the October 2001 U.S. invasion of Afghanistan, PCUSA released a statement not only condemning the American military action, but also impugning the United States as a racism-infested, terrorist nation with grossly misplaced priorities.

In December 2002, PCUSA joined with more than 70 other organizations to help organize large- and small-scale protests against America's then-probable invasion of Iraq. The group also sent its own delegation to Iraq to protest the coming war and, in effect, defend the legitimacy of Saddam Hussein's regime. PCUSA's public critisms are not aimed solely against the United States. In 2004, for instance, local chapters of the organization signed -- along with more than 200 other leftwing groups -- a letter exhorting members of the U.S. Senate to oppose Israel's construction of an anti-terrorism security barrier in the West Bank -- characterizing the barrier as an illegal "apartheid wall" that violated the civil and human rights of Palestinians.

Pax Christi USA receives financial support from the Ford Foundation and the Raskob Foundation for Catholic Activities.

PHYSICIANS FOR HUMAN RIGHTS - ISRAEL (PHR-I)

52 Golomb St.
Tel-Aviv 66171
Israel

Phone :972 3 6873718
URL: www.dundee.ac.uk Israeli health-care organization

> Consistently condemns Israeli military reprisals against terrorists, but does not denounce the Palestinian terrorist attacks

Opposing "the subjugation of medical care to political considerations of any kind," Physicians for Human Rights-Israel (PHR-I) was established in 1988 by Israeli and Palestinian doctors as "a non-partisan, non-profit organization dedicated to promoting and protecting the right to health care [for Palestinians] in Israel and in territories under Israel's effective control." "It was apparent," explains PHR-I, "says that human rights violations in the form of systematic and official denial of access to medical care, the intentional infliction of bodily injury, torture and neglect of prisoners, grossly substandard medical care and facilities in the occupied territories and East Jerusalem, administrative detention and solitary confinement were issues that demanded attention. Therefore, PHR-Israel was founded to address these very issues."

PHR-I has adopted a consistently biased stance against Israel, prompting the Israel Medical Association to sever all ties with the organization. For instance, PHR-I regularly condemns "the Israeli Occupation," drawing no moral distinction between Palestinian terrorist attacks targeting civilians, and Israeli military reprisals targeting those terrorists. Moreover, the organization contends that "the State of Israel has no authority to erect checkpoints or roadblocks as a form of total control of the movement of Palestinian residents within the West Bank and Gaza Strip."

PHR-I also opposes Israel's security fence, constructed in the West Bank for the purpose of preventing Palestinian terrorists from reaching Israeli population centers. On January 29, 2004, PHR-I took part in a demonstration "tour" (organized by the NGO Ta'ayush) in the area of Abu Dis, East Jerusalem. According to PHR-I's press release of February 1, 2004, (titled "PHR-Israel tour of the Jerusalem Stranglehold"), "The wall is just the latest step in Israel's policy of separating the East Jerusalem hospitals from the communities they serve."

PHR-I was a co-endorser of a May 19, 2004 advertisement that appeared in the newspapers *Ha'aretz* and *Al-Quds*, depicting the Israeli Defense Force's (IDF) demolition of Palestinian homes in Rafah (located in Gaza) as unconscionable violations of human rights -- making no mention of the fact that the homes in question were being used as terrorist bases. Co-sponsors of this ad included such Palestinian NGOs as Adalah, Al-Mezan Center for Human Rights, Al-Haq, HaMoked, I'lam, and the Palestinian Center for Human Rights.

Denunciations of Israeli policy constitute the dominant theme of PHR-I literature. An August 16, 2004 report on the Rafah Crossing (in the Gaza Strip) criticizes restrictions (which it terms "collective punishment") on Palestinians attempting to enter Israel through this point. However, PHR-I makes no attempt to define this concept, or to distinguish it from legitimate and necessary security measures. Similarly, a May 2004 report titled "The Bureaucracy of Occupation," produced jointly with Machsom Watch, impugns the District Coordination Offices responsible for issuing travel permits to the Palestinian population. Without mentioning Palestinian terrorism, the report states that "[t]he denial of freedom of movement is a human rights violation."

PHR-I literature also asserts that Israeli soldiers deliberately shoot at Palestinian civilians despite the existence of clear rules governing the use of live fire and a well-defined legal system to deal with any abuses of those regulations. For example, an August 31, 2004 press statement claims: "According to information given ... by Palestinian medical organizations in Gaza ... the soldiers suddenly, and with no prior warning, opened fire" on a Palestinian ambulance.

In an October 3, 2004 statement, PHR-I condemned IDF operations in the northern Gaza Strip, virtually ignoring the fact that the operation was intended to prevent the firing of Qassam missiles into Israel.

PHR-I receives funding from Christian Aid, the Ford Foundation, the European Union, and the New Israel Fund.

REBUILDING ALLIANCE

457 Kingsley Avenue
Palo Alto, CA
94301
Phone :65-325-4663
URL: http://www.rebuildingalliance.org/Raises money to rebuild Palestinian homes damaged or destroyed by the Israeli Defense Forces

Closelly allied with the International Solidarity Movement
Accuses Israel of oppressing and abusing the Palestinian people
Engages in political lobbying

Formally established in June 2003, Rebuilding Alliance (RA) raises money to finance the reconstruction of “homes and communities in regions of war and occupation” -- specifically the regions affected by the Arab-Israeli conflict. But RA does not rebuild any Israeli homes that have been destroyed by Hamas rockets fired from Gaza, or by Hezbollah rockets launched from southern Lebanon. Rather, its aid is earmarked exclusively for "Palestinian families whose homes have been unjustly demolished by the Israeli government” -- a reference to the Israeli Defense Forces' demolition of structures that terrorists were utilizing as residences or as bases of operations. RA purports to rebuild only “the homes of people who have never been accused of any security violation.”

Intimately linked to the International Solidarity Movement (ISM), RA was created in reaction to the death of Rachel Corrie, an ISM activist who, in March 2003, was crushed beneath a bulldozer in Rafah when its operator failed to see her trying to block the destruction of a Palestinian home that was concealing a tunnel through which Hamas and Islamic Jihad terrorists were receiving smuggled weapons.

Cindy Corrie, Rachel’s mother, is a Member of RA’s Board of Directors. Craig Corrie, Rachel’s father, is an Honorary Board Member. And Alison Weir, the Founder and Executive Director of If Americans Knew, is listed as an “Associate” of RA.

Rebuilding Alliance is an outgowth of the Global Campaign to Rebuild Palestinian Homes, which was formed in June 2002 as a collaborative effort by three nongovernmental organizations -- the Israeli Committee Against House Demolitions (ICAHD), the Jerusalem Center for Social and Economic Rights, and Just Peace Technologies. Fiscal sponsorship for this Global Campaign was initially provided by Global Exchange, which is headed by the pro-Castro communist Medea Benjamin. Subsequent operational expenses were shouldered personally by members of Just Peace Technologies. Publicly lauded by ICAHD Coordinator Jeff Halper, the Global Campaign raised enough money (much of it with the help of some 400 United Methodist churches in the U.S.) to rebuild six homes and a peace center in the Jerusalem area and a kindergarten in the West Bank. Additional funds were used to petition the Israeli Supreme Court to cancel specific demolitions. In October 2002 the Global Campaign was dissolved and soon reincarnated as Rebuilding Homes. The organization officially changed its name to Rebuilding Alliance on June 28, 2003.

Apart from home reconstruction, RA's major work falls into three additional categories:

(a) *Education and Outreach*: "[T]o change the unjust policies of the Israeli government -- and make the world safer for all of us -- we must reach mainstream Americans and our senators and representatives. We [RA] provide education, information, and experiences intended to reshape American views of the Middle East."

(b) *School Building*: "Villages and organizations are asking us to help build schools. Despite personal and collective tragedies, they place the education of their children as their highest priority, the key to a better future."

(c) *Legal Defense*: "We select precedent-setting building projects and defend them, all the way up to the Israeli Supreme Court."

According to RA, the Israeli government chooses to demolish Palestinian homes for four main reasons:

(1) *Land Grab*: "Over 400,000 Israelis now live in the Occupied Territories, including the settlement 'neighborhoods' in East Jerusalem. Israeli settlements were built on private land, belonging to Palestinian villagers. Through an intricate system of zoning and planning, Palestinian homes were and continue to be demolished to make way for settlements."

(2) *Population Squeeze*: "Home demolition, along with travel restrictions, curfews, blockading of towns and uprooting of trees, is one of the most brazen and cruel of Occupation policies. These policies are designed to make life so difficult for ordinary Palestinians that eventually they will give up their land and leave."

(3) *Military Action*: "Military action destroys and damages Palestinian homes. ... Since the start of Israel's Occupation in 1967 over 14,000 Palestinian homes have been demolished, resulting in the displacement of more than 100,000 people."

(4) *Collective Punishment*: "As a form of collective punishment, the Israel government demolished the homes of suspected terrorists and their extended families." According to RA, these demolitions go "far beyond mere retaliation for terrorist attacks. It is an attack on an entire people, an attempt to make the Palestinians submit to a mini-state under Israeli control."

RA's cost for rebuilding an average home of 100 square meters (980 square feet) in the Jerusalem area is $43,000; this includes $30,000 for construction expenses; $2,400 in fundraising costs; $2,100 in administrative costs; $2,500 earmarked for a legal reserve fund; and $6,000 "to tell the story of the home to people around the world with a short film, build coalitions to adopt the home, and coordinate urgent action to prevent demolition."

RA's Executive Director is Donna Baranski-Walker, the founder of Just Peace Technologies. RA's Board Chairman is Alan Kaufman, a Green Party of Michigan representative on the International Committee of the Green Party of the United States.

RA has 501(c)(3) status as a nonprofit organization with the Internal Revenue Service, a designation reserved for tax-exempt groups that operate for religious, charitable, scientific, or educational purposes. The IRS stipulates that such entities "may not attempt to influence legislation as a substantial part of its activities" and "may not participate in any campaign activity for or against political candidates," though some voter registration activities are permitted. On its 2004 and 2005 U.S. tax returns, RA declared that it had spent no money on lobbying or legislation.

Yet RA explicitly urges its members and supporters to make in-person and telephone lobbying calls (promoting pro-Arab policies) to their congressional representatives, and its website lists weekly congressional lobbying activities. In one particular "action alert," the RA website posted specific instructions on how to help prevent the passage of House Concurrent Resolution 371, a bill supporting Israel's construction of an anti-terrorism security barrier in the West Bank. On another occasion, an RA promotional campaign urged: "We're encouraging Americans to take in the personal stories of Palestinian families, to invest in their future by helping them rebuild homes and schools, and to defend their rights in court. And when bulldozers are coming, we know we can save those homes and schools when citizens call Congress to intervene." To make it easier for people to lobby effectively, RA provided a templated online letter which could be forwarded to individual congressmen.

RA's website exhorts its readers to actively oppose the American Israel Public Affairs Committee (AIPAC), an influential Israeli lobby. Soliciting money for its "AIPAC Does Not Speak for Us" campaign in 2006, RA stated: "We urge our representatives to reject the AIPAC agenda. ... During the terrible violence that engulfed Lebanon and Israel this past summer, AIPAC ... demanded unconditional [U.S.] support for the disproportionate Israeli military assault ... AIPAC urged the U.S. to rush more bombs to Israel, bombs that destroyed entire Lebanese neighborhoods. ... AIPAC pushed for the current U.S. sanctions against the Palestinian people that have created a humanitarian crisis in Gaza. ... In the West Bank, the destruction of Palestinian homes and confiscation of land goes unabated, with the full support of AIPAC. ... We demand a suspension of U.S. military aid to Israel ... until Israel abides by international law."
Moreover, RA has engaged in direct legislative lobbying with such policymakers as California Senator Barbara Boxer and Congresswoman Anna Eshoo, asking them to vote against a proposal to cut off U.S. funding for the Palestinian government while Hamas was in political control of that entity. RA also permitted a non-U.S. citizen, a Palestinian named Husam El Nounou, to lobby Senator Boxer during a telephone call. The Palestinian NGO association to which El Nounou belongs has refused to sign a declaration pledging that any funds received from organizations such as RA will not be used to fund terrorism.

RIGHTS AND DEMOCRACY

1001 de Maisonneuve Blvd. East
Suite 1100
Montreal (Quebec)
Canada H2L 4P9
Phone :514-283-6073
URL: www.dd-rd.ca Canadian human rights organization with a pro-Palestinian, anti-Israel political agenda

The Montreal-based organization Rights and Democracy (R&D), originally known as the International Centre for Human Rights and Democratic Development, was founded in 1988 by an Act of the Canadian Parliament "to encourage and support the universal values of human rights and the promotion of democratic institutions and practices around the world." R&D has consultative status with the United Nations Economic and Social Council and is on the International Labour Organization's Special List of NGOs. It also has observer status with the African Commission on Human and Peoples' Rights.

The recipient of more than $4 million per year from the Canadian government, R&D's major objectives fall under four separate categories:

Globalization, Governance & Human Rights: "To help reduce the gap between the actual practices of states and their formal adhesion to international human rights agreements."

Rights of Indigenous Peoples: "To contribute to the full recognition and implementation of the rights of indigenous peoples nationally, regionally and internationally."

Rights of Women: "To facilitate women's leadership and participation in civil society; to ensure their full contribution to peace-building processes, to seek accountability for gender crimes in transitional justice systems, and to build women's capacity to meet the challenges of fundamentalisms, militarism and the prevailing security agenda."

Democratic Development: "To contribute to the development of democratic practices, institutions and culture at the national and regional levels ..."

R&D's campaign to promote "democratic institutions in developing areas" has been used to justify a strongly pro-Palestinian, anti-Israel political agenda. The organization has approved funding grants for a number of projects conducted by highly politicized recipients, including the Palestinian Human Rights Monitoring Group (an NGO established in 1996 to "end human rights violations committed against Palestinians in the West Bank, Gaza Strip and East Jerusalem") and the International Women's House in Hares (whose mission is "to train women ... to witness, monitor, document and publicize human rights abuses; [to] peacefully intervene to prevent such abuses from taking place; and [to] support the growth in non-violent resistance to the military occupation of Palestinian lands in the West Bank and Gaza"). Both of these donees presume Israeli military activity to be not only the greatest, but the only, threat to human rights in the Palestinian territories.

In October 2000, shortly after the outbreak of the second Palestinian Intifada, R&D issued a press release characterizing the violence as a logical reaction to: "Israeli control of over 60% of land in the Occupied Palestinian Territories"; Israeli restrictions of Palestinian "control and access to their own land" through "land seizures, house demolitions and restrictions on social and economic development"; the detention of Palestinians by Israel and the alleged denial of due process; and the "excessive and indiscriminate use of force by the Israeli military." The only passage even remotely resembling a reference to Palestinian terror was an ambiguous statement of moral equivalence: "Rights & Democracy condemns all violence by all actors in Israel and the Occupied Territories, including territories under the Palestinian National Authority." The R&D statement ended with a series of demands, including: "the end of Israeli occupation in the Occupied Territories, including East Jersusalem"; "the establishment of a Palestinian state with sovereignty over borders and natural resources"; and "the right of return for the hundreds of thousands of Palestinians forced into exile since 1948."

In an open letter to Canadian Minister of Foreign Affairs Bill Graham in April 2002, R&D called for the deployment of an international peacekeeping force coupled with the "full withdrawal of Israeli occupation of the West Bank and Gaza." Added R&D: "We believe that the Israeli occupation is the root cause of the Palestinian crisis."

SABEEL ECUMENICAL LIBERATION THEOLOGY CENTER

www.**sabeel**.org

Anti-Israel NGO

Founded in 1989 and based in Jerusalem, the Sabeel Ecumenical Liberation Theology Center is directed by Naim Ateek, former Canon of St. George's Cathedral in Jerusalem. Sabeel describes itself as "an ecumenical grassroots liberation theology movement among Palestinian Christians." The organization "hopes to connect the true meaning of Christian faith with the daily lives of all those who suffer under occupation, violence, discrimination, and human rights violations," and it "encourages Christians from around the world to work for justice and to stand in solidarity with the Palestinian people." Reliable funding information is unavailable, but support for Sabeel is apparently provided by church-based groups in North America and Europe, including the Mennonite Central Committee.

Sabeel identifies its major programs as follows:

Community Building Program: "Due to ever increasing limitations on movement and freedom, the [Palestinian] community is under a great deal of economic and civic stress. ... [This program] seeks to educate the community on the political situation ... [and] foster a sense of solidarity ..."

Youth Program: "The youth of Palestine - Israel are eager to see an end to violence and to become contributing citizens of a respectful pluralistic society. [This program] seeks to provide opportunities for young people from different churches meet and get to know each other ..."

Women's Program: This program features "day trips bringing together Palestinian and Israeli Arab women for Bible study and reflection, visits to local organizations, and discussion of contemporary topics."

Clergy Program: "Palestine is the spiritual home of numerous Christian denominations, but historical and theological differences have often made difficult cooperation between denominations. [This program] seeks to nurture unity and mutual support among local clergy, [and] encourage ecumenical thought and action ..."

International Program: This program "seeks to educate the Christian community worldwide about the present reality of Palestinian Christians, provide accurate and timely interpretation of events from a Palestinian Christian perspective, and arrange opportunities for foreigners to meet and know Palestinians."

Sabeel promotes an anti-Israel agenda in Protestant churches in both North America and Europe and has supported the divestment campaign against Israel.

The extreme positions of Sabeel are given voice by its Director Naim Ateek, who has said, on various occasions: "It seems to many of us that Jesus is on the cross again with thousands of crucified Palestinians around him. [...] The Israeli government crucifixion system is operating daily"; and "Israel has placed a large boulder, a big stone that has metaphorically shut off the Palestinians in a tomb. It is similar to the stone placed on the entrance of Jesus' tomb..."

Sabeel supports a "one-state solution" to the Arab-Israeli conflict, where Israel would continue to exist, but not as a Jewish state. "As part of a democratic, binational Palestine," says Ateek, "the Jews would eventually become a minority in the country."

In 2002 the Archbishop Desmond Tutu, a Nobel Peace Laureate, signed on informally as an international patron for Sabeel in order to "assist the Palestinian Christian organization in its outreach and development work with Christian Churches around the world." Rev. John Gladwin, Bishop of Chelmsford and Chair of Christian Aid's Board of Trustees, is a patron of Sabeel's UK branch. Paul Dean, who sits on Christian Aid's Executive Committee, also participates in Sabeel activities. And Afif Safieh, the PLO representative in London, is a major supporter of Sabeel and its ideology.

In its English-language quarterly publication *Cornerstone*, Sabeel highlights its activities both locally and internationally, and presents theological reflections on contemporary social and political events.

SAVE THE CHILDREN (STC)

URL: www.**save**the**children**.org Educational resource center for teachers of Middle Eastern affairs

Holds strong pro-Palestinian militant, anti-Israel bias

Save The Children (STC) is a United Kingdom-based NGO that has an annual income of almost $700 million and is active in more than 100 countries in Africa, Europe, Asia, and Latin America and the Caribbean. STC's mission is to "fight for children in the UK and around the world who suffer from poverty, disease, injustice and violence, working with them to find lifelong answers to the problems they face."

STC's work focuses primarily on the following programs:

Emergencies: "Emergencies ... include war, refugee crises, famine, drought and floods. ... Children are particularly vulnerable in emergencies because they are physically weaker than adults and risk being separated from their families. ... We began life as an emergency relief agency. Now we respond to people's immediate needs in an emergency while prioritizing long-term recovery and development."

HIV and AIDS: "Save The Children works to prevent HIV/AIDS and support children who are affected by it. We tackle poverty, educate children about HIV/AIDS, support community care for children orphaned by AIDS, challenge prejudice against young people affected by HIV/AIDS, protect orphaned children from exploitation and abuse, and involve children in HIV/AIDS prevention and support work."

Health: "Save The Children tackles the main cause of ill-health -- poverty -- by campaigning for fairer international policies and resources, both nationally and internationally, for health services. We work with health providers, governments, other non-governmental organizations, communities and children to improve access to affordable, good quality health services."

Education: "Save The Children works to ensure that all children get access to good quality education by tackling poverty, helping communities run schools, training teachers, developing education policies and curricula, supporting flexible learning schemes, developing educational opportunities for very young children, and providing education for children caught up in emergencies."

Poverty and Economics: "The extent and severity of global poverty are directly linked to economic policies and activities that ignore children's right to a happy, healthy and secure childhood. Save The Children is pushing for more investment in key services that benefit children ..."

Exploitation and Protection: "We lobby to improve juvenile justice systems, to stop the abuse of children accused of crime. We help child workers, refugees, asylum-seekers and other excluded children get healthcare and education, and lobby internationally against child trafficking, the use of child soldiers and harmful child labor."

Equality and Rights: "The UN Convention on the Rights of the Child underpins all of Save The Children's work. All children are equal, and have human rights such as the right to food, shelter, health care, education, and protection from violence, neglect and exploitation."

Presenting a very biased, anti-Israel version of the history of the Arab-Israeli conflict, STC has failed to condemn the Palestinian exploitation of children as suicide bombers; has ignored the use of textbooks that promote Jew-hatred among Palestinian schoolchildren; and has condemned Israel's construction of an anti-terror security barrier in the West Bank.

The STC campaign against the security barrier included a 2004 presentation at the United Nations Human Rights Commission session in Geneva. Moreover, in March 2004 the British and Swedish branches of STC published a report, "Living Behind Barriers," which claimed that as a result of the barrier, Palestinian children had suffered an "alarming rise in [their] sense of insecurity and risk of violence." (By contrast, the document said nothing about the emotional fallout that Israeli children may have suffered as a result of Palestinian terror attacks.) The report also asserted that Israeli transgressions, and not hate-oriented Palestinian educational programs, were to blame for the fact that many Palestinian children equated Jews with "animals." Finally, it made unsubstantiated allegations that Israeli police routinely "torture and abuse" Palestinian minors.

In April 2006, STC criticized the United States, Canada, and the European Union for choosing to suspend aid payments to the Palestinian Authority after the newly elected Hamas government took office on March 29. STC's position on this matter was shared by such NGOs as Medecins Sans Frontiers, Oxfam, Medecins du Monde, Amnesty International (USA), Christian Aid, the International Federation for Human Rights, and KAIROS.

STC has received funding from dozens of foundations, including the Ford Foundation, the W. K. Kellogg Foundation, the Rockefeller Foundation, the Ahmanson Foundation, the Carnegie Corporation of New York, the Bill and Melinda Gates Foundation, the William and Flora Hewlett Foundation, the Andrew W. Mellon Foundation, the David and Lucile Packard Foundation, the Pew Charitable Trusts, the Surdna Foundation, and the Turner Foundation.

STUDENTS FOR JUSTICE IN PALESTINE (SJP)

email: lsjp@law.berkeley.edu
157 Boalt Hall

URL: http://www.law.berkeley.edu/students/jrnlorgs/orgs/orglist/lsjp.html

- Anti-Semitic, pro-Palestinian activist group founded at University of California's Berkeley campus in 2001
- Has chapters on more than 25 major campuses throughout the U.S.
- Advocates economic sanctions against Israel

Students for Justice in Palestine (SJP) originated on the University of California, Berkeley campus in 2001. Since then, SJP cells have spread to some 25 major campuses throughout the United States, including Yale, Princeton, Columbia, Georgetown, and the universities of Michigan and Maryland. SJP at the University of Maryland states that its mission is to pursue "freedom and self-determination for the Palestinian people," a goal predicated on ending "[t]he Israeli military occupation, with its daily humiliation, abuse and brutal violence"; "[t]he right of return and repatriation for Palestinian refugees of war and ethnic cleansing"; and "[t]he cessation of settlement activity and the dismantling of settlements built outside of Israel's pre-1967 border." Toward the advancement of these objectives, SJP demands "[d]ivestment ... from companies that invest or do substantial business in Israel," and an "end to U.S. tax-funded aid to Israel."

Calling Israel "this generation's South Africa," SJP vows to do for contemporary Palestinians what the anti-apartheid campaign did for blacks in South Africa. Toward that end, SJP exhorts college students to help punish the "Apartheid State of Israel" by demanding that their schools divest their financial assets from all companies that conduct business there. SJP has staged campus protests against Starbucks, General Electric, Disney, and scores of other companies.

SJP members, who denounce what they term the Israeli-sponsored "concentration camps" wherein Palestinians are purportedly forced to live, harass Jewish students when they emerge from campus synagogues. In one incident after a rally at San Francisco State University (SFSU), SJP supporters surrounded a small group of Jewish students and incited violence while shouting, "Too bad Hitler didn't finish the job," and other epithets. On April 9, 2002 (Holocaust Remembrance Day), pro-Palestinian groups at SFSU protested Israel's occupation of the West Bank and then circulated posters depicting Jews eating Christian babies. That same day, SJP members held a rally and a sit-in on the Berkeley campus, demanding that the university divest all its assets from companies that conducted any business in Israel. Police arrested 79 people that day, 41 of them students. Pro-Palestinian protests also erupted on several other campuses that same day, involving nearly 10,000 students at Ohio State, the University of Minnesota, University of Illinois Urbana-Champaign, and Carnegie Mellon University. In November 2002, Yale University's SJP set up a mock Israeli checkpoint on campus, harassing Jewish students with cardboard rifles.

A co-founder of the Berkeley SJP is Snehal Shingavi, a graduate student who gained notoriety in 2001 for teaching a controversial course called "The Politics and Poetics of Palestinian Resistance." Explaining that his instruction would focus on "Israel's brutal oppression of Palestine since 1948," Shingavi in the course catalog urged conservative students not to bother registering for his class.

SJP's national conference at the University of Michigan in November 2002 was sponsored by the Islamic Association for Palestine, an organization that raises money for the families of suicide bombers. The conference also featured keynote speaker Sami Al-Arian, a former professor at the University of South Florida who was the leader of Palestinian Islamic Jihad operations in North America.

In its literature, SJP demands an immediate end to the current Israeli military "occupation"; an immediate cessation of all U.S. material and political support to Israel; divestment from all corporations that conduct business in, or with, Israel; and the implementation of the right of return and the repatriation of all Palestinians.

SUSTAIN (STOP US TAX-FUNDED AID TO ISRAEL NOW)

c/o Mark Lance
P.O. Box 3720
Washington, DC
20007

URL: http://www.ndparking.com/sustaincampaign.orgViews the United States and Israel as the world's primary perpetrators of evil

Opposes U.S. military response to 9/11

Based in Washington, D.C. and presiding over more than a dozen additional chapters throughout the United States, the group Stop U.S. Tax-funded Aid to Israel Now (SUSTAIN) was established in late 2000. It describes itself as "a non-hierarchical, grassroots organization committed to supporting and sustaining the Palestinian movement for justice, human rights and self-determination."

"We are committed to building a campaign against U.S. military and economic aid to Israel so that U.S. tax-dollars do not support the [Israeli] abuse of human rights," SUSTAIN asserts. On federal Tax-Day, SUSTAIN criticizes America's financial support (with its tax revenues) of Israel. The organization has also taken rhetorical and economic action against the Caterpillar bulldozer company (to protest the Israeli Defense Force's use of that company's equipment in the demolition of Palestinian terrorists' homes); denounced the construction of Israel's security fence; and promoted divestment from Israeli corporations and economic interests.

Two weeks after the 9/11 attacks, SUSTAIN organized a "Global Justice Intifada" in Washington, D.C. to condemn "U.S. imperialism" and demand justice on behalf of "Palestinians resisting Israeli occupation" and "Iraqis fighting genocidal sanctions."

Mark Lance, a professor at Georgetown University and a founding member of SUSTAIN, wrote an article in the spring of 2002 titled "Imperialism and Anti-authoritarian Resistance after 9-11: Some Crucial Questions," in which he expressed his desire to organize "solidarity" groups within the Palestinian territories and Lebanon, while at the same time working with the terrorist organizations Hamas and Hezbollah. These groups, wrote Lance, "must be understood in terms of the role [they play]. Hamas provides the majority of social services to the people of this oppressed and overpopulated strip of land. Brutalized by Israel, and neglected by the PNA [Palestinian National Authority], Hamas has been the only group to take up the slack. Thus, organizing that rejects them out of hand or in all respects is simply impossible. This applies even more to the role of Hezbollah in the south of Lebanon."

SUSTAIN has endorsed the "Declaration Regarding Caterpillar Violations of Human Rights," a document that impugns the U.S.-based Caterpillar Corporation for selling its machinery to the Israeli army for counter-terrorism operations, as noted above.

SUSTAIN is a member organization of the United for Peace and Justice anti-war coalition, which is led by Leslie Cagan, a longtime committed socialist who aligns her politics with those of Fidel Castro's Communist Cuba.

TA'AYUSH

Phone :972-3-6914437
URL: http://www.taayush.org/

Anti-Israel NGO
Supports sanctions, boycotts, and divestment campaigns against Israel

Founded in the fall of 2000, Ta'ayush (Arabic for "life in common") is an Arab-Jewish political NGO based in Israel. Condemning the "segregation, racism, and discrimination between Jews and Arabs within Israel," this organization opposes "the walls of closure and siege encircling the Palestinians in the occupied West Bank and Gaza Strip," and portrays Israel as "an armed fortress in the heart of the Middle East." Characterizing Israel's 1948 creation as *Al Nakba* (Arabic for "The Catastrophe"), Ta'ayush participates in numerous protests against Israel's construction of its anti-terrorism barrier in the West Bank, labeling it an "Apartheid Wall."

In 2004 Ta'ayush initiated a "Not In Our Name!" petition that stated: "We, the undersigned, citizens of Israel, completely reject the Sharon government's claim that the 'Separation Fence' ... is intended to defend our safety and security. ... This is not the way to prevent suicide bombings, but rather to further aggravate the misery, despair and hatred, and to perpetuate the conflict for future generations." Ta'ayush elaborates: "The State of Israel is erecting the Separation Wall on Palestinian land out of 'security considerations,' while the true objective is to annex land west of the Wall into Israel. This provocative act ... is being carried out with all the oppressive and violent means at the disposal of the occupying IDF forces -- through shooting and killing, serious injury, beating and threats, closures and curfews, and fear and intimidation tactics."

Ta'ayush also supports anti-Israel sanctions, boycotts, and divestment initiatives in conjunction with pro-Palestinian NGOs.

Ta'ayush is currently conducting a campaign titled "Free Tali Fahima," named in honor of a longtime Tel Aviv-based activist who frequently demonstrated against Israel's "oppression" of Palestinians. Fahia was incarcerated in 2004 for her role in planning terrorist attacks against Jewish targets and for aiding Al-Aqsa Martyrs' Brigades commander Zakariya Zubeidi, her Palestinian "lover" from Jenin. Says Ta'ayush: "We appeal to women and men of conscience worldwide, especially members of the medical, psychiatric and legal professions, on behalf of Ms. Tali Fahima, an Israeli peace activist whose conditions of imprisonment in prolonged isolation ... threaten her long-term wellbeing. Having closely followed her case, we strongly believe that the legal grounds for her detention and prosecution are insubstantial and verge on the ridiculous."

U.S. CAMPAIGN TO END THE ISRAELI OCCUPATION

1101 Pennsylvania Ave. SE
Suite 204
Washington, DC

20003
Phone :202-318-1613
URL: http://www.endtheoccupation.org/Anti-Israel coalition

Advocates the termination of U.S. support for Israel

The U.S. Campaign to End the Israeli Occupation (a.k.a. End the Occupation) is a coalition of groups working together "to change those U.S. policies that both sustain Israel's ... occupation of the West Bank, Gaza, and Jerusalem, and deny equal rights for all." The Campaign holds annual conferences to bring its coalition members together. As of June 2000, some 214 local and national organizations had signed on to the Campaign. Among these were: Americans for Justice in Palestine; Global Exchange; the International Solidarity Movement; Middle East Children's Alliance; Palestine Right to Return Coalition (Al-Awda); American Muslims for Jerusalem; the American-Arab Anti-Discrimination Committee; the Institute for Policy Studies; Pax Christi USA; Students for Justice in Palestine; SUSTAIN; the American Friends Service Committee; the 8th Day Center for Justice; the International Socialist Organization; BostonToPalestine; Grassroots International; the Women's International League for Peace and Freedom; Women Against Military Madness; Jews Against the Occupation; MADRE; the National Lawyers Guild; Michael Lerner's Tikkun Community; Friends of Sabeel; If Americans Knew; Christian Peacemaker Teams; Peace Action; Jews Against the Occupation; MADRE; Palestine Media Watch; and United for Peace and Justice.

In November 2002 the Campaign published an article titled "Seeing Clearly Through a Veil of Blood," in which the author wrote that Israel owed Yasser Arafat and the Palestine Liberation Organization (PLO) a debt of gratitude for their supposedly invaluable "support for a two-state solution." The article further stated that much anti-Jewish hatred "is fueled by the injustice of Israel's occupation of Palestine."

In July 2003, at its Second U.S. Campaign Organizers Conference, End the Occupation hosted Nihad Awad, the Executive Director of the Council on American-Islamic Relations (CAIR), who has publicly declared his support for the Hamas terrorist organization.

The Campaign opposes Israel's construction of a security fence; it supports all divestment efforts intended to impose financial hardship on Israel; and it has endorsed the "Declaration Regarding Caterpillar Violations of Human Rights," a document that impugns the U.S.-based Caterpillar Corporation for selling its machinery to the Israeli army, which in turn uses that equipment to demolish Palestinian terrorists' homes and bases of operation.

The Campaign is currently working on a "Palestine Human Rights Litigation Project," whose focus is on a pair of class-action lawsuits against former Israeli military officials in U.S. federal district courts. Filed on behalf of Palestinian and Lebanese civilians, these suits allege that the officials are guilty of war crimes; crimes against humanity; cruel, inhuman, or degrading treatment; and extrajudicial killings.

The Campaign's "Legislative Project" urges Members of the U.S. Congress to adopt a pro-Palestinian position regarding the Arab-Israeli conflict.

The Campaign also works closely with Palestine Media Watch to minimize media references to Palestinian terrorism and corruption, while promoting images of Palestinians as victims of Israeli oppression.

Advisory Board members of the Campaign include Dr. Joel Beinin, Professor of Middle East History at Stanford University, and Phyllis Bennis of the Institute for Policy Studies.

The Campaign is a member organization of the United for Peace and Justice anti-war coalition, which is led by Leslie Cagan, a longtime committed socialist who aligns her politics with those of Fidel Castro's Communist Cuba.

On its website in 2006, the Campaign displayed a statement complaining that Hezbollah (a.k.a. Hizballah) had been "cast misleadingly in much media coverage" of the latter's then-recent war against Israel. "Much more than a militia," said the Campaign, "the Hizballah movement is also a political party that is a powerful actor in Lebanese politics and a provider of important social services. Not a creature of Iranian and Syrian sponsorship, Hizballah arose to battle Israel's occupation of south Lebanon from 1982-2000 and, more broadly, to advocate for Lebanon's historically disenfranchised Shi'i Muslim community. While it has many political opponents in Lebanon, Hizballah is very much of Lebanon."

In May 2007, twenty-two black American professors, writers, religious figures, and other leaders issued "a call to Black America" to join the Campaign's June 10th rally "to commemorate the 40th anniversary of the beginning of the illegal Israeli occupation of Palestinian territories." Among the signatories to this letter were Manning Marable, Cornel West, and a number of individuals affiliated with United for Peace and Justice, the Green Party USA, the Institute for Policy Studies, and the NAACP. The letter noted the need "to bring attention to this 40 year travesty of justice"; it condemned the Israeli government for having "appropriated Palestinian land in open defiance of international law"; it urged black leaders to defend the "Palestinian people's right to full self-determination"; and it expressed "outrage at the Israeli government that collaborated with the apartheid South African government ... and emulated South Africa's treatment of its Black majority in its own treatment of the Palestinian people."

UNION OF ARAB STUDENT ASSOCIATIONS

URL: http://www.angelfire.com/or/uasa/

Umbrella organization for Arab-American students
Opposes Israel's existence
Endorses the Palestine Solidarity Movement and the International Solidarity Movement
Opposes U.S. aid to Israel

Established in 1996 by Hanna Hanania, the Union of Arab Student Associations (UASA) describes itself as "a student-based organization that seeks to connect and unify local Arab-American university groups and ... educat[e] the Arab community and the general public about the culture, language, and history of the Arab world while promoting vital issues that pertain to Arabs in the United States." The Union currently has several thousand members representing more than 40 universities across the United States.

In 1999, the UASA website directed its viewers to visit the website of its affiliate "Students for Palestine," which featured a map of Israel completely covered by a Palestinian flag.

UASA endorsed the November 2003 National Conference of the Palestine Solidarity Movement, which is the collegiate arm of the pro-Hamas group International Solidarity Movement.

In January 2001, UASA established a sister organization named the Network of Arab-American Professionals (NAAP) to serve as "a channel through which alumni and professionals could step up their activism and focus their activities to reflect the experiences, needs, and resources of an older, more established working base of members." UASA deemed the new NAAP vital to helping Arab-Americans "make a long-term impact on American society -- both culturally and politically."

UASA invited Ralph Nader to be a keynote speaker at one of its national conferences.

UNION OF PALESTINIAN MEDICAL RELIEF COMMITTEES (UPMRC)

PO Box 51483
Jerusalem, Israel
URL: http://www.pmrs.ps/last/index.php

Palestinian health organization whose political agenda closely reflects the views of the Palestinian Authority

Founded in 1979, the Union of Palestinian Medical Relief Committees (UPMRC) describes itself as "a grassroots, community-based Palestinian health organization ... seeking to supplement the decayed and inadequate health infrastructure [of Palestinians] caused by years of Israeli military occupation." "Our comprehensive health programs," adds UPMRC, "focus on the needs of the most vulnerable members of Palestinian society: women, children, and the poor in rural villages, refugee camps, and urban centers." The organization's staff includes physicians, community health workers, nurses, midwives, and other health professionals, many of whom volunteer their services.

Attributing most Palestinian health problems to Israeli transgressions, UPMRC's activities fall under the following major program areas:

Community Health Centers: UPMRC operates 25 Community Health Centers in towns and villages throughout the West Bank and Gaza Strip.

Specialized Services: These include: dental services, eye care, counseling, dermatology, a "Rational Use of Drugs Program," laboratory Services, and water treatment and testing.

Mobile Clinics and Outreach: UPMRC mobile clinics "bring services to villages and towns under difficult circumstances, such as closure, curfews, and deprived and remote areas."

Medical Equipment Loan Centers: UPMRC's three Medical Equipment Loan Centers supplement the organization's services "by providing medical equipment and assistive devices to the disabled, the elderly, and the chronically ill, among others."

Health Education: This initiative "develops materials on a variety of topics, organizes interactive educational theater programs, launches health education campaigns, conducts ... discussion and support groups, and trains community members in first aid and emergency [intervention]."

School Health: This program focuses its resources on the poorest schools in the West Bank and Gaza Strip.

School of Community Health: This "non-profit educational institution ... trains qualified Community Health Workers and provides continuing education to physicians and other health care professionals."

Emergency First Aid: This training program seeks to establish "a national network of qualified First Aid providers who can respond to any emergency, whether during political struggle or in normal life."

Community-Based Rehabilitation: This project aims "to change misperceptions, education the general public about disabilities and provide disabled people with the necessary skills to become more self-sufficient and integrate into the wider community."

Chronic Diseases: This program "targets adults and focuses on screening and prevention through education, as well as treatment."

The Well-Baby and Child Health Program: This initiative "conducts screenings, vaccinations and educational programs in order to ensure that infants and children are well prepared to live health lives."

Women's Health: "Through this program, women in even the most remote villages in Palestine have access to vital services such as health education, pre-natal, post-natal and family planning care, as well as a host of other basic and specialized services ..."

Community Mobilization: These programs fund "a number of projects in villages and camps aiming at improving the infrastructure in these areas and creating job opportunities for those unemployed due to Israeli measures."

Advocacy & Public Awareness: UPMRC engages in lobbying and advocacy "with the aim to influence national policies and formulate better strategies to achieve Health for All."

UPMRC summarizes Israel's alleged influence on Palestinian health care with the following narrative:

"All aspects of the health situation in Palestine have been affected by Israeli occupation. The 1967 war marked the beginning of the Israeli occupation of the territories and its illegal annexation of Jerusalem. ... During the occupation, the Israeli administration did much to undermine health care within the Occupied Territories. Much of this was due to neglect in the form of underfunding. ... The Israelis also took active measures to cripple health institutions in Palestine. ... While crippling Palestine's health infrastructure, the Israeli governmental policies continued to create health emergencies throughout Palestine. ... [During the current *Intifada*] the Israeli government has ... imposed various collective punishment measures that have served to choke the physical, mental, political, economic and social life of Palestine."

UPMRC was a signatory to a May 15, 2002 petition calling for the creation of a Friends of the Earth "Palestine Campaign" to combat the alleged "environmental violations" of the Israeli army. The petition read, in part: "We the undersigned represent the majority of the Palestinian civil society and we are pained ... by the unprecedented violations by the [Israeli] occupation and its military. Often times, daily environmental violations such as massive land sweeping have reached proportions that equal decades of similar crimes. ... We continue to watch as our land and our future are destroyed, and we continue to engage the world—to demand for witnesses and voices—amidst our travesty."

UPMRC has a close working relationship with Physicians for Human Rights - Israel, and receives substantial funding from the Ford Foundation.

UNITED ASSOCIATION FOR STUDIES AND RESEARCH

Islamic think-tank that promotes the ideology of the Palestinian terrorist organization Hamas

Founded in Chicago in 1989 by Hamas operative Mousa Abu Marzook, the United Association for Studies and Research (UASR) is an Islamic think tank professing a commitment to "the study of ongoing issues in the Middle East, such as the Arab-Israeli conflict." It also promotes the ideology of Hamas.

Mohammad Salah, a Hamas operative who the U.S. government identified as a "specially designated terrorist," was an employee of UASR in the early 1990s. In 1993 Salah cooperated with Israeli prosecutors and provided information on Hamas activities in America. Revealing that UASR served as the base for the political command of Hamas in the United States, he identified Hamas official Ahmed Yousef as UASR's Director.

"UASR is a front organization for a terrorist group," says George Mason University professor Peter Leitner, President of the Higgins Counterterrorism Research Center. Leitner calls UASR "part of a shell game of international terrorism -- phony organizations that are really terrorist cells [and] part of the international terrorist network."

Former CIA operative Brian Fairchild asserts that "organizations like UASR" can advance the global terrorist agenda by "recruiting new members, raising funds to support international terrorism, and ... actually support[ing] a terrorist attack in the U.S."

Since late 2003, UASR has based its operations in a basement apartment located in the town of Springfield, Virginia. The windows of this basement are covered with a false brick contact paper, making it impossible to view the apartment from the outside. "From time to time," reports CNSNews.com, "day or night, the occupants emerge from the office to make cell phone calls in the parking lot. ... Government investigators say the use of prepaid disposable cell phones make it virtually impossible for them to obtain a wiretap. It all adds up, investigators say, to indications that the group may be taking a more active role in terrorist activities."

In December 2003, the U.S. Senate Finance Committee asked the Internal Revenue Service for its records on UASR and two-dozen other Muslim groups as part of an investigation into possible links between non-governmental organizations and terrorist-financing networks.

In March 2004, UASR publicly condemned Israel's targeted killing of Hamas leader Sheikh Ahmed Yassin, describing him as the "founder and spiritual leader of the Islamic Resistance Movement in Palestine." UASR demanded that Israel "end its policy of extra-judicial murders of Palestinian people, the destruction of their homes and property, and the continued illegal occupation of the Palestinian territories."United For Peace and Justice (UFPJ)

UNITED NATIONS RELIEF AND WORKS AGENCY (UNRWA)

HQ Gaza
P.O. Box 140157
Amman 11814
Jordan

Phone :972 8 677 7333
URL: http://www.un.org/unrwa/Agency of the United Nations that was created to assist Arab refugees in 1950

The United Nations Relief and Works Agency for Palestine Refugees in the Near East (UNRWA) defines itself as "a relief and human development agency, providing education, healthcare, social services and emergency aid to over 4.3 million refugees living in the Gaza Strip, the West Bank, Jordan, Lebanon and the Syrian Arab republic." With more than 27,000 staff, almost all of them refugees themselves, UNRWA is by far the largest UN operation in the Middle East. Its budget for the year 2006 was $470.9 million.

Created by the United Nations General Assembly, UNRWA began operations on May 1, 1950, with the intent that it would be disbanded fairly soon -- once the Palestinian refugee problem was solved. In the absence of a solution to that problem for well over a half-century, however, the General Assembly has repeatedly renewed the Agency's mandate.
UNRWA's major programs include the following:

Health: This program "aims to protect, preserve and promote the health of Palestine refugees and to meet their basic health needs" -- such as primary health care; nutrition and supplementary feeding; assistance with secondary health care; and environmental health in refugee camps.

Relief and Social Services: This program "supports the poorest refugee families who are unable to meet their own basic needs," offering food aid, poverty alleviation, emergency relief, shelter rehabilitation, and community development.

Education: "UNRWA operates one of the largest school systems in the Middle East and has been the main provider of basic education to Palestine refugees for nearly five decades. The Agency provides primary and junior secondary schooling free of charge for all Palestine refugee children in the area of operations. Vocational and technical training courses are given in the eight UNRWA vocational training centers. The Agency also runs an extensive teacher-training program, and offers university scholarships to qualified refugee youth."

Microfinance and Micro-Enterprise: UNRWA launched this program in the West Bank and Gaza Strip in June 1991, "in response to rapidly deteriorating economic conditions marked by high unemployment and spreading poverty following the outbreak of the first *intifadah* in 1987 and the Gulf War." The program is organized around funds that make loans to small-scale enterprises in those regions.

Ninety-six percent of UNRWA operations are financed by voluntary contributions, mostly in the form of cash, from a number of national governments. The largest donor is the United States, which provides fully one-third of the Agency's funding. The other leading donors are the European Commission and the governments of Sweden, Norway, the United Kingdom, and Canada. Saudi Arabia and the oil-rich Gulf states contribute only 2 percent of UNRWA's budget.

According to UNRWA's definition, Palestinian refugees include not only the roughly 700,000 people who actually fled their homes during the 1948 Arab-Israeli war, but all of their descendents in subsequent generations as well. UNRWA also counts, as refugees, all Arabs who have applied for relief in its camps, regardless of when they arrived or from where they came. Even when those people move out of the camps (which are more accurately described as towns) and become residents or citizens of another country (only Jordan will grant them citizenship), UNRWA continues to classify them as "Palestinian refugees." Consequently, UNRWA places the current number of such refugees at more than 4 million. Insisting that these refugees not be repatriated into their host countries, the Agency considers their true home to be "Israeli-occupied Palestine." Because of such policies, Middle East Forum director Daniel Pipes has said: "UNRWA has outlived its utility and should be dismantled."

Nearly all teachers in UNRWA schools belong to unions affiliated with terrorist organizations such as Hamas (and other groups with al Qaeda connections). As a result, these schools (and the textbooks used therein) teach children to hate Jews and Israelis and to glorify suicide bombers as "martyrs." Moreover, the refugee camps for which the Agency is responsible are major centers of Arab terrorism. This is evidenced by the fact that nearly all the missile attacks from Gaza into Israel originate in UNRWA-administered regions; the UNRWA-run camp in Jenin is one of the leading terrorist hotbeds in the world.

UNRWA frequently registers complaints with the media regarding the Israeli Defense Force's alleged humanitarian "abuses" in Gaza, which, according to the Agency's Commissioner-General Karen AbuZayd, include the siege of Gaza, the targeted killings of "suspected militants," and incursions into densely populated neighborhoods, causing terror among the civilian population. All of this, says UNRWA, "has badly shaken the society."

At a September 7, 2006 press conference, AbuZayd openly criticized the UN directive barring all staff from having any contact with Hamas. "We should engage with them [Hamas]," said AbuZayd, "and encourage them, discuss with them. This is a movement that has been more or less underground and had little contact with the outside world. It needs to hear from other people and we are discouraged from doing that."

In the summer of 2003, the Hamas organization won more than 90 percent of the vote in elections to determine who would run the UNRWA workers' union in the Arab refugee camps of Gaza. These election victories had grave implications: In October 2004, Israel's United Nations ambassador Dan Gillerman sent a letter to UN Secretary-General Kofi Annan containing documentation that Hamas was using UN ambulances to smuggle arms and terrorists through the Gaza Strip; Gillerman also demanded the dismissal of Peter Hansen from his position as Commissioner-General of UNRWA, and called for the United Nations to conduct a full investigation of the Agency.

Gillerman's charges were supported by a May 2004 televised report that armed Palestinian terrorists who had just murdered six Israeli soldiers in southern Gaza, used an ambulance owned and operated by UNRWA to flee the scene of their crime. Hamas activist Nidal 'Abd al-Fataah 'Abdallah Nizal, who worked as a UNRWA ambulance driver, confessed to also having used his official UN vehicle to bypass security and transport arms, explosives and terrorists -- as did senior UNRWA employee Nahed Rashid Ahmed Attalah. Though Peter Hansen initially denied that his organization's vehicles were being exploited in this manner, a few months later he told Canada's CBC TV: "I am sure that there are Hamas members on the UNRWA payroll, and I don't see that as a crime."

UNIVERSAL HERITAGE FOUNDATION (UHF)

223 Academy Drive
Kissimmee, FL
34744

Phone :407-518-6886
Fax :407-518-6876
URL: http://www.uheritage.org/Florida-based nonprofit corporation whose stated mission is "to serve God Almighty and His creation by promoting equality, justice, and a peaceful coexistence through education, community service, and outreach"

In 2003, held a conference inviting militant Islamists as guest speakers

A subsidiary of the Islamic Circle of North America and the Muslim American Society, the Universal Heritage Foundation (UHF) was founded on September 10, 2003 as a non-profit corporation based in Kissimmee, Florida. Located on a 31-acre campus 15 miles from Disney World, UHF's mission is "to serve God Almighty and His creation by promoting equality, justice, and a peaceful coexistence through education, community service, and outreach programs; [and] to promote a greater understanding and respect for, and among, people of all faiths, colors, and gender." UHF further professes its devotion to helping create "a society where we appreciate our diversity and common heritage, while moving forward as one humanity with respect and love for all of God's creation."

On December 19-21, 2003, UHF held its inaugural conference, titled "Islam For Humanity." Prominent among its list of guest speakers were militant Islamists with strong anti-American, anti-Israel value systems. These included:

Zulfiqar Ali Shah, UHF's current Chairman/Chief Executive Officer, and the former President of the Islamic Circle of North America
Shaikh Abdur-Rahman Al-Sudais, chief cleric of the Grand Mosque in Mecca

Muzammil Siddiqui, former President of the Islamic Society of North America

Siraj Wahhaj, a Council on American-Islamic Relations Advisory Board member who was named as a possible co-conspirator to the 1993 bombing of the World Trade Center, and who testified as a character witness for the convicted terror mastermind Omar Abdel Rahman

Sayyid Muhammad Syeed, Secretary General of the Islamic Society of North America

Talat Sultan, the current President of the Islamic Circle of North America

Abdullah Idris Ali, who served as the Islamic Society of North America's President from 1992-1997, and is a Board of Advisors member for the American Muslim Council

Sohail Ghannouchi, the Muslim American Society President who admitted to raising funds for Imam Jamil Al-Amin, a Georgia-based Muslim leader who was sentenced to life in prison for murdering a sheriff's deputy in Atlanta

Mokhtar Maghraoui, a Central Shura Member of the Islamic Circle of North America

Muhammed Younes, President of the American Muslim Union

Salah Sultan, President of Islamic American University, and the former head of the Muslim American Society's Department of Islamic Research and Studies

Ihsan Bagby, General Secretary of the Muslim Alliance in North America

Shaikh Wajdi Ghunaim, an Egyptian cleric who supports suicide bombings

Imam Abdul Malik, Muslim chaplain of the New York City Metro Transit Authority

Imam Muhammad Musri, who oversees seven mosques from the Islamic Society of Central Florida

Sheikh Alaa Ramadan, Imam of the Islamic Center of Claremont, California

Maulana Shafayat Muhammad, spiritual leader of the Florida-based Darul Aloom *madrassa* (religious school) where "dirty bomber" Jose Padilla worshipped

Imam Mohamad Bashar Arafat, Muslim Chaplain for the Baltimore City Police Department and President of the Islamic Affairs Council of Maryland

Shaikh Waleed Basyouni, Imam of the Ta'leemul Islaam Masjid in Houston, and an instructor at American Open University

Tariq Rasheed, Imam of the Jama' Masjid spiritual center in Orlando, Florida (Rashid defended Palestinian-American businessman Jesse Maali, who federal authorities claim "financially supported terrorist groups" and wrote "an essay and poems [expressing] sympathy for suicide bombers in Israel.")

Altaf Ali, the Council on American-Islamic Relations' Florida Director who wavered on the question of whether or not the people who had died in the World Trade Center on 9/11 were innocent, and who used a joint press conference with the FBI to defend Khalid Sheikh Mohammed, the mastermind of 9/11.

UNIVERSITY OF CALIFORNIA DIVESTMENT CAMPAIGN

Seeks to coerce Israel to change its policies by having universities withdraw all their investments in Israel and so undermine that nation's economy

Initiated in 2001 by the UC Berkeley branch of Students for Justice in Palestine, the University of California Divestment Campaign seeks to coerce Israel to change its policies vis a vis the Palestinian people by spearheading a movement among universities nationwide to withdraw all their investments in Israel and thereby undermine that nation's economy. Modeled on the 1980s divestment effort against the apartheid government in South Africa, this anti-Israel campaign spread quickly to an estimated 50 universities across the United States, including eight other University of California (UC) campuses. Condemning "Israel's systematic human rights violations [and] its ongoing apartheid system," the movement gained added traction when professors at Princeton, Harvard, MIT, and UC Berkeley launched faculty divestment campaigns in May and June of 2002.

The Divestment Campaign traces its beginnings to a November 30, 2000 lecture by Francis A. Boyle at Illinois State University. Boyle, a legal adviser to Yasser Arafat's Palestine Liberation Organization, delivered his address at the request of political science professor Jamal Nassar. The UC Berkeley chapter of SJP quickly responded to Boyle's call for divestment and launched its campaign. Boyle helped organize a similar movement with Palestinian students at the University of Illinois.

The online version of the Divestment Campaign petition had collected 2,023 signatures by December 21, 2003, some 229 of which were from UC faculty members. Berkeley's SJP claims to have collected 6,000 signatures on a similar petition circulated by hand. Notably, the words "peace" and "reconciliation" are do not appear in the Divestment Petition, which states: "We, the undersigned -- horrified by the human rights abuses of Palestinians at the hands of the Israeli government, the continual military occupation and colonization of Palestinian territory by Israeli forces and settlers, the forcible eviction from and demolition of Palestinian homes, the refusal to allow Palestinian people the right to return to their homes and properties, and the continual violation of international law and UN Resolution 194 in the racist policies of Israel -- lend our support to the Palestinian people and call on the UC Regents to end its financial ties to Israel by divesting from companies with subsidiaries in Israel and/or substantial financial commitments (over 5 million dollars) to the Israeli economy."

UC Divestment sponsors a steady stream of teach-ins and protests. Guest speakers regularly visit campuses under the auspices of Middle East education to support the campaign. The speakers most important to the movement are University of California faculty and staff members. The UC Divestment web page displays a number of pro-divestment quotes from UC professors, who use their positions as publicly funded educators to promote their political views.

The Divestment Campaign works closely with the International Socialist Organization, the Maoist International Movement, the Revolutionary Anti-Imperialist League, the International Solidarity Movement, the Palestine Solidarity Movement, and Al-Awda. Prominent figures such as Archbishop Desmond Tutu and the late professor Edward Said have been among the Campaign's supporters.

URUKNET

Ass. Uruknet
c/o TEV
Via Sauli 9
Milano, Italy
20127

URL: http://www.uruknet.info/Pro-Baathist, anti-American website

> Views the United States as an evil nation whose invasion of Iraq was motivated by a lust for oil and empire

Based in Italy, Uruknet.info is a pro-Baathist, pro-Saddam Hussein website that posts the anti-American compositions of numerous Arab and Western writers, Muslim and non-Muslim alike. Uruknet depicts Israel as an "apartheid state," and the U.S. as the world's leading supporter of terrorism. Notable contributors to Uruknet include the following writers:

> *Kurt Nimmo*: This New Mexico-based blogger (who also writes for CounterPunch) wrote a June 2006 Uruknet piece predicting that President Bush, because of his declining popularity, would soon launch a frivolous, unwarranted invasion of Iran. "Bush and the neocons," wrote Nimmo, "... have nothing but contempt for the American people, who they consider clueless peons, little more than expendable pawns in their global game of domination, beginning in the Middle East." In order to persuade Americans "to do their murderous bidding," he explained, lackeys of President Bush have more than once coordinated and staged "gruesome acts of false flag terrorism" (i.e., they have tried to rally the public by committing or provoking acts of terror and then blaming innocent foreigners for those deeds).
>
> In a 2005 article that appeared on Uruknet, Nimmo defended British Member of Parliament George Galloway as "one of the last principled men in the whole of the British government." In a July 2006 piece, Nimmo opined that "the neocons" in the Bush administration were privately delighted to see "millions of enraged Muslims taking up arms against the United States" — because that frightening image "will force a reluctant and usually peaceful population ... to donate their sons and daughters to a horrific war" which seeks "the eradication (or at minimum submission) of the Muslim hordes."

Norman Solomon: In a March 2007 article posted on Uruknet, this founder and Executive Director of the Institute for Public Accuracy characterized as "ultimately destructive" a recent congressional decision "to refuse to do the one thing that the Constitution empowers Congress to do to halt a U.S. war—stop appropriating taxpayer money for it."

Kevin Zeese: Also in March 2007, this Director of Democracy Rising and co-founder of Voters For Peace similarly blasted congressional Democrats for not being steadfast enough in pushing for an immediate U.S. troop withdrawal from what he viewed as an immoral and unjustified war in Iraq.

Stephen Lendman: In a March 2007 Uruknet article, this Chicago-based blogger wrote that the Islamic terrorist threat facing America was sparked entirely by U.S. aggression. "Ending the [terrorist] threat is simple," he explained. "... Stop attacking them, and they won't hit back." According to Lendman, America's military ventures in both Iraq and Afghanistan were equally "willful and malicious acts of illegal aggression."

Dave Lindorff: A writer for CounterPunch and a supporter of cop-killer and leftist icon Mumia Abu Jamal, Lindorff wrote in a March 2007 Uruknet article: "We know now that when Dick Cheney makes a foreign policy or war policy decision regarding Iraq or Iran or Saudi Arabia, he is really thinking about what it will do for Halliburton and Dubai—and for Dick Cheney."

Jason Miller: Administrator of the blog *Thomas Paine's Corner, Miller describes himself as "a wage slave of the American Empire who has freed himself intellectually and spiritually." In one Uruknet article, he* condemned Americans for being "perverse" and "audaci[ous]" enough "to call ourselves a 'Christian nation' as we rape, pillage, and plunder the rest of the world via military and economic weapons." In a separate composition, Miller declared that "by and large, those labeled 'terrorists' by the Bush administration ... are people who are simply using 'asymmetrical warfare' to resist the ongoing oppression, exploitation and subjugation of an imperialist aggressor." In Miller's estimation, America is a "foreign occupier" whose "invading hordes" have been "waging genocide against the Iraqi people since the Gulf War."

Robert Weitzel: This Wisconsin-based writer has been published in CommonDreams and the *Milwaukee Journal Sentinel*. As he sees things, the contemporary Western-Islamic conflict "is not a clash of ideology or religion, nor is it to spread democracy or to fight the long war on terrorism. It is about the immoral war profiteering of the U.S. military-industrial complex ... It is about the maiming and killing [by America] of civilians who are not yet born."

Jane Cutter: This organizer for International ANSWER wrote a 2007 Uruknet article denouncing "U.S. imperialism"; deriding "the role of the bought-and-paid-for corporate media in selling the Bush administration's lies" that led the U.S. to war in Iraq; and asserting that "all the justifications for the invasion have been proven to be lies."

Manuel Valenzuela: Born in Mexico City and now splitting his time between Spain and the United States, Mr. Valenzuela is an Internet columnist who, in an April 2007 Uruknet article, wrote that the U.S. government was: deviously fabricating "new Pearl Harbors leading to perpetual war and perpetual fear for perpetual profit, power and control"; embarking on "a century-long war on concocted dark skinned enemies from alien lands"; exploiting "the purposeful murder of their fellow countrymen as the marketing ploy by which empire seekers unleash hell on Earth"; and using "America's rural and urban poor" as "cannon fodder for their corporatist masters." Valenzuela further asserted that "9/11 was designed, like the Reichstag fire in 1930s Nazi Germany, and as other false flag operations throughout history, as the first salvo in a war of propaganda and fear upon the American people"; that 9/11 turned Americans into "crazed and hypnotized warmongers" who allowed "criminals and murderers in government to invade, attack and occupy lands that had no reason for attack"; and that the Twin Towers were in fact brought down by the American government.

Rina Palta: This San Francisco-based writer also contributes to *Mother Jones* magazine, the *San Francisco Weekly*, and AlterNet. She is a supporter of Barbara Ehrenreich, honorary chairwoman of the Democratic Socialists of America.

Other occasional contributors to Uruknet include writers affiliated with the Traprock Peace Center, Democracy Now, and Electronic Intifada.

WAR ON WANT (WOW)

Fenner Brockway House
37-39 Great Guildford Street
London
SE1 OES

Phone :0845 193 1952
URL: http://www.waronwant.org/Human rights NGO that works closely with the Union of Palestine Medical Relief Committees

Its motto is, "The only war worth fighting is the war on poverty."

Based in London, War On Want (WOW) is dedicated to "fighting for a world without poverty" and ridding the earth of military conflict. "The only war worth fighting is the war on poverty," says the organization's motto.

WOW's roots can be traced back to February 1951, when the British publisher and socialist Victor Gollancz published a letter in *The Guardian* asking people to join an international struggle against poverty, calling for a negotiated settlement to the Korean War, and advocating the creation of an international fund "to turn swords into ploughshares." Gollancz asked all those who supported his vision to send him a postcard with the simple word "yes" printed on it; he received some 5,000 replies. One of the respondents was future Prime Minister Harold Wilson, who coined the name "War On Want" for the fledgling movement.

In the early 1960s, WOW's attention was focused on its campaign for the forgiveness of Third World debt.

In the 1970s the organization campaigned for workers' rights on tea plantations and for the end of South African apartheid. It also "helped to expose the scandal of baby foods companies marketing powdered milk as a healthier option than breast milk to mothers in the developing world." According to WOW, such milk substitutes were "a more dangerous and expensive option for these mothers who had no access to safe drinking water and sterilization facilities."

In the 1980s WOW focused on the role of women in the developing world and supported "the liberation movements in Eritrea, South Africa and Western Sahara."

In the 1990s War On Want's major concern was "the need to respond to issues raised by globalization." Favoring a socialist economic model, WOW "worked in partnership with progressive governments and organizations to ... deliver a more equal distribution of wealth." In 1999 War on Want representatives marched at the World Trade Organization (WTO) meeting in Seattle, demanding "fair access for goods from developing countries to the [W]est."

War On Want's current programs include the following:

Trade Justice: "[T]he rules of the global economy have been set up to serve the interests of big business, not people's needs. ... We need a rules-based system for world trade, but it must serve the interests of the poorest and most vulnerable, not lead to their increased marginalization as the WTO negotiations are now doing."

Corporate Accountability: "The globalization of the world's economy means corporations have gained more and more power. Too often, multinational companies harm local communities, damage the environment and violate workers' rights ... Business is ethically unequipped to deliver for people and the environment." WOW singles out for reprobation three companies in particular: (a) Caterpillar, which sells bulldozers to the Israeli army, which in turn "uses them in the illegally occupied territories ... 'to destroy [Palestinian] agricultural farms ... as well as numerous homes and sometimes human lives'"; (b) Wal-Mart, which "[bases its] business strategy ... on low prices, but it achieves these low prices by forcing down working conditions for its employees, adopting anti-union policies and squeezing suppliers in developing countries"; and (c) Coca-Cola, which "has built a global empire ... [but] has been accused of dehydrating local communities in its pursuit of water resources to feed its own plants, drying up farmers' wells and destroying local agriculture."

Corporations and Conflict: "Multinational corporations are complicit in wars throughout the world, putting profit before people and often legitimizing and fueling the conflict ... whether through supplying military hardware to armed forces or running mercenary armies on behalf of combatant states."

Palestine: "Palestine is in the grip of a humanitarian catastrophe. ... This crisis is a direct result of Israel's military occupation of Palestine and its recent intensification of action against the Palestinian people. Israel is tightening its noose around Palestinians living in the West Bank through the continued expansion of settlements and the construction of the Separation Wall on occupied Palestinian land."

Western Sahara: "On 31 October 1975, Morocco and Mauritania invaded Western Sahara as Spain (the former colonial power) looked on. The Saharawi people were expelled from their homes by force, including the use of napalm. Most fled to the Algerian desert. Mauritania withdrew its claim to Western Sahara in 1979 and left. But Morocco stayed. The Saharawi people declared their own Republic in exile, which is now recognized by 60 other states. Yet the world still refuses to uphold international law and bring the Occupation to an end."

Privatization: "The privatization of public services in developing countries is hampering the global fight against poverty. The evidence shows that the poor are denied access to essential services when multinationals take over. Private companies have failed to extend services to ensure that the poorest people can access them ... Governments are best placed to provide public services on the scale needed to tackle poverty and ensure access and affordability for all."

War On Want's Chairperson is Pat Ingram, formerly a member of the National Executive Committee and the International Committee of UNISON (Britain's largest trade union). WOW's Chief Executive is Louise Richards, who said in November 2005: "People have increasingly come to realize the Iraq war was about oil, profits and plunder. ... [O]ur report gives detailed evidence to show Iraq's oil profits are well within the sights of the oil multinationals."

WOW's most notable former official is British Member of Parliament George Galloway, who served as the organization's General Secretary from 1983 to 1987.

War On Want considers the Union of Palestine Medical Relief Committees to be one of its partner organizations.

WHEELS OF JUSTICE

740 Round Lake Road
Luck, WI
54853

URL: http://justicewheels.org/Identifies Israeli and American militarism and oppression as "the root injustices" that give rise to such phenomena as the Iraqi insurgency and Palestinian terrorism

Offers "eyewitness accounts" of the suffering in Iraq and in Palestinian villages
Has addressed audiences in hundreds of cities and thousands of venues

Founded in July 2003, Wheels of Justice (WOJ) is a bus tour that "canvasses the United States with education, outreach, training, active non-violent resistance, and network/community-building." Ceylon Mooney, the tour's co-coordinator and one of its booking agents, has described the WOJ bus as "a mobile classroom" that "comes complete with teachers and a wide range of instructional materials: videos, photographs, essays, fact sheets, etc." WOJ's "instructors" are activists who give "eyewitness accounts" of the suffering they have witnessed during visits to Iraqi and Palestinian villages. They identify Israeli and American militarism and oppression as "the root injustices" that give rise to such phenomena as the Iraqi insurgency and Palestinian terrorism.

From 2003 through 2006, WOJ activists addressed audiences in hundreds of cities and thousands of venues, including more than 1,500 middle schools, high schools, colleges, and universities. WOJ is sponsored by the International Solidarity Movement (ISM), Al-Awda, Voices in the Wilderness, and the

Middle East Children's Alliance. Most of the activists traveling with the tour have spent time in Iraq as members of Voices in the Wilderness, or in Israel as volunteers with the ISM. Their efforts are funded primarily by merchandise sales and private donations. Among WOJ's featured speakers are ISM activist Brian Avery; If Americans Knew founder Alison Weir; and Al-Awda co-founder Mazin Qumsiyeh.

With regard to the Arab-Israeli conflict in particular, WOJ charges that virtually every social, economic, medical, and spiritual ill afflicting the Palestinians can be attributed to Israel's policies of "colonization, occupation, displacement, [and] apartheid." Calling for an immediate end to all American aid to Israel, WOJ condemns the "effects of war and occupation on civilians in Palestine/Israel ... including house demolitions, armed conflict, apartheid laws, collective punishment, and degrading humanitarian conditions." According to WOJ, "[T]he Israeli military occupation continues a legacy that began in 1947 with the ethnic cleansing of Palestinians to make room for the State of Israel."

Vis a vis the war in Iraq, WOJ asserts: "The cultural, political and economic institutions of Iraq belong to the Iraqis, not to Washington; the hijacking of Iraq's culture and resources by a foreign power exacerbates and prolongs the consequences of the ... U.S.-led war, and the ordinary people of Iraq still have no self-governance."

"The consequences of these [American and Israeli] wars and occupations," says WOJ, "fall upon the shoulders of the poor and oppressed, the refugees and the marginalized, and those in our own communities whose needs are neglected by government's costly pursuit of foreign wars."

Reasoning that the violence in Iraq and in "Palestine/Israel" is "supported by our tax dollars and by our elected officials," WOJ claims that: "Americans bear a great responsibility. The people of the world know this, and U.S. government policy provokes rage and retaliation against Americans. ... To break the cycle of violence we must change our roles in these conflicts; as individuals and as a nation, we must move from instigator to negotiator, from enabler to resister."

WOJ likens the allegedly brutal policies of the U.S. and Israel to those that historically promoted "the dispossession and oppression of other peoples, including American Indians, African Americans, South African blacks under Apartheid, etc."

WOJ's recommended reading materials for its members and supporters include books authored or edited by: Naseer H. Aruri (Dartmouth professor and former Board member of both Human Rights Watch and Amnesty International); the late Ibrahim Abu-Lughod (a former member of the pro-Arafat Palestine National Council, which in the 1960s established the PLO as the political representative of the Palestinian people); Noam Chomsky (Massachusetts Institute of Technology linguistics professor); Norman Finkelstein (DePaul University political science professor); the late Simha Flapan, (the first National President of the pro-Soviet, pro-Stalin party called Mapam); Tanya Reinhart (a post-Zionist Israeli linguist whose thesis supervisor was Noam Chomsky, and who sees Israel's immediate withdrawal from all occupied territories as the key to peace with the Palestinians); Roane Carey, (author of *The New Intifada: Resisting Israel's Apartheid*); the late Edward Said (Columbia University professor of comparative literature); and four so-called "new historians" who place all blame for the Arab-Israeli conflict on Israel -- Ilan Pappe, Avi Shlaim, Benny Morris, and Tom Segev.

WOJ implores its ideological supporters to engage in some form of nonviolent protest against Israeli and/or American wrongdoing. "Nonviolence," the organization says, "can be interpositioning yourself between Israeli tanks and Palestinian civilians, or standing with Iraqi families as their backyards become a proving ground for the most powerful military machine the world has ever seen." Less perilous measures, adds WOJ, "can also take form in speaking truth to the power of a state's legal system, refusing to accept one people as fundamentally 'evil' and another as 'good,' and refusing to bankroll war, terror and occupation."

Other activities suggested by WOJ include: (a) organizing public teach-ins, lectures, presentations, vigils, protests, movie screenings, slide shows, and poetry events; supporting "bands against bombs" concerts and musical performances; (b) participating in "religious services for justice and peace in Iraq and Palestine/Israel"; (c) attending campaign rallies and events featuring elected and selected public officials; and (d) participating in protests against companies that "indirectly or directly participate in war/occupation and related activities" -- companies such as Boeing (which manufactures weapons, aircraft, and intelligence and surveillance systems); Bechtel (which handled reconstruction projects in post-invasion Iraq); Lockheed-Martin (a maker of missile and missile-defense systems); and Caterpillar (which manufactures bulldozers that are used by the Israeli Defense Forces to raze the homes of Palestinian terrorists).

WOJ also encourages blood-drive participants to donate their blood "in the name of Iraqi or Palestinian civilians killed/wounded by U.S. weapons."

Organizations that formally endorse WOJ include Pax Christi USA, Jews Against the Occupation, September 11th Families for Peaceful Tomorrows, the Traprock Peace Center, Veterans for Peace, and Fellowship for Reconciliation.

WORLD ASSEMBLY OF MUSLIM YOUTH (WAMY)

P.O. Box 10845
Riyadh 11443
Saudi Arabia
Phone :966 14641669
URL: http://www.wamy.co.uk/Saudi-based Islamic organization with chapters in 55 countries

Founded by Osama bin Laden's nephew
Holds conferences and distributes literature promoting *jihad* and anti-Semitism
Raises funds for Palestinian terrorist groups, including Hamas
Has been linked to both the 9/11 attacks and the 1993 World Trade Center bombing

A non-governmental youth and student group affiliated with the United Nations, the World Assembly of Muslim Youth (WAMY) was founded in 1972. It defines itself as "an independent organization and Islamic forum that supports the work of Muslim organizations and needy communities the world over." While WAMY's international headquarters are located in Saudi Arabia, the organization also maintains satellite chapters in 55 additional countries and is affiliated with some 500 other Muslim youth groups on five continents.

Specifically, WAMY aims to achieve the following: "Preserve the identity of Muslim youth and help overcome the problems they face in modern society"; "educate and train them in order for them to become active and positive citizens in their countries"; "introduce Islam to non-Muslims in its purest form as a comprehensive system and way of life"; "establish a relationship of dialogue, understanding and appreciation between Muslim organizations and the western societies"; and "provide assistance to Muslim and non-Muslim organizations to fulfil [sic] these goals through training and cooperation."

Toward these ends, WAMY holds regional and local Muslim youth and student camps; helps to establish Muslim scout groups; organizes conferences, symposia, workshops and research circles "to address youth and students issues"; publishes books, brochures, reports, and exhibition material "that best introduce Islam to non-Muslims in its holistic vision"; organizes exchange visits, Hajj and Umra trips; and provides training and support to Muslim youth organizations around the world. These activities have earned WAMY the designation of "humanitarian and relief-works organization" from the United Nations.

The World Assembly of Muslim Youth is also one of the vehicles through which the Saudi Wahhabi government funds Islamic extremism and international terrorism. WAMY was co-founded by Kamal Helwabi, a former senior member of the Egyptian Muslim Brotherhood, and by Osama bin Laden's nephew, Abdullah bin Laden (who served as WAMY's President through 2002 and is now its Treasurer). WAMY raises funds for the terrorist group Hamas, and in October 2002 made Hamas leader Khaled Mash'al an "honored guest" at a Muslim youth and globalization conference held in Riyadh. WAMY also helps finance the Kashmir insurgency against India, characterizing it as a "liberation" movement.

A Saudi opposition group reports that WAMY disseminates literature encouraging "religious hatred and violence against Jews, Christians, Shi'a and Ashaari Muslims." As WAMY puts it, this literature is expressly designed "to teach our children to love taking revenge on the Jews and the oppressors, and teach them that our youngsters will liberate Palestine and Jerusalem when they go back to Islam and make *jihad* for the sake of Allah." Some WAMY publications have included interviews with Saudi clerics such as Ayed al-Qarni, an adviser to Saudi Prince Fahd. In one such interview, al-Qarni stated that he prays for America's destruction daily, that he encourages students to go to Iraq to fight against U.S. forces, and that those who cannot go should at least contribute money to the cause. Another WAMY publication features a list of "martyrs" who have attacked and murdered Israelis; one of the individuals on this list is a man who drove 14 bus passengers off a cliff as a member of the group "Heroes from Palestine."

Investigations of the 1993 bombing of the World Trade Center uncovered, in an apartment of one of the terrorists, an envelope marked "WAMY" along with a training manual on how to set up terrorist cells in other countries and stage attacks.

WAMY came under FBI scrutiny after 9/11, when it was determined that a radiologist, Dr. Al Badr al-Hamzi, whose credit card was found among the possessions of the hijackers, was receiving funding from the organization. The Senate Finance Committee requested that the IRS examine WAMY's U.S. branch for links to terrorism. WAMY was also named in a trillion-dollar lawsuit by the families of the victims of 9/11. In May 2004, federal law-enforcement, immigration, and anti-terrorism agents raided WAMY's Alexandria, Virginia office, seizing all of its computers and hard drives, and arresting a volunteer board member, Ibrahim Abdullah, on immigration charges. WAMY had been operating out of the office of Jamal Barzinji, who was involved with a total of seven organizations that were raided by federal agents in connection with terrorist financing. After the raid on its office, WAMY likened itself to the YMCA, saying that it was interested only in "youth education, youth development, and serving the Muslim community."

Though WAMY's activities in the United States were derailed, its operations elsewhere in the world continue unabated -- in many instances with the help of other, likeminded organizations. For example, WAMY's efforts in Somalia are supported by the "Christian charities" Novib and Oxfam, which are based in the United Kingdom and Holland, respectively.

One of WAMY's closest affiliates is the European Council for Fatwa and Research, which aims to spread fundamentalist Islam and implement *Shari'a* (Islamic Law) worldwide. Another organization with intimate ties to WAMY is the Muslim Students' Association of the U.S. and Canada. And four directors of the International Institute of Islamic Thought (IIIT) -- including Anwar Ibrahim, a terror-supporting Malaysian Islamist who co-founded IIIT -- are trustees of WAMY.

In December 1999, WAMY announced at a press conference in Saudi Arabia that it "was extending both moral and financial support to the Council on American-Islamic Relations (CAIR) "to help it construct its $3.5 million headquarters in Washington, D.C." WAMY also agreed to "introduce CAIR to Saudi philanthropists and recommend their financial support for the headquarters project." In 2002, CAIR and WAMY jointly announced, again from Saudi Arabia, their collaboration on a $1 million public-relations campaign.

Islam scholar Stephen Schwartz calls WAMY "the Saudi equivalent of the Hitler Youth: a hate-mongering, ultra-extremist group preaching, among other niceties, that Shia Muslims are not real Muslims, but products of a Jewish conspiracy." The website Militant Islam Monitor characterizes the organization as "part of the Saudi Wahhabist 'Jihad through conversion' drive."

WORLD ISLAM STUDY ENTERPRISE

www.csidonline.org

- Founded in 1991 as an "Islamic think-tank" by Sami Al-Arian, Mazen al Najjar, Khalil Shikaki, and Ramadan Abdullah, all of whom are leaders of Palestine Islamic Jihad
- Sponsored events that featured radical Islamic speakers, including Sheik Omar Abdul Rahman, who was convicted in connection with the 1993 World Trade Center bombing
- Was shut down in 1995 by federal authorities; all the principals are either in jail, deported, or in terrorist cells in the Middle East

The World Islam Study Enterprise (WISE) was established as an "Islamic think tank" in 1991 by four professors at the University of South Florida (USF): Sami Al-Arian, his brother-in-law Mazen al Najjar, Khalil Shikaki, and Ramadan Abdullah Shallah. Abdullah left WISE (before it was shut down by federal authorities in 1995) to become head of the terrorist organization Palestinian Islamic Jihad (PIJ). Khalil Shikaki is the brother of Fathi Shikaki, the founder of PIJ. When Fahti Shikaki was assassinated, his replacement as PIJ's military head was Ramadan Abdullah Shallah.

Another WISE board member, Tarik Hamdi, was known by U.S. authorities to have personally met with Osama bin Laden in Afghanistan in May 1998, giving him a satellite telephone and battery pack to facilitate the latter's orchestration of terrorist activities.

During its four-year existence, WISE sponsored numerous public events such as lectures given by: Islamic Group leader Sheik Omar Abdel Rahman, who was later convicted in connection with the 1993 bombing of the World Trade Center; Rashid-el-Ghanoushi, a Tunisian who was considered a terrorist by the U.S. State Department; and Hassan Turabi, who is generally considered the real leader of the terrorist Sudanese government. According to Oliver Revell, the FBI's former top counterterrorism official, "anybody who brings in Hassan Turabi is supporting terrorists."

An FBI raid of WISE offices yielded no fewer than 500 videotapes of Al-Arian's conferences in mosques across the United States, where he raised funds for PIJ. At these events, Al-Arian proudly accepted introductions as "the President of the Islamic Committee for Palestine ... the active arm of the Islamic *Jihad* Movement." The videos further showed a number of individuals at these rallies praising the killing of Jews and Christians. The WISE raid also turned up a letter written by Al-Arian in Arabic praising a Palestinian Islamic Jihad suicide bombing that caused the deaths of 19 Israeli soldiers in 1995.

Both Al-Arian and Al Najjar were eventually arrested on charges of supporting terrorism. When discussing the indictment of these WISE leaders, then-Attorney General John Ashcroft stated that they each played "a substantial role in international terrorism" and were involved in all aspects of "finance, extolling, and assisting acts of terror."

WORLD VISION INTERNATIONAL (WVI)

Partnership Offices
800 West Chestnut Avenue
Monrovia, CA 91016-3198
USA
web: wvi.org/
International Liaison Office
6 Chemin de la Tourelle
1209 Geneva
Switzerland

Regional Offices

Africa
P.O. Box 50816
Karen Road, Off Ngong Road
Karen
Nairobi
Kenya
web: wvafrica.org/

Asia-Pacific
P.O. Box 956, Phrakhanong Post Office
SSP Tower, 19th floor
555 Sukhumvit 63 (Soi Ekamai)
Klongton-Nua, Wattana
Bangkok 10110
Thailand
web: worldvision.com.au/asiapacific/content.asp

Latin America and Caribbean
Apartado 133-2300 - Curridabat
2300 Curridbat
San Jose

Costa Rica
web: visionmundial.org/

Middle East and Eastern Europe
P.O. Box 28979
2084 Nicosia
Cyprus
web: meero.worldvision.org/

Christian relief and development organization
Condemns Israel's defense measures, while turning a blind eye to the Palestinian terrorism that necessitated it

Established in 1950 to care for orphans in Asia, World Vision International (WVI) is active in nearly 100 countries on six continents, making it one of the largest Christian relief and development organizations in the world. WVI describes itself as "a global partnership conducting child-focused emergency relief, sustainable community development, and advocacy." Its mission is "to follow our Lord and Saviour Jesus Christ in working with the poor and oppressed to promote human transformation, seek justice and bear witness to the good news of the Kingdom of God." Viewing capitalism as an instrument of societal injustice, greed, and exploitation, WVI favors an economic model based on socialism and the redistribution of wealth.

WVI identifies the following set of core values as its own:

We are Christian: "We seek to follow Jesus -- in his identification with the poor, the powerless, the afflicted, the oppressed, and the marginalized ... in his challenge to unjust attitudes and systems; in his call to share resources with each other ..."

We are committed to the poor: "We are called to serve the neediest people of the earth; to relieve their suffering and to promote the transformation of their wellbeing. ... We seek to facilitate an engagement between the poor and the affluent that opens both to transformation."
We value people: "We give priority to people before money, structure, systems, and other institutional machinery."
We are stewards: "The resources at our disposal are not our own. They are a trust from God through donors on behalf of the poor. ... We ensure that our development activities are ecologically sound."
We are partners: "We are members of an international World Vision partnership that transcends legal, structural, and cultural boundaries."
We are responsive: "We are responsive in a different sense where deep seated and often complex economic and social deprivation calls for sustainable, long-term development."

WVI divides its activities into the following categories:

Transformational Development: "... [H]ealth care, agriculture production, water projects, education, micro-enterprise development, advocacy and other programs are carried out by the community with the support of World Vision."

Emergency Relief: "People whose lives are endangered by disasters or conflict need immediate, skilled assistance. World Vision is committed to respond to any major emergency around the world, through our own programs or in co-operation with partner agencies. For example, World Vision has responded to famine in Ethiopia and North Korea, hurricanes in Central America, earthquakes in El Salvador and India Taiwan and Turkey, and war refugees in Kosovo, Chechnya, Sierra Leone, Angola, and East Timor."

Promotion of Justice: "World Vision International has endorsed the Universal Declaration of Human Rights and the United Nations Convention on the Rights of the Child as fundamental expressions of the freedoms and responsibilities that should exist in every country. Whenever possible, World Vision seeks opportunities to help reduce the level of conflict and to contribute to peaceful resolution and reconciliation."

Strategic initiatives: "World Vision invites Christian leaders to participate in conferences, consultations, training programmes and various educational opportunities."

Public Awareness: "World Vision encourages people to care about the needs of others, to understand the causes of poverty, and to offer a compassionate response. These efforts include collaboration with media and community participation in fundraising."

Witness to Jesus Christ: "World Vision believes that God, in the person of Jesus Christ, offers hope of renewal, restoration, and reconciliation. ... At the same time, World Vision is respectful of other faiths. It does not engage in proselytism or religious coercion of any kind."

In its treatment of Middle Eastern affairs, WVI is decidedly supportive of the Palestinian cause and condemnatory of Israel. The organization's political perspective was given voice in its January and May 2004 press releases regarding Israeli military operations in the Gaza Strip; these documents made unsubstantiated allegations against Israeli soldiers, and no mention of the Palestinian terror that had necessitated those operations.

In its "country profile" of the West Bank, Gaza, and Israel, WVI engages in major historical distortions and misrepresentations. For example, it states: "In 1948 a war broke our resulting in the establishment of Israel on 77% of historic Palestine. For Palestinians, this event is known as the *Nakba* (great catastrophe). Over 700,000 Palestinians were made refugees." This narrative does not mention that the war was started when, on May 15, 1948 (the very day of Israel's creation), troops from eight Arab dictatorships -- Lebanon, Syria, Jordan, Iraq, Egypt, Saudi Arabia, Yemen, and Morocco -- attacked Israel in an effort to destroy the nascent Jewish state. Moreover, *Nakba* is an Arab term that is invariably used in reference to Israel's *creation* - not, as WVI implies, to the war, nor even to the resultant refugee crisis.

WVI's account of the Six Day War of 1967 is equally misleading: "In 1967 Israel occupied the West Bank and East Jerusalem and the Gaza Strip." Absent is any mention of the fact that the war was started when Egypt, Syria, and Jordan massed their troops on Israel's borders in preparation for yet another war of attempted annihilation.

WVI's narrative of Arab-Israeli affairs also includes the following: "Israel began its policy of building Jewish settlements on occupied Palestinian land. Since 1967 another mass Palestinian refugee problem was created by displacing persons within the West Bank and Gaza Strip and sending refugees to neighboring Arab countries as well as throughout the world. Year[s] under Israel occupation culminated in the first intifada (uprising) that began in December 1987. ... As the 1990's ended, a sense of disillusionment in the Occupied Territories set in due to ... Israeli policies, for example, accelerated settlement expansion, house demolitions, land confiscations and human rights abuses. The sense of disillusionment ... sparked a new intifada in September 2000, known as the Al Aqsa Intifada. ... Israeli security forces have re-entered many Palestinian-controlled areas in the name of security and are practicing a policy of sealing entries and exits to cities, villages, and towns as a form of collective punishment of the Palestinian population. This policy has severely affected the Palestinian infrastructure, economy and general social fabric and has created a humanitarian crisis."

About 80 percent of WVI's funding comes from private sources -- individuals, corporations and foundations. The rest comes from governments and multilateral agencies, including major grants from the U.S. and Australia for projects in the Palestinian Authority (2000-2003). WVI has been the beneficiary of grants from the Bill and Melinda Gates Foundation, the W. K. Kellogg Foundation, the Ahmanson Foundation, and the Rockefeller Foundation.

ZAYED CENTER FOR COORDINATION AND FOLLOW-UP (ZCCF)

Abu Dhabi
United Arab Emirates

Official think-tank for the League of Arab States until it ceased operations in 2003
Promoted an anti-Semitic and anti-American message through its speakers and publications

Defunct since 2003, the Zayed Center for Coordination and Follow-Up (ZCCF) was founded in 1999 in the United Arab Emirates (UAE) as the official think tank for the League of Arab States, an association of 22 Arab nations. ZCCF was principally funded by the late UAE President Sheikh Zayed bin Sultan Al Nahayan. His son, H.H. Sheikh Sultan Bin Zayed al Nahayan, the Deputy Prime Minister of the UAE, was the organization's Founding Chairman.

ZCCF regularly published literature and hosted speakers whose themes were strongly anti-Semitic and anti-American. Some of the organization's notable lectures and symposiums over the years included the following:

May 20, 2003: Rami Tahbob, advisor to Al Quds' File on Arab Affairs, alleged that "Israel police not only use [chemical] drugs for getting information [from Palestinians], but also for changing social structures in Palestinian society." He further claimed that "some sterilizing drugs were found in water reservoirs used by some Palestinian schools."

May 1, 2003: Saudi "economic expert" Yussuf Abdallah Al Zamel blamed the Iraq War on "radical Zionist and right-wing Christian ... powers planning behind the scenes to push the American government towards destructive wars."

April 13, 2003: Dr. Shawqi Shaath, an "Archaeology and Heritage Expert" for the Arab League, accused Israel of seeking to "wipe out Palestinian, Arab and Islamic archaeological and historical landmarks" in its own territory as well as in "Syria, Lebanon and Iraq," in order to "confer [historical] legitimacy on the Zionist Entity." He claimed that Solomon's Temple in Jerusalem never existed, and disputed Jewish historical connection to the land of Israel. "On the contrary," he said, "scientific findings prove that Palestine and its people are Arabs who have been living in it since thousands of years."

April 9, 2003: Dr. Umayma Jalahma, a professor of Islamic Studies at Saudi Arabia's King Faysal University, told a ZCCF audience that the U.S. invasion of Iraq had been timed to coincide with the Jewish holiday Purim; that "the invading [American]forces have begun to distribute the spoils and booties in Iraq, disregarding the painful cries and woes of the Iraqi children"; that "no one can curb the Zionist ambitions to establish a world state whose economic and political aspirations have no limits"; and that "Zionism and some Western circles have been active to defame the Arab and Muslim image."

April 6, 2003: Former Jordanian Information Minister Saleh Al Qallab declared that influential "rabbis" in the Bush administration were seeking to "reshape the world" through American military intervention, and suggested that the political leadership in Washington should be "removed."

April 5, 2003: Dr. Gad Taha, Professor of History at Ain Sham University, claimed that "in every Western country" there is an agent of "international Zionism" whose job is to "impose support for Israel and raise funds and aid for it."

March 11, 2003: American anti-Semite Michael Collins Piper claimed that the Jewish conspiracies for world domination described in the anti-Semitic forgery *Protocols of the Elders of Zion*, are "not a theory but a real fact." He called President Bush a "classic fanatic Zionist"; accused Israel of developing an "ethnic bomb" that will "eliminate the whole Arab race"; asserted that Israel controls the American media and government; and blamed Israel and the Mossad for the assassination of John F. Kennedy, the Watergate scandal, and the Monica Lewinsky affair.

August 28, 2002: A Zayed Center symposium on "Semitism" labeled the Holocaust a "false fable" perpetuated by Israel, and accused Israel of "spreading lies and exaggerations about holocaust [sic] in order to squeeze out huge sums of money from European countries through worst [sic] forms of blackmail."

June 19, 2002: Archimandrite Father Atallah Hanna of the Greek Orthodox Church in Jerusalem praised Palestinian "martyrdom or suicide bombing" as a strategy that serves "the continued *Intifada* for freedom." According to Hanna, "the Israeli Zionist regime" is "committing genocide in Palestine" and the Palestinians have the right "to defend themselves from the Israeli barbarism and atrocities."

June 2002: A Zayed Center conference, titled "The Middle East as a Strategic Crossroad," featured a presentation by Lyndon LaRouche, who told listeners that the 9/11 attacks "could not have happened without the connivance of something inside, very high level, inside the United States military command." Specifically, LaRouche blamed the "Zionist lobby," "Jewish gangsters," and "Christian Zionists."

April 2002: The Zayed Center hosted a talk by author Theirry Meyssan, who claims that the U.S. military, and not Arab terrorists, were responsible for the 9/11 attacks. The Zayed Center translated Meysann's book on this topic, *The Appalling Fraud*, into Arabic in July 2002.

March 2, 2002: Religious scholar Mohamed Saeed Al Bouti, Islamic Studies Professor at Damascus University, stated that "all military operations done by Palestinian militants" should be "classified as martyr operations and not suicidal operations."

January 2002: Hassan Ali Khater, a Palestinian researcher and editor of the *Al Quds Al-Sharif Encyclopedia*, suggested that the Temple of Solomon never actually existed, and claimed that "Israelis are falsifying history" by carving "Jewish inscriptions on rocks" and then "calling international experts to rediscover" the rocks "as Jewish monuments."

Some notable ZCCF publications include the following:

American Media and the Arab Israeli Conflict (April 14, 2003): Author Michael Collins Piper condemns what he considers to be Jewish/Zionist domination of U.S. foreign policy.

Oil in the American Foreign Policy: Oil Calculations in the War on Iraq (March 26, 2003): This publication says that America seeks "domination of the world" -- and that the U.S. invaded Iraq in order to seize its oil resources.

Policy of Domination and Contemporary World Tensions (March 24, 2003): ZCCF calls Israel a "diabolical" nation working in concert with the U.S. to "re-shape the Middle East" in accordance with Israeli "expansionist ambitions" and American dreams of "hegemony."

Jenin: Massacre against Humanity (January 21, 2003): This publication alleges that in April 2002 in the town of Jenin, the Israeli Defense Force (IDF) massacred innocent Palestinians *en masse*, in cold blood: "Hundreds of Palestinians civilians were killed, many crushed as their homes were demolished while they were still inside. [IDF] removed bodies in trucks, buried them in mass graves and many remained under the piles of debris. ... Even in the worst wars and military confrontations, massacres of this scale hadn't taken place." ZCCF ignored the fact that Israel's Jenin incursion was a response to a massive wave of Palestinian terrorist activity that had originated in that town. The organization further failed to acknowledge that the "massacre" accusations aimed at Israel had been proven to be false. The Palestinian Authority itself placed the official death toll from the Jenin battle at 56, of whom 48 were armed combatants.

Chasing History: Israel and Palestinian Antiquities (August 2002): This screed accuses Israel of plotting to demolish the Al Aqsa Mosque "to build their so-called Solomon Temple."

Role of the Jews in Distorting Arab Image in the Western Culture (July 2002): This publication claims that Zionists control most of America's print and electronic media, using it to distort Americans' image of Arabs.

The Battle of Armageddon and the End of the Arab-Israel Conflict as Viewed by Some American Circles (July 2002): According to this booklet, Zionists confidently expect that an impending nuclear apocalypse will be followed by the establishment of a worldwide Jewish theocracy.

Al Buraq Wall, Not Wailing Wall (December 2001): This publication calls "simply baseless" the "Zionist alleged rights to the [Western] Wall," claiming that the Al Aqsa Mosque was built "more than a thousand years before [King] Solomon."

The Zionist Movement and its Animosity to Jews (October 2001) contends that "the Zionists," not the Nazis, "were the people who killed the Jews in Europe"; that Zionists murdered fellow Jews and sent them to die in Nazi concentration camps so other Jews would be terrorized into migrating to Israel; and that the Nazis supplied weapons to "the Zionist army in Palestine."

Does Israel Rule the World? (August 2001): This publication claims that "the Jewish lobby" in the United States "controls the media, the Congress and monopolies."

Criticized extensively for its connections to such radical publications and guest speakers, the Zayed Center was shut down in August of 2003.

IMPORTANT INFORMATION AND MATERIALS

THE ARAB POPULATION IN THE U.S.

In December 2003, the U.S. census bureau released data for the first time on the Arab population of the United States. The data is from the 2000 census. For information on the Jewish population, see Demographics. The census does not break down the figures by religion, but the Arab-American Institute estimates that about 77% of Arab-Americans are Christians (42% Catholic, 23% Orthodox, 12% Protestant) and 23% Muslim.

In 2000, 1.2 million people reported an Arab ancestry in the United States, up from 610,000 in 1980 (when data on ancestry were first collected in the decennial census) and 860,000 in 1990. The Arab population increased over the last two decades: 41 percent in the 1980s and 38 percent in the 1990s. Arabs represented 0.42 percent of the U.S. population in 2000, compared with 0.27 percent in 1980.

More than one-third of those reporting an Arab ancestry were Lebanese (37 percent, see Table 1), including both people who indicated that they were only Lebanese and those who reported being both Lebanese and another ancestry, which might or might not also be Arab.6 The next largest specific groups were Syrian and Egyptian (12 percent each). Among the nearly half-million people who reported other specific Arab ancestries, the largest proportion was Palestinian (6.1 percent of the total Arab population). The Jordanian, Moroccan, and Iraqi populations were also sizable (3.3 percent, 3.3 percent, and 3.2 percent, respectively).

The largest number of Arabs lived in New York City. In 2000, 70,000 people of Arab ancestry lived in New York, making it the city with the largest number of Arabs. Six of the ten largest cities in the United States were also among the ten places with the largest Arab populations (New York, Los Angeles, Chicago, Houston, Detroit, and San Diego.

NEWEST CENSUS FIGURES PORTRAY A GROWING, AFFLUENT AND PROFESSIONAL

Arab Americans have lower than average unemployment, higher income and education than their mainstream American counterparts, according to the most recent U.S. Census figures.

The Arab American community has continued to grow, both in number and affluence through the 1990s, according to newly released figures from the U.S. Census taken in 2000.

The survey figures, which have just been made available regarding the Arab American community, paint a picture of a population that continues to integrate itself into the national mosaic of American life. It is a vibrant community that is growing, well educated and relatively prosperous compared to the rest of Americans. At the same time, Arab Americans boast a higher entrepreneurial bent while reporting a lower unemployment rate, according to the Census.

Significantly, the most recent data also found that an increasing number of Arab Americans identify themselves as being of Arab descent rather than by country of origin. . This appears to reflect a trend towards pan-ethnic identities, similar to Latinos, and is more prevalent among the U.S.-born. It also suggests a more fertile ground for unified Arab American political, cultural and social organizational efforts.

INCOMPLETE COUNT

Every ten years, the Census takes the demographic pulse of the U.S. population, collecting information ranging from family size and citizenship to education, income, and occupation. Among the questions is one on the "ancestry" or ethnic origin of participants. Answers to this question allow demographers and analysts to gain a snapshot of the Arab American community, or those who trace their roots to an Arabic-speaking country.

Historically, only a portion of the population with ancestors who come from an Arab country are captured by the ancestry question, resulting in a numeric undercount. Limitations of the sampling methodology combined with non-response by some, under-response (only two ethnic backgrounds are tabulated and reported), and reporting ancestry as race result in a relatively higher under reporting of Arab Americans.

While the 2000 Census accounted for some 1.25 million persons who self-identify with an Arabic-speaking origin, our estimates (based on research done by the Zogby International polling and marketing firm) place the population at more than 3.5 million.

The following profile, hence, is derived from this self-identified group and gives us useful, if not comprehensive, insights into the residential patterns, achievements, and identity of Arab Americans.

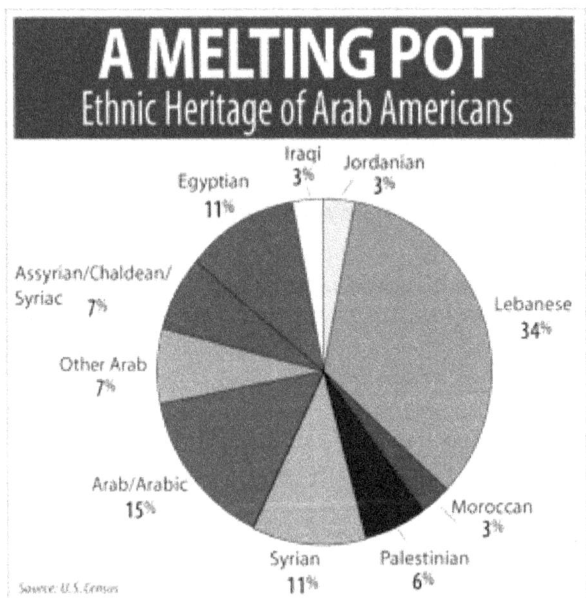

Primary Identity

Of the 1.25 million Arab Americans counted by the Census, roughly one in three claim Lebanese heritage, with 11% indicating roots in Egypt and Syria, 6% as Palestinian and 10% as Iraqi, Chaldean or Assyrian. Because ancestry is an open-ended question (unlike the race options) we learn that one in six self-identify not by a country of origin, but generically as Arab, Arabian or Arabic. This trend has increased since 1990 when less than 10% of Arab respondents indicated a generic identity.

When looking at where subgroups tend to live, we learn that those of Lebanese heritage dominate in most states, with the exception of New Jersey - where those of Egyptian heritage are the largest Arab group - and Rhode Island where persons of Syrian descent exceed other Arab Americans.

The state with the largest number of people tracing their roots to Palestine was Illinois, which also claims a large number of Arab Americans of Iraqi and Assyrian/Chaldean background. Michigan and California similarly counted a large number of Arab Americans of Iraqi and Assyrian/Chaldean heritage.

Persons from Morocco now represent 3% of the Arabic-speaking population, a new immigrant community that resides primarily along the eastern seaboard between Massachusetts and Virginia.

AGE, GENDER AND FAMILY STATUS

Like most groups with significant foreign-born segments, Arab ancestry respondents are younger than the average American, with a median age of 30.8 compared to 35.4 years in the total population.

TAKING CHARGE

Occupation Breakdown for Arab American and U.S. Population Totals

(Employed Civilian Population 16 years and over)

	U.S. Totals	Arab American Totals
Management	34%	42%
Sales, Office and Administrative Support	15%	31%
Service	27%	12%
Production, Transportation and Material Moving	9%	10%
Construction, Extraction and Maintenance	15%	5%

Source: U.S. Census

AN AFFLUENT COMMUNITY

Income (1999) by Arab American and U.S. Total Population

	U.S. Totals	Arab American Totals
Less than $10,000	10%	10%
$10,000 to $24,999	19%	16%
$25,000 to $49,999	29%	26%
$50,000 to $74,999	19%	19%
$75,000 to $99,999	10%	11%
More than $100,000	12%	18%

Source: U.S. Census

Also common among younger ethnic communities is a higher male to female ratio (1.12/1 among Arab Americans compared to .96/1 for all Americans). Arab Americans have a slightly higher percentage of persons now married (57% vs. 54% overall) and a slightly lower rate of persons currently divorced (7% compared with 10% in the general population).

Average household size among Arab ancestry respondents is 3.16 persons compared with 2.59 persons in the average American household, and more than one third (35%) have four or more members, compared to one fourth in the general population.

Citizenship and Place of Birth

Contrary to popular assumptions and the current political climate that foments suspicions about Arab American loyalties, more than eight in ten Arabs living in the United States are citizens, with a higher rate of naturalization (54%) than the overall foreign born population (40%). Of those who identify an Arab ancestry, about six in ten are U.S. born, although estimates of the native-born ratio (accounting for the fourth and fifth generation descendents of the first immigrant wave) are as high as 75%.

Growth by new immigration was significant, with more than one in four foreign-born Arabs entering the U.S. in the decade since 1990. The agency formerly known as the Immigration and Naturalization Service (INS) estimates that more than 300,000 Arabs immigrated to America in this period, with the peak year at 1996.

Changes in immigration policy since the mid 1990s has caused a decline, which is certain to be exacerbated by post September 11, 2001 visa delays and excess scrutiny.

A WELL-EDUCATED AND BILINGUAL CONSTITUENCY

One of the most impressive findings of Census data is the educational achievement of Americans of Arab descent. More than four out of ten of the Arab ancestry population have a bachelor's degree or higher, compared to 24% of Americans at large.

Nearly twice as manyArab Americans have a post-graduate degree (17%) as the average American (9%), a trend that continues to increase.
Half of the Arab ancestry population is also bilingual, revealing trends of Arabic language retention among the U.S.-born offspring of immigrants. In a separate tabulation on foreign language propensity, the Census reports that roughly 615,000 Americans speak Arabic, including close to 125,000 school-aged children. Arabic is ranked seventh among all foreign languages spoken by American children in this age group. While there is some evidence of linguistically isolated households among Arab immigrants, a full 88% of those who speak Arabic also speak English well.

EMPLOYMENT

According to the 2000 Census, Arab Americans have the same rate as other Americans of employment in the civilian labor force (64%), with only a slightly lower unemployment rate at the time the Census was conducted (5% vs. 6%).
Trends in occupational achievement also show significant differences and reflect the professional mobility offered by high educational attainment. More than four in ten working age Arab Americans are in professional or management jobs (42%) compared with roughly one third of the country as a whole (34%).

The proportion of Arab ancestry respondents in retail or administrative jobs (31%) is double the national average (15%), while only half as many in the Arab ancestry group are employed in service jobs (12%) as Americans overall (27%).

INCOME

Not surprisingly, educational achievement and occupational mobility in management and professional fields have resulted in higher than average incomes for Arab Americans.

While income levels are not even in every area of Arab American concentration, the average Arab American is better off financially than the average American at large. Close to 30% of Arab ancestry respondents report annual household income of more than $75,000 compared with 22% of all Americans. Mean household income among Arab respondents ($67,680) in 1999 exceeded the national average ($56,644) by more than $10,000.

GROWTH AND GEOGRAPHIC TRENDS

The number of Americans nationwide who identify with an Arabic-speaking ancestry grew by roughly 45% since the last Census taken in 1990. In six states, the Arab ancestry population at least doubled, including Virginia, North Carolina, Connecticut, Alabama, and New Mexico.

Among the top ten concentrated states, Arab ancestry identification increased by at least one third, with most growth occurring in Illinois, New Jersey, Pennsylvania and Michigan. General residential trends since the 1980s remain with two thirds of all Americans who identify with Arab ancestry living in 10 states, with one third residing in California, Michigan and New York.

States in which Arab ancestry rates went down in the last decade include Maryland, Rhode Island, Louisiana, West Virginia and Mississippi, trends which could correspond with intra-state migration, lower immigration rates and an aging American-born population. By contrast, some states with lower new immigration experienced significant rates of ancestry growth, indicating higher rates of ethnic identification since 1990. Indiana, Connecticut, Alabama, Washington and Missouri are examples of these.

Arab ancestry concentration within states also varies. The overwhelming majority of Americans who identify with an Arab ancestry reside in a metropolitan area (94%) compared with 80% of the general population. In some states, the population is densely clustered in urban areas: Michigan, Florida, Virginia and Texas are examples.

In states like Ohio, New York, California and Pennsylvania, Arab Americans can be found in most counties, even though the majority still resides near big cities.
The top six U.S. metropolitan areas ranked by Arab American population are: Detroit, Los Angeles, New York, Chicago, Washington, D.C. and northeast New Jersey.

FOOTNOTE: When the Census Bureau presents its data on Arab ancestry, it excludes some subgroups from countries that are part of the Arab League, such as Somalia, Sudan and Mauritania as well as Assyrians and Chaldeans. We have included them whenever possible.)

ARAB AMERICAN DEMOGRAPHICS[1]

Arab-Americans Well-Educated, Diverse, Affluent & Highly Entrepreneurial
Over 4 Million Americans Trace Ancestry to Arab Countries

The vast majority of Arab-Americans are citizens of the United States. They are very much like other Americans, except younger, more educated, more affluent and more likely to own a business. Like any other immigrant group, Arab-Americans want to enjoy America's riches while preserving the important parts of their native culture.

Though Arab-Americans are the least-studied ethnic group in the United States, they receive considerable publicity associated with political and economic events, a good example of which has been the intense focus on the community in the aftermath of the Sept. 11 terrorist attacks in New York, Washington and Pennsylvania. While this attention may be of grave political and diplomatic importance, it overshadows Arab-Americans' financial and social impact in the United States.

More importantly, such attention - including the current focus on the community - points out a longstanding problem: Very little is actually publicized and discussed about the make-up of the community. The lack of information, coupled with the media's tendency to use broad strokes to associate Arab-Americans with Arabs in the Middle East, has at times put the community in a defensive position. This article, which is based

[1] By Samia El-Badry

on the 1990 U.S. Census (which is the most recent available information) addresses the lack of information by providing a demographic and economic picture of the community.

COUNTING ARAB-AMERICANS

The 1990 U.S. Census found 870,000 Americans who list "Arab" as one of their top two ancestries. This census definition is inconsistent, however, and not necessarily reliable. Before 1920, census records lumped Arabs together with Turks, Armenians, and other non-Arabic speaking people. Moreover, until recently, non-Syrian Asian Arabs were counted as "other Asians," and others categorized as "other Africans." Palestinians, the main postwar group, were counted as refugees, Israelis or nationals of their last country of residence.

If the census undercount were adjusted and if Arab-Americans filled out census forms, their number today might be as large as three million.

Census data show that 82 percent of Arab-Americans are U.S. citizens, with 63 percent born in the United States. Fifty-four percent of Arab-Americans are men, compared with 49 percent of the total U.S. population. This is partly because men of all nationalities typically immigrate before women do.

The Arab-American population as a whole is quite young; again, probably because younger people are more likely to immigrate. Many Arab-Americans are in their childbearing years, or are native-born children or teenagers.

In general, Arab-Americans are better educated than the average American. More of them attend college, and they earn masters or higher degrees at twice the average rate. Because they tend to be well educated and of working age, their work force rates are high. Eighty percent of Arab-Americans aged 16 and older were employed in 1990, compared with 60 percent of all Americans. In addition, only 7 percent of Arab-American entrepreneurs receive public assistance, compared with 1.7 percent of non-Arab-Americans.

In a volatile economy, with many large companies laying people off, Arab-Americans --who often are entrepreneurs or self-employed (14 percent versus 8 percent) -- may be less vulnerable to company layoffs.

ARAB-AMERICAN ENTREPRENEURS

The sample includes all entrepreneurs 16 years of age or older. The census defines entrepreneurs as people who report themselves to be "self-employed" in their "own incorporated" or "non-incorporated business," "professional practice," or "farm." The 1990 census data show 73,829 Arab-American and 13,408,206 non-Arab-American entrepreneurs. Sixty-four percent of self-employed Arab-Americans own incorporated businesses, compared with only 27 percent of other entrepreneurs. *See Table 1*

Citizenship and Immigration

Most Arab-American entrepreneurs are United States citizens, either by birth (47.0 percent) or naturalization (36.3 percent). Arab migration to the United States dates to the late 19th and early 20th centuries. Early migrants typically were Syrian or Lebanese merchants pursuing economic interests. Legal and political restrictions, the Depression and World War II curbed Arab migration between 1925 and 1948.

Arabs immigrating since World War II have tended to be from capitalist classes -- landed gentry and influential urban-based families -- replaced by new leadership in their various home countries. Many post-war immigrants were Palestinians displaced when Israel was established in 1948. Others were Egyptians whose land was appropriated by the Nasser regime; Syrians overthrown by revolutionaries; and Iraqi royalists fleeing the Republican regime. They often had attended Western or westernized schools, spoke fluent English, and identified themselves as members of a professional class.

Immigration from the Middle East increased dramatically in the late 1960s. By 1990, more than 75 percent of foreign-born Arab-Americans in had immigrated after 1964, compared with 52 percent of the total U.S. foreign-born population. The largest share (44 percent) of these arrived between 1975 and 1980, compared with 24 percent of all other foreign-born persons.

Many Arabs immigrated during this period because of constant turmoil in the Middle East: the 1967 war, the civil war in Lebanon, the Kurd-Iraqi War of the 1960s and the violence in Iraq and Iran after 1978 all were trigger points. These coincided with the U.S. Immigration Act of 1965, which ended the quota system favoring immigrants from Europe. Many in this migration flow were Muslim, with even higher educations and incomes than their predecessors. This group's socioeconomic attainment pattern also greatly surpassed that of other immigrant group, and the American population as a whole.

RELIGION

Before 1960, as many as 90 percent of Arab immigrants were Christians, but recent immigrants are mostly Muslim. There were several prominent sects within the Christian population: Maronite Christians from Lebanon, Coptic Christians from Egypt and Chaldeans from Iraq.

The new immigrants settled in or near established Arab-American communities. The Detroit metropolitan region, especially Dearborn, attracted a steady stream of Arab immigrants after 1965 and may have the largest number of recent Arab immigrants. Most came from a variety of occupational backgrounds and found work in the auto industry or in other working-class employment, although not all Detroit Arabs sought such employment.

Christian Chaldeans, an Iraqi minority in a Muslim country, were among the first to take advantage of the 1965 immigration act. About one thousand lived in Detroit before passage of the act. After 1965 their numbers increased, until by 1974 they accounted for approximately one-seventh of Detroit's estimated 70,000 Arab-Americans. They opened grocery stores and established a reputation in that business similar to that of Korean grocers. By 1972 the Chaldeans were running about 278 stores in Detroit, and assisting others in the United States.

Another large Arab-American settlement in Brooklyn had attracted earlier Lebanese and Syrian migrations. Los Angeles lured many Coptic Christians from Egypt, part of the Egyptian immigrant wave after the 1967 Arab-Israeli War.

WHERE DO WE LIVE?

Today, Arab-Americans -- like many minority groups -- are geographically concentrated. Over two-thirds live in ten states; one-third in California, New York, and Michigan. They are also more likely than other Americans to live in metropolitan areas. Thirty-six percent of Arab-Americans are found in ten cities, primarily Detroit, New York, or Los Angeles.

Entrepreneurs in the United States, whether or not they are Arab-American, most often live in the Pacific, South Atlantic, East North Central, or Mid-Atlantic regions. The regional distribution of Arab-American entrepreneurs is similar to that of non-Arab-American entrepreneurs.

AGE, SEX AND MARITAL STATUS

Both groups of entrepreneurs - Arab-American and non-Arab-American -- tend to be between the ages of 25 and 44, and their age distributions are similar, with Arab-Americans generally younger than their non-Arab-American counterparts in most age categories, which may reflect the large proportion of self-employed Arab-American workers. Studies of other ethnic groups show that businesses tend to be established by newer immigrants, and Arab immigrants are, for the most part, young.

Entrepreneurship in the United States is male-dominated. Regardless of ancestry, 67.4 percent of entrepreneurs are male, 32.6 percent female. The ratio of male to female entrepreneurs is slightly larger for Arab-American than for non-Arab-American entrepreneurs. Entrepreneurs of all ancestries in the United States are likely to be married (74.3 percent for non-Arab-Americans and 73.6 percent for Arab-Americans). It is interesting to note, however; that close to 16 percent of Arab-American entrepreneurs are never-married singles (compared to 11.7 percent for non-Arab-Americans).

EDUCATION

In general, Arab-Americans are better educated than the average American. A greater percentage attends college, and those who earn master's degrees or higher do so at twice the national average. While most entrepreneurs in the United States have only a high school diploma or some college experience, Arab-American entrepreneurs are more likely to attend college and have college and postgraduate degrees.

These patterns remain the same when broken down by sex. Male entrepreneurs are more likely than females to have postgraduate degrees, however, and women entrepreneurs are more likely to have only a high school diploma or some college experience. (See Chart 4)

OCCUPATIONS

The occupational distribution between Arab-American entrepreneurs and their non-Arab counterparts is quite striking. The top five occupational categories for both groups are:

Executive/ administrative/managerial
Professional specialty
SalesServices (not personal domestic or protective),
andPrecision repair

Sales comprises the largest percentage of both Arab-American and non-Arab-American entrepreneurs, although the rate of Arab-Americans in sales (33.4 percent) is almost double that of non-Arabs (17.9 percent). Moreover, non-Arab-American entrepreneurs are much more evenly distributed across other occupations such as farming, fishing or forestry.
The top four industries attracting Arab-American and non-Arab-American entrepreneurs are:

Retail Trade
Construction
Finance/insurance/real estate, and
Professional industries

Consistent with the sales figures cited above, Arab-American entrepreneurs overwhelmingly work in retail trade (34.6 percent), followed by the professional industries (17.1 percent). Few are engaged as miners, administrators or in the agricultural/forestry/fishing fields. The same can be said for the entertainment/recreation field (although some notable exceptions apply).

Non-Arab-American entrepreneurs are more evenly distributed across industries, but most are also in the professions (19.5 percent) and retail trade (16 percent); the fewest work in entertainment/recreation (1.8 percent) and transport/commerce/utilities **(3.7 percent)**.

WHERE WE WORK

This occupational and industrial distribution varies according to region. Arab-American entrepreneurs in executive/managerial occupations concentrate in the Mid-Atlantic, Pacific, or South Atlantic regions, while those in the professions gravitate toward the East North Central and, less so, the Mountain regions. Arab-Americans in sales favor the Pacific; in service occupations, the East North Central and South Atlantic; and, in precision repair, the Pacific and Mid-Atlantic regions.

By comparison, non-Arab-American entrepreneurs in executive/managerial occupations and sales typically live in the Pacific and South Atlantic, while those in professional occupations are most likely to be found in the Pacific and Mid-Atlantic regions, and those in retail trade tend to live in the South Atlantic and Pacific, and are least likely to live in the East South Central and New England regions.

The industries among the top four for Arab-American entrepreneurs are distributed regionally as follows: Arab-Americans in construction overwhelmingly locate in the Pacific, South Atlantic, and Mid-Atlantic

regions, with the greatest concentration of non-Arabs in construction in the South Atlantic and Pacific, and a few in the Mountain region. The finance/insurance/real estate category is the only industrial arena where both groups, with similar proportions of workers, are most likely to live in the Pacific or South Atlantic regions and least likely in East South Central.
Among those industries not ranking in the top four for non-Arab-American entrepreneurs, those in professional health are concentrated in the Pacific and Mid-Atlantic, with few in the Mountain and East South Central regions, but Arab-American entrepreneurs in this industry reside primarily in the Pacific region and less often in the East South Central and New England.

Similarly, most non-Arab-American entrepreneurs in health and education can be found in the Pacific and Mid-Atlantic, with the fewest in the Mountain and East South Central regions, while Arab-American entrepreneurs in these industries are concentrated in New England, the South Atlantic and Mid-Atlantic.

THE PROFESSIONAL ELITE

The relationship between education and occupation is not surprising. Entrepreneurs in professional occupations often have post-graduate degrees. Close to 80 percent of Arab-American entrepreneurial professionals 25 years of age and older have higher degrees, compared to nearly 55 percent of their non-Arab counterparts. Entrepreneurs of every ancestry in executive, precision repair, and sales occupations commonly have some college experience, while most in service occupations have not gone beyond high school.

While the groups share similar patterns in education and industrial distribution, the variance between them is quite striking. For example, entrepreneurs in the professional health industries will more likely have postgraduate degrees, while those in finance/insurance/real estate usually have some college experience. But the proportion of Arab-Americans holding degrees in both fields is at least 20 percent higher.

HOW MUCH WE MAKE

As occupation and industry vary, so does income. The average Arab-American entrepreneur may have a higher personal and household income than a non-Arab-American counterpart in most regions of the United States.

Median household income is strikingly higher for Arab-Americans in the Pacific, Northeast, New England, and South Atlantic regions, exceeding $50,000 annually. Arab-Americans in the Mountain region have higher household, but lower personal, incomes. In the Pacific region incomes of the two groups are similar, with non-Arab-American entrepreneurs having lower household but slightly higher personal incomes.

When median personal income is broken down by sex, many of the above-noted patterns are repeated. Arab-American female and male entrepreneurs earn more than their non-Arab-American counterparts in New England, West North Central, South Atlantic, and East South Central. Non-Arab-American male and female entrepreneurs tend to have higher personal incomes in the Mountain region. All women, regardless of ancestry, earn very little, but Arab-American female entrepreneurs typically earn more than non-Arab-American females in all regions except West South Central and Mountain. Males of all ancestries typically earn more than females in every region.

A MISUNDERSTOOD GROUP

Arab-Americans are numerous, affluent and often misunderstood. Like many other ethnic or minority groups, they suffer from stereotyping and negative press. Yet they represent significant and distinct niche markets.

Arab-American entrepreneurship is as old as America, and has had to endure the traditional problems of inadequate capital, federal restrictions and the failure of policy makers and educators to understand its importance in the community. A recent census estimates the receipts of Arab-American entrepreneurs to be 1 percent of the U.S. total. This figure, however, is debated by many who say that the census is only looking at small companies.

A glance through the advertising pages of Arab-American publications reveals a mix of specialized and mainstream products and services, such as medical, legal and educational services; literary works; foods; and computer and electronic products.

Ultimately, like any other immigrant group, Arab-Americans want to enjoy America's riches while preserving the important parts of their native culture.

El-Badry is a president of International Demographic and Economic Associates (IDEA), an Austin, Tx-based consulting firm. El-Badry, who is an Arab-American of Egyptian descent, also is a vice president with Teknecon Energy Risk Advisors LLC, an Austin, Tx.-based energy consulting company. She serves on the advisory board of the Secretary of Commerce's Decennial Census as a representative of the Arab-American community.

Arab American Demographics: DETROIT, MI
Metropolitan Detroit is the largest concentration of Arabs outside of the Middle East. Over 350,000 people of Arabic heritage call Metro Detroit home
The Arab community of Detroit has one of the highest educational attainments of any ethnic group. While one in five (20.3%) of all Americans has graduated from college, almost two in five Arab Americans (36.3%) have a college degree.
A recent consumer study found very high degrees of brand loyalty among Arab Americans. Over 60% of the Arab American market segment placed brand loyalty ahead of price sensitivity.
Arab-Americans own an estimated 3,000 businesses in Michigan.
Arab Americans of Michigan live primarily in Wayne and Oakland Counties in the following cities:
Dearborn
Livonia
Detroit
Warren
Flint
Saginaw
Bloomfield Hills
Farmington Hills
An Estimated 5 Million Arab Americans live in the United States with the largest concentrations in:
California (760,000)
Michigan (476,000)
Illinois
New York
New Jersey
Florida.
Over 60% of Arab-Americans are Christian.
Suorce: Zogby International / ACCESS Marketing

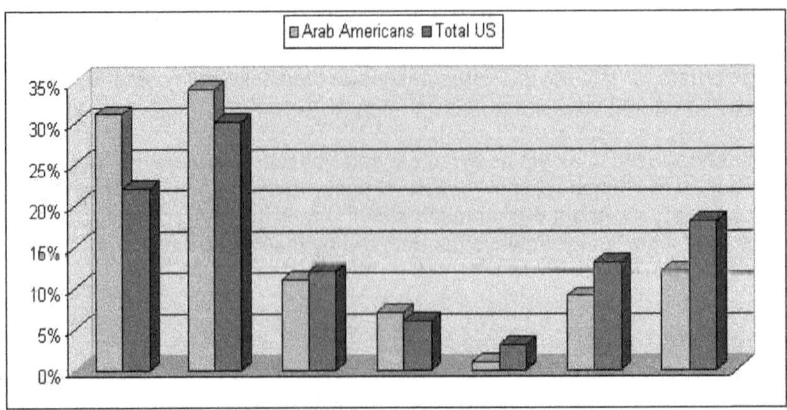

Mgt/Profl Sales/Adm Services FinanceFarming CraftLabor

22% 30% 12% 6% 3% 13% 18%

Across a variety of products,
Arab-Americans express an average
level of brand loyalty exceeding 60%
86% of Arab Americans are likely to purchase a product advertised on Arab-American Media

LARGEST ARAB AMERICAN COMMUNITIES

California	Los Angeles, Orange county, San Francisco, Marin County, San Diego, San Jose, Sacramento
Massachusetts	Boston, Newton, Brookline, Sharon, Lynn, Springfield, Framingham
New York	Brooklyn, Queens, Manhattan, Staten Island, Long Island, Westchester County, Rockland County, Albany, Rochester, Syracuse
New Jersey	Bergen County, Marlboro, Cherry Hill, Parsippany, Livingston, Manalapan, Matawan
Pennsylvania	Philadelphia, Pittsburgh, Jenkintown
Washington , DC	Baltimore, Bethesda, Rockville, Pikesville, Gaithersburg, Washington (D.C.) Arlington, Fairfax
Minnesota	Minneapolis, Hopkins, St. Paul, Woodbury, Minnetonka
Georgia	Atlanta
Washington State	Seattle, Bellevue, Redmond, Vancouver, Tacoma
Oregon	Salem, Woodburn, Portland, Oregon City, West Linn, Lake Oswego, Beaverton, Tigard, Tualatin
Colorado	Denver, Aurora, Glendale, Arvada, Parker, Littleton, Golden, Louisville, Lafayette, Boulder, Colorado Springs
Connecticut	Hartford, Stamford, New Haven
Nevada	Las Vegas, Reno
Illinois	Chicago,
Texas	Houston, Dallas, San Antonio
Michigan	Detroit, Dearborn
Florida	North Miami Beach, Hallandale, Tampa, Fort Lauderdale, Coral Springs, Orlando, St. Petersburg, Daytona Beach
California	Los Angeles, Orange county, San Francisco, Marin County, San Diego, San Jose, Sacramento
Massachusetts	Boston, Newton, Brookline, Sharon, Lynn, Springfield, Framingham
New York	Brooklyn, Queens, Manhattan, Staten Island, Long Island, Westchester County, Rockland County, Albany, Rochester, Syracuse
New Jersey	Bergen County, Marlboro, Cherry Hill, Parsippany, Livingston, Manalapan, Matawan
Pennsylvania	Philadelphia, Pittsburgh, Jenkintown
Washington , DC	Baltimore, Bethesda, Rockville, Pikesville, Gaithersburg, Washington (D.C.) Arlington, Fairfax
Michigan	Detroit, Dearborn
Minnesota	Minneapolis, Hopkins, St. Paul, Woodbury, Minnetonka
Florida	North Miami Beach, Hallandale, Tampa, Fort Lauderdale, Coral Springs, Orlando, St.

	Petersburg, Daytona Beach
Georgia	Atlanta
Washington State	Seattle, Bellevue, Redmond, Vancouver, Tacoma
Oregon	Salem, Woodburn, Portland, Oregon City, West Linn, Lake Oswego, Beaverton, Tigard, Tualatin
Colorado	Denver, Aurora, Glendale, Arvada, Parker, Littleton, Golden, Louisville, Lafayette, Boulder, Colorado Springs
Connecticut	Hartford, Stamford, New Haven
	Las Vegas, Reno
Illinois	Chicago,
Texas	Houston, Dallas, San Antonio

THE ISRAELI AND ARAB LOBBIES[2]

Reference is often made to the "Jewish lobby" in an effort to describe Jewish political influence in the United States. This term is both vague and inadequate. While it is true that American Jews are sometimes represented by lobbyists, such direct efforts to influence policy-makers are but a small part of the lobby's ability to shape policy.

Organized groups do attempt to directly affect legislation. One of these, the American-Israel Public Affairs Committee (AIPAC) is a registered lobby. Other groups do not generally engage in direct lobbying (e.g., B'nai B'rith and Hadassah), but do disseminate information and encourage their members to become involved in the political process. They also sometimes lobby on specific issues. Though they have rarely influenced policy, Christian groups have also frequently weighed in on Israel's behalf and several pro-Israel organizations are comprised entirely of non-Jews. These organizations comprise the *formal lobby.*

U.S. Middle East policy is further shaped by Jewish voting behavior and American public opinion. These indirect means of influence are the *informal lobby.*

The formal and informal components tend to intersect at several points so the distinction is not always clear-cut. Together, however, they form the Israeli (or pro-Israel) lobby. This is a more accurate label than "Jewish lobby" because a large proportion of the lobby is made up of non-Jews. This term also reflects the lobby's objective. The Israeli lobby can then be defined as *those formal and informal actors that directly and indirectly influence American policy to support Israel.*

The Israeli lobby does not have the field to itself. On any given issue, it may be opposed by a variety of interest groups unrelated to the Middle East (e.g., conservative groups that have nothing against Israel, but oppose foreign aid on principle), but its main rival is the Arab lobby, which similarly consists of those formal and informal actors that attempt to influence U.S. foreign policy to support the interests of the Arab states in the Middle East.

THE INFORMAL ISRAELI LOBBY

American Jews recognize the importance of support for Israel because of the dire consequences that could follow from the alternative. Despite the fact that Israel is often referred to now as the fourth most powerful country in the world, the perceived threat to Israel is not military defeat, it is annihilation. At the same time, American Jews are frightened of what might happen in the United States if they do not have political power.

As a result, Jews have devoted themselves to politics with almost religious fervor. This is reflected by the fact that Jews have the highest percentage voter turnout of any ethnic group. Though the Jewish population in the United States is roughly six million (about 2.3% of the total U.S. population), roughly 94% live in 13

[2] By Mitchell Bard

key electoral college states. These states alone are worth enough electoral votes to elect the president. If you add the *non-Jews* shown by opinion polls to be as pro-Israel as Jews, it is clear Israel has the support of one of the largest veto groups in the country.

The political activism of Jews forces congressmen with presidential ambitions to consider what a mixed voting record on Israel-related issues may mean in the political future. There are no benefits to candidates taking an openly anti-Israel stance and considerable costs in both loss of campaign contributions and votes from Jews and non-Jews alike. Potential candidates therefore have an incentive to be pro-Israel; this reinforces support for Israel in Congress. Actual candidates must be particularly sensitive to the concerns of Jewish voters; it follows that the successful candidate's foreign policy will be influenced, although not bound, by the promises that had to be made during the campaign.

One way that lobbyists attempt to educate politicians is by taking them to Israel on study missions. Once officials have direct exposure to the country, its leaders, geography, and security dilemmas, they typically return more sympathetic to Israel. Politicians also sometimes travel to Israel specifically to demonstrate to the lobby their interest in Israel. Thus, for example, George W. Bush made his one and only trip to Israel before deciding to run for President in what was widely viewed as an effort to win pro-Israel voters' support. While there, he also was educated and was particularly influenced by a helicopter tour given to him by a man he would later work with as a fellow head of state — Ariel Sharon. In 2005 alone, more than 100 members of Congress visited Israel, some multiple times.[1]

Jewish congressmen are naturally expected to be supportive of Israel and, with the exception of occasional odd votes, this is true. Historically, however, few Jews have held elective office or primary positions of power, even though they have always been politically active. In the past decade, however, this has gradually begun to change. Today, Jews occupy more positions of influence than ever before. For example, in the 109th Congress, 11 Senators are Jewish (11 percent) while Jewish members comprise almost 6 percent of the House.

Bill Clinton nominated two Supreme Court Justices, both Jewish. He had several Jewish Cabinet members, including National Security Adviser Sandy Berger and Agriculture Secretary Dan Glickman, and dozens of Jews held other key Administration posts. Bastions of bureaucratic opposition, and sometimes outright anti-Semitism, such as the CIA and State Department now employ Jews at the highest levels. For almost a decade, a Jew (Dennis Ross) was America's principal Mideast negotiator and Clinton appointed the first Jewish Ambassador to Israel (Martin Indyk). The George W. Bush Administration also has included many Jews in high-profile subcabinet positions

THE INFORMAL ARAB LOBBY

The disproportionate influence of the American Jewish population is in direct contrast with the electoral involvement of Arab-Americans. There are approximately 1.2 million Arabs in the United States, and roughly 38 percent of them are Lebanese, primarily Christians, who tend to be unsympathetic to the Arab lobby's goals. This reflects another major problem for the Arab lobby -- inter-Arab disunity. This disunity is reinforced by the general discord of the Arab world, which has twenty-one states with competing interests. The Arab lobby is thus precluded from representing "the Arabs."

Only about 70,000 Palestinians (6 percent of all Arab-Americans) live in the United States, but their views have received disproportionate attention because of their political activism. Similarly, a great deal of attention has focused on the allegedly growing political strength of Muslims in the United States, but fewer than one-fourth of all Arab-Americans are Muslims according to the Arab-American Institute.[2]

About half of the Arab population is concentrated in five states — California, Florida, Michigan, New Jersey, and New York — that are all key to the electoral college. Still, the Arab population is dwarfed by that of the Jews in every one of these states except Michigan.

JEWISH AND ARAB POPULATIONS IN KEY STATES[3]

State	Arab Population	Arabs as % of Total State Population	Jewish Population	Jews as % of Total State Population
CA	142,805	.48	999,000	2.9
FL	49,206	.38	628,000	3.9

MI	76,504	.82	110,000	1.1
NJ	46,381	.60	485,000	5.7
NY	94,319	.52	1,657,000	8.7

CAMPAIGN DONATIONS

Political campaign contributions are also considered an important means of influence; typically, Jews have been major benefactors. It is difficult to assess the impact of campaign giving on legislative outcomes, particularly with regard to Israel-related issues, where support or opposition may be a consequence of non-monetary factors. In addition, one does not know if a candidate is pro-Israel because of receiving a contribution, or receives a donation as a result of taking a position in support of Israel. In the past, Jewish contributions were less structured and targeted than other interest groups, but this has changed dramatically as Israel-related political action committees (PACs) have proliferated.

Initially, the Jewish community feared that post-Watergate election campaign financing reforms would reduce their influence, but the evidence so far suggests the opposite. If anything, the changes have stimulated greater political activism in the Jewish community.

The first pro-Israel PAC was formed in 1978, but there was little activity until 1982 when thirty-three pro-Israel PACs contributed $1.87 million to congressional candidates. Like other PACs, most of this money was given to incumbents and, because of the long association of Jews with the Democratic party, nearly 80 percent went to Democrats. The number of PACs more than doubled in 1984 as did their contributions. It was estimated that more than seventy pro-Israel PACs spent a little more than $4 million in 1984. By 1988, the figure was nearly $5 million. In 2004, pro-Israel PACs gave a little more than $3 million to candidates, and individuals contributed nearly $3 million more. According to the Center for Responsive Politics, pro-Israel interests have contributed $58 million in individual, PAC, and soft money contributions to national-level candidates and national party committees, but even these contributions are dwarfed by those of labor unions, lawyers, doctors, and trade associations. In fact, out of 80 “industries,” the pro-Israel contributors rank only 43rd.

The PACs' contributions became increasingly focused in 1984 and, apparently, they had a high degree of success in choosing winning candidates. In the two most expensive and publicized Senate campaigns, Percy-Simon in Illinois and Helms-Hunt in North Carolina, however, the Israeli lobby had to settle for a split decision with its preferred candidate winning only in Illinois

On the Arab lobby side, only three PACs spent a trivial sum through 1988. Between 1989 and 2004, Arab and Muslim communities combined contributed only $450,000.

The lobby took a more active and visible role than ever before in the 1984 election. The most obvious manifestation of this came in the congressional race involving seventy-six-year-old Maryland Democrat Clarence Long. Long, chairman of the House Appropriations subcommittee on Foreign Operations and a driving force behind increasing aid to Israel, was targeted by the Arab lobby: "to serve notice to members of Congress that the Arab lobby is ready and able to make life uncomfortable for Israel's friends on Capitol Hill."

Like the visible campaign undertaken in 1982 by the Israeli lobby to defeat pro-Arab Congressman Paul Findley of Illinois, the Arab lobby claimed victory when Long was defeated. As was the case in the Findley campaign, where the Congressman's district suffered from a high unemployment rate, and had been gerrymandered to his disadvantage, the reasons for Long's defeat were rooted in politics unrelated to the Middle East. In Long's case, redistricting took away a large percentage of his constituency and, after a narrow victory in 1982, he became a high priority target of the Republican National Committee.

In Jesse Jackson the Arab lobby found, for the first time, a presidential candidate receptive to their interests. Jackson had a long record of support for the Arab cause and was particularly outspoken in support of Palestinian rights, having met with Palestine Liberation Organization (PLO) chairman Yasir Arafat when it was considered politically taboo. As a result of his stands, Jackson received substantial financial support from members of the Arab lobby. The divisions of the lobby were again apparent, however, when the president of the American Lebanese League said Jackson turns his constituents off: "He seems interested in the welfare of Arab countries but not Lebanon or the United States."

Overall, the comparative impact of the two lobbies on elections was probably best summed up by Harry Truman in his frequently repeated statement to Paul Porter, a Washington attorney appointed as the ambassador to the Arab-Israeli peace talks in Geneva in 1948: "I won't tell you what to do or how to vote, but I will only say this. In all of my political experience I don't ever recall the Arab vote swinging a close election."

PUBLIC OPINION

The absence of a large voting bloc requires the Arab lobby to develop sympathies among the general public if it is to use public opinion or the electoral process as a means of influencing U.S. policy. The lobby has tried to support sympathetic American groups, such as Third World organizations, and cultivate friendships in the academic and business realms, but, as opinion polls have consistently shown, there is relatively little popular support for the Arab cause.

Since 1967, polls have found that sympathy for Israel varied between 32 and 64 percent, averaging 46 percent, while sympathy for the Arabs has oscillated between 1 and 30 percent and averaged only 12 percent. In the last several years, support for the Arabs has increased slightly, but this has not affected sympathies toward Israel.

Not only has the Arab lobby been unable to increase its standing significantly with the public, it has also failed to convince the American people that the Israeli lobby controls U.S. Middle East policy. In fact, polls indicate the public sees the Arab lobby as more of a threat than the Israeli lobby. For example, in a poll conducted several weeks after the Senate vote on the sale of AWACS to Saudi Arabia, 53 percent of the public agreed Israel has "too much influence" on American foreign policy, but only 11 percent felt the same way about American Jews. By contrast, 64 percent said Saudi Arabia had too much influence, and 70 percent believed oil companies were too influential. A March 1983 poll asking which groups have "too much" political influence found that only 10 percent of those asked said "Jews." Business corporations and unions were considered too powerful by more than 40 percent of the respondents, with Arab interests next at 24 percent.

Thus, the Arab lobby's problem is twofold; it suffers from a very negative image and Israel enjoys a very positive image. This has gradually begun to change. To combat negative Arab stereotypes, former Senator James Abourezk founded the American Arab Anti-Discrimination Committee (ADC) in 1980. The ADC is modeled after the Anti-Defamation League, but is considerably smaller and weaker.

THE FORMAL ISRAELI LOBBY

The organization that directly lobbies the U.S. government on behalf of the Israeli lobby is AIPAC. The lobby, originally called the American *Zionist* Committee for Public Affairs, was founded in 1951 by I.L. (Sy) Kenen to appeal directly to Congress for legislation to provide aid to Israel to circumvent State Department opposition. As recently as the late 1960s, the organization now considered the most powerful foreign policy lobby in Washington was essentially a one-man operation run by Kenen. In the late 1970s, AIPAC still had only a handful of staff based in Washington. Today, it has more than 100 employees with seven regional offices and a budget of more than $40 million and lobbies the Executive Branch as well as the Legislative. Because of its name, AIPAC is sometimes mistakenly thought to be a political action committee (PAC), but the organization does not rate, endorse or finance candidates.

AIPAC was not the first domestic lobby to concern itself with foreign affairs, but it is regarded as the most powerful. In 1998 and 1999, for example, *Fortune Magazine* named AIPAC the second most powerful lobby in Washington after the American Association for Retired Persons (AARP). The lobby strives to remain nonpartisan and thereby keeps friends in both parties. By framing the issues in terms of the national interest, AIPAC can attract broader support than would ever be possible if it was perceived to represent only the interests of Israel. This does not mean AIPAC does not have a close relationship with Israeli officials, it does, albeit unofficially. Even so, the lobby some times comes into conflict with the Israeli government. One of the most blatant examples occurred when AIPAC's Executive Director Thomas Dine was quoted on the front page of the *New York Times* as saying the 1982 Reagan peace plan had some good points (and many bad ones) after the Israeli government had rejected the plan in toto. Despite such disagreements, the Israeli lobby tends to reflect Israeli government policy fairly closely. Though its influence is limited primarily to issues where Congress has a say, in particular, economic matters, the organization also serves as a watchdog to deter anti-Israel policies from being adopted.

Lobbyists usually roam the halls of Congress trying to get the attention of legislators so they can explain their positions. AIPAC has the luxury of being able to call its allies in Congress to pass along information, and then leaves much of the work of writing bills and gathering cosponsors to the legislative staffs. The lobbyists themselves are mostly Capitol Hill veterans who know how to operate the levers of power.

Since it does not use stereotypical lobbying tactics, the Israeli lobby depends on the network it has developed to galvanize the Jewish community to take some form of political action. The network consists of at least seventy-five different organizations, which in one way or another support Israel. Most cannot legally engage in lobbing, but are represented on the Board of Directors of AIPAC, so they are able to provide input into the lobby's decision-making process. Equally important is the bureaucratic machinery of these organizations, which enables them to disseminate information to their members and facilitate a rapid response to legislative activity.

A second coordinating body is the Conference of Presidents of Major American Jewish Organizations. It is composed of leaders of 55 different organizations and is responsible for formulating and articulating the "Jewish position" on most foreign policy matters. The conference allows the lobby to speak with one voice in a way its opponents cannot. The conference is the main contact between the Jewish community and the executive branch, while AIPAC tends to be the conduit with the legislative branch.

Even with the Jewish population concentrated in key states, there is still only a total of about six million Jews; therefore, the Israeli lobby is dependent on the support of non-Jewish groups and actively works to form coalitions with broad segments of American society. The lobby has successfully built coalitions consisting of unions, entertainers, clergymen, scholars, and black leaders. The coalitions allow the lobby to demonstrate a broad public consensus for a pro-Israel policy.

THE ARAB LOBBY

The Arab lobby in the United States is at least as old, perhaps older than the Israeli lobby. It is composed of what I.L. Kenen called the petro-diplomatic complex consisting of the oil industry, missionaries, and diplomats. According to Kenen, there was no need for a formal Arab lobby because the petro-diplomatic complex did the Arabs' work for them.

One of the earliest activities of the petro-diplomatic complex began in 1951 when King Saud of Saudi Arabia asked U.S. diplomats to finance a pro-Arab lobby to counter the American Zionist Committee for Public Affairs (later the American Israel Public Affairs Committee -AIPAC). The Arab lobby became an official, active, and visible spokesman for the Arab cause in the wake of the oil embargo. "The day of the Arab-American is here," boasted National Association of Arab-Americans (NAAA) founder Richard Shadyac, "the reason is oil."

From the beginning, the Arab lobby has faced not only a disadvantage in electoral politics but also in organization. There are several politically oriented groups, but many of these are one man operations with little financial or popular support. Americans for Justice in the Middle East was formed by a group of Americans at the American University in Beirut after the 1967 war to combat "Zionism's virulent thirty-year campaign of hate and vindictiveness." Two Anti-Zionist Jews are also active supporters of the Arab lobby. Elmer Berger runs American Jewish Alternatives to Zionism and Alfred Lilienthal publishes his own newsletter Middle East Perspectives.

There are a number of larger and more representative groups, including the aforementioned NAAA and ADC, the Middle East Research and Information Project; the Middle East Affairs Council, Americans for Near East Refugee Aid, the Arab American Institute and the American Palestine Committee. Typically, these organizations have boards of directors composed of prominent retired government officials. Board members have included former Ambassador to Jordan, L. Dean Brown, Herman Eilts, former Ambassador to Syria and Egypt; Parker T. Hart, former Ambassador to Saudi Arabia and several others.

The formal Arab lobby is the National Association of Arab-Americans (NAAA), a registered domestic lobby founded in 1972 by Richard Shadyac. The NAAA was consciously patterned after its counterpart, the American Israel Public Affairs Committee (AIPAC). Shadyac believed the power and wealth of the Arab countries stemming from their oil reserves, would allow the Arab lobby to take advantage of the political process in the same way the Jews have been thought to. Like AIPAC, the NAAA makes its case on the basis of U.S. national interests, arguing a pro-Israel policy harms those interests. Aid to Israel is criticized as a waste of taxpayers' money, and the potential benefits of a closer relationship with the Arab states is emphasized.

The highlight of the NAAA's early efforts was a meeting between President Ford and twelve NAAA officials in 1975. Since then, the NAAA has participated in meetings with each president and obtained access to top government officials. In 1977, for example, after Sadat's historic visit to Jerusalem, the Arab lobby made its displeasure over United States support for the initiative known to President Carter, who wrote in his diary: "They [Arab-Americans] have given all the staff, Brzezinski, Warren Christopher, and others, a hard time. Although the lobby's concerns began to reach the highest levels of government, there were no perceptible changes in United States policy."

It is not only Arab-Americans who have made the lobby's case; the Arab lobby, like the Israeli lobby, has successfully built coalitions with other interest groups. As noted earlier, the pedro-diplomatic complex was the lobby until 1972, when the NAAA was formed. Even today, arguably, it is the most influential component of the lobby. Nevertheless, most of the nation's major corporations have not supported the Arab lobby. In fact, prior to the AWACS sale, oil companies were about the only corporations willing to openly identify with Arab interests. The reason is that most corporations prefer to stay out of foreign policy debates; moreover, corporations may feel constrained by the implicit threat of some form of retaliation by the Israeli lobby.

The major oil companies feel no such constraints. Exxon, Standard Oil of California (SoCal), Mobil, and Texaco have long sought to manipulate public opinion and foreign policy on the Middle East. These companies as a group comprise the Arabian American Oil Company (ARAMCO). Participation in the public relations campaign amounted to the price of doing business in the oil-producing nations.

The campaign began after the 1967 War when ARAMCO established a fund to help present the Arab side of the conflict. In May 1970, ARAMCO representatives met with Assistant Secretary of State Joseph Sisco and warned him American military sales to Israel would hurt U.S.-Arab relations and jeopardize U.S. oil supplies. The former chairman of ARAMCO testified before Congress that the United States' pro-Israel policies were harming U.S. business interests. In 1972, at Kuwait's urging, Gulf Oil joined the campaign, providing $50,000 to create a public relations firm to promote the Arab side.

The campaign took on greater urgency in 1973 after Frank Jungers, then Chairman of the Board of ARAMCO, met with Saudi King Faisal, and was pressured to take a more active role in creating a sympathetic attitude toward the Arab nations. In June, a month after the Jungers meeting, Mobil published its first advertisement/editorial in the New York Times. In July, SoCal's chairman sent out a letter to the company's 40,000 employees and 262,000 stockholders asking them to pressure Washington to support "the aspirations of the Arab people." The chairman of Texaco called for a reassessment of U.S. Middle East policy. When the October 1973 War broke out, the chairmen of the ARAMCO partners sent a memorandum to the White House warning against increasing military aid to Israel. Since 1973, ARAMCO has maintained its public relations campaign and become involved in occasional legislative fights, such as the AWACS sale, but, on the whole, the campaign has had no observable impact on U.S. policy.

Other companies outside the oil industry are involved in the Arab lobby, the most well-known being the international engineering firm Bechtel, but the Arab and Israeli lobbies have had virtually no confrontations since the AWACS fight in 1981, in part because the Israeli lobby hasn't opposed any major arms sales or other economic investments in the region that threatened U.S. corporate interests.

A relatively ignored component of the "Arab lobby" is found among the Christian community, most notably, the National Council of Churches (NCC). The NCC is composed of thirty-two Protestant denominations, including virtually all major church bodies. The Council has taken consistently anti-Israel stands, and its 1980 policy statement on the Middle East called for the creation of a PLO state. Besides passing anti-Israel resolutions, the NCC puts on seminars, radio shows, and conferences. From 1972 to 1977, it published the ARAMCO financed SWASIA (Southwest Asia) newsletter. When SWASIA ceased publication, the NCC established an Islamic desk to "enable American Christians to understand Arab Christian and Muslim attitudes." The relationship between the NCC and other Arab lobby organizations is primarily informal, with NCC leaders serving on many of their boards.

CONTRASTS

At least two major differences distinguish the Arab and Israeli lobbies. First, the Arab lobby almost always lobbies negatively; i.e., against pro-Israel legislation rather than for pro-Arab legislation. In 2004, for example, members of Congress were graded on a number of issues, including: opposition to the war with Iraq; opposition to resolutions that condemned terrorism inflicted on Israel, that supported President Bush's letter supporting Israel, that called for a halt to Saudi support for terrorism and Syrian accountability, and that supported Israel's construction of a security fence; opposition to a letter calling for the Palestinians to meet certain obligations; and a resolution expressing sympathy for an American woman who was accidentally killed protesting Israeli house demolitions.[4]

The other major difference between the two lobbies is the use of paid foreign agents by the Arab lobby. Pro-Arab U.S. government officials can look forward to lucrative positions as lobbyists, spokesmen, and consultants for the Arab cause. For example, the outspoken critic of the Israeli lobby, former Senate Foreign Relations Committee Chairman J. William Fulbright, was hired by the Saudis and the United Arab Emirates. It was the Saudis' agent, Fred Dutton, a former Assistant Secretary for Legislative Affairs and special assistant to President Kennedy, who spearheaded the AWACS campaign and reputedly conceived the "Reagan vs. Begin" angle. Other top officials who have provided their services to the Arab lobby include: Clark Clifford, President Johnson's Defense Secretary; Richard Kleindienst, President Nixon's Attorney General; and William Rogers, Nixon's Secretary of State.

Overall, the Israeli lobby is effective because it enjoys advantages in every area considered relevant to interest group influence. It has (a) a large and vocal membership; (b) members who enjoy high status and legitimacy; (c) a high degree of electoral participation (voting and financing); (d) effective leadership; (e) a high degree of access to decision-makers; and (f) public support. Moreover, for reasons at least partly attributable to the lobby's efforts, the lobby's primary objective — a U.S. commitment to Israel — has been accepted as a national interest.

MEASURING INFLUENCE

Most articles and research on the Middle East interest groups are based on anecdotes, case studies or casual observation. They either vaguely conclude the Israeli lobby has some influence some of the time or (usually in the case of works by authors hostile to Israel) assert the Israeli lobby is a powerful and dangerous influence that controls U.S. policy.

In a more rigorous study of 782 policy decisions made from 1945 to 1984, I found the Israeli lobby won; that is, achieved its policy objective, 60 percent of the time. The most important variable was the president's position. When the president supported the lobby, it won 95 percent of the time. At first glance it appears the lobby was only successful because its objectives coincided with those of the president, but the lobby's influence was demonstrated by the fact that it still won 27 percent of the cases when the president opposed its position.

One of the most surprising results, particularly in light of conventional wisdom and evidence presented in case studies, was that the president's position was not significantly affected by the electoral cycle. Although candidates may appear to pander to Jewish voters, the data indicate the electoral cycle does not affect influence success.

Lobby success also varied depending on the policy at issue. The lobby was very successful in overcoming presidential opposition on economic issues, but rarely able to defeat the president on security and political issues. The lobby was more successful on economic issues because most of those were decided in Congress where pro-Israel congressman frequently fought for increased aid levels for Israel, earmarked funds for Israel and adopted amendments to aid bills that were endorsed by the Israeli lobby.

The lobby's lack of success on political issues was most likely a result of the fact that most of these cases were decided in the executive branch where lobby influence is relatively weak. The outcome might also be explained by the tradition of congressional deference to the president on matters of security and diplomacy.

STRATEGIC AND PRACTICAL MATERIALS ON THE US LOBBYIUNG SYSTEM

THE LEGISLATIVE TRANSPARENCY AND ACCOUNTABILITY ACT OF 2006

SUMMARY AND BACKGROUND

S. 2349, the *Legislative Transparency and Accountability Act of 2006*, would, among other things, amend Senate rules governing the interaction of Senators and Senate staff with lobbyists; permit a point of order against consideration of individual provisions in a conference report that were not committed to the conferees by either House (which could be waived or suspended by a three fifths vote); and create a new Senate rule requiring that all earmarks be identified by the Senator proposing the earmark (at least 24 hours prior to consideration) along with an explanation of the essential government purpose of the earmark.

MAJOR PROVISIONS

Section 2 of **S. 2349** would:

- Permit any Senator to make a point of order against consideration of a conference report that includes any matter not committed to the conferees by either House. The point of order shall be made and voted on separately for each item alleged to be in violation of this section; and

- Permit the point of order to be waived or suspended only by an affirmative vote of three fifths of Senators duly chosen and worn. Furthermore, the Senate could appeal a ruling of the Chair on a point of order raised under this section by a three-fifths vote.

Section 3 of **S. 2349** would:

- Create a new Senate Rule XLIV regarding earmarks. Rule XLIV would define an earmark as a provision that specifies the identity of a non-federal entity to receive assistance in the form of budget authority; contract authority; loan authority; and other expenditures, or other revenue items, and the amount of the assistance; and

- Require that, before consideration of any bill, amendment or conference report could be in order, a list identifying all earmarks in the measure, along with identification of the Senator(s) who proposed them, and an explanation of the essential governmental purpose for the earmark must be made available to all Senators and posted on the Internet to the general public for at least 24 hours before its consideration.

Section 4 of **S. 2349** would:

- Amend Rule XXVIII to require that a conference report be made publicly available on the Internet 24 hours prior to consideration.

Section 5 of **S. 2349** would:

- Amend Rule XXIII to eliminate floor privileges for an ex-Senator, ex-Officer, and ex-Speaker of the House who is a registered lobbyist, foreign agent, or someone who is in the employ of any party or organization for the purpose of influencing the passage or defeat or amendment of any legislative proposal; and

- Permit the Rules Committee to promulgate regulations to allow individuals covered by this section floor privileges for ceremonial functions.

Section 6 of **S. 2349** would:

- Amend Rule XXXV to prohibit Senators from accepting a gift from a registered lobbyist or foreign agent except for meals, which would be allowed under the current dollar amount limits but must be publicly disclosed on the Senator's website within 15 days of the meal.

Section 7 of **S. 2349** would:

- Amend Rule XXXV to prohibit transportation or lodging to be paid for by a registered lobbyist or foreign agent;

- Require a Senator or Senate staff, before accepting any otherwise permissible transportation or lodging from a non-governmental entity, to obtain a written certification that the trip was not financed in whole, or in part, by a registered lobbyist or foreign agent, and that the provider did not accept funds from a registered lobbyist or foreign agent specifically earmarked for the purpose of financing the travel expenses;

- Require a Senator or Senate staff, before accepting any otherwise permissible transportation or lodging from a non-governmental entity, to provide to the Select Committee on Ethics a written, detailed itinerary of the trip, and a determination that the trip is primarily educational, consistent with the official duties of the Senator, officer, or employee, does not create an appearance of use of public office for private gain, and a has a minimal or no recreational component;

- Require a Senator or Senate staff, before accepting any otherwise permissible transportation or lodging from a non-governmental entity, to obtain written approval of the trip from the Select Committee on Ethics. Within 30 days of completing the travel, a Senator, officer, or employee would be required to file with the Select Committee on Ethics and the Secretary of the Senate a description of meetings and events attended during such travel and the names of any registered lobbyist who accompanied them, subject to limited exception on national security grounds. Such trip information must be posted on the Senator's website not later than 30 days after the completion of the travel;

- Amend Rule XXXV to require the disclosure of noncommercial air travel taken in connection with the duties of the Senator, officer, or employee (excluding a flight on an aircraft owned, operated, or leased by a government entity taken in connection with official duties), and file a report with the Secretary of the Senate, including the date, destination, and owner or lessee of the aircraft, the purpose of the trip, and the persons on the trip, except for any person flying the aircraft. Furthermore, **S. 2349** would amend the *Federal Election Campaign Act* to require disclosure of similar information for flights taken by a candidate (except for the President or Vice President) during the relevant reporting period; and

- Require the Secretary of the Senate to publicly disclose, and Senators to post on their official website, all filings required by this section within 30 days of the travel.

Section 8 of **S. 2349** would:

- Amend Rule XXXVII to prohibit for one year any former Senate senior-level employee (defined as staff who work for a Senator or committee and whose rate of pay was equal to or greater than 75% of the rate of pay of a Senator) who subsequently becomes a registered lobbyist or lobbyist employee from lobbying any Senator, officer, or employee of the Senate.

Section 9 of **S. 2349** would:

- Amend Rule XXXVII to prohibit a Senator from directly negotiating prospective private employment until after the election for his or her successor has been held, unless the Senator files a statement with the Secretary of the Senate, for public disclosure, within three business days of commencement of such negotiations, detailing the entities involved in the negotiations and the date they were commenced.

Section 10 of **S. 2349** would:

- Amend Rule XXXVII to require a Senator whose spouse or immediate family member is a registered lobbyist or employee of a registered lobbyist to prohibit all staff employed by the Senator, including staff in personal, committee, and leadership offices, from having any official contact with that family member.

Section 11 of **S. 2349** would:

- Amend Rule XLIII to prohibit a Senator from taking or withholding, or threatening to take or withhold, an official act, or to influence or offer or threaten to influence the official act of another with the intent to influence on the basis of partisan political affiliation an employment decision or employment practice of any private entity.

Section 12 of **S. 2349** would:

- Express the sense of the Senate that any applicable restrictions on Congressional branch employees should apply to the Executive and Judicial branches.

LEGISLATIVE HISTORY

On February 28, 2006, the Senate Committee on Rules and Administration marked up **S. 2349**. The measure was reported to the Senate by an 18-0 vote and was introduced in the Senate on March 1.

ADMINISTRATION POSITION

The Administration had not issued a Statement of Administration Policy on this bill.

EXPECTED AMENDMENTS

It is expected that **S. 2128**, the *Lobbying Transparency and Accountability Act of 2006*, will be offered as a substitute amendment. **S. 2128** would, among other things:

- Require "grass-roots lobbying" groups that spend more than $25,000 per quarter or $100,000 per year on grass-roots operations to disclose their expenditures and activities;

- Require registered lobbyists to file quarterly, rather than semi-annually as now required. The reports would be required to include details not required under current law, including: offices lobbied, fundraisers hosted, co-hosted, or otherwise sponsored, campaign contributions to federal candidates, political committees, and party committees, travel organized for lawmakers, aides, and executive branch officials, and any other expenses covered for members of Congress or the executive branch, including the costs of meetings, retreats, conferences or similar events. The information would have to be posted online within 48 hours;

- Prohibit a registered lobbyist from making a gift or providing travel to any Member of Congress or their staff;
- Establish a 30-day deadline for disclosure by Senators of any privately funded travel;
- Require Members of Congress and high-level executive branch officials to wait two years before lobbying their former colleagues; and
- Establish a bipartisan 10 member Commission to Strengthen Confidence in Congress.

LOBBYING IN THE UNITED STATES: STRATEGIC AND PRACTICAL INFORMATION

LOBBYING THE EXECUTIVE BRANCH: CURRENT PRACTICES AND OPTIONS FOR CHANGE[3]

Under the Lobbying Disclosure Act (LDA) of 1995, as amended, individuals are required to register with the Clerk of the House of Representatives and the Secretary of the Senate if they lobby either legislative or executive branch officials. In January 2009, Secretary of the Treasury Timothy Geithner placed further restrictions on the ability of lobbyists to contact executive branch officials responsible for dispersing Emergency Economic Stabilization Act (EESA, P.L. 110-243) funds. Subsequently, President Barack Obama and Peter Orszag, Director of the Office of Management and Budget (OMB), issued a series of memoranda between March and July 2009 that govern communication between federally registered lobbyists and executive branch employees administering American Recovery and Reinvestment Act of 2009 (P.L. 111-5) funds. Most recently, in October 2009, the White House directed executive agencies to prohibit, when possible, the appointment of federally registered lobbyists to federal advisory bodies and committees.

The Recovery and Reinvestment Act lobbying restrictions focus on both written and oral communications between lobbyists and executive branch officials. Pursuant to the President's memoranda, restrictions have been placed on certain kinds of oral and written interactions between federally registered lobbyists and executive branch officials responsible for Recovery Act fund disbursement. The President's memoranda require each agency to post summaries of oral and written contacts with lobbyists on dedicated agency websites. EESA regulations are virtually identical.

Since 1995, Congress has on three occasions approved legislation to regulate lobbyists' contacts with executive branch officials. Prior to 1995, lobbying laws only required that lobbyists contacting Members of Congress register with the Clerk of the House of Representatives and the Secretary of the Senate.[1] Under current lobbying laws, individuals are required to register with the Clerk and the Secretary when lobbying either legislative or executive branch officials. Federally registered lobbyists who wish to lobby executive branch departments and agencies regarding funds provided by the Emergency Economic Stabilization Act[2] and the American Recovery and Reinvestment Act of 2009[3] are subject to additional restrictions pursuant to a series of memoranda and guidelines issued between January and July 2009.

This report outlines the development of registration requirements for lobbyists engaging executive branch officials since 1995. It also summarizes steps taken by the Obama Administration to limit and monitor lobbying of the executive branch; discusses the development and implementation of restrictions placed on lobbying for Recovery Act and EESA funds; examines the Obama Administration's decision to stop

---

[3] Jacob R. Straus Analyst on the Congress December 1, 2009 Congressional Research Service Jacob R. Straus Analyst on the Congress jstraus@crs.loc.gov, 7-6438

appointing lobbyists to federal advisory bodies and committees; considers third-party criticism of current executive branch lobbying policies; and evaluates options for possible modifications in current lobbying laws and practices.

STATUTORY COVERAGE FOR EXECUTIVE BRANCH OFFICIALS

In 1995, the Lobbying Disclosure Act (LDA) repealed the Lobbying Act portion of the Legislative Reorganization Act of 1946[4] and created a system of detailed registration and reporting requirements for lobbyists. It included a provision requiring lobbyists to register with Congress and the disclosure of lobbying contacts with certain "covered" executive branch employees. [5] The LDA was amended in 1998 to make technical corrections, including altering the definition of executive branch officials covered by the act.[6] In 2007, the Honest Leadership and Open Government Act further amended LDA definitions on covered officials.[7]

[1] P.L. 601, 60 Stat. 839-842, August 2, 1946. Title III of the Legislative Reorganization Act of 1946 is the "Federal Regulation of Lobbying Act." These individuals are often referred to as "federally-registered" lobbyists to distinguish them from individuals who might have to register with state or local officials under non-federal laws.

[2] P.L. 110-343, 122 Stat. 3765, October 3, 2009. [3] P.L. 111-5, 123 Stat. 115, February 17, 2009. [4] Provisions contained in the Legislative Reorganization Act of 1946, for the first time, established requirements for

individuals lobbying Congress to register with and report to the House of Representatives and the Senate. The Lobbying Act, however, did not impose restrictions on lobbying activities. Instead, it merely required individuals who lobby Congress to register with the House and Senate and disclose certain activities. For more information, see *Political Activity, Lobbying Laws and Gift Rules Guide*, ed. Trevor Potter and Kirk L. Jowers, 2nd ed., vol. 1 (Little Falls, NJ: Glasser Legal Works, 1999), p. 1-7.

[5] P.L. 104-65, 109 Stat. 691, December 19, 1995. [6] P.L. 105-166, 112 Stat. 38, April 8, 1998. [7] P.L. 110-81, 121 Stat. 735, September 14, 2007.

LOBBYING DISCLOSURE ACT OF 1995

The Lobbying Act of 1946 focused on lobbyists' interactions with Congress, and was silent on lobbying the executive branch. The LDA, for the first time, included executive branch officers and certain employees by defining them as "covered officials."[8] Section 3 of LDA defines a covered executive branch official as

(A)

the President;

(B)

the Vice-President;

(C)

any officer or employee, or any individual functioning in the capacity of such an officer or employee, in the Executive Office of the President;

(D)

any officer or employee serving in a position in level I, II, III, IV, or V of the Executive Schedule, as designated by statute or Executive order;[9]

(E)

any member of the uniformed services whose pay grade is at or above O-7 under section 201 of title 37, *United States Code*;[10] and

(F)

any officer or employee serving in a position of a confidential policy-determining, policy-making, or policy-advocating character described in section 7511(b)(2) of title 5, *United States Code.*[11]

Under the LDA, lobbyists who contact these executive branch officials are now required to register with the Clerk of the House and the Secretary of the Senate, and to disclose lobbying contacts and activities. The LDA made these requirements identical for covered legislative and executive branch officials and assigned to the Clerk of the House and the Secretary of the Senate the responsibility of collecting registration and disclosure statements.[12]

LOBBYING DISCLOSURE TECHNICAL AMENDMENTS ACT OF 1998

In April 1998, the LDA was amended to make technical corrections. Part of the technical corrections was a minor change in the *U.S. Code* section cited by the LDA defining covered

[8] P.L. 104-65, 109 Stat. 692, December 19, 1995; 2 U.S.C. § 1602.

[9] For more information on the Executive Schedule and executive branch pay, see CRS Report RL34463, *Federal White-Collar Pay: FY2009 Salary Adjustments*, by Barbara L. Schwemle; CRS Report RL34380, *The Executive Schedule IV Pay Cap on General Schedule Compensation*, by Curtis W. Copeland; and CRS Report RL33245, *Legislative, Executive, and Judicial Officials: Process for Adjusting Pay and Current Salaries*, by Barbara L. Schwemle.

[10] 37 U.S.C. § 201 establishes rates of compensation for commissioned officers of the uniformed services (other than commissioned warrant officers). For more information, see also CRS Report RL33446, *Military Pay and Benefits: Key Questions and Answers*, by Charles A. Henning.

[11] P.L. 104-65, 109 Stat. 692, December 19, 1995; 2 U.S.C. § 1602. 5 U.S.C. § 7511 defines terms related to federal

employment, human resources, and pay. [12] 2 U.S.C. § 1603 defines the registration requirements for all lobbyists. For more information on the role of the Clerk of the House and the Secretary of the Senate in collecting registration and disclosure statements, see CRS Report RL34377, *Honest Leadership and Open Government Act of 2007: The Role of the Clerk of the House and the Secretary of the Senate*, by Jacob R. Straus.

officials.[13]The amendment changed the reference in the LDA from 5 U.S.C. § 7511 (b)(2) to 5

U.S.C. § 7511 (b)(2)(B) to reflect the ability to the Office of Personnel Management to exempt a position from the competitive service.[14]

HONEST LEADERSHIP AND OPEN GOVERNMENT ACT OF 2007

The Honest Leadership and Open Government Act (HLOGA) of 2007 also amended the LDA. HLOGA did not further alter the definition of a covered executive branch official but did refine thresholds and definitions of lobbying activities, change the frequency of reporting for registered lobbyists and lobbying firms, require additional disclosures, create new semi-annual reports on campaign contributions, and add disclosure requirements for coalitions and associations.[15]

OBAMA ADMINISTRATION LOBBYING POLICIES

Since its inception, the Obama Administration has focused on ethics and the potential influence of lobbyists on executive branch personnel. One of President Barack Obama's first actions was to issue ethics and lobbying guidelines for executive branch employees. These guidelines laid the foundation for formal lobbying restrictions issued in July 2009.

EXECUTIVE BRANCH ETHICS PLEDGE

On January 21, 2009, President Obama issued Executive Order 13490, "Ethics Commitments by Executive Branch Personnel."[16] The executive order created an ethics pledge for all executive branch appointments made on or after January 20, 2009;[17] defined terms included in the pledge; allowed the Director of the Office of Management and Budget (OMB), in consultation with the counsel to the President, to issue ethics pledge waivers; instructed the heads of executive agencies to consult with the Director of the Office of Government Ethics to establish rules of procedure for the administration of the ethics pledge; and authorized the Attorney General to enforce the executive order. In a press release summarizing the executive order, the White House explained the ethics pledge and the importance of following ethics and lobbying rules:

The American people ... deserve more than simply an assurance that those coming to Washington will serve their interests. They deserve to know that there are rules on the books to keep it that way. In the *Executive Order on Ethics Commitments by Executive Branch*

[13] P.L. 105-166, 112 Stat. 38, April 6, 1998. The amendment to the definition of a covered executive branch employee is found in Section 2 of the act and at 2 U.S.C. § 1603 (3)(F).

[14] 5 U.S.C. § 7511 (b)(2)(B).

[15] P.L. 110-81, 121 Stat. 735, September 14, 2007. For further analysis of HLOGA's lobbying provision changes see CRS Report R40245, *Lobbying Registration and Disclosure: Before and After the Enactment of the Honest Leadership and Open Government Act of 2007*, by Jacob R. Straus.

[16] Executive Order 13490, "Ethics Commitments by Executive Branch Personnel," 74 *Federal Register* 4673, January 26, 2009. The executive order was issued on January 21, 2009, but was not published in the *Federal Register* until January 26, 2009.

[17] The ethics pledge required for all executive branch appointments made on or after January 20, 2009, includes a ban on gifts from registered lobbyists, a two-year ban on working on particular issues involving a former employer, and a ban on lobbying the administration after leaving government service. See also Executive Order 13490, "Ethics Commitments by Executive Branch Personnel," 74 *Federal Register* 4673, January 26, 2009.

Personnel, the President, first, prohibits executive branch employees from accepting gifts from lobbyists. Second, he closes the revolving door[18] that allows government officials to move to and from private sector jobs in ways that give that sector undue influence over government. Third, he requires that government hiring be based upon qualifications, competence and experience, not political connections. He has ordered every one of his appointees to sign a pledge abiding by these tough new rules as a downpayment on the change he has promised to bring to Washington.[19]

Requirement of an ethics pledge above and beyond the general oath of office administered to all government employees reinstates a similar requirement instituted by President William Jefferson Clinton in 1993.[20] The effect of such a policy is undetermined for the recruitment and retention of governmental employees or for the barring of federally registered lobbyists from serving in executive branch positions.

RESTRICTIONS ON EMERGENCY ECONOMIC STABILIZATION ACT (EESA) FUNDS LOBBYING

On January 27, 2009, just a week after Barack Obama became President, Secretary of the Treasury Timothy Geithner announced restrictions on individuals lobbying to obtain Emergency Economic Stabilization Act (EESA) funds.[21] The guidance was designed to combat potential lobbyist influence on the disbursement of EESA funds, to remove politics from funding decisions, to offer certification to Congress that each investment decision was based "only on investment criteria and the facts of the case," and to provide transparency to the investment process.[22]

The guidance classified contacts between lobbyists and executive branch officials into two broad categories: (1) unrestricted oral communications on logistical questions and at widely attended gatherings and (2) oral communications during the period following submission of a formal application for federal assistance under EESA until preliminary approval of EESA funds.

[18] "Revolving door" regulations refer to restrictions placed on the types of jobs current federal employees may take when they leave federal service. For more information on revolving doors see CRS Report 97-875, *Post-Employment, "Revolving Door," Laws for Federal Personnel*, by Jack Maskell

[19] The White House, "Statement from the Press Secretary on the President's signing of two Executive Orders and three Memoranda," press release, January 21, 2009, http://www.whitehouse.gov/the_press_office/StatementfromthePressSecretaryonthePresidentssigningoftwoExecutiveOrdersandthreeMe/.

[20] Executive Order 12834, "Ethics Commitments by Executive Branch Appointees," 58 *Federal Register* 5911, January 22, 1993. See also 5 U.S.C. § 2903.

[21] U.S. Department of the Treasury, *Communications with Registered Lobbyists and Other Persons About Emergency Economic Stabilization Act Funds*, Washington, DC, 2009, http://www.financialstability.gov/docs/LobbyingGuidelines.pdf. [Hereafter, *EESA Lobbying Restrictions.*] The Emergency Economic Stabilization Act (EESA) was signed by President George W. Bush on October 3, 2008. P.L. 110-343, 122 Stat. 3765, October 3, 2008. For more information on the Emergency Economic Stabilization Act, see CRS Report RL34713, *Emergency Economic Stabilization Act: Preliminary Analysis of Oversight Provisions*, by Curtis W. Copeland; CRS Report RL34740, *Reporting Requirements in the Emergency Economic Stabilization Act of 2008*, by Curtis W. Copeland; CRS Report RS22969, *The Emergency Economic Stabilization Act's Insurance for Troubled Assets*, by Baird Webel; and CRS Report R40134, *"Fast Track" Procedures to Disapprove Additional Funds Under the Emergency Economic Stabilization Act*, by Christopher M. Davis. Prior to January 2009, no additional lobbying restrictions on EESA funds were in place.

[22] U.S. Department of the Treasury, "Treasury Secretary Opens Term Opens [sic] With New Rules To Bolster Transparency, Limit Lobbyist Influence in Federal Investment Decisions," press release, January 27, 2009, http://www.treas.gov/press/releases/tg02.htm.

The guidance also covers oral and written communication about EESA policy or applications for funding or pending applications.[23] Restrictions on lobbyist communication with executive branch officials are mirrored in the updated guidelines issued by OMB for the Recovery Act lobbying discussed below. As with the Recovery Act restrictions, federally registered lobbyists may ask logistical questions of executive branch officials responsible for disbursing EESA funds and speak with those officials at widely attended gatherings.[24] All other contacts between federally registered lobbyists and executive branch officials must be documented if they concern EESA policy, applications for funding, or pending applications.[25]

RESTRICTIONS ON RECOVERY ACT FUNDS LOBBYING

Following the passage of the American Recovery and Reinvestment Act of 2009, the White House was concerned about the potential ability of lobbyists to influence stimulus funds that would be allocated by the executive branch. On March 20, 2009, the White House issued a memorandum outlining proposed restrictions on federally registered lobbyists' contacts with executive department and agency officials on stimulus funds. Following a 60-day review and comment period, updated guidance was issued by the Office of Management and Budget (OMB) for communication with federally registered lobbyists regarding stimulus funds in July 2009.[26]

Presidential Memorandum

To ensure the responsible and transparent distribution of funds pursuant to the American Recovery and Reinvestment Act of 2009 (Recovery Act),[27] President Obama, on March 20, 2009, issued a memorandum to the heads of the executive departments and agencies prescribing restrictions on oral communications with lobbyists on Recovery Act funds. In the memorandum's introductory remarks, President Obama stated that,

Inimplementing the Recovery Act, we have undertaken unprecedented efforts to ensure the responsible distribution of funds for the Act's purposes and to provide public transparency and accountability of expenditures. We must not allow Recovery Act funds to be distributed on the basis of factors other than the merits of proposed projects or in response to improper influence or pressure. We must also empower executive department and agency officials to exercise their available discretion and judgment to help ensure that Recovery Act funds are expended for projects that further the job creation, economic recovery, and other purposesof the Recovery Act and are not used for imprudent projects.[28]

The President's memorandum outlined four policies for executive branch departments and agencies handing out Recovery Act funds: (1) ensuring that decision making is merit based for grants and other forms of federal financial assistance, (2) avoiding the funding of "imprudent"

[23] *EESA Lobbying Restrictions*, pp. 1-3.

[24] *EESA Lobbying Restrictions*, p. 1.

[25] *EESA Lobbying Restrictions*, p. 2. [26] The White House, "Update on Recovery Act Lobbying Rules: New Limits on Special Interest Influence," Blog Post,

May 29, 2009, http://www.whitehouse.gov/blog/Update-on-Recovery-Act-Lobbying-Rules-New-Limits-on-Speciallnterest-Influence. [27] P.L. 111-5, 123 Stat. 115, February 17, 2009.

[28] The President, "Memorandum of March 20, 2009: Ensuring Responsible Spending of Recovery Act Funds," 74 *Federal Register* 12531, March 25, 2009.

projects, (3) ensuring transparency for communications with registered lobbyists, and (4) providing OMB assistance to departments and agencies for implementation of the memorandum.[29]

To ensure transparency when executive department or agency officials are contacted by federally registered lobbyists for Recovery Act projects, section 3 of the memorandum provides five guidelines for interaction with lobbyists:

1. Executive departments and agencies cannot consider the views of lobbyists concerning projects, applications, or applicants for funding.
2. Agency officials cannot communicate orally (in-person or by telephone) with registered lobbyists about Recovery Act projects, applications, or funding applications and must inquire that the individuals or entities are not lobbyists under the Lobbying Disclosure Act of 1995.[30]
3. Written communication from a registered lobbyist must be publicly posted by the receiving agency or governmental entity on its recovery website within three business days of receipt.[31]
4. Executive departments and agencies can communicate orally with registered lobbyists if particular projects, applications, or applicants for funding are not discussed, and if that government official documents in writing and posts to the department or agency's Recovery Act website "(i) the date and time of the contact on policy issues; (ii) the names of the registered lobbyists and the official(s)

between whom the contact took place; and (iii) a short description of the substance of the communication."

5. Agency officials must reconfirm, when scheduling and prior to communications, that any individuals or parties participating in the communication are not registered lobbyists.[32]

INTERIM RECOVERY ACT GUIDANCE FOR LOBBYIST COMMUNICATIONS

On April 7, 2009, pursuant to President Obama's earlier memorandum, OMB Director Peter Orszag issued "sample interim guidance" for departments and agencies which "outlines the actions employees are required to take ... whenever they receive or participate in oral communications with any outside persons or entities regarding Recovery Act funds."[33] The

[29] Ibid., pp. 12531-12534.

[30] Pursuant to the memorandum, lobbyists may submit written comments to executive branch departments and agencies.

[31] Each agency is required to have a Recovery Act website. For example, the Department of Energy website can be found at http://www.energy.gov/recovery/. The website contains a page that lists written information provided by registered lobbyists and can be found at http://www.energy.gov/recovery/reports.htm. For a list of all cabinet level departments' recovery websites see the **Appendix**.

[32] The President, "Memorandum of March 20, 2009: Ensuring Responsible Spending of Recovery Act Funds," 74 *Federal Register* 12533, March 25, 2009. Lobbying restrictions do not apply to tax issues in Division B of the Recovery Act.

[33] Office of Management and Budget, Peter R. Orszag, Director, *Interim Guidance Regarding Communications With Registered Lobbyists About Recovery Act Funds*, M-09-16, Washington, DC, April 7, 2009, p. 1, http://www.whitehouse.gov/omb/assets/memoranda_fy2009/m-09-16.pdf. [Hereafter, Orszag, *Interim Guidance*.]

interim guidance was not designed as a ban on communications with federally registered lobbyists. Instead, "communications with Federally registered lobbyists should proceed, but in compliance with the [outlined] ... protocol."[34]

The interim guidance divided communications between executive branch employees and registered lobbyists into three categories: unrestricted oral communications, restricted oral communications, and written communications.

UNRESTRICTED ORAL COMMUNICATIONS

The Orszag memorandum does not place restrictions on employees' contact with federally registered lobbyists "concerning general questions about the logistics of the Recovery Act funding or implementation" including administrative requests.[35] Instead, the interim guidance document outlines four general topics of discussion which are not covered by the President's memorandum:

(1) how to apply for funding under the Recovery Act;

(2) how to conform to deadlines;

(3)

to which agencies or officials applications or questions should be directed, [and]

(4)

requests for information about program requirements and agency practices under the Recovery Act.[36]

In addition, the Orszag memorandum does not restrict communications or interactions with registered lobbyists at "widely attended" public gatherings.[37] Restrictions, however, "do apply to private (non-public) oral communications between Federal officials and federally registered lobbyists that may happen to occur at, or on the heals of, a widely attended gathering."[38]

Restricted Oral Communication

For oral communication between executive branch employees and federally registered lobbyists on policy matters or in support of specific Recovery Act projects or applications for funding, the contact must be documented. While executive branch employees "should ask if any person participating in the oral communication is a Federally registered lobbyist,"[39] if the contact is a federally registered lobbyist, the employee must initiate a four-step process to document the communication. If, at any point in the process, the communication ceases, the employee can suspend the collection of data. The four-step process is as follows:

[34] Orszag, *Interim Guidance.*, p. 1.

[35] Ibid.

[36] Ibid.

[37] "Widely attended gatherings" are defined in ethics regulations found at 5 C.F.R. § 2635.204 (g)(2). [38] Orszag, *Interim Guidance*, p. 2.

[39] Ibid.

1. Inform the person(s) of applicable restrictions through the use of two sample templates that can be read or provided to the federally registered lobbyist. These state:

Under the President's Memorandum, we cannot engage in any oral communications with Federally registered lobbyists about the use of Recovery Act funds in support of particular projects, applications, or applicants. All such communications by Federal lobbyists must be submitted in writing, and will be posted publicly on our agency's recovery website within 3 days.

If the oral communication is about general policy issues concerning the Recovery Act and does not touch upon particular projects, applications or applicants for funding, a Federally registered lobbyist may participate in the conversation. We will document the fact of the policy conversation in writing, including the name of the lobbyist and other participants, together with a brief description of the conversation, for public posting on our agency's recovery website within 3 days.[40]

1. If the oral communications proceeds, only logistical questions or general information about Recovery Act programs should be discussed. No discussion of particular projects, applications, or applicants for funding is permitted.[41]
2. Each in-person or telephone conversation on Recovery Act policy matters should be documented with the date of contact, the names of the parties to the conversation, the name of the lobbyist's client(s), and a one-sentence description of the substance of the conversation.[42]
3. Information about the contact should be submitted to the appropriate person in the employee's agency. "That official should review the form for completeness and forward it for posting on [the] agency's website within 3 business days of the communication."[43]

RESTRICTED WRITTEN COMMUNICATION

If executive branch employees receive written communication about Recovery Act projects, applications, or applicants from federally registered lobbyists, such communication must be forwarded to a designated agency official by e-mail. The designated agency official must then forward the communication for posting to the agency's Recovery Act website.[44]

REVISED RECOVERY ACT GUIDANCE FOR LOBBYIST COMMUNICATIONS

On July 24, 2009, OMB Director Orszag released updated guidance on communications with registered lobbyists Recovery Act funds. Changes made to the interim guidance document include expansion of restrictions to "all persons outside the Federal Government (not just federally

[40] Ibid.

[41] Ibid.

[42] Orszag, *Interim Guidance*, p. 3. [43] Ibid. See the **Appendix** for a list of Recovery Act websites for each cabinet level department. [44] Orszag, *Interim Guidance*, p. 4.

registered lobbyists) who initiate oral communications concerning pending competitive applications under the Recovery Act."[45]

Restrictions for oral communication of logistical questions and oral communications at widely attended gatherings did not change from the policies established by the interim guidance document. The updated guidance document, however, differentiates between oral communications between the submission of a formal application and the award of a grant, and oral and written communication concerning policy and projects for funding.

COMMUNICATION BETWEEN THE SUBMISSION OF AN APPLICATION AND GRANT AWARD

Communication between interested parties and executive branch employees "[d]uring the period of time commencing with the submission of a formal application by an individual or entity for a competitive grant or other competitive form of Federal financial assistance under the Recovery Act, and ending with the award of the competitive funds" is restricted. Federal employees "may not participate in oral communications initiated by any person or entity concerning a pending application for a Recovery Act competitive grant or other competitive form of Federal financial assistance, whether or not the initiating party is a federally registered lobbyist."[46] These restrictions apply unless

(i) the communication is purely logistical;

(ii) the communication is made at a widely attended gathering;

(iii) the communication is to or from a Federal agency official and another Federal Government Employee;

(iv) the communication is to or from a Federal agency official or an elected chief executive of a state, local or tribal government, or to or from a Federal agency official and the Presiding Office or Majority Leader in each chamber of a state legislature; or

(v)

the communication is initiated by a Federal agency official.[47]

If communication concerns a pending application and is not exempted, the employee is directed to terminate the conversation.[48]

OTHER ORAL AND WRITTEN COMMUNICATION

Restrictions on other oral and written communication with federally registered lobbyists about pending applications use the same thresholds for reporting as provided in the interim guidance document for "Restricted Oral Communication." This includes informing the contact that the conversation will be documented; documenting the contact by recording the contact date, names

[45] Office of Management and Budget, Peter R. Orszag, director, *Updated Guidance Regarding Communications With Registered Lobbyists About Recovery Act Funds*, M-09-14, Washington, DC, July 24, 2009, p. 1, http://www.whitehouse.gov/omb/assets/memoranda_fy2009/m09-24.pdf. [Hereafter, Orszag, *Updated Guidance.*]

[46] Orszag, *Updated Guidance*, p. 2.

[47] Ibid.

[48] Ibid., p. 3.

of parties to the conversation, the name of the lobbyist's client, a one-sentence description of the conversation, and attachments of any written materials provided by outside participants during the meeting; and submitting of the forms to the agency for posting on the Recovery Act website.[49]

RESTRICTIONS ON LOBBYISTS SERVING ON FEDERAL ADVISORY COMMITTEES

Further broadening the restrictions on lobbyists, the White House, on September 23, 2009, announced a new policy to restrict the number of federally registered lobbyists serving on agency advisory boards and commissions in an effort to "reduce the influence of special interests in Washington."[50] In October 2009, Norm L. Eisen, special counsel to the President for ethics and government reform, issued two additional blog posts[51] to clarify the White House position on federally registered lobbyists serving on federal advisory committees and to respond to criticism leveled by the American League of Lobbyists[52] and by the chairs of the Industry Trade Advisory Committees (ITAC).[53] In his response, Mr. Eisen stated the following:

While we recognize the contributions some of those who will be affected have made to these committees, it is an indisputable fact that in recent years, lobbyists for major special interests have wielded extraordinary power in Washington, DC, resulting in a national agenda too often skewed in favor of the interests that can afford their services. It is that problem that the President has promised to change, and this is a major step in implementing that change.[54]

Implementation of these recommendations are to be made by each agency during the recertification and reappointment process for each advisory committee. The White House has stated that they are not attempting to stifle lobbyists' ability to advocate on behalf of their clients, just that "industry representatives shouldn't be given government positions from which to make their case."[55]

[49] Ibid., pp. 3-4.

[50] The White House, "Lobbyists on Agency Boards and Commissions," Blog Post, September 23, 2009, http://www.whitehouse.gov/blog/Lobbyists-on-Agency-Boards-and-Commissions. For more information on

federal advisory committees see CRS Report R40520, *Federal Advisory Committees: An Overview*, by Wendy R. Ginsberg.

[51] The White House, "Why We Bar Lobbyists from Agency Advisory Boards and Commissions," Blog Post, October 21, 2009, http://www.whitehouse.gov/blog/Why-We-Bar-Lobbyists-from-Agency-Advisory-Boards-and-Commissions; and The White House, "Why We Closed the Revolving Door," Blog Post, October 28, 2009, http://www.whitehouse.gov/blog/2009/10/28/why-we-closed-revolving-door.

[52] Letter from David G. Wenhold, president, American League of Lobbyists, and Peter G. Mayberry, board of directors, American League of Lobbyists, to President Barack Obama, October 28, 2009, http://www.whitehouse.gov/files/ documents/10-09-Letter-to-WH-Advisory-Committees.pdf.

[53] Letter from Gregory Dale, director, commercial trade policy, the Boeing Company, Timothy Hoelter, vice president, government affairs, Harley-Davidson Motor Company, and Brian Petty, senior vice president, government affairs, International Association of Drilling Contractors, et al. to President Barack Obama, Gary Locke, Secretary, U.S. Department of Commerce, and Ron Kirk, United State Trade Representative, October 19, 2009, http://www.whitehouse.gov/assets/documents/Chairs_ITAC_letter_to_Obama_(2).pdf.

[54] The White House, "Why We Bar Lobbyists from Agency Advisory Boards and Commissions," Blog Post, October 21, 2009, http://www.whitehouse.gov/blog/Why-We-Bar-Lobbyists-from-Agency-Advisory-Boards-and-Commissions.

[55] Letter from Norm L. Eisen, Special Counsel to the President, to Mr. Gregory Dole, director, commercial trade policy, the Boeing Company, et al, October 21, 2009, http://www.whitehouse.gov/assets/documents/ Signed_Lobbyist_Response_Letter_(10-21-09).pdf.

THIRD-PARTY CRITIQUES OF EXECUTIVE BRANCH LOBBYING POLICIES

Critiques of the Obama Administration's policy toward federally registered lobbyists has focused on Recovery Act restrictions and lobbyists serving as members of federal advisory committees. In each instance, the American League of Lobbyists has written to the White House critiquing the programs and suggesting policy modifications.

RECOVERY ACT LOBBYING POLICIES

Criticism of executive branch policies on interactions between federally registered lobbyists and executive branch officials developed shortly after the President's March 20, 2009 memorandum outlining Recovery Act lobbying restrictions. On March 31, 2009, the American Civil Liberties Union (ACLU), Citizens for Responsibility and Ethics in Washington (CREW), and the American League of Lobbyists (ALL) sent a letter to White House Counsel Gregory Craig and, at the same time, issued a press release asking the White House to rescind the restrictions. In its letter, the groups stated their support for "efforts to ensure all American Recovery and Reinvestment Act of 2009 ('Recovery Act') funds are expended in a transparent and responsible manner," but felt that "[s]ection 3 [of the President's Memorandum], 'Ensuring Transparency of Registered Lobbyists Communications,' [was] an ill-advised restriction on speech and not narrowly tailored to achieve the intended purpose."[56]

The groups' press release emphasized that the directive was both too narrow and too broad, and it encroached on individuals' right to petition the government. The press release stated the following:

In their letter, the groups said the directive was both too narrow—because it did not apply to non-registered lobbyists such as bank vice presidents or corporate directors—and also too broad, because it incorrectly assumed that all registered lobbyists may exert improper pressure for clients seeking funding for Recovery Act projects.

Additionally, the right to petition the government is one of the main tenets of our country's founding principles. To state that one class of individuals may not participate in the same manner as all others is clearly a violation of this principle.[57]

The updated guidance document issued by the White House on July 24, 2009, included some of the changes that CREW, ACLU, and ALL had requested. The updated guidance included the expansion of restrictions to cover "all persons outside the Federal Government (not just federally

[56] Letter from Melanie Sloan, executive director, Citizens for Responsibility in Government; Carline Fredrickson, Director, Washington Legislative Office American Civil Liberties Union; and Dave Wenhold, president, American League of Lobbyists, to Gregory B. Craig, Esq., White House Counsel, March 31, 2009, http://alldc.org/pdfs/ 033109WhiteHouseLetter.pdf.

[57] Citizens for Responsibility and Ethics in Washington, the American Civil Liberties Union, and the American League of Lobbyists, "Diverse Coalition of Organizations Call for White House to Rescind Rule Restricting Lobbyist Communications on Bailout Funds: ACLU, CREW, and ALL Argue Rule Will Not Improve Transparency and Accountability," press release, March 31, 2009, http://www.alldc.org/press/pr033109.pdf.

registered lobbyists) who initiate oral communications concerning pending competitive applications under the Recovery Act."[58]

FEDERAL ADVISORY COMMITTEE MEMBERSHIP

Following the September 23, 2009 White House blog post outlining the future appointment of federally registered lobbyists to executive branch agency boards and commissions, both the lobbying community and members of the Industry Trade Advisory Committees criticized the White House's position. On October 19, 2009, the 16 chairs of the Industry Trade Advisory Committees[59] wrote a letter to the Secretary of Commerce, Gary Locke, and the U.S. Trade Representative, Ron Kirk, outlining their concerns over the new policy of prohibiting federally registered lobbyists from serving on federal advisory committees. The three substantive and procedural concerns outlined in the letter are

> that banning federally registered lobbyists from serving on federal advisory committees will "undermine the utility of the advisory committee process, the level of advice that he advisory committee provide, and, consequently, the ability of the United States to achieve balanced and effective trade policies";[60]
>
> that the "new policy will undermine the broader goals of transparency with respect to lobbying which are the hallmarks of the Advisory Committee process." In addition, "because the policy focuses on registered lobbyists, it actually incentivizes individuals who desire to remain on the Committee to de-register as a registered lobbyist under the LDA";[61] and
>
> that the illegal action of a few individuals are being used to prejudge all federally registered lobbyists.[62]

The White House, in a letter from Norm L. Eisen, special counsel to the President, responded to the Industry Trade Advisory Committee's letter on October 21, 2009, and stated that

Your arguments that only lobbyists can bring the requisite experience to provide wise counsel, or that reaching beyond the roster of industry lobbyists for appointees will result in a "lack of diversity," are unconvincing on their face. We believe the committees will benefit from an influx of businesspeople, consumers and other concerned Americans who can bring fresh perspectives and new insights to the work of government.[63]

[58] *Updated Guidance*, p. 1.

[59] For a listing of the 16 Industry Trade Advisory Committees, see U.S. Department of Commerce, International Trade

Administration, "Industry Trade Advisory Committees," http://www.trade.gov/itac/committees/index.asp. [60] Letter from Gregory Dale, director, commercial trade policy, the Boeing Company; Timothy Hoelter, vice president, government affairs, Harley-Davidson Motor Company; and Brian Petty, senior vice president, government affairs, International Association of Drilling Contractors, et al. to President Barack Obama, Gary Lock, Secretary, U.S. Department of Commerce; and Ron Kirk, United State Trade Representative, October 19, 2009, p. 4, http://www.whitehouse.gov/assets/documents/Chairs_ITAC_letter_to_Obama_(2).pdf.

[61] Ibid., p. 5.

[62] Ibid.

[63] Letter from Norm L. Eisen, Special Counsel to the President, to Mr. Gregory Dole, director, commercial trade policy, the Boeing Company, et al, October 21, 2009, http://www.whitehouse.gov/assets/documents/Signed_Lobbyist_Response_Letter_(10-21-09).pdf.

OPTIONS FOR CHANGE

Creation of restrictions on federally registered lobbyists' access to executive branch departments and agencies has already changed the relationship between lobbyists and covered executive branch officials. If desired, there are additional options which might further clarify lobbyists' relationships with executive branch officials. These options each have advantages and disadvantages for the future relationships between lobbyists and governmental decision-makers. CRS takes no position on any of the options identified in this report.

AMEND THE LOBBYING DISCLOSURE ACT

If current disclosure requirements are not determined to be sufficient to capture program level lobbying activity, or if current executive branch restrictions were made permanent, the Lobbying Disclosure Act could be amended to institute provisions similar to current executive branch lobbying restrictions. Currently, lobbyists must file quarterly disclosure reports with information on their activities and covered officials contacted. In addition, the LDA, as amended by the Honest Leadership and Open Government Act of 2007, requires federally registered lobbyists to file semi-annual reports on certain campaign and presidential library contributions.[64] The disclosure requirements might be further amended to cover program specific disbursement information. Changes to the LDA would require the introduction and passage of a bill by Congress, as well as the President's signature.

CREATE A CENTRAL EXECUTIVE BRANCH DISCLOSURE DATABASE

The White House or the Recovery Accountability and Transparency Board could create a central database to collect all Recovery Act projects and contacts by federally registered lobbyists in a single, searchable location.[65] Creating a central, searchable portal might allow for department and agencies to see which lobbyists, if any, are involved in a given project and allow individuals and groups to better understand which departments and agencies are responsible for projects of interest. A similar website has been established for stimulus fund recipients to register and disclose how funds are being spent.[66]

TAKE NO IMMEDIATE ACTION

Congress or the President might determine that the current lobbying registration and disclosure provisions, executive orders, and executive branch memoranda on Recovery Act lobbying restrictions are effective. Instead of amending the LDA, issuing additional executive orders, or issuing additional memoranda, Congress or the President could continue to utilize existing law to provide lobbyists access to covered governmental officials. Changes to the LDA or executive

[64] 2 U.S.C. § 1604.

[65] While Recovery.gov contains information on the implementation of Recovery Act programs, a central database of registered-lobbyist contacts with executive branch officials does not currently exist. Each individual department and agency is responsible for listing contacts on its respective Recovery Act website. For a list of websites see the **Appendix**.

[66] For more information see https://www.federalreporting.gov.

branch policy could be made on an as-needed basis through changes to LDA guidance documents issued by the Clerk of the House and Secretary of the Senate,[67] through executive order, or through the issuance of new memoranda by the President.

[67] For more information on the role of the Clerk of the House and the Secretary of the Senate to administer the lobbying registration and disclosure system see CRS Report RL34377, *Honest Leadership and Open Government Act of 2007: The Role of the Clerk of the House and the Secretary of the Senate*, by Jacob R. Straus.

APPENDIX. CABINET-LEVEL EXECUTIVE DEPARTMENTS RECOVERY ACT WEBSITES

Table A-1. Cabinet-Level Departments Recovery Act Websites

Department	Recovery Act Website
Department of Agriculture	http://www.usda.gov/recovery
Department of Commerce	http://recovery.commerce.gov/
Department of Defense	http://www.defenselink.mil/recovery/
Department of Education	http://www.ed.gov/recovery/
Department of Energy	http://www.energy.gov/recovery/
Department of Health and Human Services	http://www.hhs.gov/recovery/
Department of Homeland Security	http://www.dhs.gov/xopnbiz/recovery.shtm
Department of Housing and Urban Development	http://www.hud.gov/recovery/
Department of the Interior	http://recovery.doi.gov/
Department of Justice	http://www.usdoj.gov/recovery/
Department of Labor	http://www.dol.gov/Recovery/
Department of State	http://www.state.gov/recovery/
Department of Transportation	http://www.dot.gov/recovery/
Department of the Treasury	http://www.treas.gov/recovery/
Department of Veterans Affairs	http://www.va.gov/recovery/

Source: Recovery Accountability and Transparency Board, "Agency Sites and Information," Recovery.gov, http://www.recovery.gov/?q=content/agencies.

Notes: Additional agencies are also required to maintain recovery websites. These include the Agency for International Development, Corporation for National and Community Service, Environmental Protection Agency, General Services Administration, National Aeronautics and Space Administration, National Endowment for the Arts, National Science Foundation, Office of Personnel Management, Railroad Retirement Board, Small Business Administration, Smithsonian Institution, Social Security Administration, and U.S. Army Corps of Engineers.

"POLITICAL" ACTIVITIES OF PRIVATE RECIPIENTS OF FEDERAL GRANTS OR CONTRACTS[4]

As a general matter, organizations or corporate entities which receive federal funds by way of grants, contracts, or cooperative agreements do not lose their rights as organizations to use their own, private resources for what may generally be termed "political" activities because of or as a consequence of receiving such federal funds. When discussing "political activities" by such private grantees or contract recipients, this report is including the activities of lobbying or advocating for legislative programs or changes; campaigning for, endorsing, or contributing to political candidates or parties; and voter registration or get-out-the-vote campaigns.

Although (with some exceptions) organizations receiving federal grants or contracts are not, by virtue of such receipt, required to abdicate or refrain from exercising their First Amendment rights of political speech, participation, or expression with their own resources, such organizations are uniformly prohibited from using the federal grant or contract money for such "political" purposes, unless expressly authorized to do so by law. These recipient organizations must thus use private or other non-federal money, receipts, contributions, or dues for their political activities, and may not charge off to or be reimbursed from federal contracts or grants for the costs of such political activities.

Non-profit social action organizations (which are tax-exempt under Section 501(c)(4) of the Internal Revenue Code [26 U.S.C. § 501(c)(4)]) are prohibited from engaging in certain lobbying activities, even with their own funds, if they receive federal grants, but may establish affiliated social action groups through which an organization and its members may exercise First Amendment rights of advocacy and speech using non-federal resources. Additionally, under certain federal programs some restrictions or limitations may attach to the receipt of federal funds, such as the application of the part of the so-called "Hatch Act" applicable to state and local employees who are in an organization which administers or distributes federal Block Grant funds, as well as other express restrictions on using federal program funds for political or for voter registration purposes.

Certain entities, because of the nature of the organization or its tax status, may have particular limitations or restrictions on political or advocacy activities which would apply, in most instances, regardless of the entities' status as a federal grantee or contractor. Thus, for example, entities which are incorporated for charitable, educational, or religious purposes, and are tax exempt under Section 501(c)(3) of the Internal Revenue Code (26 U.S.C. § 501(c)(3)), are limited in the amount of lobbying in which the organization may engage and are prohibited from participating or intervening in any political campaigns. Corporations and labor unions are expressly prohibited from making contributions or expenditures in federal elections (2 U.S.C. § 441(b)), and federal government contractors are prohibited from making political contributions in such elections (2 U.S.C. § 441(c)), although corporations, labor unions, and federal contractors are all allowed to establish and finance separate segregated funds which may act as political action committees (PACs) to gather voluntary contributions and make political campaign expenditures.

LOBBYING AND PUBLIC ADVOCACY

There are a number of provisions of federal law or regulation which apply general, across-the-board restrictions upon the use of federal appropriations, contract, or grant funds for "lobbying" purposes, while other restrictions exist which are upon a particular program or funds. The restrictions on lobbying with federal funds generally follow only the funds themselves, restricting the use of such funds, and do not require a private recipient to forgo the exercise of First Amendment advocacy activities with one's *own*, private resources in return for or as a condition to the receipt of federal grant or contract funds.[1] There are several general, government-wide restrictions on private recipients using federal funds for lobbying purposes.

FEDERAL RESTRICTIONS ON CONTRACT AND GRANT FUNDS

OMB Circular A-122. Specific restrictions on the use of federal grant funds by non-profit organizations were adopted in 1984 as part of uniform cost principles for non-profit organizations issued by the Office of

[4] Jack Maskell Legislative Attorney American Law Division

Management and Budget (OMB) in OMB Circular A-122.[2] Under these current federal provisions, non-profit grantees of the federal government may not be reimbursed out of a federal grant for their lobbying activities, or for political activities, unless authorized by Congress. These restrictions apply to attempts to influence any federal or state legislation through direct or "grass roots" lobbying campaigns, or political campaign contributions or expenditures, but exempt any activity authorized by Congress, or when providing technical and/or factual information related to the performance of a grant or contract when in response to a documented request. Specifically, OMB Circular A-122 provides that federal grant monies may not be used for, and direct or indirect costs may not be charged to, a federal grant for the following:

25a. Notwithstanding other provisions of this Circular, costs associated with the

following activities are unallowable:

(3) Any attempt to influence: (i) The introduction of Federal or State legislation; or (ii) the enactment or modification of any pending Federal or State legislation through communication with any member or employee of the Congress or State legislature (including efforts to influence State or local officials to engage in similar lobbying

[1] *Note*, however, possible tax consequences of "lobbying" by *tax-exempt* organizations even with "non-federal" money, discussed below.

[2] *See* now OMB Circular A-122, Attachment B, para. 25, as added 49 F.R. 18276 (1984), at [http://www.whitehouse.gov/omb/circulars/a122/a122.html], and provisions incorporated by reference into the Federal Acquisition Regulations (FAR) 48 C.F.R. § 31.701 *et seq.*, for non-profits.

activity), or with any Government official or employee in connection with a decision to sign or veto enrolled legislation;

(4) Any attempt to influence: (i) The introduction of Federal or State legislation; or (ii) the enactment or modification of any pending Federal or State legislation by preparing, distributing or using publicity or propaganda, or by urging members of the general public or any segment thereof to contribute to or participate in any mass demonstration, march, rally, fundraising drive, lobbying campaign or letter writing or telephone campaign; or

(5) Legislative liaison activities, including attendance at legislative sessions or committee hearings, gathering information regarding legislation, and analyzing the effect of legislation, when such activities are carried on in support of or in knowing preparation for an effort to engage in unallowable lobbying.

Federal Acquisition Regulations. The Federal Acquisition Regulations (FAR) apply to commercial contractors and nonprofit contractors of the federal government. The FAR imposes similar rules on cost allowances concerning "lobbying" and political activities as those described for non-profit grantees in OMB Circular A-122.[3] The costs of activities of a contractor which involve lobbying, influencing public policy, public advocacy, or political activities, are similarly *not* allocable to a federal contract.

Byrd Amendment: Lobbying for Other Grants or Contracts . The so-called "Byrd Amendment" applies to a "recipient of a Federal contract, grant, or cooperative agreement" and to the subcontractors and subgrantees of that contract or grant, and includes specifically within its terms any state or local government, including local and regional authorities.[4] The statutory and regulatory restrictions prohibit the use of federal funds to "pay any person for influencing or attempting to influence an officer or employee of any agency, a Member of Congress, an officer or employee of Congress ... in connection with" governmental decisions regarding the awarding of a federal contract, the making of a federal grant, loan, or cooperative agreement. The regulations note that "influencing or attempting to influence" means "making, with the intent to influence, any communication to or appearance before an officer or employee of an agency ... or a Member of Congress ....," and thus might be intended only to reach what are considered "direct" lobbying activities, as opposed to "grass roots" activities.[5] Any "information specifically requested by an agency or Congress is allowable at any time,"[6] however, and certain other contacts may be allowable depending on the timing and nature of the communication with respect to a particular solicitation for a federal grant, contract, or agreement. When covered

[3] 48 C.F.R. § 31.205-22 (commercial contractors); 48 C.F.R. § 31.701 *et seq.*, (non-profit contractors).

[4] 31 U.S.C. §§ 1352(a)(1); 1352(h)(1)(A); 1352(g)(3); 1352(g)(5)(A); *see* common rules by major agencies, 55 F.R. 6738, February 26, 1990 (and OMB government-wide guidance, 54 F.R.52306, December 20, 1989 upon which the rules were based).

[5] 55 F.R. 6738, "common rules," § 105, definitions. *Note*, for example, distinction between covered "direct" lobbying "contacts," and non-covered grass roots communications in Lobbying Disclosure Act of 1995, 2 U.S.C. §§ 1602(8)(A), and 1602(B)(iii).

[6] 55 F.R. 6739, "common rules," § 200(b).

under the provisions of the Byrd Amendment, federal contractors or grantees have to disclose and certify when they use even their *own* funds to lobby on covered matters.[7]

While a federal grantee may not, under the Byrd Amendment, lobby with respect to the awarding or making of a federal contract or grant, this particular restriction does not in itself necessarily bar general lobbying or public policy advocacy on issues when that conduct is not involved with a "covered action," that is, the making or awarding of a grant to that entity.[8] Since it is directed at lobbying only on specified federal actions concerning the making of grants, loans, contracts and agreements, and the extensions or modifications of such agreements, loans, contracts, or grants, the Byrd Amendment would have limited application to lobbying on general program legislation. While the provision might bar the use of federal funds to lobby a Member of Congress to intervene with an agency concerning the making, extension, or modification of a grant, loan, contract or agreement, or might bar the lobbying of Congress concerning a direct, earmarked appropriation, or a specific program or spending instruction in a congressional report, the Byrd Amendment would not appear to apply to the lobbying of Congress concerning the consideration of program legislation generally.[9]

The restrictions of the Byrd Amendment, in a similar manner as the OMB Circular and Federal Acquisition Regulations, are upon the federal funds and not the recipients themselves; that is, the provisions do not prohibit recipients, grantees, or contractors from using their *own* funds, or other non-federally appropriated funds to lobby the government on any matter.[10] Under the provisions of the Byrd Amendment, if the entity has any monies or resources other than federal appropriated funds sufficient to cover lobbying activities, there is a presumption that non-federal monies were used in any lobbying effort.[11] Presumption could, of course, be overcome with evidence or admissions to the contrary.

Appropriations Law Riders. There is usually now included in appropriations law provisions, a *general* rider and restriction applicable to funds

[7] 31 U.S.C. § 1352(b).

[8] 31 U.S.C. § 1352(a)(2)(A) - (E).

[9] In "further information" and guidance to "clarify OMB's interim final guidance," the Office of Management and Budget had explained, "The prohibition on use of Federal appropriated funds does not apply to influencing activities not in connection with a specific covered Federal action. These activities include those related to legislation and regulations for a program versus a specific covered Federal action." 55 F.R. 24542, June 15, 1990. OMB proposed to revoke this further explanation in 1992 since the "exemption was interpreted too broadly" (57 F.R. 1772), but made it clear that general program lobbying in Congress was still *not* covered, even while "activities to influence the earmarking of funds for a particular program, project or activity in an appropriation, authorization or other bill or in report language would be included within the Act's restrictions." 57 F.R. 1772, January 15, 1992.

[10] *Note*, however, potential tax consequences for 501(c)(3) and 501(c)(4) organizations.

[11] OMB guidance, 55 F.R. 24542, June 15, 1990.

appropriated "in this or any other act," prohibiting the use of such federal funds for "publicity or propaganda" purposes directed at "legislation pending before Congress."[12] While this language would clearly apply to federal agencies receiving and expending appropriations, there had been questions as to whether or not the language would follow funds, which originated as federal appropriations to government agencies, even into the hands of private parties and individuals. Although funds which originate as appropriated "federal funds" might be considered to lose their character as "federal funds" once they are in private hands,[13] the Government Accountability Office ([GAO], formerly the General Accounting Office) has opined that this particular restriction and rider establishes a responsibility in the grantor federal agency to assure that the funds that it distributes even to private parties are not being used in contravention of the limitation. Thus, the general appropriations law restrictions enacted yearly have been "imputed" by the Comptroller General to apply to the grantees of federal agencies.[14] In one case the GAO found a violation of the general appropriations restriction when a local transportation authority, and grantee of the Department of Transportation, used grant funds from the agency to produce a newsletter "urging readers to write to their elected representatives in Congress to support continued funding...."[15] As explained in the appropriations treatise prepared by GAO,

Finally, in B-202975, November 3, 1981, the Comptroller General resolved the uncertainty [concerning application of the restriction to funds in the hands of a grantee] ... and concluded that:

"Federal agencies and departments are responsible for insuring that Federal funds made available to grantees are not used contrary to [the publicity and propaganda] restriction."

The case involved the Los Angeles Downtown People Mover Authority, a grantee of the Urban Mass Transportation Administration (UMTA), Department of Transportation. Fearing that its funding was in jeopardy, the Authority prepared and distributed a newsletter urging readers to write to their elected representatives in Congress to support continued funding for the People Mover

[12] P.L. 110-161, "Consolidated Appropriations Act, 2008," Division D, §§ 720, 723, 121 Stat. 2024 (2007); P.L. 109-115, "Transportation, Treasury, Housing and Urban Development, Judiciary, District of Columbia, and Independent Agencies Appropriations Act, 2006," §§ 821, 824; P.L. 108-447, "Consolidated Appropriations Act, 2005," Division H, "Transportation, Treasury, Independent Agencies, and General Governmental Appropriations Act, 2005," §§ 621, 624, 118 Stat. 3278 (2004); P.L. 108-199, "Consolidated Appropriations Act, 2004," Division F, "Transportation, Treasury, and Independent Agencies Appropriations, 2004," §§ 621, 624, 118 Stat. 355 (2004).

[13] General Accountability Office, Office of General Counsel, *Principles of Federal Appropriations Law,* at 4-220 (January 2004): "...where a grant is made for an authorized grant purpose, grant funds in the hands of the grantee largely lose their identity as federal funds and are no longer subject to many of the restrictions on the direct expenditure of appropriations."

[14] B-128938, July 12, 1976; note *Principles of Federal Appropriations Law, supra* at 4-226.

[15] *Principles of Federal Appropriations Law, supra* at 4-226, citing B-202975, November 3, 1981.

project. The Comptroller General found that this newsletter, to the extent it involved UMTA grant funds, violated the anti-lobbying statute.[16]

In the later appropriations riders of this nature, the language of the provision was changed to now expressly include "by private contractor" in the restriction on the use of federal appropriations:

No part of any appropriation contained in this or any other Act shall be used directly or indirectly, including by private contractor, for publicity or propaganda purposes within the United States not heretofore authorized by the Congress.[17]

This change may indicate an express emphasis by Congress that an agency may not accomplish indirectly through a private contractor what it may not do directly, that is, use federal appropriations for publicity or propaganda campaigns, or it may signal a broader reach to all contractor and grantor funds received from the federal government, even when the private recipient is not contracted or directed to engage in the particular questionable activity by a federal agency, but rather engages in such activity independently.

In the past, GAO has traditionally interpreted the "publicity and propaganda" restrictions (as far as they applied to federal *agencies)*, as not necessarily restricting direct communications from the agencies to legislators, but rather as limiting and prohibiting "grassroots" type of lobbying campaigns. In interpreting these types of "publicity or propaganda" restrictions, GAO has explained the following:

In interpreting "publicity and propaganda" provisions ... we have consistently recognized that any agency has a legitimate interest in communicating with the public and with legislators regarding its policies. ... An interpretation of [the anti-lobbying restriction] which strictly prohibited expenditures of public funds for dissemination of views on pending legislation would consequently preclude virtually any comment by officials on administration or agency policy, a result we do not believe was intended.

We believe, therefore, that Congress did not intend ... to preclude all expression by agency officials of views on pending legislation. Rather, the prohibition of [the anti-lobbying restriction], in our view, applies primarily to expenditures involving direct appeals addressed to the public suggesting that they contact their elected representatives and indicate their support of or opposition to pending legislation, *i.e.*, appeals to members of the public for them in turn to urge their representatives to vote in a particular manner.[18]

[16] *Id.*

[17] P.L. 110-161, supra at § 723, 121 Stat. 2025 (2007); P.L. 109-115, "Transportation, Treasury, Housing and Urban Development, Judiciary, District of Columbia, and Independent Agencies Appropriations Act, 2006," § 824.

[18] 56 Comp. Gen. 889, 890 (1977); Decisions of the Comptroller General, B-128938, July 12, 1976, at 5; B-164497(5), August 10, 1977, at 3; B-173648, September 21, 1973, at 3. See also 63 Comp. Gen. 626-627 (1984), similar language concerning federal judges.

When communications are made to the public concerning public policy matters, even if such communications give arguments for or against specific legislation, the Comptroller General found no violation of the publicity or propaganda "antilobbying" rider when the material was "essentially expository in nature" and did not urge or suggest anyone contact their representative in the legislature.[19] In one example concerning Department of Transportation expenditures for displays and pamphlets and informational material at the time Congress was considering passive restraint systems (airbags) for cars, GAO noted, "While, considering the timing and location of the displays, one would have to be pretty stupid not to see this as an obvious lobbying ploy, that did not make it illegal since there was no evidence that Transportation urged members of the public to contact their elected representatives."[20]

In addition to these general appropriations law riders, there may be more specific statutory or appropriations limitations on *particular* federal monies or on particular federal programs, which also limit the use of federal monies appropriated in a particular appropriations law for lobbying, or "publicity or propaganda" campaigns directed at Congress by private grant or contract recipients, or to use grant funds to pay the salary of one who engages in such activities.[21] As to the use of funds by grantees of federal agencies when such use is restricted by an appropriation rider, the Comptroller General has interpreted the restriction on grantees in the HHS appropriations legislation, for example, and found it to have been violated "when a local community action agency used grant funds for a mass mailing of a letter to members of the public urging them to write their Congressmen to oppose abolition of the agency."[22] The Comptroller General similarly found that the provision was "violated when a university, using grant funds received from the Department of Education, encouraged students to write to Members of Congress to urge their opposition to proposed cuts in student financial aid programs."[23]

The Comptroller General has thus interpreted this appropriations rider on grantees and contractors in a similar manner as the "publicity and propaganda" riders on federal agencies, that is, to apply to "grassroots" lobbying campaigns where the public is urged to contact their Members of Congress. It should be noted that the Office of Legal Counsel of the Department of Justice has offered an opinion that the

[19] G.A.O., *Principles of Federal Appropriations Law, supra* at 4-211, citing Comptroller General Decisions B-21639, January 22, 1985; B-212252, July 15, 1983; B-178648, December 27, 1973; B-139458, January 26, 1972.

[20] *Principles of Federal Appropriations Law, supra* at 4-211, citing Comptroller General Decision B-139052, April 29, 1980.

[21] *See e.g.,* 42 U.S.C. § 2996f(a)(5), *re* Legal Services Corporation grants; and note Departments of Labor, HHS, and Education and Related Agencies Appropriations Act, 2006, P.L. 109-149, Section 503(b), as to specific appropriations rider on salary of grant recipients.

[22] *Principles of Federal Appropriations Law, supra* at 4-224, citing B-202787(1), May 1, 1981.

[23] *Principles of Federal Appropriations Law, supra* at 4-225, citing *Improper Use of Federal Student Aid Funds for Lobbying Activities,* GAO/HRD-82-108 (August 13, 1982).

particular rider on grantees and contractors in the Labor, Education, and HHS Appropriations laws is broader than the general "publicity and propaganda" riders, and could apply even to funding communications from contractors and grantees receiving funds under that particular act directly to Members of Congress on pending legislation or appropriations.[24]

Criminal Law. The principal, permanent statutory prohibition on what is considered "lobbying with appropriated funds" is a federal criminal statute at 18

U.S.C. § 1913, which prohibits the use of federal appropriations to pay for any "personal services, advertisement, telegram, telephone, letter, printed or written matter ... intended or designed to influence" Members of Congress or other officials on a variety of programs, legislation, or appropriations. The provision at 18 U.S.C. § 1913 was amended in 2002.[25] Originally adopted in 1919, the law had always been interpreted to apply only to officers and employees of the federal government,[26] and then only to lobbying the Congress. The 2002 amendments, while eliminating the criminal penalties and substituting the civil penalties of the so-called "Byrd Amendment,"[27] substantially broadened the substantive prohibition to cover the use of federal appropriations to lobby or influence all levels of governmental authority,[28] and removed the penalties provision which had indicated an applicability only to federal officers and employees. As noted by GAO, the provisions of 18 U.S.C. § 1913 might be considered to apply now to others who use "federal appropriations" for lobbying purposes, and not just to federal employees as had been done in the past.[29]

The exact parameters of this law, adopted in 1919, are not precisely known as there appears never to have been an enforcement action or indictment returned based on the provision. Although the payment for various activities financed with federal funds is barred, § 1913 expressly exempts from the prohibition the activities of officers and employees of the federal government "communicating to members of Congress on the request of any member," or to Congress "through the proper official channels, requests for legislation or appropriations" deemed necessary for the efficient conduct of the public business. This provision of law has thus been consistently interpreted in the past by the Justice Department as permitting *direct* contacts and communications from federal executive officials and executive agencies

[24] 5 Op. O.L.C. 180 (1981).

[25] P.L. 107-273, § 205(a); 116 Stat. 1778, November 2, 2002.

[26] *See* Section 6 of the Third Deficiency Appropriations Act, FY1919, 41 Stat. 68, chapter 6, § 6, July 11, 1919. As to its applicability only to federal employees, *see Grassley v. Legal Services Corporation*, 535 F.Supp. 818, 826 n.6 (S.D. Iowa 1982). There is no indication that anyone had ever been indicted under the provision from its enactment in 1919 to its amendment in 2002.

[27] *Note* 31 U.S.C. §1352(a), concerning prohibitions on contractors and grantees using federal monies for lobbying purposes.

[28] *Note* H.Rept. 107-685, 107th Cong., 2d Sess. 177 (2002); S.Rept. 107-96, 107th Cong., 1st Sess. 11 (2001).

[29] *Principles of Federal Appropriations Law, supra* at 4-225, n. 145.

to Members of Congress concerning pending or proposed federal legislation,[30] but most likely would prohibit substantial letter-writing or other types of significant "propaganda" or publicity campaigns (also called "grass roots" lobbying campaigns) funded with appropriated monies which are directed at the general public and which specifically urge or exhort the public or individuals to write or contact their congressman on an issue before the Congress.[31]

The exemption for communications through proper official channels applies expressly only to officers and employees of the federal government, and thus it is not apparent that the permissibility of "direct communications" to law makers and policy makers would also extend to persons other than federal employees who use federal appropriations for such communications, such as federal grantees or contractors. While appropriations riders limiting propaganda and publicity have generally exempted direct communications to lawmakers on relevant subject matters, it is not clear what interpretation the Department of Justice will enforce as to grantees, although they have argued in the past that the general appropriations riders do not have an exemption for official channel communications.

TAX CODE LIMITATIONS ON LOBBYING BY NON-PROFIT ORGANIZATIONS

Depending on the provision in the tax code under which an entity holds its tax-exempt status, there may be specific restrictions and/or limitations on the amount of lobbying that the organization may do, because such activity may not be considered to be within the realm of the organization's exempt functions.

Section 501(c)(3) Charitable Organizations. Organizations which are exempt from federal income taxation under section 501(c)(3) of the Internal Revenue Code (26 U.S.C. § 501(c)(3)) are community chests, funds, corporations or foundations "organized and operated exclusively for religious, charitable, scientific, testing for public safety, literary, or educational purposes." These charitable organizations, which have the advantage of receiving contributions from private parties which are tax-deductible for the *contributor* under 26 U.S.C. § 170(a), are limited in the amount of lobbying in which they may engage if they wish to preserve this preferred federal tax-exempt status.[32]

The general rule for a charitable organization exempt from federal taxation under § 501(c)(3) is that such organization may not engage in lobbying activities

[30] 5 Op. O.L.C. 180, 185 (1981); 13 Op. O.L.C. 361 (1989). See Opinion of Assistant Attorney General of the United States, HenryJ. Miller, (1962), printed at 108 *Congressional Record* 8449-8451, May 15, 1962.

[31] *Note* legislative history of § 1913, at 58 *Congressional Record* 404, May 29, 1919; 2 Op.

O.L.C. 30 (1978); 5 Op. O.L.C. 180 (1981); 13 Op. O.L.C. 300 (1989); Office of Legal Counsel, Department of Justice, "Guidelines on 18 U.S.C. § 1913," (April 14, 1995).

[32] 26 U.S.C. §§ 501(c)(3), 501(h), 4911, 6033; see IRS Regulations at 55 F.R. 35579-35620 (August 31, 1990), 26 C.F.R. Parts 1, 7, 20, 25, 53, 56, and 602.

which constitute a "substantial part" of its activities.[33] In 1976, a so-called "safe harbor" was offered to 501(c)(3) organizations where they could elect to come within specific percentage limitations on expenditures to assure that no violations of the "substantial part" rule would occur, or they could remain under the old, unspecified "substantial part test."[34] The specific statutory limitations upon organizational expenditures for covered lobbying activities (the "expenditure test" limitations) for electing 501(c)(3) organizations are as follows:

20% of the first $500,000 of total exempt-purpose expenditures of

the organization, then

15% of the next $500,000 in exempt-purposes expenditures, then

10% of the next $500,000 in exempt-purpose expenditures, and then

5% of the organization's exempt-purpose expenditures over

$1,500,000;

up to a total expenditure limit of $1,000,000 on lobbying activities.

There is currently a separate "grass roots" expenditure limit of 25%

of the "direct" lobbying limits.[35]

The activities covered under the tax code limitations on "lobbying" by charitable organizations generally encompass both "direct" lobbying as well as "grass roots" lobbying (for which there is a separate included expense limitation). "Direct" lobbying entails direct communications to legislators, and to other government officials involved in formulating legislation (as well as direct communications to an organization's own members encouraging them to communicate directly with legislators), which refer to and reflect a particular view on specific legislation. Indirect or "grass roots" lobbying involves advocacy pleas to the general public which refer to and take a position on specific legislation, and which encourage the public to contact legislators to influence them on that legislation.

The definitions of and the specific exemptions from the term "lobbying" are important in observing the expenditure limitations on an organization's activities.

[33] 26 U.S.C. § 501(c)(3). The Supreme Court has upheld the loss of the special tax-exempt status of charitable, 501(c)(3) organizations if they engage in "substantial" lobbying. *Regan*

v. Taxation With Representation of Washington, 461 U.S. 540 (1983). The Court noted that although lobbying is a protected First Amendment right, and although the Government may not indirectly punish an organization for exercising its constitutional rights by denying benefits to those who exercise them, lobbying activities are not necessarily one of the contemplated "exempt functions" of these charitable or educational organizations for which they have received the preferred tax status. Since contributions to the 501(c)(3) organization by private individuals are eligible for a deduction from the donor's federal income tax, the Government is in effect "subsidizing" those private contributions to the organization (through loss of tax revenue), and the Court found that Congress does not have to "subsidize" such lobbying activities through preferred tax status for contributions if it does not choose to do so, as long as other outlets for the organization's unlimited, protected First Amendment expression exist. *Id.* at 544-546.

[34] Religious organizations are not permitted to make the election to come within the specific monetary lobbying guidelines under 26 U.S.C. § 501(h), 26 U.S.C. § 501(h)(5). *See* IRS Form 5768, for election to come within "expenditure test."

[35] *See* 26 U.S.C. § 4911(c)(2).

For example, not all public "advocacy" activities of an organization are considered "grass roots lobbying." As noted expressly by the IRS, "... clear advocacy of specific legislation is not grass roots lobbying at all unless it contains an encouragement to action."[36] Furthermore, not all communications to legislators are considered "direct lobbying." The definition of "lobbying" for purposes of the tax code limitations expressly *exempt* activities such as

(a) making available nonpartisan analysis, study or research involving independent and objective exposition of a subject matter, even one that takes a position on particular legislation as long as it does not encourage recipients to take action with respect to that legislation;

(b) technical advice or assistance given at the *request* of a governmental body;

(c) so-called "self-defense" communications before governmental bodies, that is, communications on those issues that might affect the charity's existence, powers, duties, tax-exempt status, or deductibility of contributions to it; and

(d) contacts with officials unrelated to affecting specific legislation, even those that involve general discussions of broad social or economic problems which are the subject of pending legislation.[37]

Section 501(c)(4) Civic Organizations. Organizations which are tax exempt under section 501(c)(4) of the Internal Revenue Code are generally described as "[c]ivic leagues or organizations not operated for profit but operated exclusively for the promotion of social welfare...." If a civic league or social welfare organization is tax exempt under § 501(c)(4) of the Internal Revenue Code, there is generally no tax consequence for lobbying or advocacy activities (as long as such expenditures are in relation to their exempt function). In fact, in upholding the limitations on lobbying by 501(c)(3) charitable organizations against First Amendment challenges, the Supreme Court noted that a 501(c)(3) organization could establish a 501(c)(4) affiliate through which its First Amendment expression could be exercised through unlimited lobbying and advocacy.[38] The 501(c)(4) affiliate should be separately incorporated, keep separate books, and spend and use resources which are not part of or otherwise paid for by the tax-deductible contributions to the 501(c)(3) parent organization.[39] While 501(c)(4) organizations' lobbying activities are generally unrestricted, if a 501(c)(4) organization receives federal funds in the form of a "grant" or loan, then there are express restrictions on its "lobbying activities," discussed below.

[36] T.D. 8308, in 1990-39 Internal Revenue Bulletin, at p. 7. A communication "encourages a recipient to take action" if it (1) states that the recipient should contact legislators; (2) provides a legislator's phone number, address, etc; (3) provides a petition, tear-off postcard, or similar material to send to a legislator; or (4) specifically identifies a legislator who is opposed, in favor, or undecided on the specific legislation, or is on the committee considering the legislation, if the communication itself is "partisan" in nature and cannot be characterized as a full and fair exposition of the issue. *Id.* at 7.

[37] 26 U.S.C. § 4911(d)(2); 26 C. F. R. § 56.4911-2(c)(1) - (4).

[38] *Regan v. Taxation With Representation of Washington, supra* at 544-546 (Opinion of the Court), see also 552-553 (Blackmun concurring).

[39] *See* discussion of a 501(c)(3) setting up a 501(c)(4) lobbying affiliate in Smucker, *The Nonprofit Lobbying Guide,* Second Edition, 68-69 (Independent Sector 1999).

501(c)(4) Organizations Receiving Federal Grants. Restrictions on "lobbying activities" by certain non-profit groups, as a condition to receiving federal grants and loans, were enacted into law in 1995. Section 18 of the Lobbying Disclosure Act of 1995[40] places statutory restrictions upon the lobbying activities of non-profit civic and social welfare organizations which are tax-exempt under section 501(c)(4) of the Internal Revenue Code. This provision, which is commonly called the "Simpson Amendment," prohibits section 501(c)(4) civic leagues and social welfare organizations from engaging in any "lobbying activities," even with their *own* private funds, if the organization receives any federal grant, loan, or award.[41]

The restrictions of the Simpson Amendment originally covered all 501(c)(4) organizations which received federal monies by way of an "award, grant, *contract*, loan or any other form."[42] The term "contract," however, was subsequently removed from the provision by P.L. 104-99, Section 129, leaving the prohibition on lobbying activities with an organization's own funds as a condition to the receipt of federal monies only upon 501(c)(4) grantees and those seeking an award or loan, but allowing unlimited lobbying activities with organizational funds for 501(c)(4) contractors of the federal government. The Simpson Amendment now reads as follows: "An organization described in section 501(c)(4) of the Internal Revenue Code of 1986 which engages in lobbying activities shall not be eligible for the receipt of Federal funds constituting an award, grant, or loan."

While there may have been some constitutional objections to the provisions of the "Simpson Amendment" and its effect on First Amendment activities funded by an organization's own private, non-federal funds, the interpretation of the provision to allow for unlimited lobbying by affiliate organizations with their own, non-federal monies, has apparently obviated legal challenges. The legislative history of the provision clearly indicates that it was intended that a 501(c)(4) organization may separately incorporate an affiliated 501(c)(4), which would not receive any federal funds, and which could engage in unlimited lobbying.[43] The method of separately incorporating an affiliate to lobby, or to receive and administer federal grants, which was described by the amendment's sponsor as "splitting," was apparently intended to place a degree of separation between federal grant money and private lobbying, while permitting an organization to have a voice through which to exercise its protected First Amendment rights of speech, expression and petition.[44] As stated by the sponsor of the provision, Senator Simpson, "If they decided to split into two

[40] P.L. 104-65, 109 Stat. 691, 703-704, as amended by P.L. 104-99, Section 129, 110 Stat.

34. [41] *See* now 2 U.S.C. § 1611. [42] P.L. 104-65, Section 18, 109 Stat. 704 (emphasis added). [43] H.Rept. 104-339, at 24 (1995). [44] *See* comments by the sponsors of provision, Senator Simpson and Senator Craig, at 141

Congressional Record 20041-20042, 20052-20053 (July 24, 1995).

separate 501(c)(4)s, they could have one organization which could both receive funds and lobby without limits."[45]

It may also be noted that while § 501(c)(4)s which receive certain federal funds may not engage in "lobbying activities," the term "lobbying activities" as used in the "Simpson Amendment" prohibition in Section 18 of the Lobbying Disclosure Act is defined in Section 3 of that legislation to include only direct "lobbying contacts and efforts in support of such contacts" such as preparation, planning, research and other background work intended for use in such direct contacts.[46] A "lobbying contact" under the Lobbying Disclosure Act is an "oral or written communication (including an electronic communication) to a covered executive branch official or a covered legislative branch official" which concerns the formulation, modification or adoption of legislation, rules, regulations, policies or programs of the federal government.[47] Organizations which use their own private resources to engage only in "grass roots" lobbying and public advocacy (including specifically any communication that is "made in a speech, article, publication or other material that is distributed and made available to the public, or through radio, television, cable television, or other medium of mass communication")[48] would, therefore, not appear to be engaging in any prohibited "lobbying activities" under this provision. The Lobbying Disclosure Act's definitions of "lobbying activities" and "lobbying contacts" exclude, and do *not* independently apply to activities which consist only of "grass roots" lobbying and public advocacy.[49]

Similarly, since the term "lobbying activities" relates only to the direct lobbying of covered *federal* officials, the "Simpson Amendment" would not appear to limit in any way an organization's use of its own private resources to lobby state or local legislators or other state or local governmental bodies or units. While direct lobbying of the Congress, or of certain high level executive branch officials, is covered under the Lobbying Disclosure Act as a "lobbying contact," and thus by definition a "lobbying activity," the acts of testifying before a congressional committee, subcommittee, or task force, or of submitting written testimony for inclusion in the public record of any such body, or of responding to notices in the Federal Register or other such publication soliciting communications from the public to an agency, or responding to any oral or written request from a government official for information,

[45] 141 *Congressional Record,* at 20045 (Senator Simpson); *see also* Senator Simpson's explanation of "splitting," 141 *Congressional Record,* at 20052, 20053.

[46] 2 U.S.C. § 1602(7), P.L. 104-65, Section 3(7).

[47] 2 U.S.C. § 1602(8), P.L. 104-65, Section 3(8).

[48] *Note* this express exception to the term "lobbying contact," at 2 U.S.C. § 1602(8)(B)(iii),

P.L. 104-65, Section 3(8)(B)(iii).

[49] Broader limitations on public "advocacy" and lobbying by organizations receiving federal grant money, and on entities wishing to do business with federal grantees, which had been considered by the House as appropriations riders in the 104th Congress (commonly known as the "Istook Amendment," *e.g.*, H.R. 2127, 104th Congress, H.J.Res. 114, 104th Congress), were not enacted into law.

are expressly exempt from the definition of a "lobbying contact," and thus in themselves cannot qualify as a "lobbying activity."[50]

REPORTING LOBBYING ACTIVITIES

Lobbying Disclosure Act of 1995, as Amended. Organizations which engage in a certain amount of lobbying activities through personnel compensated to lobby on the organization's behalf are required to register and to file disclosure reports under the Lobbying Disclosure Act of 1995, as amended.[51] Additionally, outside lobbying firms or individual lobbyists who are retained and compensated over a threshold amount to lobby for an organization/client, and who engage in the requisite lobbying contacts are required to file as lobbyists and to identify the client organizations for whom they lobby.[52] There is no general exclusion or exception from the disclosure and registration requirements for non-profit organizations who otherwise meet the threshold requirements on lobbying contacts, except for churches and their integrated auxiliaries, which are exempt from reporting and disclosure.[53]

Byrd Amendment. While federal grant law or contract law does not necessarily require a recipient organization to report details of all expenditures, such as for lobbying or advocacy that the organization conducts with its own non-federal resources,[54] such recipients of grants or contracts have to declare and certify, under the provisions of the so-called Byrd Amendment, when they use even their own funds to compensate a registered lobbyist to influence covered federal actions.[55]

Tax Law. Most tax-exempt, non-profit organizations (other than churches) having annual gross receipts of over $25,000 must file with the IRS a Form 990 which, unlike most tax filings, is open to public inspection. Charitable 501(c)(3) organizations must also file Schedule A with Form 990, providing the reporting of lobbying expenditures, that is, expenses for "influencing legislation" under the Internal Revenue Code definitions. "Electing" organizations (electing the "expenditure test" for lobbying limits for 501(c)(3)s under 26 U.S.C. § 501(h)) must also compute and allocate expenses attributable to "grass roots" lobbying, as well as to "direct" lobbying; but non-electing organizations (under the "substantial part" test)

[50] *See* 2 U.S.C. § 1602(8)(B), for list of 18 exceptions to the term "lobbying contacts."

[51] 2 U.S.C. § 1603(a)(2), note definitions in §§ 1602(10) and 1602(2).

[52] 2 U.S.C. § 1603(a)(1).

[53] Exemptions from definition of covered "lobbying contact," 2 U.S.C. § 1602(8)(B)(xviii), include those for churches and religious orders that are exempt from filing federal income tax returns under 26 U.S.C. § 6033(a)(2)(A).

[54] *See* generally, Thompson Publishing Group, *Grants Management Handbook*, at p. 42-43, Tab 460, noting that although grantees need not, and may not be required by individual agencies to, report a detailed itemization of expenditures ("object class expenditure reporting"), a federal agency, the agency's office of inspector general, and the GAO, have the right to audit and examine all grantee records, and thus detailed records must be kept to facilitate any such audits and oversight. *Id.* at 3-4. As noted above, criminal penalties may apply to certain misuse of federal funds.

[55] 31 U.S.C. § 1352(b).

must provide to the IRS a "detailed" description of their lobbying activities, information not required from "electing" organizations.

ELECTION CAMPAIGN ACTIVITIES

Similar to "lobbying" activities by groups receiving federal funds, entities which receive federal contracts or grants are not, by virtue of the receipt of such contract or grant, generally prohibited from using their *own* resources and funds for political or campaign activities. However, under both general as well as specific restrictions and limitations, recipients of federal grants and contracts may not use federal funds for political campaign purposes, nor may they charge off to or seek reimbursement from a federal contract or grant for expenses of campaign expenditures or campaign contributions.

RESTRICTIONS ON USE OF GRANT OR CONTRACT FUNDS

OMB Circular A-122. The explicit restrictions on the use of federal grant funds for "lobbying" by non-profit organizations that were adopted in 1984 as part of uniform cost principles for non-profit organizations issued by the Office of Management and Budget (OMB) in OMB Circular A-122, apply also to bar the use of grant funds for political activities, unless authorized by law. OMB Circular A-122 provides that federal grant monies may not be used for, and direct or indirect costs may not be charged to a federal grant for the following:

25a. Notwithstanding other provisions of this Circular, costs associated with the

following activities are unallowable:

(1) Attempts to influence the outcomes of any Federal, State, or local election, referendum, initiative, or similar procedure, through in kind or cash contributions, endorsements, publicity, or similar activity,

(2) Establishing, administering, contributing to, or paying the expenses of a political party, campaign, political action committee, or other organization established for the purpose of influencing the outcomes of elections....[56]

Federal Acquisition Regulations. The Federal Acquisition Regulations apply to for-profit businesses and entities contracting with the federal government, and in a similar manner and in identical wording to the OMB limitations for nonprofit grantees, prohibit the use of federal contract funds for political campaign purposes, and prohibit the writing off to a federal contract the expenses for such activities. The regulations thus expressly provide as "unallowable costs" the expenses for:

(1) Attempts to influence the outcomes of any Federal, State, or local election, referendum, initiative, or similar procedure, through in kind or cash contributions, endorsements, publicity, or similar activities;

[56] OMB Circular A-122, Attachment B, para. 25, as added 49 F.R. 18276 (1984), online at [http://www.whitehouse.gov/omb/circulars/a122/a122.html].

(2) Establishing, administering, contributing to, or paying the expenses of a political party, campaign, political action committee, or other organization established for the purpose of influencing the outcomes of elections.[57]

HATCH ACT AND GRANT RECIPIENTS

The federal law commonly known as the "Hatch Act" has provisions which apply to employees of state and local governments when their principal employment is in connection with a federally funded activity.[58] These Hatch Act provisions, which relate to the permissible political activities of a "State or local officer or employee,"[59] generally apply only to state or local *governmental* personnel, and do not apply on their face to personnel who work for private, non-profit organizations merely because they receive federal grant or contract monies.[60] Although generally applying *only* to governmental employees, there are some circumstances, under certain federal programs, where non-profit organizations which are funded under a particular federal program might be expressly designated under federal statutory law to be "state or local" governmental agencies for purposes of these "Hatch Act" provisions.

Private, non-profit agencies which receive and administer federal funds under certain social programs, for example, have at times been specifically included by law in the definition of "state or local agency" for purposes of the Hatch Act.[61] The law establishing the Community Services Block Grant Program, which supplanted much of the Economic Opportunity Act programs, for example, provides that any private non-profit agency "receiving assistance under this chapter which has responsibility for planning, developing, and coordinating community antipoverty programs shall be deemed to be a State or local agency" for the purposes of the Hatch Act at chapter 15 of title 5, United States Code:[62]

[57] 48 C.F.R. §31.205-22

[58] 5 U.S.C. § 1501 *et seq.*

[59] 5 U.S.C. § 1501(4).

[60] *See* definitions in 5 U.S.C. § 1501. A "State or local agency" under the Hatch Act is expressly defined to mean "the executive branch of a State, municipality, or other political subdivision of a State, or an agency or department thereof." 5 U.S.C. § 1501(2).

[61] *See*, for example, former provisions of law applying to community action agencies under the Economic Opportunity Act of 1964, 42 U.S.C. § 2943 (1976 ed.); former provisions of law applying to Manpower and Job Corps programs under the Comprehensive Employment and Training Act of 1973, 29 U.S.C. §§ 848(g), 990 (1976 ed.); and provisions of law applying to staff attorneys of entities receiving funds from the Legal Services Corporation, 42 U.S.C. § 2996e(e), and agencies under the Head Start program, 42 U.S.C. § 9851.

[62] P.L. 97-35, 95 Stat. 515, August 13, 1981, see 42 U.S.C. § 9904(e) (1982 Code ed.). While that original provision was repealed by the Hatch Act Amendments of 1993 (P.L. 103-94, § 6, 107 Stat. 1005, October 6, 1993), the designation for Hatch Act purposes of similar agencies under the Community Services Block Grant Program was reinstated in a similar form in 1998. P.L. 105-285, title II, § 201, 112 Stat. 2747, October 27, 1998.

For purposes of chapter 15 of Title 5, [5 U.S.C. § 1501 *et seq.*], any entity that assumes responsibility for planning, developing and coordinating activities under this chapter [42 U.S.C. § 9901 *et seq.*] and receives assistance under this chapter [42 U.S.C. § 9901 *et seq.*] shall be deemed to be a State or local agency. For purposes of paragraphs (1) and (2) of section 1502(a) of such title, any entity receiving assistance under this chapter [42 U.S.C. § 9901 *et seq.*] shall be deemed to be a State or local agency.[63]

Similarly, an agency under the Head Start program which "assumes responsibilityfor planning, developing, and coordinating Head Start programs and receives assistance" under the program is to be considered a "state or local agency" for the purposes of the application of the Hatch Act.[64] Any programs assisted under the act, that is, any grant recipients, have a specific statutory responsibility to carry out the programs and to use program funds in a manner that does not involve partisan political activities or other activities associated with a partisan candidate or political party.[65]

For those covered by the "Hatch Act" applicable to an employee of a "state or local agency," the provisions of that federal law set out three specific restrictions on political activities of employees, whether they are on or off duty, or on annual leave, sick leave, or other leave from work.[66] The first two, paragraphs (1) and (2) of § 1502(a) of title 5, United State Code, relate to coercive activities for or against candidates or in making of campaign contributions,[67] while the third relates to employees' candidacies for elective office:

[63] 42 U.S.C. § 9918(b)(1). Agencies under this federal program that receive funds and plan, develop, or coordinate program activities, are to be considered "state and local agencies" for all of the restrictions that the federal "Hatch Act" places on state and local *governmental* employees, at 5 U.S.C. § 1501(a)(1) - (3). For agencies or entities which merely receive "assistance" under the Community Services Block Grant Program (but are not responsible for planning, coordinating and/or developing community programs), the employees of such entities are only subject to the restrictions of that portion of the "Hatch Act" which prohibit the use of one's authority or influence to interfere with the results of an election, and which prohibit other coercive conduct relating to the payment of contributions for political purposes by employees of state or local agencies. 5 U.S.C. § 1502(a)(1) and (2).

[64] 42 U.S.C. § 9851(a).

[65] 42 U.S.C. § 9851(b). Voter registration and get-out-the-vote campaigns are discussed in the next section.

[66] Agencies which have responsibility for planning, developing and coordinating Head Start programs are subject to all three restrictions, including candidacy, while employees of agencies just receiving assistance under the program are subject only to the no coercion provisions of paragraphs (1) and (2) of 5 U.S.C. § 1502(a). 42 U.S.C. 9851(a).

[67] The prohibition on use of official authority to influence an election is described by the Office of Special Counsel (the agency with Hatch Act enforcement authority) as "aimed at activities such as threatening to deny a promotion to any employee who does not vote for certain candidates, requiring employees to contribute a percentage of their pay to a political fund, influencing subordinate employees to buy tickets to political fund raising dinners and similar events, and advising employees to take part in political activity." U.S. Office of Special Counsel, *Political Activity and the State and Local Employee,* at 5 (August 2000).

1. Employees may not use their "official authority or influence for the purpose of interfering with or affecting the result of an election or a nomination for office" (5 U.S.C. § 1502(a)(1));
2. Employees may not "directly or indirectly coerce, attempt to coerce, command, or advise" fellow employees to make contributions in support of a party or candidate (5 U.S.C. § 1502(a)(2));
3. Employees may not be candidates for public office in a partisan election (5

U.S.C. § 1502(a)(3); *see* § 1503, permitting candidacy in nonpartisan election).

Other than these three specific restrictions on official interference, coercion, and candidacy, "State and local employees subject to the provisions of the Hatch Act may take an active part in political management and political campaigns."[68] In addition to allowing general political activities related to candidates and elections during their free time, the Hatch Act does not generally apply to public policy activity relating to "issues" (as opposed to candidates and political parties), either legislative issues or issues that come before voters in referenda elections.[69] Furthermore, the Hatch Act (even the more restrictive portion for *federal* employees) does not apply to nonpartisan voter registration or get-out-the-vote campaigns.[70]

FEDERAL CONTRACTORS AND POLITICAL CONTRIBUTIONS

Persons who have negotiated or are negotiating a contract with the federal government are prohibited during the duration of that contract from making or offering to make political contributions to any party or candidate for public office in connection with a federal election.[71] This restriction reaches contributions made from the firms' business or partnership assets, but would permit, in the case of partnerships, donations made from the personal assets of the partners.[72] Federal government contractors which are corporations, labor unions, membership organizations, cooperatives, or corporations without capital stock, may also establish

[68] *Political Activity and the State and Local Employee, supra* at 5.

[69] U.S. Office of Special Counsel, Letter Opinion, March 18, 2003; United States Civil Service Commission, Office of the General Counsel, Letter Opinion, March 13, 1974.

[70] 5 C.F.R. §734.203; United States Office of Special Counsel [OSC], advisory opinion 2006, available at [http://www.osc.gov/documents/hatchact/federal/fha34014.pdf]; OSC, advisory opinion May 25, 2004, OSC File No. AD-04-xxx, at 1, available at [http://www.osc.gov/documents/hatchact/federal/fha-32.pdf]; OSC, Federal Hatch Act Advisory, "Voter Registration Drives in the Workplace," April 14, 2004, at 2 available at [http://www.osc.gov/documents/hatchact/federal/fha-31.pdf].

[71] 2 U.S.C. § 441c. Federal "employees," as opposed to contractors, may generally not make political contributions to their employer or employing authority. 18 U.S.C. § 603.

[72] See discussion of this restriction in U.S. Department of Justice, *Federal Prosecution of Election Offenses,* at pp. 100-101 (6th ed. January 1995).

a "separate segregated fund" to which voluntary contributions may be made, and from which political campaign contributions may be made to parties or candidates.[73]

DIVERSION OF GRANT OR CONTRACT FUNDS FOR "POLITICAL" USES

As a general matter, recipients of federal grants and contract monies must use the funds for the purposes and programs that were intended to be supported within the statutory scheme that authorized the grants or contracts.[74] It may be possible in certain contexts that concerted activity by individuals which causes federal funds from a federal program to be disbursed or used in contravention of the purposes of that program, in violation of established regulations or laws, and to be used instead for partisan or improper advocacy purposes, might entail, for example, a scheme to "impair[ ], obstruct[ ], or defeat[ ] the lawful function of any Department of the Government," such as to constitute a conspiracy to "defraud the United States" in violation of 18 U.S.C. §371.[75] As noted by the Supreme Court, a conspiracy to "defraud the United States" does not necessarily require a showing that the government was cheated out of money or property, nor does it necessarily require that an illegal act be done, as the Supreme Court found that conspiracy to defraud the United States "also means to interfere with or obstruct one of its lawful governmental functions by deceit, craft or trickery, or at least by means that are dishonest."[76]

The courts have upheld a charge of conspiracy to defraud the United States where individuals had conspired to use a federal program "to accomplish political objectives ... unrelated to legitimate Commission business," by having employees hired with funds from a federal program (CETA) work on political campaigns, in *United States v. Pintar.*[77] In *Pintar*, the court found that even though no monetary loss to the government or monetary gain to the defendants was proven, the conspiracy count of defrauding "the United States of its right to have programs of an agency financed ... by the United States Government ... administered, honestly, fairly,

[73] 2 U.S.C. § 441c.

[74] "[G]rantees are, of course, obligated to spend grant funds for the purposes and objectives of the grant and consistent with any statutory or other conditions attached to the use of the grant funds. *See, e.g.*, B-303927, June 7, 2005; 42 Comp. Gen. 682 (1963); 2 Comp. Gen. 684 (1923)." United States Government Accountability Office, Office of the General Counsel, *Principles of Federal Appropriations Law*, Third Edition, Volume II, p. 10-71 (February 2006).

[75] *See Dennis v. United States,* 384 U.S. 855, 861 (1966); *Iannelli v. United States,* 420 U.S. 770 (1975); *Blumenthal v. United States,* 332 U.S. 539 (1947); *United States v. Treadwell,* 760 F.2d 327 (D.C.Cir. 1985).

If false statements, writings, accounting or vouchers are used in furtherance of the misuses of appropriated monies, then other federal criminal laws, such as 18 U.S.C. §§ 1001, 287, may also be relevant.

[76] *Hammerschmidt v. United States,* 265 U.S. 182, 188 (1924). The obstruction or interference with the functions of a government department or agency which constitutes a scheme to "defraud the United States" has thus included schemes which thwart or interfere with the objectives and express purposes of a governmental program, or which tend to interfere with the fair and impartial administration of government programs.

[77] *United States v. Pintar,* 630 F.2d 1270, 1275 (8th Cir. 1980).

without corruption or deceit,"[78] could be sustained even with no actual harm to the Government shown, as long as some dishonest or deceitful means were demonstrated. The dishonest or deceitful means involved in that case was "a pattern of concealment" of the activity.[79]

FEDERAL LIMITATIONS BECAUSE OF THE CHARACTER OR NATURE OF THE ORGANIZATION

Corporate and Labor Union Political Contributions or Expenditures. Entities and organizations which are corporations or labor unions are prohibited by federal law from making "a contribution or expenditure in connection with any election" to a federal office.[80] Such corporate or labor union entities, while prohibited from using treasury funds for campaign purposes, are permitted, however, to use such funds to establish and maintain a "separate segregated fund" (generally referred to as political action committees [PACs]), to which voluntary contributions may be made, and from which political campaign expenditures or contributions may be made.[81] Corporations and labor unions may also make certain other expenditures relative to a federal election under limited circumstances.[82]

Tax Code Limitations on Non-Profit Organizations. If an organization is a non-profit, charitable organization which holds its tax-exempt status under Section 501(c)(3) of the Internal Revenue Code (26 U.S.C. § 501(c)(3), that is, organizations which may receive contributions which are tax-deductible for the donor), then that organization has an express restriction that it may not "participate in or intervene in (including the publishing or distributing of statements), any political campaign on behalf of (or in opposition to) any candidate for public office." There are certain activities which have been deemed to be "nonpartisan" activities related to elections (including nonpartisan voter registration activities) in which such organizations may engage and still retain their preferred tax-exempt status.[83]

VOTER REGISTRATION AND GET-OUT-THE-VOTE DRIVES

Although voter registration and get-out-the-vote drives might generally be seen as a subset of "political" or "campaign" activities, such drives when conducted on a *nonpartisan* basis are often treated differently than partisan political campaign

[78] 630 F.2d at 1275. [79] 630 F.2d at 1278-1279. [80] 2 U.S.C. § 441b. [81] 2 U.S.C. § 441(b)(2)(C). [82] For a detailed discussion of the corporate contribution and expenditure restriction, see

CRS Report RS21571, *Campaign Finance and Prohibiting Contributions by Tax-Exempt*

Corporations: FEC v. Beaumont, by L. Paige Whitaker. [83] For a detailed discussion of the tax code restrictions and limitations on non-profit organizations and campaign activity, see CRS Report RL33377, *Tax-Exempt Organizations: Political Activity Restrictions and Disclosure Requirements*, by Erika Lunder.

activities for the purposes of several federal provisions. Such activities may be considered "nonpartisan" if the organization does not distinguish, discriminate, or is not directed or focused only on a particular political party, among other political parties in registering voters or urging voters to go to the polls.[84] An activity could thus be nonpartisan even though the particular "population" or "community" at which such activities are directed may consist of persons who could conceivably, historically, or theoretically favor one political party over another.

Nonpartisan voter registration drives and the encouragement of voting are seen as more "civic minded" and beneficial activities, which increase and further participatory democracy, than merely partisan political campaigning.[85] Thus, for example, 501(c)(3) "charitable" organizations, which are *not* allowed to engage in any political campaign activities, *are* allowed to conduct nonpartisan voter registration drives and get-out-the-vote campaigns.[86] Similarly, activities which might constitute prohibited political activities under the federal "Hatch Act," specifically do *not* include nonpartisan voter registration drives,[87] and although corporations and labor organizations are not allowed to spend treasury funds to influence political campaigns, such organizations are expressly allowed to use corporate or union treasury funds to engage in nonpartisan voter registration and get out the vote campaigns targeted at a corporation's own executives or stockholders, or a labor organization's own members and their families.[88]

GENERAL LIMITATIONS ON USE OF GRANT AND CONTRACT FUNDS

Similar to "lobbying" and "campaign" activities, a business, association, corporation, organization, or other entity which receives a federal contract or a federal grant is *not* prohibited, by virtue of the receipt of such federal contract or grant, from using its *own* resources and funds for voter registration or get-out-the vote campaigns. As a general matter, and as noted above, however, federal grant monies and monies given by federal agencies under federal contracts may only be applied for the purposes provided in the underlying federal law and appropriation. As explained by the General Accountability Office,

As stated in 31 U.S.C. § 1301(a), appropriations may be used only for the

purpose(s) for which they were made. One of the ways in which this

[84] *See, e.g.*, Rev. Rul. 2007-41, 2007-25 I.R.B. 1421, discussed in CRS Report RL33377.

[85] *See, e.g.*, National Voter Registration Act, 42 U.S.C. § 1973gg, "Findings and Purposes," to increase voting registration and voter participation in elections. Under this act, state governments are required, and federal agencies are urged, to assist in facilitating the registration of eligible citizens. See also Higher Education Act which requires institutions to "make a good faith effort to distribute a mail voter registration form, requested and received from the State, to each student enrolled in a degree or certificate program and physically in attendance at the institution, and to make such forms widely available to students at the institution." 20 U.S.C. § 1094(a)(23).

[86] Rev. Rul. 2007-41, 2007-25 I.R.B. 1421, discussed in CRS Report RL33377, *supra* at 11.

[87] See footnote 70, this report.

[88] 2 U.S.C. § 441b(b)(2)(B).

fundamental proposition manifests itself in the grant context is the principle that grant funds may be obligated and expended only for authorized grant purposes. What is an "authorized grant purpose" is determined by examining the relevant program legislation, legislative history, and appropriation acts.[89]

Thus, unless the purpose of a grant, or a contract given by a federal agency, is to carry out a particular legislative directive or intent to increase voter registration generally, or to increase voter registration in a particular community or population, then the grantee or contractor would not be authorized to use such grant funds, or to be reimbursed for costs under a federal contract, for the purpose of registering voters or getting voters to the polls.

Although the more particularized restrictions on, for example, non-profit grantees in OMB Circular A-122, and on for-profit businesses in the Federal Acquisition Regulations, using federal funds for "attempts to influence the outcomes of any ... election ... through in kind or cash contributions, endorsements, publicity, or similar activity," do not expressly encompass nonpartisan voter registration activity, the general requirement to use federal grant and contract funds only for the underlying legislative purposes would appear to prohibit such activity financed with federal dollars, unless authorized by law. Furthermore, a federal agency or department, in making grants, may have specific restrictions in regulations, in "guidance" for grantees and contractors, or in the specific grant or contract agreement, which must be examined since they may contain particular and specific limitations on other activities under the particular program.[90]

STATUTORY RESTRICTIONS ON SPECIFIC PROGRAMS

There are certain federal programs which may have additional or specific statutory restrictions on the use of program funds for certain specified activities, including voter registration or get-out-the vote campaigns. The law establishing the Community Services Block Grant Program, for example, places specific restrictions on voter registration activities or assistance to voters in getting to the polls within the programs supported by federal funds under the Community Services Block Grant program. The relevant provisions of law state that:

Programs assisted under this chapter shall not be carried on in a manner involving the use of program funds, the provision of services, or the employment or assignment of personnel, in a manner supporting or resulting in the identification of such programs with —

[89] *Principles of Federal Appropriations Law, supra* at p. 10-36.

[90] Note, for example, HUD regulations at 24 C.F.R. § 570.207, " Ineligible activities," concerning activities not eligible for funding under Community Development BlockGrants; 24 C.F.R. § 1003.207, "Ineligible activities," concerning specifically activities not eligible for funding under the Community Development Block Grants for Indian Tribes and Alaska Native Villages. See also 45 C.F.R. § 1226.5, providing that "volunteers or other assistance, in any program under the Act [Corporation for National and Community Services] shall not be assigned or provided to an organization if a principal purpose or activity of the organization includes" voter registration. See also 45 C.F.R. § 2551.121; 45 C.F.R. § 2552.121; 45 C.F.R. § 2553.91.

(B) any activity to provide voters or prospective voters with transportation to the polls or similar assistance in connection with any such election; or

(C) any voter registration activity.[91]

The particular restrictions concerning the Community Services Block Grant Program thus appear to apply to the use of program funds as well as to activities within the federally assisted *program*, but do not appear to extend to organizations and their activities outside of and separate from such programs (that is, that do not use program funds, services or personnel connected to this program),[92] and particularly do *not* apply to "affiliate" or connected organizations which are not participating in the program.

Similarly, programs assisted under the Head Start statutory provisions may not use program funds and may not provide services which identify the program with any voter assistance or voter registration efforts;[93] and the provisions establishing the Corporation for National and Community Service expressly prohibit the use of the program funds or any program administered by the Corporation to be used for "any voter registration activity."[94] Attorneys engaged in legal assistance under the Legal Services Corporation provisions may not engage in any "activity to provide voters with transportation to the polls, or to provide similar assistance in connection with an election, or ... any voter registration activity."[95]

CONSTITUTIONAL ISSUES IN LEGISLATIVE ATTEMPTS TO PROHIBIT ANY ADVOCACY, LOBBYING, OR VOTER REGISTRATION ACTIVITIES BY PRIVATE ENTITIES AS A CONDITION TO RECEIVING FEDERAL CONTRACTS OR GRANTS

Efforts by the federal government to restrict private, nongovernmental entities from using their *own* private or non-federal resources to engage in any public advocacy, electioneering communications, or voter registration activities, as a condition precedent to receiving, or because the entity receives, some federal funding would raise serious First Amendment concerns. The activities involved in lobbying and political advocacy, whether by persons individually or in association with one another engaging in advocacy communications to the public or to public officials on political, social and economic issues of interest to the individuals and groups, are intertwined with and implicate

fundamental rights protected by the First Amendment to the United States Constitution, including freedom of speech and the rights of

[91] **42 U.S.C. § 9918(b)(2)**. [92] *See,* for example, discussion in *Rust v. Sullivan*, 500 U.S. 173, 196-197 (1991). [93] 42 U.S.C. §9851(b). [94] 42 U.S.C. § 5043(a). [95] 42 U.S.C. § 2996f(a)(6) and (b)(4).

association and petition.[96] In *Eastern Railroads President Conference v. Noerr Motor Freight, Inc.*, the Supreme Court ruled that because of First Amendment considerations the prohibitions of the Sherman Anti-Trust Act could *not* prohibit rival businesses from acting in concert to lobby legislatures for favorable transportation legislation. The Court noted that lobbying activities involve the "right of petition [which] is one of the freedoms protected by the Bill of Rights," and could not be restricted by statute without serious First Amendment implications.[97] The Court explained the importance of lobbying activities in our representative form of government:

In a representative democracy such as this, these branches of government act on behalf of the people and, to a very large extent, the whole concept of representation depends upon the ability of the people to make their wishes known to their representatives.[98]

Rather than a detriment to be limited and suppressed by the government, the activities involved in lobbying, public advocacy and political expression about public policy issues, government, legislation, and candidates have been found by the Supreme Court to be among the most important freedoms in preserving an open democracy, and have been characterized as activities which our nation seeks to encourage rather than discourage.[99] The Supreme Court has on numerous occasions emphasized the importance of protecting public advocacy rights, and has noted the "profound national commitment to the principle that debate on public issues should be uninhibited, robust, and wide open,"[100] and has in the past even noted that "expression on public issues 'has always rested on the highest rung of the hierarchy of First Amendment values.'"[101] The Supreme Court has therefore found that the advocacy communications involved in lobbying, political speech, and expression entail the exercise of protected First Amendment rights of association, speech and

[96] *United States v. Harriss*, 347 U.S. 612 (1954); *United States v. Rumely,* 345 U.S. 41 (1953); *Eastern Railroads President Conference v. Noerr Motor Freight, Inc.,* 365 U.S. 127, 137-138 (1961). *Note* discussion in Browne, "The Constitutionality of Lobby Reform: Implicating Associational Privacy and the Right to Petition the Government," 4:2 *William & Mary Bill of Rights Journal* 717 (1995).

[97] 365 U.S. at 138.

[98] 365 U.S. at 137.

[99] "Discussion of public issues ... are integral to the operation of the system of government established by our constitution." *Buckley v. Valeo,* 424 U.S. 1, 14 (1976). As early as 1938 Chief Justice Stone postulated on the possible stricter scrutiny under the First Amendment for "legislation which restricts those political processes which can ordinarily be expected to bring about repeal of undesirable legislation." *United States v. Carolene Products Co.,* 304 U.S. 144, 152, n.4.

[100] *New York Times v. Sullivan,* 376 U.S. 254, 270 (1964); *Garrison v. State of Louisiana,* 379 U.S. 69 (1964).

[101] *NAACP v. Clairbome Hardware Co.*, 458 U.S. 886, 913 (1982); *Carey v. Brown*, 447

U.S. 455, 467 (1980); *FCC v. League of Women Voters of California*, 468 U.S. 364, 381 (1984).

petition, and that any regulations imposed by Congress on such lobbying and advocacy activities may not unduly burden the exercise of those rights.[102]

In the area of *political* advocacy, as in the area of public policy advocacy and lobbying, the courts have been careful and deferential to the rights of private parties in terms of their freedoms of association and expression.[103] In *Buckley v. Valeo,* the Supreme Court, even while upholding limitations on political contributions to federal candidates and committees, invalidated a provision of the Federal Election Campaign Act which would have restricted the amount of money certain entities could spend independently on political advocacy concerning candidates in federal elections. The Court found that

The Act's expenditure ceilings impose direct and substantial restraints on the quantity of political speech.... It is clear that a primary effect of these expenditure limitations is to restrict the quantity of campaign speech by individuals, groups, and candidates. The restrictions, while neutral as to the ideas expressed, limit political expression "at the core of our electoral process and of the First Amendment freedoms."[104]

Even when a federal regulation on lobbying, or public policy or political advocacy involved merely a *disclosure* and reporting requirement, and not a restriction which directly limits or prohibits advocacy activities, such a regulation underwent rigorous constitutional scrutiny. Thus, although the Court has noted in First Amendment cases that disclosure seems to be the "least restrictive means" of obtaining certain permissible and important governmental objectives (such as the prevention of fraud and undue influence of monied special interests on basic governmental processes), such rigorous constitutional scrutiny of laws which merely required *disclosures* relating to political speech and advocacy were necessary since the Court recognized the "deterrent effects on the exercise of First Amendment rights" which may arise "as an unintended but inevitable result of the government's conduct in requiring disclosure."[105]

[102] *United States v. Harriss*, 347 U.S. 612 (1954); *United States v. Rumely,* 345 U.S. 41 (1953); *Eastern Railroads President Conference v. Noerr Motor Freight, Inc.,* 365 U.S. 127, 137-138 (1961).

[103] In *McConnell v. Federal Election Commission*, 540 U.S. 93, 205 (2003), the Supreme Court noted that the "'constitutional guarantee has its fullest and most urgent application precisely to the conduct of campaigns for political office,' *Monitor Patriot Co. v. Roy,* 401

U.S. 265. 272 (1971), and '[a]dvocacy of the election or defeat of candidates for federal office is no less entitled to protection under the First Amendment than the discussion of political policy generally or the advocacy of the passage or defeat of legislation.' *Buckley,* 424 U.S., at 48."

[104] *Buckley v. Valeo,* 424 U.S. 1, 39 (1976).

[105] *Buckley v. Valeo, supra*, at 65; *United States v. Harriss, supra*; *NAACP v. Button,* 371

U.S. 415 (1963).

RESTRICTIONS ON FEDERAL FUNDS

Congress clearly may limit, regulate or condition the use of the *funds* it appropriates,[106] and as noted earlier in this report, there are now under federal law and regulation several direct prohibitions and multiple restrictions on the use by private recipients of federal funds or federal subsidies for political or advocacy/lobbying purposes.[107] When legislative or regulatory provisions do not place restrictions and conditions merely upon the *use* of federal funds, nor merely attempt to control or "define" the content of a government program, but rather institute direct restrictions and prohibitions on political advocacy and expression of certain private entities with their own resources as a requisite and as a condition for those private parties to receive federal funds, then such legislation must be examined under the heightened scrutiny of First Amendment principles. The Supreme Court has noted that restrictions on otherwise constitutionally protected activities could not be "justified simply because" persons were receiving federal funds, nor was "a lesser degree of judicial scrutiny ... required simply because Government funds were involved."[108] As explained by the Supreme Court in a more recent case, "Congress cannot recast a condition on funding as a mere definition of its program in every case, lest the First Amendment be reduced to a simple semantic exercise."[109]

"UNCONSTITUTIONAL CONDITIONS" ON THE RECEIPT OF FEDERAL FUNDS

Although it is clear Congress may limit, regulate, or condition the use of the funds it appropriates, such as in the existing and detailed prohibitions on lobbying or political advocacy by private recipients with federal grant or contract funds, the Supreme Court has in the past ruled "that the government may not deny a benefit to a person because he exercises a constitutional right."[110] The principle had thus developed in a line of Supreme Court constitutional law cases that the government may not *condition* the receipt of a public benefit upon the requirement of relinquishing one's protected First Amendment rights.[111] In a lower federal court

[106] ***Cincinnati Soap Co. v. United States,* 301 U.S. 308, 321-322 (1937).**

[107] **See discussion in this report, at pp. 2-9, 14-15, and 21-22, discussing OMB Circular A**122, Attachment B, para. 25, as added 49 F.R. 18276 (1984); Federal Acquisition Regulations for commercial contractors and nonprofit contractors of the federal government, 48 C.F.R. § 31.205-22 (commercial contractors); 48 C.F.R. § 31.701 *et seq.*, (non-profit contractors); the so-called "Byrd Amendment," 31 U.S.C. §§ 1352, *see* common rules by major agencies, 55 F.R. 6738, February 26, 1990 (and OMB government-wide guidance, 54 F.R.52306, December 20, 1989 upon which the rules were based; and 18 U.S.C. § 1913 and various yearly appropriations law riders.

[108] *FCC v. League of Women Voters,* 468 U.S. 364, 401n.27 (1984).

[109] *Legal Services Corporation v. Velazquez*, 531 U.S. 533, 547 (2001).

[110] *Regan v. Taxation With Representation of Washington,* 461 U.S. 540, 545 (1983).

[111] Note "unconstitutional conditions" cases, including *Perry v. Sinderman,* 408 U.S. 593 (1972); *Speiser v. Randall,* 357 U.S. 513 (1956); *Regan v. Taxation With Representation of* (continued...)

decision (affirmed by the United States Court of Appeals) dealing specifically with lobbying by "consumer groups" that sought a state contract, for example, the court ruled that a state provision could not be interpreted to bar an entity that lobbies or hires lobbyists from being eligible for a particular government contract (thus in effect barring lobbying by state contractors with their own funds and resources), since that would place an unconstitutional condition upon the receipt of government funds in violation of the protected First Amendment public advocacy rights of those contractors:

A valid state law ... cannot be applied in a way to thwart the exercise of a right guaranteed by the Constitution ....

The Attorney General's policy burdens and deters the exercise of the first amendment right to petition the government. Persons and organizations such as plaintiffs are confronted with a dilemma: forsake lobbying or give up the right to seek contracts or subgrants from the State of Indiana.

Under the first and fourteenth amendments, a state may not directly abridge lobbying activities or indirectly abridge such activities by withholding government benefits from those persons who lobby or retain lobbyists.[112]

Although it is true that a private organization may simply choose to forego participating in or conducting political advocacy, voter registration drives, or lobbying to be eligible to participate in a particularly restricted federal program, and although no one has a "right" to participate in or receive funding provided by a federal program, the Supreme Court under the so-called "unconstitutional conditions" cases has in the past established the principle that the receipt of a federal benefit may not be conditioned upon abdicating one's constitutional rights, particularly one's First Amendment freedom of speech:

For at least a quarter-century, this Court has made clear that even though a person has no "right" to a valuable governmental benefit and even though the government may deny him the benefit for any number of reasons, there are some reasons upon which the government may not rely. It may not deny a benefit to a person on a basis that infringes his constitutionally protected interests — especially, his interest in freedom of speech. For if the Government could deny a benefit to a person because of his constitutionally protected speech or associations, his exercise of those freedoms would in effect be penalized and inhibited. This would allow the government to "produce a result which [it] could not command directly." *Speiser v. Randall,* 357 U.S. 513, 526. Such interference with constitutional rights is impermissible.[113]

In 1996 the Court recognized, under the circumstances of the case before it, "the right of independent contractors not to be terminated for exercising their First

[111] (...continued) *Washington,* 461 U.S. at 545, *see also* 461 U.S. at 552-553 (Blackman, J. concurring) (1983); *FCC v. League of Women Voters,* 468 U.S. 364, 381 (1984). *Compare* with *Rust*

v. Sullivan, 500 U.S. 173, 196 (1991).

[112] *Citizens Energy Coalition v. Sendak*, 459 F. Supp. 248, 258 (S.D. Ind. 1978), *aff'd* 594 F.2d 1158 (7th Cir. 1979).

[113] *Perry v. Sinderman,* 408 U.S. 593, 597 (1972).

Amendment rights."[114] In explicating the principles of prohibiting the denial of federal benefits for private parties who exercise their First Amendment rights of speech and advocacy, the Court noted

Our unconstitutional conditions precedents span a spectrum from government employees, whose close relationship to the government requires a balancing of important free speech and government interests, to claimants for tax exemptions, *Speiser v. Randall*, 357 U.S. 513 (1958), users of public facilities, *e.g. Lamb's Chapel v. Center Moriches Union Free School Dist.,* 508 U.S. 384, 390-394 (1993); *Healy v. James,* 408 U.S. 169 (1972), and recipients of small government subsidies, *e.g., FCC v. League of Women Voters of Cal.,* 468 U.S. 364 (1984), who are much less dependant on the government but more like ordinary citizens whose viewpoints on matters of public concern the government has no legitimate interest in repressing.[115]

Thus, while the government may place certain conditions on the recipients of federal benefits, grants or subsidies, and may refuse to subsidize or pay for one's private lobbying or advocacy activities, the participation in First Amendment expression may arguably *not* be the basis for denying a public benefit. As explained by Justice Blackman concurring in *Regan v. Taxation With Representation*, the "denial of business expense deduction for lobbying is constitutional, but an attempt to deny all deductions for business expenses to a taxpayer who lobbies would penalize unconstitutionally the exercise of First Amendment rights"; and that while "denial of welfare benefits for abortion is constitutional, ... an attempt to withhold all welfare benefits from one who exercises right to an abortion probably would be impermissible."[116] It may be noted in this regard that in *Speiser v. Randall,*[117] the Supreme Court expressly found that the state may not place a condition on eligibility even for a tax-exemption on a basis that violates one's First Amendment freedoms of speech, expression, and association: "To deny an exemption to claimants who engage in certain forms of speech is in effect to penalize them for such speech."[118]

The Supreme Court under this line of cases thus invalidated a federal law which would have placed an advocacy restriction on any recipient of particular grants from a federally funded program (public broadcasting) in *Federal Communications Commission v. League of Women Voters of California.*[119] In that case the federal statutory ban on public broadcasters "editorializing" was expressly found unconstitutional by the Supreme Court. In the original provisions establishing the Corporation for Public Broadcasting, the non-commercial broadcast stations which

[114] *Board of Commissioners v. Umbehr*, 518 U.S. 668, 686 (1996). [115] 518 U.S. at 680. [116] 461 U.S. at 552, note, discussing *Cammarano v. United States,* 358 U.S. 498 (1959);

Harris v. McRae, 448 U.S. 297, 317, n. 19 (1980) and *Maher v. Roe,* 432 U.S. 464, 474-475,

n. 8 (1977). [117] 357 U.S. 513 (1956). [118] 357 U.S. at 518. [119] 468 U.S. 364 (1984).

received any grants or funding from CPB were prohibited from "editorializing."[120] Although broadcast stations may be required in the public interest to afford opportunities for opposing viewpoints and equal time under the so-called fairness doctrine, the Court found that such broadcasters, merely because they receive some federal funding through the Corporation for Public Broadcasting, could not be prohibited from providing their own expression and opinions on matters of public interest, as the ban was not narrowly tailored to sufficiently address the government's asserted justifications for such restrictions on protected First Amendment conduct. The court found that although the government may regulate the use of its own appropriations, and need not subsidize private advocacy, the complete ban on editorializing would impermissibly prohibit the private broadcast stations from using their *own* resources and funding for such public advocacy activity.[121]

It is obvious that Congress may and does institute various conditions and requirements on the receipt of federal funds. Although the cases discussed above were found to constitute an "unconstitutional condition" on the receipt of federal funds by private parties, and on the use of the recipient's own resources for protected First Amendment advocacy, the Supreme Court has permitted the government to require a restriction on the use of a recipient's *own* funds for certain speech *within a particular program* when that program is even partially funded with federal funds. In *Rust v. Sullivan*,[122] a provision restricting programs funded by the government from providing abortion counseling was upheld by the Supreme Court. The Court did note that the restriction examined there was, however, a restriction going only to the *program* which was partially federally funded, and not a restriction on the *recipient* of the funds, who could continue separately and independently to counsel on abortion or even to perform abortions apart from the federally funded program. The Court explained that the government did not place a "condition on the recipient of the subsidy," but rather placed the restrictions on the "particular program or service" which "merely require that the grantee keep such activities separate and distinct from the" publicly funded activities.[123] As stated by the Court: "[T]he government is not denying a benefit to anyone, but is instead simply insisting that public funds be spent for the purposes for which they were authorized."[124] Chief Justice Rehnquist, writing for the Court, distinguished this situation from the "unconstitutional conditions" cases:

In contrast, our "unconstitutional conditions" cases involve situations in which the Government has placed a condition on the *recipient* of the subsidy rather than on a particular program or service, thus effectively prohibiting the recipient from engaging in the protected conduct outside the scope of the federally funded program.[125]

[120] *See* P.L. 90-129, November 7, 1967, 81 Stat. 368. [121] 468 U.S. at 399-401. [122] 500 U.S. at 173 (1991). [123] 500 U.S. at 196.

[124] *Id.*

[125] 500 U.S. at 197.

Another restriction and limitation following federal funds in the area of advocacy are the provisions of the Federal Election Campaign Act which allow for a "voluntary" expenditure limitation on campaign expenses when a candidate agrees to accept federal funds for his or her political campaign. As noted by the Supreme Court in *Buckley v. Valeo, supra*, however, that particular provision was not directly challenged by any party in the case, and the issue of its constitutionality was not before the Court.[126] The Court appeared, however, to be favorably disposed to the idea of voluntary limitations since it believed the overall provisions providing federal funds to private parties for political advocacy and campaigning enhanced, rather than restricted, opportunities to communicate and advocate to the public: "Subtitle H is a congressional effort, not to abridge, restrict or censor speech, but rather to use public money to facilitate and enlarge public discussion and participation...."[127]

GOVERNMENT SPEECH

More recently, the Supreme Court has noted that when the government funds activities and programs, it may limit, restrict and fashion the speech of those speaking *on its behalf* either as "government speech," or when the government uses "private speakers to transmit specific information pertaining to its own programs."[128] In 1995, the Court explained that "[w]hen the government disburses public funds to private entities *to convey a governmental message*, it may take legitimate and appropriate steps to ensure that its message is neither garbled nor distorted by the grantee."[129]

What might be considered an "exception" to the First Amendment, that is, allowing for government regulation of either "government speech," or some private speech within the parameters of certain government programs or government created forums, would not, in any event, extend to *all* activities and programs of individuals or private entities which receive government grants. In *Legal Services Corporation v. Velazquez,*[130] the Court overturned a restriction on the Legal Services Corporation's grantees "lobbying" for changes in welfare legislation as part of legal representation of indigent clients. The Court found that even though the legal services program was government funded, and thus the speech that the government wished to regulate and limit by statute was, in fact, within the confines of that program (as in *Rust*), the activity and speech involved, that is, lobbying the legislature on behalf of a client, could still not be considered "government speech," and thus was not subject to regulation under the government speech doctrine.[131]

[126] 424 U.S. at 87, n. 119.

[127] 424 U.S. at 92-93.

[128] *Legal Services Corporation v. Velazquez*, 531 U.S. 533, 541 (2001).

[129] *Rosenberger v. Rector and Visitors of the University of Virginia*, 515 U.S. 819, 833 (1995), citing *Rust, supra* at 196-200. Emphasis added. In the *University of Virginia* decision the Court found that providing state funds for the printing of various student publications did not constitute "Government speech" that could be regulated on a content basis so as to exclude groups with religious-based publications.

[130] 531 U.S. 533 (2001).

In light of the development of the "government speech" doctrine, the Supreme Court has engaged in a certain amount of reinterpretation of some of the previous precedents on what have been characterized as "unconstitutional conditions" cases. The Supreme Court in *Velazquez*, for example, discussed the holding in *Rust v. Sullivan* in terms of "government speech":

The Court in *Rust* did not place explicit reliance on the rationale that the counseling activities of the doctors under Title X amounted to governmental speech; when interpreting the holding in later cases, however, we have explained *Rust* on this understanding. We have said that viewpoint-based funding decisions can be sustained in instances in which the government itself is the speaker, see *Board of Regents of Univ. Of Wis. System v. Southworth*, 529 U.S. 217, 229, 235 (2000), or instances, like *Rust*, in which the government "used private speakers to transmit specific information pertaining to its programs." *Rosenberger v. Rector and Visitors of the Univ. Of Va.,* 515 U.S. 819, 833 (1995).[132]

Along a somewhat similar line as the "government speech" concept may be situations where private organizations serve as what might be described as surrogates or stand-ins for government agencies, to perform governmental functions of administering and disbursing public funds. Thus, as noted above, in some of these instances federal law has treated these organizations, for purposes of restrictions on the *partisan* political activities of their employees, as "state or local" governmental agencies under the provisions of the part of the so-called "Hatch Act" which apply to employees of state and local governments.[133]

Unlike broad restrictions on recipients using their own resources and funds to engage in protected First Amendment conduct outside of the particular federally assisted programs, the particular restrictions concerning, for example, the Community Services Block Grant Program, or the Head Start program, appear to apply only within the federally assisted *program*, and do not appear to extend to organizations and their activities outside of and separate from such programs (that is, that do not use program funds, services or personnel connected to this program). Additionally, the existing statutory restrictions on programs and funds do not apply to "affiliate" or connected organizations which are not participating in the program.

[131] 531 U.S. at 542-543.

[132] 531 U.S. at 541. The Court in *Velazquez, supra*, at 543, also reinterpreted the finding in the Public Broadcasting case in terms of "government speech," and noted that, concerning the restriction on editorializing in public radio which it found impermissible in *Federal Communications Commission v. League of Women Voters of California*, 468 U.S. 364 (1984): "The First Amendment forbade the Government from using the forum in an unconventional way to suppress speech inherent in the nature of the medium."

[133] 5 U.S.C. §§ 1501 *et seq.* See discussion in this report, *infra* at pp. 16-18.

GOVERNMENTAL INTEREST PROMOTED BY THE LEGISLATION; LEAST RESTRICTIVE MEANS OF ACCOMPLISHING OBJECTIVE

The Supreme Court has found that while First Amendment rights are "fundamental, they are not in their nature absolute."[134] The Court has increasingly resorted to "balancing" conflicting interests of the government and private parties when possible limitations on First Amendment activities are somewhat indirect; when the governmental interest in the regulation is of a compelling enough nature; and when the statute is drawn with sufficient precision. When a provision of law limits, burdens, or interferes with protected First Amendment rights, the Supreme Court will generally examine the law and its purposes to determine initially if there are significant, "overriding" or "compelling" governmental interests in the restriction that outweigh the impositions on protected First Amendment rights. If there are such governmental interests in the restrictions on First Amendment activities, then the Court will examine whether the restriction is sufficiently narrowly tailored to promote those interests asserted as the statute's justification.

In cases involving the limitation of political advocacy in campaigns and the disclosure of lobbying activities, for example, the protection of basic governmental processes by disclosing the sources of pressures and influences on the legislative process,[135] and the prevention of the corruption of the electoral process and undue influences on candidates and officeholders which may accompany large cash payments and contributions to candidates and political parties,[136] have been found to be such important governmental interests which may justify in some cases certain limitations or burdens on First Amendment activities (including voter registration activities by political parties — when funded by unregulated amounts of "soft money" — shortly before a federal election).[137] Even while such interests have been found to be significant and important, however, the Court has struck down restrictions and direct or indirect limitations on advocacy speech and political activities which were not narrowly tailored to meet the objective of preventing undue influence or the appearance of corruption.[138]

[134] *Whitney v. California*, 274 U.S. 357, 373 (1927) [*J. Brandeis* concurring]; *Terminiello v. Chicago*, 337 U.S. 1, 4 (1949).

[135] *United States v. Harriss, supra.*

[136] *Buckley v. Valeo, supra.; McConnell v. Federal Election Commission,* 540 U.S. 93, 143 (2003), as to the Government's contention that the campaign act's restrictions on "soft money" contributions and certain expenditures "were necessary to prevent the actual and apparent corruption of federal candidates and officeholders," the Court noted: "Our cases have made clear that the prevention of corruption or its appearance constitutes a sufficiently important interest to justify political contribution limits." The Court also noted the legitimate governmental interest in preventing "undue influence on an officeholder's judgment, and the appearance of such influence." *Id.* at 150.

[137] *McConnell, supra* at 161-173.

[138] In terms of public or political advocacy, the Supreme Court has struck down as overly-broad and not sufficiently connected to the legitimate interest of preventing corruption of candidates and officeholders, for example, a federal law which would have limited the (continued...)

In the instance of legislation which would restrict some private parties who receive monies from the federal government from engaging in public advocacy, voter registration, and lobbying activities with their own non-governmental resources, it does not appear that the prevention of corruption of candidates or officeholders, or undue influences on basic governmental processes are necessarily the interests that are intended to be forwarded. Rather, it appears that the principal governmental purposes in such legislation would be two-fold: one would be to prevent the use and diversion of federal government funds for private lobbying, political, and public policy advocacy activities which are not authorized by Congress; and the second would be to prevent the federal government "subsidizing" lobbying, advocacy, or voter registration activities of private parties by providing such private parties with federal dollars for *other* purposes.

As to the governmental interest of not paying for private lobbying or political activities, clearly the federal government need not "pay for" nor directly "subsidize" the lobbying or political advocacy of private entities.[139] To that end, it should be noted, as discussed earlier, that current federal law and regulations already expressly prohibit the use of contract or grant funds by any governmental contractor or grantee for lobbying and political purposes, or the paying for or "charging off" of expenses for political advocacy, activities or lobbying to any government contract or grant. The federal government may clearly limit the use of the funds it appropriates in this way for the specific public purposes it desires.[140] Similarly, the government need not "subsidize," through such things as tax exemptions or specific deductions for lobbying, the private advocacy activities of organizations or persons. In *Cammarano*

v. United States, the Supreme Court noted that the denial of a tax deduction as a business expense for the lobbying expenses of a private entity was permissible because

> Petitioners are not being denied a tax deduction because they engage in
>
> constitutionally protected activities, but are simply being required to pay for
>
> those activities entirely out of their own pockets, as everyone else engaging in

[138] (...continued) amount of money private parties may independently spend on advocating the election or defeat of a candidate, *Buckley v. Valeo, supra* at 39-51; limitations on the amount of money the candidate or the candidate's family may spend of his or her own resources, *Buckley v. Valeo, supra* at 51-54; has struck down restrictions on the expenditure of private moneys by corporations concerning referenda and ballot issues, as opposed to expenditures on candidates, *First National Bank of Boston v. Bellotti*, 435 U.S. 765 (1978); and has struck down provisions of laws and interpretations which would limit advocacy groups which are non-stock, non-profit corporations from spending money to influence the election or defeat of federal candidates, *Federal Election Commission v. Massachusetts Citizens for Life, Inc.*, 479 U.S. 238 (1986); see also interpretation in *McConnell* that BCRA limitations on expenditures do not apply to "MCFL"organizations. 540 U.S. at 209-211.

[139] *Regan v. Taxation With Representation, supra* at 544-546: "... Congress is not required by the First Amendment to subsidize lobbying." *Cammarano v. United States,* 358 U.S. 498 (1959).

[140] *See* generally, *Cincinnati Soap Co. v. United States,* 301 U.S. 308, 321-322 (1937).

> similar activities is required to do under the provisions of the Internal Revenue
>
> Code.[141]

In the case of *Regan v. Taxation With Representation of Washington, supra*, the Supreme Court similarly approved the restrictions on "charitable," 501(c)(3) organizations' lobbying as a basis for their tax exemption, and the deductibility of contributions to them from the donor's federal income tax, since "Congress has merely refused to *pay for the lobbying out of public moneys.*"[142]

If the interest of the government in a legislative restriction is merely to avoid directly subsidizing or paying for private lobbying or political activities out of public monies, then the method of restriction in any proposed legislation which barred all privately funded advocacy by grant or contract recipients might arguably, in the first instance, be considered "over-inclusive" because it reaches activities, speech and conduct paid for completely with *private, non-federal* monies, as well as privately-funded activities wholly outside of the realm of the federal program. As such, the restriction may arguably be found, with respect to otherwise protected First Amendment speech and conduct, to be unnecessarily over-broad and burdensome on such First Amendment rights. As discussed by the Supreme Court in *FCC v. League of Women Voters, supra,* it may be argued that a less restrictive means to reach this goal of not paying for private lobbying or political activities out of government funds may be to enact and enforce more effective audits, restrictions, regulations, and accounting procedures prohibiting the use of any *federal funds* for such activities. This would reach the presumed goal of limiting the use of federal funds, but would not be a potentially overlybroad restriction that would encompass within its prohibition the exercise by private recipients of protected First Amendment speech and conduct financed entirely with their own resources, and would not punish entities for entering the public debate on community, civic and national issues by engaging in protected public advocacy.

A further interest of the government forwarded by legislation might also be to prevent an "indirect" subsidy for groups who engage in political advocacy by providing such groups with federal funds for *other* non-advocacy activities, studies, or services which the government desires. As such, this purpose is distinguished from the prevention of the use of government funds directly for lobbying or advocacy, or the "subsidy" for lobbying that a tax exemption for such activities or all activities of the organization would provide. The argument is that money is "fungible" and grants and contracts for proper public purposes to private groups "frees up" other non-federal money which the private grantee may use for any purposes, including lobbying or voter registration activities.

There maybe significant questions raised, however, as to whether a government grant or contract for one specific public purpose or service performed, or product provided, by the recipient is or may be considered a "subsidy" for *other*, private activities of the grant or contract recipient which are funded wholly by private, non-federal contributions and funds. The Supreme Court, in another context, has found

[141] 358 U.S. at 513. [142] *Regan v. Taxation With Representation, supra* at 545. Emphasis added.

that such a grant is *not* a subsidy of the other, non-federally funded activities. In *Committee for Public Education and Religious Liberty v. Regan,*[143] the Supreme Court specifically found that providing grant funds to a religious organization for one (secular) purpose, does *not* constitute a federal "subsidy" of the other, private, non-federally funded religious activities of the organization. Even the fact that federal grant funds to an organization for public purposes might arguably "free up" non-federal money for other, private activities which the government does not want to fund, does not make the federal grant or payment a subsidy of those other purposes. In specifically rejecting the "fungibility" of cash argument, the Supreme Court said,

None of our cases requires us to invalidate these reimbursements simply because they involve payments in cash. The Court "has not accepted the recurrent argument that all aid is forbidden because aid to one aspect of an institution frees it to spend its other resources on religious ends." *Hunt v. McNair,* 413 U.S. 734,743 (1973).[144]

The Supreme Court has thus expressly rejected this theory as a realistic or necessary outcome or result of government assistance of *some* activities of an organization vis-a-vis other, independent activities and, therefore, it is logical to assume that it would not necessarily be recognized as a "compelling" or "overriding" interest by the Court which could justify direct restrictions on protected First Amendment conduct that a private entity engages in with its own resources, outside of the government-sponsored program.

[143] 444 U.S. 646 (1980).

[144] 444 U.S. at 658. The Government also does not appear to be "subsidizing" the First Amendment activities of private parties as had been found by the courts in the past by, for example, providing a tax deduction for private parties who make contributions to an organization (and thus subsidizing the activities of the charity by loss of tax revenue for contributions supporting those activities), or by providing a direct tax deduction for monies expended for lobbying activities. *See*, e.g., discussion in *Regan* and *Cammarano, supra*.

LOBBYING CONGRESS: AN OVERVIEW OF LEGAL PROVISIONS AND CONGRESSIONAL ETHICS RULES[5]

This report is intended to provide a brief overview and summary of the federal laws, ethical rules and regulations which may be relevant to the activities of those who lobby the United States Congress. The report provides a summary discussion of the federal lobbying registration and disclosure requirements of the Lobbying Disclosure Act of 1995, the Foreign Agents Registration Act, the propriety of contingency fees for lobbying, restrictions on lobbying with federal funds, post-employment ("revolving door") lobbying activities by former federal officials, and House and Senate ethics rules which may be relevant to contacts with private lobbyists by Members, officers and employees of Congress.

Although the term "lobbying" may have developed a somewhat sinister and pejorative connotation over the years, the activities involved in lobbying are intertwined with fundamental First Amendment rights of speech, association and petition,[1] and may facilitate the exchange of important information and ideas between the government and private parties.[2] For those who act in a representative capacity for a client, lobbying the legislature for a change in the state of the law may be an important part of the services provided to the client. However, because of the substantial potential for *undue* or *wrongful* influence from those who are paid to influence the legislative process, there has developed a body of law and rules to regulate lobbying activities, as well as to regulate the activities of public officials in their interactions with those who lobby, particularly with reference to the potentially corrupting effect of large sums of money on the legislative process.[3] There are several federal statutory laws, as well as Rules of the House and Senate, which either apply to lobbying specifically, or which may be relevant to congressional lobbyists because the provisions bear upon a Member's or employee's dealings with those who attempt to influence the legislative process.

[1]*United States v. Harriss,* 347 U.S. 612 (1954); *United States v. Rumely,* 345 U.S. 41 (1953); *Eastern Railroad Presidents Conference v. Noerr Motor Freight, Inc.,* 365 U.S. 127, 137-138 (1961); *note* generally, Hope Eastman, *Lobbying: A Constitutionally Protected Right*, American Enterprise Institute for Public Policy Research (1977).

[2]S. Rept. 99-161, 99th Cong., 2d Sess., "Congress and Pressure Groups: Lobbying in a Modern Democracy," Senate Committee on Governmental Affairs 1-14 (1986).

[3]The Supreme Court expressed concern as early as 1853 with paid lobbying activities and undue influence, finding that a secret contingency contract for lobbying was void and unenforceable as a matter of public policy because it "tends to corrupt or contaminate, by improper influences, the integrity of our ... political institutions" by "creat[ing] and bring[ing] into operation undue influences" by those "stimulated to active partisanship by the strong lure of high profit." *Marshall v. Baltimore & Ohio Railroad,* 57 U.S. 314, 333-334 (1853).

THE LOBBYING DISCLOSURE ACT OF 1995

In 1995 Congress completely rewrote the 50-year old law (the Federal Regulation of Lobbying Act of 1946) which had required certain registrations and disclosures of lobbying activities directed at Members of Congress. The new "Lobbying Disclosure Act of 1995"[4] provides more specific thresholds, and clearer and broader definitions of "lobbyist" and "lobbying" activities and contacts which will trigger the requirements for the registration and reporting of persons who are compensated to engage in lobbying.

[5] Jack Maskell Legislative Attorney American Law Division *Congressional Research Service The Library of Congress* and Congressional Ethics Rules

The Lobbying Disclosure Act of 1995 is directed at so-called "professional lobbyists," that is, those who are compensated to engage in certain lobbying activities on behalf of a client or an employer.[5] In addition to covering only those who are paid to lobby, the initial "triggering" provisions of the law cover only lobbying activities which may be described as "direct" contacts with covered officials. The law's registration requirements are not separately triggered by "grass roots" lobbying activities. That is, an organization which engages *only* in "grass roots" lobbying, regardless of the extent of "grass roots" lobbying activities, will not be required to register its members, officers or employees who engage in such activities.[6]

The Act recognizes generally two kinds of lobbyists: (1) "in house" lobbyists of an organization or business – employees of that organization or business who are compensated, at least in part, to lobby on its behalf; and (2) "outside" lobbyists – members of a lobbying firm, partnership, or sole proprietorship that engage in lobbying for "outside" clients. When registration is required from a paid "lobbyist" under the lobbying law, such registration is done by the organization or the lobbying firm. That is, a business or organization which has employees who engage in a certain amount of lobbying on its behalf ("in-house" lobbyists), must register and identify its employee/lobbyists. "Lobbying firms" or entities (including a sole practitioner) who lobby or have employees, partners or associates who lobby for "outside" clients, must file a separate registration for each client represented, identifying such things as the lobbyist, the client and the issues.

The previous lobby registration statute enacted in 1946, as interpreted by the Supreme Court in *United States v. Harriss, supra,* was criticized for employing a general and equivocal test for registration and reporting, concerning whether lobbying

[4]P.L. 104-65, December 19, 1995, 109 Stat. 691, as amended by the Lobbying Disclosure Technical Amendments Act, P.L. 105-166, April 6, 1998.

[5]*See* H. R. Rpt. 104-339, 104th Cong., 1st Sess., at 2 (1995).

[6]Once an organization has met the threshold requirements for "direct" lobbying and is registered, certain background activities and efforts "in support of" its direct "lobbying contacts," which may include activities which also support other activities or communications which are *not* lobbying contacts, such as grass roots lobbying efforts, may need to be disclosed generally as "lobbying activities." 2 U.S.C. § 1602(7). *Note* H.R. Rpt. No. 104339, 104th Cong.,1st Sess., "Lobbying Disclosure Act of 1995," 13-14 (1995). The instructions of the Clerk of the House and Secretary of the Senate also note that "Communications excepted by Section 3(8)(B) will constitute 'lobbying activities' if they are in support of other communications which constitute 'lobbying contacts.'"

was one's "main" or "principal purpose," and for providing no specific thresholds, or clear measures to trigger the requirements of the law. The new Lobbying Disclosure Act of 1995, however, provides more specific thresholds, triggering measures, and *de minimis* amounts.

Expenditure Threshold. Initially, it should be noted that there is a *de minimis* expense threshold below which the requirement for registration by organizations and lobbying groups or firms will not be triggered. Any organization which uses its own employees as lobbyists (in-house lobbyists) will not need to register if the organization's total expenses for lobbying activities do not exceed $22,500 in a six-month period.[7] A lobbying firm (including a self-employed individual) does not need to register for a particular "outside" client if its total income from that client for lobbying related matters does not exceed $5,500 in a six month filing period.[8]

Contact and Time Threshold. A "lobbyist" under the disclosure law is an organization's employee who engages in lobbying, or is someone who works on his or her own or for a lobbying firm and is retained by an organization or entity to lobby on its behalf, who makes more than one "lobbying contact," and spends at least 20% of his or her total time for that employer or client on "lobbying activities" over a six-month period.[9] A "lobbying contact" is an oral or written communication to a covered official, including a Member of Congress, congressional staff, and certain senior executive branch officials, with respect to the formulation, modification or adoption of a federal law, rule, regulation or policy. The term "lobbying activities" is broader than "lobbying contacts," and includes "lobbying contacts" as well as background activities and other efforts in support of such lobbying contacts.

Items Disclosed on Registration. Under the Act a "lobbyist" needs to be registered within 45 days after making the requisite lobbying contacts or within 45 days of being employed to make such contacts, whichever is earlier. Registration will be on identical forms filed with the Secretary of the Senate and Clerk of the House. The information on the registrations will generally include identification of the lobbyist, the client or employer, and any organizations other than the client that contribute more than $10,000 for the lobbying activities in six months and play a major role in supervising or controlling the lobbying activities; an identification of any foreign entity that owns 20% of the client, controls the activities of the client or is an interested affiliate of the client; a list of the issues on which the registrant expects to engage in lobbying, and those on which he or she has already lobbied for the client or employer.

Reports. In addition to the *registration* of lobbyists, semi-annual reports, covering January 1 - June 30, and July 1 - December 31, are required to be filed. These reports will identify the lobbyist, clients and employers, and issues upon which

[7]2 U.S.C. § 1603(a)(3)(A)(i). The threshold amount is adjusted every four years, 2 U.S.C. § 1603(a)(3)(B), and was adjusted January 1, 2001.

[8]2 U.S.C. § 1603(a)(3)(A)(ii). The threshold amount is adjusted every four years, 2 U.S.C. § 1603(a)(3)(B), and was adjusted January 1, 2001.

[9]2 U.S.C. § 1602(10).

one lobbied, and are to provide a good faith estimate of lobbying costs, rounded to the nearest $20,000 (if expenses exceed $10,000).

Oral or Written Identifications to Officials Being Lobbied. The Act expressly requires that a lobbyist, upon the request of any "covered official" during an oral contact, provide an identification of his or her client, whether or not the lobbyist is registered under the Act, and a disclosure of any interests of foreign affiliates.[10] If a written lobbying contact is made, the lobbyist is required on his or her *own* to identify any foreign entity on whose behalf the contact is being made, and any foreign entity which owns 20% of the client or organization, controls or supervises the client, or is an affiliate with a direct interest in the lobbying activities.

Registration and Filing Information. Registrations, as well as the semi-annual reports from already registered lobbyists, are made to the Clerk of the House of Representatives, Legislative Resource Center, and to the Secretary of the Senate, Office of Public Records. Forms for registration and reporting, and detailed filing instructions for lobbying firms and for organizations with lobbyists are available from the offices of the Clerk of the House and the Secretary of the Senate, and may also be accessed on the Internet for the House at [http://clerkweb.house.gov] ; and for the Senate at [http://www.senate.gov/contacting/contact_lobby.html]. The reports and registrations made to these legislative offices are maintained as public records which may be researched and examined by the press, the public, by Members' offices, and have recently been made available on-line at [http://sopr.senate.gov] .

FOREIGN AGENTS REGISTRATION ACT

In addition to the required registrations under the new federal Lobbying Disclosure Act of 1995, the provisions of the Foreign Agents Registration Act (FARA)[11] may be relevant if one is acting for or on behalf of a foreign government or a foreign political party or entity, or other foreign entity, and is engaging in "lobbying" activities as part of the representation for that foreign client. As amended by the new Lobbying Disclosure Act, if one is representing the interests of a foreign government or a foreign political party, such agent must continue to register under the Foreign Agents Registration Act, but then need not register under the Lobbying Disclosure Act. However, persons representing *private* foreign entities, and who lobby in the United States, should register under the Lobbying Disclosure Act rather than the Foreign Agents Registration Act. Those properly registered under the Lobbying Disclosure Act are exempt from registering under the Foreign Agents Registration Act.

The Foreign Agents Registration Act, as amended by the Lobbying Disclosure Act of 1995, and its amendments, provides that "agents of a foreign principal"[12] must file a registration statement not with the

Clerk of the House or the Secretary of the Senate, but with the Attorney General listing detailed financial and business

[10]2 U.S.C. § 1609. [11]*See* now 22 U.S.C. §§ 611 *et seq.* [12]22 U.S.C. § 611(b) and (c).

information,[13] must file and label all informational materials,[14] and keep detailed books and records open to inspection by public officials.[15] An "agent" is defined in the law as one who acts "at the order, request, or under the direction or control, of a foreign principal, or of a person any of whose activities are directly or indirectly supervised, directed, controlled, financed, or subsidized in whole or in part by a foreign principal ...."[16]

The types of activities on behalf of a "foreign principal" that would subject an "agent" to coverage under the Act include "political activities"; acting as a "public relations counsel," publicity agent or political consultant; collecting or disbursing contributions for the foreign principal; and representing the interests of the foreign principal "before any agency or official of the Government of the United States."[17] The term "political activities" also includes activities which may generally be characterized as among those commonly considered to be "lobbying" activities:

The term "political activities" means any activity that the person engaging in believes will, or that the person intends to, in any way influence any agency or official of the Government of the United States or any section of the public within the United States with reference to formulating, adopting, or changing the domestic or foreign policies of the United States . . . .[18]

There are several exemptions to the registration and record-keeping requirements of the Foreign Agents Registration Act, including exemptions for the official activities of diplomats and consular officers and the activities of certain officials of foreign governments; exemptions for persons engaging only in"private and nonpolitical activities in furtherance of bona fide trade or commerce" for such foreign principal; and an exemption for certain legal representation of foreign principals by attorneys in judicial or on-the-record, formal agency proceedings.[19]

CONTINGENCY FEES FOR LOBBYING

A contingency fee arrangement for "lobbying" activities before Congress is one in which the payment for such activities is contingent upon the success of the lobbying efforts to influence the legislative process to have legislation adopted or defeated in the United States Congress. There is no statute under federal law which expressly addresses the issue of contingency fees with respect to all lobbying activities before the Congress. Contingency fees may be expressly barred, however, under certain

[13]22 U.S.C. § 612. [14]22 U.S.C. § 614. The Lobbying Disclosure Act of 1995 eliminated the use of and the

definition of the term "political propaganda," now employing the more neutral term "informational material." [15]22 U.S.C. § 615. [16]22 U.S.C. § 611(c)(1). [17]22 U.S.C. § 611(c)(1)(i)-(iv). [18]22 U.S.C. § 611(o). [19]22 U.S.C. § 613.

circumstances. There is in federal law, for example, an express prohibition against contingency fee arrangements with respect to seeking certain contracts with the agencies of the Federal Government.[20] Activities which might generally or colloquially be called "lobbying," but which involve making representations on behalf of private parties before federal agencies to obtain certain government contracts, may thus be subject to the contingency prohibitions.[21]

Contingency fees are also prohibited for lobbying the Congress by persons who must register as agents of foreign principals under the Foreign Agents Registration Act. The prohibition is upon agreements where the amount of payment "is contingent in whole or in part upon the success of any political activities carried on by such agent."[22] The covered "political activities" of such agents under the Foreign Agents Registration Act include any activity which the agent "intends to, in any way influence any agency or official of the Government of the United States ... with reference to formulating, adopting, or changing the domestic or foreign policies of the United States ...," and thus includes the activities of "lobbying" Members and staff of Congress on legislation or appropriations.[23]

Although there is no general federal law expressly barring all contingency fees for successful lobbying before Congress, there is a long history of judicial precedent and traditional judicial opinion which indicates that such contingency fee arrangements, when in reference to "lobbying" and the use of influence before a legislature on general legislation, are void from their origin (*ab initio*) for public policy reasons, and therefore would be denied enforcement in the courts.[24] Explaining the reason for such policy, Justice Oliver Wendell Holmes, writing for the Court,

[20]41 U.S.C. § 254(a), 10 U.S.C. § 2306(b) (defense contracts). *Note* Federal Acquisition Regulations [FAR], 48 C.F.R. § 3.400 *et seq.* Negotiated solicitations and contracts are required to contain a contractor warranty that no contingent fees were paid. FAR, 48 C.F.R. § 52.203-5.

[21]The reason for this contingency fee ban has been explained as follows: "Contractors' arrangements to pay contingent fees for soliciting or obtaining Government contracts have long been considered contrary to public policy because such arrangements may lead to attempted or actual exercise of improper influence ...." Nash, Schooner, & O'Brien, *The Government Contract Reference Book, A Comprehensive Guide to the Language of Procurement*, Second Edition, at 119 (George Washington University 1998).

[22]22 U.S.C. § 618(h).

[23]22 U.S.C. § 611(o).

[24] "Contingent fee arrangements, conditioned on the obtaining of favorable legislation, are unenforceable in the courts." *Luff v. Luff*, 267 F.2d 643, 646 (D.C.Cir. 1959). *See Marshall*

v.

Baltimore & Ohio R.R., *supra* at 336 (1853); *Tool Company v. Norris*, 69 U.S. (2 Wall.) 45, 54 (1864); *Trist v. Child*, 88 U.S. (21 Wall.) 441 (1874); *Hazelton v. Sheckells*, 202 U.S. 71 (1906); *Noonan v. Gilbert*, 68 F.2d 775 (D.C.Cir. 1934); *Brown v. Gesellschaft Fur Drahtlose Telegraphie*, 104 F.2d 227, 229 (D.C.Cir. 1939), *cert denied* 307 U.S. 640 (1939); *Ewing v. National Airport Corporation*, 115 F.2d 859, 860 (4th Cir. 1940), *cert. denied* 312 U.S. 705 (1941); *note* also *Florida League of Professional Lobbyists, Inc.*

v.

Meggs, 87 F.3d 457 (11th Cir. 1996), upholding against constitutional challenge Florida statute barring contingency fees.

noted that it was the "tendency" in such contract agreements to provide incentives towards corruption, as such agreements "invited and tended to induce improper solicitations ... intensified ... by the contingency of the reward."[25] It should be noted that the laws of 39 States prohibit outright, and the laws of a 40th State limit the amount of, contingency fees for successful legislative lobbying,[26] and this may further limit the probability of judicial enforcement of a contingency fee contract, even one for lobbying the Congress.

While the tradition and practice has been for the courts to look disfavorably upon contingency fee arrangements for successfully influencing public officials in performing discretionary actions, it should be noted that in some instances contingency fee contracts based on the success of legislation have been upheld and enforced in a few courts when the duties contracted for were professional services that did not involve traditional, statutorily defined "lobbying" or the use of personal influence before the legislature,[27] or where the client had a legitimate claim or legal right to be asserted in a matter before the legislature (*e.g.*, "debt legislation").[28]

As noted in the instructions of the Clerk of the House and Secretary of the Senate, if contingency fees are permitted and used in a lobbying agreement with respect to lobbying before the Congress, the making of such a contract for a contingent fee "triggers a registration requirement at inception." The fee is disclosed in semi-annual reports in the period "that the registrant becomes entitled to it."

FEDERAL FUNDS SUBSIDIZING OR REIMBURSING LOBBYING

There exist general restrictions under federal law and regulations against the use of federal funds for lobbying activities. Officers and employees of the federal government are expressly barred from using funds appropriated for their agencies for the purposes of certain types of "lobbying" activities and publicity campaigns directed at influencing the Congress on pending legislation.[29] Contractors and grantees of the

[25]*Hazelton v. Sheckells,* 202 U.S. 71, 79 (1906).

[26]*Note* survey of State laws in CRS Congressional Distribution Memorandum, "Contingency Fees for Lobbying Activities," September 21, 2000.

[27]*Weinstein v. Palmer,*32 NW2d 154 (Minn. 1948); *Johnston v. J.R. Watkins Co.,* 157 P.2d 755, 757 (Okla. 1945): "A contract for purely professional services such as drafting a petition for an act, attending to the taking of testimony, collecting facts ..." is not within Oklahoma's statutory ban on "lobbying" on a contingent fee basis.

[28]As to as "debt legislation" and claims (as opposed to general or "favor legislation"), *see* discussion in *Brown v. Gesellschaft, supra* at 229; *Grover v. Merritt Development Co.,* 47

F. Supp. 309 (D.Minn. 1942); and 51 Am Jur. 2d, "Lobbying," § 4 at 995, *citing State ex rel. Hunt v. Okanogan County*, 153 Wash 399, 280 P 31; *Hollister v. Ulvi*, 199 Minn 269, 271 NW 493; *Stansell v. Roach,* 147 Tenn 183, 246 SW 520.

[29]18 U.S.C. § 1913; *note also* general rider in Treasury, Postal Service and General Governmental Appropriations Acts, and riders on individual yearly appropriations acts. Generally, such prohibited activities would not include *direct* contacts by executive officials to Members or staff of Congress, but rather may reach costly letter-writing or similar (continued...)

federal government may not be reimbursed out of federal contract or grant money for their lobbying activities, unless authorized by Congress, under the provisions of the Federal Acquisition Regulations (FAR) drafted to encompass the principles set out in an earlier circular from the Office of Management and Budget.[30]

Under the guidelines of provisions known as the "Byrd Amendment," as amended by the Lobbying Disclosure Act of 1995, federal grantees, contractors, recipients of federal loans or those with cooperative agreements with the federal government, are also prohibited by law from using federal monies to "lobby" the Congress, federal agencies or their employees with respect to the awarding of federal contracts, the making of any grants or loans, the entering into cooperative agreements, or the extension, modification or renewal of these types of awards.[31] Federal contractors, grantees and those receiving federal loans and cooperative agreements must also report lobbying expenditures from non-federal sources which they used to obtain such federal program monies or contracts.[32]

Charitable organizations, including religious organizations, which are exempt from taxation under section 501(c)(3) of the Internal Revenue Code (organizations to which contributions may be tax-deductible for the donor under § 170(c)(2)), are limited in the amount of lobbying in which they may engage if they wish to preserve this preferred tax-exempt status from the federal government.[33]

Section 18 of the Lobbying Disclosure Act of 1995 places statutory restrictions upon the lobbying activities of certain non-profit organizations which are tax-exempt under section 501(c)(4) of the Internal Revenue Code.

This provision, which is commonly called the "Simpson Amendment," prohibits section 501(c)(4) social welfare organizations from engaging in any "lobbying activities," even with their own

[29](...continued) publicity campaigns directed at the public expressly urging the public to contact Members of Congress about legislation.

[30]48 C.F.R. §§ 31.205-22; 31.701 *et seq.*; note OMB Circular A-122, ¶B21, as added 49 F.R. 18276 (1984).

[31]31 U.S.C. § 1352(a).

[32]31 U.S.C. § 1352(b). See common agency regulations implementing "Byrd Amendment," at 55 F.R. 6735-6756 (February 26, 1990).

[33]26 U.S.C. §§ 501(c)(3), 501(h), 4911, 6033; *see* IRS Regulations at 55 F.R. 35579-35620 (August 31, 1990), effecting 26 C.F.R. Parts 1, 7, 20, 25, 53, 56, and 602. The Supreme Court has upheld such loss of special tax-exempt privilege for "substantial" lobbying noting that although lobbying is a protected right, and although the government may not indirectly punish an organization for exercising its constitutional rights by denying benefits to those who exercise them, lobbying activities are not one of the contemplated "exempt functions" of these organizations for which they have received the preferred tax status, and that Congress does not have to "subsidize" such lobbying activities of private organizations through preferred tax status of receiving deductible contributions if it does not choose to do so. *Regan v. Taxation With Representation of Washington*, 461 U.S. 540, 544-546 (1983).

private funds, if the organization receives any federal grant, loan, or award.[34] The legislative history of the provision clearly indicates, however, that a 501(c)(4) organization may separately incorporate an affiliated 501(c)(4), which willnot receive any federal funds, and which could engage in unlimited lobbying.[35] The method of separately incorporating an affiliate to lobby, which was described by the amendment's sponsor as "splitting," was apparently intended to place a degree of separation between federal money and private lobbying while permitting an organization to have a voice through which to exercise its protected First Amendment rights of speech, expression and petition: "If they decided to split into two separate 501(c)(4)'s, they could have one organization which could both receive funds and lobby without limits."[36]

It may also be noted that while 501(c)(4)'s which receive certain federal funds may not engage in "lobbying activities," the term "lobbying activities" as used in that prohibition is expressly defined in that law to include only direct "lobbying contacts and efforts in support of such contacts," such as preparation, planning, research and other background work intended for use in such contacts.[37] Organizations which engage *only* in grass roots lobbying and public advocacy, and do not make direct contacts or communications with covered officials, would therefore not appear to be engaging in any prohibited "lobbying activities" as defined under this provision.

POST-EMPLOYMENT LOBBYING BY FEDERAL OFFICIALS

There are various "post-employment" or "revolving door" conflict of interest restrictions upon certain officers and employees of the Federal Government which may work to restrict their lobbying of the Congress on particular matters or for a certain period of time after such officials leave office. In addition to the "switching sides" restrictions which apply generally to all former executive branch employees representing private parties before officers and employees of the executive branch in matters on which the employee had worked or had authority over while with the Government,[38] there are certain so-called "cooling off" or "no contact" periods which may apply to *any* matter before one's former agency, department or branch of Government, regardless of whether or not one had worked on it while with the

[34]2 U.S.C. § 1611.

[35]H. R. Rpt. 104-339, *supra* at 24.

[36]141 *Congressional Record* 20045, 20053, July 24, 1995, statements of Senator Simpson.

[37]2 U.S.C. § 1602(7).

[38]All officers and employees of the executive branch are prohibited from "switching sides" on a specific case or matter, that is, they are prohibited from ever making "with the intent to influence" any communication or appearance on behalf of a private party before a federal department or agency on a particular matter involving specific parties if the employee had worked personally and substantially on that matter for the government while in its employ. 18 U.S.C. § 207(a)(1). A similar restriction on "switching sides" applies for two years to executive branch personnel who, although they did not work on the matter personally or substantially, had such particular matter involving specific parties under their official responsibility while with the government. 18 U.S.C. § 207(a)(2). See also definitions at 18

U.S.C. § 207(i)(1)(A).

Government. As to those restrictions relevant to lobbying the Congress,[39] the statute prohibits former Members of Congress from making representations, that is, appearances or communications with intent to influence, on any matter before any Member, officer or employee of the entire legislative branch of government for one year after the Member leaves office.[40] The staff of a Member, if compensated above a particular rate, may not "lobby" that Member or his or her staff for one year after leaving employment, and covered staff of committees may not lobby any Members or staff of that committee for one year after leaving employment.[41]

No federal employee or official who has participated in trade or treaty negotiations on behalf of the United States and had access to certain non-public information may, for one year after leaving office, represent, aid or advise any other person with respect to such negotiations.[42] In addition, those high level Government officials who are subject to the one-year "cooling off" or "no contact" bans, are also prohibited, for one year after leaving their positions, from lobbying for, representing, aiding, or advising any official foreign entity with the intent to influence the official actions of any officer or employee of a department or agency of the United States, including Members of Congress.[43]

CONGRESSIONAL ETHICS RULES

In addition to statutory laws applicable to lobbyists and lobbying, there are internal congressional rules in both the House and the Senate which establish and provide ethical guidelines and standards of conduct for Members, officers and employees of those bodies. While these are internal rules and are not necessarily enforceable against, nor applicable directly to private parties who lobby the Congress, these House and Senate Rules will obviously impact and influence the activities and conduct of lobbyists. Ethical guidelines and professional standards for lobbyists expressed by voluntary organizations of professional lobbyists may contain a specific requirement for compliance with congressional ethical standards. The guidelines adopted by the American League of Lobbyists, for example, provide in part that: "A lobbyist should not cause a public official to violate any law, regulation or rule

[39]Restrictions on high level executive branch officials prohibit such officials from making representational communications and appearances before their former agencies for one year after leaving the Government, and restrict for one year certain very high level officials from making representational or advocacy communications or appearances before their former agency *and* to any individual who occupies an executive level position anywhere in the executive branch. 18 U.S.C. § 207(c) and (d).

[40]18 U.S.C. § 207(e)(1).

[41]18 U.S.C. § 207(e)(2),(3). Senate Rules also still apply to Members and staff regarding one-year post-employment bans on lobbying. All staff of a Senator, if they are registered lobbyists or paid by registered lobbyists, are prohibited from lobbying that Member and staff for one year, and all such former committee staff are barred for one year after leaving from lobbying the Members and staff of that committee. Senate Rule 37, cl. 9.

[42]18 U.S.C. § 207(b).

[43]18 U.S.C. § 207(f); *note* definitions at 18 U.S.C. § 207(i)(1)(B).

applicable to such public official."[44] It is probably stating the obvious to note that conduct and pressures exerted by a lobbyist which place a Member of Congress or a congressional staffer in a compromising ethical position may in the long run be counterproductive to one's lobbying goals.

GIFTS.

Restrictive rules on the acceptance of gifts from private sources were adopted by both Houses of Congress for their Members and staff in 1995, and the House Rules were amended in 1999.[45] The Rules generally prohibit the receipt or solicitation of most gifts by Members, officers and employees of the Congress from private sources, except in those circumstances expressly permitted in the applicable Senate or House Rule. Although the general rule is that all gifts are prohibited, the House and Senate Rules list over 20 express exceptions to the gift prohibition.

The House and Senate gift rules act, in effect, as both an implementation and exceptions to the statutory gift provisions enacted into law in 1989, as part of the Ethics Reform Act of 1989, prohibiting the solicitation or receipt of gifts from any person doing business with or seeking action from one's agency, or who is affected by the performance of one's official duties.[46] Since the exceptions in the House and Senate gift rules allow for the *receipt* of gifts in certain circumstances, but do not authorize the *solicitation* of any such gifts, Members, officers and employees are still prohibited from soliciting gifts from those doing business with or seeking action from the Congress. This discussion is intended only as a summary and overview of the gift restrictions. For specific fact situations, and details on the prohibitions, reference should be made to the actual language of the applicable House or Senate Rule, and to interpretations of the House Committee on Standards of Official Conduct or the Senate Select Committee on Ethics.

General Restriction. The House and Senate Rules now provide that Members, employees and officers of the House or Senate may not accept gifts from *any* source, except in narrowly defined circumstances expressly set out in the respective Rules.

The limitations and prohibitions in these Rules apply not only to gifts given directly to the Member, officer or employee of the House or Senate, but also gifts to a family member of the Member, officer or employee, if the gift is given "with the knowledge and acquiescence" of the Member, officer or employee, and the Member, officer or employee "has reason to believe the gift was given because of" his or her official position.[47]

[44]American League of Lobbyists, "Code of Ethics," Article 2, Section 2.2, adopted on

February 28, 2000. [45]S. Res. 158, 104th Cong. (July 28, 1995); H. Res. 250, 104th Cong. (November 16, 1995), *see* H. Res. 9, 106th Cong., January 6, 1999, providing for *de minimis* exception.

[46]P.L. 101-194, Section 303, 5 U.S.C. § 7353; specifically 5 U.S.C. § 7353(b)(1). [47]House Rule 25, cl. 5(a)(2)(B)(i); Senate Rule 35, cl. 1(b)(2)(A).

Gifts From Lobbyists. While gifts from all private sources are generally covered by the prohibitions and restrictions of the House and Senate gift rules, the provisions may apply to gifts from lobbyists on an even more restrictive basis, as *some* of the exceptions made to the rules will not exempt gifts from registered lobbyists or from agents of foreign principals registered under the Foreign Agents Registration Act. Specifically, while a lobbyist or foreign agent may be a "relative" or a "personal friend" of a Member, officer and employee, and may thus fit within one of those two exceptions to the gift ban, the "personal hospitality" of a lobbyist or a foreign agent is *not* separately exempt from the rules prohibitions, and thus Members and employees may not accept meals or lodging in the home of a lobbyist solely under the "personal hospitality" exemption.[48] Similarly, while contributions to an authorized legal defense fund are permitted from anyone as an express exemption to the gifts rules, such contributions may *not* be received from lobbyists or foreign agents under that exemption;[49] nor may necessary travel or transportation expenses for "fact finding" or other such events in connection with official duties be accepted from lobbyists or from foreign agents.[50]

Lobbyists and agents of foreign principals are expressly prohibited from providing anything to an entity or organization that is "maintained or controlled" by a Member, officer or employee;[51] are prohibited from making charitable contributions on the basis of a recommendation or designation of a Member, officer or employee (other than a contribution in lieu of an honorarium if properly reported within 30 days);[52] and may not make any contribution or expenditure relating to a conference or retreat or the like sponsored by or affiliated with an official congressional organization for or on behalf of Members, officers or employees.[53]

De Minimis Exception. Both the House and Senate Rules provide a *de minimis* exception for gifts from private sources, and allow for the acceptance of a gift (including the gift of a meal) if the gift has a value of less than $50.[54] Gifts aggregating $100 or more in a year from any one source, however, may not be accepted. Any gift of $10 or more will be counted toward the yearly aggregate, but no specific accounting or formal record keeping for all such gifts of $10 or more is expressly required by the Rules. Certain items of "nominal value" or with "little intrinsic value," such as greeting cards, baseball caps and T-shirts, are also expressly exempt from the gifts limitation.[55]

[48]House Rule 25, cl. 5(a)(3)(P); Senate Rule 35, cl. 1(c)(17); *see infra* p. 14. [49]House Rule 25, cl. 5(a)(3)(E) and cl. 5(c)(3); Senate Rule 35, cl. 1(c)(5) and cl. 3(c). [50]House Rule 25, cl. 5(b)(1)(A); Senate Rule 35, cl. 2(a)(1). [51]House Rule 25, cl. 5(c)(1); Senate Rule 35, cl. 3(a). [52]House Rule 25, cl. 5(c)(2) and (d); Senate Rule 35, cl. 3(b) and 4. [53]House Rule 25, cl. 5(c)(4); Senate Rule 35, cl. 3(d). [54]House Rule 25, cl. 5(a)(1)(B); Senate Rule 35, cl. 1(a)(2). [55]House Rule 25, cl. 5(a)(3)(W); Senate Rule 35, cl. 1(c)(23).

Exception for Gifts from Family and Friends. One of the major categories of exemption from the strict gifts prohibitions are gifts from one's relatives, and gifts from personal friends. The House and Senate gift bans, seeking not to unduly interfere with normal family and personal relationships, allow the receipt and exchange of gifts from and between family members.[56]

Similarly, Members, officer and employees may continue to exchange gifts with or receive gifts from personal friends.[57] If a gift from a personal friend is to exceed $250 in value, however, the Member, officer or employee must get a written determination from the House Committee on Standards of Official Conduct in the House, or the Senate Select Committee on Ethics in the Senate, that the exception still applies.[58] In an effort not to create too large a potential "loophole" within the gifts rules by allowing one to merely claim that any gift-giver is a "friend," the rules establish certain criteria or factors to be considered in determining whether one qualifies as a personal "friend," including whether the Member, officer or employee has a history of personal friendship and gift exchange with this individual; whether the individual in question paid personally for the gift, or was reimbursed or claimed a tax deduction for it; whether the Member, officer or employee knew that similar gifts were given by this individual to other Members, officer or employees.[59]

A person who is a lobbyist by profession, but is also a relative or a personal friend (as defined) of a Member of Congress or of a congressional staffer, may therefore continue to participate in normal gift giving and gift exchanges based on that personal relationship with his or her relative, friend or fiance(e).

Meals, Food and Refreshments. A meal provided to the Member, officer or employee is considered a "gift" to that Member, officer or employee, and may not be accepted unless it meets other specific exceptions.[60] Since there is a general exemption for gifts of less than $50, however, a meal may generally be accepted as long as the value of the meal is below that amount (and does not exceed the $100 yearly aggregate from that one source). When food or refreshments are offered simultaneously (same time and place) to both a Member, officer or employee and his or her spouse or dependent, only the food provided to the Member, officer or employee will be considered a "gift" for the purpose of figuring the amount of such a gift under the Rules.[61]

It should be noted also that under both the House and Senate Rules refreshments and food of "nominal value," when not part of a meal, are expressly exempt from the

[56]Family member is defined in the Ethics in Government Act to include a wide variety of relatives and specifically the fiance(e) of the Member, officer or employee. 5 U.S.C.A. App. 6, § 109(16). House Rule 25, cl.5(a)(3)(C); Senate Rule 35, cl. 1(c)(3).

[57]House Rule 25, cl. 5(a)(3)(D)(i); Senate Rule 35, cl. 1(c)(4)(A). [58]House Rule 25, cl. 5(a)(5); Senate Rule 35, cl. 1(e). [59]House Rule 25 cl.5(a)(3)(D)(ii)(I)-(III); Senate Rule 35,cl. 1(c)(4)(B)(i)-(iii). [60]*See* definition of "gift," House Rule 25, cl. 5(a)(2)(A); Senate Rule 35, cl. 1(b)(1). [61]House Rule 25, cl. 5(a)(2)(B)(ii); Senate Rule 35, cl. 1(b)(2)(B).

gifts restriction and may be accepted without violation of the gift rules.[62] This exception would appear to allow one to partake of refreshments, appetizers, or hors d'oeuvres commonly served at receptions and parties, without regard to the gift prohibition, and without regard to whether the sponsor is a "lobbyist," a lobbying organization, or an entity which employs lobbyists.

Although meals are generally included in the definition of a "gift," and although free meals from private individuals or organizations are not in themselves exempt from the gift ban, there are a number of situations and instances where a Member, officer or employee may accept such a meal under the House and Senate gift rules, even without regard to the $50 *de minimis* limitation. Members, officers, and employees would be able to accept such gifts of meals when in connection with attendance at a political fundraising event sponsored by a political organization;[63] from family and personal friends;[64] in connection with outside, private business employment activities, employment discussions with a prospective employer, or when provided by a political organization in connection with a campaign event sponsored by the political organization;[65] in the course of permissible "training" events when served to all attendees as an integral part of the event;[66] when an individual provides "personal hospitality" at his or her personal or family residence (but a registered lobbyist or agent of a foreign principal does not qualify for the personal hospitality exemption);[67] in connection with the permissible attendance at "widely attended" gatherings, including charitable events, when taken in a group setting;[68] or in connection with the acceptance of necessary expenses for approved "fact-finding" or officially connected conference expenses.[69]

Exception for Personal Hospitality. In addition to the exceptions for gifts from relatives and gifts made on the basis of "personal friendship," the House and Senate gift rules also exempt from the gift prohibitions certain gifts of "personal hospitality" provided by an individual who is not a registered lobbyist nor an agent of a foreign principal.[70] The personal hospitality must be provided by an individual, and not a corporation or an organization, for a non-business purpose at the personal residence or on property or facilities owned by the individual or his or her family.

Exception for Attendance at Widely Attended Gatherings. Members, officers or employees are expressly permitted, as an exception to the gift rules, to accept an offer of free attendance at a "widely attended" gathering, such as a

[62]House Rule 25, cl. 5(a)(3)(U); Senate Rule 35, cl. 1(c)(22). [63]House Rule 25, cl. 5(a)(3)(B); Senate Rule 35, cl. 1(c)(2). [64]House Rule 25, cl. 5(a)(3)(C) and (D); Senate Rule 35, cl. 1(c)(3) and (4). [65]House Rule 25, cl. 5(a)(3)(C)(i)-(iii); Senate Rule 35, cl. 1(c)(7)(A)-(C). [66]House Rule 25, cl. 5(a)(3)(L); Senate Rule 35, cl. 1(c)(13). [67]House Rule 25, cl. 5(a)(3)(P); Senate Rule 35, cl. 1(c)(17). [68]House Rule 25, cl. 5(a)(4); Senate Rule 35, cl. 1(d). [69]House Rule 25, cl. 5(b); Senate Rule 35, cl. 2. [70]House Rule 25, cl. 5(a)(3)(P); Senate Rule 35, cl. 1(c)(17).

"convention, conference, symposium, forum, panel discussion, dinner, viewing, reception, or similar event," when the free attendance is offered by the sponsor of the event, and when the Member, officer or employee is either to "participate" in the event, or, if the Member, officer or employee is not participating, when the event is deemed "appropriate to the performance of the official duties" or the representative function of the Member, officer or employee attending.[71] A House Member, officer or employee may also bring an accompanying individual to such an event,[72] and a Senator, officer or employee of the Senate may also bring an accompanying individual if others in attendance will be so accompanied, or when appropriate to assist in the representation of the Senate.[73] When permitted to attend, the "free attendance" which one may accept is intended to include the waiver of the conference or other fee, local transportation, and food, refreshments, entertainment and instructional material provided to all the attendees as an integral part of the event. The acceptance of entertainment or food collateral to the event, or not taken in a group setting, is not permitted as part of the exception, and would be considered as a gift and therefore within the gift limitations.[74]

Exception for Charitable Events. The attendance of a Member, officer or employee at a charitable event is generally treated as attendance at a "widely attended" gathering. That is, it appears that Members, officers and employees were intended to be able to accept (for themselves and an accompanying individual) free attendance at charitable events, including the waiver of entrance or other such fees, and the provision of meals, food, and entertainment provided as an integral part of the event to all attendees. In the House, the Member, officer or employee, however, is expressly prohibited from accepting "reimbursement for transportation or lodging" expenses (other than for local transportation) in connection with such event.[75] In the Senate, when a charitable event is *not* substantially recreational in nature (that is, when the event is not, for example, a celebrity golf, tennis, or ski event or the like), and when the Senator, officer or employee meets the requirements for "necessary" expenses for travel regarding "fact-finding" or other officially connected events, such "necessary" expenses may be accepted for charitable fund-raising events.[76]

Exception for Necessary Travel Expenses for "Fact-Finding" Events and Conferences. Members, officers and employees of the House and Senate may, under certain conditions and restrictions, continue to accept (from other than lobbyists or agents of a foreign principal) reimbursement or payment in kind for "necessary transportation, lodging and related expenses for travel" for such things as fact-finding trips, meetings, speeches, conferences or similar events "in connection

[71]House Rule 25, cl. 5(a)(3)(Q) and cl. 5(a)(4)(A)(i) and (ii); Senate Rule 35, cl. 1(c)(18) and

cl. 1(d)(1)(A) and (B). [72]House Rule 25, cl. 5(a)(4)(B). [73]Senate Rule 35, cl. 1(d)(2). [74]House Rule 25, cl. 5(a)(4)(D); Senate Rule 35, cl. 1(d)(4). [75]House Rule 25, cl.5(a)(4)(C). [76]Senate Rule 35, cl. 1(d)(3), and Senate Rule 35, cl. 2(a)-(e).

with the duties of the Member, officer or employee as an officeholder."[77] Such reimbursement, since it is in connection with the official duties of a Member or employee, is considered in theory to be a reimbursement to the House of Representatives or to the Senate, rather than a prohibited personal gift to the Member, officer or employee, when certain conditions and restrictions are observed.

Employees of the House or Senate must receive advance approval to accept any such reimbursements; and Members, officers and employees must provide a detailed disclosure of the expenses reimbursed within 30 days after the travel is completed.[78] In the House of Representatives, transportation expenses may not be accepted for travel for more than 4 days within the United States or 7 days exclusive of travel time outside of the United States, unless approved in advance by the House Committee on Standards of Official Conduct;[79] while in the Senate travel expenses for such events are authorized only for up to 3 days for travel within the United States and 7 days for foreign travel.[80]

The permission to accept "necessary" travel expenses for events "in connection with the duties of a Member, officer or employee as an officeholder" does not apply to any events "which are substantially recreational in nature."[81] The permissible expenditures which may be reimbursed under the exception are limited to "reasonable expenditures" for "transportation, lodging, conference fees and materials, and food and refreshments," and expressly do *not* extend to expenditures for "recreational activities," nor for expenditures for entertainment "other than that provided to all attendees as an integral part of the event."[82] In the House of Representatives, Members, officers and employees mayaccept permissible reimbursement expenses for such officially connected events for an accompanying spouse or child,[83] and in the Senate acceptable expenses may include the expenses for a Member's, officer's or employee's spouse or child if attendance is "appropriate to assist in the representation of the Senate."[84]

Other Exceptions. Other exceptions to the strict prohibition on the receipt of any gifts include: anything for which fair market value is paid or anything not used and promptly returned; political contributions or attendance at political fundraisers sponsored by a political organization; payments to legal defense funds (other than those from lobbyists and foreign agents); gifts from another Member, officer or employee of the Senate or House; food, refreshments, lodging, transportation and

[77]House Rule 25, cl. 5(b)(1), Senate Rule 35, cl. 2(a).

[78]House Rule 25, cl. 5(b)(1)(A)(i) and cl. 5(b)(2) and (3); Senate Rule 35, cl. 2(a)(1)(A) and

(B), cl. 2(b) and (c).

[79]House Rule 25, cl. 5(b)(4)(A).

[80]Senate Rule 35, cl. 2(d)(1).

[81]House Rule 25, cl. 5(b)(1)(B); Senate Rule 35, cl. 2(a)(2).

[82]House Rule 25, cl. 5(b)(4)(B) and (C); Senate Rule 35, cl. 2(d)(2) and (3).

[83]House Rule 25, cl. 5(b)(4)(D).

[84]Senate Rule 35, cl. 2(d)(4).

other benefits resulting from outside business or employment activities, from prospective employers, or provided by a political organization in connection with a fundraiser or campaign event; pensions and similar benefits from a former employer; informational materials sent to a Member's office in the form of books, articles, periodicals, written material, or tapes; awards or prizes in events open to the public; honorary degrees and nonmonetary awards for public service; training if in the interest of the House of Representatives or the Senate; bequests and inheritances; items which may be received under the Foreign Gifts and Decorations Act,[85] the Mutual Educational and Cultural Exchange Act,[86] or other statute; anything paid for by federal, State, or local government; opportunities and benefits generally available to the public or to a group of federal or government employees; a plaque, trophy or commemorative item; anything for which the House Committee on Standards of Official Conduct or the Senate Select Committee on Ethics provides a waiver; and home-State products donated to the Member primarily for promotional purposes such as display or free distribution, and which are of minimal value to any individual recipient.

HONORARIA, PRIVATE COMPENSATION.

It had been a somewhat common practice in the past, although subject to much criticism, for a "special interest" or lobbying group, or a group or organization represented by a lobbyist, to invite a Member of Congress or a senior staffer to speak or appear before the group in connection with subject matters of interest to the organization, and to offer the Member or congressional staffer an "honorarium" for the speech or personal appearance. Under ethics provisions in House and Senate Rules, however, the practice of receiving an "honorarium" for a speech, article, or an appearance is now flatly prohibited for all Members of the House and the Senate, Senate staff, and for senior House employees and officers.[87]

The honoraria prohibitions in the House and Senate exclude the costs of "actual and necessary" travel expenses provided or reimbursed by the sponsor of the event, that is, transportation and subsistence expenses incident to the event provided to the official and his or her spouse or family member may be accepted. In the Senate, a Senator may bring an employee acting as an aide to an event rather than a family member. A contribution to charity of up to $2,000 may generally be made by the

[85]5 U.S.C. § 7342.

[86]22 U.S.C. § 2458a.

[87]House Rule 25, cl. 1(a)(2); Senate Rule 36. House officers and employees compensated less than 120% of the minimum pay for a GS-15 may receive an honorarium if the subject matter is not directly related to their official duties, the payment is not made because of their status as House officials or employees, and the offering entity does not have interests substantially affected by the performance or non-performance of their official duties. Although the statutory honoraria ban was found unconstitutional for federal employees in *United States v. N.T.E.U.*, 513 U.S. 454 (1995), and although the Department of Justice has ruled that it will not enforce the statutory ban against any officer or employee even in the legislative or judicial branches of Government (*see* Office of Legal Counsel Opinion, February 26, 1996), Members and employees of the House and Senate still come within and are subject to the prohibitions in House and Senate Rules.

sponsor of the event in lieu of the payment of an honorarium to the member or employee, without violation of this provision or the new gift rule.[88]

The receipt of any outside earned income or compensation from private parties by Members and staff of Congress will encounter other restrictions and limitations. As a general standard, the congressional rules in the House and in the Senate prohibit a Member or an employee from receiving any compensation or allowing any compensation "to accrue to his beneficial interest from any source, the receipt of which would occur by virtue of influence improperly exerted from his position in Congress."[89] Other restrictions exist on the receipt of outside income, such as prohibitions on receiving any compensation (or certain gifts) from foreign governments;[90] Member of Congress contracts with the Federal Government or receipt of any benefits out of Federal Government contracts;[91] receiving compensation for representational services before federal agencies;[92] and tax restrictions concerning "self dealing" with "private foundations," which are the subject of certain tax restrictions.[93]

Earned income rules and restrictions enacted into law and provided for in House and Senate Rules provide that all Members of Congress and certain senior staff[94] are subject to an outside earned-income cap which is equal to 15% of the official salary of a level II in the Executive Schedule; and they may not (1) affiliate with a firm to provide compensated professional services involving a fiduciary relationship; (2) allow any such firm to use one's name; (3) practice a profession which involves a fiduciary relationship for compensation; (4) serve for compensation as an officer or board member of any association or corporation; or (5) receive compensation for teaching without prior approval of the Standards of Official Conduct Committee.[95] Income received over certain amounts, as well as certain gifts, and reimbursements for travel, must be publicly disclosed by the recipient official in annual personal financial

[88]Senate Rule 36, *see* §§ 501(c) and 505(3) of the Ethics in Government Act of 1978, as added by the Ethics Reform Act of 1989; Senate Rule 35, cl. 4; House Rule 25, cl. 1(c), and House Rule 25, cl. 4(b) and cl. 5(d).

[89]House Rule 23, cl. 3; Senate Rule 37, cl. I.

[90]Constitution, Article I, Section 9, Clause 8.

[91]18 U.S.C. §§ 431, 432; 41 U.S.C. § 22.

[92]18 U.S.C. § 203.

[93]26 U.S.C. §§ 4941, 4946.

[94]The limitations apply to non-career employees in the government who are compensated at a rate equal to or more than 120% of the base salary for a GS-15. 5 U.S.C. App., - Ethics in Government Act, § 501(a); House Rule 25, cl. 4(a); Senate Rule 36.

[95]5 U.S.C. App., -Ethics in Government Act, §§ 501(a), 502. Senate staff earning in excess of $25,000 are subject to somewhat similar limitations by Senate Rules, and may not affiliate with a firm or partnership to provide professional services for compensation; may not permit one's name to be used in such a form; may not practice a profession for compensation "to any extent" during regular office hours of the Senate; and may not be an officer or board member of any publicly held or regulated corporation, financial institution or business entity (does not include non-profit, tax-exempt organizations). Senate Rule 37, cl. 5 and 6.

disclosure statements required by the Ethics in Government Act of 1978, as amended.[96]

UNWRITTEN STANDARDS OF CONDUCT AND PROPRIETY.

It should be kept in mind that in addition to express written rules, either the House or the Senate may exercise its constitutional authority for the self-protection and integrity of the institution by disciplining a Member or employee of that body for conduct which violates no express House or Senate Rule or law, but which is found contrary to acceptable ethical norms and/or which tends to bring the institution into dishonor or disrepute.[97] The Senate, for example, has censured a Senator for placing a paid lobbyist for a trade association with interests in particular tariff legislation, on the staff of the committee considering such legislation, with access to the confidential committee material. In this censure of Senator Bingham in 1929 for conduct which violated no express rule or law, the resolution noted that the action of the Senator "while not the result of corrupt motives on the part of the Senator from Connecticut, is contrary to good morals and senatorial ethics and tends to bring the Senate into dishonor and disrepute ...."[98] The House of Representatives has disciplined Members based in part on violations of provisions of the "Code of Ethics for Government Service" which states, among other provisions, that an elected or appointed official in the government should not accept favors or benefits "under circumstances which may be construed by reasonable persons as influencing the performance of his government duties."[99]

Members, staff and those who deal with them on a professional basis must thus be cognizant not only of express ethics rules, regulations and statutory provisions, but must also be sensitive to the perceptions and appearances of impropriety, special access or favoritism that may result from particular transactions and activities.

OTHER STATUTORY CONSIDERATIONS

CAMPAIGN CONTRIBUTIONS.

Lobbyists are not as a class prohibited from making campaign contributions to the campaign of a Member of Congress, nor are there specific limitations on federal campaign contributions because one is a "lobbyist." However, with respect to campaign contributions in a federal election generally, it should be noted that cash

[96]5 U.S.C. App., Ethics in Government Act, §§ 101 *et seq.;* House Rule 26; Senate Rule 34.

[97]Constitution, Article I, Section 5. *Note* H.R.Rpt. 90-27, 90th Cong., 1st Sess. 24-26, 29 (1967); House Rule 23, cl. 1; *Ethics Manual for Members, Officers and Employees of the*

U.S. House of Representatives, 102d Cong., 2d Sess. 12-16 (1992); S. Res. 338, 88th Cong., 2d Sess., Sec. 2(a) (1964), Standing Orders of the Senate, *Senate Manual*, § 79; S.Rept. 832508, 83rd Cong., 2d Sess. 22 (1954); *Senate Ethics Manual,* 106th Cong., 2d Sess. 12-14 (2000).

[98]S. Res. 146, 71st Cong. (1929). *Note* S. Doc. No. 92-7, 92d Cong., 1st Sess., "Senate Election, Expulsion and Censure Cases from 1793 to 1972" (1972).

[99]72 Stat. Part II, B12, ¶5.

contributions over $100 are prohibited by federal law;[100] that political contributions from the treasury funds of corporations, national banks, labor unions, or from federal government contractors are prohibited by federal law;[101] that campaign contributions are prohibited from foreign nationals,[102] or by one in the name of another;[103] that there are limitations on amounts that may be contributed to federal candidates of $1,000 per election, primary or run-off from individuals, and $5,000 per election, primary or runoff from political action committees (multi-candidate committees);[104] that political contributions to federal candidates are required to be publicly reported by the recipient campaign committee;[105] and that no campaign contributions may be converted by a Member of Congress to personal use.[106]

BRIBERY, ILLEGAL GRATUITIES.

Whenever things of value are offered to a public official, consideration should be given to the federal criminal law provisions which concern bribery and illegal gratuities. Under the bribery law, a federal official may not "corruptly" receive or solicit, and no one may corruptly offer or give, anything of value "in return for ... being influenced in the performance of any official act."[107] The "corrupt" nature of the transaction is part of the required intent which is characteristic of a "bribe." This element of the offense – a corrupt agreement or bargain – has been described as requiring some express or implied *quid pro quo* involved in the transaction, that is, something given in exchange for something else.[108] The bribe under these circumstances must be shown to be the thing that is the "prime mover or producer of the official act" performed or agreed to be performed.[109] Even a campaign contribution could be the "thing of value" given in a bribe, since the recipient public official need not benefit personally from a bribe that is received by a third party, such as a campaign committee. In *United States v. Anderson,*[110] the court upheld the conviction of a registered lobbyist for a mail-order company for bribing a Senator with "campaign contributions" to vote on certain postal rate legislation, when the evidence was sufficient to indicate a "corrupt intent" to influence by means of such payments, as opposed to the permissible activity of merely giving "campaign

[100]2 U.S.C. § 441g. [101]2 U.S.C. §§ 441b, 441c. [102]2 U.S.C. § 441e. [103]2 U.S.C. § 441f. [104]2 U.S.C. § 441a. [105]2 U.S.C. § 434. [106]House Rule 23, cl. 6; Senate Rule 38, cl. 2; *note* 2 U.S.C. § 439a. [107]18 U.S.C. § 201, *see* specifically 18 U.S.C. § 201(b). [108] *United States v. Sun-Diamond Growers of California*, 526 U.S. 398, 404 (1999); *United*

States v. Brewster, 506 F.2d 62, 72 (D.C.Cir. 1974); *United States v. Arthur,* 544 F.2d 730, 734, 735 (4th Cir. 1976); *United States v. Tomblin,* 46 F.3d 1369, 1379 (5th Cir. 1995). [109]*United States v. Brewster, supra* at 72, 82. [110]509 F.2d 312 (D.C.Cir. 1974), *cert. denied,* 420 U.S. 991 (1975).

contributions inspired by the recipient's general position of support on particular legislation."[111]

In addition to the bribery clause, the so-called "illegal gratuities" section of the same statute prohibits the giving or the receipt of something of value, other than as provided by law, "for or because of" an official act done or to be done.[112] Campaign contributions given for a political candidate who is a federal officeholder are unlikely to be involved in the case of illegal gratuities, since the thing of value given in the case of an illegal gratuity (unlike for a bribe) must be received for the official "personally" or for himself.[113]

However, as to personal gifts to a public official, it should be noted that the "illegal gratuities" clause is less exacting than the bribery clause as to the required intent. The "illegal gratuities" section does not require a specific "corrupt" intent, nor a corrupt bargain or *quid pro quo* such that the gift or other thing of value is the "motivator" or the influence for the official act, as is required in the bribery provision.[114] Rather, the illegal gratuities provision requires merely that the thing of value given or received was "other than as provided by law," and was given or received "for or because of" some identifiable official act. Since the illegal gratuity need not be the motivator of an official act, nor is it required that the illegal gratuity be intended to influence an official act, an illegal gratuity may even be given *after* an act has already been performed, as a "thank you" or in appreciation for the official act. The Supreme Court explained the differing intents required in the two clauses as follows:

The distinguishing feature of each crime is its intent element. Bribery requires intent "to influence" an official act or "to be influenced" in an official act, while illegal gratuity requires only that the gratuity be given or accepted "for or because of" an official act. In other words, for bribery there must be a *quid pro quo* – a specific intent to give or receive something of value *in exchange* for an official act. An illegal gratuity, on the other hand, may constitute merely a reward

[111]*Id.* at 330-331. Political contributions to entities do not in themselves constitute bribes "even though many contributors hope that the official will act favorably because of their contributions." *United States v. Tomblin, supra* at 1379.

[112]18 U.S.C. § 201(c).

[113]*United States v. Brewster, supra* at 77. The statute was amended in 1986, P.L. 99-646, §46(f),(g), 100 Stat. 3601-3604, to provide technical amendments to the criminal code, including changing the terms "for himself" to "personally." There is no indication of an intent to change the substance of the elements of the offense. If facts are developed that contributions, ostensibly made to a third party or entity "for or because of" official acts done or to be done by a public official, were in fact used or expended in a manner to financially enrich or financially benefit the official personally, then it might be argued that such funds were received "personally" or "for himself." Contributions to a campaign committee, therefore, which are wrongfully converted to personal use and are used, for example, to pay for personal living expenses of a

public official, or other personal expenses such as transportation, clothing, or food, might arguably be considered payments received "personally" for the official.

[114]*Brewster, supra* at 72; *United States v. Sun-Diamond Growers, supra* at 404 - 405.

for some future act that the public official will take (and may have already

determined to take), or for a past act that he has already taken.[115]

Although no specific illegal bargain, or "corrupt" intent, in giving or receiving an illegal gratuity need be shown, there is nevertheless a criminal intent requirement embodied in the characterization "illegal gratuity" (the criminal receipt of a payment) as distinguished from a mere "gift" unrelated to any official act. That intent has been described as knowingly being compensated or rewarded (or intending to compensate or reward an official), other than as provided by law for one's salary, for an official governmental act already performed or to be performed in the future by the official.[116] While some cases in the circuits had gone so far as to find that a specific official act need not be contemplated or identified for a payment or gift to constitute an "illegal gratuity," as long as the payment or gift was given to a recipient who is in a "position to use his authority in a manner which could affect the gift giver,"[117] the Supreme Court in the *Sun-Diamond* case confirmed that such so-called "status gifts," unconnected to any identified official act, were not violative of the criminal illegal gratuities provision.[118] Such so-called "status gifts," without the requisite criminal intent of a connection to any official act, are regulated and controlled by federal regulations and administrative provisions for executive branch officers and employees,[119] and in the case of Members and employees of Congress are governed by the House and Senate Rules discussed above.

FURTHER ETHICAL CONSIDERATIONS FOR ATTORNEYS

As a profession, attorneys may be called upon more often than others to provide legislative representational services for clients. When lobbying the Congress, as in providing other professional services for a client, there are certain ethical rules, guidelines, and considerations which are unique to and need to be recognized and observed by attorneys.

The American Bar Association has promulgated *Model Rules of Professional Conduct*, which have been adopted in one form or another within the various jurisdictions. These rules discuss ethical considerations and norms for attorneys in not only representing clients before courts, but also in representing clients in nonadjudicatory matters, such as before a legislature:

[115]*United States v. Sun-Diamond Growers, supra* at 404 - 405.

[116]*United States v. Brewster, supra* at 81, 82, quoting earlier Supreme Court decision in *United States v. Brewster,* 408 U.S. 501, 527 (1972);*United States of Irwin*, 354 F.2d 192, 196 (2d Cir. 1965), *cert. denied,* 383 U.S. 967 (1966).

[117]*United States v. Niederberger*, 580 F.2d 63, 69 (3rd Cir. 1978), *cert. denied,* 439 U.S. 980 (1978); *United States v. Allessio*, 528 F.2d 1079, 1082 (9th Cir. 1976), *cert. denied,* 426

U.S. 94 (1976).

[118]*United States v. Sun-Diamond Growers, supra* at 406 -410. *See* also *United States v. Brewster,* 506 F.2d 62 (D.C.Cir. 1974).

[119]5 C.F.R. §§ 2635.201 *et seq.*, 5 U.S.C. § 7353.

RULE 3.9: Advocate in Non-adjudicative Proceedings

A lawyer representing a client before a legislative or administrative tribunal in a non-adjudicative proceeding shall disclose that the appearance is in a representative capacity and shall conform to the provisions of Rules 3.3(a) through (c), 3.4(a) through (c), and 3.5.

COMMENT:

In representation before bodies such as legislatures, municipal councils, and executive and administrative agencies acting in a rulemaking or policy-making capacity, lawyers present facts, formulate issues and advance argument in the matters under consideration. The decision-making body, like a court, should be able to rely on the integrity of the submissions made to it. A lawyer appearing before such a body should deal with the tribunal honestly and in conformity with applicable rules of procedure.

Lawyers have no exclusive right to appear before non-adjudicative bodies, as they do before a court. The requirements of this Rule therefore may subject lawyers to regulations inapplicable to advocates who are not lawyers. However, legislatures and administrative agencies have a right to expect lawyers to deal with them as they deal with courts.

The ethical rules referenced in Rule 3.9 concern, among other items, duties of attorneys not to knowingly make false statements, or to fail to disclose a material fact to a tribunal when such non-disclosure may further a fraud or criminal act of the client (Rule 3.3), as well as specific prohibitions on improper and undue influence of an officer (Rule 3.5). The Model Rules of Professional Conduct also note that it is "professional misconduct" for a lawyer to "state or imply an ability to influence improperly a government agency or official" (Rule 8.4(e)).

Attorneys should also be aware that in addition to federal post-employment "revolving door" laws, under the American Bar Association Model Rules after a lawyer leaves public employment he "shall not represent a private client in connection with a matter in which the lawyer participated personally and substantially as a public officer or employee, unless the appropriate government agency consents after consultation."[120] This may in some instances limit the representational activities of attorneys for clients before Congress when the attorneys have left public employment; the issue would most likely not arise in the context of general lobbying activities by the attorney, but rather in his or her capacity as counselor for someone subject to such proceedings as committee investigatory proceedings and hearings.[121]

[120] ABA Model Rules of Professional Conduct, Rule 1.11.

[121] *See* discussion, for example, of former rule as it applied to litigation in *General Motors Corp. v. City of New York*, 501 F.2d 639, 648-651 (2d Cir. 1974); *Laker Airways Ltd. v. Pan Am World Airways*, 103 F.R.D. 22 (D.D.C. 1984).

LOBBYING REFORM: BACKGROUND AND LEGISLATIVE PROPOSALS

In the decade since enactment of the Lobbying Disclosure Act of 1995 (LDA), concerns have been raised about the capacity of Congress to oversee the activities of professional lobbyists. Lobbyists and others who seek to participate in public policy activities through the formation of coalitions and associations whose members may not be identifiable, and the use of grassroots campaigns that attempt to mobilize citizens to advance the message of a lobbyist's client have also raised concerns. Some lobbying activities have also been linked to campaign finance practices, congressional procedures regarding the acceptance of gifts from lobbyists, and the inclusion of earmarks advocated by lobbyists in appropriations legislation.

In the 109th Congress, legislative proposals related to lobbying focus on six broad areas, including (1) enhanced requirements for electronic filing of lobbying reports and semiannual reports required under LDA; (2) redefinition of the term "client" under the statute; (3) more detailed disclosure by lobbyists of which groups and entities are funding coalitions and associations they represent; (4) more detailed disclosure by lobbyists of the individuals in Congress and the executive branch they contact; (5) congressional Rules regarding the interactions of Members and staff with lobbyists; and (6) the Federal Election Campaign Act of 1971, as amended, as it relates to lobbying activities.

Legislative proposals addressing some or all of those concerns introduced in the House thus far in the 109th Congress include H.R. 4975; H.R. 4948; H.R. 4920; H.R. 4682; H.R. 4799; H.R. 4787; H.R. 4738; H.R. 4696; H.R. 4671; H.R. 4670; H.R. 4667; H.R. 4658; H.R. 4575; H.R. 2412; H.R. 1302; H.R. 1304; and H.Res. 81. Measures related to lobbying issues introduced in the Senate include S. 2349, S. 2265, S. 2261, S. 2233, S. 2186; S. 2180; S. 2128; S. 1972; and S. 1398.

Floor consideration of S. 2349 was begun in the Senate by unanimous consent on March 6, 2006. A cloture motion on S. 2349 was presented on March 8 by Senator Bill Frist. Cloture on the bill was not invoked by a vote of 51 - 47 on March

9. Further consideration of S. 2349, as amended, and amendments that were pending when cloture was voted on, remain pending in the Senate. It has been reported that the Senate could take up consideration of S. 2349, as amended, during the week of March 27.

The regulation of lobbying disclosure is governed by the Lobbying Disclosure Act of 1995 (LDA),[1] as amended by the Lobbying Disclosure Technical Amendments Act of 1998.[2] LDA requires any lobbyist who is compensated for his actions, whether an individual or firm, to register and to file with the Clerk of the House and the Secretary of the Senate semiannual reports of their activities. These reports identify the name of the registrant lobbyist, client, and the broad issue areas in which lobbying was carried out. In the decade since the enactment of the LDA, concerns have been raised about the capacity of Congress to oversee lobbying activities of professional lobbyists who seek to participate in public policy activities through the formation of coalitions and associations whose members maynot be identifiable, and the use of grassroots campaigns that attempt to mobilize citizens to advance the message of a lobbyist's client.

Concerns related to the efficacy of current lobbying disclosure practices have also been linked to other activities carried out by lobbyists. These include campaign finance practices,[3] congressional rules regarding the acceptance of gifts and support from lobbyists,[4] and the inclusion of earmarks advocated by lobbyists in appropriations legislation.[5]

In the American political system, the pursuit of private interests through adoption and amendment of public policy dates back to the founding of the republic. Writing in support of the new Constitution, James Madison identified interest groups, or factions — groups of citizens united by a common impulse of passion or of interest — as a cornerstone of the American regime.[6] In 1803, Alexis de Tocqueville observed that "in no country in the world has the principle of association been more successfully applied ... than in America."[7] The First Amendment provides opportunity for these groups to exist by prohibiting laws abridging freedom of speech, the right of the people to peaceably assemble, and to petition the government for a redress of grievances.[8]

[1] P.L. 104-65, Lobbying Disclosure Act of 1995 (109 Stat. 691, 2 U.S.C. 1601).
[2] P.L. 105-166, Lobbying Disclosure Technical Amendments Act of 1998 (112 Stat. 38, 2 U.S.C. 1601 note)
[3] See CRS Issue Brief IB87020, *Campaign Finance*, by Joseph E. Cantor.
[4] For further analysis, see CRS Report RL33234, *Lobbying Disclosure and Ethics Proposals Related to Lobbying Introduced in the 109th Congress: A Comparative Analysis*, by R. Eric Petersen; and CRS Report RL33237, *Congressional Gifts and Travel, Legislative Proposals for the 109th Congress*, by Mildred Amer.
[5] See CRS Report RL33295 *Comparison of Selected Senate Earmark Reform Proposals*, by Sandy Streeter; and CRS Report 98-518, *Earmarks and Limitations in Appropriations Bills*, by Sandy Streeter.

For the past 40 years, observers have noted a steady increase in the number of organized interest groups, including associations, public interest groups, and professional organizations. Additionally, these observers note a change in the types of activities in which these organizations engage to advance their interests.[9] In addition to longstanding lobbying techniques of establishing personal ties with Members of Congress, their staff and executive branch officials, and testifying at congressional and administrative hearings, interest groups are also using direct mail, public relations, newspaper advertisement, and other marketing techniques to generate public interest in public policies and programs. These activities can include engaging citizens to lobby on their behalf to persuade a government official regarding legislation or executive agency action. Some of these organized efforts, which are not currently subject to disclosure under LDA, are also accompanied by sophisticated media campaigns to advance the causes of a group.[10] Widespread lobbying campaigns may be targeted to citizens, journalists, lawmakers, executive agency personnel, and other groups with interests similar to those of the organization on whose behalf the campaign is mounted.[11] This practice is sometimes referred to as "grassroots" advocacy to identify its appeal to the general public. Some observers, noting the use of marketing techniques and alleging that a connection to the general public is lacking, sometimes refer to such efforts as "astroturf" lobbying.[12]

[6] See Federalist Number 10, in *The Federalist* by Alexander Hamilton, James Madison, and John Jay, edited by Benjamin Fletcher Wright, (Cambridge, MA: The Belknap Press of Harvard University Press, 1961), pp. 129-136.
[7] Alexis de Tocqueville, *Democracy in America* (New York: Colonial Press, 1989), vol. I,
[8] For a broad overview of the roles and activities of groups that lobby Congress, see U.S. Senate, Committee on Governmental Affairs, Subcommittee on Intergovernmental Relations, *Congress and Pressure Groups: Lobbying in a Modern Democracy*, 99th Cong., 2nd sess. (Washington: GPO, 1986), pp. 1-40.
[9] See H. R. Hood, *Interest Group Politics in America: A New Intensity* (Englewood Cliffs, NJ: Prentice Hall, 1990).
[10] Darrell M. West and Burdett A. Loomis, *The Sound of Money: How Political Interests Get What They Want* (New York: W. W. Norton and Company, 1998), pp. 16-20; and R. Kenneth Godwin, "Money Technology and Political Interests: The Direct Marketing of Politics," in Mark P. Petracca, ed., *The Politics of Interests: Interest Groups Transformed* (Boulder, CO: Westview Press, 1992), pp. 308-325.
[11] West and Loomis, *The Sound of Money*, pp. 45-64.
[12] Nicholas Confessore, "Meet the Press," *Washington Monthly*, Dec. 2003, available at [http://www.washingtonmonthly.com/features/2003/0312.confessore.html].

In addition to the expanded scope and breadth of lobbying campaigns, some observers have noted that many lobbying campaigns involve increased reliance by interest groups on anonymous, or "stealth" campaigns, in which the lobbying activities directed to the public or policy makers are organized through coalitions and associations. Some of these coalitions and associations form alliances with other groups, or serve as groups which exist solely to advance a campaign for or against a specific policy action.[13] Political scientists Darrell West and Burdett Loomis assert that anonymous campaigns are carried out in voter education efforts, and electoral, legislative, and rulemaking settings, and that "the key in each of these efforts is that the actual sponsor is masked by front organizations that make it difficult for the public to see who really is funding the activity. Stealth campaigns are consciously designed to fly under the radar of press and public oversight."[14]

Anonymous campaigns to sway public opinion and affect public policy are not new. Writing a series of articles that became known generally as the Federalist Papers, Alexander Hamilton, James Madison, and John Jay,[15] sought to sway the general public in the 13 United States, and New York residents in particular, to press their leaders for ratification of the U.S. Constitution. In 1787 and 1788, 85 articles authored by the trio appeared in newspapers throughout the country under the pseudonym "Publius," as part of what has been described as the "most significant public-relations campaign in history."[16] In the articles, the three authors made no mention of their close association with the Constitutional Convention that drafted and approved the document.

Presently, however, concern has been expressed that entities that use anonymous lobbying activities and public relations campaigns might circumvent the process of public consideration of lawmaking and regulatory activities. Observers suggest that current lobbying disclosure laws, described below, allow interested entities to shield their lobbying activities through the use of ostensibly separate, independent coalitions and associations.[17] Proposals to require more detailed disclosure of lobbying clients, the government officials who have been lobbied, and expenditures dedicated to lobbying have followed. Those supporting more detailed disclosure might argue that such efforts could afford greater transparency and a broader understanding of the effects of private interests in the public policy making process. From their perspective, such a change might also instill greater accountability. Those opposing changes to current lobbying disclosure practices might maintain that expanding disclosure could have a potential adverse impact on constitutionally protected rights of assembly, association, and to petition the government, particularly the longstanding tradition of carrying out these activities without the necessity of self-identification. Additionally, opponents might assert that such a change could increase the administrative burden associated with reporting on their lobbying efforts under LDA.

[13] For examples of anonymous lobbying, see Jeffrey H. Birnbaum, "Lobbying Under The Cloak Of Invisibility," *Washington Post*, Mar. 7, 2005, p. E1, retrieved through nexis.com.
[14] West and Loomis, *The Sound of Money*, pp. 69-70.
[15] Hamilton, Madison and Jay went on to become the first Secretary of the Treasury, a Representative in the First through Fourth Congresses and fourth President, and the first Chief Justice of the United Sates, respectively.
[16] The Federalist Papers website, [http://www.law.ou.edu/hist/federalist/].
[17] Josephine Hearn, "Dems Want to Change Congressional Rules," *The Hill*, July 14, 2004, p.3; and Alison Mitchell, "Loophole Lets Lobbyists Hide Clients' Identity," *New York Times*, July 4, 2002, p. A1.

CURRENT LOBBYING DISCLOSURE LAW: A SUMMARY OF POTENTIALLY AFFECTED PROVISIONS OF LDA

LDA requires any lobbyist, whether an individual or firm, whose lobbying expenses exceed certain thresholds[18] to register with the Secretary of the Senate and the Clerk of the House of Representatives within 45 days after the lobbyist first makes a lobbying contact with covered officials in the legislative and executive branches of the federal government on behalf of a client.[19] The law requires lobbyists to file with the Clerk and the Secretary semiannual reports of their activities. These reports identify the name of the registrant, lobbyists the registrant employs, client, and the broad issue areas in which lobbying was carried out. In addition, the disclosure must include

* a good faith estimate, by broad category, of the total amount of lobbying-related income from the client, or expenditures by an organization lobbying in its own behalf, during the semiannual period. Expenditures may be estimated at less than $10,000 or in increments of $20,000;

* the specific issues that were the subject of a lobbyist's efforts, including "to the maximum extent practicable" a list of bill numbers;

[18] If the total income for matters related to lobbying activities on behalf of a client represented by a lobbying firm does not exceed $5,000, or total expenses in connection with the lobbying activities an organization whose employees engage in lobbying activities on its own behalf do not exceed $20,000, then no registration and disclosure is required.

[19] Legislative branch officials covered under LDA include Members of Congress; elected officers of either chamber; any employee of a Member, committee, leader or working group organized to provide assistance to Members; and any other legislative branch employee serving in a position that is compensated at a rate of 120% of the basic pay for GS 15 of the General Schedule.

Executive branch covered officials include the President; the Vice President; any officer or employee in the Executive Office of the President; any officer or employee serving in a position compensated through the Executive Schedule; any member of the uniformed military services whose pay grade is at or above O-7 under 37 U.S.C. 201 (In the United States Army, Air Force, and Marine Corps, this is a brigadier general. In the United States Navy and Coast Guard the equivalent rank is rear admiral.); and any officer or employee serving in a position of a confidential, policy-determining, policy-making, or policy advocating character that the Office of Personnel Management has excepted from the competitive service under 5 U.S.C. 7511(b)(2)(b).

a statement of the houses of Congress and the federal agencies contacted by the lobbyist; and

a list of the employees of the registrant who acted as lobbyists on behalf of the client, and a declaration of any previous employment as a covered executive branch or legislative branch official in the two years prior to registration.

LDA defines a lobbyist as any individual compensated by a client for services that include more than one lobbying contact, within certain limits.[20] A "client" is defined as any person or entity that employs and compensates another person to conduct lobbying activities on their behalf.[21] A coalition or association may also be listed as a client. LDA does not require information on the specific membership of these groups. Under the current guidance issued by the Clerk of the House and Secretary of the Senate, such members of informal coalitions may optionally be viewed as separate clients for disclosure purposes.[22] **Table 1** summarizes the number of registrants, clients and lobbyists registered with the Secretary of the Senate since LDA took effect.

[20] An individual whose lobbying activities constitute less than 20% of the time engaged in the services provided to a client over a six month period is exempt from LDA disclosure requirements.

[21] Under LDA, groups that carry out lobbying activities on their own behalf must also register with the Clerk and the Secretary.

[22] Office of the Clerk of the House of Representatives and Office of the Secretary of the Senate, *Lobbying Disclosure Act Guidance and Instructions*, p. 11. The document is also available through the Senate website at [http://www.senate.gov/pagelayout/legislative/ g_three_sections_with_teasers/lobbyingdisc.htm].

Table 1. Registrants, Clients and Lobbyists Registered Under the Lobbying Disclosure Act of 1995, 1996-2004

Yeara	Registrants		Clients		Lobbyists	
	Total	Annual change	Total	Annual change	Total	Annual change
1996	3,557	—	8,118	—	10,798	—
1997	4,051	13.89%	10,013	23.34%	14,946	38.41%
1998	4,422	9.16%	16,873	68.51%	18,589	24.37%
1999	4,813	8.84%	13,793	-18.25%	21,279	14.47%
2000	4,774	-0.81%	13,865	0.52%	16,342	-23.20%
2001	5,160	8.09%	15,941	14.97%	18,854	15.37%
2002	5,536	7.29%	17,575	10.25%	21,089	11.85%
2003	6,005	8.47%	15,317b	-12.85%	24,872	17.94%
2004	6,231	3.76%	19,758	28.99%	30,402	22.23%

Source: Data from the Secretary of the Senate, Office of Public Records and CRS calculations.

Notes: Except for 2000, data reflect all records available on September 30. Data for 2000 reflect only active registrations, clients and lobbyists.

a. As of Sept. 30 for each year. LDA became effective Jan. 1, 1996, and data for that year cover nine months.
b. Total reflects Senate Office of Public Records efforts to regularize differences in various client names.

LDA ENFORCEMENT

Whoever knowingly fails to rectify an incomplete disclosure report following notification of the error by the Clerk of the House or Secretary of the Senate, or who otherwise does not comply with the requirements of LDA, may be liable for a civil fine of up to $50,000.[23] The clerk and secretary must refer alleged incidents of noncompliance to the United States Attorney for the District of Columbia. The number of such referrals made since LDA became effective on January 1, 1996, is not publicly available. During a hearing to examine procedures to make the legislative process more transparent before the Senate Committee on Rules and Administration, however, Senator Christopher Dodd stated that "[s]ince 2003, the

[23] For further discussion of LDA and other laws, rules, and regulations affecting those who lobby Congress, see CRS Report RL31126, *Lobbying Congress: An Overview of Legal Provisions and Congressional Ethics Rules*, by Jack Maskell.

Office of Public Records has referred over 2,000 cases to the Department of Justice, and nothing's been heard from them again."[24]

The Department of Justice has reportedlyclaimed that between September 2003 and September 2005, it has received around 200 referrals involving possible LDA violations and has pursued 13 of those cases for further enforcement action. Of that total, media accounts claim that seven are still open, three have been closed without further action by the department, and three have been settled. No public announcements by the department regarding the settlements have been identified, but it has been reported that the three cases were settled for fines totaling $47,000 and other considerations including periods during which some registrants were prohibited from conducting federal lobbying. It is not known whether these cases comprise the total LDA enforcement effort. Attorneys for the Department of Justice reportedly contend that the details of any settlements of violations under LDA are protected from public disclosure by the Privacy Act.[25]

CURRENT LEGISLATIVE PROPOSALS

In the 109th Congress, legislative proposals related to lobbying focus on six broad areas, including

redefinition of the term "client" under LDA;

enhanced requirements for electronic filing of lobbying reports and semiannual reports required under LDA;[26]

[24] Senator Christopher Dodd, remarks during the Senate Committee on Rules and Administration hearing to examine procedures to make the legislative process more transparent, Feb. 8, 2006, retrieved through cq.com, at [http://cq.com/display.do?dockey=/cqonline/prod/data/docs/html/transcripts/congressional/109/congressionaltranscripts109000002046780.html@committees&metapub=CQ-CONGTRANSCRIPTS&searchIndex= 0&seqNum=1].

[25] Kenneth P. Doyle, "Senate Passed 2,000 Possible LDA Violations To DOJ, Dodd Reports; DOJ Pursued 13 Cases," *BNA Money and Politics Report*, Feb. 14, 2006; Kenneth P. Doyle, "DOJ Refuses to Disclose Settlements With Those Who Violate Lobbying Law," *BNA Daily Report for Executives*, June 20, 2005; and Kenneth P. Doyle, "Justice Department Reveals First Cases Settled Under Lobbying Disclosure Statute,"*BNA Daily Report for Executives*, Aug. 16, 2005, retrieved from the BNA website.

[26] The Office of the Clerk in Dec. 2004 inaugurated a voluntary electronic filing system for those required to file under LDA. Pursuant to a directive issued by Rep. Bob Ney, chairman of the Committee on House Administration, the Clerk will only accept electronic filing of LDA materials after Jan. 1, 2006 (Bob Ney, chairman, Committee on House Administration, "Electronic Filing of Disclosure Reports," dear colleague letter, June 29, 2005, at [http://www.house.gov/cha/dearcolleaguejune29-05.htm]; see also the Clerk's website at [http://clerk.house.gov/pd/index.html]). For some time, the Senate Office of Public Records has maintained a voluntary program of electronic filing "for the purpose of minimizing the burden of filing" LDA materials (Senate Office of Public Records, "Frequently Asked Questions," at [https://opr.senate.gov/faq.html]). Additionally, the Senate makes LDA (continued...)

more detailed disclosure of which groups and entities are funding coalitions and associations;

more detailed disclosure by lobbyists of the individuals in Congress and the executive branch whom they contact;

congressional Rules regarding the interactions of Members and staff with lobbyists; and

the Federal Election Campaign Act of 1971 (FECA), as amended.[27] as they relate to lobbying activities.

Several measures, addressing issues related principally to lobbying, and described below, have been introduced in the 109th Congress. Three measures that have received committee consideration and have been subsequently reported either to the House or Senate. These measures are

S. 2349, the Legislative Transparency and Accountability Act of 2006, introduced by Senator Trent Lott;

S. 2128, the Lobbying Transparency and Accountability Act of 2006, introduced by Senator John McCain; and

H.Res. 648, to eliminate floor privileges and access to Member exercise facilities for registered lobbyists who are former Members or officers of the House, introduced by Representative David Dreier.

For further information and analysis of proposals to reform congressional rules governing ethics and legislative procedures, see CRS Report RL33234, *Lobbying Disclosure and Ethics Proposals Related to Lobbying Introduced in the 109th Congress: A Comparative Analysis*, by R. Eric Petersen; CRS Report RL33237, *Congressional Gifts and Travel, Legislative Proposals for the 109th Congress*, by Mildred Amer; CRS Report RL33295, *Comparison of Selected Senate Earmark Reform Proposals*, by Sandy Streeter; and CRS Report RL32954, *527 Political Organizations: Legislation in the 109th Congress*, by Joseph E. Cantor and Erika Lunder.

HOUSE MEASURES

MEASURES CONSIDERED

H.Res. 648. On January 31, 2006, Representative David Dreier, chairman of the Committee on Rules introduced H.Res. 648. On February 1, 2006, the House adopted the measure under suspension of the Rules, by a vote of 379 - 50, 1 present. H.Res. 648 amended House Rule IV to deny floor privileges to former Representatives, House officers, parliamentarians or former minority employees nominated as an elected officer of the House if they: are a registered lobbyist or agent of a foreign principal; have any direct personal or pecuniary interest in any legislative measure pending before the House or reported by a committee; or are employed or represent any entity for the purpose of influencing, the passage, defeat, or amendment of any legislative proposal.

The measure also amended House Rule IV to deny access to Member exercise facilities to any former Member, officers, or their spouses, who is a registered lobbyist.[28]

[28] In addition to H.Res. 648, five other measures with provisions regarding access to House facilities by former Representatives or other former officials who have floor privileges who become lobbyists have been introduced in the 109th Congress. H.Res. 646, introduced on Jan. 31, 2005, by Rep. Walter B. Jones, would deny admission to the Hall of the House to former Members who are lobbyists. The measures was referred to the Committee on Rules. No further action has been taken at the time of this writing. H.Res. 663, introduced on Jan. 31, 2005, by Rep. Vic Snyder, would also deny floor privileges to former Representatives who lobby. Additionally, the measure would deny former Members who are registered lobbyists services or facilities provided in House office buildings that are operated for the exclusive use of Members and former Members. H.Res. 663 was refereed to the Committees on Rules and House Administration. No further action has been taken at the time of this writing. H.Res. 659, introduced by Rep. David Obey on Jan. 31, 2006, would require former officials with floor privileges to sign a statement that the have no direct personal or pecuniary interest in any legislative measure pending before the House or reported by a committee; that they are not employed as a lobbyist or represent any party or organization for the purpose of influencing legislation in the House; and that they will not lobby for the passage, amendment, or defeat of any legislative measure pending before the House, reported by a committee, or under consideration in any of its committees or subcommittees. The measure was referred to the Committee on Rules, and in addition to the Committee on Standards of Official Conduct, for a period to be subsequently determined by the Speaker, in

each case for consideration of such provisions as fall within the jurisdiction of the committee concerned. H.R. 4682, the Honest Leadership and Open Government Act of 2006, introduced Feb. 1, 2006, by Rep. Nancy Pelosi, and described in greater detail below, would amend House Rule IV to deny floor privileges to former Representatives, House officers, parliamentarians or former minority employees nominated as an elected officer of the House if they are a registered lobbyist or agent of a foreign principal; have any direct personal or pecuniary interest in any legislative measure pending before the House or reported by a committee; or are employed or represent any entity for the purpose of influencing, the passage, defeat, or amendment of any legislative proposal. The measure would also amended House Rule IV to deny access to Member exercise facilities to any former Member who is a registered lobbyist. No further action has been taken at the (continued...)

OTHER MEASURES INTRODUCED

H.R. 4975. H.R. 4975, the Lobbying Accountability and Transparency Act of 2006, was introduced by Representative David Dreier on March 16, 2006. Representative Dreier, who is chairman of the Committee on Rules, was designated by the Speaker to develop legislation related to lobbying and ethics provisions on behalf of the House majority.[29] The measure would amend LDA to require quarterly, instead of semiannual, filing of lobbying disclosure reports;

reduction of the thresholds for which registration and disclosure is required, from $5,000 to $2,500 for a lobbying firm and from $20,000 to $10,000 for an an organization whose employees engage in lobbying activities on its own behalf;

reduction of the increments in which lobbying expenditures may be estimated, from less than $10,000 to less than $5,000, or in larger increments, from $20,000 to $10,000;

electronic filing of lobbying registrations and disclosure reports;

creation and maintenance by the Clerk and the Secretary of a searchable, sortable, and downloadable database containing LDA registration and disclosure information, made available through the Internet;

disclosure by registered lobbyists of all past executive branch and congressional employment in the past seven years.

H.R. 4975 would amend LDA to require disclosure by lobbyists of any contributions made to federal candidates, officeholders, leadership PACs, political party committees or other entity which would be subject to disclosure under FECA. Lobbyists would also be required to disclose any gifts that count toward the annual gift limit established by House rules. The measure would increase the civil penalty

[28] (...continued) time of this writing. H.R. 4696, introduced by Rep. Mike Rogers of Michigan on Feb. 1, 2005, and described below, would also suspend floor privileges to former Members who are registered as lobbyists. The measure was referred to the Committees on Government Reform, House Administration, Rules, and Resources, for a period to be subsequently determined by the Speaker, in each case for consideration of such provisions as fall within the jurisdiction of the committee concerned. No further action has been taken at the time of this writing.

[29] "House Speaker Hastert and Rep. Dreier Hold News Conference on Lobbying Reform," transcript, *CQ.com*, Jan. 17, 2006, at [http://www.cq.com/display.do?dockey=/ cqonline/prod/data/docs/html/transcripts/newsmaker/109/ newsmakertranscripts109-000002036139.html@committees&metapub=CQ-TRANSCRI PTS&searchIndex=1&seqNum=15].

for failure to comply with lobbying disclosure requirements up to $100,000. Registered lobbyists would be prohibited from traveling in corporate aircraft on which a Member of the House travels.

H.R.

4975 would authorize the Inspector General of the House to audit LDA disclosure information, and to refer potential violations of the act to the Department of Justice. The measure provides for ongoing reviews and annual reports by the inspector general on activities carried out by the Clerk of the House under LDA.[30]

H.R.

4975 was referred to the Committee on the Judiciary, and in addition to the Committees on House Administration, Rules, Government Reform, and Standards of Official Conduct, for a period to be subsequently determined by the Speaker, in each case for consideration of such provisions as fall within the jurisdiction of the committee concerned. No further action has been taken at the time of this writing.

H.R.

4948. H.R. 4948, the Ethics Reform Act of 2006, was introduced by Representative Earl Blumenauer on March 14, 2006. The measure would amend LDA to

transfer authority to receive LDA registrations and reports from the Clerk and the Secretary to an independent ethics commission in the legislative branch created by the measure;[31]

[30] In addition to provisions related to lobbying, H.R. 4975 would require notification by the House to former Members, officers and senior staff of the beginning and ending date of post employment restrictions mandated under 18 U.S.C. 207. A Member of the House who is negotiating for prospective employment in which he or she has a conflict of interest, or for which there is the appearance of a conflict of interest, must make a statement within five days after commencing such negotiations to the Committee on Standards of Official Conduct. Members of the House, House officers, and employees would be prohibited from wrongfully influencing, on a partisan basis, any entity's employment decisions or practices. Privately funded travel would be suspended under the measure, and the Committee on Standards of Official Conduct required to develop guidelines regarding the use of such travel in the House. House gift rules would be amended to include requirements for the valuation of tickets to sporting and entertainment events. Frequent and comprehensive training on ethics would be required for existing and new house staff, with Members of the House encourages to participate in such training. H.R. 4975 would require the biennial publication of an ethics manual. See CRS Report RL33234,

Lobbying Disclosure and Ethics Proposals Related to Lobbying Introduced in the 109th Congress: A Comparative Analysis, by R. Eric Petersen; and CRS Report RL33237, *Congressional Gifts and Travel, Legislative Proposals for the 109th Congress*, by Mildred Amer. The measure would rescind pensions accrued by a Member of Congress during their time in office upon a conviction of certain offenses that occurred while the Member served in Congress.

The measure also makes changes to provisions of FECA related to 527 organizations. See CRS Report RL32954, *527 Political Organizations: Legislation in the 109th Congress*, by Joseph E. Cantor and Erika Lunder.

[31] H.R. 4948 would also terminate the Committee on Standards of Official Conduct. The commission would investigate any alleged violation of chamber rules or other standards of conduct by Members of the House or House employees; provide advisory opinions on ethics (continued...)

require quarterly, instead of semiannual, filing of lobbying disclosure reports; and

require electronic filing of LDA registrations and reports, and for those reports to be made available to the public through the Internet.

H.R.

4948 was referred to the Committee on House Administration, and in addition to the Committees on Rules, and the Judiciary, for a period to be subsequently determined by the Speaker, in each case for consideration of such provisions as fall within the jurisdiction of the committee concerned. No further action has been taken as of the time of this writing.

H.R.

4920. H.R. 4920, the Accountability and Transparency in Ethics Act, was introduced on March 9, 2006 by Representative Michael Castle. The measure would amend LDA to transfer responsibility for receiving LDA registrations and reports from the Clerk to the Committee on Standards of Official Conduct;

require quarterly, instead of semiannual, filing of lobbying disclosure reports;

require electronic filing of LDA registrations and reports, and for those reports to be made available to the public through the Internet; and

establish a civil fine of not more $50,000 for any registrant or lobbyist who attempts to offer a gift to a Member of the House in violation of House gift rules.

The measure would also prohibit former Members officers, or employees of Congress from lobbying any current Member, officer or employee for a period of one year after they leave office or terminate employment.[32] H.R. 4920 was referred to the Committee on the Judiciary, and in addition to the Committees on House Administration and Rules, for a period to be subsequently determined by the Speaker,

[31] (...continued) matters to Members of the House and their staff, and establish an office on advice and education.

[32] In addition to the lobbying provisions, H.R. 4920 would create an independent ethics commission within the legislative branch to investigate any alleged violation of chamber rules or other standards of conduct by Members of the House or House employees. The measure would make changes in House rules regarding the duties of the Committee on Standards of Official Conduct, and require annual ethics training for Members and staff of the House. H.R. 4920 would amend House rules to require advanced authorization by the Standards Committee of any privately funded travel to be undertaken by a Member of the House.

in each case for consideration of such provisions as fall within the jurisdiction of the committee concerned. No further action has been taken as of the time of this writing.

H.R. 4799. H.R. 4799, to establish a legislative branch office of public integrity, was introduced by Representative Christopher Shays on February 16, 2006. The measure would establish an office of public integrity within the legislative branch, overseen by a director appointed jointly by the Speaker and minority leader of the House, and the majority and minority leaders of the Senate. The office would

receive, monitor, and oversee financial disclosure and other reports filed by Members, congressional officers, and their staff under the Ethics in Government Act of 1978[33], and reports filed by registered lobbyists under LDA;

investigate any alleged violation, of any rule or other standard of conduct;

present a case of probable ethics violations to the Committee on Standards of Official Conduct of the House of Representatives or the Senate Select Committee on Ethics, as appropriate;

make recommendations to the appropriate ethics committee that it report any substantial evidence of a violation by a Member, officer, or employee of the House or the Senate of any law applicable to the performance of his duties that may have been disclosed in an investigation by the office;

provide information and informal guidance to Members, congressional officers, and their staff regarding any rules and other standards of conduct applicable in their official capacities;

give consideration to the request of any Members, congressional officers, and their staff for a formal advisory opinion, subject to the review of the Committee on Standards of Official Conduct of the House of Representatives or the Senate Select Committee on Ethics, as appropriate, with respect to the general propriety of any current or proposed conduct;

conduct periodic and random reviews and audits of reports filed with it to ensure compliance with all applicable laws and rules; and

provide informal guidance to lobbying registrants of their responsibilities under LDA.

Under the measure, the office would have authority to refer potential violations of LDA to the Department of Justice, and to audit LDA registrations and disclosure reports. LDA would be amended to require electronic filing of registration and

[33] Ethics in Government Act of 1978, 5 U.S.C. Appendix Sec. 401.

disclosure reports, which would be made available in a searchable database accessible through the Internet.[34]

H.R.

4799 was referred to the Committee on House Administration, and in addition to the Committees on Rules and the Judiciary, for a period to be subsequently determined by the Speaker, in each case for consideration of such provisions as fall within the jurisdiction of the committee concerned. No further action has been taken as of the time of this writing.

H.R.

4787. H.R. 4787, the Truth-in-Lobbying Disclosure Act, was introduced by Representative John Doolittle on February 16, 2006. The measure would amend LDA to require the disclosure of any federal funds received through grants, contracts, or other sources by a client other than a state, during a semiannual reporting period. Any funds received by reason of a provision in an appropriations act that specifies the entity and the amount received, or specifies a project in a state or congressional district would also be subject to LDA disclosure. H.R. 4787 was referred to the House Committee on the Judiciary. No further action has been taken at the time of this writing.

H.R.

4738. H.R. 4738, the Commission to Strengthen Confidence in Congress Act of 2006, was introduced by Representative Mark Udall on February 8, 2006. A similar measure, S. 2186, described below, was introduced in the House by Senator Norm Coleman on January 25, 2006. H.R. 4738 would not change current lobbying laws and regulations, but would establish a commission to strengthen confidence in Congress through an evaluation of current congressional rules related to congressional interactions with various lobbying activities. A bipartisan, 10 member commission would be appointed by the majority and minority leadership of each chamber. The commission would be charged to

evaluate and report the effectiveness of current congressional ethics requirements;

weigh the need for improved ethical conduct with the need for lawmakers to have access to expertise on public policy issues;

determine and report minimum standards relating to official travel for Members of Congress and staff;

evaluate the range of gifts given to Members of Congress and staff, determine and report the effects on public policy, and make recommendations for limits on gifts;

[34] In addition to provisions affecting lobbying disclosure, H.R. 4799 would also make several changes to current procedures for consideration of ethics complaints against Members of Congress, including an expansion of who may file a complaint, processes for investigating claims of chamber rules violations, and interactions between the office and the House Committee on Standards of Official Conduct and the Senate Select Committee on Ethics.

evaluate and report the effectiveness and transparency of congressional disclosure laws and recommendations for improvements;

assess and report the effectiveness of the ban on Member of Congress and staff from lobbying their former office for one year and make recommendations for altering the time frame;

make recommendations to improve the process whereby Members of Congress can earmark priorities in appropriations acts, while still preserving congressional power of the purse;

evaluate the use of public and privately funded travel by Members of Congress and staff, violations of congressional rules governing travel, and make recommendations on limiting travel; and

investigate and report to Congress on its findings, conclusions, and recommendations for reform.

H.R. 4738 was referred to the Committee on House Administration. No further action has been taken at the time of this writing.

H.R. 4696. Representative Mike Rogers of Michigan introduced H.R. 4696, the Restoring Trust in Government Act, on February 1, 2006. The measure proposes

creation of an independent commission on lobbying and in the legislative branch composed of four members, with the Speaker and minority leader of the House, and the majority and minority leaders of the Senate each appointing one for a term of two years;

development of a fee-based funding process under which LDA registrants would be required to pay reasonable fees to cover the estimated costs of operating the commission;

requirements that each LDA registrant file with the commission monthly reports in electronic form that cover lobbying activities that relate to Congress, and that the commission post those disclosures on the Internet; and

enactment of a four-year ban on former federal employees lobbying Congress after they terminate their government employment.

H.R. 4696 would extend current statutory provisions that prevent Members of Congress from lobbying any Member or committee for one year to all senior legislative branch staff. The measure would amend LDA to impose a prison term of up to one year for failing to comply with disclosure requirements. H.R. 4696 would also suspend House floor privileges for former Members who become lobbyists subject to LDA registration. The measure was referred to the Committee on the Judiciary, and in addition to the Committees on Government Reform, House Administration, Rules, and Resources, for a period to be subsequently determined by the Speaker, in each case for consideration of such provisions as fall within the jurisdiction of the committee concerned. On February 9, the Committee on Resources requested executive comment on sections of the bill that are unrelated to lobbying law.[35] No further action has been taken at the time of this writing.

H.R. 4682. Representative Nancy Pelosi, who is the House Minority Leader, introduced H.R. 4682, the Honest Leadership and Open Government Act of 2006 on February 1, 2006. The measure would amend LDA to require

quarterly, instead of semiannual, filing of lobbying disclosure reports;

electronic filing of lobbyist registrations and disclosure reports filed with the Secretary of the Senate or the Clerk of the House of Representatives;

reduction of the increments in which lobbying expenditures may be estimated in larger increments, from $20,000 to $1,000;

disclosure by registered lobbyists of all past executive branch and congressional employment;

establishment and maintenance by the Clerk and Secretary of lobbying disclosure information in an electronic database that directly links lobbying disclosure information to the information disclosed in reports filed with the Federal Election Commission (FEC) under FECA, and made available to the public free of charge through the Internet, and to make those reports available within 48 hours of filing;

disclosure by registrants, and their employees who work as lobbyist, of any contributions made under FECA; and

disclosure of grassroots lobbying communications by paid lobbyists and itemized disclosure of expenditures on grassroots lobbying activities. In the event that a grassroots lobbyist receives or spends $250,000 or more for grassroots lobbying activities, an additional report must be made within 20 days.

H.R. 4682 would require members of coalitions or associations that employ a lobbyist, and not the coalition or association, to be listed as the clients of the registrant lobbyist. H.R. 4682 provides an exception for tax-exempt associations and for some members of a coalition or association if those members expect to contribute less than $500 per any quarterly period to the lobbying activities of the coalition.

[35] In addition to the lobbying-related proposals, H.R. 4696 would amend congressional financial disclosure regulations to permit random audits, and create an independent commission to approve all congressional travel. The measure also address matters related to Indian gambling and campaign finance statutes.

The measure would also require registrants to certify that the registrant and lobbyists they employ have not provided a gift, directly or indirectly, to a Member of the House in violation of House Rule XXV; a contribution to an event to honor a covered legislative branch official or an entity named after or controlled by a covered official in the legislative or executive branches; or to pay the costs of a retreat or other gathering of more than one covered official from the legislative or executive branches.

H.R. 4682 would establish an Office of Public Integrity within the House Office of Inspector General. The office would receive LDA registrations and disclosure reports, and conduct audits and investigations necessary to ensure compliance with LDA. A director of the office would be appointed by the Inspector General. The office would have the authority to refer violations of LDA to the United States Attorney for the District of Columbia for disciplinary action.

H.R. 4682 would eliminate floor privileges and access to Member exercise facilities to former Representatives who become lobbyists. The measure would increase the civil penalty for failure to comply with lobbying disclosure requirements up to $100,000.[36] In addition, H.R. 4682 would establish criminal penalties for noncompliance with LDA. Knowing and willful failure to comply with registration requirements would be punishable by fines, a term of imprisonment up to five years, or both. Whoever knowingly willfully, and corruptly fails to comply with LDA disclosure requirements would be subject to fines, a term of imprisonment up to 10 years, or both. H.R. 4682 would extend the ban preventing former senior executive personnel, former Members of Congress, and legislative branch personnel from lobbying the entity in which they previously served from one to two years. The measure was referred to the Committee on the Judiciary, and in addition to the Committees on Rules, Government Reform, Standards of Official Conduct, Armed Services, and House Administration, for a period to be subsequently determined by the Speaker, in each case for consideration of such provisions as fall within the

[36] S. 2180 would require a number of other changes to laws and rules governing congressional ethics that are not directly related to lobbying disclosure. These include requiring public disclosure by Members of Congress of employment negotiations; the establishment of fines and penalties for Member of Congress who wrongfully influence, on a partisan basis, any entity's employment decisions or practices; amendments to Senate Rules to prohibit favoritism; requiring the Senate Select Committee on Ethics to develop and revise guidelines on reasonable expenditures for official government travel; requiring certification that congressional travel meets certain conditions, and establishing civil fines for false certifications.

jurisdiction of the committee concerned.[37] No further action has been taken at the time of this writing.

H.R.

4671. H.R. 4671, the Clarity in Lobbying Act, was introduced by Representative Scott Garrett on January 31, 2006. The measure would require LDA registrants to disclose any gifts given to a covered legislative branch official. H.R. 4671 was referred to the Committee on the Judiciary. No further action has been taken at the time of this writing.

H.R.

4670. H.R. 4670, the Keep Lobbying Clean act, was introduced by Representative Scott Garrett on January 31, 2006. The measure would prohibit anyone convicted of a felony under federal, state or local law from lobbying. Failure to abide by the prohibition would be subject to imprisonment for up to one year and a civil fine up to $50,000 or the amount of compensation which the person received or offered for the prohibited conduct, whichever is greater. H.R. 4670 was referred to the Committee on the Judiciary. No further action has been taken at the time of this writing.

H.R.

4667. H.R. 4667, the Lobbying Transparency and Accountability Act of 2006 was introduced by Representative Michael Fitzpatrick on January 31, 2006. The measure would amend LDA to require

quarterly, instead of semiannual, filing of lobbying disclosure reports;

electronic filing of lobbyist registrations and disclosure reports filed with the Secretary of the Senate or the Clerk of the House of Representatives;

reduction of the thresholds for which registration and disclosure is required, from $5,000 to $2,500 for a lobbying firm and from $20,000 to $10,000 for an an organization whose employees engage in lobbying activities on its own behalf;

[37] H.R. 4682 requires a number of other changes to laws and rules governing congressional ethics that are not directly related to lobbying disclosure. These include requiring public disclosure by Members of Congress of employment negotiations; the establishment of fines and penalties for Member of Congress or employees of the House who wrongfully influence, on a partisan basis, any entity's employment decisions or practices; amendments to the House Code of Official Conduct to prohibit favoritism; requiring the House Committee on Standards of Official Conduct to develop and revise guidelines on reasonable expenditures for official government travel; requiring certification that congressional travel meets certain conditions, and establishing civil fines for false certifications. Additionally, H.R. 4682 would require changes in House operations elated to the congressional legislative workweek, time to read measures before they are considered on the floor and procedural changes in conference committees. Finally, H.R. 4682 would establish minimum requirements for executive branch appointees in certain public safety positions, and make changes to public contracting provisions.

reduction of the increments in which lobbying expenditures may be estimated, from less than $10,000 to less than $5,000, or in larger increments, from $20,000 to $10,000;

disclosure by registered lobbyists of all past executive branch and congressional employment;

establishment and maintenance of lobbying disclosure information in an electronic data base which directly links lobbying disclosure information to the information disclosed in reports filed with the FEC under FECA, and made available to the public free of charge through the Internet; and

disclosure of grassroots lobbying communications by paid lobbyists and itemized disclosure of expenditures on grassroots lobbying activities.

H.R.4667 would amend LDA to redefine the term “client” as any person or entity that employs a lobbyist on behalf of that person or entity. The measure requires that firms and other entities that are members of coalitions or associations that employ a lobbyist, are to be considered clients, along with the coalition or association, if their total contribution related to lobbying activities is greater than $10,000.

The measure would increase the civil penalty for failure to comply with lobbying disclosure requirements up to $100,000. H.R. 4667 provides for reviews and semiannual reports by the Comptroller General on activities carried out by the Clerk of the House and the Secretary of the Senate under LDA. Additionally, a current ban on former senior executive personnel, former Members of Congress, and legislative branch personnel, preventing them from lobbying the entity in which they previously served, would be extended from one to two years.[38]

H.R. 4667 was referred to the Committee on the Judiciary, and in addition to the Committees on Standards of Official Conduct, Rules, Resources, and Government Reform, for a period to be subsequently determined by the Speaker, in each case for consideration of such provisions as fall within the jurisdiction of the committee concerned.[39] No further action has been taken at the time of this writing.

[38] H.R. 3623, introduced by Rep. Robert Andrews on July 29, 2005, would increase the "cooling off"period to five years after the Member leaves office during which former Members of Congress may not lobby, or appear or communicate with intent to influence any matter before any Member, officer or employee of the entire legislative branch. The measure was referred to the Committee on the Judiciary.

[39] H.R. 4667 would require a number of other changes to laws and rules governing congressional ethics that are not directly related to lobbying disclosure. These include requiring public disclosure by Members of Congress of employment negotiations; a ban on privately funded travel for Members of Congress, and enhanced disclosure requirements regarding gifts given by lobbyists to Members of Congress and congressional staff. (continued...)

H.R. 4575. On December 16, 2005, Representative Christopher Shays introduced H.R. 4575, the Lobbying Transparency and Accountability Act of 2005, which would require

quarterly, instead of semiannual, filing of lobbying disclosure reports;

reduction of the thresholds for which registration and disclosure is required, from $5,000 to $2,500 for a lobbying firm and from $20,000 to $10,000 for an an organization whose employees engage in lobbying activities on its own behalf;

disclosure by registered lobbyists of all past executive branch and congressional employment;

reduction of the increments in which lobbying expenditures may be estimated, from less than $10,000 to less than $5,000, or in larger increments, from $20,000 to $10,000;

electronic filing of lobbyist registrations and disclosure reports filed with the Secretary of the Senate or the Clerk of the House of Representatives;

establishment and maintenance of lobbying disclosure information in an electronic database that directly links lobbying disclosure information to the information disclosed in reports filed with the FEC under FECA and made available to the public free of charge through the Internet; and

disclosure of grassroots lobbying communications by paid lobbyists and itemized disclosure of expenditures on grassroots lobbying activities. In the event that a grassroots lobbyist receives or spends $250,000 or more for grassroots lobbying activities, an additional report must be made within 20 days.

H.R.

4575 would amend LDA to redefine the term "client" as any person or entity that employs a lobbyist to carry out lobbying or grass roots lobbying activities on behalf of that person or entity. The measure requires that firms and other entities that are members of coalitions or associations that employ a lobbyist are to be considered clients, along with the coalition or association, if their total contribution related to lobbying activities is greater than $10,000.

H.R.

4575 would increase the civil penalty for failure to comply with lobbying disclosure requirements up to $100,000. The measure provides for reviews and

[39] (...continued) Additionally, the measure would institute House Rules changes related to the use of earmarks and the availability of measures pending floor consideration , and clarify statutes regarding the use of federal funds for political activity.

semiannual reports by the Comptroller General on activities carried out by the Clerk of the House and the Secretary of the Senate under LDA. Additionally, the ban on former senior executive personnel, former Members of Congress, and legislative branch personnel preventing them from lobbying the entity in which they previously served would be extended from one to two years.[40] H.R. 4575 was referred to the Committee on the Judiciary, and Committees on Standards of Official Conduct, Rules, and Resources for a period to be subsequently determined by the Speaker, in each case for consideration of such provisions as fall within the jurisdiction of the committee concerned. No further action has been taken at the time of this writing.

H.R. 2412. H.R. 2412, the Special Interest Lobbying and Ethics Accountability Act of 2005, was introduced by Representative Martin Meehan on May 17, 2005.[41] The measure would amend LDA to require

quarterly, instead of semiannual, filing of lobbying disclosure reports;

electronic filing of lobbyist registrations and disclosure reports filed with the Secretary of the Senate or the Clerk of the House of Representatives;

establishment and maintenance of lobbying disclosure information in an electronic data base which directly links lobbying disclosure information to the information disclosed in reports filed with the FEC under FECA, and made available to the public free of charge through the Internet;

identification of each executive branch official and Member of Congress with whom lobbying contacts are made, on an issue-byissue basis, for each covered official contacted;

disclosure by registered lobbyists of all past executive branch and congressional employment; and

disclosure of grassroots lobbying communications by paid lobbyists and itemized disclosure of expenditures on grassroots lobbying activities.

[40] H.R. 4575 requires a number of other changes to laws and rules governing congressional ethics that are not directly related to lobbying disclosure. These include requiring public disclosure by Members of Congress of employment negotiations; and increased disclosure of travel by Members of Congress. The measure also specifies the valuation of tickets to sporting and entertainment events provided to covered executive and legislative branch officials.

[41] A section-by-section discussion of the provisions of H.R. 2412 is available in CRS Report RS22226, *Summary and Analysis of Provisions of H.R. 2412, the Special Interest Lobbying and Ethics Accountability Act of 2005*, by Jack Maskell.

H.R.

2412 would amend LDA to redefine the term "client" as any person or entity that employs a lobbyist on behalf of that person or entity. The measure requires that firms and other entities that are members of coalitions or associations that employ a lobbyist, are to be considered clients, along with the coalition or association, if their total contribution related to lobbying activities is greater than $10,000.

The measure would increase the civil penalty for failure to comply with lobbying disclosure requirements up to $100,000. H.R. 2412 provides for reviews and semiannual reports by the Comptroller General on activities carried out by the Clerk of the House and the Secretary of the Senate under LDA. Additionally, a current ban on former senior executive personnel, former Members of Congress, and legislative branch personnel, preventing them from lobbying the entity in which they previously served, would be extended from one to two years.

H.R. 2412 was referred to the Committee on the Judiciary, the Committees on Standards of Official Conduct, and the Committee on Rules, for a period to be subsequently determined by the Speaker, for consideration of those provisions that fall within the jurisdiction of each committee.[42] No further action has been taken at the time of this writing.

H.R. 1302 and H.R. 1304. On March 15, 2005, Representative Lloyd Doggett introduced H.R. 1302, and H.R. 1304, both entitled the Stealth Lobbyist Disclosure Act of 2005. H.R. 1302 would amend LDA to redefine the term "client" as any person or entity that employs a lobbyist on behalf of that person or entity. The measure would require members of coalitions or associations that employ a lobbyist, and not the coalition or association, to be listed as the clients of the registrant lobbyist. H.R. 1302 provides an exception for tax-exempt associations and for some members of a coalition or association if those members expect to contribute less than $1,000 per any semiannual period to the lobbying activities of the coalition. The measure was referred to the Committee on the Judiciary, Subcommittee on the Constitution. No further action has been taken at the time of this writing.

H.R. 1304 would amend the Internal Revenue Code to treat any coalition or association that is identified as a client on an LDA registration as a tax-exempt political organization. Any such coalition or association would be required to notify the Secretary of the Treasury of its existence within 72 hours after one of its lobbyists

[42] H.R. 2412 requires a number of other changes to laws and rules governing congressional ethics that are not directly related to lobbying disclosure. These include requiring public disclosure by Members of Congress of employment negotiations; the establishment of fines and penalties for Member of Congress or employees of the House who wrongfully influence, on a partisan basis, any entity's employment decisions or practices; amendments to the House Code of Official Conduct to prohibit favoritism; requiring the House Committee on Standards of Official Conduct to develop and revise guidelines on reasonable expenditures for official government travel; requiring certification that congressional travel meets certain conditions, and establishing civil fines for false certifications. Finally, H.R. 2412 would require the appointment of a bipartisan ethics task force in the House to make recommendations on strengthening ethics oversight and enforcement, and providing the resources necessary to accomplish that goal.

makes an initial contact, and to report any change in its membership within 72 hours. Reports to the Secretary of the Treasury would include a general description of the business or activities of each member of the coalition or association, and the amount each coalition member is expected to contribute to influencing legislation. H.R. 1304 would exempt from the disclosure requirements public charities and other tax-exempt organizations which have substantial exempt activities other than lobbying, and coalition or association members who contribute less than $2,000 per year for lobbying activities. Finally, the measure would impose a penalty tax for failure to give the required notices. H.R. 1304 was referred to the Committee on Ways and Means. No further action has been taken at the time of this writing.

H.Res. 81. H.Res. 81, introduced by Representative Mark Green on February 2, 2005, would require the Clerk of the House of Representatives to post on the Internet lobbying registration and reports filed with the Clerk under the Lobbying Disclosure Act of 1995.[43] The measure was referred to the Committee on the Judiciary, and subsequently to the Subcommittee on the Constitution. No further action has been taken at the time of this writing.

SENATE MEASURES

MEASURES CONSIDERED

S. 2349, Senate Consideration. Floor consideration of S. 2349 was begun in the Senate by unanimous consent on March 6, 2006. During debate, Senator Trent Lott offered S.Amdt. 2907. The amendment was a substitute for S. 2349 consisting of the text of S. 2349, as reported, as Title I, and S. 2128, as reported, as Title II. S.Amdt. 2907 was adopted by unanimous consent, and was considered a part of the original text of the bill for any further amendments. S. 2349, as amended was subsequently further amended before a cloture motion was presented on March 8 by Senator Bill Frist. Cloture on the bill was not invoked by a vote of 51 - 47 on March

9. Further consideration of S. 2349, as amended, and two amendments that were pending when cloture was voted on, remain pending in the Senate. For detailed discussion and analysis of the consideration of S. 2349, see CRS Report RL33293,

Lobbying and Related Reform Proposals: Consideration of Selected Measures, 109th Congress, by R. Eric Petersen. It has been reported that the Senate could take up consideration of S. 2349, as amended, during the week of March 27.[44]

S. 2349, Committee Consideration. On February 28, 2006, the Senate Committee on Rules and Administration marked up an original measure, the

[43] The Senate Office of Public Records, an entity within the Office of the Secretary of the Senate, provides access to LDA registration and semiannual reports through the Internet at [http://sopr.senate.gov/].

[44] Kenneth P. Doyle, "As House Bill Introduced, Frist Says Senate Will Return to Reform Debate," *BNA Money and Politics Report*, Mar. 20, 2006, at [http://pubs.bna.com/ip/bna/mpr.nsf/eh/A0B2N2F8Z2]; and Tory Newmyer, "Ethics Bill Set for Brief Return Next Monday," *Roll Call*, Mar. 20, 2006, at [http://www.rollcall.com/issues/51_99/news/12614-1.html].

Legislative Transparencyand Accountability Act of 2006. The measure was reported to the Senate by an 18-0 vote. Introduced in the Senate on March 1, and numbered

S. 2349, the measure amends Senate rules governing the interaction of Senators and Senate staff with lobbyists, and makes several changes regarding Senate procedures thought to be subject to influence by lobbyists. As reported by the committee, S. 2349 would

amend Senate rules to prohibit for one year any former Senate senior-level employee[45] who served on the staff of a Senator or of a Senate committee, and who subsequently becomes a registered lobbyist or lobbyist employee for the purpose of influencing legislation, from lobbying any Senator, officer, or employee of the Senate;

require a Senator to file with the Secretary of the Senate, a statement for public disclosure that he or she is negotiating or has any arrangement concerning prospective employment if a conflict of interest or the appearance of a conflict of interest may exist. The disclosure would be required to file a disclosure within three days of commencing such negotiation or arrangement;

require a Senator or Senate staff member to obtain written certification before undertaking any travel that the trip was not financed in whole, or in part, by a registered lobbyist or foreign agent, and that the provider did not accept funds from a registered lobbyist or foreign agent specifically earmarked for the purpose of financing the travel expenses. A Senator would be required to provide the Select Committee on Ethics a written, detailed itinerary of the trip; and a determination that the trip is primarily educational; consistent with the official duties of the Member, officer, or employee; does not create an appearance of use of public office for private gain; and has a minimal or no recreational component;

require written approval of privately funded travel from the Select Committee on Ethics. Within 30 days of completing the travel, a Senator, officer, or employee would be required to file with the Select Committee on Ethics and the Secretary of the Senate a description of meetings and events attended during such travel and the names of any registered lobbyist who accompanied them, subject to limited exception on national security grounds. The measure would require that trip information be posted on the Senator's official website not later than 30 days after the completion of the travel;

[45] The proposal would affect Senate staff who worked for a Senator or Senate committee and whose rate of pay was equal to or greater than 75 percent of the rate of pay of a Senator for more than 60 days in a

calendar year. Senators are paid $165,200. Senate staff who earned more than $2,382.69 or more per week for more than nine weeks, or $123,900 per year, would be subject to the post employment restriction proposal.

amend Senate rules to require the disclosure of noncommercial air travel taken in connection with the duties of the Member, officer, or employee, and file a report with the Secretary of the Senate, including the date, destination, and owner or lessee of the aircraft, the purpose of the trip, and the persons on the trip, except for any person flying the aircraft;

amend Senate rules to prohibit Senators from accepting gifts from lobbyists. Senators and Senate staff could accept a meal or other food from lobbyists subject to gift rule limits. Any food gift accepted would be subject to public disclosure through the Senator's website;

amend Senate rules to revoke floor privileges from any former Senator, Senator-elect, Secretary of the Senate, Sergeant at Arms of the Senate, or Speaker of the House who is a registered lobbyist or agent of a foreign principal, or is an employee or representative of any party or organization for the purpose of influencing, the passage, defeat, or amendment of any legislative proposal; and

require a Senator whose spouse or immediate family member[46] is a registered lobbyist or employees of a registrant under LDA for the purpose of influencing legislation to prohibit all staff employed by the Senator, including staff in personal, committee, and leadership offices, from having any official contact with the family member.

S. 2349 would also allow any Senator to make a point of order against consideration of a conference report that includes any matter not committed to the conferees by either House. The point of order could be made and voted on separately for each item alleged to be in violation. The point of order could be waived or suspended by an affirmative vote of 3/5 of the Members, duly chosen and sworn. The Senate could appeal a ruling of the Chair on a point of order raised under this measure by a 3/5 vote.

Additionally, the measure would amend Senate rules, creating Rule XLIV regarding earmarks. An earmark would be defined as a provision that specifies the identity of a non-federal entity to receive assistance in the form of budget authority; contract authority; loan authority; and other expenditures; or other revenue items, and the amount of the assistance. Before consideration of any bill, amendment or conference report could be in order, a list identifying all earmarks in the measure, along with identification of the Senator(s) who proposed them, and an explanation of the essential governmental purpose for the earmark must be made available, along with any joint statement of managers associated with the measure, to all Senators and made available on the Internet to the general public for at least 24 hours before

[46] Under the measure, immediate family member would mean the son, daughter, stepson, stepdaughter, son-in-law, daughter-in-law, mother, father, stepmother, stepfather, mother-in-law, father-in-law, brother, sister, stepbrother, or stepsister of the Senator.

its consideration. Similarly, S. 2349 would amend Senate rules to require that conference reports be available on the Internet 24 hours before consideration.

The measure would also amend Senate rules to prohibit a Senator from taking or withholding, or threatening to take or withhold an official act, or to influence or offer or threaten to influence the official act of another with the intent to influence on the basis of partisan political affiliation an employment decision or employment practice of any private entity. Finally, S. 2349 would establish the sense of the Senate that any restrictions on legislative branch employees should apply to the executive and judicial branches.

S. 2128, Committee Consideration. On March 2, 2006, the Senate Committee on Homeland Security and Governmental Affairs marked up S. 2128, the Lobbying Transparency and Accountability Act of 2005 Introduced by Senator John McCain, and voted 13-1 to report the measure as amended to the Senate. As reported, S. 2128 would amend LDA to further define a client as any person or entity that participates in a substantial way in planning, supervision or control of lobbying activities. Disclosure would not be required if a connection between the person or entity and the client is public knowledge, unless the person or entity plans supervises or controls lobbying activities;

further define lobbying activities to include paid efforts to stimulate grassroots lobbying but that do not include grassroots lobbying;

define grassroots lobbying to mean the voluntary efforts of members of the general public to communicate their views on an issue to federal officials, or to encourage other Members of the public to do the same;

define grassroots lobbyist to mean any individual who is retained by a client to engage in grassroots lobbying, and who is paid $25,000 or more in each quarterly period;

define paid efforts to stimulate grassroots lobbying as any paid attempt in support of lobbying contacts on behalf of a client to influence more than 500 members of the general public to contact one or more covered official to urge those officials (or Congress) to take specific action on an issue. The measure excludes communications from an entity to its members, employees, officers, or shareholders;

require quarterly, instead of semiannual, filing of lobbying disclosure reports;

require disclosure by registered lobbyists of all past executive branch and congressional employment;

require electronic filing of lobbyist registrations and disclosure reports filed with the Secretary of the Senate or the Clerk of the House of Representatives;

reduce of the thresholds for which registration and disclosure are required from $5,000 to $2,500 for a lobbying firm, and from $20,000 to $10,000 for an an organization whose employees engage in lobbying activities on its own behalf;

reduce the increments in which lobbying expenditures may be estimated, from less than $10,000 to less than $5,000, or in larger increments, from $20,000 to $10,000. Grassroots lobbyists would be subject to disclosure ranges of less than $10,000, less than $25,000, and increments above $25,000, rounded to the nearest $20,000;

require good faith estimates of the proportion of the total amount spent on grassroots lobbying activities, and within that amount, the total amount specifically relating to grassroots lobbying through paid advertising;

require electronic filing of lobbyist registrations and disclosure reports filed with the Secretary of the Senate or the Clerk of the House of Representatives;

require the establishment and maintenance of lobbying disclosure information in an electronic database that directly links lobbying disclosure information to the information disclosed in reports filed with the FEC under FECA and made available to the public free of charge through the Internet;

require registrants and lobbyists to file a report disclosing their name, employer, and the name of each federal candidate or officeholder, leadership PAC, or political party committee to whom a contribution of $200 or more was made, or for whom a fund-raising event was hosted or otherwise sponsored;

require disclosure within 30 days of travel the name of each covered official for whom a registrant or lobbyist employee provided or arranged any payment or reimbursement for travel, including an itemization of payments or reimbursements provided the purpose and final itinerary of the trip, the names of registrants or employees who were on the trip, the identity of the trip sponsor, and the identity of any person or entity other than the sponsor who provided direct or indirect payment for the travel;

require disclosure of the date, recipient, and amount of funds contributed or arranged by a registrant or registrant employee to pay the costs of; an event to honor or recognize a covered legislative branch official or covered executive branch official; contributions to, or on behalf of, an entity that is named for a covered legislative branch official or covered executive branch official, or to a person or entity in recognition of such official; an entity established, financed, maintained, or controlled by a covered legislative branch official or covered executive branch official, or an entity designated by such official; or to pay the costs of a meeting, retreat, conference or other similar event held by, or for the benefit of one or more covered official; and

prohibit a registered lobbyist from making a gift or providing travel to any Member of Congress or their staff.

S. 2128 as reported would require the Clerk and the Secretary to provide semiannual reports to the House Committee on Government Reform and Senate Committee on Homeland Security and Governmental Affairs listing the number of lobbyists and lobbying firms referred to the United States Attorney for the District of Columbia for noncompliance. The measure would require the United States Attorney for the District of Columbia to report on a semiannual basis the number of enforcement actions and the amount of any fines to the House Committees on Government Reform and the Judiciary, and the Senate committees on Homeland Security and Governmental Affairs and the Judiciary. S. 2128 as reported would increase the civil penalty for noncompliance with LDA to up to $100,000. The measure would require the Comptroller General to audit annually registrations and reports filed under LDA to determine the extent of compliance by lobbyists and their clients and to report to Congress by April 1. Additionally, the ban on former senior executive personnel, former Members of Congress, and legislative branch personnel, preventing them from lobbying the entity in which they previously served, would be extended from one to two years.

OTHER MEASURES INTRODUCED

S. 2265. S. 2265, the Pork Barrel Reduction Act, was introduced by Senator John McCain on February 9, 2006. The measure would amend LDA to require recipients of federal funds to file a report identifying the name and amount paid to any lobbyist registered under LDA whom the recipient retained to lobby on behalf of the recipient to receive the federal funding.[47]

S. 2261. S. 2261, the Transparency and Integrity in Earmarks Act of 2006, was introduced by Senator Barack Obama on February 8, 2006. The measure would amend LDA to require recipients of federal funds to file a report identifying the name

[47] S. 2265 would also make changes to Senate procedures for considering appropriations legislation, and conference reports. Additionally the measure would prohibit the obligation of funds for appropriations earmarks that are included only in congressional reports, and would require the disclosure by Senators of any proposed earmarks or unauthorized appropriations.

and amount paid to any lobbyist registered under LDA whom the recipient retained to lobby on behalf of the recipient to receive the federal funding.[48]

S. 2259. S. 2259, the Congressional Ethics Enforcement Commission Act of 2006, was introduced by Senator Barack Obama on February 8, 2006. The measure would create an independent office of public integrity in the legislative branch overseen by a congressional ethics enforcement commission. The office would

investigate lobbying disclosures filed with the Senate and the House;

investigate Senators and Senate staff who violate restrictions on interactions with lobbyists;

conduct research concerning governmental ethics and implement any public educational programs it considers necessary; and

report annually to the Senate Select Committee on Ethics and the House Committee on Standards of Official Conduct on the commission's activities, and make recommendations on matters within the its jurisdiction.

The measure provides for a nine-member commission, with the Speaker and minority leader of the House, and the majority and minority leaders of the Senate each appointing two, and the final member appointed on the concurrence of at least three of the chamber leaders. After an initial two-year appointment following enactment of the measure, commission members would serve four-year terms. The commission would conduct investigations of alleged violations of lobbying and chamber rules on the sworn complaint of any U.S. citizen. Investigations by the commission would be in lieu of any preliminary investigation by the ethics committees of either chamber. During any investigation the commission could refer the matter to the Attorney General if it finds evidence of criminal acts.

At the conclusion of its investigation, S. 2259 provides that the commission could terminate its investigation if it does not find probable cause to proceed. In the event that the commission has probable cause to believe that a violation has occurred, upon a majority vote it may: initiate a private reprimand of the violator, if the alleged violation did not result in significant economic advantage or gain by the alleged violator, significant economic loss to the state, or significant impact on public confidence in government; or initiate an adjudicatory proceeding to determine whether to present a case to the Select Committee on Ethics of the Senate or the Committee on Standards of Official Conduct of the House of Representatives as to whether there has been a violation. The measure provides for fines up to $10,000 and or imprisonment for up to one year for anyone who knowing files or encourages the filing of a frivolous complaint before the commission.

[48] S. 2261 would also make to Senate procedures regarding the inclusion and consideration of appropriations earmarks.

S. 2259 was referred to the Committee on Homeland Security and Governmental Affairs. No further action has been taken at the time of this writing.

S. 2233. S. 2233, the Lobbyist Reform Act of 2006, introduced by Senator Dianne Feinstein on February 1, 2006, would

extend the cooling off period required under 18 U.S.C. 207 to two years, and would extend provisions that currently bar former Members of Congress from lobbying any Member, officer, or staff member of either chamber to all employees of Congress;

prohibit the acceptance of gifts from lobbyists by Senators and Senate staff;

prohibit the acceptance by Senators and Senate staff of privately funded travel by lobbyists or entities that are affiliated with any group that lobbies; and

prohibit registered lobbyists from serving on political committees authorized by FECA.

S. 2233 was referred to the Committee on Rules and Administration. A hearing was held by the committee on February 8, 2006. At the conclusion of the hearing, it was announced that a markup of proposals related to lobbying within the jurisdiction of the committee could be held during the week of February 27.

S. 2186. S. 2186, the Commission to Strengthen Confidence in Congress Act of 2006, was introduced by Senator Norm Coleman on January 25, 2006. A similar measure, H.R. 4738, described above, was introduced in the House by Representative Mark Udall on February 8, 2006. S. 2186 would not change current lobbying laws and regulations, but would establish a commission to strengthen confidence in Congress through an evaluation of current congressional rules related to congressional interactions with various lobbying activities. A bipartisan, 10-member commission would be appointed by the majority and minority leadership of each chamber. The commission would be charged to

evaluate and report the effectiveness of current congressional ethics requirements;

weigh the need for improved ethical conduct with the need for lawmakers to have access to expertise on public policy issues;

determine and report minimum standards relating to official travel for Members of Congress and staff;

evaluate the range of gifts given to Members of Congress and staff, determine and report the effects on public policy, and make recommendations for limits on gifts;

evaluate and report the effectiveness and transparency of congressional disclosure laws and recommendations for improvements;

assess and report the effectiveness of the ban on Member of Congress and staff from lobbying their former office for one year and make recommendations for altering the time frame;

make recommendations to improve the process whereby Members of Congress can earmark priorities in appropriations Acts, while still preserving congressional power of the purse;

evaluate the use of public and privately funded travel by Members of Congress and staff, violations of Congressional rules governing travel, and make recommendations on limiting travel; and

investigate and report to Congress on its findings, conclusions, and recommendations for reform.

S. 2186 has been referred to the Committee on Rules and Administration. A hearing was held by the committee on February 8, 2006. At the conclusion of the hearing, it was announced that a markup of some of the proposals related to lobbying within the jurisdiction of the committee could be held during the week of February

27. No further action has been taken at the time of this writing.

S. 2180. On January 20, 2006, Senator Harry Reid, who is Senate Minority Leader, introduced S. 2180, the Honest Leadership and Open Government Act of 2006. The measure would amend LDA to require

quarterly, instead of semiannual, filing of lobbying disclosure reports;

reduction of the increments in which lobbying expenditures may be estimated in larger increments, from $20,000 to $1,000;

disclosure by registered lobbyists of all past executive branch and congressional employment;

electronic filing of lobbyist registrations and disclosure reports filed with the Secretary of the Senate or the Clerk of the House of Representatives;

establishment and maintenance by the Clerk and Secretary of lobbying disclosure information in an electronic database made available to the public free of charge through the Internet, and to make those reports available within 48 hours of filing; and disclosure of grassroots lobbying communications by paid lobbyists and itemized disclosure of expenditures on grassroots lobbying activities. In the event that a grassroots lobbyist receives or spends $250,000 or more for grassroots lobbying activities, an additional report must be made within 20 days.

S. 2180 would require the disclosure of any entity, other than the client, who participates in the planning, supervision, or control of lobbying activities. S. 2180 would not require disclosure if an entity's affiliation with the client is publicly available knowledge, or if any funding for the client is publicly disclosed by the entity. The measure would not require the disclosure of any information about individuals who are members of, or donors to, an entity treated as a client by LDA.

The measure would establish a Senate Office of Public Integrity. The office would receive LDA registrations and disclosure reports, and conduct audits and investigations necessary to ensure compliance with LDA. A director of the office would be appointed by the President pro tempore, based on recommendations of the Senate majority and minority leaders. The office would have the authority to refer violations of LDA to the Senate Select committee on Ethics and the Department of Justice for disciplinary action.

S. 2180 would ban Senate floor privileges to former Senators who become lobbyists. The measure would increase the civil penalty for failure to comply with lobbying disclosure requirements up to $100,000.[49] In addition, S. 2180 would establish criminal penalties for noncompliance with LDA. Knowing and willful failure to comply with registration requirements would be punishable by fines, a term of imprisonment up to five years, or both. Whoever knowingly willfully, and corruptly fails to comply with LDA disclosure requirements would be subject to fines, a term of imprisonment up to 10 years, or both. S. 2180 would extend the ban preventing former senior executive personnel, former Members of Congress, and legislative branch personnel from lobbying the entity in which they previously served from one to two years. S. 2180 was referred to the Committee on Homeland Security and Governmental Affairs. No further action has been taken at the time of this writing.

S. 2128, as Introduced. Senator John McCain introduced S. 2128, the Lobbying Transparency and Accountability Act of 2005, on December 16, 2005. Similar in nature to H.R. 4575, the measure would have amended LDA to require

quarterly, instead of semiannual, filing of lobbying disclosure reports;

[49] S. 2180 would require a number of other changes to laws and rules governing congressional ethics that are not directly related to lobbying disclosure. These include requiring public disclosure by Members of Congress of employment negotiations; the establishment of fines and penalties for Member of Congress or employees of the House who wrongfully influence, on a partisan basis, any entity's employment decisions or practices; amendments to Senate Rules to prohibit favoritism; requiring the Senate Select Committee on Ethics to develop and revise guidelines on reasonable expenditures for official government travel; requiring certification that congressional travel meets certain conditions, and establishing civil fines for false certifications.

reduction of the thresholds for which registration and disclosure are required from $5,000 to $2,500 for a lobbying firm, and from $20,000 to $10,000 for an an organization whose employees engage in lobbying activities on its own behalf;

reduction of the increments in which lobbying expenditures may be estimated, from less than $10,000 to less than $5,000, or in larger increments, from $20,000 to $10,000;

disclosure by registered lobbyists of all past executive branch and congressional employment;

electronic filing of lobbyist registrations and disclosure reports filed with the Secretary of the Senate or the Clerk of the House of Representatives;

establishment and maintenance of lobbying disclosure information in an electronic database that directly links lobbying disclosure information to the information disclosed in reports filed with the FEC under FECA and made available to the public free of charge through the Internet; and

disclosure of grassroots lobbying communications by paid lobbyists and itemized disclosure of expenditures on grassroots lobbying activities. In the event that a grassroots lobbyist receives or spends $250,000 or more for grassroots lobbying activities, an additional report must be made within 20 days.

S. 2128, as introduced, would amend LDA to redefine the term "client" as any person or entity that employs a lobbyist to carry out lobbying or grass roots lobbying activities on behalf of that person or entity. The measure would have required that firms and other entities that are members of coalitions or associations that employ a lobbyist are to be considered clients, along with the coalition or association, if their total contribution related to lobbying activities is greater than $10,000.

S. 2128, as introduced, would increase the civil penalty for failure to comply with lobbying disclosure requirements up to $100,000. The measure would have provided for reviews and semiannual reports by the Comptroller General on activities carried out by the Clerk of the House and the Secretary of the Senate under LDA. Additionally, the ban on former senior executive personnel, former Members of Congress, and legislative branch personnel preventing them from lobbying the entity in which they previously served would have been extended from one to two years.[50]

S. 1972. On November 7, 2005, Senator Rick Santorum introduced S. 1972, the Terrorist Lobby Disclosure Act of 2005. The measure would amend LDA to require Members of Congress and legislative branch employees to disclose to the Secretary of State any contacts with representatives or officials of governments that have been designated as state sponsors of terrorism by the Department of State. S. 1972 would require the Secretary to issue a report listing those who have had such contacts to the Senate Committee on Foreign Relations, the Senate Subcommittee on State, Foreign Operations, and Related Programs of the Committee on Appropriations, the House Committee on International Affairs, and the House Subcommittee on Foreign Operations, Export Financing, and Related Programs of the Committee on Appropriations. S. 1972 was referred to the Committee on Homeland Security and Governmental Affairs. No further action has been taken at the time of this writing.

S. 1398. S. 1398, the Lobbying and Ethics Reform Act of 2005 was introduced by Senator Russell Feingold on July 14, 2005. Similar in nature to H.R. 2412, the measure would amend LDA to require

quarterly, instead of semiannual, filing of lobbying disclosure reports;

electronic filing of lobbyist registrations and disclosure reports filed with the Secretary of the Senate or the Clerk of the House of Representatives;

establishment and maintenance of lobbying disclosure information in an electronic data base which directly links lobbying disclosure information to the information disclosed in reports filed with the FEC under FECA and made available to the public free of charge through the Internet;

identification of each executive branch official and Member of Congress with whom lobbying contacts are made, on an issue-byissue basis, for each covered official contacted;

disclosure by registered lobbyists of all past executive branch and congressional employment; and

[50] S. 2128 requires a number of other changes to laws and rules governing congressional ethics that are not directly related to lobbying disclosure. These include requiring public disclosure by Members of Congress of employment negotiations and increased disclosure of travel by Members of

Congress. The measure also specifies the valuation of tickets to sporting and entertainment events provided to covered executive and legislative branch officials.

disclosure of grassroots lobbying communications by paid lobbyists and itemized disclosure of expenditures on grassroots lobbying activities.

The measure would amend LDA to redefine the term "client" as any person or entity that employs a lobbyist on behalf of that person or entity. The measure requires that firms and other entities that are members of coalitions or associations that employ a lobbyist, are to be considered clients along with the coalition or association if their total contribution related to lobbying activities is greater than $10,000.

S. 1398 would increase the civil penalty for failure to comply with lobbying disclosure requirements up to $100,000. The measure provides for reviews and semiannual reports by the Comptroller General on activities carried out by the Clerk of the House and the Secretary of the Senate under LDA. Additionally, the ban on former senior executive personnel, former Members of Congress, and legislative branch personnel, preventing them from lobbying the entity in which they previously served, would be extended from one to two years. Finally, S. 1398 would revoke any benefit or privilege extended to former Members of Congress, including floor privileges, from former Members who are registered lobbyists.[51] S. 1398 was referred to the Committee on Homeland Security and Governmental Affairs. Hearings regarding lobbying proposals were held by the committee on January 25, 2006. No further action has been taken at the time of this writing.

[51] S. 1398 requires a number of other changes to laws and rules governing congressional ethics that are not directly related to lobbying disclosure. These include requiring public disclosure by Members of Congress of employment negotiations; the establishment of fines and penalties for Member of Congress or employees of the House who wrongfully influence, on a partisan basis, any entity's employment decisions or practices; amendments to the House Code of Official Conduct and the standing Rules of the Senate to prohibit favoritism; requiring the House Committee on Standards of Official Conduct to develop and revise guidelines on reasonable expenditures for official government travel; requiring certification that congressional travel meets certain conditions, and establishing civil fines for false certifications.

S. 1398 would also institute a ban on gifts from lobbyists to members of Congress and their staff. In the House, Rep. George Miller introduced H.R. 3177 on June 30, 2005 to ban gifts from lobbyists. Both measures also would amend the rules of the respective chambers in which they were introduced to prohibit Members from accepting gifts from lobbyists.

H.R. 3177 was referred to the House Committee on the Judiciary. No further action has been taken at the time of this writing.

FURTHER RESOURCES

Lobbying

CRS Current Legislative Issues page on Lobbying Disclosure and Ethics Reform, at [http://beta.crs.gov/cli/cli.aspx?PRDS_CLI_ITEM_ID=2405].

CRS Report RL33293, *Lobbying and Related Reform Proposals: Consideration of Selected Measures, 109th Congress*, by R. Eric Petersen.

CRS Report RL33234, *Lobbying Disclosure and Ethics Proposals Related to Lobbying Introduced in the 109th Congress: A Comparative Analysis*, by R. Eric Petersen.

CRS Report RS22226, *Summary and Analysis of Provisions of H.R. 2412, the Special Interest Lobbying and Ethics Accountability Act of 2005*, by Jack Maskell.

CRS Report RS22209, *Executive Lobbying: Statutory Controls*, by Louis Fisher.

CRS Report 96-809, *Lobbying Regulations on Non-Profit Organizations*, by Jack

H. Maskell.

CRS Report RS20725, *Lobbyists and Interest Groups: Sources of Information*, by Mari-Jana "M-J" Oboroceanu.

Congressional Ethics Rules

CRS Report RL33237, *Congressional Gifts and Travel: Proposals in the 109th Congress*, by Mildred Amer.

CRS Report RL33047, *Restrictions on the Acceptance of "Officially Connected" Travel Expenses From Private Sources Under House and Senate Ethics Rules*, by Jack Maskell.

CRS Report 97-875, *"Revolving Door," Post-Employment Laws for Federal Personnel*, by Jack Maskell.

CRS Report RS22231, *The Acceptance of Gifts of Free Meals by Members of Congress*, by Jack Maskell.

CRS Report RL31126, *Lobbying Congress: An Overview of Legal Provisions and Congressional Ethics Rules*, by Jack Maskell.

Congressional Procedures

CRS Report RL33295, *Comparison of Selected Senate Earmark Reform Proposals*, by Sandy Streeter.

Campaign Finance

Campaign Finance and Regulation of 527 Organizations, at
[http://beta.crs.gov/cli/cli.aspx?PRDS_CLI_ITEM_ID=529]

CRS Report RL32954, *527 Political Organizations: Legislation in the 109th Congress*, by Joseph E. Cantor, and Erika Lunder.

SUPPLEMENTS

ETHNIC INTEREST GROUPS IN THE UNITED STATES

MOST RECOGNIZED ETHNIC INTEREST GROUPS

The following ethnic interest groups as the most recognized in the United States:

1. Ancient Order of Hibernians (Irish)
2. German-American Heritage Foundation of the USA (Germans)
3. National Italian American Foundation (Italians)
4. Serbian Unity Congress (Serbs)
5. Albanian American Civic League (Albanians)
6. Sons of Norway (Norwegians)
7. German American National Congress (Germans)
8. Cuban-American National Foundation (Cubans)
9. TransAfrica (Africans)
10. Assembly of Turkish Americans (Turks)
11. United Macedonian Diaspora (Macedonians)
12. National Association of Arab-Americans (Arabs)
13. American Israel Public Affairs Committee (Israelis)
14. Armenian Assembly of America (Armenians)
15. Armenian National Committee of America (Armenians)
16. American Hellenic Institute Public Affairs Committee (Greeks)
17. National Association for the Advancement of Colored People (African Americans)
18. Institute of Caribbean Studies (Caribbeans)
19. Japan Society of America (Japanese)
20. Mexican American Legal Defense and Educational Fund (Mexicans)
21. League of United Latin American Citizens (Hispanics/Latinos)
22. National Iranian American Council (Iranians)
23. Anti-Defamation League (American Jews)
24. National Congress of American Indians (Native Americans)
25. English-Speaking Union (Anglo-Americans of British origin)
26. League of the South (Anglo-Americans of Southern USA origin)

LETTER FROM MEMBERS OF CONGRESS

More than 250 members of Congress have signed on to a declaration reaffirming their commitment to "the unbreakable bond that exists between [U.S.] and the State of Israel", in a letter to Secretary of State Hillary Clinton.

Dear Secretary Clinton:

We are writing to reaffirm our commitment to the unbreakable bond that exists between our country and the State of Israel and to express to you our deep concern over recent tension. In every important relationship, there will be occasional misunderstandings and conflicts.

The announcement during Vice President Biden's visit was, as Israel's Prime Minister said in an apology to the United States, "a regrettable incident that was done in all innocence and was hurtful, and which certainly should not have occurred." We are reassured that Prime Minister Netanyahu's commitment to put in place new procedures will ensure that such surprises, however unintended, will not recur.

The United States and Israel are close allies whose people share a deep and abiding friendship based on a shared commitment to core values including democracy, human rights and freedom of the press and religion. Our two countries are partners in the fight against terrorism and share an important strategic relationship.

A strong Israel is an asset to the national security of the United States and brings stability to the Middle East. We are concerned that the highly publicized tensions in the relationship will not advance the interests the

U.S. and Israel share. Above all, we must remain focused on the threat posed by the Iranian nuclear weapons program to Middle East peace and stability.

From the moment of Israel's creation, successive U.S. administrations have appreciated the special bond between the U.S. and Israel.

For decades, strong, bipartisan Congressional support for Israel, including security assistance and other important measures, have been eloquent testimony to our commitment to Israel's security, which remains unswerving.

It is the very strength of this relationship that has, in fact, made Arab-Israeli peace agreements possible, both because it convinced those who sought Israel?s destruction to abandon any such hope and because it gave successive Israeli governments the confidence to take calculated risks for peace.

In its declaration of independence 62 years ago, Israel declared: "We extend our hand to all neighboring states and their peoples in an offer of peace and good neighborliness, and appeal to them to establish bonds of cooperation and mutual help with the sovereign Jewish people settled in its own land."

In the decades since, despite constantly having to defend itself from attack, Israel has repeatedly made good on that pledge by offering to undertake painful risks to reach peace with its neighbors.

Our valuable bilateral relationship with Israel needs and deserves constant reinforcement.

As the Vice-President said during his recent visit to Israel: "Progress occurs in the Middle East when everyone knows there is simply no space between the U.S. and Israel when it comes to security, none. No space."

Steadfast American backing has helped lead to Israeli peace treaties with Egypt and Jordan. And American involvement continues to be critical to the effort to achieve peace between Israel and the Palestinians.

We recognize that, despite the extraordinary closeness between our country and Israel, there will be differences over issues both large and small.

Our view is that such differences are best resolved quietly, in trust and confidence, as befits longstanding strategic allies. We hope and expect that, with mutual effort and good faith, the United States and Israel will move beyond this disruption quickly, to the lasting benefit of both nations.

We believe, as President Obama said, that "Israel's security is paramount" in our Middle East policy and that "it is in U.S. national security interests to assure that Israel?s security as an independent Jewish state is maintained."

In that spirit, we look forward to working with you to achieve the common objectives of the U.S. and Israel, especially regional security and peace.

Sincerely,
STENY HOYER ERIC CANTOR
HOWARD L. BERMAN ILEANA ROS-LEHTINEN
GARY ACKERMAN DAN BURTO

RES. 1734 [111TH]: REAFFIRMING CONGRESSIONAL OPPOSITION TO THE UNILATERAL DECLARATION OF A PALESTINIAN STATE

November 29, 2010

Mr. POE of Texas (for himself, Ms. BERKLEY, Ms. ROS-LEHTINEN, Mr. WEINER, Mr. BURTON of Indiana, and Mr. ACKERMAN) submitted the following resolution; which was referred to the Committee on Foreign Affairs

RESOLUTION

Reaffirming Congressional opposition to the unilateral declaration of a Palestinian state, and for other purposes.

Whereas a true and lasting peace between Israel and the Palestinians can only be achieved through direct negotiations between the parties;

Whereas the leadership of the Palestinian Authority (PA) and the Palestine Liberation Organization (PLO) have repeatedly refused to negotiate directly with the Government of Israel, demanding unprecedented preconditions from Israel in exchange for their return to direct negotiations;

Whereas Palestinian leaders have repeatedly threatened to unilaterally declare a Palestinian state and to seek recognition of a Palestinian state by the United Nations and other international forums;

Whereas Palestinian leaders are reportedly holding high-level discussions on pursuing recognition of a Palestinian state by the United Nations and other international forums;

Whereas UN Special Coordinator for the Middle East Peace Process Robert Serry on October 26, 2010, expressed his support for recognition of a Palestinian state by the United Nations;

Whereas, on March 11, 1999, the Senate adopted Senate Concurrent Resolution 5, and on March 16, 1999, the House of Representatives adopted House Concurrent Resolution 24, both of which resolved that 'any attempt to establish Palestinian statehood outside the negotiating process will invoke the strongest congressional opposition.';

Whereas Secretary of State Hillary Rodham Clinton stated on October 20, 2010, that 'There is no substitute for face-to-face discussion and, ultimately, for an agreement that leads to a just and lasting peace.';

Whereas Secretary Clinton stated on November 10, 2010, that 'Negotiations between the parties is the only means by which all the outstanding claims arising out of the [Israeli-Palestinian] conflict can be resolved. . . . So we do not support unilateral steps by either party that could prejudge the outcome of such negotiations.';

Whereas, on November 10, 2010, the Israeli Knesset adopted a resolution 'reject[ing] entirely the threats of some Palestinian leaders to declare unilateral Palestinian statehood . . . [affirming] that all points of dispute must be debated only within the framework of direct negotiations . . . [and] call[ing] on the Palestinian leadership to return to the negotiating table.';

Whereas Prime Minister Benjamin Netanyahu of Israel, in a speech at Bar Ilan University in Israel on June 14, 2009, stated that '[A] fundamental prerequisite for ending the conflict is a public, binding and unequivocal Palestinian recognition of Israel as the nation state of the Jewish people. . . . Therefore, today we ask our friends in the international community, led by the United States, for what is critical to the security of Israel: Clear commitments that in a future peace agreement, the territory controlled by the Palestinians will be demilitarized. . . . If we receive this guarantee regarding demilitarization and Israel's security needs, and if the Palestinians recognize Israel as the State of the Jewish people, then we will be ready in a future peace agreement to reach a solution where a demilitarized Palestinian state exists alongside the Jewish state.';

Whereas efforts to bypass negotiations and to unilaterally declare a Palestinian state or to appeal to the United Nations or other international forums for recognition of a Palestinian state would clearly and fundamentally violate the underlying principles of the 1993 Oslo Accords and the Middle East peace process, and represent another instance of the Palestinian leadership's noncompliance with its commitments under existing agreements; and

Whereas United States opposition to any unilateral Palestinian declaration of statehood or related measures should be reaffirmed strongly and unequivocally: Now, therefore, be it

Resolved, by the House of Representatives that Congress--

(1) reaffirms its strong opposition to any attempt to establish a Palestinian state outside the negotiating process;

(2) strongly and unequivocally opposes any attempt to seek recognition of a Palestinian state by the United Nations or other international forums;

(3) calls upon the Administration to continue its opposition to the unilateral declaration of a Palestinian state;

(4) calls upon the Administration to affirm that the United States would deny any recognition, legitimacy, or support of any kind to any unilaterally declared 'Palestinian state' and would urge other responsible nations to follow suit, and to make clear that any such unilateral declaration would constitute a grievous violation of the principles underlying the Oslo Accords and the Middle East peace process;

(5) calls upon the Administration to affirm that the United States will oppose any attempt to seek recognition of a Palestinian state by the United Nations or other international forums and will veto any resolution to that end by the United Nations Security Council;

(6) calls upon the President and the Secretary of State to lead a high-level diplomatic effort to encourage the European Union and other responsible nations to strongly and unequivocally oppose the unilateral declaration of a Palestinian state or any attempt to seek recognition of a Palestinian state by the United Nations or other international forums; and

(7) supports the resolution of the Israeli-Palestinian conflict and the achievement of a true and lasting peace through direct negotiations between the parties.

BASIC TITLES ON THE UNITES STATES

Title	ISBN
United States Banking & Financial Market Handbook	1438751052
United States Business and Investment Opportunities Yearbook Volume 1 Strategic Information and Opportunities	143877821X
United States Business Law Handbook - Strategic Information and Basic Laws	1438771320
United States Business Law Handbook - Strategic Information and Basic Laws	1438771320
United States Chambers of Commerce Directory, Vol.1 Alaska, Arkansas, Arizona	1438751060
United States Clothing & Textile Industry Handbook	1438751079
United States Congress Guide	1438751087
United States Country Study Guide - Strategic Information and Developments Volume 1 Strategic Information and Developments	1438775865
United States Ecology & Nature Protection Handbook	1438751095
United States Energy Policy, Laws and Regulations Handbook	1438751109
United States Healthcare Sector Organization, Management and Payment Systems Handbook - Strategic Information, Programs and Regulations	9781433086045
United States Industrial and Business Directory	1438751117
United States Internet and E-Commerce Investment and Business Guide - Strategic and Practical Information: Regulations and Opportunities	1438751125
United States Investment and Business Guide - Strategic and Practical Information	1438769040
United States Investment and Business Guide Strategic and Practical Information	1438769040
United States Justice System and National Police Handbook	1438751133
United States Medical & Pharmaceutical Industry Handbook	1438751141

Title	ISBN
United States Mineral & Mining Sector Investment and Business Guide - Strategic and Practical Information	143875115X
United States Oil & Gas Sector Business & Investment Opportunities Yearbook	1438751168
United States Privatization Programs and Regulations Handbook	1438751176
United States Recent Economic and Political Developments Yearbook	143306233X
United States Research & Development Policy Handbook	1433062909
United States Telecommunication Industry Business Opportunities Handbook	1438751184
United States: How to Invest, Start and Run Profitable Business in United States Guide - Practical Information, Opportunities, Contacts	9781433084843
United States: Importacion a los Estados Unidos	1433068826
United States: Starting Small Business In the US Handbook	1433068834
US - Korea North: Political and Economic Cooperation Handbook	9781577515517
US - Utah Investment & Business Guide	1433057972
US - Utah Small Business Assistance and Programs Handbook	1433057980
US "Green Card" How to Become US Permanent Resident Handbook	1433054035
US "War on Terror" Handbook	1433061465
US "War on Terror" Handbook	1433061465
US "War on Terror" Handbook	1433061465
US "War on Terror" Military Strategy Handbook	1433054043
US & Canada Literary Agents and Publishers	1433054051
US & International Economic Assistance to Palestine Handbook	143875244X
US & International Economic Assistance to Palestine Handbook	143305406X
US A "Spy" Guide - Strategic Information and Developments	1433054078
US A Spy" Guide"	1438752458
US Aerospace and Space Doctrine Handbook	1433068869
US Affordable Healthcare Act Handbook - Strategic Information and Implementation	9781433086045
US African Development Fund Handbook	1438752466
US African Development Fund Handbook	1433054086
US AGENCY FOR INTERNATIONAL DEVELOPMENT BUSINESS OPPORTUNITIES HANDBOOK	1438752474
US AGENCY FOR INTERNATIONAL DEVELOPMENT BUSINESS OPPORTUNITIES HANDBOOK	1433054094
US Agency for International Development Handbook	1438752482
US Agency for International Development Handbook	1433054108
US Air Force Academy Handbook	1438752490
US Air Force Academy Handbook	1433054116
US Air Force Air University Handbook	1438752504
US Air Force Air University Handbook	1433054124
US Air Force Base Conversion Agency Handbook	1438752512
US Air Force Base Conversion Agency Handbook	1433054132
US Air Force Handbook	1438752520
US Air force Handbook	1433060558
US Air Force Handbook	1433054140
US Air force Handbook	1433060558
US Air force Handbook	1433060558
US Air Force in Europe Handbook	1438752539
US Air Force in Europe Handbook	1433054159
US Air force or the Future Handbook Volume 1	1433061066
US Air force or the Future Handbook Volume 1	1433061066

Title	ISBN
US Air Force or the Future Handbook Volume 1	1433061066
US Air force or the Future Handbook Volume 2	1433061074
US Air force or the Future Handbook Volume 2	1433061074
US Air Force or the Future Handbook Volume 2	1433061074
US Air force or the Future Handbook Volume 3	1433061228
US Air force or the Future Handbook Volume 3	1433061228
US Air force or the Future Handbook Volume 3	1433061228
US Air Force or the Future Handbook Volume 4	1433061090
US Air force or the Future Handbook Volume 4	1433061090
US Air force or the Future Handbook Volume 4	1433061090
US Air Force Special Operations School Handbook	1438752547
US Air Force Special Operations School Handbook	1433054167
US Air Transportation Business Law Handbook - Strategic Information and Basic Laws	1438752555
US Air Transportation Business Law Handbook - Strategic Information and Basic Laws	1433054175
US Air Transportation Handbook: Regulations and Business Opportunities	1438752563
US Air Transportation Handbook: Regulations and Business Opportunities	1433054183
US Airport Improvement Program Handbook	1438752571
US Airport Improvement Program Handbook	1433054191
US Airports Handbook: Regulations and Business Opportunities	143875258X
US Airports Handbook: Regulations and Business Opportunities	1433054205
US Airpower and Space Security Doctrine Handbook	1433068877
US Alabama Business Registration and Incorporation Guide	1433000350
US Alabama Investment & Business Guide	1433000369
US Alabama Small Business Assistance and Programs Handbook	1433000377
US American Indians Business Opportunities Handbook	1433061856
US American Indians Business Opportunities Handbook	1433061856
US American Indians Business Opportunities Handbook	1433061856
US and Canada Literary Agents and Publishers Handbook	1438752431
US Anti SPAM Laws and Regulations Handbook	1438752598
US Anti SPAM Laws and Regulations Handbook	1433054213
US Anti Terrorism Handbook: Strategy, Operations, Programs	1438752601
US Anti Terrorism Handbook: Strategy, Operations, Programs	1433054221
US Anti-Gambling Laws and Regulations Handbook	9781577515524
US Arms Control and Disarmament Agency Handbook	143875261X
US Arms Control and Disarmament Agency Handbook	143305423X
US Arms Control and International Security Policy Handbook	1438752628
US Arms Control and International Security Policy Handbook	1433054248
US Arms Export Policy and Control Procedures Handbook	1438752636
US Arms Export Policy and Control Procedures Handbook	1438752644
US Arms Export Policy and Control Procedures Handbook	1433054256
US Arms Export Policy and Control Procedures Handbook	1433054264
US Arms Sales to Foreign Countries Handbook	1438752652
US Arms Sales to Foreign Countries Handbook	1433054272
US Army Future Combat Systems Handbook	1433062925
US Army Future Combat Systems Handbook	1433062925
US Army Future Combat Systems Handbook	1433062925
US Army Handbook	1433060701

Title	ISBN
US Army Handbook	1433060701
US Army Handbook	1433060701
US Army Modernization Plans Handbook	1433062917
US Army Modernization Plans Handbook	1433062917
US Army Modernization Plans Handbook	1433062917
US Army National Guards Handbook	1438752660
US Army National Guards Handbook	1433054280
US Army New Weapon Systems Handbook	1433062046
US Army New Weapon Systems Handbook	1433062046
US Army New Weapon Systems Handbook	1433062046
US Army Security Assistance Command Handbook	1438752679
US Army Security Assistance Command Handbook	1433054299
US Army Security Assistance Training Management Organization Handbook	1438752687
US Army Security Assistance Training Management Organization Handbook	1433054302
US Army Weapon Systems Handbook	1438752695
US Army Weapon Systems Handbook	1433054310
US Assistance to Afghanistan Handbook	1438752709
US Assistance to Afghanistan Handbook	1433054329
US Assistance to Albania Handbook	1438752717
US Assistance to Albania Handbook	1433054337
US Assistance to Angola Handbook	1438752725
US Assistance to Angola Handbook	1433054345
US Assistance to Armenia Handbook	1438752733
US Assistance to Armenia Handbook	1433054353
US Assistance to Azerbaijan Handbook	1438752741
US Assistance to Azerbaijan Handbook	1433054361
US Assistance to Bangladesh Handbook	143875275X
US Assistance to Bangladesh Handbook	143305437X
US Assistance to Belarus Handbook	1438752768
US Assistance to Belarus Handbook	1433054388
US Assistance to Benin Handbook	1438752776
US Assistance to Benin Handbook	1433054396
US Assistance to Bolivia Handbook	1438752784
US Assistance to Bolivia Handbook	143305440X
US Assistance to Bosnia-Herzegovina Handbook	1438752792
US Assistance to Bosnia-Herzegovina Handbook	1433054418
US Assistance to Brazil Handbook	1438752806
US Assistance to Brazil Handbook	1433054426
US Assistance to Bulgaria Handbook	1438752814
US Assistance to Bulgaria Handbook	1433054434
US Assistance to Burundi Handbook	1438752822
US Assistance to Burundi Handbook	1433054442
US Assistance to Cambodia Handbook	1438752830
US Assistance to Cambodia Handbook	1433054450
US Assistance to Colombia Handbook	1438752849
US Assistance to Colombia Handbook	1433054469
US Assistance to Croatia Handbook	1438752857
US Assistance to Croatia Handbook	1433054477
US Assistance to Cuba Handbook	1438752865

Title	ISBN
US Assistance to Cuba Handbook	1433054485
US Assistance to Cyprus Handbook	1438752873
US Assistance to Cyprus Handbook	1433054493
US Assistance to Czech Republic Handbook	1438752881
US Assistance to Czech Republic Handbook	1433054507
US Assistance to Dominican Republic Handbook	143875289X
US Assistance to Dominican Republic Handbook	1433054515
US Assistance to DR Congo Handbook	1438752903
US Assistance to DR Congo Handbook	1433054523
US Assistance to East Timor Handbook	1438752911
US Assistance to East Timor Handbook	1433054531
US Assistance to Ecuador Handbook	143875292X
US Assistance to Ecuador Handbook	143305454X
US Assistance to Egypt Handbook	1438752938
US Assistance to Egypt Handbook	1433054558
US Assistance to El Salvador Handbook	1438752946
US Assistance to El Salvador Handbook	1433054566
US Assistance to Eritrea Handbook	1438752954
US Assistance to Eritrea Handbook	1433054574
US Assistance to Ethiopia Handbook	1438752962
US Assistance to Ethiopia Handbook	1433054582
US Assistance to FYR of Macedonia Handbook	1438752970
US Assistance to FYR of Macedonia Handbook	1433054590
US Assistance to Georgia Handbook	1438752989
US Assistance to Georgia Handbook	1433054604
US Assistance to Ghana Handbook	1438752997
US Assistance to Ghana Handbook	1433054612
US Assistance to Guatemala Handbook	1438753004
US Assistance to Guatemala Handbook	1433054620
US Assistance to Guinea Handbook	1438753012
US Assistance to Guinea Handbook	1433054639
US Assistance to Guyana Handbook	1438753020
US Assistance to Guyana Handbook	1433054647
US Assistance to Haiti Handbook	1438753039
US Assistance to Haiti Handbook	1433054655
US Assistance to Honduras Handbook	1438753047
US Assistance to Honduras Handbook	1433054663
US Assistance to India Handbook	1438753055
US Assistance to India Handbook	1433054671
US Assistance to Indonesia Handbook	1438753063
US Assistance to Indonesia Handbook	1438753071
US Assistance to Indonesia Handbook	1433054698
US Assistance to Indonesia Handbook	143305468X
US Assistance to Ireland/Northern Ireland (UK) Handbook	143875308X
US Assistance to Ireland/Northern Ireland (UK) Handbook	1433054701
US Assistance to Jamaica Handbook	1438753098
US Assistance to Jamaica Handbook	143305471X
US Assistance to Jordan Handbook	1438753101
US Assistance to Jordan Handbook	1433054728

Title	ISBN
US Assistance to Kazakhstan Handbook	143875311X
US Assistance to Kazakhstan Handbook	1433054736
US Assistance to Kenya Handbook	1438753128
US Assistance to Kenya Handbook	1433054744
US Assistance to Kosovo Handbook	1438753136
US Assistance to Kosovo Handbook	1433054752
US Assistance to Kyrgyzstan Handbook	1438753144
US Assistance to Kyrgyzstan Handbook	1433054760
US Assistance to Laos Handbook	1438753152
US Assistance to Laos Handbook	1433054779
US Assistance to Lebanon Handbook	1438753160
US Assistance to Lebanon Handbook	1433054787
US Assistance to Liberia Handbook	1438753179
US Assistance to Liberia Handbook	1433054795
US Assistance to Lithuania Handbook	1438753187
US Assistance to Lithuania Handbook	1433054809
US Assistance to Madagascar Handbook	1438753195
US Assistance to Madagascar Handbook	1433054817
US Assistance to Malawi Handbook	1438753209
US Assistance to Malawi Handbook	1433054825
US Assistance to Mali Handbook	1438753217
US Assistance to Mali Handbook	1433054833
US Assistance to Mexico Handbook	1438753225
US Assistance to Mexico Handbook	1433054841
US Assistance to Moldova Handbook	1438753233
US Assistance to Moldova Handbook	143305485X
US Assistance to Mongolia Handbook	1433054868
US Assistance to Morocco Handbook	1438753241
US Assistance to Morocco Handbook	143875325X
US Assistance to Morocco Handbook	1433054876
US Assistance to Morocco Handbook	1433054884
US Assistance to Mozambique Handbook	1438753268
US Assistance to Mozambique Handbook	1433054892
US Assistance to Myanmar Handbook	1438753276
US Assistance to Myanmar Handbook	1433054906
US Assistance to Namibia Handbook	1438753284
US Assistance to Namibia Handbook	1433054914
US Assistance to Nepal & Pakistan Handbook	1438753292
US Assistance to Nepal & Pakistan Handbook	1433054922
US Assistance to Nicaragua Handbook	1438753306
US Assistance to Nicaragua Handbook	1433054930
US Assistance to Nigeria Handbook	1438753314
US Assistance to Nigeria Handbook	1433054949
US Assistance to Panama Handbook	1438753322
US Assistance to Panama Handbook	1433054957
US Assistance to Paraguay Handbook	1438753330
US Assistance to Paraguay Handbook	1433054965
US Assistance to Peru Handbook	1438753349
US Assistance to Peru Handbook	1433054973

Title	ISBN
US Assistance to Philippines Handbook	1438753357
US Assistance to Philippines Handbook	1433054981
US Assistance to Poland Handbook	1438753365
US Assistance to Poland Handbook	143305499X
US Assistance to Romania Handbook	1438753373
US Assistance to Romania Handbook	1433055007
US Assistance to Russia Handbook	1438753381
US Assistance to Russia Handbook	1433055015
US Assistance to Rwanda Handbook	143875339X
US Assistance to Rwanda Handbook	1433055023
US Assistance to Senegal Handbook	1438753403
US Assistance to Senegal Handbook	1433055031
US Assistance to Serbia and Montenegro Handbook	1438753411
US Assistance to Serbia and Montenegro Handbook	143305504X
US Assistance to Sierra Leone Handbook	143875342X
US Assistance to Sierra Leone Handbook	1433055058
US Assistance to Slovak Republic Handbook	1438753438
US Assistance to Slovak Republic Handbook	1433055066
US Assistance to Somalia Handbook	1438753446
US Assistance to Somalia Handbook	1433055074
US Assistance to South Africa Handbook	1438753454
US Assistance to South Africa Handbook	1433055082
US Assistance to Sri Lanka Handbook	1438753462
US Assistance to Sri Lanka Handbook	1433055090
US Assistance to Sudan Handbook	1438753470
US Assistance to Sudan Handbook	1433055104
US Assistance to Tajikistan Handbook	1438753489
US Assistance to Tajikistan Handbook	1433055112
US Assistance to Tanzania Handbook	1438753497
US Assistance to Tanzania Handbook	1433055120
US Assistance to Turkey Handbook	1438753500
US Assistance to Turkey Handbook	1433055139
US Assistance to Turkmenistan Handbook	1438753519
US Assistance to Turkmenistan Handbook	1433055147
US Assistance to Uganda Handbook	1438753527
US Assistance to Uganda Handbook	1433055155
US Assistance to Ukraine Handbook	1438753535
US Assistance to Ukraine Handbook	1433055163
US Assistance to Uzbekistan Handbook	1438753543
US Assistance to Uzbekistan Handbook	1433055171
US Assistance to Vietnam Handbook	1438753551
US Assistance to Vietnam Handbook	143305518X
US Assistance to West Bank/ Gaza Handbook	143875356X
US Assistance to West Bank/ Gaza Handbook	1433055198
US Assistance to Yemen Handbook	1438753578
US Assistance to Yemen Handbook	1438753586
US Assistance to Yemen Handbook	1433055201
US Assistance to Yemen Handbook	143305521X
US Assistance to Zambia Handbook	1438753594

Title	ISBN
US Assistance to Zambia Handbook	1433055228
US Assistance to Zimbabwe Handbook	1438753608
US Assistance to Zimbabwe Handbook	1433055236
US Aviation and Aerospace Industry Handbook Vol 2 Military Equipment	1433053616
US Aviation and Aerospace Industry Handbook Volume 1 BASIC TRENDS AND REGULATIONS	1438753616
US Aviation and Aerospace Industry Handbook Volume 1 BASIC TRENDS AND REGULATIONS	1433055244
US Aviation Industry Strategic Developments and Statistics Yearbook	1433068885
US Banking & Financial Market Handbook	1433052458
US Bankruptcy Regulations and procedures Handbook	1438753624
US Bankruptcy Regulations and procedures Handbook	1433055252
US Banks Handbook	1438753632
US Banks Handbook	1433055260
US Book Distributors Directory vol2	1438753640
US Book Distributors Directory vol2	1433055279
US Brazil Diplomatic and Political Cooperation Handbook	1438751516
US Budgeting Process Handbook	1433068893
US Business and Investment Opportunities Yearbook	1438753659
US Business and Investment Opportunities Yearbook	1433055287
US Business for Sale and Franchises Opportunities Handbook: Information by State	1433068907
US Business Intelligence Handbook	1438753667
US Business Intelligence Handbook	1433055295
US Business Intelligence Report - Practical Information, Opportunities, Contacts	1438753675
US Business Intelligence Report - Practical Information, Opportunities, Contacts	1433055309
US Business Law Handbook - Strategic Information and Basic Laws	1438753683
US Business Law Handbook - Strategic Information and Basic Laws	1433055317
US Buying and Financing Residential Real Estate in the US Handbook	1433004925
US Buying or Selling a Business in the US Handbook	1433004941
US California Business Registration and Incorporation Guide	1433004976
US California Government Handbook - Practical Information and Contacts	1433002353
US California Investment & Business Guide	1433004984
US California Small Business Assistance and Programs Handbook	1433004992
US Catalog of Federal Domestic Assistance Handbook	9781577515531
US CENTRAL INTELLIGENCE AGENCY (CIA) HANDBOOK	1438753691
US CENTRAL INTELLIGENCE AGENCY (CIA) HANDBOOK	1433055325
US Chambers of Commerce Directory, Vol.1 Alaska, Arkansas, Arizona	1433052466
US Chambers of Commerce Directory, Vol.3 Florida	1438753705
US Chambers of Commerce Directory, Vol.3 Florida	1433055333
US Chemical and Biological Weapon Strategy Handbook	1433060493
US Chemical and Biological Weapon Strategy Handbook	1433060493
US Chemical and Biological Weapon Strategy Handbook	1433060493
US Citizenship, Naturalization Regulation and Procedures Handbook: Practical Information and Contacts	9781577515548
US Civil Rights Policy Handbook	1438753713
US Civil Rights Policy Handbook	1433055341
US Clothing & Textile Industry Handbook	1433052474
US Coastal Guards Handbook	1438753721
US Coastal Guards Handbook	143305535X

Title	ISBN
US Commercial insurance Modernization Handbook	1433062933
US Commercial insurance Modernization Handbook	1433062933
US Commercial insurance Modernization Handbook	1433062933
US Commodity Futures Trading Commission Handbook	143875373X
US Commodity Futures Trading Commission Handbook	1433055368
US Companies in Russia Directory	1438753748
US Companies in Russia Directory	1433055376
US Company Laws and Regulations Handbook Volume 1 Corporate Laws and Regulations Basics	1433070804
US Company Laws and Regulations Handbook Volume 2 Non Profits	1433070820
US Congress Guide	1438753756
US Congress Guide	1433055384
US Congress Guide	1433052482
US Congress Joint Committee on Printing Handbook	1433056526
US Congress Joint Committee on Taxation Handbook	1433056534
US Congress Joint Economic Committee Handbook	1433056542
US Congressional Budget Office Handbook	1438753764
US Congressional Budget Office Handbook	1433055392
US Counterintelligence Handbook	1438753772
US Counterintelligence Handbook	1433055406
US Counterintelligence Operations against Cuba Handbook	1438753780
US Counterintelligence Operations against Cuba Handbook	1433055414
US Country Study Guide - Strategic Information and Developments	1438753799
US Country Study Guide - Strategic Information and Developments	1433055422
US Customs Broker Handbook: Regulations, Procedures, Opportunities	1433068915
US Customs Brokers Directory	1433068923
US Customs Regulations Handbook	1438753802
US Customs Regulations Handbook	1433055430
US Customs, Trade Regulations and Procedures Handbook	1438753810
US Customs, Trade Regulations and Procedures Handbook	1433055449
US Defense Advanced Research Projects Agency Handbook	1438753829
US Defense Advanced Research Projects Agency Handbook	1433055457
US Defense Agencies and Organizations Handbook	1438753837
US Defense Agencies and Organizations Handbook	1433055465
US Defense and Intelligence Abbreviations and Acronyms Handbook	1438753845
US Defense and Intelligence Abbreviations and Acronyms Handbook	1433055473
US Defense and Military Strategy Handbook	1433060973
US Defense and Military Strategy Handbook	1433060973
US Defense and Military Strategy Handbook	1433060973
US Defense Information Systems Agency Handbook	1438753853
US Defense Information Systems Agency Handbook	1433055481
US Defense Intelligence Agency Business Guide	1438753861
US Defense Intelligence Agency Business Guide	143305549X
US Defense Intelligence Agency Handbook	143875387X
US Defense Intelligence Agency Handbook	1433055503
US Defense Policy Handbook	1438753888
US Defense Policy Handbook	1433055511
US Defense Security Service Handbook	1438753896
US Defense Security Service Handbook	143305552X

Title	ISBN
US Defense Threat Reduction Agency Handbook	143875390X
US Defense Threat Reduction Agency Handbook	1433055538
US Department of Agriculture Business Opportunities Handbook	1438753918
US Department of Agriculture Business Opportunities Handbook	1433055546
US Department of Agriculture Handbook	1433055554
US Department of Commerce Handbook	1438753926
US Department of Commerce Handbook	1433055562
US Department of Defense Handbook	1438753934
US Department of Defense Handbook	1433055570
US Department of Energy Business Opportunities Handbook	1438753942
US Department of Energy Business Opportunities Handbook	1433055589
US Department of Energy Handbook	1438753950
US Department of Energy Handbook	1433055597
US Department of Health and Human Services Handbook	1438753969
US Department of Health and Human Services Handbook	1433055600
US Department of Homeland Security Handbook	1438753977
US Department of Homeland Security Handbook	1433055619
US Department of Housing and Urban Services Handbook	1438753985
US Department of Housing and Urban Services Handbook	1433055627
US Department of Interior Handbook	1438753993
US Department of Interior Handbook	1433055635
US Department of Justice Handbook	1438754000
US Department of Justice Handbook	1433055643
US Department of Labor Handbook	1438754019
US Department of Labor Handbook	1433055651
US Department of State Handbook	1438754027
US Department of State Handbook	143305566X
US Department of the Air Force Handbook	1438754035
US Department of the Air Force Handbook	1433055678
US Department of the Army Handbook	1438754043
US Department of the Army Handbook	1433055686
US Department of the Navy Handbook	1438754051
US Department of the Navy Handbook	1433055694
US Department of the Treasury Handbook	143875406X
US Department of the Treasury Handbook	1433055708
US Department of Transport Handbook	1438754078
US Department of Transport Handbook	1433055716
US Department of Veteran Affairs Handbook	1438754086
US Department of Veteran Affairs Handbook	1433055724
US Diplomatic Handbook - Strategic Information and Developments	1438754094
US Diplomatic Handbook - Strategic Information and Developments	1433055732
US Drug and Medical Devices Export-Import Regulations Handbook	1438754108
US Drug and Medical Devices Export-Import Regulations Handbook	1433055740
US Ecology & Nature Protection Handbook	1433052490
US Ecology & Nature Protection Laws and Regulation Handbook	1433075210
US E-Commerce Business Guide	1438754116
US E-Commerce Business Guide	1433055759
US E-Commerce Business Law Handbook - Strategic Information and Basic Laws	1438754124
US E-Commerce Business Law Handbook - Strategic Information and Basic Laws	1433055767

Title	ISBN
US Economic and Political Assistance to Macedonia Handbook	1438754132
US Economic and Political Assistance to Macedonia Handbook	1433055775
US ECONOMIC ASSISTANCE TO RUSSIA Handbook	1438754140
US Economic Assistance to Russia Handbook	1433055783
US Education System and Policy Handbook	1433068796
US El Salvador Diplomatic and Political Cooperation Handbook	1438751648
US Emission Trading Laws, Regulations and Programs Handbook	9781577515555
US Energy Policy, Laws and Regulation Handbook	1433072971
US Energy Policy, Laws and Regulations Handbook	1433052504
US Environmental Protection Agency Handbook	1438754159
US Environmental Protection Agency Handbook	1433055791
US Export Guide: How to Export Products and Services from the United States	1438754167
US Export Guide: How to Export Products and Services from the United States	1433055805
US Export Programs Guide	1438754175
US Export Programs Guide	1433055813
US Export-Import Bank Handbook	1438754183
US Export-Import Bank Handbook	1433055821
US Export-Import Trade and Business Directory	143305583X
US Export-Import, Investment & Financial Assistance Handbook	1438754191
US Export-Import, Investment & Financial Assistance Handbook	1433055848
US Farmers Markets Directory	1433062038
US Farmers Markets Directory	1433062038
US Farmers Markets Directory	1433062038
US Farmers Markets Directory – Volume 2 Ohio-Wyoming	1433068931
US FDA Cosmetics Products Control and Regulations Handbook	1438754205
US FDA Cosmetics Products Control and Regulations Handbook	1433055856
US FDA Drug Products Control and Regulations Handbook	1438754213
US FDA Drug Products Control and Regulations Handbook	1433055864
US FDA Food Products Control and Regulations Handbook	1438754221
US FDA Food Products Control and Regulations Handbook	1433055872
US FDA Medical Devices Control and Regulations Handbook	143875423X
US FDA Medical Devices Control and Regulations Handbook	1433055880
US Federal Bureau of Investigation (FBI) Academy Handbook	1433055899
US Federal Bureau of Investigation (FBI) Business Opportunities Handbook	1438754248
US Federal Bureau of Investigation (FBI) Business Opportunities Handbook	1433055902
US Federal Bureau of Investigation (FBI) Handbook	1438754256
US Federal Bureau of Investigation (FBI) Handbook	1433055910
US Federal Business Opportunities Handbook	1438754264
US Federal Business Opportunities Handbook	1433055929
US Federal Communication Commission Handbook	1438754272
US Federal Communication Commission Handbook	1433055937
US Federal Depository Libraries Directory	1438754280
US Federal Depository Libraries Directory	1433055945
US Federal Election Commission Handbook	1438754299
US Federal Election Commission Handbook	1433055953
US Federal Energy Sector Regulations Handbook	1438754302
US Federal Energy Sector Regulations Handbook	1433055961
US Federal Executive Government Handbook	1438754310
US Federal Executive Government Handbook	143305597X

Title	ISBN
US Federal Government Directory	1438754329
US Federal Government Directory	1433055988
US Federal Grant Management Handbook	1438754337
US Federal Grant Management Handbook	1433055996
US Federal Law Enforcement Training Center Handbook	1438754345
US Federal Law Enforcement Training Center Handbook	1433056003
US Federal Maritime Commission Handbook	1438754353
US Federal Maritime Commission Handbook	1433056011
US Federal Maritime Commission Handbooks	1438754361
US Federal Maritime Commission Handbooks	143305602X
US Federal Mine Safety and Health Commission Handbook	143875437X
US Federal Mine Safety and Health Commission Handbook	1433056038
US Federal Reserve System Handbook	1438754388
US Federal Reserve System Handbook	1433056046
US Federal Trade Commission Handbook	1438754396
US Federal Trade Commission Handbook	1433056054
US Financial Crimes Enforcement Regulations Handbook	1433060450
US Financial Crimes Enforcement Regulations Handbook	1433060450
US Financial Crimes Enforcement Regulations Handbook	1433060450
US Financial Crimes Prevention Handbook for Everybody	1433060590
US Financial Crimes Prevention Handbook for Everybody	1433060590
US Financial Crimes Prevention Handbook for Everybody	1433060590
US Fire-Safe Hotels Directory: Fire-Safe Hotels by States	9781577515562
US Food and Drug Administration Handbook	143875440X
US Food and Drug Administration Handbook	1433056062
US Food Assistance to Russia Handbook	1438754418
US Food Assistance to Russia Handbook	1433056070
US Foreign Embassies, Representations and Consulate Offices in the US Handbook	143306894X
US Foreign Policy & Government Guide	1438754426
US Foreign Policy & Government Guide	1433056089
US Foreign Trade Sanctions Handbook	1438754434
US Foreign Trade Sanctions Handbook	1433056097
US Foreign Trade Zones Handbook	1438754442
US Foreign Trade Zones Handbook	1433056100
US Free Trade Agreements with Foreign Countries Handbook	1433068958
US Free Trade and Investment Agreements and Associations Handbook	1438754450
US Free Trade and Investment Agreements and Associations Handbook	1433056119
US Free Trade and Investment Agreements and Associations with Foreign Countries Handbook	1438754469
US Free Trade and Investment Agreements and Associations with Foreign Countries Handbook	1433056127
US Future Combat & Weapon Systems Handbook	1438754477
US Future Combat & Weapon Systems Handbook	1433056135
US Gabling Industry Investment and Business Guide - Strategic and Practical Information	1438754485
US Gabling Industry Investment and Business Guide - Strategic and Practical Information	1433056143
US Gaming Industry Investment and Business Guide - Strategic and Practical Information	1438754493
US Gaming Industry Investment and Business Guide - Strategic and Practical	1433056151

Title	ISBN
Information	
US Gaming Industry Investment and Business Guide - Strategic and Practical Information	1433056178
US Gaming Industry Investment and Business Guide - Strategic and Practical Information Volume 1	1438754515
US Gaming Industry Law and Regulations Handbook	1438754507
US Gaming Industry Law and Regulations Handbook	143305616X
US Gaming Industry Laws and Regulations Handbook	1438754523
US Gaming Industry Laws and Regulations Handbook	1433056186
US General Service Administration Handbook	1438754531
US General Service Administration Handbook	1433056194
US George W. Bush President of the US (Leadership Vision Reforms)	1433016974
US Gourmet Food Distributors Directory vol 1	1433056208
US Gourmet Food Distributors Directory vol 2	1433056216
US Gourmet Food Distributors Directory vol 3	1433056224
US Gourmet Food Distributors Directory vol 4	1433056232
US Gourmet Food Distributors Directory vol 5	1433056240
US Gourmet Food Distributors Directory vol 6	1433056259
US Gourmet Food Distributors Directory Volume 1	143875454X
US Gourmet Food Distributors Directory Volume 2	1438754558
US Gourmet Food Distributors Directory Volume 3	1438754566
US Gourmet Food Distributors Directory Volume 4	1438754574
US Gourmet Food Distributors Directory Volume 5	1438754582
US Gourmet Food Distributors Directory Volume 6	1438754590
US Government and Business Contacts Handbook	1438754604
US Government and Business Contacts Handbook	1433056267
US Government and Special Subsidized Housing Buying Programs Handbook	1438754612
US Government and Special Subsidized Housing Buying Programs Handbook	1433056275
US GOVERNORS FEDERAL LEGISLATIVE AGENDA HANDBOOK	1438754620
US GOVERNORS FEDERAL LEGISLATIVE AGENDA HANDBOOK	1433056283
US GOVERNORS GUIDE	1438754639
US GOVERNORS GUIDE	1433056291
US GOVERNORS STATE-TO-THE STATE ANNUAL ADDRESSES AND BUDGET PRESENTATIONS YEARBOOK	1438754647
US GOVERNORS STATE-TO-THE STATE ANNUAL ADDRESSES AND BUDGET PRESENTATIONS YEARBOOK	1433056305
US Green Card" How to Become US Permanent Resident Handbook"	1438752415
US Hedge Finds Handbook	1438754655
US Hedge Finds Handbook	1433056313
US House Committee on Agriculture Handbook	1438754663
US House Committee on Agriculture Handbook	1433056321
US House Committee on Appropriations Handbook	1438754671
US House Committee on Appropriations Handbook	143305633X
US House Committee on Armed Services Handbook	143875468X
US House Committee on Armed Services Handbook	1433056348
US House Committee on Education and the Workforce Handbook	1438754698
US House Committee on Education and the Workforce Handbook	1433056356
US House Committee on Energy and Commerce Handbook	1438754701
US House Committee on Energy and Commerce Handbook	1433056364

Title	ISBN
US House Committee on Financial Services Handbook	143875471X
US House Committee on Financial Services Handbook	1433056372
US House Committee on Government Reform Handbook	1438754728
US House Committee on Government Reform Handbook	1433056380
US House Committee on House Administration Handbook	1438754736
US House Committee on House Administration Handbook	1433056399
US House Committee on International Relations Handbook	1438754744
US House Committee on International Relations Handbook	1433056402
US House Committee on Resources Handbook	1438754752
US House Committee on Resources Handbook	1433056410
US House Committee on Rules Handbook	1438754760
US House Committee on Rules Handbook	1433056429
US House Committee on Science Handbook	1438754779
US House Committee on Science Handbook	1433056437
US House Committee on Small Business Handbook	1438754787
US House Committee on Small Business Handbook	1433056445
US House Committee on Standards of Official Conduct Handbook	1438754795
US House Committee on Standards of Official Conduct Handbook	1433056453
US House Committee on Taxation Handbook	1438754809
US House Committee on Taxation Handbook	1433056461
US House Committee on the Budget Handbook	1438754817
US House Committee on the Budget Handbook	143305647X
US House Committee on the Judiciary Handbook	1438754825
US House Committee on the Judiciary Handbook	1433056488
US House Committee on Transportation and Infrastructure Handbook	1438754833
US House Committee on Transportation and Infrastructure Handbook	1433056496
US House Committee on Veterans Affairs Handbook	1438754841
US House Committee on Veterans Affairs Handbook	143305650X
US House Committee on Ways and Means Handbook	143875485X
US House Committee on Ways and Means Handbook	1433056518
US House Joint Committee on Printing Handbook	1438754868
US House Joint Committee on Taxation Handbook	1438754876
US House Joint Economic Committee Handbook	1438754884
US House of Representatives Ethics Manual	1433068966
US House Permanent Select Committee on Intelligence Handbook	1438754892
US House Permanent Select Committee on Intelligence Handbook	1433056550
US Idaho Business Registration and Incorporation Guide	1433022672
US Idaho Investment & Business Guide	1433022680
US Idaho Small Business Assistance and Programs Handbook	1433022699
US Illinois Business Registration and Incorporation Guide	1433022702
US Illinois Investment & Business Guide	1433022710
US Illinois Small Business Assistance and Programs Handbook	1433022729
US Immigration Policy and Programs Handbook Vol. 1 Basic Information and Legislation	1438754906
US Immigration Policy and Programs Handbook Vol. 1 Basic Information and Legislation	1433056569
US Immigration Policy and Programs Handbook Vol. 2 Procedures, Regulations, Application Forms	1433056577
US Immigration Policy Handbook	1438754914

Title	ISBN
US Immigration Policy Handbook; Strategic and Practical Information	1433056585
US Importing Products into the US Market Guide	1433022737
US Income Tax Treaties with Foreign Countries Handbook	1438754922
US Income Tax Treaties with Foreign Countries Handbook	1433056593
US Income Tax Treaties with Foreign Countries Handbook. Vol 2	1433056607
US Income Tax Treaties with Foreign Countries Handbook. Vol 3	1433056615
US Income Tax Treaties with Foreign Countries Handbook. Vol 4	1433056623
US Income Tax Treaties with Foreign Countries Handbook. Vol 5	1433056631
US Income Tax Treaties with Foreign Countries Handbook. Volume 2	1438754930
US Income Tax Treaties with Foreign Countries Handbook. Volume 3	1438754949
US Income Tax Treaties with Foreign Countries Handbook. Volume 4	1438754957
US Income Tax Treaties with Foreign Countries Handbook. Volume 5	1438754965
US Indian Gaming Laws and Regulations Handbook	1433061457
US Indian Gaming Laws and Regulations Handbook	1433061457
US Indian Gaming Laws and Regulations Handbook	1433061457
US Indian Reservations Casino Gaming Industry Investment and Business Guide - Strategic and Practical Information	1433056658
US Indian Reservations Casino Gaming Investment and Business Guide - Strategic and Practical Information	1438754973
US Indian Reservations Casino Gaming Investment and Business Guide - Strategic and Practical Information	143305664X
US Indian Tribal Leaders Directory	1433061449
US Indian Tribal Leaders Directory	1433061449
US Indiana Business Registration and Incorporation Guide	1433023229
US Indiana Investment & Business Guide	1433023237
US Indiana Small Business Assistance and Programs Handbook	1433023245
US Industrial and Business Directory	1433052512
US Industrial and Business Directory	1433056666
US Information Agency Handbook	1438754981
US Information Agency Handbook	1433056674
US Initial Public Offering Regulations Handbook	143875499X
US Initial Public Offering Regulations Handbook	1433056682
US Intelligence and Counterintelligence History Handbook Vol.1 American Revolution, Civil War, World War 1, Between the Wars	1433061384
US Intelligence and Counterintelligence History Handbook Vol.1 American Revolution, Civil War, World War 1, Between the Wars	1433061384
US Intelligence and Counterintelligence History Handbook Vol.2 World War 2	1433061392
US Intelligence and Counterintelligence History Handbook Vol.2 World War 2	1433061392
US Intelligence and Counterintelligence History Handbook Vol.3 Cold War Counterintelligence, 1960s,70s,80s, end of 20th Century	1433061406
US Intelligence and Counterintelligence History Handbook Vol.4 Military and Nuclear Technology, Russian Spies in the US, Defense Industry	1433061414
US Intelligence and Counterintelligence History Handbook Vol.4 Military and Nuclear Technology, Russian Spies in the US, Defense Industry	1433061414
US Intelligence and Counterintelligence Laws and Regulations Handbook	1433061430
US Intelligence and Counterintelligence Laws and Regulations Handbook	1433061430
US Intelligence and Counterintelligence Laws and Regulations Handbook	1433061430
US Intelligence Community Handbook	1438755007
US Intelligence Community Handbook	1433056690
US Intelligence Community Legal Reference Book	9781577515579

Title	ISBN
US Intelligence Community Legal Reference Handbook	9781577515586
US Intelligence Policy Handbook	1438755015
US Intelligence Policy Handbook	1433056704
US Internal Revenue Service Handbook	1438755023
US Internal Revenue Service Handbook	1433056712
US International Telephone Traffic Report	1433068974
US Internet and E-Commerce Investment and Business Guide - Strategic and Practical Information: Regulations and Opportunities	1438755031
US Internet and E-Commerce Investment and Business Guide - Strategic and Practical Information: Regulations and Opportunities	1433056720
US Internet and E-Commerce Investment and Business Guide - Strategic and Practical Information: Regulations and Opportunities	1433052520
US Investment and Business Guide - Strategic and Practical Information	143875504X
US Investment and Business Guide - Strategic and Practical Information	1433056739
US Investment and Trade Laws and Regulations Handbook	1433076837
US Investment and Trade Laws and Regulations Handbook	1433076810
US Investors' Fraud Prevention Handbook	1438755058
US Investors' Fraud Prevention Handbook	1433056747
US Iowa Business Registration and Incorporation Guide	1433023989
US Iowa Investment & Business Guide	1433023997
US Iowa Small Business Assistance and Programs Handbook	1433024004
US Iraq Strategy Handbook: new developments	1433060469
US Iraq Strategy Handbook: new developments	1433060469
US Iraq Strategy Handbook: new developments	1433060469
US Justice System and National Police Handbook	1433052539
US Largest Commercial Banks Handbook (Banks with 300+ Mill Dol. Assets)	1438755066
US Largest Commercial Banks Handbook (Banks with 300+ Mill Dol. Assets)	1433056755
US Laws for Regulation of Therapeutic Goods in the United States Handbook	9781577515593
US Legislative Process Handbook Vol. 1 House of Representatives	1433068982
US Legislative Process Handbook Vol. 2 Senate	1433068990
US Libraries and Information Science National Commission Handbook	1438755074
US Libraries and Information Science National Commission Handbook	1433056763
US Marine Corp Handbook	1433061058
US Marine Corp Handbook	1433061058
US Marine Corp Handbook	1433061058
US Marketing and Advertising Regulations Handbook	1438755082
US Marketing and Advertising Regulations Handbook Volume 1 Ecommerce and Internet Marketing Regulations	1433056771
US Medical & Pharmaceutical Industry Handbook	1433052547
US Medical Drugs Development and Approval Process Handbook	9781577515609
US Michigan Life Sciences Business Opportunities and Programs Handbook	1433069008
US Military Base Structure and Location Handbook	1433060507
US Military Base Structure and Location Handbook	1433060507
US Military Base Structure and Location Handbook	1433060507
US Military Cooperation with African Countries Handbook	1438755090
US Military Cooperation with African Countries Handbook	143305678X
US Military Cooperation with Asian Countries Handbook	1438755104
US Military Cooperation with Asian Countries Handbook	1433056798
US Military Cooperation with China Handbook	1438755112

Title	ISBN
US Military Cooperation with China Handbook	1433056801
US Military Cooperation with Eastern European Countries Handbook	1438755120
US Military Cooperation with Eastern European Countries Handbook	143305681X
US Military Cooperation with Russia Handbook	1438755139
US Military Cooperation with Russia Handbook	1433056828
US Military Forces Recruitment Handbook	143306104X
US Military Forces Recruitment Handbook	143306104X
US Military Forces Recruitment Handbook	143306104X
US Military Intelligence Handbook	1438755147
US Military Intelligence Handbook	1433056836
US Military Intelligence Interrogation Techniques Handbook	1438755155
US Military Intelligence Interrogation Techniques Handbook	1433056844
US Military Policy Toward Iraq Handbook	1438755163
US Military Policy Toward Iraq Handbook	1433056852
US Mineral & Mining Sector Investment and Business Guide - Strategic and Practical Information	1433052555
US Mining Industry Technology, Equipment and Financial Services Directory	1438755171
US Mining Industry Technology, Equipment and Financial Services Directory	1433056860
US Mining Laws and Regulations Handbook	1433078430
US Missile Defense Agency Handbook	143875518X
US Missile Defense Agency Handbook	1433056879
US Missile Defense Glossary Handbook	9781577515616
US Mobile Telecom & Data Companies Directory	1438755198
US Mobile Telecom & Data Companies Directory	1433056887
US Mortgage and Financial Companies Directory	1433056895
US Mortgage Market Handbook	1438755201
US Mortgage Market Handbook	1433056909
US Mortgage System Handbook Vol.1 : How to Obtain Mortgages for Foreigners	1433062941
US Mortgage System Handbook Vol.1 : How to Obtain Mortgages for Foreigners	1433062941
US Mortgage System Handbook Vol.1 : How to Obtain Mortgages for Foreigners	1433062941
US Mortgage System Handbook Vol.2 : How to Obtain Mortgages in the US	143306295X
US Mortgage System Handbook Vol.2 : How to Obtain Mortgages in the US	143306295X
US Mortgage System Handbook Vol.2 : How to Obtain Mortgages in the US	143306295X
US National Academy of Science and Research Policy Handbook	143875521X
US National Academy of Science and Research Policy Handbook	1433056917
US National Academy of Science Handbook	1438755228
US National Academy of Science Handbook	1433056925
US National Aeronautics and Space Administration Handbook	1438755236
US National Aeronautics and Space Administration Handbook	1433056933
US National Border Protection Strategy Handbook	1433069016
US National Counter Terrorism Center Handbook	1433061376
US National Counter Terrorism Strategy Handbook	1433061236
US National Counterterrorism Center Handbook	1433061376
US National Counterterrorism Center Handbook	1433061376
US National Counterterrorism Strategy Handbook	1433061236
US National Counterterrorism Strategy Handbook	1433061236
US National Cyber Security Strategy and Programs Handbook - Strategic Information and Developments	9781577515623
US National Drug Control Policy Handbook	1438755244

Title	ISBN
US National Drug Control Policy Handbook	1433056941
US National Educational & Social Development Policy Handbook	1433035391
US National Educational and Social Development Policy Handbook Volume 2 Social Policy	9781577515630
US National Emergency Response and Rescue Training Programs Handbook	1438755252
US National Emergency Response and Rescue Training Programs Handbook	143305695X
US National Export Strategy and Regulations Yearbook	1433069024
US National Fire Fighting Training Handbook - Strategic Information and Contacts	1438755260
US National System of Fire Fighting Handbook - Strategic Information and Contacts	1433056968
US National Governors Association Handbook	1438755279
US National Governors Association Handbook - Organization, Strategy, Contacts	1433056976
US National Guard and Reserve Management Policy Handbook	1433060477
US National Guard and Reserve Management Policy Handbook	1433060477
US National Guard and Reserve Management Policy Handbook	1433060477
US National Guard Handbook	1433061031
US National Guard Handbook	1433061031
US National Guard Handbook	1433061031
US National Homeland Security Strategy Handbook	1433060523
US National Homeland Security Strategy Handbook	1433060523
US National Homeland Security Strategy Handbook	1433060523
US National Import Strategy and Regulations Yearbook	1433069032
US National Import Strategy Handbook	1433069040
US National Institute of Health Handbook	1438755287
US National Institute of Health Handbook	1433056984
US National Plan of Integrated Airport Systems Handbook	1438755295
US National Plan of Integrated Airport Systems Handbook	1433056992
US National Science Foundation Handbook	1438755309
US National Science Foundation Handbook	143305700X
US National Security Handbook	1438755317
US National Security Handbook	1433057018
US National Security Policy Handbook	1438755325
US National Security Policy Handbook	1433057026
US National Security Strategy Handbook	1433060531
US National Strategy on Combating Terrorism Handbook	1433060515
US Naval Intelligence Handbook	1438755333
US Naval Intelligence Handbook	1433057034
US Naval Postgraduate School Handbook	1438755341
US Naval Postgraduate School Handbook	1433057042
US Navy Defense Industry Handbook	143875535X
US Navy Defense Industry Handbook	1433057050
US Navy Enlisting Handbook Vol 1 Navy Enlisted Occupational Standards	1433069059
US Navy Enlisting Handbook Vol 2 Navy Enlisted Classifications	1433069067
US Navy Handbook	1433061015
US Navy Seals Handbook	1438755368
US Navy Seals Handbook - Strategic Information and Contacts	1433057069
US Navy Total Manpower Requirements Handbook	1433069075
US Nonproliferation, Arms Control, and International Security Handbook	1438755376
US Nonproliferation, Arms Control, and International Security Handbook	1433057077
US Nuclear Energy Development Strategy: Programs and Projects Handbook	9781577515647

Title	ISBN
US Nuclear Energy Sector Laws and Regulations Handbook	9781577515708
US Nuclear Industry Handbook	1438755384
US Nuclear Industry Handbook	1433057085
US Nuclear Industry Investment and Business Guide - Strategic and Practical Information	1438755392
US Nuclear Industry Investment and Business Guide - Strategic and Practical Information	1433057093
US Nuclear Power Facilities and Power Stations Handbook	1438755406
US Nuclear Power Facilities and Power Stations Handbook	1433057107
US Nuclear Power Facilities Handbook	1438755414
US Nuclear Power Facilities Handbook	1433057115
US Nuclear Regulatory Commission Handbook	1438755422
US Nuclear Regulatory Commission Handbook	1433057123
US Ocean Transportation Companies Directory	1438755430
US Ocean Transportation Companies Directory	1433057131
US Office of Management and Budget Handbook	1438755449
US Office of Management and Budget Handbook	143305714X
US Office of Personnel Management Handbook	1438755457
US Office of Personnel Management Handbook	1433057158
US Oil & Gas Companies Directory	1433069083
US Oil & Gas Sector Business & Investment Opportunities Yearbook	1433052563
US Oil and Gas Exploration Laws and Regulation Handbook	1433079089
US Overseas Private Investment Corporation Programs Handbook	1438755465
US Overseas Private Investment Corporation Export Subsidies System Handbook	1433057166
US Pacific Air Force Handbook	1438755473
US Pacific Air Force Handbook	1433057174
US Pacific Regional Strategy Handbook	1438755481
US Pacific Regional Strategy Handbook	1433057182
US Paging and Messaging Telecom Companies Directory	143875549X
US Paging and Messaging Telecom Companies Directory	1433057190
US Payphone Telecom Service Providers Directory	1438755503
US Payphone Telecom Service Providers Directory	1433057204
US Peace Corp Handbook	1438755511
US Peace Corp Handbook	1433057212
US Policy and Legislation on Cuba Handbook	143875552X
US Policy and Legislation on Cuba Handbook	1433057220
US Political Intelligence Handbook	1438755538
US Political Intelligence Handbook	1433057239
US Ports Handbook: Structure, Location, Operation	1433057247
US Ports of Entry Handbook: Airports and Ports	1433069091
US Postal Service Handbook	1438755546
US Postal Service Handbook	1433057255
US President George W. Bush Handbook	1438755554
US President George W. Bush Handbook	1433057263
US Presidential Doctrines Handbook - Reagan, Carder, Clinton, Bush, Obama	9781577515890
US Prison Privatization Handbook: Strategic Information, Regulations, Developments	9781577515920
US Private Security Contractors in Afghanistan and Iraq Handbook - Strategic Information and Regulations	9781577515937
US Private Security Forces Regulations Handbook - Strategic Information, Basic Laws	9781577515944

Title	ISBN
and Regulations	
US Privatization Programs and Regulations Handbook	1438755562
US Privatization Programs and Regulations Handbook	1433057271
US Privatization Programs and Regulations Handbook	1433052571
US Privatization Yearbook: Major Programs and Projects	1433069105
US Privatizations Consulting Companies Directory	1433069113
US Professional Internet Advertising Handbook	1438755570
US Professional Internet Advertising Handbook	143305728X
US Racing Industry Laws and Regulations Handbook	1438755589
US Racing Industry Laws and Regulations Handbook	1433057298
US Radio Broadcasting Business Opportunities and Regulations Handbook	1438755597
US Radio Broadcasting Business Opportunities and Regulations Handbook	1433057301
US Real Estate Market Business Law Handbook - Strategic Information and Basic Laws	1438755600
US Real Estate Market Business Law Handbook - Strategic Information and Basic Laws	143305731X
US Real Estate Markets Analysis and Investment Opportunities Yearbook	1438755619
US Real Estate Markets Analysis and Investment Opportunities Yearbook	1433057328
US Recent Economic and Political Developments Yearbook	143306233X
US Recent Economic and Political Developments Yearbook	143306233X
US Research & Development Policy Handbook	1433062909
US Research & Development Policy Handbook	1433062909
US Residential Real Estate Investment Guide for Everybody	1438755627
US Residential Real Estate Investment Guide for Everybody	1433057336
US Residential Real Estate Investment Guide for First Time Buyers	1438755635
US Residential Real Estate Investment Guide for First Time Buyers	1433057344
US Residential Real Estate Investment Guide for Foreigners	1438755643
US Residential Real Estate Investment Guide for Foreigners	1433057352
US Residential Real Estate Investment Guide for Permanent Residents	1438755651
US Residential Real Estate Investment Guide for Permanent Residents	1433057360
US Satellite Communication Companies Directory	143875566X
US Satellite Communication Companies Directory	1433057379
US Science and Technology Policy Handbook	1438755678
US Science and Technology Policy Handbook	1433057387
US Sea and River Ports Handbook	1438755686
US Sea and River Ports Handbook	1433057395
US Sea And River Ports Handbook Vol. 2 North Carolina-Wisconsin	1433069121
US Secret Service Handbook	1438755694
US Secret Service Handbook	1433057409
US Securities and Exchange Commission Handbook	1438755708
US Securities and Exchange Commission Handbook	1433057417
US Security and Anti Terrorism Legislation Handbook	1438755716
US Security and Anti Terrorism Legislation Handbook	1433057425
US Security Cooperation Agency Handbook	1438755724
US Security Cooperation Agency Handbook	1433057433
US Security Cooperation Education and Training Center Handbook	1438755732
US Security Cooperation Education and Training Center Handbook	1433057441
US Senate Agriculture, Nutrition, And Forestry Committee Handbook	1438755740
US Senate Agriculture, Nutrition, And Forestry Committee Handbook	143305745X

Title	ISBN
US Senate Appropriations Committee Handbook	1438755759
US Senate Appropriations Committee Handbook	1433057468
US Senate Armed Services Committee Handbook	1438755767
US Senate Armed Services Committee Handbook	1433057476
US Senate Banking, Housing, And Urban Affairs Handbook	1438755775
US Senate Banking, Housing, And Urban Affairs Handbook	1433057484
US Senate Budget Committee Handbook	1438755783
US Senate Budget Committee Handbook	1433057492
US Senate Commerce, Science, And Transportation Handbook	1438755791
US Senate Commerce, Science, And Transportation Handbook	1433057506
US Senate Committee On Indian Affairs Handbook	1438755805
US Senate Committee On Indian Affairs Handbook	1433057514
US Senate Energy And Natural Resources Committee Handbook	1438755813
US Senate Energy And Natural Resources Committee Handbook	1433057522
US Senate Environment And Public Works Committee Handbook	1438755821
US Senate Environment And Public Works Committee Handbook	1433057530
US Senate Finance Committee Handbook	143875583X
US Senate Finance Committee Handbook	1433057549
US Senate Foreign Relations Committee Handbook	1438755848
US Senate Foreign Relations Committee Handbook	1433057557
US Senate Governmental Affairs Committee Handbook	1438755856
US Senate Governmental Affairs Committee Handbook	1433057565
US Senate Guide vol1	1438755864
US Senate Guide vol1	1433057573
US Senate Guide VOLUME 2. United States Senators Biographic Information and Contacts	1433061112
US Senate Health, Education, Labor And Pensions Committee Handbook	1438755872
US Senate Health, Education, Labor And Pensions Committee Handbook	1433057581
US Senate Joint Committee On Taxation Handbook	1438755880
US Senate Joint Committee On Taxation Handbook	143305759X
US Senate Joint Economic Committee Handbook	1438755899
US Senate Joint Economic Committee Handbook	1433057603
US Senate Judiciary Committee Handbook	1438755902
US Senate Judiciary Committee Handbook	1433057611
US Senate Rules And Administration Committee Handbook	1438755910
US Senate Rules And Administration Committee Handbook	143305762X
US Senate Select Committee On Ethics Handbook	1438755929
US Senate Select Committee On Ethics Handbook	1433057638
US Senate Select Committee On Intelligence Handbook	1438755937
US Senate Select Committee On Intelligence Handbook	1433057646
US Senate Small Business Committee	1438755945
US Senate Small Business Committee	1433057654
US Senate Special Committee On Aging Handbook	1438755953
US Senate Special Committee On Aging Handbook	1433057662
US Senate Veterans' Affairs Committee Handbook	1438755961
US Senate Veterans' Affairs Committee Handbook	1433057670
US Small Business Administration Handbook	143875597X
US Small Business Administration Handbook	1433057689
US Small Business Support Guide: 50 States of the United States	143306913X

Title	ISBN
US South Africa Diplomatic and Political Cooperation Handbook	1438752156
US Space Programs and Exploration Handbook	1438755988
US Space Programs and Exploration Handbook	1433057697
US Spain Diplomatic and Political Cooperation Handbook	1438752199
US Special Combat Forces Handbook	1438755996
US Special Combat Forces Handbook	1433057700
US Special Operations Command Handbook	1438756003
US Special Operations Command Handbook	1433057719
US Special Operations Forces Handbook vol 1	1433061023
US Special Operations Forces Handbook vol 2	1433061023
US Special Operations Forces Handbook vol 3	1433057727
US Special Operations Forces Handbook vol 4	1433061023
US Starting Business (Incorporating) in the US Guide	1433047209
US Starting Business (Incorporating) in....Guide	1433069148
US Starting Business (Incorporating) in....Guide	143306880X
US STATE GOVERNMENTS KEY ECONOMIC AND POLITICAL ISSUES AND PROGRAMS HANDBOOK	1438756011
US STATE GOVERNMENTS KEY ECONOMIC AND POLITICAL ISSUES AND PROGRAMS HANDBOOK	1433057735
US Stem Cell Research Policy & Programs Handbook	143875602X
US Stem Cell Research Policy & Programs Handbook	1433057743
US Submarine Force Handbook	1438756038
US Submarine Force Handbook	1433057751
US Subsidized Housing Buying Programs Handbook	1438756046
US Subsidized Housing Buying Programs Handbook	143305776X
US Tax Guide - Corporate Taxation	1433057778
US Tax Guide-Corporate Taxation	1438756054
US Taxation Laws and Regulations Handbook	1433081261
US Telecom Companies Directory	1433057786
US Telecom Laws and Regulations Handbook vol 1	1433082632
US Telecom Laws and Regulations Handbook vol 2	1433082659
US Telecommunication Industry Business Opportunities Handbook	1438756062
US Telecommunication Industry Business Opportunities Handbook	143305258X
US Telecommunication Industry Business Opportunities Handbook	1433057794
US Terrorism Prevention Regulations Handbook	1433069156
US Trade & Export Sanctions Handbook	1438756070
US Trade & Export Sanctions Handbook	1433057808
US Trade and Development Agency Handbook	1438756089
US Trade and Development Agency Handbook	1433057816
US Trade Industrial and Business Show Handbook	1438756097
US Trade Industrial and Business Show Handbook	1433057824
US Trade Representative Office Handbook	1438756100
US Trade Representative Office Handbook	1433057832
US Transportation Policy and Regulations Handbook	1433068818
US TV Broadcasting Business Opportunities and Regulations Handbook	1438756119
US TV Broadcasting Business Opportunities and Regulations Handbook	1433057840
US War Against International Terrorism Handbook	1438756127
US War Against International Terrorism Handbook	1433057859
US War Against Iraq Handbook: Political Strategy and Operations	1438756135

Title	ISBN
US War Against Iraq Handbook: Political Strategy and Operations	1433057867
US War on Terror" Military Strategy Handbook"	1438752423
US Wine Industry Investment and Business Opportunities Yearbook	1433069164
US Wireless Telecom & Data Companies Directory	1433057875
US Yugoslavia Economic and Political Cooperation Handbook	1438752407
US: Importing into the Unites States Practical Guide	1433069172
US: State of Georgia Business Financial Assistance Programs Handbook	1433069180
USA Constitution and Citizenship Laws Handbook - Strategic Information and Basic Laws	1438780168
USA Immigration Laws and Regulations Handbook - Strategic Information and Basic Laws	1438783760
USA Insolvency (Bankruptcy) Laws and Regulations Handbook - Strategic Information and Basic Laws	9781433085758
USA Labor Laws and Regulations Handbook - Strategic Information and Basic Laws	1438781962
USA Land Ownership and Agriculture Laws Handbook	143876023X
US-Argentina Diplomatic and Political Cooperation Handbook	1438751389
US-Argentina Diplomatic and Political Cooperation Handbook	1433052792
US-Argentina Economic and Political Cooperation Handbook	1438751397
US-Argentina Economic and Political Cooperation Handbook	1433052806
US-Armenia Diplomatic and Political Cooperation Handbook	1433052814
US--Armenia Diplomatic and Political Cooperation Handbook	1438751400
US-Armenia Economic and Political Cooperation Handbook	1433052822
US--Armenia Economic and Political Cooperation Handbook	1438751419
US-Australia Diplomatic and Political Cooperation Handbook	1438751427
US-Australia Diplomatic and Political Cooperation Handbook	1433052830
US-Australia Economic and Political Cooperation Handbook	1438751435
US-Australia Economic and Political Cooperation Handbook	1433052849
US-Austria Diplomatic and Political Cooperation Handbook	1438751443
US-Austria Diplomatic and Political Cooperation Handbook	1433052857
US-Austria Economic and Political Cooperation Handbook	1438751451
US-Austria Economic and Political Cooperation Handbook	1433052865
US-Azerbaijan Diplomatic and Political Cooperation Handbook	1433052873
US-Azerbaijan Economic and Political Cooperation Handbook	143875146X
US-Azerbaijan Economic and Political Cooperation Handbook	1433052881
US-Belgium Diplomatic and Political Cooperation Handbook	1438751478
US-Belgium Diplomatic and Political Cooperation Handbook	143305289X
US-Belgium Economic and Political Cooperation Handbook	1438751486
US-Belgium Economic and Political Cooperation Handbook	1433052903
US-Bosnia & Herzegovina Diplomatic and Political Cooperation Handbook	1438751494
US-Bosnia & Herzegovina Diplomatic and Political Cooperation Handbook	1433052911
US-Bosnia & Herzegovina Economic and Political Cooperation Handbook	1438751508
US-Bosnia & Herzegovina Economic and Political Cooperation Handbook	143305292X
US-Brazil Diplomatic and Political Cooperation Handbook	1433052938
US-Brazil Economic and Political Cooperation Handbook	1433052946
US-Bulgaria Diplomatic and Political Cooperation Handbook	1438751524
US-Bulgaria Diplomatic and Political Cooperation Handbook	1433052954
US-Bulgaria Economic and Political Cooperation Handbook	1438751532
US-Bulgaria Economic and Political Cooperation Handbook	1433052962
US-Canada Diplomatic and Political Cooperation Handbook	1438751540

Title	ISBN
US-Canada Diplomatic and Political Cooperation Handbook	1433052970
US-Canada Economic and Political Cooperation Handbook	1438751559
US-Canada Economic and Political Cooperation Handbook	1433052989
US-Chile Diplomatic and Political Cooperation Handbook	1438751567
US-Chile Diplomatic and Political Cooperation Handbook	1433052997
US-Chile Economic and Political Cooperation Handbook	1438751575
US-Chile Economic and Political Cooperation Handbook	1433053004
US-Chile Free Trade Agreement Handbook	1433069199
US-China Diplomatic and Political Cooperation Handbook	1438751583
US-China Diplomatic and Political Cooperation Handbook	1433053012
US-China Economic and Political Cooperation Handbook	1433053020
US-Costa Rica Diplomatic and Political Cooperation Handbook	1433053039
US-Costa Rica Economic and Political Cooperation Handbook	1438751591
US-Costa Rica Economic and Political Cooperation Handbook	1433053047
US-Croatia Diplomatic and Political Cooperation Handbook	1438751605
US-Croatia Diplomatic and Political Cooperation Handbook	1433053055
US-Croatia Economic and Political Cooperation Handbook	1433053063
US-Cuba Political and Economic Relations Handbook	1433053071
US-Czech Republic Diplomatic and Political Cooperation Handbook	1438751613
US-Czech Republic Diplomatic and Political Cooperation Handbook	143305308X
US-Czech Republic Economic and Political Cooperation Handbook	1438751621
US-Czech Republic Economic and Political Cooperation Handbook	1433053098
US-Egypt Diplomatic and Political Cooperation Handbook	143875163X
US-Egypt Diplomatic and Political Cooperation Handbook	1433053101
US-Egypt Economic and Political Cooperation Handbook	143305311X
US-El Salvador Diplomatic and Political Cooperation Handbook	1433053128
US-El Salvador Economic and Political Cooperation Handbook	1438751656
US-El Salvador Economic and Political Cooperation Handbook	1433053136
US-Estonia Diplomatic and Political Cooperation Handbook	1438751664
US-Estonia Diplomatic and Political Cooperation Handbook	1433053144
US-Estonia Economic and Political Cooperation Handbook	1438751672
US-Estonia Economic and Political Cooperation Handbook	1433053152
US-Finland Diplomatic and Political Cooperation Handbook	1438751680
US-Finland Diplomatic and Political Cooperation Handbook	1433053160
US-Finland Economic and Political Cooperation Handbook	1438751699
US-Finland Economic and Political Cooperation Handbook	1433053179
US-France Diplomatic and Political Cooperation Handbook	1438751702
US-France Diplomatic and Political Cooperation Handbook	1433053187
US-France Economic and Political Cooperation Handbook	1433053195
US-Georgia Diplomatic and Political Cooperation Handbook	1438751710
US-Georgia Diplomatic and Political Cooperation Handbook	1433053209
US-Georgia Economic and Political Cooperation Handbook	1438751729
US-Georgia Economic and Political Cooperation Handbook	1433053217
US-Germany Diplomatic and Political Cooperation Handbook	1438751737
US-Germany Diplomatic and Political Cooperation Handbook	1433053225
US-Germany Economic and Political Cooperation Handbook	1438751745
US-Germany Economic and Political Cooperation Handbook	1433053233
US-Greece Diplomatic and Political Cooperation Handbook	1433053241
US-Greece Economic and Political Cooperation Handbook	1438751753

Title	ISBN
US-Greece Economic and Political Cooperation Handbook	143305325X
US-Hungary Diplomatic and Political Cooperation Handbook	1438751761
US-Hungary Diplomatic and Political Cooperation Handbook	1433053268
US-Hungary Economic and Political Cooperation Handbook	143875177X
US-Hungary Economic and Political Cooperation Handbook	1433053276
US-India Diplomatic and Political Cooperation Handbook	1433053284
US-India Economic and Political Cooperation Handbook	1438751788
US-India Economic and Political Cooperation Handbook	1433053292
US-Indonesia Diplomatic and Political Cooperation Handbook	1438751796
US-Indonesia Diplomatic and Political Cooperation Handbook	1433053306
US-Indonesia Economic and Political Cooperation Handbook	143875180X
US-Indonesia Economic and Political Cooperation Handbook	1433053314
US-Iran Political & Economic Relations Handbook	1438751818
US-Iran Political & Economic Relations Handbook	1433053322
US-Iraq Political & Economic Relations Handbook	1438751826
US-Iraq Political & Economic Relations Handbook	1433053330
US-Israel Diplomatic and Political Cooperation Handbook	1438751834
US-Israel Diplomatic and Political Cooperation Handbook	1433053349
US-Israel Economic and Political Cooperation Handbook	1438751842
US-Israel Economic and Political Cooperation Handbook	1433053357
US-Italy Diplomatic and Political Cooperation Handbook	1438751850
US-Italy Diplomatic and Political Cooperation Handbook	1433053365
US-Italy Economic and Political Cooperation Handbook	1433053373
US-Japan Diplomatic and Political Cooperation Handbook	1438751869
US-Japan Diplomatic and Political Cooperation Handbook	1433053381
US-Japan Economic and Political Cooperation Handbook	143305339X
US-Jordan Free Trade Agreement Handbook	1433069202
US-Kazakhstan Diplomatic and Political Cooperation Handbook	1438751877
US-Kazakhstan Diplomatic and Political Cooperation Handbook	1433053403
US-Kazakhstan Diplomatic and Political Relations Handbook	1438751885
US-Kazakhstan Diplomatic and Political Relations Handbook	1433053411
US-Kazakhstan Economic and Political Cooperation Handbook	1438751893
US-Kazakhstan Economic and Political Cooperation Handbook	143305342X
US-Korea South Diplomatic and Political Cooperation Handbook	143305373X
US-Korea South Economic and Political Cooperation Handbook	1433053748
US-Kuwait Diplomatic and Political Cooperation Handbook	1438751907
US-Kuwait Diplomatic and Political Cooperation Handbook	1433053438
US-Kuwait Economic and Political Cooperation Handbook	1433053446
US-Kyrgyzstan Diplomatic and Political Cooperation Handbook	1438751915
US-Kyrgyzstan Diplomatic and Political Cooperation Handbook	1433053454
US-Kyrgyzstan Economic and Political Cooperation Handbook	1438751923
US-Kyrgyzstan Economic and Political Cooperation Handbook	1433053462
US-Latvia Diplomatic and Political Cooperation Handbook	1438751931
US-Latvia Diplomatic and Political Cooperation Handbook	1433053470
US-Latvia Economic and Political Cooperation Handbook	143875194X
US-Latvia Economic and Political Cooperation Handbook	1433053489
US-Lithuania Diplomatic and Political Cooperation Handbook	1438751958
US-Lithuania Diplomatic and Political Cooperation Handbook	1433053497
US-Lithuania Economic and Political Cooperation Handbook	1438751966

Title	ISBN
US-Lithuania Economic and Political Cooperation Handbook	1433053500
US-Mexico Diplomatic and Political Cooperation Handbook	1438751974
US-Mexico Diplomatic and Political Cooperation Handbook	1433053519
US-Mexico Economic and Political Cooperation Handbook	1438751982
US-Mexico Economic and Political Cooperation Handbook	1433053527
US-Moldova Diplomatic and Political Cooperation Handbook	1438751990
US-Moldova Diplomatic and Political Cooperation Handbook	1433053535
US-Moldova Economic and Political Cooperation Handbook	1433053543
US-New Zealand Diplomatic and Political Cooperation Handbook	1433053551
US--New Zealand Diplomatic and Political Cooperation Handbook	1438752008
US-New Zealand Economic and Political Cooperation Handbook	143305356X
US--New Zealand Economic and Political Cooperation Handbook	1438752016
US-Norway Diplomatic and Political Cooperation Handbook	1438752024
US-Norway Diplomatic and Political Cooperation Handbook	1433053578
US-Norway Economic and Political Cooperation Handbook	1438752032
US-Norway Economic and Political Cooperation Handbook	1433053586
US-Peru Diplomatic and Political Cooperation Handbook	1438752040
US-Peru Diplomatic and Political Cooperation Handbook	1433053594
US-Peru Economic and Political Cooperation Handbook	1438752059
US-Peru Economic and Political Cooperation Handbook	1433053608
US-Philippines Diplomatic and Political Cooperation Handbook	1438752067
US-Philippines Economic and Political Cooperation Handbook	1433053624
US-Poland Diplomatic and Political Cooperation Handbook	1438752075
US-Poland Diplomatic and Political Cooperation Handbook	1433053632
US-Poland Economic and Political Cooperation Handbook	1438752083
US-Poland Economic and Political Cooperation Handbook	1433053640
US-Portugal Diplomatic and Political Cooperation Handbook	1438752091
US-Portugal Diplomatic and Political Cooperation Handbook	1433053659
US-Portugal Economic and Political Cooperation Handbook	1438752105
US-Portugal Economic and Political Cooperation Handbook	1433053667
US-Russia Cooperation Against Terrorism Handbook	1438756143
US-Russia Cooperation Against Terrorism Handbook	1433057883
US-Russia Diplomatic and Political Cooperation Handbook	1438752113
US-Russia Diplomatic and Political Cooperation Handbook	1433053675
US-Russia Economic & Financial Cooperation Handbook	1438756151
US-Russia Economic & Financial Cooperation Handbook	1433057891
US-Russia Economic and Political Cooperation Handbook	1438752121
US-Russia Economic and Political Cooperation Handbook	1433053683
US-Russia Military Cooperation Handbook	143875616X
US-Russia Military Cooperation Handbook	1433057905
US-Russia Political Cooperation Handbook	1438756178
US-Russia Political Cooperation Handbook	1433057913
US-Russia Scientific & Technological Cooperation Handbook	1438756186
US-Russia Scientific & Technological Cooperation Handbook	1433057921
US-Russia Scientific Cooperation Handbook	1438756194
US-Russia Scientific Cooperation Handbook	143305793X
US-Russia Space Cooperation Handbook	1438756208
US-Russia Space Cooperation Handbook	1433057948
US-Saudi Arabia Diplomatic and Political Cooperation Handbook	143875213X

Title	ISBN
US-Saudi Arabia Diplomatic and Political Cooperation Handbook	1433053691
US-Saudi Arabia Economic and Political Cooperation Handbook	1438752148
US-Saudi Arabia Economic and Political Cooperation Handbook	1433053705
US-Serbia Diplomatic and Political Cooperation Handbook	1438752393
US-South Africa Diplomatic and Political Cooperation Handbook	1433053713
US-South Africa Economic and Political Cooperation Handbook	1438752164
US-South Africa Economic and Political Cooperation Handbook	1433053721
US-South Korea Diplomatic and Political Cooperation Handbook	1438752172
US-South Korea Economic and Political Cooperation Handbook	1438752180
US-Spain Diplomatic and Political Cooperation Handbook	1433053756
US-Spain Economic and Political Cooperation Handbook	1438752202
US-Spain Economic and Political Cooperation Handbook	1433053764
US-Sri Lanka Diplomatic and Political Cooperation Handbook	1438752210
US-Sri Lanka Diplomatic and Political Cooperation Handbook	1433053772
US-Sri Lanka Economic and Political Cooperation Handbook	1433053780
US-Sweden Diplomatic and Political Cooperation Handbook	1433053799
US-Sweden Economic and Political Cooperation Handbook	1438752229
US-Sweden Economic and Political Cooperation Handbook	1433053802
US-Switzerland Diplomatic and Political Cooperation Handbook	1438752237
US-Switzerland Diplomatic and Political Cooperation Handbook	1433053810
US-Switzerland Economic and Political Cooperation Handbook	1438752245
US-Switzerland Economic and Political Cooperation Handbook	1433053829
US-Taiwan Diplomatic and Political Cooperation Handbook	1433053837
US-Taiwan Economic and Political Cooperation Handbook	1438752253
US-Taiwan Economic and Political Cooperation Handbook	1433053845
US-Turkey Diplomatic and Political Cooperation Handbook	1433053853
US--Turkey Diplomatic and Political Cooperation Handbook	1438752261
US-Turkey Economic and Political Cooperation Handbook	1433053861
US--Turkey Economic and Political Cooperation Handbook	143875227X
US-Turkey Economic and Political Relations Handbook	1438756216
US-Turkey Economic and Political Relations Handbook	1433057956
US-Turkmenistan Diplomatic and Political Cooperation Handbook	1438752288
US-Turkmenistan Diplomatic and Political Cooperation Handbook	143305387X
US-Turkmenistan Economic and Political Cooperation Handbook	1438752296
US-Turkmenistan Economic and Political Cooperation Handbook	1433053888
US-UK Diplomatic and Political Cooperation Handbook	143875230X
US-UK Diplomatic and Political Cooperation Handbook	1433053896
US-UK Economic and Political Cooperation Handbook	1438752318
US-UK Economic and Political Cooperation Handbook	143305390X
US-Ukraine Diplomatic and Political Cooperation Handbook	1433053918
US-Ukraine Economic and Political Cooperation Handbook	1438752326
US-Ukraine Economic and Political Cooperation Handbook	1433053926
US-Ukrainian Business Contacts Directory	1433069210
US-Uruguay Diplomatic and Political Cooperation Handbook	1438752334
US-Uruguay Diplomatic and Political Cooperation Handbook	1433053934
US-Uruguay Economic and Political Cooperation Handbook	1438752342
US-Uruguay Economic and Political Cooperation Handbook	1433053942
US-Uzbekistan Diplomatic and Political Cooperation Handbook	1438752350
US-Uzbekistan Diplomatic and Political Cooperation Handbook	1433053950

Title	ISBN
US-Uzbekistan Economic and Political Cooperation Handbook	1433053969
US-Venezuela Diplomatic and Political Cooperation Handbook	1433053977
US--Venezuela Diplomatic and Political Cooperation Handbook	1438752369
US-Venezuela Economic and Political Cooperation Handbook	1433053985
US--Venezuela Economic and Political Cooperation Handbook	1438752377
US-Vietnam Diplomatic and Political Cooperation Handbook	1433053993
US-Vietnam Economic and Political Cooperation Handbook	1438752385
US-Vietnam Economic and Political Cooperation Handbook	1433054000
US-Yugoslavia Diplomatic and Political Cooperation Handbook	1433054019
US-Yugoslavia Economic and Political Cooperation Handbook	1433054027
Utah Business Registration and Incorporation Guide	1438756224
Utah Business Registration and Incorporation Guide	1433057964
Utah Investment & Business Guide	1438756232
Utah Small Business Assistance and Programs Handbook	1438756240

US GOVERNMENT LIBRARY

TITLE *	ISBN
Overseas Private Investment Corporation (OPIC) Handbook	0739731835
THE FBI ACADEMY HANDBOOK	0739731858
The White House Handbook	0739731815
US African Development Fund Handbook	073973184X
US AGENCY FOR INTERNATIONAL DEVELOPMENT BUSINESS OPPORTUNITIES HANDBOOK	0739731866
US Agency for International Development Handbook	0739731874
US Arms Control and Disarmament Agency Handbook	0739739832
US CENTRAL INTELLIGENCE AGENCY (CIA) HANDBOOK	0739732757
US Civil Rights Policy Handbook	073976201X
US Commodity Futures Trading Commission Handbook	0739762028
US Congressional Budget Office Handbook	0739762036
US Defense Intelligence Agency Handbook	0739711709
US Department of Agriculture Business Opportunities Handbook	0739762044
US Department of Agriculture Handbook	0739762052
US Department of Air Force Handbook	0739762060
US Department of Commerce Handbook	0739762079
US Department of Defense Handbook	0739762087
US Department of Energy Business Opportunities Handbook	0739762095
US Department of Energy Handbook	0739762109
US Department of Health and Human Services Handbook	0739762117
US Department of Housing and Urban Services Handbook	0739762125
US Department of Interior Handbook	0739762133
US Department of Justice Handbook	0739762141
US Department of Labor Handbook	073976215X
US Department of State Handbook	0739762168
US Department of the Army Handbook	0739762176
US Department of the Navy Handbook	0739762184
US Department of the Treasury Handbook	0739762192
US Department of Transport Handbook	0739762206
US Department of Veteran Affairs Handbook	0739762214
US Environmental Protection Agency Handbook	0739762222

TITLE *	ISBN
US Export-Import Bank Handbook	0739762230
US Federal Bureau of Investigation (FBI) Business Opportunities Handbook	0739762370
US Federal Bureau of Investigation (FBI) Handbook	073976246X
US Federal Communication Commission Handbook	0739733494
US Federal Election Commission Handbook	0739762400
US Federal Energy Sector Regulations Handbook	0739762419
US Federal Executive Government Handbook	0739731823
US Federal Maritime Commission Handbook	0739762427
US Federal Mine Safety and Health Commission Handbook	0739762435
US Federal Reserve System Handbook	0739762532
US Federal Trade Commission Handbook	0739762451
US Food and Drug Administration Handbook	0739762397
US Food Assistance to Russia Handbook	0739762478
US Information Agency Handbook	0739762486
US Intelligence Policy Handbook	0739762494
US Internal Revenue Service Handbook	0739762508
US Libraries and Information Science National Commission Handbook	0739762516
US National Academy of Science and Research Policy Handbook	0739762524
US National Aeronautics and Space Administration Handbook	0739762249
US National Drug Control Policy Handbook	0739762389
US National Institute of Health Handbook	0739762443
US National Science Foundation Handbook	0739762362
US National Security Policy Handbook	0739762354
US Navy Seals Handbook	0739762540
US Office of Management and Budget Handbook	0739762346
US Office of Personnel Management Handbook	0739762338
US Peace Corp Handbook	073976232X
US Postal Service Handbook	0739762311
US Science and Technology Policy Handbook	0739762303
US Securities and Exchange Commission Handbook	073976229X
US Small Business Administration Handbook	0739762281
US Special Operation Forces Handbook	0739762001
US Trade and Development Agency Handbook	0739762273
US Trade Representative Office Handbook	0739762265
WORLD BANK BUSINESS OPPORTUNITES HANDBOOK	0739762257
US Homeland Security Handbook	073976277X
US Air Force Academy Handbook	0739762753
US Pacific Air Force Handbook	0739762788

NEW! WORLD OFFSHORE TAX GUIDES

Price: $149.95 each

1.	Andorra Offshore Tax Guide
2.	Anguilla Offshore Tax Guide
3.	Bahamas Offshore Tax Guide
4.	Barbados Offshore Tax Guide
5.	Belize Offshore Tax Guide
6.	Bermuda Offshore Tax Guide
7.	British Virgin Islands Offshore Tax Guide
8.	Cayman Islands Offshore Tax Guide
9.	Cook Islands Offshore Tax Guide
10.	Costa Rica Offshore Tax Guide
11.	Cyprus Offshore Tax Guide
12.	Dubai Offshore Tax Guide
13.	Gibraltar Offshore Tax Guide
14.	Grenada Offshore Tax Guide
15.	Guernsey Offshore Tax Guide
16.	Hong Kong Offshore Tax Guide
17.	Ireland Offshore Tax Guide
18.	Isle of Man Offshore Tax Guide
19.	Jersey Offshore Tax Guide
20.	Labuan Offshore Tax Guide
21.	Liechtenstein Offshore Tax Guide
22.	Luxembourg Offshore Tax Guide
23.	Madeira Offshore Tax Guide
24.	Malta Offshore Tax Guide
25.	Mauritius Offshore Business and Investment Opportunities Handbook
26.	Mauritius Offshore Tax Guide
27.	Monaco Offshore Tax Guide
28.	Nauru Offshore Tax Guide
29.	Netherlands Antilles Offshore Tax Guide
30.	Panama Offshore Tax Guide
31.	Seychelles Offshore Tax Guide
32.	Switzerland Offshore Tax Guide
33.	Turks & Caicos Islands Offshore Tax Guide
34.	Vanuatu Offshore Tax Guide

www.ingramcontent.com/pod-product-compliance
Lightning Source LLC
Chambersburg PA
CBHW081113021225
36210CB00032B/473